Praise for *Sexuality in Greek and Roman Culture,* Second Edition

"My upper-level students enjoyed Skinner's frank and engaging style, and appreciated her ability to navigate through contentious theoretical issues with discretion and clarity. The new features of the second edition further increase the value of what is by far the best survey of the subject available."

Anthony Corbeill, University of Kansas

"This book delivers but also exceeds what I'd hoped for in the second edition. In addition to an updated text and bibliography positioning the book in relation to scholarly developments, Skinner has added textboxes to stimulate class debate, and end-of-chapter 'discussion prompts' to encourage students' reflection upon our relationship with/estrangement from ancient sexuality."

Susan Deacy, University of Roehampton

"Skinner's revised and expanded second edition increases the chief pleasure of her first—to see a true scholar at work, formidably informed. Her scope of erudition embraces all manner of ancient testimony, from Greek romances to gravestones."

Micaela Janan, Duke University

"Thoroughly revised and with new sections and illustrations in each chapter, this book remains a landmark study of a complex yet fascinating subject. Written by a global authority in the field, it delivers rigorous, up-to-date scholarship in a style appealing to the non-specialist reader."

Konstantinos P. Nikoloutsos, Saint Joseph's University

"A breathtaking synthesis of cutting edge research, this superb second edition of Skinner's magisterial overview of ancient sexuality combines sophistication with accessibility and remains an indispensable resource for students, teachers, and scholars."

Yurie Hong, Gustavus Adolphus College

Ancient Cultures

These enjoyable, straightforward surverys of key themes in ancient culture are ideal for anyone new to the study of the ancient world. Each book reveals the excitement of discovering the diverse lifestyles, ideals, and beliefs of ancient peoples.

Published

Ancient Babylonian Medicine
Markham J. Geller

The Spartans
Nigel Kennell

Sport and Spectacle in the Ancient World
Donald G. Kyle

Food in the Ancient World
John M. Wilkins and Shaun Hill

Greek Political Thought
Ryan K. Balot

Theories of Mythology
Eric Csapo

Sexuality in Greek and Roman Culture, second edition
Marilyn B. Skinner

In preparation

Science in the Ancient World
Daryn Lehoux

Ethnicity and Identity in the Ancient World
Kathryn Lomas

Roman Law and Society
Thomas McGinn

Economies of the Greek and Roman World
Jeremy Paterson

Economies of the Greco-Roman World
Gary Reger

The City of Rome
John Patterson

Sport and Spectacle in the Ancient World, second edition
Donald G. Kyle

SEXUALITY *in* GREEK *and* ROMAN CULTURE

MARILYN B. SKINNER

SECOND EDITION

WILEY Blackwell

This second edition first published 2014
© 2014 John Wiley & Sons, Inc.

Edition history: Blackwell Publishing Ltd (1e, 2005)

Wiley-Blackwell is an imprint of John Wiley & Sons, formed by the merger of Wiley's global Scientific, Technical and Medical business with Blackwell Publishing.

Registered Office
John Wiley & Sons Ltd, The Atrium, Southern Gate, Chichester, West Sussex, PO19 8SQ, UK

Editorial Offices
350 Main Street, Malden, MA 02148-5020, USA
9600 Garsington Road, Oxford, OX4 2DQ, UK
The Atrium, Southern Gate, Chichester, West Sussex, PO19 8SQ, UK

For details of our global editorial offices, for customer services, and for information about how to apply for permission to reuse the copyright material in this book please see our website at www.wiley.com/wiley-blackwell.

The right of Marilyn B. Skinner to be identified as the author of this work has been asserted in accordance with the UK Copyright, Designs and Patents Act 1988.

Library of Congress Cataloging-in-Publication Data

Skinner, Marilyn B.
  Sexuality in greek and roman culture / Marilyn B. Skinner. – 2nd Edition.
     pages   cm. – (Ancient cultures; 2621)
  Includes bibliographical references and index.
    ISBN 978-1-4443-4986-3 (pbk.: alk. paper) – ISBN 978-1-118-61108-1 (epub) –
ISBN 978-1-118-61092-3 (mobi) – ISBN 978-1-118-61081-7 (epdf)   1. Sex customs–Greece–
History–To 1500–Textbooks.   2. Sex customs–Rome–History–Textbooks.   I. Title.
  HQ13.S535 2013
  306.70937′6–dc23
                                                   2013018151

A catalogue record for this book is available from the British Library.

Cover image: Detail of Sleeping Hermaphrodite, Roman marble copy of original Hellenistic sculpture. © Araldo de Luca/Corbis
Cover design by Simon Levy

Set in 10/12.5pt Rotation by SPi Publisher Services, Pondicherry, India

1 2014

Housman: Actually, "*trochos*" *is* Greek, it's the Greek word for hoop, so when Horace uses "*Graecus trochus*" it's rather like saying "French *chapeau*". I mean he's laying it on thick, isn't he?

Jackson: Is he? What?

Housman: Well, to a Roman, to call something *Greek* meant – very often – sissylike, or effeminate. In fact, a hoop, a *trochos*, was a favourite gift given by a Greek man to the boy he, you know, to his favourite boy.

Jackson: Oh, beastliness, you mean?

Tom Stoppard, The Invention of Love

Tondo of a red-figure cup by the Pedieus Painter, c.510 BCE

Contents

Illustrations and Maps

Illustrations

Maps

Preface to the Second Edition

Publication of a second edition of *Sexuality in Greek and Roman Culture* gives me the opportunity to correct shortcomings noted by reviewers and readers of the first edition, incorporate new findings and update an ever-increasing bibliography, expand treatment of several topics, add more images, restructure the final chapters chronologically, and carry the narrative of ancient sexual ethics down to the Christian era. Students, I hope, will welcome a few features to make the work more user-friendly: for each chapter, the inclusion of a text box containing intriguing facts tangential to the main topic and the addition of discussion prompts and further readings at the end, as well as a glossary at the back defining boldfaced terms employed in the text. Many of these changes were suggested by respondents to electronic surveys conducted by the publisher. I deeply appreciate the thoughtful feedback those participants provided; as a teaching tool the book has benefited greatly.

While I have preserved all of the original content, I have rewritten entire portions of text, especially in the introduction, the chapters on classical Athens and the Hellenistic period, and the concluding chapters on imperial Rome. Perceptive reviewers observed that the previous edition was as much about gender as it was about sexuality. Indeed, it is almost impossible to disentangle the two, even conceptually. The introduction has been enlarged, then, by a theoretical explanation of relationships among the terms "sex," "gender," and "sexuality" as they will be encountered here. Though finding it hard to cover all the material I wished to include, I have added longer discussions of Aeschines' speech *Against Timarchus*, the historical backdrop to Alexander the Great's conquests, polygamy within the Argead dynasty, and the influence of Egyptian sexual customs and religion upon Greek writings produced in Ptolemaic Alexandria, as all seemed germane to main chapter themes. Finally, I have separated my account of sexual mores under the Caesars into two parts: one chapter on changing elite attitudes, Greek and Roman, toward the human body and the marriage bond, using literature and official public art as my chief witnesses, and the other on conditions and trends affecting the populace as a whole, presenting a fuller context for studying the rise of Christianity and its focus upon sexual denial. Although that last chapter is still eclectic, I believe it is more cohesive, and I trust that in providing detailed economic, legal, and demographic information I have not strayed too far from my goal of showing how an ascetic movement underpinned by eschatology might fit into the big sociological picture.

Because this book is a textbook, I have used commonly transliterated forms of proper names: "Aeschylus" instead of "Aiskhylos." Exceptions are gods and mythic heroes, as students ought to know both Greek and Roman alternatives, and technical terms: *hetairai*, not "hetaeras." Instructors might like to have my reason for supplying what I term "discussion prompts." Initially I planned to include a set of review questions with factual answers to help students prepare for examinations. That practical notion became unfeasible, however, as I realized that I did not know what a teacher would emphasize in a given chapter and what she might prefer to leave out, depending on the level and size of the course, the length of the instructional period, and the various uses to which an assigned textbook might be put. The prompts I devised instead can function in numerous ways. Because they permit open-ended responses, classmates may debate them in breakout sessions or blog about them. They offer a choice of topics for short writing assignments. In combination with primary sources they can be used for open-book tests. Finally, ingenious students will doubtless be able to recast some of them as pick-up lines. Whatever the situation, prompts, as the noun implies, invite reflection upon personal experiences while one is seeking to grasp the workings of a foreign set of gender and sexual protocols. Whether such a process will render readers more comfortable with antiquity, I do not know. I suspect, though, that it will render them less comfortable with their own habits of thinking, and that is a good thing.

As before, I am indebted to colleagues who generously commented on drafts and offered timely assistance. On the subject of demographic projections Bruce Frier gave invaluable advice. Kristina Milnor sent a chapter of her forthcoming monograph on Pompeian graffiti. Konstantinos Nikoloutsos helped me look at Alexander through the eyes of a queer theorist. Gil Renberg supplied a bibliographic reference that complicated my view of the Warren Cup. On behalf of the Troy Project, C. Brian Rose authorized re-use of a drawing by Nurten Sevinç originally published in *Studia Troica* (1996). Archaeological illustrator Christina L. Kolb produced a detailed rendering of a much discussed scene on the so-called "Getty Birds" vase. Once more, my apologies if I have overlooked mentioning someone's scholarly contribution to the finished volume.

My thanks as well to those associated with Wiley-Blackwell who worked hard with me to produce an improved second edition: Haze Humbert, Acquisitions Editor, for commissioning the undertaking and soliciting suggestions from instructors; Ben Thatcher, Project Editor, for guiding me through the maze of getting permissions – again; Nora Naughton of NPM Ltd, the project production manager; Doreen Kruger, the meticulous copyeditor; and Elizabeth Saucier, Editorial Assistant, and her marketing staff for the arresting cover design. Finally, my express gratitude once again to Jeff Carnes for preparing an even more complicated index this time around.

Preface to the First Edition

The immediate decade has seen an explosion of curricular interest in ancient sexuality, a topic once warily neglected in the classroom. Undergraduate courses on gender and sexuality in Greece and Rome are now regularly offered by a large number of college and university classics programs in the United States, Canada, Great Britain, and Australia. They have proven enormously popular, and not just because their subject matter is intrinsically fascinating. Students who encounter the strange ways in which the educated classes of antiquity spoke about themselves as men and women and the odd cultural meanings they imposed on what takes place in the bedroom cannot help but begin to reconsider their own assumptions about themselves as members of a (supposedly) given sex and actors in a (supposedly) universal tragicomedy of desire and mating. Learning to view intimate matters from an alien perspective is a scary experience, particularly for young adults. This textbook is designed to help undergraduates engage with ancient sexuality in all its otherness. It is also designed for the general reader, who may have heard rumors about exciting new questions being broached in a proverbially conservative discipline.

As an academic field of study, Greco-Roman sexuality has only just become legitimate, to say nothing of trendy. Already, though, the literature is enormous and continues to grow, so that giving an overview of current thinking necessarily attempts to hit a moving target. The intellectual energy of specialists and the cutting-edge quality of their research guaranteed that the study changing the way everyone looked at a particular issue inevitably appeared just weeks after my own discussion of that issue was written. I have tried to keep abreast of developments as much as possible. For that reason, the bibliography is weighted heavily toward work published in the past ten or fifteen years. Instructors who wish to present this material in the context of more traditional accounts of social and political history may need to assign short readings from standard reference works. They may also want to select an accompanying sourcebook, although I have incorporated fairly lengthy chunks of ancient texts. All translations of Greek and Roman primary sources, except where indicated, are my own.

In composing what is, to my knowledge, the first overall survey of ancient sexuality, I have employed two different approaches to contemporary scholarship. As an expositor, I have attempted to compile and synthesize conclusions drawn from recent analyses and, in dealing with controversial questions, to explain the point of contention and present arguments from both sides. As a practicing investigator, however, I have sometimes taken positions when a given account appears to me the more plausible one. Because discussion in certain areas is intensely focused, and fundamental assumptions about the symbolic content of Greek and Roman sexual discourses are not always expressly articulated, I have formulated general observations on the semiotics of ancient sexuality that may themselves be starting points for further debate. I welcome such disagreement. As I maintain throughout this volume, the field is in its infancy – a textbook written for courses taught years from now will take for granted concepts that have not yet occurred to present-day researchers. Debate is the matrix of new understanding.

While writing this book, I realized that I was uniquely equipped to tell the story of how our picture of ancient sexual mores has changed in the past quarter-century, not because of any greater depth of erudition but rather thanks to two generations' worth of hindsight. My college years fell in the late 1950s and early 1960s, before the cultural watersheds of the sexual revolution, the Vietnam War, and the second wave of feminism. I went to school, as young women of my background did in those days, to find a man to provide for me and my offspring and graduated four years later with no husband and a solid liberal arts education, which has served me in much better stead. During the next decade I was in a position, first as an adjunct instructor and then as a doctoral student, to observe how female undergraduates, not too much younger than I, were coming of age in a cultural landscape that had meantime changed dramatically, how they were confronting the world with wholly different expectations about their future. The sense of dislocation I experienced guaranteed a lasting emancipation from prior habits of thought: I would never again assume that notions of sex and gender were intrinsically correct just because they had been drummed into me when I was a child growing up in sheltered suburbia. Agnosticism and inquisitiveness subsequently attracted me, as a freshly degreed college professor, to the revolutionary domain of women and gender studies and finally into the history of sexuality. There I have had a privileged opportunity to indulge the kind of curiosity that, as Michel Foucault proclaimed in *The Use of Pleasure*, is "worth acting upon with a degree of obstinacy: not the curiosity that seeks to assimilate what it is proper for one to know, but that which enables one to get free of oneself" (1986: 8). It is in that spirit that this textbook is written: to arouse in younger persons the same impulse to think alternatively, especially about their own intimate experiences.

The difficulties that this large project presented were made easier through the assistance of many colleagues, associates, and friends. First, I wish to thank the editorial staff of Blackwell Publishing. Simon Alexander, the Publishing Coordinator for Classics, kept me working to deadline and thoughtfully replied to my proposals about cover design. Al Bertrand, the Commissioning Editor, thoroughly critiqued chapter after chapter, offering invaluable advice and support. Editorial Controller

Angela Cohen helped keep track of permissions requests and supplied counsel on many technical problems of book preparation. The suggestions of several anonymous readers who responded to the initial book proposal aided me considerably as I subsequently revised the outline. Finally, my special thanks to Laura McClure, the Press referee who reviewed the entire manuscript, for her warm enthusiasm and generous assistance.

Several fellow classicists read individual excerpts from the book or provided me with work-in-progress. Elizabeth Belfiore offered expert bibliographical and scholarly advice on Greek tragedy and Plato and allowed me to consult her forthcoming study of the Platonic representation of Socrates in the *Symposium*. Jeffrey Carnes sent me a draft of his paper on ancient sexuality and recent Supreme Court decisions, a presentation that has become even timelier as the legal dispute over gay marriage intensifies. Laura McClure provided advance proofs of the opening chapters of *Courtesans at Table: Gender and Greek Literary Culture in Athenaeus* (2003) and responded thoughtfully to my discussion of the courtesan figure. Kristina Milnor gave permission to cite her working paper no. 14, "No Place for a Woman? Critical Narratives and Erotic Graffiti from Pompeii," available from the University of Michigan Institute for Research on Women and Gender. Amy Richlin sent her own provocative survey of imperial Roman sexuality prepared for a forthcoming Blackwell's Companion volume; as always, it has been a cognitive delight to grapple with her ideas. Brian Rose supplied me with an offprint of the first publication of the Polyxena Sarcophagus and helped me contact the author, Dr Nurten Sevinç, for permission to reproduce her illustration of the find. My apologies to anyone if I have inadvertently overlooked mentioning his or her intellectual contribution to the volume.

Needless to say, this textbook reflects the feedback of students who have been exposed to my thinking in various courses on Roman literature and women and gender in antiquity. I owe a particular debt of gratitude to the undergraduates in my Fall 2001 Freshman Colloquium CLAS 195, "Encounters with Classical Antiquity," and the graduate students in my Spring 2002 seminar CLAS 596, "Greek and Roman Sexuality," for serving as willing guinea pigs in thought experiments about the ancient world. Students at Carleton College in Northfield, Minnesota, Macalester College in St Paul, Minnesota, and members of the Department of Classical and Near Eastern Studies at the University of Minnesota peppered me with insightful questions when I presented parts of the book on a lecture tour in April, 2004. Holly Cohen, my research assistant, spent hours in the library probing into strange byways of ancient culture. Serpil Atamaz Hazar, a doctoral student in the History Department, translated my letters to Dr Sevinç into Turkish and her replies into English. To all of them, and to my long-suffering colleagues in the Department of Classics at the University of Arizona, let me express my deep gratitude.

Acknowledgments

The author and publisher gratefully acknowledge the permission granted to replicate the copyright material in this book:

Faber & Faber Ltd for non-USA permission to reproduce in print and electronically an excerpt from "Annus Mirabilis" from *High Windows* by Philip Larkin. Copyright © 1974 by Philip Larkin.

Farrar, Straus and Giroux, LLC, for United States permission to reproduce in print and electronically an excerpt from "Annus Mirabilis" from *Collected Poems* by Philip Larkin. Copyright © 1988, 1989 by the Estate of Philip Larkin. Reproduced by permission of Farrar, Straus and Giroux, LLC.

Faber & Faber Ltd for UK and British Commonwealth permission to reproduce in print and electronically an excerpt from *The Invention of Love* by Tom Stoppard. Copyright © 1997 by Tom Stoppard.

Grove/Atlantic Inc. for United States permission to reproduce in print and electronically an excerpt from *The Invention of Love* by Tom Stoppard. Copyright © 1997 by Tom Stoppard.

The Penguin Group for permission to use passages from pp. 61–2, 337, and 340–1 of Trevor J. Saunders's translation of *The Laws* by Plato (Harmondsworth, Middlesex, England: Penguin Books, 1970). Copyright © Trevor J. Saunders, 1970. Reproduced in print and electronically by permission of Penguin Books Ltd.

Every effort has been made to trace copyright holders and to obtain their permission for the use of copyright material. The publisher apologizes for any errors or omissions in the above list and would be grateful if notified of any corrections that should be incorporated in future reprints or editions of this book.

Abbreviations

Abbreviations of the names of ancient authors and their works follow, whenever possible, the practice of the *Oxford Classical Dictionary*, 4th edition (2012). Otherwise, Greek authors and titles are abbreviated as in Liddell and Scott, *Greek–English Lexicon*, 9th edition, revised by H. Stuart Jones and supplemented by various scholars (1968), referred to as *LSJ*. Latin authors and titles are abbreviated as in the *Oxford Latin Dictionary* (1982), commonly cited as *OLD*. Names of authors or works in square brackets [—] indicate spurious or questionable attributions. Numbers in superscript following a title indicate the number of an edition (e.g., *OCD*[4]). Abbreviations and descriptions of works of secondary scholarship are also usually taken from *OCD*[4].

General

ad loc.	*ad locum*, at the placed being discussed in the commentary
ap.	*apud*, within, indicating a quotation contained in another author
c.	*circa*, about or approximately
cf.	compare
ch.	chapter
ff.	following pages
fig., figs.	figure, figures
fl.	flourished
fr., frr.	fragment, fragments
ibid.	*ibidem*, in the same work cited above
inv.	inventory number
n., nn.	note, notes
pass.	*passim*, throughout
pl.	plural
pr.	preface

Greek Authors and Works

Ael.	Aelian
VH	*Varia Historia*
Aeschin.	Aeschines
Andoc.	Andocides
Anth. Pal.	*Palatine Anthology*
Antiph.	Antiphon
Ap. Rhod. *Argon.*	Apollonius Rhodius, *Argonautica*
Ar.	Aristophanes
Ach.	*Acharnians*
Eccl.	*Assemblywomen*
Eq.	*Knights*
Lys.	*Lysistrata*
Ran.	*Frogs*
Thesm.	*Women at the Thesmophoria*
Arist.	Aristotle
[*Ath. pol.*]	*Constitution of the Athenians*
Eth. Eud.	*Eudemian Ethics*
Eth. Nic.	*Nichomachean Ethics*
Gen. an.	*On the Generation of Animals*
Metaph.	*Metaphysics*
[*Oec.*]	*On Household Management*
Pol.	*Politics*
[*Pr.*]	*Problemata*
Rh.	*Rhetoric*
Arr.	Arrian, Anabasis *of Alexander*
Artem.	Artemidorus, *Oneirokritika*
Ath.	Athenaeus, *Deipnosophistae*
Callim.	Callimachus
Aet.	*Aetia*
Hymn 5	*Hymn to Athena*
Cass. Dio	Cassius Dio
Dem.	Demosthenes
Din.	Dinarchus
Diod. Sic.	Diodorus Siculus
Diog. Laert.	Diogenes Laertius
Epict.	Epictetus
Disc.	*Discourses*
Epicurus	Epicurus
RS	*Principal Doctrines*
Sent. Vat.	*Vatican Sayings*
Eub.	Eubulus
Eur.	Euripides
Alc.	*Alcestis*

Hipp.	*Hippolytus*
Gal.	Galen
Ars med.	*Art of Medicine*
Libr. propr.	*On My Own Books*
PHP	*On the Doctrines of Hippocrates and Plato*
UP	*On the Use of the Parts of the Body*
Hdt.	Herodotus
Hermesian.	Hermesianax
Hes.	Hesiod
Op.	*Works and Days*
Theog.	*Theogony*
Hipp. *Haer.*	Hippolytus, *Refutation of All Heresies*
[Hippoc.]	Hippocrates
Genit.	*On Generation*
Loc. Hom.	*Places in Man*
Mul.	*Diseases of Women*
Nat. Hom.	*On the Nature of the Human Being*
Hom.	Homer
Il.	*Iliad*
Od.	*Odyssey*
Hymn. Hom. Ap.	*Homeric Hymn to Apollo*
Cer.	*Homeric Hymn to Demeter*
Ven.	*Homeric Hymn to Aphrodite*
Hyp.	Hyperides
Iambl. *VP*	Iamblichus, *Life of Pythagoras*
Isae.	Isaeus
Isoc.	Isocrates
[Longinus] *Subl.*	[Longinus], *On the Sublime*
[Luc.] *Am.*	[Lucian], *Affairs of the Heart*
Lucian *Eun.*	Lucian, *The Eunuch*
Lucill.	Lucillius
Lys.	Lysias
Men.	Menander
Sam.	*Samia*
Muson.	Musonius Rufus
Nic.	Nicander
NT	New Testament (Authorized Version)
1 Cor.	First Epistle to the Corinthians
Rom.	Epistle to the Romans
OT	Old Testament (Authorized Version)
Lev.	Leviticus
Parth. *Amat. narr.*	Parthenius, *Sufferings in Love*
Paus.	Pausanias, *Description of Greece*
Philostr.	Philostratus
VS	*Vitae sophistarum* (*Lives of the Sophists*)

Pind.	Pindar
Ol.	*Olympian Odes*
Pl.	Plato
Criti.	*Critias*
Leg.	*Laws*
Men.	*Meno*
Min.	*Minos*
Phdr.	*Phaedrus*
Prot.	*Protagoras*
Resp.	*Republic*
Symp.	*Symposium*
Ti.	*Timaeus*
Plut.	Plutarch
Alex.	*Life of Alexander*
Amat.	*Dialogue on Love*
Caes.	*Life of Caesar*
Cat. Mai.	*Life of the Elder Cato*
Cic.	*Life of Cicero*
Crass.	*Life of Crassus*
De cupid. divit.	*On the Desire for Riches*
De Is.	*On Isis and Osiris*
De mul. vir.	*On the Virtues of Women*
Lyc.	*Life of Lycurgus*
Mor.	*Moralia*
Per.	*Life of Pericles*
Pomp.	*Life of Pompey*
Sol.	*Life of Solon*
Polyb.	Polybius
Porph. *Abst.*	Porphyry, *On Abstinence*
Pythag. *Ep.*	*Letters of Pythagoras and the Pythagoreans*
Sor. *Gyn.*	Soranus, *Gynecology*
Stob.	Stobaeus
Str.	Strabo
Theoc. *Id.*	Theocritus, *Idylls*
Theophr.	Theophrastus
Char.	*Characters*
Thuc.	Thucydides
Xen.	Xenophon
[Ath. pol.]	*Constitution of the Athenians*
Lac.	*Constitution of the Spartans*
Mem.	*Recollections of Socrates*
Oec.	*On Household Management*
Symp.	*Symposium*

Roman Authors and Works

Apul.	Apuleius
Apol.	*Apologia*
Fl.	*Florida*
Met.	*Metamorphoses*
Aug. *RG*	Augustus, *Res Gestae (Things Accomplished)*
August.	Augustine
Conf.	*Confessions*
De civ. D.	*City of God*
Aur. Vict. *Caes.*	Aurelius Victor, *Lives of the Caesars*
Cael. Aur. *Morb. Chron.*	Caelius Aurelianus, *On Chronic Diseases*
Catul.	Catullus
Cic.	Cicero
Att.	*Letters to Atticus*
Cael.	*On Behalf of Caelius*
Dom.	*On his House*
Fam.	*Letters to his Friends*
Fin.	*On the Supreme Good and Evil*
Inv. rhet.	*On Devising a Speech*
Marcell.	*On Behalf of Marcellus*
Nat. D.	*On the Nature of the Gods*
Off.	*On Duties*
Phil.	*Philippics*
Planc.	*On Behalf of Plancius*
Rosc. Am.	*On Behalf of Sextus Roscius of Ameria*
Top.	*Topica*
Tusc.	*Tusculan Disputations*
Columella, *Rust.*	Columella, *On Agriculture*
Curt.	Q. Curtius Rufus, *History of Alexander*
Dig.	*Digest of Roman Law*
Gai. *Inst.*	Gaius, *Institutes*
Gell. *NA*	Aulus Gellius, *Attic Nights*
Hor.	Horace
Carm.	*Odes*
Sat.	*Satires*
Jer. *Adv. Iovinian.*	Jerome, *Against Jovinian*
Just. *Epit.*	Justin, *Epitome* (of Trogus)
Just. *Inst.*	Justinian, *Institutes*
Juv.	Juvenal
Liv.	Livy
Lucr. *DRN*	Lucretius, *On the Nature of Things*
Macrob. *Sat.*	Macrobius, *Saturnalia*
Mart.	Martial

Nep.	Cornelius Nepos
NT	New Testament
1 Cor.	First Epistle to the Corinthians
Rom.	Epistle to the Romans
OT	Old Testament
Lev.	Leviticus
Ov.	Ovid
Am.	*Amores*
Ars am.	*Art of Love*
Fast.	*Fasti*
Her.	*Heroides*
Met.	*Metamorphoses*
Pont.	*Letters from Pontus*
Tr.	*Tristia*
Passio Perp.	*The Passion of Saints Perpetua and Felicity*
Paulus *Sent.*	Iulius Paulus, *Sententiae*
Petron.	Petronius
Sat.	*Satyricon*
Plaut.	Plautus
Aul.	*The Pot of Gold*
Plin. *HN*	Pliny (the Elder), *Natural History*
Plin. *Ep.*	Pliny (the Younger), *Letters*
Prop.	Propertius
Quint. *Inst.*	Quintilian, *Institutes of Oratory*
Sall.	Sallust
Cat.	*Catiline*
Sen.	Seneca (the Elder)
Controv.	*Controversiae*
Sen.	Seneca (the Younger)
Ep.	*Moral Epistles*
Helv.	*Letter to Helvia*
Q Nat.	*Natural Questions*
SHA	Scriptores Historiae Augustae (*Lives of the Later Emperors*)
Alex. Sev.	*Severus Alexander*
Hadr.	*Hadrian*
Heliogab.	*Heliogabalus*
Suet.	Suetonius
Div. Aug.	*Life of the Deified Augustus*
Calig.	*Life of Caligula*
Div. Claud.	*Life of the Deified Claudius*
Dom.	*Life of Domitian*
Galb.	*Life of Galba*
Div. Iul.	*Life of the Deified Julius*

Ner.	*Life of Nero*
Tib.	*Life of Tiberius*
Tac.	Tacitus
Agr.	*Agricola*
Ann.	*Annals*
Hist.	*Historiae*
Tert.	Tertullian
Apol.	*Apology*
De praescr. haeret.	*Prescription against Heretics*
Tib.	Tibullus
Ulp.	Ulpian
Varro, *Rust.*	Varro, *On Agriculture*
Verg.	Vergil
Aen.	*Aeneid*
G.	*Georgics*

Works of Secondary Scholarship

ABV	J. D. Beazley, *Attic Black-figure Vase Painters* (1956)
AE	*L'Année Épigraphique*, published in *Revue Archéologique* and separately (1888–)
ARV²	J. D. Beazley, *Attic Red-figure Vase Painters*, 2nd edn. (1963)
Coll. Alex.	J. U. Powell (ed.), *Collectanea Alexandrina* (1925)
CIG	A. Boeckh (ed.), *Corpus Inscriptionum Graecarum* (1828–77)
CIL	*Corpus Inscriptionum Latinarum* (1863–)
CLE	F. Bücheler and E. Lommatzsch (eds.), *Carmina Latina Epigraphica* (1895–1926)
CR Acad. Inscr.	*Comptes rendus de l'Académie des Inscriptions et Belles-lettres*
DK	H. Diels and W. Kranz (eds.), *Fragmente der Vorsokratiker*, 6th edn (Berlin, 1952)
FGrH	F. Jacoby (ed.), *Fragmente der griechischen Historiker* (1923–)
Gow	A. S. F. Gow (ed.), *Machon: The Fragments* (1965)
GP	A. S. F. Gow and D. L. Page (eds.), *The Greek Anthology: Hellenistic Epigrams*, 2 vols. (1965)
IG	*Inscriptiones Graecae* (1873–)
IL Jug	*Inscriptiones Latinae quae in Iugoslavia .... repertae et editae sunt* (Ljubljana 1963–86)
ILS	H. Dessau, *Inscriptiones Latinae Selectae* (1892–1916)
Kock	T. Kock, *Comicorum Atticorum Fragmenta* (1880–8)
Kühn	K. G. Kühn, *Medicorum Graecorum Opera*

Littré	E. Littré, *Oeuvres complètes d'Hippocrate*, 10 vols. (1839–61)
Lutz	C. E. Lutz, *Musonius Rufus: "The Roman Socrates"* (1947)
Marx	F. Marx, *C. Lucilii Carminum Reliquiae* (1904–5)
Nauck[2]	A. Nauck (ed.), *Tragicorum Graecorum Fragmenta*, 2nd edn. (1889)
Pack	R. A. Pack (ed.), *Artemidori Daldiani onirocriticon libri* V (1963)
PColon.	*Kölner Papyri* (1976–)
PDidot.	*Papyrus Firmin-Didot*, H. Weil, *Un Papyrus Inédit* (1879)
Pf.	R. Pfeiffer (ed.), *Callimachus*, 2 vols (1949–53)
PKöln	*Kölner Papyri* XI (2007)
PMG	D. L. Page (ed.), *Poetae Melici Graeci* (1962)
POxy.	*Oxyrhynchus Papyri* (1898–)
PSI	*Papiri Greci e Latini, Pubblicazioni della Società italiana per la recerca dei papiro greci e latini in Egitto* (1912–)
S-M	B. Snell and H. Maehler (eds.), *Pindari carmina cum fragmentis* (1987–8)
Suppl. Hell.	H. Lloyd-Jones and P. Parsons (eds.), *Supplementum Hellenisticum*, Texte und Kommentare no. 11 (1983)
Suppl. Mag.	R. W. Daniel and F. Maltomini (eds.), *Supplementum Magicum*, Papyrologica Coloniensia 16/1–2, 2 vols. (1989–91)
SVF	H. von Arnim, (ed.), *Stoicorum Veterum Fragmenta* (1903–)
Us.	H. Usener (ed.), *Epicurea* (1887)
V	E.-M. Voigt (ed.), *Sappho et Alcaeus: Fragmenta* (1971)
van der Horst	P. W. van der Horst, *Chaeremon: Egyptian Priest and Stoic Philosopher* (1984)
West[2]	M. L. West (ed.), *Iambi et Elegi*, 2nd edn. (1989)
Wimmer	F. Wimmer (ed.), *Theophrasti Eresii opera* (1931)

Chronological Charts

Greece

Period	Date CE	Political Events	Cultural Events
BRONZE AGE	1450–1200	Mycenaean civilization at its zenith	
DARK AGE	1184	Traditional date of fall of Troy	
	*c.*800		Invention of Greek alphabet
	776		First Olympic games
	*c.*750	Rise of the *polis* Overseas colonization begins	Homer
ARCHAIC AGE	*c.*700	Development of oligarchic symposium culture	Hesiod; *Homeric Hymns* Archilochus Sappho
	594	Archonship of Solon	Anacreon
	560–514	Pisistratid dynasty rules Athens	
	*c.*530		Pythagoras emigrates to Croton
	525		Red-figure pottery technique
CLASSICAL PERIOD	490	Battle of Marathon	Pindar
	458		Aeschylus' *Oresteia*
	451/50	Pericles' Citizenship Law	

Period	Date CE	Political Events	Cultural Events
	431–404	Peloponnesian War	
	431		Euripides' *Medea*
	429	Death of Pericles	
	428		Euripides' *Hippolytus*
	411		Aristophanes' *Lysistrata*
	399	Trial and execution of Socrates	
	c.399–347		Plato's dialogues
	c.350		Praxiteles' Aphrodite of Cnidus
	338	Battle of Chaeronea	
	336	Philip II of Macedon assassinated	
	335		Aristotle founds the Lyceum
	331	Battle of Gaugamela	
	323	Death of Alexander the Great	
HELLENISTIC PERIOD	321–292		Career of Menander
	306		Epicurus founds the Garden
	305	Ptolemy I Soter king of Egypt	
	301		Zeno founds the Stoa
	283–246	Reign of Ptolemy II Philadelphus	Apollonius, Callimachus, Theocritus
	c.100		Meleager's *Garland*
	30	Death of Cleopatra VII	

Rome

Period	Date CE	Political Events	Cultural Events
ARCHAIC PERIOD	753	Traditional date of the founding of Rome	
	6th century	Etruscan domination of Rome	
	510–509	Expulsion of Tarquins and founding of the Republic	
REPUBLIC	218–201	Second Punic War	
	c.205–184		Career of Plautus
	186	Suppression of Bacchic rites	Scipionic Circle of
	149–146	Third Punic War	P. Cornelius
	146	Sack of Corinth	Scipio Aemilianus Terence, Lucilius, Polybius
	133	Tribunate of Tiberius Gracchus	
	123–121	Tribunates of Gaius Gracchus	
LATE REPUBLIC	106	Birth of Cicero	
	100	Birth of Julius Caesar	
	90–88	Social War: revolt of Rome's Italian allies	
	87–82	Civil wars of Marius and Sulla	
	63	Consulship of Cicero; suppression of Catilinarian conspiracy	
	60	Formation of First Triumvirate	
	c.57–54		Career of Catullus
	c.54		Lucretius' *On the Nature of Things*
	49	Caesar crosses Rubicon	
	48	Pompey defeated at Pharsalus	
	44	Caesar assassinated	
	44–42	Civil wars between Brutus and Cassius and Marc Antony and Octavian	
	c.39–38		Vergil's *Eclogues* published
	31	Battle of Actium	
	c.35–30		Publication of Horace's *Satires*

Period	Date CE	Political Events	Cultural Events
AUGUSTAN AGE	c.29–23		Books 1–3 of Propertius' elegies
	27	Augustus (Octavian) invested with supreme powers by Senate	
	after 27		Tibullus' elegies
	23		Horace's *Odes*
	19		Deaths of Tibullus and Vergil; publication of Vergil's *Aeneid*
	18	Julian laws on marriage and adultery	
	16		Propertius' fourth book
	9		Dedication of *Ara Pacis*
	8		Relegation of Ovid
	14	Death of Augustus	
ROMAN EMPIRE	14–37	Reign of Tiberius	Career of Seneca the Elder
	37–41	Reign of Caligula	
	41–54	Reign of Claudius	
	54–68	Reign of Nero	Petronius; Seneca the Younger; Musonius Rufus
	60–230		Second Sophistic; Greek novels
	69	Year of the Four Emperors	
	69–79	Reign of Vespasian	
	79	Eruption of Vesuvius	Death of Pliny the Elder
	81–96	Reign of Domitian	
	93	Persecution of Stoic opposition	
	98–117	Reign of Trajan	Pliny the Younger, Tacitus, Martial
	117–138	Reign of Hadrian	Juvenal, Plutarch, Herodes Atticus
	130		Death of Antinous
	c.155–180		Career of Apuleius
	157–216		Career of Galen
	161–180	Reign of Marcus Aurelius	
	165/6–189	Antonine Plague	

Period	Date CE	Political Events	Cultural Events
	193–211	Reign of Septimius Severus	Tertullian
	212	Roman citizenship extended to all free persons in empire	
	218–222	Reign of Elagabalus	
	235–270, 275–284	Periods of civil disorder	
	284–305	Reign of Diocletian	
LATE ANTIQUITY	313	Edict of Milan; religious toleration for Christians	
	320	Abolition of Julian penalties for celibacy	
	342	Outlawing of passive sexual conduct for males	
	c.390		Composition of *Historia Augusta*
	533	Sanctions against active male homoeroticism	

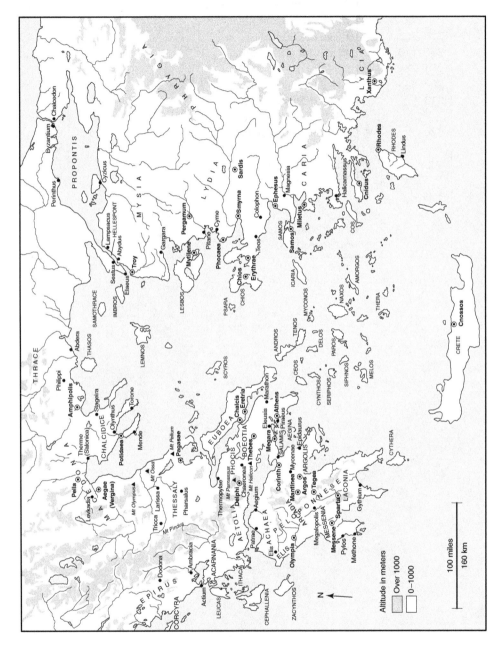

Map 1 Greece and the Aegean World

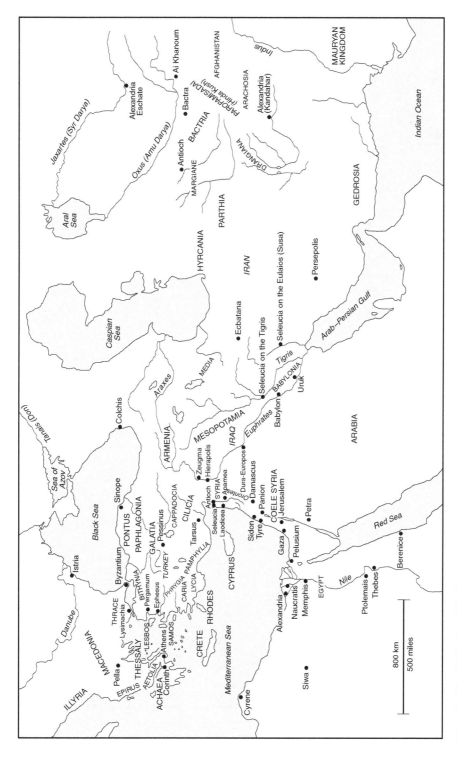

Map 2 The Hellenistic World

Map 3 Italy

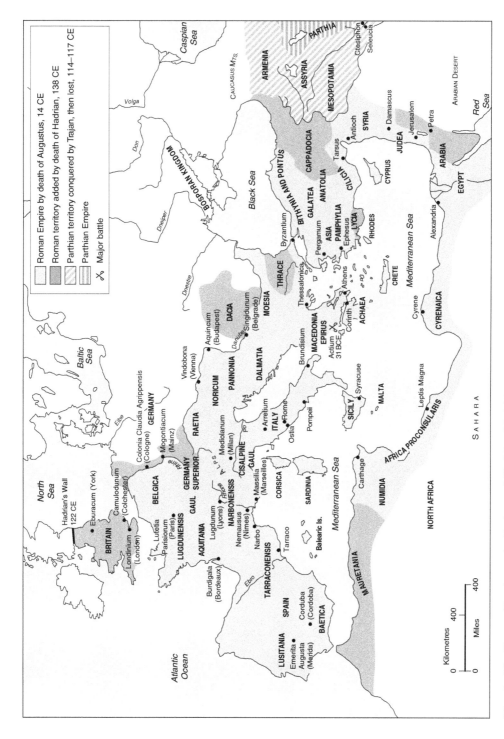

Map 4 The Roman Empire under Trajan and Hadrian 98–138 CE

Introduction: Why Ancient Sexuality? Issues and Approaches

Lawyers have little time for Platonic love. In a trial in America that attracted nationwide media attention, however, one point of constitutional law turned on arguments involving pronouncements about sex by the fourth-century BCE philosopher **Plato**. Plaintiffs in *Evans* v. *Romer*, heard in a Colorado district court in October 1993, were attempting to invalidate an amendment to the Colorado state constitution, Amendment 2, approved by referendum a year before. This amendment prohibited public agencies, municipalities, and school districts from adopting laws or policies granting protected status on the basis of sexual orientation. Its opponents argued that putting gays, lesbians, and bisexuals at such specific disadvantage violated their right to equal protection of the laws under the Fourteenth Amendment to the United States Constitution because it did not serve legitimate government interests and placed unique burdens on their ability to participate equally in the political process. Plaintiffs also challenged it on First Amendment grounds, including violation of the prohibition against the establishment of religion. Since many Christian denominations take the position that homosexual acts are morally wrong without exception, Amendment 2, they alleged, was an intrusion of fundamentalist Christian bias against homosexuals into secular law.

Here is where Plato enters the courtroom. To refute the latter contention, the state called in John M. Finnis, a specialist in moral philosophy, as an expert witness. In an affidavit, Finnis asserted that condemnation of homosexual activity had its basis in **natural-law theory**, the notion that human morality is governed by inherent principles evident to reason, and was clearly articulated by the founders of the Western tradition of rational philosophy: "All three of the greatest Greek philosophers, **Socrates**, Plato and **Aristotle**, regarded homosexual conduct as intrinsically shameful, immoral, and indeed depraved or depraving" (Finnis 1994: 1054). Appearing for the plaintiffs, Martha Nussbaum, an authority on Greek philosophy, contested that claim. Finnis's understanding of the Greek classical tradition was based on an

Sexuality in Greek and Roman Culture, Second Edition. Marilyn B. Skinner.
© 2014 John Wiley & Sons, Inc. Published 2014 by John Wiley & Sons, Inc.

erroneous reading of poorly translated texts, she maintained; there was no evidence that ancient philosophers considered same-sex erotic attachments immoral. Condemnation of such relationships "as a violation of natural law or the natural human good" was therefore "inherently theological" (Expert Witness Summary at 2, quoted by Clark 2000: 4). By inference, then, it was an establishment of religion.

As an example of what she said were the misleadingly translated passages that had given Finnis the wrong impression, Nussbaum cited the 1926 Loeb Library version of Plato's last treatise, the *Laws*. There, the philosopher several times appears to condemn same-sex copulation explicitly, at 636c and again at 836c and 841d, as "contrary to nature." She testified, however, that the translator, R. G. Bury, had rendered the Greek in keeping with the shame and embarrassment about homosexuality commonly felt at that time, giving it a far more negative cast than was appropriate. In a subsequent article defending her testimony, Nussbaum explained that Plato repeatedly expresses fears about the threat posed to rational judgment by all the physical drives – hunger and thirst as well as sex. He focused on the dangers of same-sex relations in the *Laws* not because he viewed them as wrong, but because they were "especially powerful sources of passionate stimulation" (Nussbaum 1994: 1580). As for the statements that homosexuality is "contrary to nature," that is, to the practices of the animal kingdom, Nussbaum noted that they occurred each time in imaginary public pronouncements and construed them as rhetorical devices for convincing the ordinary man. Appeals to animal nature would carry little weight with Plato himself because he would say that a rational being cannot be guided by the behavior of nonrational creatures (1994: 1576–7, 1631, 1633, 1639).

After Nussbaum had finished her direct testimony, Robert George, a political scientist from Princeton, was brought in on rebuttal. Ensuing controversy dealt with the correct translation of certain passages of Plato's *Laws* and, in fact, upon the single word *tolmêma* ("act of daring") at 636c, which Nussbaum asserted was morally neutral and her opponent claimed to be pejorative. Both sides based their arguments for the meaning of the word upon the entry given in the most authoritative dictionary of ancient Greek, though they relied upon two different editions of the same dictionary. There is no need to go into all the philological technicalities, or all the courtroom charges and countercharges, whose repercussions continued on in print as fiercely argued follow-up discussions by participants appeared in academic and legal journals. Eventually, both the Colorado District and Supreme Courts found for the plaintiffs, and the United States Supreme Court ruled in 1996 that Amendment 2 was unconstitutional.

None of the judicial opinions issued by the various courts cited evidence from Greek texts in making a determination. Nevertheless, the philosophical and ethical issues raised in the Amendment 2 case indicate that informed discussion of Greco-Roman sexual protocols has the potential to shed valuable new light on modern controversies about sexuality. What was unfortunate about *Evans* v. *Romer*, as observers have since pointed out, was that the actual courtroom exchanges focused narrowly on Plato's attitude toward male–male *copulation*, which is, indeed, of a piece with his distrust of all forms of sexual pleasure, including that provided by heterosexual acts. His well-known insistence that sublimated homoerotic *affect*, divorced from physical expression, can be an impetus toward moral and intellectual good was not given any weight in testimony, despite the fact that "Platonic love," as an ideal, is affirmed not only in his earlier dialogues the *Phaedrus* and the *Symposium* but also at *Laws* 837d, where it is stipulated that "the love belonging to virtue and desiring that a young man be as good as possible" should operate in his model state. But homoerotic feelings are completely beyond the scope of the law, which can only take cognizance of acts (Mendelsohn 1996: 43–4). Thus the two discourses – that of the academy, where ancient texts are interpreted, and that of the courtroom – are, in a sense, inexorably fated to disagree with one another.

Provided it is done in a less adversarial setting, however, bringing a historical consciousness of Greek and Roman sexuality to discussions of public policy does open up broader perspectives on a given question. Reflecting upon the lessons of *Evans* v. *Romer*, Randall B. Clark points out that the *Laws* "offers its readers a provocative presentation of the problematic character of both homosexual desire and the family, as well as a thoughtful consideration of the appropriate governmental role in the regulation of both – pressing issues still" (2000: 6). He foresees an investigation of Plato's moral position on same-sex eroticism serving as the starting point for timely inquiry into the overall relationship between personal behavior and the public good. What is true in this instance for Platonic doctrine seems no less valid for Greek and Roman sexuality as a whole field of knowledge. Studying the sexual values and practices of the ancient world with the goal of arriving at a more accurate understanding of them is not a frivolous undertaking but a matter of genuine practical concern.

Thinking about Sexuality

Under the entry "**sexuality**," the *Oxford English Dictionary Online* lists four related definitions: first, "the quality of being sexual or having sex"; second, "possession of sexual powers, or capability of sexual feelings"; third, "recognition of or preoccupation with what is sexual"; and, finally, "appearance distinctive of sex."[1] In current academic parlance, however, the word is often employed in two additional, more theoretical, senses. First, it can denote the meanings placed upon human sexual physiology, sexual sensations, and sexual behavior within a particular community, "the cultural interpretation of the human body's erogenous zones and sexual capacities" (Halperin et al. 1990: 3). Second, it can also designate the dominant role that sexual inclinations, particularly object preference, are thought to play in the shaping of subjective identity. This last definition of "sexuality" has emerged only recently in the contemporary Western world, and, in gaining recognition, has acquired a troubled history.

The ancient Greeks, who had a specialized word for so many other things, had none for what we mean by "sexuality." The nearest parallel in the Greek language is the collective expression *ta aphrodisia*, "the matters of Aphrodite" (Dover 1973: 59; 1978: 63–4). What Greek culture regarded as the preserve of the goddess of love was an ensemble of separate but closely related physical phenomena – sexual acts, urges, and pleasures. Although Latin, like Greek, had a rich vocabulary, both direct and metaphoric, for sexual organs and sexual acts, it too lacked an encyclopedic concept of the sexual. This explains why Adams's 1982 study of Latin sexual terminology confines itself to terms for the body parts and the activities associated with them.

That difference in conceptualization is thought to mark a profound cultural difference. The historian of sex **Michel Foucault** distinguishes *ta aphrodisia* from "sexuality" in this way: "Our idea of 'sexuality' does not just cover a wider area; it applies to a reality of another type, and it functions quite differently in our morals and knowledge" (1986: 35). Whereas modern English speakers can form an abstract idea of human sexual behavior, Greeks and Romans supposedly viewed it in more concrete terms. For them, what was sexual was presumably limited and self-evident, as opposed to our notion of a broadly diffused and often masked biological and psychological drive. In addition, they appear to have attached a very different set of moral weights to certain expressions of sexuality, most notably same-sex eroticism. Whether this formulation is entirely accurate or not is one of the issues to be considered in this book.

In ancient Greek and Latin, the name of a divinity may be a metonymy, or verbal substitute, for what he or she oversees. So "**Aphrodite**" or "**Venus**," her Roman equivalent, can euphemistically mean "sex." As the name Aphrodite is hard to fit into meter, Greek poetry usually refers to the goddess as "**Cypris**," a title derived from her traditional birthplace, Cyprus, a large island lying south of the Turkish peninsula. Another deity who watches over the sphere of physical wants and satisfactions is **Eros** ("Desire"), often identified as Aphrodite's son; his Roman name is "**Cupid**" (from *cupido* "desire"). While Eros, the god, is connected mainly with sexual passion, which he arbitrarily inflicts upon divinities and mortals, the semantic range of the abstract noun *erôs* extends well beyond the sexual. Homeric heroes, for example, have an appetite, *eros*, for food and drink (*Il.* 1.469, etc.).[2] Similarly, *himeros* and *pothos*, both translated as "yearning," can be used to express a sentimental or sad longing that may or may not be sexual in nature. In **Aristophanes'** *Frogs* the god **Dionysos** confesses a *pothos* to **Heracles**, who immediately asks whether it is for a woman or a boy; no, the god of theater explains, it is for the recently deceased tragedian **Euripides** (55–67). Like Eros, the affective states of *himeros* and *pothos* can be personified, but only as an artistic convention, because their divine personalities are never fully realized. Finally, *erôs* as "desire" must be carefully distinguished from ***philia***, the love we bestow on those close to us, family members and friends. In this book, the name of the god Eros will be capitalized and not italicized; the Greek noun *erôs* should be understood to mean a form of sexual passion or obsession; and feelings of *philia* will be termed "affection."

Sex Changes

In the late 1950s and early 1960s, open discussion of intimate matters was seldom conducted in university classrooms. Yet, even after the most cursory reading of certain texts, Classics majors at American colleges and universities were aware that many ancient authors took sex for granted and spoke frankly about it, making casual references to forms of desire, behavior, and acts then deemed "unnatural" by all but a relatively small minority of the population.[3] Those students could not help but acknowledge that in Greece and Rome, the two foundational cultures of Western Europe, there existed a set of moral standards quite distinct from the ones by which they had been raised. While it would have been impossible then to bring up that fact in the classroom, consciousness of it *as fact*, and a predictable curiosity, were enough to motivate future scholars within their ranks to investigate ancient sexual notions enthusiastically once the academic climate permitted it.

Meanwhile, in a paradigm shift originating after the First World War and gaining great momentum around the middle of the twentieth century, cultural institutions central to industrialized Western society underwent radical structural changes. In particular, the attitudes, beliefs, values, and practices associated with gender and sexuality found themselves subjected to considerable transformation. In America, the reasons why a prior emphasis on restraint was replaced by a new sexual liberalism are complicated, but D'Emilio and Freedman (1988: 239–74) identify a number of issues that contributed to this development. In 1960, approval of the oral contraceptive pill by the Food and Drug Administration gave women the freedom to make their own reproductive choices, including postponing marriage and motherhood while being sexually active. Besides the accessibility of a reliable contraceptive, larger contributing factors included the spread of a youth subculture and an increased preoccupation with sexual satisfaction among middle-class married couples. The same phenomenon was occurring across the Atlantic, throughout Europe but perhaps most visibly in England during the "Swinging Sixties," a period later labeled "the permissive era" (Weeks 1989: 249–72). Philip Larkin's deeply ironic take upon the behavior of English young people at that time sums up the reaction of many witnesses to the onset of such an extraordinarily sudden adjustment of British mores:

> Sexual intercourse began
> In nineteen sixty-three
> (Which was rather late for me) –
> Between the end of the *Chatterley* b~~
> And the Beatles' first LP.
> Up till then there'd only been
> A sort of bargaining,
> A wrangle for a ring,
> A shame that started at sixteen
> And spread to everything.
> Then all at once the quarrel sank:
> Everyone felt the same,
> And every life became
> A brilliant breaking of the bank,
> A quite unlosable game.[4]

Experience of what is still popularly termed a "sexual revolution" suggested to many observers even then that cultural expressions of sex required much more in the way of explanation than a mere appeal to universal biological processes.

Under the motto "the personal is political," radical feminists in the United States, educated in activist theory and tactics by their participation in the civil rights and anti-war movements of the 1960s, began analyzing heterosexual relations as the expression of a social power imbalance between men and women. Second-wave feminist theorists started from the premise that, for women, the so-called "revolution" was not a vehicle of emancipation and, in fact, had opened up additional opportunities for sexual exploitation by men. They proceeded to define medical and psychological explanations of woman's nature and needs, along with rape and other forms of physical aggression against women, as strategies of gender oppression (Shulman 1980; Eisenstein 1983: 5–41; Donovan 1985: 141–69). Feminist anthropologists and sociologists followed suit by inquiring into the apparent universality of female subordination and the socialization of women into gender roles (Ortner 1974 and other essays in the same volume; see also the collection edited by Reiter 1975). Lesbian theorists questioned whether heterosexuality itself is a strictly biological or a culturally imposed phenomenon (Rubin 1975; Rich 1980). Notions that "natural features of gender, and natural processes of sex and reproduction, furnish only a suggestive and ambiguous backdrop to the cultural organization of gender and sexuality" and that "sexuality is socially shaped and, in the course of this, inevitably curbed" (Ortner and Whitehead 1981: 1, 25) were very much in the air during the late 1970s, largely due to feminist analysis of the interrelationship of social systems and sexual practices.

Within this climate of intellectual dispute over long-held assumptions about sex and gender, the timely appearance of two ground-breaking investigations of sexuality commanded immediate scholarly attention. Published in France in 1976, and in English translation two years later, the first volume of Michel Foucault's projected six-volume *History of Sexuality* supplied a fresh theoretical perspective for the analysis of sexual experience. In undertaking to write an account of sexuality, the French historian and philosopher was not concerned with what people have actually been doing in and out of bed, but rather with how such activities have been classified by those endowed with medical, legal, and scientific authority. Foucault argued that modern societies have developed whole new disciplines aimed at promoting analytical discussion of sex, as well as whole new categories of persons fundamentally defined by their sexual practices and object choices. By encouraging people to get at the obscure "truth" of their private sexuality through therapies such as psychoanalysis, present-day systems of government are able to regulate the behavior of individuals more efficiently, often with their full cooperation. Foucault was by no means the first to propose that the forms sexuality takes in a given society are closely linked to the ways in which power is organized. Nevertheless, his exploration of the tactics used in recent times to convert sexuality into a "technology" capable of regulating the activities of individuals and entire populations sparked off keen interest in the question of whether, at other historical moments, societies had developed different kinds of frameworks for categorizing sexual behaviors and attaching significance to them.

As if in response to that very question, in the same year in which the English translation of Foucault's *History of Sexuality, Volume I* appeared, **K. J. Dover**'s *Greek Homosexuality* (1978) was published. Occasional discussions of sexual behavior in antiquity had been published before, either privately or under a pseudonym. These, however, were tendentious: authors assembled information about Greek and Roman sexual conduct for sensational purposes or in order to make a political point and were not interested in studying the topic for its own sake (Halperin et al. 1990: 7–13). Dover's was the first empirical book-length scholarly investigation of the social conventions governing same-sex eroticism among ancient Greek males. He could not go into the "facts" of personal relationships, for we lack trustworthy information about the feelings and activities of individuals. Instead, he intended to define the cultural values surrounding homosexuality in the classical Greek world and to analyze how accepted homosexual and heterosexual behaviors were integrated with one another (1978: 2).

Having examined textual evidence drawn from comedy, forensic speeches, philosophical discourses, and poetry, together with visual evidence from Athenian vases of the sixth and fifth centuries BCE, Dover concluded that erotic relationships between adult Athenian men and adolescent boys, not just slaves but freeborn citizen youths, were regarded as normal, natural, and even commendable, provided certain social rules were properly observed. Sexual desire for a boy was spoken of in terms no different from those in which desire for a woman was expressed. A man might readily turn from a love object of one sex to one of the other; alternatively, a strong preference for one sex over the other was thought simply a matter of taste. Finally, and most crucial of all for subsequent work on ancient sexuality, Dover argued that the Greeks conceptualized any act of sexual congress involving at least one adult male as a dominance–submission relationship in which the adult male was expected to assume the "active" role of penetrator; conve
trated, whether woman, boy, or other adult male, was a
"passive" female status (1978: 100–9). Athenian sexuality
along the same hierarchical lines as Athenian society. The in
adult citizen male to females, prostitutes of both sexes, slav
and those men alleged to prefer the passive role was conf
bodies for his own gratification, while their social inferiori
accessibility as sexual objects. This is the so-called "**penetr**
sexuality.

Although Dover's study was addressed to fellow classi
reputation outside his own discipline because the findings
tailed so neatly with a newly emerging method of looking a
phenomenon. Responding to the theoretical model sketch
Foucault's *History of Sexuality*, researchers had begun
changes in patterns of sexual conduct. They identified two
the organization of sexuality throughout classical antiqui
contemporary Western world. Sex relations were structur
trast to our ideal of equality between the partners, and the gender roles of active and passive partner were not tied to sex – for the person in the submissive role, at

least, structural "femininity" was the consequence of lower status, not sex. The foreignness of ancient sexual arrangements became the standard case in point for the controversial assertion that sexual identity and sexual practices are products of local circumstances and thus an argument for replacing biologically determinist assumptions about sexuality with those grounded on historical difference.

Checking the Right Box

At this point we ought to sort out another set of classification terms readily confused in daily life: sex, gender, and sexuality. "**Sex**" as a category of identification is no doubt the simplest of these, for it designates the (usually straightforward) physiological result of a combination of XX or XY chromosomes, the possession of female or male primary and secondary physical characteristics. On the other hand, "**gender**," originally a linguistic expression, was appropriated by feminists in the 1970s to mean the social and cultural constructions of masculinity and femininity associated with biological sex (West and Zimmerman 1987: 125–6). This distinction between bodily, primarily genital and reproductive, differences and the abstract system of expected traits and behaviors imposed upon them has been deemed the single most crucial advance contributed by late twentieth-century feminism to social theory (Flax 1990: 21; Sedgwick 1990: 27–8). Once gender had been identified as a cultural production, it was seen to mask an asymmetrical relation between social identities, one in which the disadvantaged position of the female might coolly be explained away as a consequence of "nature." Throughout this book, accordingly, we will frequently employ gender as an analytical tool when trying to grasp how ancient notions of "masculinity" and "femininity" served as placeholders for organizing experience. What we will *not* do is to adopt the bureaucratic practice of using "gender" as a putatively less crude synonym for "sex." Reducing gender to the binary opposition of "M" or "F" regularly encountered when filling in paperwork does not reflect the realities of ancient sexual protocols, or of contemporary ones, for that matter. To cite one commonplace instance: though the word "transsexual," as generally used, specifies a person living a sex other than the one assigned at birth, "transgender" can refer to a much wider range of departures from established sexual norms (Wilchins 2004: 21–31). "Gender" is thus a very fuzzy variable.

The ancients had no abstract notion of gender. Their idea of sexual binarism was not the same as ours, either.[5] For one thing, the word "unisex" would be hard to explain to a Greek or a Roman. That men and women lived for the most part in separate spheres was taken for granted. Similarly, "transsexual" and "transgender" are easily thinkable within our own cultural frameworks; that is, we have a medical understanding of those rare individuals born with the physical characteristics of both sexes, and we ourselves can imagine, even if we have never met, a person whose gender subjectivity is not aligned with her/his sexual category. Ancient society drew firmer lines. In our text we will regularly encounter stereotypes of androgynous *conduct*, men behaving in a womanish fashion or women thought to take the manly role in sex. Crossing boundaries of deportment was only too easy and was evidence of moral failings. Dual sexuality, or the possession of both sets of primary sexual characteristics, was quite another matter. In classical Greek and Roman thought systems, those creatures, known as **hermaphrodites**, violated the law of nature, which draws absolute distinctions between the sexes; accordingly, they were prodigies, indications of divine displeasure, and at certain periods legally condemned to exposure (Brisson 2002: 14–15). In the Hellenistic age, however, artists began to visualize the hermaphrodite as a mortal youth ideally combining the distinct beauties of masculinity and femininity. Hence the Louvre Hermaphrodite, whose profile and upper arm grace our cover, and whom you probably took for a girl until you noticed the biceps. (Nowadays everyone wants solid biceps, but up until very recently only men were supposed to have them.) Such a figure belonged to the realm of fantasy, like our unicorns.

"Sexuality," as we have already observed, encompasses a group of meanings no less broad than that of gender. Moreover, when "sex" is utilized as the equivalent of "sexuality," as it often is, to mean the entire assortment of acts, codes, desires, fantasies, pleasures, and role playing involved in human sexual conduct, additional difficulties arise. As Eve Kosofsky Sedgwick notes, the semantic field of "sex/sexuality" in this latter sense "is all over the experiential and conceptual map" because it takes in the extremes of both the biological and the cultural together with much in between (1990: 29). Clarifying the further entanglement of "sex/sexuality" with gender requires still more analytic precision, for the complexity of these multiple frames of reference ensures that some aspects of sex and gender will be aligned with each other at the biogenetic end of the spectrum, others united at the cultural end, while still others may prove completely autonomous, or even opposed. Yet in current work on the history of sexuality it is very tempting to conflate sexuality and gender because of a scholarly preoccupation with the dichotomy of heterosexual/homosexual orientation as it may or may not manifest itself in surviving records. To see why that problem is so central to an investigation of ancient sexuality, we need to examine past and present debate over the theoretical stances of **essentialism** and **constructionism**.

During most of the twentieth century, approaches to the topic of sex/sexuality assumed an "essentializing" point of view. Whether they attempted an empirical description of values and practices as found in given societies or an explanation of its psychic mechanisms, they envisioned sex, in Jeffrey Weeks's words, as "a driving, instinctual force, whose characteristics are built into the biology of the human animal, which shapes human institutions and whose will must force its way out, either in the form of direct sexual expression or, if blocked, in the form of perversion or neuroses" (1989: 2). This quasi-Freudian notion of sexual psychodynamics dominated the thinking of academics and the general public through the middle decades of the twentieth century and still enjoys some popular acceptance, though its tenets have been repeatedly questioned, first by feminists and then by Foucault and his disciples.[6] Another generalizing account of sexuality is the sociobiological, which identifies supposedly basic, universal patterns of male and female behavior and explains them as evolutionary strategies for procreative success: through processes of natural selection, it hypothesizes, gender-specific conduct has been "hardwired" into the human brain. To cite one passage from a recent British description of human sexuality aimed at the lay reader:

> We have inherited a behavioural legacy from the lifestyle of our hunter-gatherer ancestors, which continues to mould much of our behaviour. Men are more driven by the immediate, short term gratification of sexual intercourse, although they often love and invest in the children they father. Women have evolved to be driven by a broader range of strategies for producing surviving offspring, networking with one another and with a special ability to juggle the many demands of raising a family. (Potts and Short 1999: 235)

Anthropological observations and historical records do show large congruencies in gendered behavior across cultures and centuries, such as the existence of a "double standard" for men and women. Yet, according to researchers whose thinking has been shaped by feminist, gay, and lesbian investigations of sex and gender, neither Freudianism nor genetic determinism can satisfactorily explain the multiplicity of culturally unique patterns sex takes.[7] Both accounts, it is obvious, leave little room for variation from compulsory heterosexuality. Though Freud himself did not consider same-sex desire "degenerate," he saw heterosexual object choice as the preferred outcome of the maturation process begun at puberty (1962: 1–14, 95–6). Meanwhile, **sociobiology**, with its focus on reproductive advantage, cannot offer a plausible evolutionary reason for homoerotic inclination.

During the past three decades, therefore, scholars espousing a "constructionist" approach to human sexuality have attempted to demonstrate that there are relatively few underlying features of sex so embedded in nature that they may be deemed constant. Sexuality, from this historical and critical perspective, is so shaped by cultural forces and mediated by factors such as language that it must be seen as exclusively the product of a particular society (Weeks 1989: 1–6). Indeed, Foucault actually proposed, in one of his most drastic formulations, that the abstract idea of "sex" was itself a construct, a by-product of the nineteenth-century deployment of "sexuality" as a technology of social control. Sex does not underlie sexuality; the reverse is true (Foucault 1980: 152–7; cf. Halperin 2002: 87–9).

For a historian, then, the key problem at issue is the emergence of "homosexual" and its corollary "heterosexual" as categories of personal identity. Although individuals with a dominant or exclusive attraction to members of their own sex have probably always existed, scientific, medical, and layman's discourses categorizing them as a deviant social group and obliging them to acquiesce in that description of themselves arose only at the end of the nineteenth century (Foucault 1980: 42–3). From an extreme constructionist point of view, then, there were no "homosexuals" prior to the actual invention of the term; there were only homosexual acts. Consequently, the theory that homosexual desire is a learned response to environmental conditioning that reflects changing social and economic conditions is an assumption with which Foucault's name is very often associated. He himself never took an explicit position on the question of whether homosexuality is caused by biological or social factors and at least once refused to commit himself when pressed about the topic (Halperin 1995: 4).

That disagreement between proponents of "essentialist" and "constructionist" approaches to sex is not a mere academic controversy remote from daily life; it has immediate political repercussions. If patterns of human sexuality are a biologically determined certainty, it could be argued that homosexuality is innate and not a matter of personal choice; this would allow us "to consider sexual orientation in the same deterministic frame of reference that we have been accustomed to use for race" and confer the same set of ethical and legal protections upon it (Nye 1999: 6). However, an essentializing perspective might equally well be employed in order to demonstrate the intrinsic superiority of heterosexual marriage to other kinds of social arrangements, to justify different ways of treating men and women in the workplace, and even to allow disparate access to resources based solely upon gender. Suspicion that a theoretical acceptance of "natural" sexual arrangements can only further the repressive political agenda of social conservatives has given essentialist approaches to sex a bad name among feminists and queer theorists.

Constructionist thinking, on the other hand, presupposes that sexuality, not being underpinned by nature, is inherently unstable and its continuity of organization more apparent than real: new configurations of economic, political, and social power necessarily elicit new paradigms of gender and sexuality. Such assumptions mandate flexibility and relativism in weighing sexual behaviors, especially those that might be considered marginal or "**queer**" in relation to prevailing social standards. This stance, too, has practical implications that certain groups have found threatening. Some feminists object that constructionism dismisses the "noncoincidental" recurrence of similar patterns of gender oppression in unrelated cultures (Richlin 1992: xix–xx), while gay historians fear that it renders gay history impossible (Boswell 1989: 20). Insistence that "**Greek love**" had nothing in common with modern-day homosexuality could be taken as a repudiation of the iconic place of Greece (and, to a lesser extent, Rome) in the dawning gay activist movement of the 1950s and 1960s (Richlin 2005) and might even be construed as fundamentally homophobic, in so far as it denies the permanent reality of homoerotic orientation (Davidson 2007: 149–51). Other progressive academics can counter those protests by maintaining that a focus on change rather than inescapable continuity makes resistance to present modes of oppression more viable.

In the discipline of classical studies, scholarly debate over the validity of strict essentialist or constructionist approaches peaked in the early 1990s, the period of the "sexuality wars," when adherents of a given position resorted to abrasive, often *ad hominem*, reviews of work with which they disagreed. The fracas had a chilling effect on both research and collegiality. Since then, new theoretical postulates have suggested that the opposition of essentialism to constructionism may itself be too rigid. One significant factor in tempering the dispute has been the growing acceptance of **Judith Butler**'s contention that subjects, via their material bodies, constantly enact their gender identities: gender is performed rather than passively worn like a costume (Butler 1990, 1993). Another was the insight that "homosexuality" is not one coherent and stable category but instead encompasses several kinds of gender deviance other than that characterized by exclusive object-choice and permanent orientation (Sedgwick 1990: 44–8; Halperin 2002: 104–37). Present-day "heterosexuality" is no less polyvalent. As a historicist benchmark dividing "now" from "back then," the "homo/heterosexual" antithesis is not as clear-cut as it was once thought to have been. Hence "essentialism vs. constructionism" might well seem like a false dichotomy.

Not all current work is ready to move on, however. In 2007 James Davidson published *The Greeks and Greek Love*, a volume of over 600 pages ostensibly aimed at a general reading audience, although its length might well daunt the casual browser. The complexity of the subject, he argued, dictated the scope of the inquiry, since "Greek love," though a single phenomenon, had to be understood within an array of contexts. While Davidson did not affirm an essentialist position, he dismissed the idea that the ancient Greeks had no sexual orientations at all as "hard to believe" (2007: 4). At the same time, his furious effort to discredit the "penetration model," its proponents Dover and Foucault, and the cultural anthropology to which it owed its origins came across as an all-out war against social constructionism. Furthermore, his depiction of Greek same-sex affiliations seemed suspiciously akin to popular culture images of present-day gay male partnerships. To charges that he had distorted historical facts in order to draw a more appealing picture of Greek behaviors, the author responded acrimoniously and the old controversy opened up again, now facilitated by the technological advances of online reviewing and blogging.[8]

Davidson and his Critics

For James Davidson, an overwhelming emphasis on "sodomania," his label for an unhealthy preoccupation with forced anal sex as literal or symbolic aggression, dominates current scholarship on Greek sexuality (2007: 101–66). Davidson's "radical reappraisal" of homoerotic relationships stresses instead their communal value in forging social networks and their ideology of passionate romantic friendship. Such beneficial but often overlooked features of "Greek love" indeed demand more attention and will receive it in this book. To certain reviewers, though, Davidson's efforts to explain away its disquieting aspects fly in the face of the evidence (Jope 2008; Hubbard 2009). Assertions that the "boys" pursued by adult males were actually in their late teens to early twenties; that younger adolescents were protected by law; that puberty itself arrived later in antiquity than it does in the modern Western world; and that publicly acknowledged pair-bonding was not uncommon, especially in military units, appear to "overmuch sanitize and romanticize" ancient male same-sex desire (Verstraete 2009). While we cannot evaluate all these claims at length, we should observe that the Athenian vase paintings discussed in Chapter 3 illustrate a wide age range of courted partners, from early adolescence up to and including young manhood, and that assignment of legal penalties, including the death penalty, to molestation of under-age boys does seem to go beyond the data (Ormand 2009). I myself am skeptical about a so-called pre-industrial "puberty shift." If ancient Greek boys matured later than they do today because of dietary limitations, as Davidson thinks, this would have been even more true of girls, who were often less well nourished. In medical texts, however, the socially determined age of female puberty was set at fourteen, the period at which blood began to accumulate in the body prior to **menarche** (first menstruation) and hence the proper time for marriage (Dean-Jones 1994: 50–1). Reasons for hastening social maturation for one sex while postponing it for the other are hard to seek; consequently this drastic suggestion requires further examination before being adopted. Yet by reminding us that "Greek love" had its deeply emotional side, Davidson makes a considerable contribution and corrects a tendency to dwell upon inequalities in its power structure.

The lesson to be learned from this newest irruption of a seething issue in gay identity politics is that the longing to uncover continuities in the past rather than alterities goes deep. Though himself intellectually opposed to a "homosexual essentialism" inviting gay men to seek their counterparts in the Greeks, David Halperin can still find positive things to say about that impulse:

> Identification is desire ... Identification gets at something, something important: it picks out resemblances, connections, echo effects. Identification is a form of cognition. (2002: 15)

At the same time, psychic identification poses its dangers. Since intergenerational homoerotic relationships were the characteristic feature of institutionalized "Greek love," historians' wish to distinguish ancient liaisons with boys from what might seem the predatory exploitation of minors is pressing (Verstraete and Provencal 2005a: 3; Buffière 2007: 9–24; for a divergent outlook, Hubbard 2000). It is patently one of Davidson's motives for insisting, rightly or wrongly, on both late physiological maturation and strict rules of age in courtship (2007: 68–71). Classical Athens is thus a limit case for both essentialist perceptions of uniformity and constructionist tolerance of the unfamiliar. It is easy to go along with the former; let us see how the latter might work out in practice.

The Language and Ethos of Boy-love

Recent charges that Roman Catholic clergy, in America and elsewhere, have committed sexual offenses against children, subsequently covered up by those in authority, have stunned the general public all over the world and provoked angry protests from American Catholics. Erotic attachments between adults and adolescents, even when viewed from a historical distance, are a sensitive issue capable of arousing intense feeling in the classroom. Before we embark on a discussion of Greek **pederasty**, therefore, we need to clarify the sense of that word as it will be used in the present book by differentiating it from its common meaning in English, as well as from the expressions **pedophilia** and *homosexuality*, often used in the same general context.

We can begin by distinguishing *pedophilia* from pederasty. Pedophilia, derived from the ancient Greek words for "child" (*pais*) and "affection" (*philia*), denotes an attraction to prepubescent or pubescent children as sexual objects. Whether the subject acts on that drive or only fantasizes about it (by consuming child pornography, for example), such an inclination is deemed morally reprehensible by the vast majority of people in our society and is viewed by psychiatrists as an abnormal sexual proclivity. This is, then, the appropriate term for the sexual offenses alleged to have been committed in the diocese of Boston and elsewhere. The pedophile may be male or female and the object of his or her desire may be a girl or a boy; in neither case is the noun sex-specific. In contrast, the word pederasty, as used in ordinary English, specifies the desire felt by an adult male for a boy, or the concomitant sexual act, with the word "boy" usually understood to mean "preadolescent." Thus pederasty is by definition homosexual, although "homosexuality" commonly implies consenting sexual behavior among adults, while both "pedophilia" and "pederasty" as labels for present-day sexual conduct designate the abuse of a victim below the age of consent.

When classical scholars utilize the noun "pederasty," however, they draw an even finer set of distinctions. Pederasty designates the social custom whereby adult male Greeks courted citizen youths, as sexual objects but also, at least notionally, as protégés; in fact, our Anglicized word "protégé," with its very slight nuance of indelicacy (especially in the feminine), comes close to suggesting that twofold objective. However, we do not as a rule apply "mentor" and "protégé" to the partners in the relationship, preferring the technical terms used by the ancient Greeks themselves: **erastês** ("lover") for the adult male and **erômenos** ("beloved") for the youth. The title of Dover's pioneering study notwithstanding, most scholars nowadays also distinguish the term "pederasty" from "homosexuality" by restricting the latter word to the modern Western category of sexual orientation; when they wish to emphasize the same-sex aspect of pederasty, they have recourse to the descriptive adjective "**homoerotic**."

"Youth," of course, is a vague expression, but it is generally assumed that adolescent Greek males became objects of open admiration from the time of the appearance of secondary sex characteristics at puberty until the growth of the full beard, an approximate age range of fifteen or sixteen to eighteen. Younger boys, though, were not off-limits. In the *Symposium*, Plato's speaker Pausanias, who articulates the conventional aristocratic ideology of boy-love, states that the better sort of admirer refrains from loving boys who have not yet begun to possess intelligence (*nous*), which coincides with the onset of the beard (181d). This implies that some adults did court younger boys; it also indicates that such behavior was frowned upon not because it was deemed "abnormal" or "contrary to nature," but because the boy was thought not yet mature enough mentally to make fully rational choices.[9] We differ from the Greeks, then, not just in our moral condemnation of the employment of prepubescent children for sexual purposes, but also in fixing the age of consent well beyond puberty.

Yet ancient Greek society was ambivalent even about the risks of ostensibly innocent social interchange between adults and youths, as one episode from Plato's dialogue *Charmides* indicates. Socrates, the first-person speaker, has just arrived back in Athens from military service during the first year of the Peloponnesian War (433 BCE). He tells of stopping by the wrestling school of Taureas and asking whether any of the current crop of young men has shown himself outstanding "in wisdom, or beauty, or both." Critias, a man of distinguished family, proudly mentions his relative Charmides. When this boy enters, Socrates at once acknowledges his beauty. Informed that he is also interested in philosophy and writes poetry, the philosopher expresses a desire to meet him and asks Critias to call him over. "Even if he were younger," Socrates says, "there's nothing shameful about my conversing with him in your presence, since you're both his guardian and his cousin" (155a). The two men concoct an excuse: Socrates supposedly knows a cure for the headaches the boy has been experiencing. After Charmides is seated beside him, and the surrounding crowd presses up against them, Socrates confesses to catching a glimpse of what he should not have seen (155d–e):

> Right then, my good man, I saw what was beneath his cloak and I burst into flame and was no longer in command of myself and thought the poet Cydias wisest in respect to erotic matters, who, speaking of a beautiful boy, advises someone: "Take care not to be seized as a ration of meat, a fawn coming before a lion." For I seemed to myself to have been caught by such a creature.

Of course, Socrates quickly recovers his aplomb and turns the talk back to questions of virtue. His frank admission of physical temptation kindled through a single inadvertent glance needs to be kept in mind, though, especially by readers saturated, as we are, with media images of sex. We might also think carefully about his discretion in assuring Critias that a conversation with Charmides would not be construed as improper provided an adult kinsman was present, and about the fact that he and Critias needed to invent a pretext for summoning Charmides to meet him. This is a culture at once more candid about young men's sexual appeal for older men and much more prudish about it.

Understanding why erotic relationships between men and youths were permitted will be possible only if we step back to survey other cultural factors, including the ethical climate. It may be useful, then, to undertake a constructionist thought experiment in which we attempt to comprehend the ethics of Athenian pederasty from the perspective of the Greeks themselves.[10] Making an effort at the outset to grasp one of the most perplexing features of classical Greek sexuality should give us good practice in thinking ourselves into an alien mindset – a skill required of all historians. As a convenient guide, we can follow the line of inquiry outlined in the second volume of Foucault's *History of Sexuality*, published in English under the title *The Use of Pleasure* (1986). The reader should be aware, however, that employing Foucault's account of Greek sexuality for this purpose does not amount to a blanket endorsement of it. Later on, we will engage with criticism of his thinking by expert Greek and Roman social historians.

First, some background. As we have already noted, the accepted age of sexual maturity in the ancient world was a few years lower than ours. Puberty marked the beginning of sexual activity for an ancient Greek girl as well as her brother: soon after its onset, at the age of thirteen or fourteen, she was married off – with medical justification and encouragement – to a man who might easily be twice as old as she was. Boswell observes that romantic dealings between men and boys were thus part of a large pattern of cross-generational erotic relations (1989: 32). For both sexes, too, the years between the end of childhood and full maturity were a period of gradual socialization, marked by discrete stages of development. Virgin girls did not become women (**gynaikes**) immediately upon the wedding night, but instead remained in a kind of liminal state, halfway between maiden and wife, until the birth of their first child. Adolescent boys were successively admitted to their clan-group or *phratry* at the age of sixteen and to membership in a tribe, with accompanying legal rights, upon reaching eighteen. Only at nineteen or twenty were they able to particilate in public affairs as full members of the citizen body, probably after completing two years of informal military schooling or, from the late fourth century BCE on, compulsory service as trainees, ***ephêboi*** ([Arist.] *Ath. pol.* 42).

During this transitional period, older mentors coached them in the gender-related activities they would perform for the rest of their lives. Such instruction took place, for the most part, outside the natal home. The teenage bride frequently moved into a household (***oikos***) in which the groom's widowed mother already lived and was taught domestic arrangements by her mother-in-law. Under special circumstances, the husband might undertake her training; in the treatise *On Household Management* by the essayist **Xenophon**, the principal speaker Ischomachus educates his fourteen-year-old bride in domestic science (*Oec.* 7.5–6). Boys of the same age learned to conduct themselves as men by attending all-male banquets, ***symposia***, in the company of relatives and by imitating older peers at the gymnasium. As Plato's speaker Pausanias emphasizes (*Symp.* 184d–e), the good example of an *erastês* was thought to be instrumental in developing traits of character. Hence, social historians of ancient Greece often describe the phenomenon of institutionalized pederasty as a gender-specific mode of **initiation**: in classical Athens it would have been the masculine analogue to marriage, the girl's rite of passage. Whether its origins can be traced back to prehistoric initiation rituals is a question to be discussed in Chapter 2.

Though we cannot recover the actual experiences of persons involved, we must bear in mind that for the younger partner in such an erotic relationship the liaison may not always have been a positive experience. Let us again compare that boy with his recently married sister. The code of conduct expected of a new bride, stressing modesty, self-control, and submissiveness, was straightforwardly articulated by the culture. Boys courted by male lovers, on the other hand, found themselves subject to conflicting directives: a well-behaved youth was expected to resist the physical advances of any suitor but might (or might not) be commended for gratifying at last a patient, generous, and morally deserving *erastês*. Dover notes the close parallel with the rules prescribed for the woman, up until recently, in modern heterosexual courtship (1978: 88–90). Exactly like girls of my generation, then, adolescent Greek boys were given mixed messages about the conduct expected of them.

Athenian brides were also in a somewhat better position to turn to their elders for advice. The girl had married with her family's consent. Though she now belonged to another household, her mother and other female relatives might still live in close proximity. Sympathetic and experienced women would consequently be around to help her adjust to her circumstances and offer guidance on matters of sex and pregnancy. To be sure, some *erômenoi* may have received equally good counseling and supervision; in Xenophon's *Symposium*, the young athlete Autolycus attends a dinner at his admirer's house while chaperoned by his father. However, the boy's family could also create difficulties for both parties. If under eighteen, the youth was still subject to the authority of his father, who might put his son in the charge of a slave attendant (***paidagôgos***) to discourage the attentions of suitors (Pl. *Symp.* 183c). While no Athenian law specifically prohibited an adult male from having sex with a boy of citizen status, David Cohen (1991: 176–80) has suggested that a family could prosecute it as a violation of the boy's honor under the law of **hybris**, which punished any action that gratified the perpetrator by shaming another person – man, woman, child, free or slave – intentionally (Arist. *Rh*. 1378b.23–9; cf. Aeschin. 1.15).

Lack of certainty about what was expected of them and potential tensions between *erastês* and kindred were circumstances that might have made youths vulnerable to psychological manipulation. During the banquet conversation in Xenophon's *Symposium*, Socrates observes that an unscrupulous lover who verbally seduces a young man "corrupts [*diaphtheirei*] the soul of the one persuaded" (8.20). Negative physical consequences of forced sexual relations in early adolescence were also recognized. In the *Nichomachean Ethics*, Aristotle states that a disposition to sexual passivity can be created through habituation, "as in the case of those violated in youth" (1148b.27–9). The same opinion is expressed in a treatise falsely attributed to the philosopher, *Problemata* 4.26, where repeated penetration at the time of adolescent "ripeness" (**hêbê**) is said to create a quasi-natural desire through the recollection of pleasure (Dover 1978: 169–70; J. J. Winkler 1990: 67–9). Since the Greeks themselves were not unaware of the emotional and physiological hazards of pederasty, their approval of it as a social practice constitutes, as one early discussion called it, "a problem in Greek ethics."[11]

It was the ethical aspect of ancient sexuality that had begun to preoccupy Michel Foucault during the eight years between the publication of the first and the second volumes of the *History of Sexuality*. As he tells us in the introduction to the long-delayed second volume, he had arrived at the conclusion that understanding how modern individuals could conceive of themselves as persons of a given "sexuality" required a preliminary analysis of how Western man had already, in antiquity, come to look upon himself as subject to certain desires and to examine his own responses to such desires (1986: 5–6). Accordingly, Foucault undertook the study of ancient Greek concerns about appropriate sexual behavior, considering them within a broader context of overall social values. The kind of evidence he chose to consult was more limited than Dover's, for he deliberately concentrated on prescriptive texts addressed to men that dealt with the conduct expected of freeborn male citizens (1986: 22–3). In Athens, this was the only group of individuals recognized as fully accountable legal and moral agents.[12]

Democratic Athens invested each **kyrios**, or male citizen who headed a household, with patriarchal authority. This meant that the *kyrios* was himself responsible for the conduct of all other members of that household, its women, children, and slaves, and acted as their legal guardian and representative in the public sphere. At the same time, he also performed his civic duties by attending popular assemblies, voting, holding office, serving on juries, and defending the city-state in wartime. Competence to supervise the private economy of an *oikos*, to deliberate prudently on affairs of state, to manage public business, and to conduct oneself bravely on the battlefield depended upon self-mastery, **enkrateia**. The man properly in control of himself did not wholly abstain from bodily pleasures, which served as practical tests of his resolve. Instead, through meticulous training in virtue beginning in boyhood, he had become skilled in using pleasure wisely, never allowing desire, however keen, to overcome rational judgment. "Governing oneself, managing one's estate, and participating in the administration of the city were three practices of the same type," and only someone who had achieved the first objective was duly prepared to take on responsibilities in each of the other two areas (1986: 75–7).

The pleasures connected with sex posed the most difficulty. From a medical and ethical standpoint, sex was both natural and necessary, but the gratification it brought, being so intense, was open to misuse. Thus the two chief forms of immorality associated with sex were "excess and passivity" (1986: 47). For an adult male physically to assume the role of receptive partner was to surrender masculine status and assimilate oneself to the inferior female. But passivity could also be understood in a metaphoric sense, as capitulation to brute appetite in the case of someone who habitually overindulges in food, drink, or sex and becomes enslaved (we would say "addicted") to pleasure. In abandoning moderation (*sôphrosynê*), he behaves in a womanish manner; hence the paradox, from our point of view, of a habitual adulterer being thought "effeminate."[13] The courtship activities involved in a pederastic relationship with a citizen boy were therefore a prime occasion for display of self-control by the *erastês*: he had to temper his passion with reason in order to show due respect for the boy's civic status and personal autonomy.

For his part, the *erômenos* was expected to pay scrupulous attention to the distinction between honor and shame, since his youth was a preparation for manhood and he was being evaluated by onlookers for his potential to assume domestic and civic responsibilities. "By not yielding, not submitting, remaining the strongest, triumphing over suitors and lovers through one's resistance, one's firmness, one's moderation … the young man proves his excellence in the sphere of love relations" (1986: 210). Manifesting such confidence and strength of character while yet a boy, particularly in a scenario theoretically casting him as the subordinate player, augured well for his future leadership qualities. Accordingly, an *erômenos* could not define himself in his own mind as an object of pleasure; there was, in fact, a cultural reluctance to imagine him participating in enjoyment of the act. Xenophon preserves a recollection of Socrates' banquet conversation in which he voices what was apparently a common assumption: "A youth does not share in the pleasures of sex with the man, as a woman does, but soberly looks upon the other drunk with passion" (*Symp.* 8.21). He must not even feel desire himself: instead, he complies with his lover's requests only out of esteem and gratitude, in anticipation of a lifelong friendship (*philia*) once the older man's ardor has cooled. As the underlying ethical preoccupation of Greek pederasty, this question of "how to make the object of pleasure into a subject who was in control of his pleasures" (1986: 225) ultimately became the catalyst of the "Socratic-Platonic" definition of *erôs* as the means by which both partners arrive at philosophical truth through strict asceticism, totally abstaining from carnal satisfaction (1986: 229–46).

Apparently originated by Socrates,[14] then greatly elaborated in two of Plato's major dialogues, the *Symposium* and the *Phaedrus*, this erotics draws an absolute distinction between love of the body and love of the soul. All admirers of beauty are naturally kindled by the physical charms of a youth, but the true lover is even more warmly attracted to his beloved by the boy's integrity of character and potential for growth in virtue. He therefore seeks, in the well-known imagery of the *Symposium*, to "beget" wisdom in the other and so engender offspring that are immortal (208b–209e). Physical consummation of *erôs* is, however, incompatible with the pursuit of spiritual goodness, and the lover must forcibly check his baser impulses like a charioteer restraining an unruly horse. Inspired by the older man's example, the beloved himself develops a passion for truth; he begins to take an active part in the philosophic quest, responding to his lover's *erôs* with a reciprocal *anterôs* (*Phdr.* 255e.1). From that lover, now his teacher, the young man learns the practices of self-restraint and rational inquiry that will allow him to participate as an equal partner in the lifelong pursuit of wisdom.

This combination of altruistic devotion, sexual asceticism, and the quest for mystic experience enjoyed a long afterlife in the Christian West – although, as Foucault notes (1986: 229–30), under Christianity the Greek homoerotic relationship was transformed into a union of male and female and featured feminine embodiments of temptation (Morgan le Fay in the *Morte d'Arthur*) and redemption (Beatrice in Dante's *Divine Comedy*). Whether the object of desire is a boy or a woman, however, the fundamental ideology remains the same: steadfast mutual desire, *erôs*, becomes the means by which both partners, through suffering and perseverance, achieve mastery over their ignoble passions and arrive at the highest good – a rational understanding of absolute Being or a redemption bestowed through divine grace.

According to Foucault's analysis, then, the Greek institution of pederasty indeed posed a problem in ethics. Yet the actual moral issue was framed differently from the way in which members of our own culture would conceive of it. From our perspective, the wrongdoing in pederastic relations involves the unjust exploitation of a trusting or helpless victim by someone in a position of power. The Greeks regarded the adolescent citizen boy as a self-sufficient human being able to make a rational decision about sex and quite capable of behaving with dignity and honor in a homoerotic relationship. Nevertheless, the young man's susceptibility to persuasion due to relative lack of experience created an area of cultural anxiety, largely because of the negative effect any impression of dishonorable conduct would later have on his civic and social status. Because a Greek pederastic relationship, as ideally conceived, conformed to the dominance–submission paradigm of sexual intercourse, yet constituted a privileged venue for the mutual exhibition of virtuous self-mastery, interaction between the partners was invested with peculiar moral tensions that we, approaching it with an opposed set of assumptions, find ourselves at something of a loss to reconstruct.

If the ancient Greeks, like the very rich, are different from you and me – and not just in their sexual customs – ancient Romans, on the other hand, are often thought to resemble us far too closely. Yet a quick glance at the kind of jokes they laughed at will demonstrate that they, too, had some very unusual notions about sex.

Foul Mouths

Analogies between imperial Rome and the modern world have always been popular in Hollywood. During the Cold War era several big-budget films used the situation of an oppressive Roman government persecuting devout Christians to moralize on the place of the man or woman of good conscience within a totalitarian system (for example, *Quo Vadis* [1951], *The Robe* [1952], *Demetrius and the Gladiators* [1954], *Ben-Hur* [1959]). Rome's decline has long served as a cautionary tale for the United States (Galinsky 1992: 53–70), and disquieting concerns about America's vulnerability as a superpower were evoked in Anthony Mann's 1964 motion picture *The Fall of the Roman Empire* (M. M. Winkler 1995: 138–46). The Oscar-winning epic *Gladiator* (2000), which pays considerable homage to the Mann film, stunningly explores one overriding social question of the new millennium: the impact of violent spectacle on an entertainment-hungry populace.

One reason why comparisons between ancient Rome and contemporary America are so readily made is that a great deal of Roman first-person literature seems quite accessible to the modern reader. Composed by authors trained in rhetoric, it is written for oral delivery and generates an immediate emotional response when it professes to communicate feeling candidly. Thus Roman love elegy invites us to identify with a passionately enamored speaker whose subjective experiences seem the same as our own because they are depicted with considerable psychological acumen. Here, for example, is **Sulpicia**, the only Roman woman whose poetry survives, tangling herself up in her own syntax as she shamefacedly apologizes to her lover for standing him up ([Tib.] 3.18 = 4.12):

> May I not be to you now, my love, the same burning obsession
>   that I seem to have been just a few days ago,
> if I have committed anything in my whole stupid youth
>   of which I should confess I have repented more
> than that I left you alone last night
>   wanting to conceal my own passion.

And here is **Ovid**, the self-styled *praeceptor amoris* ("love guru") counseling a young man in his advice manual *The Art of Love* about courting a girl (1.707–18):

> Alas, a youth has too much confidence in his own looks
>   if he waits until she asks him first.
> Let the man approach first, let the man speak imploring words:
>   she will receive flattering entreaties courteously.
> To gain her favors, ask: she's just hoping to be asked;
>   state the grounds for your appeal, and when it all began …
> But if you sense that the request is arousing smug conceit,
>   cease your efforts and step back.
> What flees, many women desire: they despise what is in front of them;
>   by coming on more gently, stop them from getting bored with you.

Such extracts from erotic lyric and elegy can give the impression that nothing has really changed in two thousand years, not even the rules of dating.

Yet, at the pole furthest from the romantic fantasies of love elegy, we find Latin graffiti, rhetorical invective, and satire packaging fierce antagonism beneath a veneer of obscene wit. Amy Richlin demonstrated in her pathbreaking study *The Garden of Priapus* that in these genres humanity is divided into two camps: "us" (the speaker and his audience) and "them" (women, foreigners, the lower classes, sexual deviants). The humorist creates comic pleasure for his readers by displacing their insecurities on to such objects of ridicule (1992: 57–70). These texts respond to widespread fears permeating upper-class Roman society, fears triggered by the competitive scrutiny of peers, built-in inequalities in the omnipresent patronage system, and the uncertainties of political life. They are our best evidence for what the Romans considered kinky, unwholesome, and disgusting. Consequently, they demand a great deal of background knowledge about underlying sexual assumptions before a reader can grasp their implications, let alone their wit.

One revealing example is a short poem by the epigrammatist **Martial** (10.40):

> Since people were always telling me
> that my Polla was spending time in secret with a *cinaedus*,
> I broke in on them, Lupus. He wasn't a *cinaedus*.

To understand what is going on here, we have to start with a definition of **cinaedus**. This is one of two derogatory terms in Latin (the other is **pathicus**) used to designate adult males who were thought to prefer receptive anal sex. In Rome, in which the conceptual scheme of sexual relations is even more macho and phallocentric than that of classical Greece, such persons were objects of scathing ridicule (Richlin 1992: 220–2, 1993; Williams 2010: 191–7). Because Polla herself cannot penetrate the *cinaedus* anally, the speaker wonders what the pair is up to.

Holt Parker, whose translation I quote, explains how our way of thinking is likely to lead us astray at this point. When Martial tells us the fellow was not after all a *cinaedus*, we naturally assume the two were found having intercourse (if not "homosexual," then "heterosexual"). Martial's audience would reach a different conclusion: if not a *cinaedus*, something much worse. The one category of sexual acts more demeaning than passive anal sex was oral sex, and the foulest thing of all was to perform it on a woman. Oral sex was repulsive because it contaminated the mouth through association with the disgusting genitalia (Richlin 1992: 26–7), and cunnilingus may have seemed particularly nauseating because of a misogynistic revulsion at menstrual blood (Williams 2010: 223). Polla's friend is therefore unmasked as a man who dirties his mouth by applying it to a woman's vagina. "Perhaps few things," Parker comments, "show the differences between our sexual system and the Romans' more vividly than these three lines" (1997: 57).

In contrast to our system of sexual identities defined by the biological sex of the partner, Roman culture built its sexual taxonomy – its method of assigning identity – upon discrete practices (Parker 1997; Williams 1992: 259–64, 2010: 178–9). The vocabulary for those practices is very specific, each verb designating only one mode of genital or oral contact. When a man, playing the role of penetrator, inserts his penis into the vagina (*futuere*), the mouth (*irrumare*), or the anus (*pedicare*) of someone else, he performs a "normal" sexual act. All other acts are abnormal and vile because the performer degrades himself in proffering his own orifice to give someone else pleasure, though, as noted, they differ in the degree of contempt attached. Roman sexual ideology also assumed that men who derived gratification from deviant sexual conduct might be inclined to one practice and therefore could categorize persons according to their preferred activity: a *pathicus* craves anal intercourse; a *fellator* enjoys performing oral sex on a man; a *cunnilingus* pleasures women. However, the term *cinaedus* was so broad in its extension that it could be applied to those who performed oral sex on men or women (or both) and even, as Craig Williams reminds us, to womanizers (2010: 224–30). Transcending the distinction of active and passive roles, this label served as an all-purpose indicator of gender deviance.

What may be even odder than this set of pigeonholes is the fact that Roman authors took such glee in sticking real or make-believe persons into them, while audiences rejoiced at seeing it done. Writing in the last decade of the Roman Republic, the poet **Catullus** labels prominent statesmen, including **Julius Caesar**, *cinaedi* (57.1–2). **Cicero**, ex-consul and leading orator, slyly insinuates in a speech before the Roman priestly college that his political opponents are given to oral sex (*Dom.* 25). During the empire, when it became imprudent to attack actual dignitaries by name, Catullus' imitator Martial published twelve books of epigrams, many of which conclude, often by way of a clever argument, that a certain fictitious target is guilty of this or that appalling habit.

The Roman man in the street might get mischievous satisfaction when a powerful figure like Caesar was slandered, but why were Martial's epigrams about made-up sexual criminals so popular among the educated classes? Ancient Roman society prescribed firm rules of correct appearance and conduct for upper-class men, who were expected to maintain a cool, imposing demeanor, self-consciously avoiding whatever might seem "feminine" in gaze, walk, gesture, or dress (Gleason 1995). This highly stratified society, where rank was designated by clothing and other visible markers, associated social standing with moral repute (the political term *boni* meant both "virtuous men" and "upper-class men"). Naturally it was obsessed with possible gaps between external appearance and inner disposition. This mindset then aroused suspicions that outwardly "manly" men were secretly effeminate, together with a corollary fear that an inadvertent look or motion, however innocent, might spell "pathic" to an acute observer. Such anxiety, Williams suggests, "surfaces in various jokes at the expense of men who give every appearance of an unimpeachable masculinity, but who are actually *cinaedi*" (2010: 212). When he assumes the stance of the investigator who uncovers dirty secrets and reveals them to the world, Martial offers readers the opportunity to join him in performing the exposé. It does not matter that his comic butts are fictitious; the reassuring message communicated to the audience is that "we are both on the proper side."

Martial's epigrams turn an implicit power struggle between individuals into entertainment. Readers project themselves imaginatively into the character of the satiric speaker, enjoying his malicious humor and the skill with which he skewers his opponent. Gladiatorial games operate on much the same principle, although audience response to man-to-man combat may have been more complex, involving identification with vanquished as well as victor (Barton 1993: 15–25). Richlin provocatively suggests that gratification from watching the degradation of the weaker by the stronger is fundamental to the thought patterns of Roman society (1992: 210). For the Romans, hostility and sexuality would therefore be two sides of the same coin. Configured hierarchically, with its gender roles prearranged upon an axis of dominance and submission, sexuality provided a handy symbolic code for making light of status differentials, threats to social standing, and the underlying fears that accompanied them.

Conclusion

On both sides of the great cultural schism in our society, there are educated men and women of strong convictions who wish to appropriate the classical past in order to justify their own principles, courses of action, and objectives. *Evans* v. *Romer*, the lawsuit discussed at the beginning of this chapter, illustrates the problems with trying to do so. True, an informed grasp of Greco-Roman social history can indeed contribute to a discourse on citizenship. It is even possible that ancient sexual protocols may be germane to public policy. However, arriving at a consensus about the correct meaning of such protocols is not easy even for trained philologists and philosophers. In attempting to fathom the evidence correctly, we can be led astray by a natural tendency to impose our own presuppositions upon a concept that seems tantalizingly akin to one with which we are familiar. Examining Athenian pederasty and Roman sexual humor as cases in point has shown why we must be sensitive to the surrounding conceptual framework of the society. Extracting strands of belief or practice from the complex fabric of ancient sexuality in order to thrust them into present debate as supposedly clinching examples is counterproductive. Any manifest lack of fit between antiquity and now will only provoke further disagreement – and some lack of fit is inevitable.

In surveying Greek and Roman sexuality, this book therefore assumes an objective and nonjudgmental stance. For the purposes of historical inquiry, it also adopts a constructionist approach, postulating that ancient sexual behaviors were socially determined responses to the overall cultural environment. Our method of study involves analyzing relationships between social institutions and prevailing attitudes to sex and gender and studying the effect of modifications to those institutions upon cultural definitions of "good" and "bad" or "normal" and "abnormal" conduct. Elements of sexual ideology indigenous to Roman culture are carefully differentiated from those characteristic of classical and Hellenistic Greece. We focus upon what is distinctive and remarkable about the sexual thinking of the ancient world, contrasting it with the beliefs about sex that most of us share today. That last strategy requires, of course, that we keep an open mind about what we learn.

Provided we allow the Greeks and Romans to remain neutral in our culture wars, looking back at antiquity may help us to gain a more balanced perspective on the twentieth century's drastic shift in sexual mores. One well-recognized justification for studying ancient Mediterranean gender systems is that they offer a *historically distanced* model for understanding how social constructions of masculinity and femininity necessarily reflect a wide array of other cultural assumptions. Sexual beliefs and values are components of more extensive gender systems. If we confront the Greco-Roman paradigm of sexuality within its own cultural setting and without passing judgment, pro or con, on the forms of expression it took, we will be better equipped to recognize presuppositions about sex that we ourselves take for granted and to determine what contemporary social purposes they may serve.

Discussion Prompts

1. The anthropologist Pierre Bourdieu coined the expression "symbolic capital" to refer to intangible resources such as prestige or honor. When lawyers (or political pundits, or professors) appeal to the examples of ancient Greece or Rome as a precedent, what symbolic capital possessed by those cultures enables speakers to do so?
2. Societies with "traditional" gender arrangements, in which men are the providers, women the domestic caretakers, and the sexuality of females is closely guarded, were until quite recently the norm in the Western world, as they still are elsewhere. What advantages do such traditional societies provide for the population as a whole? (Note: you are not being asked whether they are good or bad.)
3. Why are Freudian explanations of human sexual behavior less popular now than they were fifty years ago? What makes sociobiological explanations popular today?
4. During the Cold War era epic films set in Rome mirrored tensions between the West and the Communist bloc. What facets of imperial Roman culture as generally perceived make it useful as a cinematic model for reflecting upon the position of the United States or Great Britain in the twenty-first century?

Notes

1 "Sexuality, *n.*" *Oxford English Dictionary*, 2nd edn., ed. J. A. Simpson and E. S. C. Weiner (Oxford: Clarendon Press, 1989). *OED Online* (Oxford University Press, April 17, 2001: http://oed.com/cgi/entry/00221321).

2 One minor problem is that the abstract noun can be spelled either with an omicron (*eros*) or an omega (*erôs*). Since they mean the same, I use whichever spelling appears in the ancient text.

3 I am drawing upon my own recollections as an undergraduate student in that era. Rumors that the innocuous selections from Catullus assigned in a Latin survey course during my freshman year (fall 1957) were not fully representative of the author inspired me to purchase Merrill's complete edition and attempt to translate the less innocent poems. Trying to discover what was going on with the help of a tame translation and a noncommittal dictionary was maddening, though ultimately rewarded by shocked enlightenment. See Halperin (1990: 2–3) for an autobiographical account of studying

the same poet in the early 1970s; while he and his fellow-students were then allowed to read Catullus' obscene and pederastic texts, the lexical information needed to grasp them fully was available only as "a body of subterranean lore which circulated informally among classical scholars and was communicated from like-minded professor to student in the course of private conversations outside the classroom" (1990: 3). A textbook to be used in an undergraduate course on ancient sexuality would even at that time have been unthinkable.

4 "Annus Mirabilis," from *High Windows* (New York: The Noonday Press, Farrar, Straus and Giroux, 1974), p. 34.

5 The relationship of the contemporary idea of gender to ancient notions of sexual difference and the sexed body is examined in Holmes 2012, which appeared too late for its conclusions to be fully incorporated here.

6 I employ the term "quasi-Freudian" because Freud's own concept of the sexual drive is more

complex: though an innate, elementary psychic force, in the mature adult it is repressed by the super-ego and can be sublimated into socially beneficial kinds of expression, such as art (1930: 36–45; 1962: 104–5). Because channels of repression and sublimation are culturally specific, sexual subjectivity is shaped in part by historical circumstances; there is a sense, then, in which even the Freudian model of human sexual desire is "constructed" (Sissa 2008: 201–2).

7   For a classical scholar's critique of biological reductionism as an unsatisfactory approach to studying ancient (and modern) sex/gender systems, see Parker (2001: 330–8). The author employs anthropological theory to "defamiliarize" Greek and Roman gender categories, which, as he shows, are integral to the larger cultural system and cannot be assimilated to modern Western categories.

8   See the comments on the *Bryn Mawr Classical Review* blog (www.bmcreview.org/) regarding reviews and responses posted as *BMCR* 2008.07.20, *BMCR* 2009.09.61, *BMCR* 2009.11.03, and *BMCR* 2009.11.15.

9   A cup in Oxford by the Brygos Painter (*ARV*² 378/137; illustrated as no. R520 in Dover 1978 and Kilmer 1993) shows a mature, bearded man about to have sex with an apparently prepubescent boy. The second-century CE epigrammatist Strato celebrates the allure of a twelve-year-old, though he increases his praise of the charms of each successive year up through seventeen (*Anth. Pal.* 12.4). Twelve, then, may be the absolute minimum age at which a boy, for the Greeks, became sexually desirable. It was also felt that girls ought not to have sexual activity before puberty – even if they were prostitutes ([Dem.] 59.22).

10 Dover 1973 is a short and very accessible survey of classical Greek attitudes toward various kinds of sexual behavior between members of the same sex and between those of opposite sexes.

11 John Addington Symonds, *A Problem in Greek Ethics, being an inquiry into the phenomenon of sexual inversion, addressed especially to medical psychologists and jurists*. Symonds, a classicist, wrote his study of ancient Greek homosexuality in 1873; a decade later, it made its first appearance in a private edition of only ten copies. After his death, a revised version was appended to the first edition of Havelock Ellis's *Sexual Inversion* (1897), but Symonds's executor bought out the entire printing and prohibited any reference to the essay in the second edition (which, in turn, was suppressed by the British government). A limited edition of 100 copies finally appeared in 1901 (Halperin 1990: 4).

12 The Neopythagoreans, Hellenistic followers of the precepts of the sixth-century BCE philosopher Pythagoras, considered women moral subjects and wrote advice treatises directed especially to them, but Foucault does not take those writings into account.

13 In Greek thought, as we will see in Chapter 1, women are by nature more susceptible to passion and less capable of mastering their desires. The medical model of female physiology in the Hippocratic corpus actually denies them any control over their sexual appetites (Dean-Jones 1992).

14 The question of how far "Socrates," the speaker in Plato's dialogues, expresses opinions that can be attributed to the historical Socrates is a very difficult one. However, both Plato and Xenophon present us with a Socrates who enjoins abstinence from sexual pleasure in love affairs and proclaims the superiority of spiritual to carnal love; while these portraits are fictionalized, then, it is likely that the Socrates who inspired them advocated similar views.

References

Adams, J. N. 1982. *The Latin Sexual Vocabulary*. Baltimore, MD: The Johns Hopkins University Press.

Barton, C. A. 1993. *The Sorrows of the Ancient Romans: The Gladiator and the Monster*. Princeton, NJ: Princeton University Press.

Boswell, J. 1989. "Revolutions, Universals, and Sexual Categories." In M. B. Duberman, M. Vicinus, and G. Chauncey, Jr., (eds.), *Hidden from History: Reclaiming the Gay and Lesbian Past*. New York: New American Library. 17–36.

Brisson, L. 2002. *Sexual Ambivalence: Androgyny and Hermaphoditism in Graeco-Roman Antiquity*. Trans. J. Lloyd. Berkeley, Los Angeles, and London: University of California Press.

Buffière, F. 2007. *Éros adolescent: La pédérastie dans la Grèce antique*. Paris: Les Belles Lettres.

Butler, J. 1990. *Gender Trouble: Feminism and the Subversion of Identity*. New York: Routledge.

——. 1993. *Bodies that Matter: On the Discursive Limits of "Sex."* New York: Routledge.

Clark, R. B. 2000. "Platonic Love in a Colorado Courtroom: Martha Nussbaum, John Finnis, and Plato's *Laws* in *Evans* v. *Romer*." *Yale Journal of Law and the Humanities* 12.1: 1–38.

Cohen, D. 1991. *Law, Sexuality, and Society: The Enforcement of Morals in Classical Athens*. Cambridge: Cambridge University Press.

D'Emilio, J. and Freedman, E. B. 1988. *Intimate Matters: A History of Sexuality in America*. New York: Harper & Row.

Davidson, J. N. 2007. *The Greeks and Greek Love: A Radical Reappraisal of Homosexuality in Ancient Greece*. London: Weidenfeld & Nicolson.

Dean-Jones, L. A. 1992. "The Politics of Pleasure: Female Sexual Appetite in the Hippocratic Corpus." *Helios* 19: 72–91.

—— 1994. *Women's Bodies in Classical Greek Science*. Oxford: Clarendon Press.

Donovan, J. 1985. *Feminist Theory: The Intellectual Traditions of American Feminism*. New York: Frederick Ungar.

Dover, K. J. 1973. "Classical Greek Attitudes to Sexual Behavior." *Arethusa* 6: 59–73.

—— 1978. *Greek Homosexuality*. London: Duckworth.

Eisenstein, H. 1983. *Contemporary Feminist Thought*. Boston: G. K. Hall.

Finnis, J. M. 1994. "Law, Morality, and 'Sexual Orientation.'" *Notre Dame Law Review* 69: 1049–76.

Flax, J. 1990. *Thinking Fragments: Psychoanalysis, Feminism, and Postmodernism in the Contemporary West*. Berkeley, CA: University of California Press.

Foucault, M. 1980. *The History of Sexuality, vol. 1: An Introduction*. Trans. R. Hurley. New York: Vintage Books. [Orig. pub. as *La Volenté de savoir*. Paris: Gallimard, 1976.]

—— 1986. *The History of Sexuality, vol. 2: The Use of Pleasure*. Trans. R. Hurley. New York: Vintage Books. [Orig. pub. as *L'Usage des plaisirs*. Paris: Gallimard, 1984.]

Freud, S. 1930. *Civilization and Its Discontents*. Trans. J. Strachey. New York: W. W. Norton.

—— 1962. *Three Essays on the Theory of Sexuality*. Trans. and rev. J. Strachey. New York: Basic Books.

Galinsky, K. 1992. *Classical and Modern Interactions: Postmodern Architecture, Multiculturalism, Decline, and Other Issues*. Austin: University of Texas Press.

Gleason, M. 1995. *Making Men: Sophists and Self-Presentation in Ancient Rome*. Princeton, NJ: Princeton University Press.

Halperin, D. M. 1990. *One Hundred Years of Homosexuality and Other Essays on Greek Love*. New York: Routledge.

—— 1995. *Saint Foucault: Towards a Gay Hagiography*. Oxford: Oxford University Press.

—— 2002. *How to Do the History of Homosexuality*. Chicago and London: The University of Chicago Press.

——, Winkler, J. J., and Zeitlin, F. I. (eds.). 1990. "Introduction." In Halperin et al. (eds.), *Before Sexuality: The Construction of Erotic Experience in the Ancient Greek World*. Princeton, NJ: Princeton University Press.

Holmes, B. 2012. *Gender: Antiquity and Its Legacy*. Oxford: Oxford University Press.

Hubbard, T. K. 2000. "Pederasty and Democracy: The Marginalization of a Social Practice." In T. K. Hubbard (ed.), *Greek Love Reconsidered*. New York: William Hamilton Press. 1–11.

—— 2009. Review of J. Davidson, *The Greeks and Greek Love*. H-Histsex (February 2009): http://h-net.msu.edu/cgi-bin/logbrowse.pl?trx=vx;list=H-Histsex;month=0902;week=b;msg=Ug%2BYuljwHAbsmjyw%2BhMXhQ (accessed February 20, 2011).

Jope, J. 2008. Review of J. Davidson, *The Greeks and Greek Love*. *Gay and Lesbian Review* 15.3 (May–June): 38–9.

Kilmer, M. F. 1993. *Greek Erotica on Attic Red-figure Vases*. London: Duckworth.

Mendelsohn, D. 1996. "The Stand: Expert Witnesses and Ancient Mysteries in a Colorado Courtroom." *Lingua Franca* 6.6 (Sept./Oct.): 34–46.

Nussbaum, M. C. 1994. "Platonic Love and Colorado Law: The Relevance of Ancient Greek Norms to Modern Sexual Controversies." *Virginia Law Review* 80: 1515–651.

Nye, R. A. 1999. "Introduction: On Why History is So Important to an Understanding of Human

Sexuality." In R. A. Nye (ed.), *Sexuality*. Oxford: Oxford University Press. 3–15.

Ormand, K. 2009. Response to J. Davidson in *Bryn Mawr Classical Review* 2009.11.03

Ortner, S. B. 1974. "Is Female to Male as Nature is to Culture?" In M. Z. Rosaldo and L. Lamphere (eds.), *Woman, Culture, and Society*. Stanford: Stanford University Press. 67–87.

—— and Whitehead, H. 1981. "Introduction: Accounting for Sexual Meanings." In S. B. Ortner and H. Whitehead (eds.), *Sexual Meanings: The Cultural Construction of Gender and Sexuality*. Cambridge: Cambridge University Press. 1–27.

Parker, H. N. 1997. "The Teratogenic Grid." In J. P. Hallett and M. B. Skinner (eds.), *Roman Sexualities*. Princeton, NJ: Princeton University Press. 47–65.

—— 2001. "The Myth of the Heterosexual: Anthropology and Sexuality for Classicists." *Arethusa* 34.3: 313–62.

Potts, M. and Short, R. 1999. *Ever Since Adam and Eve: The Evolution of Human Sexuality*. Cambridge: Cambridge University Press.

Reiter, R. R. (ed.). 1975. *Toward an Anthropology of Women*. New York: Monthly Review Press.

Rich, A. 1980. "Compulsory Heterosexuality and Lesbian Existence." *Signs* 5: 631–60.

Richlin, A. 1992. *The Garden of Priapus: Sexuality and Aggression in Roman Humor*, rev. edn. Oxford: Oxford University Press.

—— 2005. "Eros Underground: Greece and Rome in Gay Print Culture, 1953-65." In B. C. Verstraete and V. Provencal (eds.), *Same-Sex Desire and Love in Greco-Roman Antiquity and in the Classical Tradition of the West*. Binghamton, NY: Harrington Park Press (co-published simultaneously as *Journal of Homosexuality* 49 nos. 3/4 [2005]). 421–61.

Rubin, G. 1975. "'The Traffic in Women': Notes on the 'Political Economy' of Sex." In Reiter (ed.), *Toward an Anthropology of Women*, 157–210.

Sedgwick, E. K. 1990. *Epistemology of the Closet*. Berkeley, CA: University of California Press.

Shulman, A. K. 1980. "Sex and Power: Sexual Bases of Radical Feminism." In C. R. Stimpson and E. S. Person (eds.), *Women: Sex and Sexuality*. Chicago: University of Chicago Press. 21–35.

Sissa. G. 2008. *Sex and Sensuality in the Ancient World*. Trans. G. Staunton. New Haven and London: Yale University Press.

Verstraete, B. 2009. Review of J. Davidson, *The Greeks and Greek Love*. *Bryn Mawr Classical Review* 2009.09.61: http://bmcr.brynmawr.edu/2009/2009-09-61.html (accessed February 20, 2011).

Verstraete, B. C. and Provencal, V. 2005a. "Introduction." In Verstraete and Provencal (eds.), *Same-Sex Desire and Love*.

Weeks, J. 1989. *Sex, Politics and Society: The Regulation of Sexuality since 1800*, 2nd edn. London: Longman.

West, C. and Zimmerman, D. H. 1987. "Doing Gender." *Gender and Theory* 1: 125–51.

Wilchins, R. 2004. *Queer Theory, Gender Theory: An Instant Primer*. Los Angeles: Alyson.

Williams, C. A. 1992. "Homosexuality and the Roman Man: A Study in the Cultural Construction of Sexuality." Unpublished PhD thesis, Yale University.

—— 2010. *Roman Homosexuality*. 2nd edn. Oxford: Oxford University Press.

Winkler, J. J. 1990. *The Constraints of Desire: The Anthropology of Sex and Gender in Ancient Greece*. New York: Routledge.

Winkler, M. M. 1995. "Cinema and the Fall of Rome." *Transactions of the American Philological Association* 125: 135–54.

Further Reading

Dover, K. J. 1978. *Greek Homosexuality*. Cambridge, MA: Harvard University Press. Essential for understanding both the basic features of institutionalized pederasty and the development of work on ancient sexuality.

Halperin, D. M. 1990. *One Hundred Years of Homosexuality*. New York and London: Routledge. Highly influential expansion of Dover's key ideas.

—— 2002. *How to Do the History of Homosexuality*. Chicago and London: The University of Chicago Press. Collection of essays dealing with specific theoretical issues involved in writing the history of homosexuality from a constructionist perspective.

Holmes, B. 2012. *Gender: Antiquity and Its Legacy*. Oxford: Oxford University Press. Groundbreaking survey of the ways in which the classical past has been employed in order to formulate modern conceptions of gender.

Hubbard, T. K. 2003. *Homosexuality in Greece and Rome: A Sourcebook of Basic Documents*. Berkeley, Los Angeles, and London: University of California Press. Compiles essential Greek and Latin materials on the topic in English translation.

Johnson, M. and Ryan, T. (eds.). 2005. *Sexuality in Greek and Roman Society and Literature: A Sourcebook*. London and New York: Routledge. Greek and Roman sources in translation, arranged thematically in order to provide a comparative perspective. Covers topics such as marriage, prostitution, sex, and violence.

Joshel, S. R., Malamud, M., and McGuire, Jr., D. T. (eds.). 2001. *Imperial Projections: Ancient Rome in Modern Popular Culture*. Baltimore and London: Johns Hopkins University Press. Essay collection exploring the ways ancient Rome has been portrayed in contemporary popular culture, especially film, and how images of Rome are deployed in present-day debates over politics and sexuality.

McClure, L. K. 2002. *Sexuality and Gender in the Classical World*. Oxford and Malden, MA: Blackwell. Useful selection of primary sources and reprinted articles, including several cited in this volume.

Ormand, K. 2009. *Controlling Desires: Sexuality in Ancient Greece and Rome*. Westport, CT: Praeger. Ormand's introduction treats many of the same questions raised in the present chapter.

Richlin, A. 2013. "Sexuality and History." In N. Partner and S. Foot (eds.) *The SAGE Handbook of Historical Theory*. London: Sage Publications. 294–310. Highly recommended survey article of work on the history of sexuality that asks provocative questions about how "history" and "sexuality," as areas of academic knowledge, intersect with each other.

1

The Homeric Age: Epic Sexuality

In traditional agricultural societies, like those of ancient Greece, sexual beliefs and practices are closely bound up with cult attached to fertility deities, mainly female. Greek women's own fecundity authorized them to intercede with powerful goddesses such as Artemis, Demeter, and Hera; wives and mothers played a leading role in rites promoting the fruitfulness of crops and animals. At female-only festivals, the celebrants' activities might include using obscene speech or handling replicas of sexual organs, because in a ritual context indecency that is otherwise taboo is charged with procreative energy (Dillon 2002: 109–38). For women in particular, then, certain facets of human sexuality possessed a numinous quality, and we must bear this in mind when reading the amatory verse of Sappho or viewing vase paintings of women tending sacred *phalloi* (models of male genitalia) as part of the Haloa festival. Although we will not deal with the ritual element in ancient sexuality at much length – that topic is more conveniently treated in a book on Greek and Roman religion – we should remember that seasonal commemorations of the erotic in human life were an important part of ordinary people's devotional experience.

Study of ancient discourses about sexuality properly begins with the archaic oral poets **Homer** and **Hesiod** and their followers who composed the **Homeric Hymns**. In the **epic** (narrative) works the *Iliad* and the *Odyssey*, Homer offers intimate glimpses of mortal and immortal couples and alludes to numerous unions of gods with mortals. Hesiod's **didactic** (instructional) poems the *Theogony* and the *Works and Days* contain important accounts of the origins of the gods Aphrodite and Eros and the first woman, **Pandora**. In the later *Homeric Hymn to Aphrodite*, the story of the goddess's seduction of **Anchises** reveals early Greek notions of the pleasures and dangers associated with sexual activity. Epic passages supplied basic models for many later Greek and Roman narratives dealing with erotic relationships. Since these poems were performed orally long before they were written

Sexuality in Greek and Roman Culture, Second Edition. Marilyn B. Skinner.
© 2014 John Wiley & Sons, Inc. Published 2014 by John Wiley & Sons, Inc.

down, and were therefore widely accessible, it is likely that they deeply influenced men's and women's perceptions of themselves as gendered beings.

For their subject matter, Hesiod and Homer drew upon myths and motifs that had been circulating since at least the third millennium BCE not only among Greek-speaking peoples of the mainland but, with variations, all over the Eastern Mediterranean world. Archaeological finds indicate that the inhabitants of Bronze Age Greece, the **Mycenaeans**, whose civilization reached its zenith between 1450 and 1200 BCE, participated fully in the commercial and artistic exchanges of the Eastern Mediterranean. Parallels, thematic and even verbal, between archaic Greek poetry and Near Eastern texts imply that the early Greeks borrowed many ingredients of their religious and cultural heritage from the centralized and long-established Semitic and Egyptian states with which they traded (West 1997: 10–59). For this reason, much current work on the Greek system of gender and sexuality locates it within a larger Mediterranean environment and looks to ancient Near Eastern societies for close structural parallels.

However, religion is one of the most conservative features of any society. When cult practices developed by one culture come into contact with a different system of beliefs, the recipients are sometimes able to integrate such practices into their own religious framework only by changing their meanings radically. During the formative years of classical Greek civilization, in the eighth and seventh centuries BCE, Hellenic peoples of the mainland and the settlements on the eastern shore of the Mediterranean were attempting to define their religious identity by purging borrowed myths and rituals of disagreeable constituents (Garrison 2000: 59–88). Epic poetry was vital to this process because it fixed the natures and attributes of the Olympic divinities in the popular imagination: thus the sixth-century philosopher Xenophanes, criticizing erroneous theological beliefs, blamed Homer and Hesiod for popularizing the notion that gods might be capable of theft, adultery, and deception (fr. 11 DK).

Prominent among the deities imported into Greek religious life from the Near East may have been the powerful Semitic goddess of love and war variously known as Inanna, Ishtar, or Astarte. If she was incorporated into the Greek pantheon as Aphrodite, it was well before Homer's time. In literature, though, the disposition of the Greek goddess is quite different from that of her oriental cousins, for Hesiod and Homer concentrate almost exclusively upon the sensual and enticing aspects of her divine personality. Yet traces of her more formidable Eastern character are present elsewhere; in archaic and classical Sparta, for example, she was worshipped as a martial deity, an unexpected side of her persona that intrigued later Greeks (Budin 2010).

The Golden Goddess

Aphrodite's origins continue to be disputed. One influential school of thought regards her as a doublet of Ishtar-Astarte directly adopted from the Near East (Burkert 1985: 152–3; Breitenberger 2009: 7–20). Conversely, some scholars have attempted to make a case for her indigenous Greek background, drawing parallels with deities in other Indo-European pantheons (Boedeker 1974). However, her name does not appear in proto-Greek Linear B tablets from Mycenaean sites, as we might expect had she arrived with the earliest Greek-speaking settlers. Lately she has been traced to Cyprus, where a goddess cult heavily influenced by Levantine traditions flourished in the late Bronze Age (Budin 2003: 131–79). Whatever her remote antecedents, there has obviously been extensive cross-cultural contamination. Even if Aphrodite is not originally Cypriot – or Palestinian, as the historian **Herodotus** (1.105) and the travel writer Pausanias (1.14.7) assert – her cult does show close links with that of Ishtar-Astarte, including the use of incense and dove sacrifices; the descriptive title *Ourania*, "Heavenly," which corresponds to Astarte's designation "Queen of Heaven"; and associations with war, gardens, the sea, and, especially at Corinth, sacred prostitution, though the historical reality of the last item is questioned. The epithet *chryseê*, "golden," is restricted to her and used in epic verse more often than any other formulaic term: numerous passages describe her wearing golden jewelry. Although it was naturalized into Greek quite early, the word for "gold" is a Semitic borrowing, and the motif of a goddess adorning herself with jewels as she prepares to deploy her sexuality for manipulative purposes can be traced back to the Mesopotamian myth of Inanna and her mortal lover Dumuzi (Brown 1997: 31). These resemblances, though arresting, still do not convince everyone, and the debate goes on with little hope of resolution (Cyrino 2010: 18–19).

In Hesiod's *Theogony* Aphrodite's birth results from the castration of the sky god Ouranos. Urged by his mother, the earth goddess Gaia, to punish Ouranos for imprisoning his siblings, their son Kronos lops off his father's genitals with a sickle and throws them into the ocean. "They were borne along the open sea a long time," Hesiod recounts, "and from the immortal flesh a white foam [*aphros*] rushed, and in this a girl was nurtured" (190–2). Bypassing the island of Cythera, off the coast of southern Greece, and arriving at Cyprus, she steps forth on land, grass springing up as she walks. She is called by several names: Aphrodite since she was born of foam, Cytherea and Cyprogenes from Cythera and Cyprus, her first ports of call, and Philommêdês ("genital-loving") because she originated from Ouranos' members. Eros and Himeros, "Desire" and "Yearning," are her attendants, and her assigned realm of interest (*moira*) is "maidens' banter and smiles and deceits and sweet delight and lovemaking and gentleness" (205–6).

Scholars agree that the story of Ouranos' castration, bizarre and horrific even by Greek standards, is derived from the Near East: parallels with the Babylonian cosmological epic *Enūma eliš* are especially striking (West 1997: 277, 280–3). Aphrodite's birth, however, is an independent narrative stemming from another source. This was possibly a Cypriot cult myth, for a terracotta figurine found at Perachora near Corinth in Greece, dated to the mid-seventh century BCE and showing obvious Oriental influence, depicts a female figure emerging from what appears to be the male genital sac (Sale 1961: 515). Surprisingly, the figure, though given long hair and breasts and clad in a woman's dress or *peplos*, is depicted as bearded and must therefore be androgynous: the excavators connect it with "the bisexual

Aphrodite of the Orient and Cyprus" (Payne et al. 1940: 232). This may also be an early representation of Aphrodite in her aspect as Ourania, "Heavenly Aphrodite," who governed the transmission of the manly way of life by example through the cultural institution of pederasty and whose most salient characteristic was masculinity (Ferrari 2002: 109–11). At the same time, the Hesiodic myth of origins attempts to explain Aphrodite's name, which is most likely non-Greek, by associating it with the Greek word *aphros*, which can mean both "semen" and "froth of the sea." It may imply that the semen issuing from Ouranos' severed member was transformed into sea-foam, a familiar phenomenon of the natural world (Hansen 2000). Appropriately, then, the goddess of love would come into being out of a matrix at once supernatural and earthly.

Since the Greeks conceived of the universe as animate and thought of the world and its physical features in biological terms, ancient cosmology endows the divinities who arouse desire with the vital function of creative intermediaries: by inspiring beings to mate and procreate, they bring new entities into existence. Consequently, Aphrodite is portrayed as older than the other Olympian gods, for she emerges as a stimulus to union in the previous generation, immediately after the sky and the earth are forcibly separated. Her placement outside the genealogical scheme of the *Theogony* indicates that she is not altogether subject to the same rules as the Olympians. The *Homeric Hymn to Aphrodite* affirms that just three goddesses – **Athena**, Artemis, and Hestia – are immune from her power, and that she even deceives **Zeus** himself, the king of the gods, whenever she pleases (*Hymn. Hom. Ven.* 7–39).

Homer's portrayal of Aphrodite ignores those exotic origins, welcoming her into the Olympian family by making her a daughter of Zeus, born of the goddess Dione. Early in the *Iliad*, she displays her intimidating side when she urges **Helen** to go to **Paris'** bedchamber after he has been vanquished by Menelaus. Helen refuses, but Aphrodite frightens her into submission by threatening to withdraw her protection and leave her exposed to the wrath of Greeks and Trojans alike (3.383–420). Shortly thereafter, though, the goddess herself becomes an object of ridicule when she attempts to rescue her son **Aeneas** on the battlefield and is wounded in the hand by the Greek warrior Diomedes (5.311–430). She flees sobbing to Olympus, where Zeus, her father, sternly advises her that "the deeds of war have not been given to you" (5.428). Hellenic Aphrodite is thus dissociated from her Asiatic counterparts, who are redoubtable battle-goddesses.

In the famous episode of Zeus' deception (14.153–351), **Hera**, the queen of the gods, contrives to borrow Aphrodite's decorated breast-band (*himas kestos*) in order to make herself sexually irresistible to her husband. Homer describes the sash in this way:

> ... From her breasts she [Aphrodite] loosed the fretted band,
> ornate, and there on it all kinds of spell have been worked:
> thereupon is lovemaking, and yearning, and bantering persuasion,
> which steals away the mind of even those who think prudently.

Normally, Homer uses *himas* to denote a leather strap, such as a chin-strap; thus he seems to envision the abstract elements "lovemaking," "yearning," and "persuasion" as anthropomorphic personifications tooled onto the sash. Figurines found in Turkey and Iran, dated to the end of the third millennium BCE, depict a nude goddess with a single strap or a double crossed strap across her breasts and carefully stylized pubic hair calling attention to her sexuality (Garrison 2000: 75, with figs 3.3a–b and 3.4). However, actual examples of Near Eastern and Greek magical spells dating from the classical period involve the wearing of knotted cords to gain mastery of another, erotically or for some other purpose (Faraone 1990: 220–9). It appears that the love-goddess's emblem, a very old symbol of her control over fertility, has been given an ominous significance through association with the unwholesome use of love magic.[1]

In the *Odyssey*, the blind singer Demodocus sings of Aphrodite's adultery with the war-god Ares (8.266–366). The tale is cast as comic entertainment, for it accompanies a display of skilled dancing by the young men of Phaeacia intended to mollify Odysseus, who has been insulted by one of their number. Hephaestus, the lame divine craftsman who is Aphrodite's husband, is informed of this liaison by the sun-god Helios. He goes to his smithy, forges unbreakable chains too delicate to be seen, hangs them in place around his bed, and then pretends to go off to Lemnos. When Aphrodite and Ares take advantage of his supposed absence to make love, they entangle themselves in the chains. Hephaestus summons all the gods to witness their indignity, demanding the return of the courtship gifts he had given to his father-in-law Zeus. Poseidon, Zeus' brother, negotiates the freedom of the adulterous couple by guaranteeing payment of the fine for adultery (*moichagria*, 332) that Ares will owe. Since Greek custom makes the male the responsible party in cases of infidelity, Aphrodite's susceptibility to seduction is determined by her female weakness as well as her character as a love-goddess. Yet, apart from her humiliation at being exposed to the laughter and joking of the male Olympians (the female gods remain home out of modesty), she suffers no unpleasant consequences. Her impunity contrasts sharply with the brutal punishments inflicted upon mortal heroines who yield to passion.

Homeric epic thus appears to make a conscious effort to dissociate Aphrodite from the transcendent nature of the Eastern goddesses of war and fertility, to foreground the negative implications of her powers, and to limit her sphere of activity to the bedroom. It is revealing that Hesiod's epithet *philommêdês*, explicitly glossed in the *Theogony* as having to do with the genitals, appears in Homeric poetry as a creative mispronunciation, refashioned into the much more innocent *philommeidês*, "laughter-loving."

But early Greek audiences remained very much aware of Aphrodite's dangerous aspect. The *Homeric Hymn to Aphrodite*, composed by an anonymous oral poet possibly in the seventh century BCE, tells of the goddess's affair with the Trojan prince Anchises. The child of their union, whose birth is foretold in the final lines of the poem, was Aeneas, who led the survivors of the Trojan War to Italy and became the ancestor of the Romans. In this account, Aphrodite's relationship with a young mortal lover corresponds to that of the Near Eastern goddesses Inanna and Ishtar and their respective mortal consorts, Dumuzi and Tammuz. It also has parallels in other Greek myths, such as that of the dawn-goddess Eos, who sought immortality for her beloved Tithonus but forgot to ask for eternal youth. In the *Hymn*, the tale of Eos and Tithonus serves as a negative paradigm – a cautionary tale – for Aphrodite and Anchises' tryst.

Paradoxically, the poem celebrates Aphrodite's power by recounting how she herself fell victim to a degrading obsession. To punish her for the many times she had driven gods to mate with mortals, Zeus gives her a taste of her own medicine, instilling longing (*himeros*) in her heart for the handsome Anchises. One glance at him as he tends his father's cattle on Mount Ida and Aphrodite is smitten; she rushes to her temple at Paphos in Cyprus, bathes and decks herself out in all her gold and finery, and hurries back to Ida. As she proceeds, wolves, lions, bears, and leopards follow her, fawning, and she puts the desire to mate in all of them. Aphrodite has assumed the character of the awesome Phrygian fertility goddess Cybele, worshiped in that region as the Mountain Mother and mistress of wild beasts (Burkert 1985: 154).

When she arrives at Anchises' hut, Aphrodite disguises herself as a young, richly clad maiden. Though he is at once gripped by passion (*eros*, 91), Anchises perceives intuitively that she may be a divinity – what would a real girl be doing out in the wilds? Aphrodite disarms his natural fear and suspicion by saying that she is a Phrygian princess kidnapped and brought there by the divine messenger **Hermes**, who told her she was destined to be Anchises' wife. Then she works her seductive wiles by throwing herself upon the young man's mercy (131–42):

> But I implore you by Zeus and your worthy parents,
> for dishonorable folk would not get such a son as you,
> bring me, virginal and inexperienced in love
> and present me to your father and your diligent mother
> and to your brothers born of the same blood.   135
> I'll be no unseemly daughter-in-law, but a suitable one.
> And send a messenger quickly to the swift-mounted Phrygians
> to tell my father and my mother, who is grieving greatly;
> they will send you gold in abundance and woven clothing.
> Receive the many excellent bridal gifts, and having done so,   140
> prepare the feast for the longed-for marriage,
> honorable in the sight of men and immortal gods.

"So speaking," we are told, "the goddess cast sweet desire into his heart" – another way of saying that these words fuel Anchises' prior infatuation. He recklessly replies (145–54):

> If you are mortal, and a woman was the mother that bore you,   145
> and the famous Otreus is your father, as you tell me,
> and you are here through the power of the immortal messenger Hermes,
> and you will be called my wife all your days,
> then not one of the gods or mortal men
> will hold me back at this point, before I have lain in love with you   150
> right now. Not even if Apollo himself, the far-shooter,
> should send dreadful missiles from his silver bow.
> I would be willing thereafter, woman resembling the goddesses,
> to go down to Hades, having mounted your bed.

Anchises then takes the unprotesting "maiden" to his couch, removes her jewelry and clothing one piece at a time – the four-line description of disrobing is meant to titillate – and has intercourse with her. "He didn't clearly know what he was doing," the narrator carefully notes (167), but subtle psychological dynamics are at work. When he pounces upon the supposedly helpless girl lost in the wild without a protector, Anchises assumes the position of a god like Zeus or Apollo, "given to surprising virgins in just such secluded locations as this" (Brown 1997: 34). The sexual exploits of such gods doubtless encapsulate archaic Greek male fantasies. In addition, the prospect of delaying gratification until the appropriate ceremonies have been performed proves too much for our hero. He wants to possess his prize at once.

At evening, Aphrodite, in her true form, wakes Anchises. He panics. "As soon as I saw you, goddess, I knew you were divine, but you didn't tell me the truth." Then he begs her to show pity, and not leave him to survive in a weakened state – "a man who sleeps with immortal goddesses is not a strong man thereafter" (185–90). Anchises means this literally. Male sexual energy is thought of as liquid force (**menos**). When a human male fraternizes with a goddess, natural gender hierarchy is disrupted because the greater power of the goddess saps the vitality of the mortal.

Aphrodite kindly reassures Anchises. Yet she also confesses her intense shame at disgracing herself by sleeping with a mortal man and (as she knows immediately) getting herself pregnant by him (247–55). She will take measures, then, to ensure that the baby's parentage is kept secret. After his birth, he will be reared by woodland nymphs on Mount Ida; when he turns five, she will bring him to live with his father. The cover story Anchises must tell is that his son is the child of a nymph. If he ever boasts that he has slept with Aphrodite, Zeus will strike him with a thunderbolt. Then the goddess takes her departure. Though the hymn ends there, every Greek would have known the rest of the story. Anchises *was* foolish enough to let the truth slip (he'd been drinking). Zeus' retaliatory thunderbolt disabled him for life. Long before Freud, ancient mythmakers represented castration as lameness, so his punishment is both a kind of poetic justice and a reflection of the actual physical danger posed to men by inordinate sexual relations. Too much sex weakens the body and causes impotence.

Though it may seem to cast Aphrodite in a negative light, this song was composed to honor the goddess. It glorifies her by showing the irresistible might of her eroticism in action, even as it warns us of the threat she poses. Her tricking of Anchises to serve her own selfish needs is a basic fact of nature. This, to the archaic Greek mind, is the way sex operates.

Dynamics of Desire

> … Chaos first came into being, and after that
> broad-breasted Gaia, eternally fixed seat of all the immortals
> who inhabit the peaks of snowy Olympus,
> and murky Tartarus in the depths of Earth with its broad ways,
> and Eros, who is most beautiful among the immortal gods,

> the limb-loosener, who overpowers both mind and wise intent
> in the breasts of all the gods and all mankind.
>
> Hesiod, *Theogony* 116–22

In Greek mythology, personified Desire was initially a cosmic principle of generation. When he describes the coming-into-being of the universe, Hesiod makes Eros spontaneously arise from the primordial abyss, Chaos, along with Gaia the earth goddess and Tartarus the shadowy underworld. Gaia then brings forth her male consort, Ouranos or Sky, from her own depths. From that point on, Hesiod's archaic cosmos functions biologically, as other divinities are born of the physical union of Sky and Earth, two sexually differentiated partners. To start the process of creation going, then, Eros must be present. But his job is not to bring the sexes together, for Earth's male partner, Sky, does not yet exist. Instead, by inducing Earth to draw her consort out of herself, he causes a rift within an original unity, giving rise to duality (Vernant 1990: 465–6). "**Orphic**" literature, a term applied by modern scholars to a set of religious texts circulating among sixth- and fifth-century adherents of purification cults, may have subsequently elaborated on this notion. In Aristophanes' comedy *Birds*, produced at Athens in 414 BCE, the chorus of birds proudly proclaims that Eros, creator of the immortals, was hatched from a wind-egg (693–702). Aristophanes' joke is thought to parody Orphic doctrine; if so, the egg, traditionally a symbol of the perfect whole, is an appropriate source from which the principle of cosmic fission must emerge. Along the same lines, Pherecydes of Syros, a mythographer active in the middle of the sixth century BCE, apparently claimed that Zas (Zeus) transformed himself into Eros in order to create the cosmos.[2]

It is only later, after Aphrodite is born of Ouranos' severed members, that Hesiod assigns Eros his more familiar role of bringing sexual partners together so that they may produce other beings in turn. His status is altered, for, as we have seen, he is now reduced to working, along with Himeros, as a subordinate agent of the divinity who oversees relations between male and female. Moreover, he operates in a "fallen world," where an original harmony has been disrupted and the techniques of Aphrodite must come into play because men and women are naturally estranged from one another (duBois 1992: 101). We will understand why the sexes are forever alienated after we have studied Hesiod's myth of Pandora.

The god Eros is a personification of the instinctive drive to mate and reproduce. Greek culture viewed this biological compulsion as both positive and necessary. To civilized harmony, however, the power of Eros posed an unruly threat – witness the carnage of the Trojan War, supposedly provoked by a single act of adultery. While preoccupation with the fecundity of plants, animals, and women made sexuality central to both religious and community life, Greeks of the eighth and seventh centuries BCE dwelt, for the most part, in a subsistence economy, where resources of all kinds, including human fertility, had to be husbanded. Raw sexuality was also deemed a phenomenon belonging to the sphere of nature, ***physis***. This word – in contrast to our anthropomorphic cliché "Mother Nature" – did not summon up visions of an unspoiled refuge from civilization's stresses, nor was it associated with healthful products, as in "natural organic foods." Especially when used together with its notional opposite, ***nomos*** or "law, convention," *physis* was firmly linked to what could not be radically changed by human agency, but only rendered less destructive. Hence *erôs* had to be controlled through various cultural mechanisms, or "technologies," so that it could be exploited for the benefit of the population as a whole (Thornton 1997: 1–7, 139–60). The mechanisms for harnessing sexual energy were chiefly rites of passage, male and female, leading up to the pivotal institution of marriage (Calame 1999 [1992]: 91–129). Eros' importance in being the reason that such social institutions existed explains his prominence in archaic and classical Greek poetry both lyric and dramatic. However, representations of the god in later poetry, especially that sung at drinking parties or *symposia*, differ markedly from his portrayal in Hesiod and the Orphic hymns, for he is figured there not as a creative demiurge but rather as a violent and arbitrary force. In Homer, however, he does not appear in either capacity, for, while the noun *eros* occurs frequently, it is never personified.

The Baneful Race of Women

Most of us, when still children, heard the story of Pandora, the Greek Eve, and how curiosity tempted her to open the box from which all kinds of human misery escaped. This myth comes down to us from Hesiod, who tells it twice, once in the *Theogony* (535–612) and again in the *Works and Days* (42–105).[3] Because it is given such a principal place in his two didactic poems, it must have expressed meanings important to his contemporaries. In Hesiod, however, the story has a significance much bleaker than the simple moral we now assign it, for it explains in each case why the human condition makes no sense and the labors of mankind are doomed to everlasting futility.

"Mankind" is the operative word here. In the *Works and Days* the Pandora myth disrupts chronological sequence. Hesiod has not yet told us when and how humanity originated; its existence alongside the gods is simply taken for granted. (His account of the Five Ages of Man, with the successive creations of the Gold, Silver, and so on, races, immediately follows that of Pandora, *Op.* 106–201.) At this point in the mythic scenario, before the creation of the first woman, human beings are exclusively male. Although they were living in a kind of Golden Age – free from evils, from hard labor and sickness (*Op.* 90–2) – they did not eat the flesh of animals and had no access to technology. Prometheus, one of the immortal Titans, took up their cause. First, as described in the *Theogony*, he instituted animal sacrifice, tricking Zeus into accepting bones and fat rather than meat as the gods' portion; then he stole the fire that would allow mortals to control their environment. Zeus, in retaliation, resolved to give mankind "an evil thing [*kakon*] in exchange for fire, in which they may delight themselves, embracing their own evil" (*Op.* 57–8). He ordered Hephaestus to fashion a maiden from earth and water; Athena, patroness of women's crafts, to teach her weaving; Aphrodite to bestow grace upon her; and Hermes to put in her "the mind of a bitch and a thieving nature" (*Op.* 60–68). Hermes also endowed her with speech and a name, *Pandora*, or "all-gift." The narrator of the *Works and Days* explains that she was so called because each of the gods gave her a gift, although the Greek could just as easily mean that she was a gift from all the gods.[4]

When Pandora is ready, Hermes brings her as a present to Prometheus' stupid brother Epimetheus. This is a Hesiodic joke: *Prometheus* means "forethought,"

Epimetheus "afterthought." Although Prometheus had sternly warned him against taking any gifts from Zeus, Epimetheus forgets and joyfully accepts her. Pandora subsequently removes the lid of the storage jar (*not* a box – we will see why in a moment) in which sufferings, labor, and sicknesses are contained and scatters them all over the earth. Because Hesiod states plainly that "she devised [*emêsato*] miserable cares for human beings" (*Op*. 95), it appears she does so maliciously, not through ignorance. By Zeus' design, however, Hope (*Elpis*) remains trapped in the jar, underneath the lid. Hope's continued presence there is no consolation, for she too counts among potential plagues because of her capacity to delude (Pucci 1977: 104–5; Clay 2003: 124–5). Thanks to Pandora, then, "the earth is full of evils and the sea is full" and diseases bring suffering to men silently, by day and night (*Op*. 100–4).

In the *Theogony*, the pattern of events is much the same, but Hesiod is at greater pains to underscore that Zeus' gift constituted the first woman, or rather Wife (Clay 2003: 102). He traces "the race of women" (*genos … gynaikôn*, *Theog*. 590) back to her and compares them to drones in beehives, who consume the honey produced by bees "into their own belly [**gastêr**]" while making no contribution to the household themselves. Wives are thus a drag upon men's endeavors. Yet a man must marry in order to have children. And he *must* have children, for otherwise there will be no one to care for him in his old age, and no one to inherit, intact, the fruits of a lifetime of hard work. Even so – best-case scenario – if he marries a good wife, he may produce bad children. Thus, Hesiod concludes fatalistically, "it is not possible to deceive or to bypass the mind of Zeus" (*Theog*. 613, cf. *Op*. 105).

If we take this account at face value, it is outrageously misogynistic, not least because it ignores the vital economic role wives played as stewards of family property and producers of woven goods, a major source of domestic wealth in archaic Greece. But let us try giving it a broader frame of reference by assuming that Pandora stands for something more than just "Wife" or "Woman." In creating her, Zeus causes two sexes to exist where there was only one. This means that sexual intercourse has now become an inescapable part of human existence. Pandora is therefore a doublet of Aphrodite, whose emergence from the sea, after the forced separation of the primal parents Sky and Earth, introduces the duality of the sexes into the cosmic order. Hesiod underscores that parallelism between divine and human by giving Pandora a "robing scene" similar to those of Hera preparing to seduce Zeus in *Iliad* 14 and Aphrodite beautifying herself for Anchises (Bergren 1989: 10–14). In both poems, he relates that Pandora was decked out in elaborate finery by Athena. In the *Works and Days*, the Graces and Persuasion put gold necklaces upon her, and, in the *Theogony*, Hephaestus fashions for her a golden crown embossed with figures of beasts. Here we are reminded of the radiant robes and golden ornaments donned by each of the two Olympians, and perhaps of Aphrodite's magic sash as well. Like Hera and Aphrodite, then, Zeus' gift to mankind presents herself as a vision of dazzling, if superficial, beauty. The goddesses, moreover, are exploiting their sexual appeal in order to deceive, and Pandora too is endowed with "lies and wheedling words and a thieving character" by Hermes (*Op*. 77–8). Such a combination of elegant, "golden" allure and falsity suggests that Pandora is an allegory of sexuality itself, and so another embodiment of the potential risks to a man involved in dealings with Aphrodite and Eros.

What are these risks? Even if he steers clear of goddesses, sex with mortal women can endanger a man because there are physical limits upon his potency. In a later passage of the *Works and Days*, Hesiod advises (582–8):

> But when the thistle flowers and the shrill cicada,
> sitting in a tree, pours down his clear song without pause
> from beneath his wings, in the season of toilsome heat,
> then goats are fattest and wine tastes best,
> women are horniest, but men most debilitated,
> because the Dog-star dries up head and knees
> and the flesh is parched by heat.

That women are lusty and men impotent during the dog-days of summer was a widespread folk belief. Approximately a century later, Alcaeus of Lesbos cast this passage of the *Works and Days* into lyric verse for performance at drinking parties (fr. 347V). He speaks even more bluntly of the physiological response of each sex to summer heat: "and now women are most polluted [*miarôtatai*] and men insubstantial [*leptoi*]." For a scientific explanation of these alleged facts, we can turn to the author of the pseudo-Aristotelian *Problemata* (4.25). Men are by nature hot and dry, he says, and women moist and chilled. During winter, the moisture and warmth in men are strong enough to produce seed and arouse desire, while in women lack of heat inside and out causes their own moisture to congeal. In summer, the degree of heat in women is in balance, but for men it is excessive, and that surplus heat saps their vitality. Hence the two sexes are diametrically opposed to each other in terms of their bodily constitution, one reason why Hesiod could figure them as originating separately and literally belonging to distinct species.

Such convictions shaped Greek ideas of how females respond to sexual arousal. Since *erôs* has a softening and liquefying effect, they were thought more susceptible to passion than men, whose dryer constitutions enabled them better to resist erotic impulse. That is why more blame attaches to the male partner in cases of adultery. Furthermore, they had no physiological need to curb their appetites, since their capacity for sex, unlike that of men, was bottomless (Carson 1990: 137–45). A sex-hungry woman was a threat, then, not only because she might be prone to make demands during summer, the wrong time of year, but also because she consumed *menos*, a man's vital fluid. Her womb (*gastêr*) was an unplumbed abyss into which he poured his limited resources of semen. Pandora's storage jar containing all the evils that plague men is a metaphor for that same *gastêr*, or womb/belly.

Consequently, Hesiod cautions the man planning to marry that, while there is nothing better than a good wife, there is nothing worse than a bad one, "a dinner-trapper who, no matter how stalwart he is, singes him without a torch and gives him to raw old age" (*Op.* 704–5). The warning contained in these two lines should again be taken literally. Since the same word can mean both "belly" and "womb," the wife's sexual rapacity is described as gluttony. Her appetite affects her husband in exactly the same way as summer heat by scorching him and drying him out. Eventually he succumbs to premature senility, for she has sucked away the *menos* that ensures youth as well as vigor. It is for this reason, too, that the race of women who descend from Pandora are portrayed as greedy drones. Lack of reciprocity is inscribed into the sexual act, in which male energy goes to nourish female fecundity. Even intercourse for the purpose of begetting children is a gamble from the masculine point of view: in financial terms, a precious commodity, sperm, must be invested with no assurance that long-run dividends, in the form of a comfortable old age, will be returned. Those are the economics, so to speak, of human sexuality in Hesiod.

Love under Siege

Illicit sexuality underpins the plot of Homer's *Iliad*, for the original cause of hostility between the Greeks and the Trojans was Paris' abduction of Helen, at that time the wife of the Spartan king Menelaus. The overriding themes of the poem, the inevitability of death and the value of everlasting fame in the face of human mortality, are movingly underscored by frank reminders – often put in the mouth of Helen, who constantly blames herself for what has happened – that all this suffering on both sides has been the outcome of irresponsible behavior on the part of two individuals. Yet Homer does not make Helen, or even Paris, into cardboard villains; each is a complex character. And, although we are given only brief glimpses of their marriage, we realize soon enough that it is an unhappy one: on Helen's part, a powerful sexual attraction to her present husband vies with shame, regret, and anger at his fecklessness when he blithely ignores the moral consequences of his actions. The self-centered preoccupations of the lovers are in turn offset by the graver concerns of Paris' brother Hector, commander of the Trojan army, and his wife Andromache, and the essentially comic tryst of Zeus and Hera. It is disconcerting that these various involvements, which provide an emotional backdrop for the bloody carnage around Troy, are presented merely as short interludes in the dominant business of killing.

Earlier we spoke of the scene in *Iliad* 3 in which Aphrodite, in the guise of an old servant, compels Helen to go to Paris' bedchamber. Helen's reluctance to do so is motivated by embarrassment at his poor performance as a warrior, which she had witnessed from Troy's walls. As the armies were advancing to meet each other, Paris burst from the Trojan ranks. Wearing a leopard skin and brandishing two javelins – showy trappings, well suited to his personality – he had challenged any man of the Greeks to single combat. But when Menelaus, Helen's former husband, eagerly took him up on it, Paris, losing his nerve, backed off "like a man seeing a snake." Only a cutting rebuke from Hector could make him stand his ground. Seizing upon the opportunity to end the war, once and for all, through a fair fight between the two principals, both sides, represented by their kings Agamemnon of Mycenae and Priam of Troy, arranged the terms of the competition and formally ratified them with a sacrifice. Helen and her possessions would belong to the man who won;

afterward, the remaining Greeks and Trojans would swear an oath of friendship, and the Greeks would return home. Unfortunately, the outcome of the combat left the issue unresolved. When Menelaus, who was getting the better of Paris, attempted to deal the death-blow, his sword shattered. He then grabbed his opponent by the helmet and tried to drag him away, but Aphrodite broke the chin-strap, caught up Paris and hid him in a mist, and carried him off to his bedchamber. She had saved his life at the price of his heroic stature (such as it was), for he was not even allowed to die honorably.

Helen is humiliated, and once she and Paris are face to face she lets him know it. "I wish you had died on the battlefield," she complains. "So much for your boasting that you were a better man than Menelaus. Go back and challenge him to fight again – no, don't: he could very well kill you" (3.428–36). But Paris feels no chagrin whatsoever. If Menelaus won, he retorts, it was with Athena's help; next time it will be *his* turn, as "we have gods on our side too." (He is doubtless thinking of Aphrodite, although she, as we have seen, is no fighter.) Then he coaxes, "But come now, let's both go to bed and enjoy ourselves in making love [*philotêti*]." Never before, he adds, has *erôs* shrouded his heart this much, not even when on the island of Cranae he first "joined [*emigên*] with you on a bed in love" after their elopement (3.441–6). He leads the way to the marital couch, and she meekly follows. We are not told whether she gives in primarily because of desire or because she fears the wrath of Aphrodite.

In this scene, it is the erotic language itself, as opposed to the behavior of the two characters, that offers insight into what Homer's audience ideally expected of sexual intercourse. The word *philotês*, properly meaning "friendship, love, affection," is regularly used in epic verse to denote not just the act of sex but, associated with it, the feelings of intimacy it should foster. Similarly, with the verb *eunaô* "go to bed," Paris uses the dual, a grammatical ending in ancient Greek distinct from the singular and the plural, applied only to natural pairs like a yoke of oxen. The idea of reciprocity is understood: he assumes that Helen actively consents to sex and will experience as much pleasure in it as he himself will. This assemblage of vocabulary and grammatical constructions is formulaic in scenes of human lovemaking, which suggests that the epic model of sexual relations is one of mutual participation and enjoyment. At the same time, similar language also occurs in genealogical accounts and so implies that the act of intercourse described might be likely to produce offspring (although Paris and Helen themselves have no children). Homeric archetypes of human eroticism therefore attempt to balance the carnal, the procreative, and the affective aspects of sex (Calame 1999 [1992]: 39–43). Yet we should note that, although the elements of consent and reciprocity might characterize any sexual union, the factor of potential reproduction restricts the ideal erotic encounter to that of a heterosexual, if not necessarily married, couple.

Helen and Paris' actual relationship falls short of the ideal, however, because, apart from strong physical attraction and the bond forged by mutual guilt, little enough keeps them together. In Paris, Homer has drawn an intriguing portrait of a man who lives by and for his charm and sex appeal. His brother Hector calls him *gynaimanês*, "woman-crazy" (*Il.* 3.39), and reproaches him for his unwillingness to stand up against the man whose wife he had stolen. "Your lyre and the gifts of

Aphrodite, your hair and looks, won't help you when you're joined with the dust," he remarks (3.44–5), sarcastically using the same verb, *meignumi*, employed as an euphemism for the act of intercourse. Paris acknowledges the fairness of this reprimand, but adds, in his own defense, that gifts bestowed by the gods themselves cannot be cast aside, since no one would choose them willingly (3.65–6). His rationalization puts the blame on Aphrodite: she has made him who he is, and to go against his temperament would be to insult her. Several books later, in a much admired simile, Paris is likened to a stallion at liberty (6.506–14):

> As when a stabled horse overfed at the manger
> breaks his ties and runs pounding over the plain,
> accustomed to bathe himself in the well-flowing river,
> full of himself; he carries his head high,
> and over his shoulders his mane tosses;   510
> lightly his knees bear him, burnished proud,
> to the familiar pasture of the herd; so Paris, son of Priam,
> descended from steep Pergamus, shining in his armor like the bright sun,
> laughing loudly, and his swift feet carried him on.

The comparison is psychologically acute. There is nothing more eye-catching than a horse bursting with energy and unexpectedly on the loose. Thus "all the qualities of masculine sexuality well used are evoked by the simile" (Beye 1966: 27). Nevertheless, a Greek audience would also be well aware of the danger a runaway stallion, oblivious to his surroundings, poses to himself, other horses, and anyone trying to catch him. Homer drives the point home by inserting this description of Paris right after one of the most poignant scenes in the epic: Hector has just bidden farewell to his wife Andromache, who was tearfully urging him to remain within the city walls. Hector's grim commitment to duty marks the sharpest possible contrast with his brother's insouciance, while Andromache's overriding concern for her husband's safety is touchingly at odds with Helen's frustration at Paris' dishonorable conduct.

Why is Helen so preoccupied with the shame his lack of integrity brings upon her? From antiquity onwards, audiences have perceived that she, the prize for which Greeks and Trojans are fighting, is an emblem of the *kleos*, the immortal fame, earned by whoever proves himself the best warrior at Troy. Since poetry is the vehicle of such fame, Helen is to some degree a personification of epic values: she self-consciously voices the heroic perspective of the poet. When Iris, messenger of the gods, summons her to attend the single combat between Paris and Menelaus, Helen is weaving a great double-folded cloth on which are figured "the many contests the horse-taming Trojans and bronze-corseleted Achaeans had endured for her sake" (*Il.* 3.125–8). In this weaving project Homer has mirrored himself composing the plot of his song. Subsequently, addressing Hector, Helen speaks of Paris and herself as "subjects of song for future generations" (6.358). Homer, it has been observed, creates a Helen who articulates her own poetic function in two distinct ways: within the epic scenario she recognizes her guilt as the cause of the war, and she also expresses the bard's sense of his cultural importance as preserver and transmitter of the past (Clader 1976: 8–9). Yet, trapped as she is into depending upon a man whose fixation on lust and its gratification precludes sensitivity to the opinion of peers and posterity, Helen is forced to deny her symbolic identity. This is the dilemma imposed on her by her dual role as spokesperson for Homer and pawn of Aphrodite.

Receptions of Helen

Helen's centrality to the *Iliad* has earned her a place among the most celebrated figures of classical mythology, her name synonymous with "beauty" even to those who have not read a word of Greek literature. From Homer onward she accrued even richer metaphoric coloring when her elopement became attached to radical critiques of human knowledge and free agency. The lyric poet Steisichorus (*c*.600 BCE) devised a revisionist account, his so-called *Palinode* or "Recantation" denying that Helen ever sailed to Troy (*PMG* 192 *ap*. Pl. *Phdr*. 243a–b). Expanding the story, Herodotus put her in Egypt, a Greek fantasy land, for the duration of the war (2.112–20). In his drama *Helen* Euripides makes Greeks and Trojans fight over a phantom (*eidôlon*), the "false and dishonorable sign" of their folly (Austin 1994: 112), while Helen's presence beside the Nile introduces doubts about the reliability of accepted mythic "truths" (Wright 2005: 133–57). Finally the sophist Gorgias, Socrates' contemporary, attempted to exonerate her in his *Encomium of Helen*: she indeed went to Troy, Gorgias concedes, but perhaps as the helpless victim of Fortune or the gods, or else her accountability was lessened through duress, or persuasive speech, or love. In antiquity, then, nothing about this heroine, not even her contribution to the Trojan War, can be taken for granted. Ambiguity, moral and existential, is key to her mythic nature (Worman 2001).

Laden with allegorical meaning, Helen was afterward integrated into the Western literary and artistic tradition. Courtly love lyric recalls her as a precursor to the poet's idealized beloved; medieval and early modern Troy narratives treat her as the incarnation of passion's destructive force (Gumpert 2001: 116–20, 137–8). In those works, too, she finds both detractors and defenders.

For the Renaissance Faust legend she is Faust's paramour and the final cause of his damnation – in Marlowe's tragedy *Doctor Faustus* the famous speech beginning: "Was this the face that launched a thousand ships …?" is in actuality spoken to a demon who has assumed her form (Wootton 2005: xvii–xviii in reference to *DF* V.1.1357–76). Conversely, Goethe's Romantic celebration of Faust's quest for experience treats the pairing of Faust and Helen as a "union of literatures, of eighteenth-century Europe and classical Greece" (Maguire 2009: 159). Following the lead of poets, European oil painters (e.g. Guido Reni in his *Abduction of Helen* [1631; fig. 1.1] and Jacques-Louis David in the *Love of Paris and Helen* [1789], both now in the Louvre) depicted her affair in a grandiose fashion, full of pageantry and sentiment. Though losing none of her ethical complexity, Helen became a badge of the classical sublime.

The advent of the novel in the nineteenth century and film in the twentieth might have supplied venues for even more searching treatments of her myths. So far, though, the products have been disappointing. Helen makes only a token appearance in serious fiction; thus in Christa Wolf's *Cassandra* (1984) the fact that she is *not* in Troy (a variation on the "phantom Helen" motif) is a closely guarded secret as the city prepares for war on the pretext of defending her. Popular historical novels (such as George 2006) attempt to justify her flight from Sparta by depicting her marriage to Menelaus as a loveless one. Hollywood, too, faces the dilemma of condoning adultery if it handles her sympathetically. Hence, films that set the elopement with Paris at the heart of the plot motivate it (in the absence of Aphrodite, since modern-day viewers require psychologically realistic explanations) by having

(Continued)

Receptions of Helen — Continued

Fig. 1.1   Guido Reni (1575–1642). "The Abduction of Helen," 1641. Location: Louvre. Source: © RMN-Grand Palais/Art Resource, NY.

him chivalrously rescue her from an intolerable marriage. Apart from being a brute, which is bad enough, Menelaus is also demoted to a puppet in the hands of his scheming brother Agamemnon, keen for any excuse to attack wealthy Troy (M. M. Winkler 2009: 211–13, 217–23). Cinematic exoneration of Helen, required to make her palatable to audiences, consequently diminishes her. She did not cause the war, and her fabled beauty, the source of her erotic power, is reduced to a vapid prettiness (Blondell 2009). In the closing scenes of Wolfgang Petersen's *Troy* (2004), Paris, insisting upon his duty to join the fight, leaves her to flee the burning city alone. By choosing, however belatedly, a good higher than Helen, he destabilizes the romantic premise that love must conquer all and allows Achilles and Briseis to supplant him and his erstwhile beloved as the film's tragically doomed couple. In the process of whitewashing Helen, Hollywood has accomplished what countless Greek, Roman, medieval, and early modern narratives could not: at last she is rendered totally transparent. And bland.

The Beguilement of Zeus

"What high immortals do in mirth / is life and death on Middle Earth," observed W. H. Auden. He was not necessarily thinking of Homer (nor, for that matter, of Tolkien), but his couplet accurately sums up the interactions of divine personalities in the *Iliad*. In the petty rivalries of the Olympians grave human concerns are burlesqued. Sexuality, of course, emerges as one of those chief concerns.

The tragic events of the *Iliad* are set in motion by Zeus' decision to honor **Achilles**, whom Agamemnon, his king and overlord, had grievously insulted. To show the Greeks that they cannot win without Achilles' help, Zeus allows the Trojan forces to gain the upper hand while Achilles withdraws to his tent, refusing to participate in combat. Hera is a partisan of the Greeks, and her clever seduction of her husband comes very close to thwarting that objective. She schemes with Hypnos, the god of sleep, to render Zeus unconscious after lovemaking. This, in turn, permits her favorites to regain mastery of the field and, in the process, seriously to disable the Trojan champion Hector.

When she approaches Zeus, bathed, perfumed, and dressed to kill, Hera's coy demeanor is reminiscent of those other supernatural seductresses Aphrodite and Pandora. Upon seeing her, Zeus reacts as impulsively as Paris and Anchises. "As soon as he saw her, *eros* shrouded his shrewd heart," the narrator says, "even as when they first joined in love [*emisgesthên philotêti*], going, the two of them, to bed without the knowledge of their parents" (14.294–6). The sexual terminology and grammatical duals will already be familiar from Paris' speech to Helen in *Iliad* 3. Paradigms of human passion are thereby applied to the erotic experience of divinities: a rush of desire overwhelms the mind, more intense than what was felt the first time the partners made love. Zeus' response to this urge is a masterpiece of comic invention, however, for he presses his suit by embarking upon a catalogue of his prior conquests. "Come, let us go to bed and turn to lovemaking," he pleads,

> for never before did desire for goddess or mortal woman   315
> so overflood and master the heart within my breast,
> not when I fell in love with the wife of Ixion,
> who bore Peirithous, a counselor equivalent to the gods,
> nor when I loved fair-ankled Danaë, Acrisius' daughter,
> who bore Perseus, most renowned of all warriors,   320
> nor when I loved the daughter of widely-famed Phoenix,
> who bore to me both Minos and godlike Rhadamanthys,
> nor even when I loved Semele or Alcmene in Thebes,
> she who brought forth Heracles, her stouthearted son,
> while the other, Semele, bore Dionysos, a delight to mortals;   325
> nor when I loved Demeter, the splendid-haired queen,
> nor when I loved glorious Leto, nor whenever I loved you yourself,
> as much as I want you now, and sweet longing seizes me.

The "never before … as now" formula, so flattering on the lips of Paris, has been reduced to sheer absurdity: one can only guess at the thoughts that might have passed through Hera's mind as Zeus rambles on reminiscing. Furthermore, though he employs the formulaic expression "go to bed" (*eunêthente*), the king of the gods cannot in fact wait until they have returned to their bedchamber, as propriety demands (Zeitlin 1995: 124). Thus all the motifs found in the earlier paradigmatic scene between Helen and Paris are ironically burlesqued.

Whatever Hera's secret feelings, she represses them and pretends to be scandalized. Make love *here*? What a thought! Suppose another god were to happen along and see us? I'd be *mortified*! If that's really what you want, let's go back home (14.329–40). Again, as with Anchises, the love-object's feigned resistance only fans the flames of desire. Zeus, the cloud-gatherer, pledges to surround Hera with a golden mist, so that not even Helios, the sun-god, will be able to perceive them. Then he takes his wife in his arms. Since a bed is required by the formulaic language, the earth sends up a patch of fresh grass for them to lie upon, sprinkled thickly and softly with lotus, crocus, and hyacinth, while the promised dewy golden cloud covers them. So the plan of Hera was accomplished.

In the entire poetic tradition, Hera is the only being, immortal or mortal, who ever triumphs over Zeus even for a moment, and her sneaky victory is retold with appropriate gusto. Humorous as this episode is, however, it has implications for the political stability of the cosmos, for it is of a piece with the recurrent rebellions of Gaia and other female figures in Hesiod's *Theogony*. Zeus' roll-call of past loves reminds us of what the mythological record makes only too clear: "[His] omniscience fails in the face of his desire. Invincible and all-knowing, he is nevertheless baffled by eros" (Holmberg 1995: 110–11). In a universe that comes into existence through spontaneous generation, rather than the creative act of a demiurge, and continues to function on biological principles even under a rational Olympian regime, Hera's seductive wiles pose a challenge to the established order, for they create, if only temporarily, a lapse of direction, a failure of Zeus' will, that might well culminate in a return to primeval chaos. Zeus wakes before any permanent damage is actually done, but the plot of the *Iliad* has come close to being subverted.

Alternatives to Penelope

It is an axiom of scholarship on the *Odyssey* that all its female figures, human and divine, are "foils," or substitute models, for its heroine **Penelope**. Implied contrasts with Clytemnestra, Helen, Calypso, Nausicaa, **Circe**, and Arete delicately illuminate various facets of Penelope's character, such as her chastity, steadfastness, intelligence, and capacity for queenship. Yet **Odysseus'** transactions with other types of the feminine also serve an ideological purpose, for they point up the negative consequences of allowing female sexual desire to range freely without restraint. Odysseus' own objective of resuming his position as king and husband on Ithaca is expressly endorsed by the poem, while female sexuality is depicted throughout as a major impediment to that goal (Holmberg 1995: 108).

The *Odyssey* is, as Wohl neatly puts it, "a charter for the transition from the warrior society of the *Iliad* to the *polis* culture of fifth-century Athens" (1993: 19).

Odysseus' homecoming to an Ithaca completely changed from the one he left mirrors the degree to which Greek society itself changed during the Dark Age, the twelfth to eighth centuries BCE. For example, the queens Helen and Arete join their menfolk dining with visitors in the central hall of the Homeric palace; epic poetry takes it for granted that noble women will participate in hospitality. This assumption may reflect the relative accessibility of one-room private residences during the immediate post-Mycenaean period. Archaeological remains indicate, however, that residential architecture was subsequently modified to provide greater privacy for the inhabitants: starting around 700 BCE, rooms began to be clustered around an interior courtyard with a single door giving admission from the street (Morris 2000: 280–6). This new layout, which soon became the norm and continued to prevail in the classical Greek city-state or **polis**, emphasized the wife's role as guardian of the domestic interior, as opposed to the husband's function of representing the household to the outside world. Indeed, a corresponding literary tendency to gender the interior area of the house as feminine, dissociating the physical space of women from the larger public realm, surfaces for the first time in Hesiod's *Works and Days* (519–25) and is therefore contemporaneous with this architectural revolution.

If the single-family household, the *oikos*, is destined to be the basic unit of society in the city-state, the man and woman who together manage it must be well suited in character and abilities for their respective tasks, and must also exhibit **homophrosynê**, "like-mindedness," in supervising its dependants and expending resources. Odysseus' brawn and courage complement Penelope's fidelity, and they possess an equal amount of **mêtis** or practical intelligence. This makes them ideal partners in such an enterprise. They are, then, the epic archetype of marital excellence. Odysseus' encounters with other females, conversely, test alternative models of relations between the sexes and demonstrate why they are unsuited to the emerging *polis* society.

The goddesses Calypso and Circe are examples of sexually autonomous females. Each lives alone on an island that seems a paradise of lush fertility, and each hankers after Odysseus as her mortal lover. At the beginning of the poem, Calypso has been holding the hero prisoner for seven years. When Hermes arrives bringing Zeus' direct order to release him, she bitterly complains that male divinities, who regularly consort with mortals, grudge their female counterparts the right to do the same (5.118–29). But if Homer allows Calypso to point out the unfairness of the Olympian double standard, it is only to make her own ethical position the more untenable: she herself has been detaining Odysseus against his will, compelling him to sleep with her by force (*anangkêi*, 5.155). Furthermore, like the loutish Cyclops, she dwells in a cave, on an island in the midst of the formless sea; her environment is "distant from all forms of social, political, or religious normativeness" (Peradotto 1993: 176). The very meaning of her name, "Concealer," hints at both death and the oblivion that is the antithesis of everlasting fame. When Calypso offers Odysseus immortality as a bribe to remain with her, we realize that life as the goddess's companion would be tantamount to extinction for the epic hero. The Calypso episode questions whether the subjection of female libido is both proper and necessary and gives an unambiguously affirmative answer.

Circe poses an even more dangerous threat to male sexuality, for her secret weapons are drugs, **pharmaka**, and she employs them, together with her magic wand, to change Odysseus' men into swine after they have eaten and drunk with her. Female independence is automatically equated with female domination, which strips men of their essential humanity and reduces them to the level of beasts. To be a man, conversely, is to keep women's sexuality properly in check. Odysseus is able to withstand the power of Circe's potion by relying on a counter-herb, the mysterious plant *moly* given to him by Hermes; he then gains mastery over the goddess by drawing his sword and threatening her with violence (10.321–2). Realizing that he is Odysseus, whose arrival Hermes had already predicted, Circe pleads with him to put away his blade and make love: "then let us both go up to bed, so that, mingling in affection on the bed, we may have faith in each other" (333–5). This is a particularly clear expression of the idea that intercourse should foster intimacy and trust between the sexes. Yet Odysseus, nevertheless, fears that Circe, once he is naked, will render him unmanly (*anênora*, 341) and agrees to sex only after she swears a great oath to do him no further harm. Once she has restored his comrades to their proper human shape, however, and they are all settled in her palace as her guests, Odysseus stays with her a full year and decides to leave only after his men become impatient. Supposedly benign, Circe still remains capable of delaying his homecoming.

Although Phaeacia, Odysseus' first landfall after leaving Calypso's island, is a civilized, even hyper-civilized, society, it is entirely cut off from other peoples. The Trojan War, which had created such a political cataclysm throughout the Mediterranean world, has reached its inhabitants only as the subject of song. It is also an inbred society: Arete, the wife of king Alcinous, is at the same time his niece, whom he married when he succeeded his brother on the throne (7.63–8). Her status as the former king's only child, through whom the royal bloodline would doubly pass, might explain the unusual political influence she is said to possess. Both her daughter Nausicaa and the disguised goddess Athena hint to Odysseus that the queen is the real decision-maker in the palace.

It seems odd, then, that Arete only speaks three times in the epic, once when she recognizes the clothing Odysseus wears and asks where he got it (7.237–9), again when she sensibly advises him to knot the ties to a chest she has just given him (8.443–5), and, finally, when she praises his account of the mythic heroines he had seen in the underworld (11.336–41). There, indeed, she refers to him as "*my* guest," although she quickly adds that all the other Phaeacian nobles share in that honor. Otherwise, her husband Alcinous is the one to give orders for Odysseus' entertainment, to plan his homecoming, propose gifts, and even, in an unexpected move – considering that he does not yet know his visitor's identity – hint at offering him Nausicaa's hand in marriage (7.311–15). When Echeneus, spokesman for the elders of the community, endorses Arete's call for additional gifts to Odysseus, he pointedly states that the king has the final say: "the action and the word depend on Alcinous here" (11.346). Yet appearances may be deceiving. Nausicaa's and Athena's independent testimony to Arete's authority raises the possibility that the fine speeches of Alcinous, who seems rather defensive about his right to command, and the deference to him shown by the elders are fictions masking his wife's genuine though publicly unacknowledged rule (Wohl 1993: 30–1).

If Nausicaa's mother is the actual power behind the throne, that could account for the unusual poise and self-possession her daughter displays when she comes upon Odysseus, shipwrecked and naked, in Book 6. Homer's tact in alluding to matters sexual is at its most diplomatic in this episode, as his listeners would be quite aware of implicit parallels with stock scenes of maiden abduction. First, the meeting of hero and adolescent girl takes place on a beach, often a venue for rape or seduction: in the false tale Odysseus tells the swineherd Eumaeus, his nurse is seduced by a Phoenician sailor while washing clothes (15.520–2). Again, the mythic motif of girls carried off while dancing or playing with their companions is only too familiar – Hades' seizure of Demeter's daughter Persephone comes immediately to mind (*Hymn. Hom. Cer.* 4–32). Before playing ball, Nausicaa and her companions cast off their veils, the symbol of female modesty (6.100). As Odysseus emerges from his hiding place, he is compared to a ravenous lion stalking his prey through rain and wind (6.130–4): the simile does not externalize his own mental state, but instead conjures up the impression he makes upon the maidens. When her companions scatter, Nausicaa is left alone to confront the stranger.[5] Given these parallels with mythic rape scenes, it is wholly unexpected of her to stand up to him bravely instead of passively submitting to whatever might befall her.

Nausicaa is unusual in other ways as well. Critics have noted her precocious sexuality (Wohl 1993: 28–9). In later Greek literature, virgins often blush at the very suggestion of marriage, but she anticipates it with some eagerness. Although she is ashamed to mention it in front of her father (6.66–7), she speaks frankly about it to her maidens and even to Odysseus, whom she has barely met. In lines 275–88, she explains why he should dissociate himself from her party before they enter the city:

> And then some common fellow, coming upon us, might say thus: 275
> "Who's this tall and handsome stranger following after Nausicaa?
> Where'd she find him? He's going to be her husband.
> Either she's got herself off his ship some traveler from a faraway people –
> since nobody lives near us – or else in answer to her prayers
> the god she longed for came down from the sky, and she'll have him   280
> all her life. Better so, if she herself went and found somebody elsewhere.
> For she turns up her nose at these Phaeacians among her people
> though there are many excellent young men courting her."
> That's what they would say, and this would bring shame on me.   285
> And I would blame a girl who did such things,
> and who, going against the will of her father and mother,
> would sleep with men before being publicly married.

In just a few lines, Nausicaa brings up, through an imaginary third party, the notion of Odysseus marrying her, informs him that she is not averse to it, for she is not particularly interested in the several suitors who pursue her now, but also insists that it is marriage or nothing, because she is not the kind of girl who sleeps around.

Her seamless segue from talk of marriage to talk of relations with a man before marriage is especially worthy of note. Nausicaa may be a sheltered princess, but she possesses a keen sense of how to play the flirting game, implying that she has already devoted a good deal of private daydreaming to it.

Just as he had previously turned down the opportunity to live as an immortal with Calypso, Odysseus rejects the option of marrying the king's daughter, for the *Odyssey* is not a conventional fairy-tale. For all her charm and intelligence, Nausicaa may not be quite suited to serve as mistress of an *oikos* in the real world, as opposed to the storybook land of Phaeacia. Her opening conversation with her father (6.57–70), in which she pointedly avoids reference to her own impending need for clean clothing at her wedding, indicates that she can be devious. This impression is confirmed in her speech to Odysseus, which, for all its apparent common sense, attempts to set a personal agenda. While her efforts to exert subtle control over older men are part of the humor, that precocity could interfere with the *homophrosynê* that, as Odysseus himself tells her (6.180–5), is the most essential ingredient of a successful marriage. Putting this another way, Nausicaa is as yet too lighthearted and too self-absorbed to be able to use her wits as Penelope does, in scheming to keep Odysseus' household as intact as possible while bearing up under a painful weight of uncertainty.

The most troubling stand-in for Penelope is Helen, once again restored to her erstwhile position as queen of Sparta. Entertaining the young Telemachus in Book 4, she initiates the telling of stories about the exploits of Odysseus in Troy – after first drugging the wine with a *pharmakon* that will allow those present to relive the past without pain.[6] In her own account of how, while in Troy, she recognized Odysseus in disguise and was eventually taken into his confidence, she portrays herself as his equal in cunning and secretly loyal to the Greeks. Her husband Menelaus then counters with a story of how she almost exposed the device of the Trojan Horse by walking around it imitating the voices of the wives of the warriors inside; Odysseus alone prevented them from answering (4.235–89). While the paired narratives agree in crediting Odysseus with extraordinary achievements, they likewise underscore the ambiguity of Helen's position as a "multiple, inconclusive, and dangerous figure, whose reputation fluctuates repeatedly between praise and blame" (Worman 2001: 20). Like Aphrodite in Demodocus' song, but unlike her sister Clytemnestra, she enjoys full immunity from the consequences of adultery, while her store of mind-altering medications permits her to exert a form of psychic control over the men in her company. In the *Iliad*, Helen had embodied a fascination both awesome, "dreadfully like that of immortal goddesses" (*Il.* 3.158), and terrifying. Though in the *Odyssey* her sexual allure is supposedly disciplined, she remains an imposing and very unsettling presence. Hence Menelaus' prophesied fate – to dwell with Helen forever in the Elysian fields (*Od.* 4.561–70) – must appear, on reflection, a "less than unequivocally blissful" one (Suzuki 1989: 63).

The problem of gender on which the plot of the *Odyssey* turns is the weakness in the organization of *polis* society created by the wife's capacity to betray her absent spouse. Corollary tales present contrasting resolutions of that domestic and political dilemma. Clytemnestra, who, after cheating on her husband Agamemnon, conspired to murder him, is opposed throughout to the faithful Penelope, constantly reminding us that female loyalty can never be presupposed. The adultery of Ares and Aphrodite, like the deception of Zeus in the *Iliad*, burlesques the epic action by shifting it to Olympus and transposing it into a comic mode. In allowing Hermes and Apollo to joke roguishly about the sorry predicament of the lovers, it momentarily subverts the gravity of the central thematic issue (Olson 1989: 141–3; Peradotto 1993: 178–81). Yet the parallels between Hephaestus, the wronged husband, and Odysseus himself, especially in his disguise as a beggar, underscore the seriousness of those concerns on the human plane. Hephaestus is physically lame, and Odysseus feigns a limp, supporting himself on a staff; each triumphs over potential or actual violators of his household primarily through cunning; each is a master craftsman (Newton 1987). While Hephaestus forges magic chains to trap the adulterous couple, Odysseus constructs the very bed whose secret of manufacture proves his identity. Male virility – called into doubt by the kind of physical disability inflicted as punishment upon Anchises – is reaffirmed when the husband asserts authority over the *lechos*, the marital bed.

This, then, is the reason Penelope plays the "bed trick" on the stranger professing to be Odysseus. Readers often wonder why she continues to resist even after the nurse Eurycleia and Telemachus have both vouched for his identity. When Odysseus, faced with her lack of cooperation, finally gives up and tells Eurycleia to prepare a bed for him, Penelope takes the cue (23.174–80). She is not being unreasonable, she says: "I know very well how you looked [*mala d' eu oid' hoios eêstha*] when you left Ithaca." Then she confirms the order: fix a bed for him outside the bedchamber, "that very bed he himself made [*ton rh' autos epoiei*]." In revealing that she has in fact recognized him, she catches Odysseus off-guard. Aghast at the possibility that some man had hacked through the trunk of the olive tree that formed one of the bed's supports, rendering it portable, he abandons discretion and blurts out the secret of its manufacture, proving beyond doubt who he is. Critics have rightly noted that the immovability of the bed is symbolic of not only the permanence of marriage (a meaning already obvious to ancient audiences)[7] but, more to the point, the wife's continuing fidelity, and, by extension, the steadfastness of her resolve (J. J. Winkler 1990: 157–8; Doherty 1995: 144; Zeitlin 1995: 123–4). Because the bed is a concrete emblem of the sexual act itself, its fixed position within the innermost chamber of the house epitomizes the fundamental role of marital sexuality in stabilizing the *oikos*. Moreover, its metaphoric function as the defining token of Odysseus' identity may also imply that sexual experience was felt to play a vital part in developing a consciousness of oneself as unique.

Achilles in the Closet?

Perhaps the most significant feature of sexuality as it is represented in the Homeric epics is their meaningful silence about what later Greek civilization took for granted. There is no explicit mention of pederasty or any other form of same-sex eroticism in either the *Iliad* or the *Odyssey*. When the abduction of the Trojan boy Ganymede is mentioned, "the gods" as a group are held responsible; nothing is said of Zeus' own infatuation with him (*Il.* 20.232–5). Hermes appears to mortals in the guise of an adolescent with his first growth of beard, "the most attractive time of young manhood" (*Il.* 24.348, *Od.* 10.279), but the adjective *charieis*, "graceful, elegant, beautiful," describes what is visually pleasing in general and need not imply an erotic response. Finally, nowhere is it actually stated that Achilles and Patroclus are anything more than comrades, although commentators ancient and modern have claimed that the phrasing of a few lines, even if formulaic, hints that a more intimate bond is to be understood.

Although the interaction between Nestor's son Pisistratus and Odysseus' son Telemachus is handled casually, references to their sleeping in close proximity have raised suspicion that the relationship should be understood as a pederastic one (Clarke 1978: 383). We can deal with this suggestion quickly, since the passages on which it rests are few. Accompanied by Athena in the guise of his father's associate Mentor, Telemachus sails to Pylos on the west coast of Greece seeking news of Odysseus, and then proceeds overland to Sparta escorted by Pisistratus. At Pylos, king Nestor invites him to spend the night in the palace rather than on his ship, and he is given a bed in the portico alongside Pisistratus, who, we are informed in the next line, is "still a bachelor" (*Od.* 3.397–401). However, Homer is not telling us about his erotic inclinations but instead explaining why he customarily sleeps there; if Pisistratus were married, he would occupy a bedchamber with his wife. While the two young men are staying at Sparta, they bed down in the forecourt of the palace, and they may be lying alongside one another, since Telemachus wakes Pisistratus by kicking his foot (*lax podi kinêsas*, 15.45). On the other hand, he could also do that while standing above him, and the action, in any case, is not terribly romantic. Between themselves, Pisistratus and Telemachus show none of the fervent affection that Achilles and Patroclus feel for one another; when they part company (15.193–216); Telemachus characterizes their relationship as that of hereditary guest-friends (*xenoi*) and youths of the same age (*homêlikes*). Their like-mindedness (*homophrosynê*), which he also acknowledges, is a desirable thing in future rulers and allies as well as man and wife. On balance, the two princes seem simply to be travel buddies who have shared a memorable adventure.

With Achilles and Patroclus it is different. After giving Patroclus permission to wear his armor into battle as a ruse to assist the Greeks, Achilles expresses a wish that both armies, Trojans and Greeks alike, would perish, so that the two of them by themselves might capture Troy (*Il.* 16.97–100). The apparent callousness and egotism of the remark shocked ancient scholars, who excised it on the grounds that it was a later insertion by someone who thought the pair were lovers (Clarke 1978: 384–5). Yet the grim fancy suits Achilles' aggrieved mood, for he is still seething over Agamemnon's insult. Although it would hardly be reflective of his ordinary state of mind, it shows that at this critical juncture, when he is so caught up in bitter resentment, Patroclus is the only other person who still exists for him. The hero's subsequent hysterical reaction to the news of his friend's death, his fanatical thirst for revenge, and his persistent grief and sleeplessness even after Patroclus is buried seemed no less excessive to ancient critics. Modern readers are also struck by his constant embracing and touching of the corpse, his self-confessed longing (*pothos*, 19.320–1, a word often found in erotic contexts) for the dead man, his stubborn refusal of food and drink, and his mother Thetis' consoling advice: "it is good even to mingle with a woman in love" (24.130–31), where the phraseology might mean either that "even having sex," along with eating and sleeping, or that "having sex even with a woman," as opposed to a man, is a good thing. At the very least, the intensity of Achilles' passion goes far beyond the emotional attachments other males in the epics feel not just for their fellow soldiers but for their blood kin.

In classical Athens, numerous persons familiar with Homer had no doubts about the nature of the friendship. In his lost play *Myrmidons*, the tragedian Aeschylus represented the distraught Achilles speaking of Patroclus' thighs (*mêrôn*) and of their many kisses (frr. 135 and 136 Nauck²); Phaedrus in Plato's *Symposium* praises Achilles for being a devoted *erômenos* who avenges his lover's death (179e–180b); and in a forensic speech before a jury the orator **Aeschines** cites the pair as models of temperate and noble love, as opposed to the unrestrained and violent lusts of men like his opponent (1.141–50). However, the Socrates of Xenophon's *Symposium* vigorously attacks the presumption of pederasty, saying that Achilles avenges "not a boyfriend but a companion" (*hetairos*, 8.31). We should also note a real confusion over who was the *erastês* and who the *erômenos* among those who inferred such a relationship. Nestor recalls Patroclus' father advising him to give Achilles good counsel, since he, Patroclus, was the older (11.786); Plato's Phaedrus therefore chastises Aeschylus for portraying Achilles as the lover. Yet Achilles is clearly the dominant figure in Homer, a fact that absolutely contradicts the protocols of the mentor–protégé relationship on which pederasty was conceptually grounded.[8] Halperin (1990: 86–7) points out that classical Athenians were obviously attempting, with great difficulty, to impose a notional framework of man–boy relations familiar to them upon the alien patterns of emotion and behavior displayed by the Homeric heroes. In a sense, their grasp of what is going on between Achilles and Patroclus was as incomplete as ours.

Conclusion

In the preceding sections we have surveyed the representation of sexual encounters, divine and human, in the foundational poetry of ancient Greece – the epic narratives that shaped central social institutions, such as marriage and the *oikos*, by instilling and reinforcing conventional gender expectations. Except for our closing glance at male–male relationships in Homer, the focus has been on unions between male and female partners. Because these myths reflect the experience of an agricultural economy for which propagation is crucial, they are not concerned with sexuality that is nonreproductive by definition. Instead, Hesiodic epic concentrates upon the ordering of the cosmos through generational succession, Homeric epic upon the social division of labor and the proper performance of gendered tasks. Sex in this scheme of things is, as we have observed earlier, even-handed in terms of anticipated pleasure, rather than solely aimed at gratifying the dominant partner. Furthermore, it operates in conjunction with a sensuality conditioned by the polar dimorphism of male and female bodies (Sissa 2008: 5–8). Although the loves of the gods are a special case, epic human *erôs* is overwhelmingly an attraction of equals and opposites.

No one will deny, meanwhile, that Homer recognizes the reality of strong homoerotic affect between two adult males. But the lack of any explicit mention of physical relations has been taken as evidence that the practice of institutionalized pederasty was not yet established in Greece (Dover 1978; Percy 1996: 36–41). Some ancient readers had a different explanation for Homer's reticence. Aeschines, in the speech mentioned above, claims that the relationship of Achilles and Patroclus is not called by its real name because any educated listener would understand the situation. Yet that begs the question of why direct reference would be suppressed in the first place. The absence of any overt recognition of pederasty in epic is thought-provoking in view of the prominence it will soon assume in lyric poetry of the Greek archaic age, for that period falls roughly between 700 and 500 BCE; that is, it begins scarcely a century after Homer. During that time, literary treatment of *erôs* undergoes a great shift in focus, with boy-love becoming one of its central motifs. Does this change reflect a genuine alteration in social practice – the sudden appearance of pederasty as an institutionalized custom, at least among the elite – or can it be explained simply by the emerging popularity of other genres of poetry, composed for a different audience? Or are both factors involved? To gain a broader perspective on this question, we will need to examine the recitation of explicitly pederastic poetry in the context of elite male drinking parties (*symposia*) and the social purpose of such gatherings. So in the next chapter we turn to the Greek symposium, an occasion considerably more convivial than its modern scholarly namesake.

Discussion Prompts

1. While Aphrodite displays some attributes common to Near Eastern war goddesses, Homer explicitly denies her any skills on the battlefield. The only Olympian goddess associated with warfare is the virgin Athena, who defends the city and its people. These facts suggest that Greek culture perceived tension between mature female sexuality and the sphere of combat. Since Athena is female, that tension cannot be explained by gender alone but must have more complex roots. Discuss.

2. The mythic origins of the Greek cosmos are biological: beings are produced from the physical coupling of a male and a female parent. Contrast the Greek creation myth with the process described in *Genesis*, in which a supreme power, God, brings all things into existence out of nothing. Are there structural differences between a biologically generated universe and a divinely created one?

3. Pandora is given to mankind in retaliation for Prometheus' theft of fire, which enables human beings to master nature. In what way does the sexuality she represents serve as a brake on human aspiration?

4. In the *Iliad* and the *Odyssey* we encounter various kinds of sexual relationships between partners both human and divine. What is the purpose of treating the lovemaking of divinities (Zeus and Hera, Ares and Aphrodite) in comic fashion? Compare the unions of the goddesses Calypso and Circe with Odysseus to the seduction of Anchises by Aphrodite. What is different in terms of the divine vs. human balance of power?

Notes

1 A much later nude female figurine from Cyprus (Garrison 2000: 79, fig. 3.5) shows a goddess with a knotted strap crossed over her breasts, standing upon a toad. Toads as archaic-age votive offerings at Corinth and in the sanctuary of Artemis Orthia at Sparta may have been dedicated to prevent barrenness or ensure safe pregnancy (Gimbutas 1982: 177).

2 This detail is preserved by Proclus, a fifth-century CE philosopher, in his commentary on Plato's dialogue *Timaeus*. Because it is very late testimony, it may not be wholly reliable (Kirk-Raven-Schofield 1983: 62 and fr. 54).

3 Hesiod's two accounts of the rivalry between Zeus and Prometheus culminating in the manufacture of Woman agree in broad outline, although each contains elements not included in the other. Thus Zeus' gift is anonymous in the *Theogony* and named Pandora only in the *Works and Days*. Clay (2003: 104–5, 116–20) contrasts the perspectives from which the two narratives are told: humanity in the first poem is viewed through divine eyes as a potential antagonist, while in the second the focus is on the tragic human lot. When summarizing the main events, I follow the version in the *Works and Days*, as it is more detailed.

4 It is possible that the name *Pandora* was originally an epithet of the earth goddess, meaning "she who brings all gifts [to mortals]." If so, this would be another example of alterations to the religious content of a myth in response to changed ideological concerns of a society (Garrison 2000: 85).

5 Fifth-century vases by the Nausicaa Painter (Munich 2322, *ARV²* 1107/2) and Aison (Boston 04.18, *ARV²* 1177/48) graphically illustrate this moment, making the girls' fear of a possible sexual threat on the part of Odysseus quite clear (Shapiro 1995: 156–9).

6 The drug, which Helen obtained in Egypt, is said to prevent the drinker from grieving even if a mother or father should die, or a brother or son were slaughtered before his own eyes (4.222–6). Given Helen's association with epic in the *Iliad*, critics have suggested that her *pharmakon* is a symbol of poetry, itself an antidote for pain (Clader 1976: 33; Bergren 1981). However, the sinister properties of a drug that can induce such emotive numbness seem to cast doubt upon the moral quality of both Helen and the poetry she represents (Suzuki 1989: 57–91, esp. 70–1).

7 A learned commentator on *Od.* 23.288 remarks that the bed's solidity is a figure for the indissoluble marriage bond (noted by Zeitlin 1995: 121).

8 The lyric poet Pindar compares the instruction the boy boxer Hagesidamus, winner at the Olympics, received from his trainer Ilas to that which Patroclus received from Achilles (*Ol.* 10.16–19). Because the relations of trainers and young athletes are often depicted in a pederastic light (Scanlon 2002: 211–26), Pindar is, like Aeschylus, representing Achilles as Patroclus' *erastês* (Hubbard 2002: 264 with n. 25, and 2003).

References

Austin, N. 1994. *Helen of Troy and Her Shameless Phantom*. Ithaca, NY: Cornell University Press.

Bergren, A. L. T. 1981. "Helen's 'Good Drug': *Odyssey* IV 1–305." In S. Kresic (ed.), *Contemporary Literary Hermeneutics and Interpretation of Classical Texts*. Ottawa: University of Ottawa Press. 201–14.

—— 1989. "*The Homeric Hymn to Aphrodite*: Tradition and Rhetoric, Praise and Blame." *Classical Antiquity* 8: 1–41.

Beye, C. R. 1966. *The "Iliad," the "Odyssey," and the Epic Tradition*. Garden City, NY: Anchor Books.

Blondell, R. 2009. "'Third Cheerleader on the Left': from Homer's Helen to Helen of *Troy*." *Classical Receptions Journal* 1.1: 4–22. Downloaded from crj.oxfordjournals.org on March 29, 2011.

Boedeker, D. D. 1974. *Aphrodite's Entry into Greek Epic*. Leiden: E. J. Brill.

Breitenberger, B. 2009. *Aphrodite and Eros: The Development of Erotic Mythology in Early Greek Poetry and Cult*. New York and London: Routledge.

Brown, A. S. 1997. "Aphrodite and the Pandora Complex." *Classical Quarterly* 47: 26–47.

Budin, S. L. 2003. *The Origin of Aphrodite*. Bethesda, MD: CDL Press.

—— 2010. "Aphrodite *enoplion*." In A. C. Smith and S. Pickup (eds), *Brill's Companion to Aphrodite*. Leiden and Boston: E. J. Brill. 79–112.

Burkert, W. 1985. *Greek Religion*. Trans. J. Raffan. Cambridge, MA: Harvard University Press.

Calame, C. 1999 [1992]. *The Poetics of Eros in Ancient Greece*. Trans. J. Lloyd. [Orig. pub. as *I Greci e l'eros: Simboli, pratiche e luoghi*, Roma-Bari: Gius. Laterza & Figli, 1992.] Princeton, NJ: Princeton University Press.

Carson, A. 1990. "Putting Her in Her Place: Woman, Dirt and Desire." In D. M. Halperin, J. J. Winkler, and F. I. Zeitlin (eds.), *Before Sexuality: The Construction of Erotic Experience in the Ancient Greek World*. Princeton, NJ: Princeton University Press. 135–69.

Clader, L. L. 1976. *Helen: The Evolution from Divine to Heroic in Greek Epic Tradition. Mnemosyne* supp. 42. Leiden: E. J. Brill.

Clarke, W. M. 1978. "Achilles and Patroclus in Love." *Hermes* 106: 381–96.

Clay, J. S. 2003. *Hesiod's Cosmos*. Cambridge: Cambridge University Press.

Cyrino, M. S. 2010. *Aphrodite*. New York and London: Routledge.

Dillon, M. 2002. *Girls and Women in Classical Greek Religion*. London: Routledge.

Doherty, L. E. 1995. *Siren Songs: Gender, Audiences, and Narrators in the* Odyssey. Ann Arbor: University of Michigan Press.

Dover, K. J. 1978. *Greek Homosexuality*. London: Duckworth.

duBois, P. 1992. "Eros and the Woman." *Ramus* 21: 97–116.

Faraone, C. A. 1990. "Aphrodite's ΚΕΣΤΟΣ and Apples for Atalanta: Aphrodisiacs in Early Greek Myth and Ritual." *Phoenix* 44: 219–43.

Ferrari, G. 2002. *Figures of Speech: Men and Maidens in Ancient Greece*. Chicago: University of Chicago Press.

Garrison, D. H. 2000. *Sexual Culture in Ancient Greece*. Norman: University of Oklahoma Press.

George, M. 2006. *Helen of Troy*. New York: Penguin.

Gimbutas, M. 1982. *The Goddesses and Gods of Old Europe, 6500–3500 BC: Myths and Cult Images*. Berkeley, CA: University of California Press.

Gumpert, M. 2001. *Grafting Helen: The Abduction of the Classical Past*. Madison: University of Wisconsin Press.

Halperin, D. M. 1990. *One Hundred Years of Homosexuality and Other Essays on Greek Love*. New York: Routledge.

Hansen, W. 2000. "Foam-born Aphrodite and the Mythology of Transformation." *American Journal of Philology* 121: 1–19.

Holmberg, I. 1995. "The *Odyssey* and Female Subjectivity." *Helios* 22: 103–22.

Hubbard. T. K. 2002. "Pindar, Theoxenus, and the Homoerotic Eye." *Arethusa* 35: 255–96.

—— 2003. "Sex in the Gym: Athletic Trainers and Pedagogical Pederasty." *Intertexts* 7: 1–26.

Kirk, G. S., Raven, J. E., and Schofield, M. 1983. *The Presocratic Philosophers: A Critical History with a Selection of Texts*. 2nd edn. Cambridge: Cambridge University Press.

Maguire, L. 2009. *Helen of Troy: From Homer to Hollywood*. Malden, MA, and Oxford: Wiley-Blackwell.

Morris, I. 2000. *Archaeology as Cultural History: Words and Things in Iron Age Greece*. Oxford: Blackwell.

Newton, R. M. 1987. "Odysseus and Hephaestus in the *Odyssey*." *Classical Journal* 83: 12–20.

Olson, S. D. 1989. "Odyssey 8: Guile, Force and the Subversive Poetics of Desire." *Arethusa* 22: 135–45.

Payne, H., et al. 1940. *Perachora: The Sanctuaries of Hera Akraia and Limenia*. Oxford: Clarendon Press.

Peradotto, J. 1993. "The Social Control of Sexuality: Odyssean Dialogics." *Arethusa* 26: 173–82.

Percy, W. A., III. 1996. *Pederasty and Pedagogy in Archaic Greece*. Urbana, IL: University of Illinois Press.

Pucci, P. 1977. *Hesiod and the Language of Poetry*. Baltimore, MD: The Johns Hopkins University Press.

Sale, W. 1961. "Aphrodite in the *Theogony*." *Transactions of the American Philological Association* 42: 508–21.

Scanlon, T. F. 2002. *Eros and Greek Athletics*. Oxford: Oxford University Press.

Shapiro, H. A. 1995. "Coming of Age in Phaiakia: The Meeting of Odysseus and Nausicaa." In B. Cohen (ed.), *The Distaff Side: Representing the Female in Homer's "Odyssey"*. Oxford: Oxford University Press. 155–64.

Sissa, G. 2008. *Sex and Sensuality in the Ancient World.* Trans. G. Staunton. New Haven and London: Yale University Press.

Suzuki, M. 1989. *Metamorphoses of Helen: Authority, Difference, and the Epic.* Ithaca, NY: Cornell University Press.

Vernant, J.-P. 1990. "One … Two … Three: Erôs." In Halperin et al. (eds.), *Before Sexuality.* 465–78.

West, M. L. 1997. *The East Face of Helicon: West Asiatic Elements in Greek Poetry and Myth.* Oxford: Clarendon Press.

Winkler, J. J. 1990. *The Constraints of Desire: The Anthropology of Sex and Gender in Ancient Greece.* New York: Routledge.

Winkler, M. M. 2009. "Helen of Troy: Marriage and Adultery according to Hollywood." In *Cinema and Classical Texts: Apollo's New Light.* Cambridge and New York: Cambridge University Press. 210–50.

Wohl, V. J. 1993. "Standing by the Stathmos: The Creation of Sexual Ideology in the *Odyssey.*" *Arethusa* 26: 19–50.

Wootton, D. (ed.) 2005. *Christopher Marlowe: Doctor Faustus with the English Faust Book.* Indianapolis: Hackett.

Worman, N. 2001. "This Voice Which Is Not One: Helen's Verbal Guises in Homeric Epic." In A. Lardinois and L. McClure (eds.), *Making Silence Speak: Women's Voices in Greek Literature and Society.* Princeton, NJ: Princeton University Press. 19–37.

Wright, M. 2005. *Euripides' Escape-Tragedies: A Study of* Helen, Andromeda, *and* Iphigenia among the Taurians. Oxford and New York: Oxford University Press.

Zeitlin, F. I. 1995. "Figuring Fidelity in Homer's *Odyssey.*" In Cohen, (ed.) *The Distaff Side.* 117–52.

Further Reading

Austin, N. 1994. *Helen of Troy and Her Shameless Phantom.* Ithaca, NY: Cornell University Press. Full exploration of the alternative myth in which Menelaus' wife remains in Egypt while war is waged over a "phantom Helen."

Breitenberger, B. 2009. *Aphrodite and Eros: The Development of Erotic Mythology in Early Greek Poetry and Cult.* New York and London: Routledge. Distinguishes the divine personalities of Aphrodite and her accompanying helpers, the Charities and Peitho, from that of Eros and examines the literary relationships among these deities.

Clay, J. S. 2003. *Hesiod's Cosmos.* Cambridge: Cambridge University Press. Critical interpretation of Hesiod's *Theogony* and *Works and Days* as corresponding mythic descriptions of order on the divine and human planes, with special attention to the two stories of Prometheus and the creation of Woman.

Carter, J. B., and Morris, S. P. (eds.). 1995. *The Ages of Homer.* Austin: University of Texas Press. Illuminating collection of essays on the archaeological, historical, and poetic contexts of Homer and the reception of the epics in later antiquity.

Cohen, B. (ed.). 1995. *The Distaff Side: Representing the Female in Homer's "Odyssey".* Oxford: Oxford University Press. Essays by various authors on aspects of gender and femininity in the epic. Not surprisingly, there is no comparable volume for the *Iliad.*

Cyrino, M. S. 2010. *Aphrodite.* New York: Routledge. Presents an accessible introduction to Aphrodite as a cosmic power as well as a goddess of beauty and sexual desire.

Foley, H. P. 2009. "Women in Ancient Epic." In J. M. Foley (ed.), *A Companion to Ancient Epic.* Oxford and Malden, MA: Wiley-Blackwell. 105–18. Cross-cultural survey of the major roles of female figures in this genre.

Maguire, L. 2009. *Helen of Troy: From Homer to Hollywood.* Malden, MA, and Oxford: Wiley-Blackwell. Thematically-organized account of the function of Helen of Troy in literature from antiquity to the present.

Thornton, B. S. 1997. *Eros: The Myth of Ancient Greek Sexuality.* Boulder, CO: Westview Press. Controversial discussion of ancient perceptions of sexual desire as a dangerous natural force.

2

The Archaic Age: Symposium and Initiation

Archaic Greece was a song culture. Whether performed publicly in a ritual context where it was complemented by choral dancing, or privately at a gathering of friends by a single artist, music was the chief medium of popular entertainment. The librettos of songs, bereft of their melodies, are mainly the texts that survive, often only in snippets and papyrus fragments. Metrically, they fall into two main categories: **elegiac** poetry, composed of recurrent couplets of unequal length (a line of six metrical feet followed by one of five) and accompanied by the *aulos*, a kind of double flute; and **lyric** poetry, arranged in various kinds of stanzas made up of short rhythmic phrases, sung, as the name indicates, to the lyre. Thematically, the genre to which a song belongs is determined by the occasion of performance: paeans are hymns of praise to Apollo, dithyrambs are choral songs for Dionysos, *skolia* are after-dinner songs, **parterheneia** are songs for maiden choruses, **iambs** are poems of slander and abuse, and so forth (Fowler 1987: 90–101).

Since the use of writing was extremely limited, music was learned by ear. **Solon**, the leading Athenian statesman of his time (he served as *archôn* or chief official in 594/3 BCE), heard his nephew play a song of **Sappho** at a party and asked the boy to teach it to him, "so that," he said, "I may learn it and die" (Ael. *ap.* Stob. 3.29.58). Access to literary culture, as distinct from formal education, was more catholic because literacy was not a requirement for artistic appreciation. Non-elites, slaves, and women would all have had access to myths, songs, and oral lore transmitted by word of mouth. Still, we have to imagine circumstances of performance quite different from those we associate with today's mass-media entertainment. No electronic amplification, no CDs or MP3 files, no downloading from the Internet, of course, but also no mega-concerts with crowds of raucous fans in attendance. If poetry was sung before a large audience, the dignity of the event, almost always religious, guaranteed solemnity. Solo songs, or monodies, were performed in a more intimate venue, the dining room of a wealthy private house or a ruler's palace, with only a group of invited companions present. Probably the nearest modern analogy to hearing a Sappho or an **Alcaeus** sing on those occasions

Sexuality in Greek and Roman Culture, Second Edition. Marilyn B. Skinner.
© 2014 John Wiley & Sons, Inc. Published 2014 by John Wiley & Sons, Inc.

would be the experience of listening to a folk guitarist in a small coffee house with a regular clientele. The artist knows many members of her audience personally, draws energy from their rapport with her, and tailors her recital to their interests and preferences. If she writes her own material, she may mention in her lyrics something familiar to her listeners. Such exclusive references do not limit the song's popularity: when another folk singer incorporates one of her numbers into his own repertoire, he will usually preserve those allusions, even though his own audience may have to guess at their meaning. Thus songs still travel from artist to artist across the country, retaining elements of their original performance setting in re-performance, just as they did in antiquity.

Although the poetry of the archaic age could deal with many different subjects – warfare, religion, politics, philosophy, among others – love, and most frequently pederastic love, was its dominant concern. Our chief textual sources for the sexual attitudes and values of the archaic age are the lyrics of its love songs. They evoke the contradictory facets of *erôs*, its complex moods and sentiments, its mingled delights and pains, with metaphors that reverberate forcefully even when translated into an alien language. As scholarly evidence, though, this corpus of material presents serious difficulties. For example, we cannot take poets' statements about themselves as autobiographical. The artist speaks of himself or herself in the first person, but in doing so steps into a role, taking on the *persona* of a "Sappho" or "Alcaeus" and re-enacting the utterances of that character (Nagy 1996: 216–23). Thus the "Sappho" whom Aphrodite accosts in Sappho fr. 1 V is a fictive construct, not the composer. Because it was meant to captivate and excite audiences, moreover, love lyric presents emotional suffering in grandiose terms, and because it assumes its listeners are of the same social position, with common values and experiences, it provides no historical framework for its content. Other materials that might help to fill in the contextual gap are lacking: contemporary historical accounts are non-existent and later testimony may be inaccurate, inscriptional evidence is scanty and the archaeological record contested. Yet we know that momentous social changes, including the rise of the *polis*, colonization and expansion of trade, new contacts with the Orient, the introduction of writing and coinage, fierce competition among elites for political power, and bitter class conflict all occurred during this 300-year period.

The first question we consider in the present chapter, then, is how such external factors affected the expression of erotic feelings in a sympotic setting, especially when the lover was speaking to his *erômenos*. A second, and closely related, question has to do with the privileged status of the pederastic bond in the archaic period. Why does it suddenly take on the importance it does in the poetry of the time? This requires us to examine the controversial thesis that posits a link between homoerotic relations and initiatory, or coming-of-age, rituals.

When the Cups Are Placed

According to a commentator on Plato's *Symposium*, the phrase "wine and truth" was proverbial for those who talked frankly while inebriated. To illustrate, he quotes the opening line of a poem by Alcaeus: *oinos, ô phile pai, kai alathea*, "wine, o dear boy, and truth" (fr. 366 V). Here, in a nutshell, is the essence of the early Greek *symposium* or drinking party: alcohol, candor in the presence of trusted companions, and a young man being coached in proper behavior by older members of the group. In these surroundings, poetry performed an educational function by affirming collective values, often through direct address, as in the two books of elegies attributed to **Theognis** of Megara (composing *c*.550–540 BCE). What must strike modern readers as odd is that the framework for such elegiac instruction is pederastic; the addressee – sometimes called "**Cyrnus**," sometimes anonymous – is the speaker's beloved, and many of the verses harp on the fidelity owed to one's lover. Sympotic lyric can likewise address an *erômenos*, although it puts emphasis upon the speaker's desire and longing rather than sending an overtly didactic message. Before we turn to examining the content and formulas of archaic love poetry, though, we must locate the symposium within its political context.

The origins of the sympotic gathering are plausibly traced back to the Homeric age (Murray 1983). Local kings competed for honor by entertaining lesser nobles with sumptuous feasts and giving them valuable gifts. Members of the propertied class repaid their hosts' generosity by equipping a band of followers to accompany them on military expeditions. During the late eighth and early seventh centuries, as the *polis* society emerged, certain features of that Homeric way of life were transformed. Armies of heavily armored foot soldiers or **hoplites**, drawn from the citizenry, replaced elite troops, depriving the aristocracy of its primary civic function. Founding of overseas colonies brought about an expansion of trade, which in turn enriched a new social class of merchants and artisans. The introduction of coinage in the sixth century and its integration into the Greek economy was just as subversive of the preexisting state of affairs as foreign commerce, for it allowed low-status persons to acquire prestige goods by saving up money (Schaps 2003: 132). Coinage issued by city-states accordingly prevented wealthy nobles from monopolizing the circulation of precious metals through gift exchange (Kurke 1999: 6–23).

Over time, largely as a result of intermarriage, the nobility had acquired a disproportionate share of agricultural land, and, with it, political hegemony. With some exceptions, early archaic Greece was ruled by oligarchies, small blocs of wealthy landowning families. Sympotic culture arose in response to agitation against oligarchic privilege. As the urban middle class began to exercise its growing economic power, oligarchic families closed ranks, forming a tightly knit leisured class whose marriage and friendship affiliations crossed *polis* boundaries. Its political stance was conservative, hostile to developing democratic tendencies. The symposium became central to its cultured lifestyle. Special dining rooms were constructed in private houses, with space for between fourteen and twenty-two men, all facing each other to assist conversation. Here members of a **hetaireia** or private drinking club would discuss common political concerns while modeling masculine conduct for their *erômenoi*. The most famous visual depiction of a sympotic milieu actually comes to us from southern Italy (fig. 2.1). Painted on the inside walls of a stone sarcophagus at Paestum are scenes of drinkers reclining, playing *kottabos* (a game in which the dregs in the wine cup were thrown at a target), singing to the music of an *aulos*, and embracing.[1]

Fig. 2.1 The funeral banquet. Greek wall painting from the Tomb of the Diver, early fifth century BCE. Location: Museo Archeologico Nazionale, Paestum. Source: © Erich Lessing/Art Resource, NY.

Within sympotic culture, some historians contend, two belief systems began to compete for authority. One was a "middling ideology" encapsulated in Hesiod's *Works and Days* and propounded by iambic poets like **Archilochus** and Hipponax or moralizing elegists like Solon (Morris 1996: 28–31, 2000: 161–71; Kurke 1999: 25–7). The ideal member of the community is the *metrios* or "middling man," the self-sufficient landowner and head of household. Although he mistrusts the poor, he likewise avoids greed, for excessive wealth breeds arrogance, lack of restraint, and disdain for the rights of others – the cardinal social and religious offense of *hybris*. This ideology, subsequently the source of Athenian democratic values (Morris 1996: 40–2), opposed itself to an elitist tradition of conspicuous consumption, for the beleaguered rich who felt threatened by social developments were demonstrating their pre-eminence through the use of expensive goods imported from the Near East. Imitating Oriental potentates, symposiasts lay on couches rather than sitting at table and delighted in vessels, perfumes, and finery of Lydian manufacture. Their poets celebrated a "cult of **habrosynê**," or luxury infused with a refined sensuality (Kurke 1992). Eroticism became politicized, for the ostentatious diversion of energies and resources into appearance, dress, manners, and appreciation of the transient beauty of flowers and the human form, indulgences denied to the pragmatic middle class, found its natural sexual manifestation in nonreproductive congress (Morris 2000: 178–85). Thus this group of nobles escaped class tensions and reaffirmed among themselves their superiority to the **dêmos**, the "ordinary people," through shared meals, drinking, song, and sex in a protected sympotic ambience (Arthur 1984: 42–3).

Once the aristocracy lost its military function, it turned to sport as its main focus of physical competition. The archaic age was the period when the great Panhellenic athletic festivals were instituted, beginning with the traditional founding of the Olympic Games in 776 BCE. Games were introduced at local festivals as well; the poet **Pindar** (518–438 BCE), who composed celebratory odes for victorious athletes, mentions some twenty such regional contests (Scanlon 2002: 29). Athletic pursuits were not confined to the elite: during the sixth century, many Greek communities laid out exercise grounds so that *hoplites* might keep themselves fit for battle. These were the forerunners of the **gymnasium** with its *palaistra* or wrestling court. However, the expense of intensive training ensured that participation in athletic contests, especially on the Panhellenic level, remained the province of the well-to-do until the classical era. Though the gymnasium was open to all citizens, then, its popularity as a site for elite pastimes, including pederastic courtship, explains its close association in Plato and other classical Greek authors with the aristocratic symposium.

One last consequence of the rise of the *polis* was the proliferation of unconstitutional dictators, whom the Greeks, borrowing a foreign word, called **tyrannoi**. The "tyrants" of the archaic age were not necessarily despots conducting a reign of bloody terror. Fierce rivalry for power and prestige among oligarchic factions within the state prompted successful coups by strongmen capable of putting a stop to civic violence, at least temporarily. Once established in power, many, like Pisistratus, who controlled sixth-century Athens, turned out to be benevolent rulers who respected traditional institutions and sought to promote the welfare of the citizens. To add luster to their communities, they sponsored religious festivals, undertook civic works projects, and invited leading artists, musicians, and philosophers to enjoy their hospitality. The sixth-century poets Ibycus of Rhegium and **Anacreon** of Teos were guests at the court of the tyrant Polycrates of Samos, and Anacreon was later patronized by the **Pisistratid** dynasty. In a manner reminiscent of Homer's bard Demodocus, these poets provided banquet entertainment for the tyrant and his friends. Ibycus' and Anacreon's lyrics are characteristically sympotic in their focus on wine and love, but they lack the topical political commentary of Alcaeus' and Sappho's songs, which were composed for strictly private functions.

Fields of Erotic Dreams

Because the language of Greek lyric evokes images as readily as emotions, many of its most compelling descriptions of love are visually metaphoric, with emblematic details taken primarily from the natural world. One of the commonest figurative spaces within which Aphrodite and Eros operate is the flowery meadow (Bremer 1975: 268–74; Calame 1999 [1992]: 153–7). Hera and Zeus' rendezvous on the grassy slope of Mount Ida furnished the Homeric archetype for all such topographic descriptions. Many later episodes using a verdant meadow as backdrop do not feature consensual sex, however, but instead tell of adolescent girls forcibly inducted into womanhood. In the *Homeric Hymn to Demeter*, for example,

Hades finds Persephone gathering flowers on the plain and snatches her up as she reaches for a beautiful narcissus (*Hymn. Hom. Cer.* 6–14). Meadows can be employed as a setting for rape or seduction because they belong to the realm of nature yet are accessible from the *polis*, situated as they are on its outskirts. In addition, they are the grazing-ground for domesticated beasts, especially horses. Properly the verb for "breaking" or "taming" a horse, *damazein* is the regular euphemism for defloration: virgins were considered "wild" because their sexual potential had not yet been harnessed, as it were, to producing children.[2] Lastly, the heavily scented roses, hyacinths, and narcissi plucked by maidens in those surroundings are emblematic of the fates of unhappy youths who failed to make the transition from late adolescence to adulthood – such as Hyacinthus, Apollo's beloved whom he killed by accident, or Narcissus, who wasted away after he fell in love with his own reflection.

Whenever a lyric composer alludes to a grassy or flowering field, that whole system of symbolic resonances is brought into play. Even without an explicit mention of *erôs*, then, the language is likely to have hidden sexual implications. One well-recognized instance is Sappho fr. 2 V, an invocation summoning Aphrodite to attend a festive celebration. Elsewhere the poet expresses deep yearning for several of her female friends, whom she refers to collectively as her "companions" (*hetairai*, fr. 160 V, cf. frr. 126, 142). Here the setting is a temple precinct and what remains of the text describes it in lush detail. First, we hear of a grove of apple trees and altars fragrant with incense, both to be expected near shrines of the goddess. Other natural features, however, mark the site as unique and blessed (5–11):

> There cold water plashes through apple boughs,
> and all the place is shadowed with roses,
> and from the shivering leaves deep
> sleep slips down,
> and there a horse-pasturing meadow
> blooms with spring flowers, and breezes
> blow softly …

Apples, incense, roses, horses, the flowering meadow – each bears some relation to the cult of Aphrodite. All occupy a place in a network of erotic metaphors alluding to or symbolizing parts of the female body (Wilson 1996: 38). Thus the fleshy fruit of the apple (*mêlon*) and the folded petals of the rose can be used as analogues for the female genitalia, which explains their frequent occurrence in wedding songs. In Sappho's poem, these concrete natural objects are brought into conjunction with a special mode of sleep (***kôma***), a trance-like state often induced by supernatural means (Page 1955: 37). This is the slumber Hypnos sheds upon Zeus after he has made love to Hera: "I have wrapped a soft *kôma* about him," the god informs Poseidon (*Il.* 14.359). Through an imaginative, polysemous appeal to the senses of touch, smell, and sight, the description of the temple precinct evokes the corporal pleasures of lovemaking and repose after sex, becoming "an extended and multi-perspective metaphor for women's sexuality" (Winkler 1990: 186).[3]

Two lyrics by Anacreon illustrate how these tropes can also be deployed for invective purposes. In the first, the speaker addresses a reluctant girl, whose "skittish mind," the commentator tells us, "he allegorizes as a horse" (*PMG* 417):

> Thracian filly, why do you,
>   looking at me with suspicious eyes,
> evade me pitilessly, and assume
>   that I have no skills?
> Listen to me: I could easily throw
>   a bridle upon you
> and working the reins bend you
>   around the limits of the course.
> As it is, you graze in the meadows
>   and frisk, lightly prancing,
> for you don't have an expert rider upon you,
>   one who knows horses.

Riding is a standard ancient metaphor for sexual intercourse. Under cover of this extended conceit, then, the speaker is boasting about his masculine prowess. By comparing the girl who refuses his attentions to an untrained filly, he suggests that she does so from virginal modesty. Yet his addressee is obviously a prostitute, as her foreign origin indicates. While a respectable virgin in a meadow exposes herself to the threat of rape, the horse that ranges freely across the pastures of *erôs* is a figure for the woman already given over to promiscuity (Gentili 1988 [1985]: 186–94). The humor of the poem, then, is generated by maintaining two opposed readings of the girl's conduct and character in play through one set of images. The same contrast between prostitute and virgin seems to function in a patchy and much-supplemented papyrus text (*PMG* 346 fr. 1):

> … and your mother believes that
> she nurtures you, keeping you
> penned in the house.
> But you […] browse upon
> the fields of hyacinth
> where Cypris has tethered
> the … mares freed
> from the yoke-straps …

In ancient Greek, as in English, horses yoked together are a metaphor for wedlock. Here the addressee's companions in the flowering field are mares unyoked and set to graze by Aphrodite. Their liberty is that of the female who belongs to no one man and is sexually available to all.

For Sappho, woman's sensuality blooms in the meadow, whereas male poets treat the presence of a desirable young woman in such surroundings as a blatant provocation. One of the earliest texts capitalizing upon these nuances in order to create a puzzle for its audience is the so-called "Cologne Epode" (*PColon.* inv. 7511.1–35 = fr. 196A West²) of the seventh-century BCE poet Archilochus. A native of the island of

Paros, Archilochus was especially known in antiquity as the creator of virulent iambic, or "blame," poetry. Instead of articulating the ideals of the *hetaireia* in a positive manner, iambic verse ridiculed outsiders, real or fictional, for acting in ways that offended collective values. Group solidarity was affirmed by scapegoating an Other, usually through scurrilous and obscene allegations. Archilochus' fragments contain many coarse references, some quite bizarre: in one, a woman bending forward to fellate a man is compared to a Thracian or Phrygian slurping beer through a straw (fr. 42 West[2]).[4] He was most notorious, however, for his attacks upon a fellow citizen, Lycambes, and his daughters, one of whom was named Neobule.[5] Supposedly, Lycambes first promised Neobule to Archilochus in marriage, then broke the pledge, and Archilochus retaliated with a series of vicious attacks upon father and daughters that drove the latter to suicide. The Hellenistic epigrammatists Dioscorides and **Meleager** gallantly wrote protests on behalf of the dead girls, making them claim the allegations were untrue: "we never even *saw* Archilochus, we swear by gods and demigods, either in the streets or in the great precinct of Hera" (*Anth. Pal.* 7.351.7–8, cf. 7.352). This reference to a temple of Hera suggests that the Cologne Epode was set in its vicinity (Gentili 1988 [1985]: 185–7).

So much later tradition can tell us, but until 1974 we had very little idea of how Archilochus himself might have handled that scenario. With the publication of the new papyrus, we discovered that there, at least, he used the technique of first-person narrative to give his report a lively immediacy. The incomplete text begins with a young woman countering what was certainly a sexual proposition on the speaker's part. He ought to curb his passion completely, she says, until she is of the proper age to marry. But if his desire is too pressing, he might consider taking as a substitute another girl from her household, "a beautiful and tender virgin who greatly longs for wedlock" (3–6). Like Nausicaa negotiating with Odysseus, the maiden is anxious to define her bargaining position: she welcomes the stranger's hint at marriage but will not consent to premarital sex. By dangling the other girl, who she insists is both attractive and eligible, before his eyes, she is attempting to distract him from a worse option, rape.

"Daughter of Amphimedo," the speaker formally replies, addressing her as the child of her deceased mother, "for young men there are many delights of the goddess apart from the divine thing [*to theion chrêma*]; one of these will suffice" (10–15). At our leisure, he goes on, you and I will discuss this at further length; meanwhile, I will obey your bidding. What is meant by "the divine thing"? Even ancient readers having the complete poem in front of them were perplexed by this circumlocution, which could refer either to marriage as a divinely sanctioned state or, as a Greek lexicographer glossed it, to sexual intercourse, so described because its pleasures are godlike (Van Sickle 1976: 137–43). If "the divine thing" is construed as marriage, he must be promising to wed her later provided she cooperates now; if sexual intercourse is meant, he is apparently proposing a substitute course of action.

Several cryptic, broken lines follow (14–16):

> ... up from below the cornice and beneath the gates ...
>   don't grudge me, sweetheart, for I will check at the grass-bearing
>   gardens ...

As for the second girl, Neobule, he continues, let some other man take her. "She's ripe twice over, her virginal bloom and grace (**charis**) are long gone, she's mad for sex and can't stop herself." Popular beliefs about women's insatiable nature would make such assertions credible. After the first taste of carnal pleasure, it was thought, they soon became addicted. Too much sexual activity, however, also caused women to age quickly. So Neobule's desirability was short-lived, and, while still avid, she is now unappealing. To hell with her, says the speaker. With such a wife, I'll be the laughing stock of the neighborhood. It's *you* I want, for you're not untrustworthy and treacherous. She's just too hungry (*oxyterê*, literally "eager") and makes too many "friends." Jumping the gun in haste, he fears he produced, like the proverbial bitch, "a blind and premature litter." Though he appears to accept blame for his part in the earlier fiasco, the canine allusion is one last dig at Neobule, since bitches were also proverbial for shamelessness.

Tirade over, the anecdote progresses to its logical finale (42–53):

> Taking the girl, I laid her down
> in the luxuriant flowers. Having wrapped her in my soft cloak,
> supporting the nape of her neck with my elbow …
> … she ceased … like a fawn …
> and gently touched her breasts with my hands
> … revealed her skin fresh with the approach of youth …
> and stroking her beautiful body all over,
> I loosed my vitality [*menos*], touching her blond hair.

What the narrator does may seem obvious on first reading, but it is not that clear, and divergent interpretations of the poem hinge upon how one reads these closing lines.

If the man who tells the story actually did have full intercourse with the daughter of a citizen, and one not yet of marriageable age at that, he would have also wronged her father Lycambes, who was the girl's *kyrios* or guardian. Recall that Anchises in the *Homeric Hymn to Aphrodite* does not do as the disguised Aphrodite bids him – respect her pretended virginity, turn her over to his parents for safekeeping, and contact her relatives to propose honorable wedlock – but instead rushes her into bed. Had she been telling the truth, he would have committed an act of *hybris* with grave political repercussions, for he is a Trojan prince and she was ostensibly the daughter of a king. Anchises thus shows himself the kind of rash fool impetuous enough to reveal the secret of his son's origins later. The bedroom scene in the *Hymn* is clearly designed to give voyeuristic pleasure, so it is arguable that Archilochus' account was also aimed at exciting his all-male audience with a racy description of plucking forbidden fruit.[6] The narrator would then come across as a wily, smooth-talking rascal who achieves his immediate goal without quite making a permanent commitment – he has his way with the girl but postpones consideration of "the divine thing," marriage, to some indefinite time. In the process, he also evens the score against his personal enemy Lycambes. Since Archilochus' culture placed a high value on cleverness and verbal fluency and also understood revenge to be a man's moral duty, such a twofold success might have been applauded by a Greek audience, no matter how much it offends our own sensibilities.[7]

An alternative interpretation of events, however, is equally possible, provided we allow for sexual double-entendre in the scrappy lines 14–16 translated above. "Cornice" and "gates" might be additional metaphors for the female sexual organs (in the context, it is hard to conceive of another explanation for their presence, as the narrator is surely not commenting on the temple architecture). What else could checking at "grass-bearing gardens" connote, then, but a promise to confine himself to the pubic hair, without entering the vagina? That would be one of the unspecified delights of the goddess available to him apart from the "divine thing," full sexual intercourse. On that assumption, his addressing the girl with the **matronymic** (i.e., identifying her as her mother's daughter, rather than using the father's name for filiation, which was the ordinary procedure) is suggestive, because that was common practice for women speaking to each other privately, at least in the Hellenistic period (Skinner 1987; cf. Ogden 1996: 94–6).[8] Confidential information about sexual techniques was reputedly the sort of thing women shared among themselves.[9] In the absence of her mother, who is dead, the speaker tells the girl what she needs to know, doing so tactfully, through euphemism, as an older female friend would. When he looses his *menos* at the poem's end, then, true to his word, he ejaculates outside her body, his penis touching her pubic hair. In so far as his act does not involve penetration, it may not have qualified as sex per se, even though orgasm was achieved. Counterintuitive as that argument may appear, we will shortly see why it can be made.

Which of these two scenarios is the correct one? Given the poem's mutilated state, it is almost impossible to resolve that issue, and it is also conceivable that we were never meant to know. Archilochus, some have surmised, is playing games with his audience, leading it to anticipate a foreseeable outcome only to be taken by surprise. Having adopted a "feminine" *persona* to bargain with the girl he wants, the narrator reaches an apparent compromise with her, creates eager expectancy by his detailed description of amorous foreplay, then phrases the last words of his account so ambiguously that one cannot tell whether he has actually behaved as a "real" man in that situation would or should have done. In the end, then, the performer "eludes all the reactions that he has solicited in the course of performance" (Stehle 1997: 245, cf. Slings 1987: 50–1). If this is indeed the case, the witty representation of masculine prowess in the Cologne Epode is far more complex than corollary depictions of aggressive or victimized male gender identity in archaic lyric and elegy.

Singing as a Man …

In sympotic love poetry, ordinary masculinity takes two forms. One is embodied in a "rhetoric of control," in which the first-person speaker exercises his will over a second party. Whether he is carefully instructing a boy in the correct behavior for a trusty companion or castigating childish fickleness, the poetic *ego* speaking in this mode reflects his listeners' conviction of their innate superiority to others in body, mind, and temper as members of a socially advantaged economic and gender class. An alternative construction of male identity, however, casts the speaking subject as the helpless target of repeated violence by Eros, whose blows he is incapable of resisting, or paradoxically transfers ascendancy in the relationship to the nominally submissive beloved. Each model inscribes the male subject into an asymmetrical grid of power relations: as a spokesman for the attitudes of his elite companions, he shares their rank, participates in their privileges, and derives prescriptive authority from them, but as a mortal inferior to the gods and susceptible to the sight of youthful beauty he is at the mercy of powerful extrinsic forces. This dual presentation of manhood incorporates the full range of tensions within symposium culture.

The elegiac verse of the Theognidean corpus is permeated with the rhetoric of control employed by the lover to dictate to his beloved. Normally the *erastês* addresses his companion like a preceptor, sometimes encouragingly, at other times sternly, always professing to have the boy's best interests in mind. Here, for example, he applies strong psychological pressure in the guise of ethical training (1235–8):

> Boy, master your feelings and listen to me. I will make a statement
>   neither unpersuasive nor unpleasing to your heart.
> Make yourself grasp this word with your mind: it is not necessary
>   to do what is not in accordance with your desire.

With this guarantee of moral autonomy, the speaker paves the way for convincing the youth that he yields of his own free will. The related perils of treating a lover condescendingly, listening to false friends, and disregarding good advice are recurrent pedagogical themes in these elegies. At one point the speaker threatens a headstrong beloved with the fate of certain Greek cities of Asia Minor subdued by the Persians, presumably because they paid no heed to circumstances until it was too late (1103–4):

> Arrogance [*hybris*] destroyed both Magnesia and Colophon
> and Smyrna. Rest assured, Cyrnus, it will destroy you.

Finally, even as it pleads for the boy's fidelity, another quatrain voices the suspicion and fear of the lower classes felt by those whose privileges are slowly being eroded (1238a–40):

> Never send away your present friend and seek after another,
>   persuaded by the words of base-born men.
> Often, you know, they will say groundless things against you to me,
>   and likewise against me to you. Take no notice of them.

In these last two couplets, anxiety about the personal conduct of the *erômenos* tellingly shades into concern about larger political realities.

A related dynamic is at work in poems where the speaker, rejected by an attractive boy or girl, retaliates with some kind of disparaging sexual innuendo. In the Cologne Epode, Neobule is figured as overripe, fly-bitten fruit. Fickle *erômenoi* in Theognis' elegies are compared to birds of prey veering with every wind (1261–2) and horses indifferent to whoever rides them (1267–70). Anacreon too employs the flightiness associated with horses to insinuate that the girls he targets are incapable of behaving modestly. Listeners who can appreciate the clever implications of these metaphors are being invited to join the disappointed lover in mocking the object of ridicule. When an artist creates literary effects demanding such cultural sophistication on the part of the audience, he appeals to its sense of superiority: "models and metaphors for erotic relationships can function as part of a collective supremacist rhetoric involving the whole sympotic group" (Williamson 1998: 78). Poetry that provides an opportunity to participate vicariously in the experience of putting down a lower-status individual reaffirms elite privilege in the face of encroachment by other social orders. Fundamentally, then, it is a vehicle of tendentious political discourse.

When the male speaker is exerting dominance over another, his own bodily integrity is necessarily secure. In another poetic construction of masculinity, though, the boundaries of his selfhood lie exposed to Eros' disruptive physical effects. Love as a kind of tangible affliction is a motif already implicit in epic narrative but developed to its fullest extent in archaic lyric. There it is identified as an elemental force of nature and characterized by epithets signifying its destructiveness (Thornton 1997: 11–47). Because the archaic Greeks regarded sensations of consciousness and feeling as corporeal and originating in specific organs, passion could be conceptualized as doing bodily harm in the manner of a crippling injury or a mental or physical illness (Cyrino 1995: 168). Masculinity is at stake when love invades the body's perimeters, dissolving restraint and forcing its unwilling object to succumb to "womanish" longing. Calling upon this set of associations, Archilochus applies the epic language of combat death to the effects of love, which stabs him as an enemy would (fr. 193 West[2]):

> ... wretchedly I lie wrapped in desire,
> faint, by the gods' will pierced through the bones
> with racking pains ...

or simply overpowers him: "but, comrade, limb-loosening desire masters me" (fr. 196 West[2]). In both fragments the speaker suffers not only injury but also the shame of defeat by a stronger combatant. Similarly, Ibycus visualizes Eros rushing upon him like the north wind and forcibly pummeling his senses to the core (*PMG* 286), or casting him into the inescapable nets of Aphrodite (*PMG* 287). In what is perhaps the most imaginative use of "battering" imagery, Anacreon portrays Eros striking him like a blacksmith with a powerful sledgehammer and then plunging him into an icy winter torrent (*PMG* 413). Such images fuse excruciating physical pain with mental disorientation: in his distress, the speaker is unable to comprehend fully, much less articulate, what has befallen him (Cyrino 1995: 117). Loss of control over the rational self is complete.

When the lover is so consumed by his obsession, the hierarchical power positions of the pederastic relationship are reversed: it is the *erômenos*, not the *erastês*, who is now acknowledged as the dominant figure. Anacreon provides one revealing example (*PMG* 360):

> Boy with the virginal glance,
> I court you, but you pay no heed,
> unaware that you drive
> the chariot of my heart.

Corresponding descriptions of the lover as the suppliant or even the slave of the younger partner are found in Athenian philosophic discourse, while courtship scenes from Attic vase paintings of the late archaic and early classical periods show an older man urgently beseeching the favors of a younger one. This paradoxical exchange of functions de-emphasizes the subordination of the boy, indicating that his junior standing within the company is a transitional one and thereby distinguishing him from permanent inferiors, such as slaves and women (Golden 1984: 312–17). Adult members of the audience are meanwhile invited to participate imaginatively in the suffering of the poetic *ego*. Identifying with his despair and self-pity might afford maudlin pleasure at a particular stage of drunkenness, and reaffirming group solidarity through shared sentiment would also diffuse erotic rivalries threatening to create hostilities within the *hetaireia*. Although the conventional motif of the *erastês* as love's puppet and fool may appear to invalidate the asymmetry assigning the partner of superior social status the dominant role in the relationship, this temporary and largely symbolic reversal could actually serve as an exception that proved the rule.

One of the commonest formulas in the surviving corpus of archaic Greek verse is the combination of "Eros ... me ... again [*dêute*]" forming the opening statement of a new poem. Far from learning from one bad experience, the lyric speaker constantly finds himself in the same predicament over and over again. **Alcman**, composing at Sparta in the second half of the seventh century BCE, is quoted as beginning a love song with "Eros again, by the will of Aphrodite sweetly flooding down, softens my heart" (*PMG* 59a). The fragment of Ibycus paraphrased above starts with the god "again looking upon me with his eyes meltingly from beneath dark eyelids" as he entangles the lover in Aphrodite's nets. Anacreon employs the identical motif no fewer than five times: when golden-haired Eros hits him again with a purple ball (*PMG* 358); when he dives again, drunk with Eros, into the sea to cure his passion (*PMG* 376); when the hammer of Eros the blacksmith smites him again; when, in flight from Eros, he turns to Pythomander again (*PMG* 400); and when, combining "Eros" and "me" into the first-person verb *ereô*, he preposterously pronounces himself "again in love and not in love, mad and not mad" (*PMG* 428). Recurrent susceptibility to frustrated desire is yet another symptom of the lover's fecklessness. Still, the ability to recognize such a tendency in himself implies a measure of emotive detachment: he "must necessarily possess some degree of objectivity and perspective on his current state" (Mace 1993: 338). This consideration intimates that the formula is being employed for self-referential or comic purposes, and the mocking ironies of Anacreon lend that notion plausibility. When the speaker speaks of himself as hammered and doused by Eros *again* or as attempting a suicidal leap to cure his passion *again*, it is obvious that a poetic conceit is being parodied. For this reason, too, the reader ought to suspect that the ideological construct of the male lover as victim of Eros is not meant to be taken as gravely as might be suggested by the extravagant language in which it is couched.

Against all such contrived laments over the harshness of love, we should set the elegist Mimnermus' evocation of the alternative. Composing in Ionia on the eastern shore of the Mediterranean during the seventh century, Mimnermus was renowned for his two books of elegies. One, entitled *Nanno*, was reportedly dedicated to his mistress of that name, a girl flute-player. Hellenistic and Roman writers valued the sweetness and gentleness of his love poetry (Callim. *Aet.* 1.11–12; Prop. 1.9.9–10). The following elegy (Stob. 4.20.16 = fr. 1 West²), which may be complete in itself, shows why. In ten lines, densely permeated with Homeric vocabulary, Mimnermus voices a distinctly un-Homeric sentiment:

> What is life, what is pleasure, without golden Aphrodite?
>   May I die when these things no longer matter:
> secret intercourse and soothing gifts and bed,
>   which are flowers of youth to be plucked
> by men and women. But when painful old age comes on one,
>   which makes a man both shameful and sordid,
> evil cares always oppress his heart,
>   nor does he enjoy beholding the light of the sun;
> instead he is hateful to boys, contemptible to women.
>   So bitter a thing the god made old age.

… and Singing as a Woman

Plutarch affirms that the art of poetry is the same whether practiced by an Anacreon or a Sappho (*De mul. vir.* 243b). In composing for an audience of women, Sappho treats the same erotic themes as her male counterparts and employs familiar literary formulas and imagery in equivalent ways. Like them, she envisions sexual desire as a violent natural phenomenon ("and Eros shook my heart like a wind in the mountains falling upon oaks," fr. 47 V). Desire is also, familiarly enough, "limb-loosening," and, in a straightforward application of the *dêute* formula, it again makes her tremble – although in the next line it is further described, strangely, as a "bittersweet uncontrollable crawling thing" (fr. 130 V). Among all the lyric poets, finally, Sappho provides the most clinical description of erotic pathology, characterizing the effect of glimpsing the beloved as a progressive breakdown of one bodily faculty after another, verging at last upon death (fr. 31 V).

Despite these and other similarities, however, Sappho's concept of female sexual experience does not resemble paradigms of sexuality in male-authored poetry: contemporary feminist critics trace out a different configuration of eroticism in her lyrics. In contrast to the male *erastês*' adversarial relationships with his love object and with the god afflicting him, her dealings with both mortals and divinities seem mutually rewarding. Most obviously, her speaker does not attempt to impose her will upon the person she loves, but instead, through engaging appeals, tries to elicit a corresponding response from her (Stehle [Stigers] 1981; Skinner 1993: 133–4; Greene 1996 [1994], 2002).[10] Often, the poems are addressed to another desiring person whose feelings are given lyric expression through the speaker's empathy. Williamson explains this as a "circulation" of desire in which the difference between "I" and "you" as subject and object is elided (1995: 128–31, 1996: 253–63). Lastly, Sappho's personal contacts with Aphrodite are warm and intimate, and poems 2 and 96 show the goddess participating actively in the celebrations of the Sapphic circle. Elsewhere in the sympotic tradition, as well as in Homer and Hesiod, Aphrodite's gifts are valued, but she herself is a dangerous entity. Only in Sappho's lyrics does she enjoy a comfortable companionship with mortals.

In the "Ode to Aphrodite," Sappho's only wholly surviving poem (fr. 1 V), Aphrodite's behavior resembles, and may well be modeled upon, Athena's assistance to her favorite warriors in Homer (Winkler 1990: 166–76). Divinity and mortal share a moment of rapport, while the self-conscious use of *deûte* is taken to amusing lengths. The speaker begins by appealing to Aphrodite's mercy and reminding her of a previous epiphany. In response to Sappho's cries on that occasion, Aphrodite had descended in her sparrow-drawn chariot and requested a briefing (13–24):

> ... and you, blessed lady,
> with a smile on your immortal countenance,
> asked what I suffered *again* [*deûte*] and why
> I called on you *again* [*deûte*],
>
> and what I most wished to happen to me
> in my maddened heart. "Whom do I persuade *again* [*deûte*]
> [...] into your friendship? Who, Sappho,
> wrongs you?
>
> For if she flees, soon she will pursue,
> if she does not receive gifts, she will give them,
> if she does not love, soon she will love,
> even unwilling." (emphasis added)

In addressing the speaker as "Sappho," Aphrodite engages her not as a repeatedly frustrated lover but as a poet who uses the *deûte* formula, implying that her repertoire "includes a regular litany of love complaints of the form 'Eros ... me ... again'" (Mace 1993: 359–61). The poem thus becomes a programmatic "signature piece" neatly reprising the singer's characteristic themes. When Aphrodite is asked to return, in the concluding stanza, to accomplish Sappho's present objective and to become her *symmachos* ("fellow-fighter"), she is being enlisted as both helper in love and creative ally, an equivalent of the Muse. In this ode, consequently, homoerotic desire is a stimulus to artistic invention (Skinner 2002: 66–9). This is atypical, for elsewhere in the archaic literary tradition song may indeed be a balm and consolation for love's suffering, but the pangs of desire, an unwanted intrusion on male self-possession, cannot generate anything as constructive as art.

We have virtually no textual evidence for archaic social conditions on Sappho's native island of Lesbos, situated in the eastern Mediterranean just off the coast of modern Turkey. Elsewhere in mainstream Greek culture a male-centered, patriarchal gender ideology was so entrenched that it is not easy to imagine a milieu that could give rise to this seemingly unorthodox, female-oriented construction of sexuality. As it tenders near-contemporary iconographic evidence for women's private dining, however, a recent archaeological discovery, the "Polyxena Sarcophagus," helps us visualize Sappho performing in a similar kind of setting.[11] Made by Greek artists for Persian patrons, the sarcophagus was excavated in 1994 from a tumulus in the northern Troad, in the same geographical region as Lesbos, which would in fact have been the closest major site of Greek occupation. It is late archaic in date and may therefore have been carved between fifty and seventy-five years after Sappho's death, since she is conventionally assigned to the end of the seventh and beginning of the sixth centuries BCE.

Two faces of the sarcophagus deal with the sacrifice of Priam's daughter Polyxena. On the principal long side, four men participate in her killing, while six women look on making gestures of grief; on the short side to the right, Hecuba, her mother, mourns with two companions. The second long side depicts a funerary celebration, dominated by a seated woman in the center, who may represent the deceased. Four women surround her and two bring gifts to her. At the right of the same scene, two female musicians play while four armed warriors dance; they are watched, in turn, by four additional women. Sevinç, the discoverer of the sarcophagus, remarks upon the high visibility of women in the scene: "the men are relegated to the status of performers, whose movements follow the rhythms made by female musicians" (1996: 262).

It is the picture on the fourth side that is most germane to the present discussion. That it is pendant to the funerary celebration is indicated by the parallel relationship of the Hecuba scene to that of Polyxena's sacrifice. Five women are grouped in a convivial situation (fig. 2.2). One, at the far left, raises one hand toward her face while touching the back of a second woman with the other. She, in turn, is seated upon a dining-couch (*klinê*), sharing it with a third woman, the most prominent of the group. The two are having an animated conversation: the woman on the right makes an explanatory motion, while the other, raising her mantle and gesturing with the palm of her hand, expresses delighted astonishment.[12] To their right, two women look on: one holds an egg in her right hand and a dish in her left; the other holds a pitcher in her right hand, a mirror in her left. The egg and mirror connect this scene to the previous one of the funerary meal, where a bowl of eggs and a mirror are presented to the central figure. Mirrors are characteristic attributes of women in a domestic setting and eggs, a symbol of immortality, are appropriate grave offerings (Sevinç 1996: 262).[13] The symposium scene may therefore be a continuation of the depiction of the funerary banquet, or it might reflect a prior moment in the earthly existence of the deceased. In either case, the sarcophagus, which has no contemporary parallels in Greek art, affords evidence of women's sympotic activities from a geographical locale and a time period not far removed from those of Sappho. In such a private, hospitable environment, desire and music might well accompany each other as parallel and interrelated expressions of female subjectivity.

Fig. 2.2   Polyxena sarcophagus, *c*.525–500 BCE. Short side at right of funerary celebration: women at symposium. Source: Drawing by Dr Nurten Sevinç. Originally published in *Studia Troica* 6 (1996), p. 261. Reproduced by permission of Dr. C. Brian Rose on behalf of the Troy Project.

Boys into Men

Until now we have been speaking of the symposium as though it was all of a piece, but it actually was divided into three parts, according to classical Athenian sources. First came the dinner, consisting of bread, the staple, and what was put atop it: cheese, oil, vegetables, and, as a special delicacy, fish, for meat was consumed only on sacrificial occasions (Davidson 1997: 3–35). Food is central to depictions of symposia in Attic comedy, but archaic elegy and lyric instead concentrate on rituals of drinking (Wilkins 2000: 203). Those activities were conducted separately; only after the meal was concluded did the communal drinking, the symposium proper, begin. Since it had a high alcohol content, wine was tempered with water in a mixing bowl (**krater**), and scholars calculate that the resulting mixture was equal in potency to modern beer. Guests were served the same quantity in order. At a restrained, temperate symposium, the *krater* was filled no more than three times, enough to enliven conversation and leave guests feeling mellow; further refills, warns the god Dionysos in a comic fragment, successively lead to violence, shouting, routs, black eyes, summonses to court, vomiting, madness, and throwing furniture around (Eub. *ap*. Ath. 2.36b–c). If drinking continued, the symposium was likely to end in a ***kômos***, a noisy procession through the streets to demonstrate group solidarity. As Plato tells it, the decorous philosophic gathering at Agathon's house is interrupted, first by an inebriated Alcibiades and a few of his guests, and then by a second group of revelers who find the door open, stumble in, and make themselves at home carousing (*Symp.* 212c–e, 223b). If Plato is not distorting the historical picture, the closest analogue to Athenian streets after dark might be a university district after a Big Game victory. In his dialogues, though, drunkenness carries a great deal of symbolic weight, so we should not treat the *Symposium* as sociological evidence for the frequency of loud public disturbances.

Other kinds of men's gatherings, while designed, like the symposium, to foster comradeship and group loyalty, were more closely bound up with the military responsibilities of male citizens. Most noteworthy among these was the **Dorian** habit of communal dining. The inhabitants of Crete, an island in the central Aegean, and those of Sparta, whose territory lay at the southern tip of mainland Greece, both spoke Doric, a Greek dialect, and preserved similar archaic institutions, attributed in each case to a mythic lawgiver, Minos of Crete and Lycurgus of Sparta.[14] Spartan men ate in *syssitia*, eating clubs composed of fifteen members each. All members were expected to contribute a fixed amount of food and drink each month to the common mess, although the wealthier might provide more than was required. If a man became too poor to contribute his monthly ration, he could not exercise his rights of citizenship (Arist. *Pol.* 1271a.29–32, 1272a.12–16). Food was nutritious but not plentiful; wine was served, but drunkenness was branded as shameful. The dining arrangements of the Cretans were similar: adult males partook of vegetables, meat, and well-watered wine in the ***andreion***, "men's house." Drunkenness, Plato tells us, was there prohibited by law (*Min.* 320a). Unlike at Sparta, however, meals were subsidized by the state. Aristotle, to whom we owe the latter fact, also states that the custom of dining in common originated with the Cretans and was then brought to Sparta (*Pol.* 1271a.1–3), a belief shared by many other classical authors.

Xenophon, who spent twenty years among the Spartans and observed their institutions at first hand, praises the moderation and temperance encouraged by communal meals, where the mix of ages ensured that elders would restrain their juniors from overindulgence (*Lac.* 5.4–7). In the *Laws*, however, Plato's spokesman, a stranger from Athens, shocks his two walking companions, Cleinias, a Cretan, and the Spartan Megillus, with his declaration that their zero-tolerance policy against drunkenness is an impediment to rational self-control, since it does not allow for practice in overcoming temptation (647a–650b).[15] More crucial to our inquiry, he identifies the gymnasium and the common meal as institutions that promote physical relations between members of the same sex (nothing is said about private symposia), and notes that Crete and Sparta are jointly held responsible for introducing the custom of pederasty to Greece. This passage (636b–d), which, as we saw earlier, has even found its way into a constitutional legal brief, is foundational to the scholarly claim that pederasty has a basis in initiation rites. The ethical issues raised here furthermore suggest that approaching Greek homoeroticism as a collective expression of social behavior is more illuminating than regarding it as the product of individual inclination, motivated by pleasure – our own usual context for erotic acts.

When the **Athenian Stranger** asks for examples of Dorian rituals that educate youth in courage and self-restraint, Megillus replies that communal dining and gymnastic exercises encourage both virtues. The Athenian objects. Such institutions are the breeding-ground for civil strife, he declares, and, what is more,

> the very antiquity of these practices seems to have corrupted the natural pleasures of sex, which are common to man and beast. For these perversions, your two states may well be the first to be blamed, as well as any others that make a particular point of gymnastic exercises. Circumstances may make you treat this subject either light-heartedly or seriously; in either case you ought to bear in mind that when male and female come together in order to have a child, the pleasure they experience seems to arise entirely naturally. But homosexual intercourse and lesbianism seem to be unnatural crimes of the first rank, and are committed because men and women cannot control their desire for pleasure. It is the Cretans we all hold to blame for making up the story of Ganymede: they were so firmly convinced that their laws came from Zeus that they saddled him with this fable, in order to have a divine "precedent" when enjoying that particular pleasure.[16]

Let us put aside for the moment the question of what the Athenian Stranger means by describing same-sex copulation as "unnatural" (*para physin*), in contrast to heterosexual relations; we will take up that issue when we discuss the development of a philosophical discourse on sex and marriage during the Hellenistic period. Here we are interested in the Stranger's claims about its origins.[17] We must bear in mind that he is talking about pederasty as an *institutionalized* social activity, for it was the *overt* recognition of pederasty as a legitimate social practice, within certain parameters, that set the Greeks apart from other peoples (Dover 1988: 115). The Athenian makes three assertions: the educational system of Crete and Sparta, with its emphasis on all-male dining and gymnastic exercise, promotes homoerotic sex; the antiquity of that system has given rise to the belief that pederasty originated in those two states; the Cretans are further thought to have invented the myth of Ganymede's abduction as a justification for the custom, which implies that they themselves saw a need to justify it.

Other ancient evidence seems to support the connection Plato is drawing between the upbringing of boys, as carried out in Dorian states, and pederasty. We can begin by summarizing what three more writers, Xenophon, Aristotle, and Plutarch, have to say about the *agôgê* or age-based educational system of archaic and classical Sparta. The Spartans felt themselves constantly exposed to threats of an uprising posed by former inhabitants of the surrounding territory whom they had conquered and reduced to slavery. Therefore their whole social organization had the single objective of producing first-rate combat troops, and the *agôgê* was essential to that purpose.

Over a period of thirteen years, young citizen males passed through three stages of instruction defined by age, acquiring more rights and responsibilities in each. Socialization (*paideia*) began at seven, when boys were removed from the home and placed in a band of age mates (*agela*, literally "herd"). From that point on they ate, slept, and were schooled in common. The boys were trained in song and choral dance, but lessons in reading and writing were kept to a minimum. Starting at twelve, they cropped their hair, wore no tunics and were given just a single cloak each year. In athletics and mock fighting, they competed strenuously with each other and against other *agelai*, enduring cold, hunger, and physical hardships, including severe whippings. At twenty, after gaining combat experience as reservists or guerrilla fighters, youths graduated from the *agôgê*, were admitted to a *syssition*, and became entitled to marry. Yet they were still required to bunk with their messmates: conjugal visits to the bride's home were infrequent and clandestine.[18] When they reached thirty, they could finally leave the barracks and live in their own households, but they continued to dine with their eating group into old age. This arduous program of socialization was designed to instill conformity, obedience, courage, and stamina – traits highly valued in Spartan society.

Xenophon locates pederasty firmly within the context of the state-sanctioned instructional system, remarking, by way of introduction, that it is "related in some way to *paideia*" (*Lac.* 2.12). The lawgiver Lycurgus, he tells us, approved of a decent man attempting to befriend and associate with a boy whose soul he admired; this he deemed "the noblest form of education" (*kallistên paideian*). The infamy attached to carnal intercourse ensured that physical relations with the beloved were avoided no less than incest (2.13). Xenophon fears, though, that people will doubt his word because the laws in many *poleis* do not forbid sex with boys. Although Aristotle too appears to deny that the Spartans approve of intercourse between males (*tên pros tous arrenas sunousian*), in contrast to the Celts who do, he is probably speaking there of two adult men, as the statement occurs in a discussion of men's dealings with their wives (*Pol.* 1269b.26–27).

Plutarch – writing more than four centuries after Xenophon, but having access to many earlier sources now lost – says nothing in his *Life of Lycurgus*, which contains his fullest treatment of the *agôgê*, about whether or not pederastic relationships were physically consummated. He does, however, provide many other particulars about such involvements not found in Xenophon's account. Boys began to receive the attentions of *erastai* from among the young men of good reputation when they were twelve (17.2). Individuals under thirty, the age of full maturity, did not go to the marketplace but instead had their daily needs supplied by kinsfolk and lovers (25.1), which may imply that pederastic associations at Sparta were prolonged well past the age at which they customarily ended in other Greek states. Although discipline was communal, and elder men as a group had the right to chastise any younger male, the *erastês* was expected to act as a surrogate father, for he himself was held responsible if the boy behaved poorly (18.4). Cartledge identifies this as an instance of "displaced fathering," a phenomenon found in many other cultures (1981a: 22).

Parallels with Spartan usages can flesh out information about the education of young men in fourth-century BCE Crete. Our informant is Ephorus, who dealt with the Cretan constitution in the fourth book of his lost *Histories*, probably composed soon after Plato's death in 347 (Morrow 1993 [1960]: 21–5). Ephorus' account of Cretan *paideia* is excerpted by the early imperial Roman geographer Strabo in considerable detail (10.4.20). In Crete, too, we are told, youths were classified into age-grades. Prepubescent sons were taken to the men's halls, where they waited on their fathers and the other adult diners; when they themselves ate, they sat together on the ground, not at table.[19] Both in summer and winter they only wore scant shabby cloaks, like their Spartan counterparts. In Crete the classroom curriculum also consisted of elementary reading and writing, together with musical instruction. At seventeen, the adolescent joined an *agela* where he participated in organized activities such as hunting, athletics, and mock combat. Either at this time or upon leaving the *agela* at twenty, he was given the right to attend the public gymnasium. Marriage, finally, was both compulsory and age-related: all youths leaving the *agela* were ceremonially married at the same time, although the groom did not take the bride home right away but waited until she was old enough to manage a household. This is because the legal age of marriage for Cretan girls was twelve – unlike Sparta, where the Lycurgan code prescribed that girls marry in their late teens, so they would be mature enough to bear healthy children.

With some minor variations, then, the experience of passing from boyhood to adulthood in Sparta and Crete seems comparable: it was formally structured by age-group, it emphasized physical education and the development of combat skills, and its progress was marked by obvious rites of transition, like the cutting of hair or marriage en masse. One custom of maturation, however, is peculiar to Crete – at least we have no evidence that it ever happened anywhere else, and Strabo himself thinks it strange (*idion*). It involves the ritual abduction of the boy and is described as follows (10.4.21):

> The lover announces to the boy's relatives three or more days in advance that he is going to make the abduction. For them to hide the boy or not let him walk along the appointed road is deeply disgraceful, because they would be admitting that he does not deserve to get such a lover. When the parties come together, if the abductor is the boy's equal or superior in rank and other matters, those kindred rush at and grapple with him, but only as a token gesture to satisfy custom; then they gladly turn the boy over to him to lead off.

A perfunctory chase follows, which ends at the door of the lover's *andreion*. The pair then goes off to a remote area in the wilderness, where, accompanied by friends, they remain for two months, feasting and hunting. When they return to the city,

> the boy is let go after receiving as gifts a military outfit, an ox, and a drinking cup[20] [these are the gifts prescribed by law] and other things so numerous and costly that his kinfolk chip in because of the sum of expenses. The boy sacrifices the ox to Zeus and entertains those who came back with him, and then he gives an account of his relations with his lover, whether he was satisfied with them or not. The law permits him this so that, if any force was brought to bear upon him in the course of the abduction, he is empowered to avenge himself at this point and get rid of the offender. For those who are attractive to look at and of prominent ancestry it is disgraceful not to obtain lovers, since the assumption is that they suffer this because of their character. But the "ones who stand beside" [*parastathentes*], for so they call the abductees, receive distinction, because in both the choruses and the races they have the most honorable positions, and they are permitted to dress differently from their peers in

the outfit they were given by their lovers, and not only then but after becoming
adults they wear conspicuous clothing to indicate that each was "renowned" [*kleinos*],
for they call the beloved *kleinos* and the lover *philêtôr*.

Although the act of boy-abduction, which probably happened at puberty, has
obvious equivalents in myth – Ganymede was carried off by Zeus, Pelops by
Poseidon, and Chrysippus by Laius, the father of Oedipus – its only historical Greek
analogue is the well-known staged capture of the Spartan bride, which Plutarch also
refers to as a *harpagê* or abduction (*Lyc.* 15.3). The parallels are indeed striking, for
the Spartan ceremony must also have involved a token show of force. Both the kidnapping of the boy and the mock-seizure of the bride would allow a prospective
lover or groom to display his physical skills and mental and moral capacities to the
relatives of his intended, so proving himself worthy to ally with them – a vital
consideration in a warrior society (Patzer 1982: 82–3).[21]

Yet, according to several scholars, the analogy between the two rites ought not to
be pressed too far. Bride-abduction was a symbolic token of the groom's desire,
which the Lycurgean code promoted in the belief that passionate intercourse would
produce more vigorous infants. Institutionalized pederasty, on the other hand, was
a survival of a prehistoric procedure of ritual initiation for young males.[22] Copulation
with boys, according to this theory, had the same function as in rituals of maturation
reported for certain modern tribal cultures of the southwestern Pacific region. There
anthropologists have amply documented the existence of a belief that semen is the
physical medium through which adult masculinity is transmitted. The sex-segregated
warrior communities of Melanesia are worried about the proper gender development
of youths, who may have been subjected to dangerous feminine influence during
childhood contact with the mother.[23] In order to become men, boys must consequently be inseminated, whether through oral or anal genital contact or by having
seminal fluid applied to incisions.[24] Bremmer argues that this same notion, if not
universal among pre-literate cultures, was a common assumption of Indo-European
peoples (1980: 290). Greek ritual pederasty was therefore a means of socialization
to which the lover's sexual gratification was purely incidental.

Because it was rooted in the earliest historical period of proto-Greek civilization,
only the conservative, archaizing societies of Crete and Sparta are thought to have
preserved pederasty in what was closest to its original form. Apart from historical
reports of the custom in those two areas, traces of its formerly widespread existence
are claimed to subsist in a broad array of myths, set in various geographical areas of
Greece, that account for the origin of homosexuality in a given locale. The antiquity
of so many of these narratives, especially those concerned with pupils and their
divine or human teachers (Apollo and Hyacinthus, Poseidon and Pelops, Hylas and
Heracles, to name three), suggests that rites of initiation involving pederasty were
numerous in the pre-*polis* era (Sergent 1986: 259–69).

Initiatory elements certainly seem to feature in the Cretan custom of abduction.
It is demonstrably a "rite of passage" involving separation from a previous existence,
spending of a certain period of time in a liminal state, and final reincorporation into
the community, at which point the subject's new status is acknowledged (Van Gennep

1961: 21, 65–115). Carrying off the boy to the lover's *andreion* imposes a break with his past life, and the sojourn in the wild, where he receives instruction in hunting, a manly skill, can be regarded as a "betwixt-and-between" phase of existence. After coming back to civilization, the boy is given gifts that correspond to his altered circumstances: the warrior's clothing marks his new responsibilities as a defender of society; the ox sacrificed to Zeus, whose meat is shared with companions, is an emblem of his future religious duties as head of a household; and the wine cup is a token of his admission to the men's feasts, since boys' consumption of wine, in Crete as generally throughout Greece, was strictly monitored (Sergent 1986: 16–20).[25] Ephorus' account of this custom, which was already almost obsolete in his day, is therefore the primary text most cited as evidence by proponents of the initiatory hypothesis.

In other parts of the Greek world, pederastic courtship, according to the same theory, gradually lost its initiatory purpose and became an activity engaged in by the aristocracy for its own sake, with youthful beauty the main attraction and the lover's eventual gratification its objective. Yet it never entirely lost its association with training in adult citizenship, which explains why instruction in **aretê**, "manly virtue," remained such a prominent aspect of the ideal relationship of lover and beloved in classical Athens (Patzer 1982: 111–14). Similarly, the role in the initiatory process once played by all-male dining clubs is reflected in the attention still given to pederasty in poetry created for the archaic and classical symposium, the gathering that eventually took the place of the *syssition* or *andreion* (Bremmer 1990: 137).

Some archaeological discoveries have been interpreted as supporting this hypothesis of origins. The Chieftain Cup, a carved **Minoan** drinking vessel found at Ayia Triada in Crete and dated to approximately 1550–1450 BCE, pictures two youthful male figures of unequal height, armed with weapons, facing each other. Because of their distinct and unusual hair styles, which in Minoan art seem to indicate differences in age and status, the cup is thought to illustrate the actual rite described by Ephorus: supposedly, it shows the *philêtôr*, the taller figure, handing over the three designated gifts to the *kleinos*. The rural sanctuary of Hermes and Aphrodite at Kato Syme yielded two dedications that may forge continuity of practice between Minoan Crete and the Greek archaic age. A bronze figurine of the eighth century BCE depicts two helmeted nude males standing side by side holding hands; they are again of different heights, and each has an erect penis. In a bronze relief plaque from the middle or late seventh century now in the Louvre, an adult bearded man faces and grasps the arm of a younger man carrying a wild goat, possibly an allusion to the two months the boy and his captor spent hunting. In the absence of any written records, these images are difficult to interpret; if they have been explained correctly, however, they seem to indicate that boy-abduction was a Minoan ritual taken over by later Dorian invaders (Koehl 1986: 107–8 and plate VIIb). Though the Minoans' ethnic affiliations are mysterious, many scholars believe they originally came from Anatolia (modern Turkey), while, at the height of their prosperity around 1700 BCE, they maintained strong cultural ties with the Near East and Egypt. Tracing the practice of initiatory pederasty back to Minoan Crete thus creates a problem for those who would define it as an Indo-European survival.

Inscriptional evidence has also been brought to bear on the problem. Found in a house at Phaistos, a storage jar from the Geometric period (750–30 BCE) bears an incised graffito that identifies it as belonging to "Erpetidamus, son of a lover of boys [*paidop(h)ilas*]."[26] Along with the bronze votives mentioned above, this is the earliest support for the argument that pederasty was institutionalized in the Greek world before 700. Mid-sixth-century graffiti from the Spartan colony of Thera, an island near Crete, praise the beauty and dancing skills of boys, and some mention sexual acts. The inscriptions were found on a rock wall and other locations in the vicinity of both a later Hellenistic gymnasium and a temple of Apollo Carneius, who at Sparta was one of two divinities most concerned with the upbringing of the young.[27] When, in *IG* XII 3.537, we read that "by [Apollo] Delphinios, here Crimon mounted a boy, the brother of Bathycles," the writer's appeal to the god to bear witness may indicate that these are "ritual inscriptions, designed to celebrate the completion of initiation ceremonies" (Cantarella 1992: 7; cf. Graf 1979: 13). Still, they could just as easily be secular boasts and taunts (Dover 1978: 122–3; 1988: 125–6), and some considerations strengthen that possibility. The verb *oiphein* used in the above graffito as well as others is a Doric dialect expression for "have intercourse," blunt though not offensive (Bain 1991: 73–4). Yet we would expect a sacral pronouncement to resort to euphemism when speaking of the act. Again, one other inscription (*IG* XII 3.540) designates a Crimon, probably the same person, as "first in the Konialos," evidently the name of an obscene dance associated with an **ithyphallic** divinity (Scanlon 2002: 85–6).[28] Finally, and most problematic for the "religious inscription" reading, there was a firm Greek taboo against having sex in a sacred place, so it is very unlikely that ceremonial intercourse would occur, as the graffiti attest, within Apollo's very precinct.

Despite the explanatory appeal of the initiatory hypothesis and the supposed existence of much corroboratory evidence, vigorous objections to it have been raised by K. J. Dover (1988: 115–34). Dover questions whether the beliefs of geographically remote contemporary peoples can cast light upon archaic Greek cultural systems. Among other objections, he denies the supposed universality of primitive faith in the "masculinizing" power of semen and in ritualized homosexuality as an initiatory practice.[29] He also points to the complete absence of any recognition of homosexuality in Homer, Hesiod, Archilochus, and even in Tyrtaeus, a Spartan war poet (last half of the eighth century BCE) who, if anyone, might have had something to say about "the *erastês* setting an example of valour to his *erômenos*" (1988: 131). Consequently, he proposes that homosexuality, both male and female, was, as he puts it, brought "out of the closet" around 600 BCE by "Greek poets, artists, and people in general" – that is, that it was rendered acceptable and popularized by opinion-makers of the time. Myths, which still circulated orally, were reinterpreted in the telling to conform with new audience expectations: the rape of Ganymede, for example, was now attributed to Zeus rather than the Olympians as a collective group and given a sexual motive previously lacking.[30] What we observe in the late archaic age is, to summarize Dover's position, the *invention* of romantic pederasty – its introduction into Greek discourses on *erôs* as an acceptable pattern of social conduct. As a recognized institution it had previously been nonexistent, despite the likelihood that individual private acts of sex with boys would have taken place often enough.

The silence of epic is Dover's best argument. True, there may be reasons for that omission other than absence of the corresponding reality. In non-literate Homeric society, epic poetry recited on public occasions served as an educational medium, encoding social norms in easily remembered narrative form and thereby transmitting values from one generation to the next. Because its purpose was communally oriented, it might not have dealt with all sides of human life but instead concentrated upon relationships that reproduce social institutions and ensure family survival. That may be why Homer and Hesiod are exclusively concerned with sexuality in the context of marriage, procreation, and inheritance of an estate, as well as with the negative social consequences of deviant heterosexuality. Other kinds of sexual activity could have been engaged in covertly or openly with their existence simply ignored by early poets. Nevertheless, the want of references, even cautionary or derogatory ones, to any kind of same-sex relationship in the Hesiodic corpus or in Archilochus, who is quite blunt about sex with women, does seem peculiar if ritual pederasty was as much an element of maturation throughout the prehistoric Greek world as the initiatory hypothesis requires it to be.

Assuming, for the sake of discussion, that Dover is right, what cultural factors would have awakened interest in a type of sexual behavior of which literature had previously made no mention? Dover himself refuses to speculate, but historians swayed by his overall argument have tried to fill the explanatory gap by extrapolating from known phenomena. Scanlon, for example, hypothesizes a gradual escalation of interest in both athletics and pederasty from the eighth to the sixth centuries, spurred on by "heightened social competition for status" (2002: 68). Aesthetic admiration for the physical form of the boyish contestant, coupled with the spread of athletic nudity from Sparta to other communities, would account for a "likely cooperative evolution between the gymnasium and the popular acceptance of pederasty" (2002: 212). But that seems a secondary consequence rather than a root cause.

Demographics has become a favored historical explanation. One well-known archaeological theory that seeks to account for a surge of new cultural developments after 800 BCE holds that what amounted to a massive population explosion put a large strain on agricultural productivity and forced more intensive use of arable land. Political centralization, frequent wars, and a great wave of overseas colonization were indirect responses to problems of overpopulation (Snodgrass 1977, 1987: 188–210). Pederasty, some argue, was one strategy adopted as a remedy: men were encouraged to delay marriage and form relations with boys as a substitute (Sallares 1991: 166–71). From Crete, where the aristocracy was unable to provide adequate land for descendants, the new institution spread to the mainland (Percy 1996: 62, 69–72). This suggestion is based on Aristotle's contention (*Pol.* 1272a.24) that the Cretans had recourse to segregating women and promoting homoerotic liaisons "in order not to overpopulate." Aristotle's testimony has been questioned, however, on the grounds that the Cretan oligarchy was actually threatened by low birth rates in historical times and resorted to measures – such as early and mandatory marriage for young men – to further the production of citizen offspring. Unlike the population of Greece as a whole and Sparta in particular, Crete's population therefore remained stable, and may even have slightly increased, during Aristotle's lifetime and later (Spyridakis 1979). In and of itself, then, demographic data, though suggestive, does not appear to provide a complete explanation for the societal change hypothesized.

Unearthing the root cause for the emergence of institutionalized pederasty, if it did indeed "come out" in the seventh and sixth centuries, is far beyond the scope of this chapter. However, we can postulate a reason for its seemingly abrupt materialization as a leading theme in sympotic poetry by drawing an imaginary parallel with the so-called "sexual revolution" of the 1960s. Suppose all the newspaper and TV archives, home videos, diaries, and other documentary materials produced in the past sixty years perished in some cataclysm, and in the year 2713 what survived from that period were a couple of late-1950s Doris Day movies and several episodes of *Sex and the City* preserved in a bank vault. Researchers would be as hard pressed to understand how our culture moved so quickly from one construction of female sexuality to the other as we are to understand the reasons why pederasty, formerly unmentioned in literature, suddenly became a key preoccupation of archaic song. In each case, we would be inferring a societal transformation from a striking change in fictive treatments of sex without contextual knowledge of the circumstances those fictions supposedly mirrored.

Now, as a matter of fact, premarital intercourse, parenthood out of wedlock, living together before or instead of marriage, homosexual pair-bonding, and related patterns of activity were not unknown before the 1960s. At that time, however, they were definitely not publicized. Persons so involved kept their situation secret from all but a few trusted friends, unless they were part of a fringe community, which itself would try to maintain a low profile. Today nonconformist lifestyles are still targeted for condemnation by social conservatives, but their acceptance in the popular media is taken for granted, indeed deplored by moralists. The increasingly matter-of-fact stance assumed in movies, television, music, and other vehicles of popular culture over the past few decades toward what had been regarded as reprehensible conduct better not mentioned aloud may be more interesting as an analytical problem for historians than any increase in the conduct itself.

This is because modifications in the content of public discourses on sex, as Foucault demonstrated in the first volume of the *History of Sexuality*, are indicative of strategic shifts in how a society regulates individuals. When we are confronted with a drastic change in the prevailing discourse – in the post-industrial Western media, growing tolerance for previously marginalized behaviors and, in archaic Greece, an unprecedented poetic celebration of boy-love as a pursuit of the aristocracy – we would do well, following Foucault, to inquire how the collective ideology is responding to broad social trends by adjusting sexual protocols so as to retain some control over personal lives. Sociologists are currently exploring the effects of such factors as the proliferation of mass media, the spread of AIDS, globalization, and computerization on the way sex is presently conceptualized. One credible reason for today's increased acceptance of non-marital sexuality may be, paradoxically, to deactivate extremist momentum: by coming to terms with certain less threatening elements of the sexual revolution, liberal democracy tempers protest (Ludwig 2002: 112–13). The development of a *polis* society, a political transformation comparable in its scope and its impact on the individual to the recent transition from an industrial to a service economy, undoubtedly gave a strong impetus to the institutionalization of pederasty by converting the private dinner and drinking party into an enclave of elite self-affirmation and thus a major venue of literary performance. The unexplained turnaround from complete silence about homoerotic love to obsession with it in our sources might be a reflex of wider dissemination of verse addressing the socialization of younger males, which became a more urgent issue after the expansion of symposium culture.

Girls into Women

"This sort of love," says Plutarch, speaking of male pederasty, "was so esteemed among them [the Spartans] that fair and noble women also loved maidens" (*Lyc.* 18.4). This is our single item of ancient testimony to a parallel institution of female pederasty being found anywhere in archaic Greece. In discussing the possibility of its existence, I will use the word "homoeroticism" because "pederasty" strictly implies a man–boy liaison, and if we call the relationship "lesbianism" we could inaccurately be imposing a modern sexual construct upon the past. Although Plutarch's comment has been pressed for all it is worth, especially by supporters of the initiatory hypothesis, it is not as probative as it might appear. If such a custom was in force at Sparta, we would expect it to be situated within a nexus of other corresponding social realities, but that does not seem to be the case.

Did Spartan girls, for example, also participate in an age-structured system of *paideia*, which for boys, as we have seen, was closely integrated with erotic bonding? Like their brothers, young women were definitely required to perform strenuous physical exercise so as to become fit for childbearing (Xen. *Lac.* 1.4; Plut. *Lyc.* 14.2), and were also trained in basic reading and writing, music and dance. Pindar speaks of a Spartan girls' chorus as a "herd of maidens," using the same technical term, *agela*, applied to the boys' regiments (fr. 112 S-M). Most scholars therefore accept the premise that an official *agôgê* for girls already existed in archaic times, as it certainly did during the Roman period.[31] Yet girls did not leave home to sleep in barracks, but continued to live with their parents – or, more precisely, with their mothers, because their fathers were frequently away fighting and, even if not on campaign, still exercised, drilled, and dined with fellow soldiers. It has been suggested that living in an all-female home environment might promote homoerotic attachments (Cartledge 1981b: 90–1). Possibly, but the continued presence of the girl's biological mother in her life would also preclude the need for a surrogate parent, one crucial role filled by the male *erastês*. Since the household was the place for girls to learn how to care for a child by practicing on younger siblings, their acculturation into adulthood took place mostly in the domestic sphere. Obviously, then, no outside sponsors would have been required to instruct them in, say, the etiquette of public dining.

Yet many believe that choral compositions by Alcman show unquestionable evidence of socially sanctioned homoerotic attachments among adolescent girls. Alcman was engaged, probably by Spartan magistrates or religious authorities, to compose *partheneia*, "maiden songs," for choruses to perform at religious festivals. The sacred character of these songs, along with Sparta's general cultural conservatism, ensured their being handed down without alteration from one generation to the next, with each cohort of chorus members theatrically re-enacting the roles of its predecessors, until the verses were finally committed to writing (Pomeroy 2002 : 143–5).[32] It is therefore conceivable that these poems accurately reflect, if not the actual feelings of the adolescents who first sang them – those, of course, we cannot know – at least the feelings toward each other that Alcman's contemporaries would have expected them to express.

Taking their words at face value, we learn that the maidens of Alcman's first *Partheneion* are awed by the beauty of their chorus leaders, Agido and Hagesichora.[33] Agido, they sing, is like the sun (40–1) and the girl who is her closest rival in appearance will trail her as a second-rate horse runs behind one of superior breed (58–9). They reserve their highest praise, though, for her colleague Hagesichora (64–77):

> For there is no abundance of purple cloth
> sufficient to protect us,   65
> nor a stippled snake bracelet
> of purest gold,
> nor a Lydian cap, adornment
> of tenderly glancing girls,
> nor the hair of Nanno,   70
> nor Areta, who resembles a goddess,
> nor yet Thylacis and Cleêsithêra,
> nor, going to Ainesimbrota's house, will you say:
> "May Astaphis be mine,
> let Philylla glance my way,   75
> and Damareta and lovely Vianthemis" –
> no, Hagesichora weakens me with longing.

The text permits only a provisional reconstruction of the situation, and most of the following points are disputed. The chorus is probably composed of the eight girls mentioned by name, together with their leaders; later they say they were formerly eleven and are now ten. (What happened to the extra girl is unclear.) They compete against a rival chorus, the *Peleiades*, called after the star-cluster (Page 1951: 52–7). Ainesimbrota is the woman, possibly an official of the state religion, who may have trained them in music and dance. The occasion is a feast of Ortheia (or Orthria), one of the major divinities of Sparta, who presided over several rituals of maturation, including the ceremonial scourging of youths so often mentioned in imperial Roman sources (see Kennell 1995: 149–61). It may also be a prenuptial rite, since the girls are bearing a robe (*pharos*, 61) to Ortheia, and such a gift is attested as a votive offering at the time of a girl's marriage.[34] The girls are concerned that neither their ceremonial costumes of purple dress, Oriental bonnets, and gold ornaments, nor their own appeal as members of the rank and file, are enough to prevent defeat by the other chorus. Only Hagesichora's beauty will redeem them.

In the fragmentary third *Partheneion*, the chorus speaks even more candidly of their attraction to another chorus leader, Astymeloisa: "and with limb-loosening desire [*lusimelei te posôi*], and more meltingly than sleep and death she looks at me ..." (61–2); and, later, "if somehow she might love me, and drawing near take me by the soft hand, quickly even I would become her suppliant ..." (79–81). This is highly charged language. In describing the birth of Eros, Hesiod had characterized the god as "limb-loosening," relaxing the knee-joints of his victim (*Theog.* 121). Desire, it was thought, saps the physical and mental strength of the person who experiences it; that is why Hagesichora, in the first *Partheneion*, is said to "weaken" her companions. "Meltingly" (*takerôtera*) conveys the effect of glancing at the beloved, which deprives the beholder of his or her senses: Sappho too confesses herself "little short of dying" whenever she looks upon her addressee (fr. 31.15–16 V) and Pindar "melts" (*takomai*) like wax when he sees the fresh-limbed youthfulness of boys (fr. 123 S-M). Greek ideas of sleep and death overlap with desire conceptually, for all are temporary or permanent conditions that fall upon someone unexpectedly. The common element among the three is the loss of autonomy and sense of disintegration felt by the subject. Since their victim is greatly tempted to surrender voluntarily to the lassitude they bring rather than struggle against it, each is as alluring as it is frightening (Vermeule 1979: 145–77). Finally, the chorus members affirm that they would worship Astymeloisa like a divinity if she would show them favor, a form of congratulatory hyperbole known as *makarismos* in which a mortal is addressed as though she or he were a god – ordinarily a risky thing to do, but tolerated in special circumstances such as celebrating a wedding or an Olympic victory. The sentiments expressed in these lines (although we should emphasize again that the sequence of thought is scrappy and disconnected) seem to go far beyond mere admiration of a friend.

Whether or not these passages from Alcman have an intentional erotic significance, they were unquestionably sung in public, under the auspices of a religious ceremony. Why should a community condone, let alone sanction, youthful female homoeroticism? Claude Calame's response to that question has heavily influenced recent work on both Alcman and Sappho. He posits that choral training for girls in archaic Sparta was part of a complex of initiation rituals similar to those of boys and designed, like theirs, to instill proper awareness of impending adult responsibilities (1977: 32–40). Since the adult woman's function in the Spartan community was domestic and reproductive, female initiation rites imparted an understanding of marriage, sex, and motherhood through myth and song, while gymnastic exercises simultaneously prepared juvenile bodies for childbearing. Hence the focus of musical activity was educational: instruction in singing and dancing, along with gymnastics, was provided to groups of age-mates organized in an *agela*. Both the song composer and the chorus leader (the same person could perform both tasks, of course) were recognized as teachers. Indeed, the poet who created the libretto and music for the dance occupied an intermediary position between the chorus and the community because he or she transmitted the cultural patrimony – the ethical values and the mythological heritage on which the fabric of community life was based (1977: 399).

Within this pedagogical ambience, the yoking power of *erôs* gave the group its cohesion as the choristers collectively expressed their yearning for their leader. If desire among members was physically consummated, the pleasurable experience would alleviate future anxiety over intercourse at the time of marriage. Institutionalized female homoeroticism was therefore a vehicle for negotiating the treacherous passage between "wild" prenubile virginity, the domain of Artemis, and "domesticated" marital sex, the province of Hera and Aphrodite (1977: 400–20). From the perspective of the community as a whole, love between women was a good thing because it facilitated the physical and emotional transition between asexuality and heterosexuality, with intimacy between husband and wife its ultimate goal.

Calame argues that a similar institution for girls obtained just a generation or so later on Lesbos. Sappho's female addressees, he believes, came to her for musical instruction prior to marriage from places as far away as Asia Minor; under her direction, they involved themselves in cult-related activities similar to, if not identical with, those of Spartan girls' choruses (1977: 372). Because her companions placed themselves under the patronage of Aphrodite and the Muses, they are often characterized by other scholars as a **thiasos** or female religious community, although Calame insists that group organization was not that formal. In addition to music, the girls cultivated grace (*charis*) and beauty. In so far as *charis* is the hallmark of the nubile maiden, its acquisition was another step in preparing for marriage. However, this brand of education was probably voluntary, as opposed to the Spartan system of compulsory instruction: it produced good wives but not necessarily good citizens (1977: 401–4). Homoeroticism was an integral part of preparation for adulthood, but erotic relationships usually took the more familiar form of an attachment between the older mentor, Sappho, and one of her pupils. Such attachments facilitated the learning process, though they inevitably ended in separation when the girl left her friends to marry. Once again, then, the pedagogical system for girls looked toward domestic heterosexuality as its fulfillment; within it, the temporary experience of homoerotic companionship was a means to that end.

Calame's model of initiatory female eroticism has been challenged on several grounds. For a start, some deny the very presence of homoerotic affect in the songs of Alcman or those of Sappho. If the audience for Alcman's *partheneia* included young men – and Plutarch (*Lyc.* 14.3) says that they were present at certain festivals when maidens danced and sang – the community, employing the voice of the chorus-members, could be presenting the girls enacting the roles of Agido and Hagesichora to suitable bachelors as potential brides (Stehle 1997: 30–9, 73–93). Speaking for the entire populace, the choristers would advertise their leaders (and, by extension, themselves as well) as erotically desirable. They were assigned this public function because only women can praise other women's physical allure without creating jealousy and resentment on the part of men who have an interest in their sexuality. In addition, their own self-consciousness as objects of the spectators' erotic gaze would reinforce their perception of themselves as gendered bodies and accustom them to accept as natural a male-defined code of gender relations (Clark 1996). Parallel claims have been made for Sappho: by paying tribute to the loveliness and grace of her charges, she may have been enhancing the confidence in their own appearance required for marriageable young women in a culture that valued beauty in both sexes to an extraordinarily high degree (Hallett 1996 [1979]). In each case, the speaker would not be expressing her private sensibility but instead modeling for audiences an appropriate response to the sight of a nubile virgin.

Questions have also been raised about the applicability of Calame's construction of homoerotic desire. Does it really fit the facts of women's relationships that can be extracted from Alcman's and Sappho's fragments? Here conflicting readings have been imposed upon the same bits of evidence. Many gay historians and some classicists have argued that Sappho's sexuality is, notwithstanding the differences noted, identical at least in principle to lesbian sexuality in the contemporary Western world. Insofar as her love poetry assumes a woman-centered perspective, treats female relationships as paramount and sexual attraction between women as normal and natural, and presents a female speaker acting independently of male authority, it is "lesbian" by modern definitions (Snyder 1997a: 14–25). Other scholars draw an absolute distinction between the hierarchical structure of pederasty and what they perceive to be the egalitarian companionship of the Spartan *agela* and the Sapphic circle. Whereas the didactic framework of pederasty assumed the boy's physical and intellectual inferiority to his *erastês*, the girls in Alcman's poetry are in love with others of their own age. This also seems true of liaisons among Sappho's companions: in one fragment (22 V), the speaker bids one woman, Abanthis, to sing of another, Gongyla, "for her dress passionately excited you when you saw it," and in a second she consoles Atthis by imagining that her beloved, now far away in Lydia, still remembers her (96 V). Even Sappho's own confessions of love seem to contain the hope of reciprocated desire, a passion denied by convention to the *erômenos*. Although homoerotic relations occurred during the transitional period when the girl changed status from virgin to wedded wife, that does not necessarily make them a tool of socialization into marriage, and the fact that they took place between age-mates casts doubt on their educational function (Cantarella 1992: 83–4).

Holt Parker (1993) has recently challenged the entire set of premises on which Sappho's alleged career as "schoolmistress" rests. The notion that Sappho directed a girls' academy derives, according to Parker, from a pronouncement by the early twentieth-century philologist Wilamowitz, who drew an anachronistic comparison with German single-sex boarding schools of his own day. Nowhere in Sappho's fragments is there an indication that she teaches anything. An ancient commentator of a much later period does speak of her as "educating" (*paideuousa*) upper-class women from Lesbos and Ionia, but he may have been guessing. When other late Greek and Roman writers describe her companions as "girls," they are restructuring female social interaction to correspond to the familiar male institution of pederasty, just as the comradeship of Achilles and Patroclus was made to conform to that pattern. Finally, Sappho's group does not fit the blueprint of a *thiasos* or religious community and more closely resembles the *hetaireia* of male friends who entertained each other at symposia. It is likely, Parker concludes, that she, too, composed for aristocratic women's sympotic gatherings and that, as some fragments suggest, the objects of her affection were adult women (1993: 341–6). Such an interpretation of her life and activities departs from the tradition of segregating her by sex, as though her unique position as a *woman* poet required a distinct explanation, and brings her creative pursuits into conjunction with those of male colleagues whose presence at banquets and drinking parties is well attested.

If Calame's premises are questionable, what has induced so many authorities to accept his explanation of ancient female homoeroticism as preparation for womanhood? First, religion was the major domain in which Greek women's sexuality was publicly acknowledged, although strictly only as it pertained to the fertility of households and crops. The notion of the Sapphic circle as a *thiasos* organized around ritual initiation continues to command assent because it offers a tenuous connection to social practices existing elsewhere. Second, and even more important, it supplies a plausible answer to the problem raised above – why ancient society should allow such activity to flourish openly.

As a line of inquiry, though, that question may be misleading, for it assumes that Greek males saw ties of affection between women as a threat to marriage. That would have been true only if they viewed female same-sex relations as fundamentally antithetical to opposite-sex relations. But our modern dichotomy of "homosexual" and "heterosexual" did not exist for them, and fear of women's aberrant sexual behavior was concentrated upon premarital or adulterous heterosexual relations, which threatened the integrity of the community by disrupting lines of descent and inheritance. Sexual practices that could have no reproductive consequences perhaps flew beneath the moral radar screen. Technically, that would mean that they did not result in loss of maidenhood nor would they be considered adulterous if a partner was married, as tradition informs us Sappho was. Certainly there is no evidence for any outright prohibition at this time against sexual contact between women. If, with one or two exceptions, female homoeroticism does not show up in the literary record again until the Hellenistic period, it may simply have been ignored by men speaking to men. It is conceivable, then, that both sexual intercourse within marriage and homoerotic relations, before and possibly even after marriage, were put into the same conceptual category of good, or at least permissible, sex – as opposed to illicit heterosexual intercourse outside of marriage. Not coincidentally, anxiety about and disgust over women having sex with women does surface just when Greek writers begin to take a greater interest in females as potential emotional partners.

Sappho on the Lips of Men

If public discourses in archaic Greece were so largely preoccupied with masculine concerns, you may be wondering how Sappho's songs managed to survive at all, let alone circulate rapidly throughout the Panhellenic world. The answer is that they were appropriated by male symposium culture and performed in private dining rooms, generation after generation, along with the works of poets who had composed for just such a setting. To speculate about their peculiar cross-gender appeal under those circumstances is tempting, but, apart from frequent references to the grace and charm of the lyrics, we have no personal testimony about their emotive effect upon the men and boys who sang them. Nevertheless, two fresh discoveries show

(Continued)

Sappho on the Lips of Men — Continued

us respectively, first, how Sappho's verse was tailored to its new milieu, and, second, how Athenian symposiasts in the early fifth century BCE imagined its author as poet and lover.

In a 2004 find that made headlines everywhere, experts at the University of Cologne in Germany recovered a virtually complete twelve-line Sappho poem, one of three short poems in a fragmentary third-century BCE anthology, from scraps of papyrus (*PKöln* inv. 21351 and 21376) previously used to wrap a mummy. In this poem, now known as "the new Sappho," the elderly female speaker, addressing a group of children, first enumerates the miseries of old age and then reminds herself, citing Tithonus as an example, that no mortal can escape the effects of time, not even one wed to a goddess. That stern concluding appeal to the Tithonus myth, conceivably as listeners knew it from the *Homeric Hymn to Aphrodite*, prompted one noted British scholar to deem the poem itself "a small masterpiece" (West 2005). However, the right-hand line endings of this poem were already known from another papyrus (*POxy.* 1787 = fr. 58 V) that continued on for four more verses after mentioning Tithonus and closed with the affirmation that the beauty of the sun, and thus of life itself, compensates for other losses.

Which of those versions is the "genuine" one? We cannot recover Sappho's original as she actually composed it. Both versions should be regarded, however, as recital scripts. They may be equally authentic, then, in so far as they belong to different performance traditions (Boedeker 2009: 72–6; Lardinois 2009: 47–8; Nagy 2009: 186). Depending on the occasion, a musician might choose to terminate with a pointed reminder of human fragility or a consolatory expression of hope – just as a folk singer may decide to expand a popular ballad one evening and omit stanzas the next. Each version would have been taken as a valid interpretation of "Sappho." The coexistence of two adaptations of the same song reminds us that performed works, as opposed to transcripts on the printed page, are everlastingly fluid, and questions of correct or incorrect rendering simply do not apply (Nagy 1996: 7–38).

The homoerotic tenor of the poems apparently posed no barrier to sympotic reception and may, in fact, have promoted acceptance, if another piece of evidence has been read correctly. It involves two painted images on a fifth-century Attic vase now housed in the museum collection of the Ruhr-Universität Bochum in northwestern Germany. This is one of four such vases on which a female figure holding a musical instrument (or, in one case, a scroll) is expressly labeled "Sappho." Although these representations of the author were studied previously (Snyder 1997b), no one had looked at them in relation to other images on the same vessel. The Bochum vase is a *kalyx krater*, a piece of specialized ware produced for the rituals of drinking. On its primary side (the obverse), Sappho is portrayed holding a lyre in her left hand and a *plêktron*, or pick, in her right; her right arm is outstretched behind her, her head is turned in that direction so that she gazes backward, and her right foot inclines forward, slightly raised, as if she were just completing a dance step. On the reverse, another female figure wrapped completely in a cloak also looks behind her as she walks; since, like Sappho, she turns her head away, their glances will never meet. Above her an inscription has been just found and published: it reads *hê pais*, "the girl" (*pais*, "child," may be used of either sex, but the article is feminine). Since that publication (Yatromanolakis 2005) the vase has already received considerable attention (Nagy 2007: 239–40, 2009: 193–5; Yatromanolakis 2007: 88–90, 103–10). Whatever the precise implications of the linked images, the overall scheme, including the inscription, evokes "the sociocultural institution of pederasty" and assimilates Sappho into a "pederastic paradigm" (Yatromanolakis 2005: 27). The *kalyx krater* informs us, in other words, that for its viewers female expressions of love and longing for companions were seen as no different, in terms of gender or sexuality, from the desire for beautiful youths enshrined in the pederastic code. In our society, where lesbians, gays, bisexuals, transgenders, and other "queer folk" are assumed to have distinct agendas even as they share overriding goals, that finding gives us something to think about.

We can draw out these speculations a bit further, though we are now venturing upon very heated theoretical ground. For most, but not all, scholars in the field, the prevailing ethos of sexuality in archaic and classical Greece, as based upon the analyses of Dover and Foucault, may be equated with phallic penetration of an inferior being – woman, boy, foreigner, slave – by a hierarchical superior. Sex is accordingly characterized as a "zero-sum competition" in which points are scored at the expense of the passive partner: the dominant figure, the adult citizen male, achieves gratification not only from orgasm but also from the subjugation of the other participant, who in being penetrated takes on a feminized and subordinate role.[35] This "penetration model" has been challenged as overly reductionist because it imposes a uniform, one-sided dynamic upon the complex transactions of sex and does not take other factors into account – such as the power exercised by the beloved during courtship or the benefits, including pleasure, that she or he may derive from performing the receptive role in the sexual act (Davidson 1997: 178–9; Hubbard 1998: 70–72).

Genital activity between women is one kind of ancient sexuality this model cannot account for. Since it did not involve penetration, Page duBois asks (1995: 14), was it even thought of as "sex"? Perhaps not. References in literature and art to **dildoes**, leather phalluses used for masturbation, indicate that Greek men found it hard to imagine women pleasuring themselves without a penis-substitute.[36] Manual or other forms of stimulation simply might not have counted. Scholars also point to vases showing pairs of women making subtle gestures of familiarity (Rabinowitz 2002: 146–50), and to the easy banter about physical attributes among respectable housewives in Aristophanes' *Lysistrata* 78–92 (Konstan 1995: 57–9), as evidence of artists' consciousness that "women have a different sexual style from that of men," a more diffuse and inclusive eroticism. Furthermore, if the narrator of the "Cologne Epode" did confine himself to grassy gardens, or even if the complete text merely flirted with that option, as it appears to do, we may be confident that the "penetration model," though the prevailing one, did not exhaust the patterns of male sexual conduct available for representation in Greek art and literature.

Conclusion

After that tiresome survey of learned controversy, you may suspect that we really possess very little firm knowledge about the cultural background of Greek eroticism in the archaic age. You are unfortunately correct – much theorizing has been grounded on uncertain information. Nevertheless, it is better to recognize the limits of our understanding than to approach the poetry of that time carrying the baggage of questionable assumptions. It is also good to recall once more that the academic investigation of ancient sexuality is still in an early phase, and a great deal of data remains to be collected and assembled. At some future time archaeological discoveries or new papyrus fragments may finally clarify the hazy picture presented here. In the meantime, the songs performed at archaic symposia have allowed us to survey some of the ways in which the forces of passion, whether heterosexual or homoerotic, could be poetically celebrated within festive and intimate surroundings.

The erotic world conjured up in archaic Greek lyric and elegy is unlike Homer's or Hesiod's in being largely an imaginative terrain. Because sympotic poetry is an art-form practiced by an exclusive group and performed in an artificial, highly stylized setting, very little in it corresponds to daily reality. Even the iambic abuse of an Archilochus or his successor Hipponax, who both revel in outrageous sexual narratives, partakes of edgy fantasy: what is manifestly obscene is divested of shock value and rendered funny by over-the-top reportage. Consequently, we could not mine the surviving texts to unearth historical facts even if they were complete, since the aim of the poetry was diversion and pleasure rather than realistic description. What we can perceive, if we approach it as a form of coded statement, is an underlying social ideology: its messages are as much about the collective importance of the *hetaireia*, whether made up of men or women, as they are about desire for one or another of the participants. As time passed, though, discourses of moderation – which in Athens took the form of male democratic equality – began to counter the self-aggrandizing customs of the aristocratic symposium, including the cult of pederasty, and discussion of the proper integration of *erôs* within the well-run *polis* assumed civic urgency.

Discussion Prompts

1. Although today's popular music is chiefly marketed by the recording industry for commercial consumption, there are aspects of production that resemble the way songs were composed in the early Greek world (we still expect groups to write their own material), and some purposes served by music nowadays resemble the functions of music in the *hetaireia* (such as defining its audience as a cohesive age or ethnic group with shared values). From your personal experience, draw other parallels.

2. Compare and contrast the way in which the young male object is portrayed in the elegies of Theognis and the lyric poetry of Anacreon. In each of these genres, how are the power dynamics of the lover and beloved relationship sketched out?

3. In Chapter 1 we observed Aphrodite interacting with the mortals Anchises and Helen. What is different about the way she engages with the speaker in Sappho's "Ode to Aphrodite" (fr. 1 V)?

4. Explaining Greek acceptance of homoerotic relations, male or female, between adults and younger persons as a vestige of initiation rites is attractive to scholars for one obvious reason: it distances sexual gratification as a motive and assigns the practice a social meaning instead. Why is that preferable? Discuss.

Notes

1 The Tomb of the Diver (so named because on its stone lid a diver is represented plunging from a high platform into water, possibly symbolizing the soul's transition from one world to the next) presents a fascinating archaeological puzzle. Dated to around 480 BCE, it combines the Etruscan and Lucanian traditions of a painted stone tomb with Greek subject matter. Many details of the symposium scene have close parallels in Attic red-figure vase painting (Napoli 1970: 109–47). Pythagorean influence has been detected in the symbolism (Warland 1998).

2 "Defloration" is possibly a misleading term, as scholars debate whether Greek medicine in the classical period recognized the existence of the hymen. Sissa (1990a: 109–16, 1990b) argues that neither the Hippocratics nor Aristotle were aware of a membrane closing off the virgin girl's vagina, but Hanson (1990: 324–30) claims that the imagery of a closed jug applied to the mouth of the uterus implies the breaking of a seal. Dean-Jones (1994: 50–5) presents evidence that the Hippocratics confused the blood shed when the hymen was broken with menstrual blood stored in the womb and released upon penetration.

3 For fuller discussion of allusions to female sexuality in Sappho's imagery, see Winkler (1990: 180–7 and Wilson (1996: 186–201).

4 This is a double whammy: Thracians and Phrygians were the quintessential barbarians (cf. the "Thracian filly"), and beer (*bryton*) was thought an uncivilized beverage that could lay someone flat drunk on his back (Arist. *ap*. Ath. 10.447a–b).

5 The name "Lycambes" contains the elements *lyk-* "wolf," a traditional symbol of the outsider (like our proverbial "lone wolf"), and *-amb-*, as in the word "iambic." "Neobule" means "new plan," (i.e., a change of mind). The fact that the names of father and daughter are so suited to their parts raises the suspicion that they are "stock characters in a traditional entertainment with some (perhaps forgotten) ritual basis" (West 1974: 27). This would mean that the "Archilochus" of the fragment is playing a conventional role himself. West further speculates that *iambi* as a genre were poetic monologues that often included tales of sexual adventures along with abusive mockery (1974: 32–3).

6 Xenophon's *Symposium* party concludes with a steamy ballet on the myth of Dionysos and Ariadne that sexually excites the guests (9.3–7). Judging by scenes of mixed singing and coition on Attic vases, one might guess that verse with ribald subject matter was enthusiastically welcomed as banquet entertainment.

7 Believing that the Cologne Epode was autobiographical – so that Archilochus himself would be admitting to using a young girl as a means of payback and then blackening her name publicly – one of the two first editors of the papyrus branded the poet "a cruel psychopath" (Merkelbach and West 1974: 113). Cogent objections to approaching Archilochus' poem in this way are voiced by Lefkowitz (1976).

8 Ogden thinks that courtesans probably used this form of address, for their children, conceived in liaisons with clients, would have no recognized fathers; but the speaker in the Cologne Epode is accosting a girl of good family, since marriage is (at least theoretically) on the table.

9 Semonides, another writer of iambics, states that the ideal wife, whom he compares to a bee, "doesn't enjoy sitting among the women when they talk about sex" (fr. 7.90–91 West²).

10 Not all scholars agree that Sappho's eroticism is marked by reciprocity. Giacomelli (1980) and Calame (1999 [1992]: 25–7) contend that asymmetry is as evident in her love relationships as in those of other lyric poets. Their key piece of evidence is fragment 1, the "Ode to Aphrodite" (see below), in which the goddess assures a lovelorn Sappho that her beloved will soon feel as she does. Because Aphrodite does not say that the woman will feel love for Sappho herself, her words are taken, according to this reading, as a prophecy of erotic revenge as opposed to reconciliation. Similarly, the military metaphors in this poem suggest to duBois (1995: 9) that "Sappho participates more in the aristocratic drive for domination, in the agonistic arena of Greek social relations, than in some projected vision of nonviolent eros." Greene observes, however, that the egalitarianism of the proposed alliance between the speaker and Aphrodite and the goddess's explicit promise to use persuasion

in achieving the desired end together imply a pattern of complementary response in which each woman, as an erotic subject, pursues the other and is pursued in turn (2002: 84–91).

11   Burton (1998: 150–54) collects a variety of literary references to respectable women gathering among themselves to dine and drink, but they date from a later period.

12   On the meaning of the palm-up-and-open gesture, see Kilmer (1993: 61 and 111).

13   In a fragment of a red-figure Attic cup by the painter Douris, two women exchange a flower and an egg. Rabinowitz infers that these are love gifts because flowers are clear tokens of affection in heterosexual courting scenes (2002: 113). A second fragment of the same cup (Leipsic T 550, *ARV²* 438/139; fig. 5.2 a, b in Rabinowitz 2002) shows another pair of women giving each other flowers.

14   The Dorians were a linguistic and religious subgroup of Greeks, conscious of themselves as distinct in their customs from other populations, especially the Ionians (to which tribe the Athenians belonged). Tradition held that they entered Greece at a late date, displacing earlier Greek settlers in the Peloponnese (the southern part of the Greek peninsula) and the Aegean islands. However, the historical date and facts of the so-called "Dorian invasion" continue to generate much controversy.

15   The *Laws* is a utopian treatise theorizing about the code of laws by which an ideal colony should be governed. Three elderly men, the unnamed Athenian Stranger and his two friends, hike at a leisurely pace from the Cretan city of Cnossos to the Cave of Zeus on Mount Ida. This is a distance of some twenty miles as the crow flies and it allows for twelve books' worth of political reflection. Megillus and Cleinias are doubtless in good physical shape because of their strict military training in adolescence; the fact that their companion, who did not undergo that youthful regimen, can keep up – and indeed do most of the talking en route – makes a neat point. At the beginning of the *Laws*, the Athenian, a surrogate for Plato himself, subjects the Cretan and Spartan ways of life to harsh scrutiny. The passages we are examining occur in that context.

16   The translation used for all passages from the *Laws* is that of Saunders (1970). Textual problems in the first sentence are discussed at length in England's authoritative commentary (1976 [1921]: I. 230–31). Because of uncertainties about the text, grammatical ambiguities, and disputed meanings of certain words, the sense of Plato's Greek is not always easy to pin down, and translators have to make hard choices. Students should bear in mind that there can often be no absolute certainty about what a Greek or Roman author really wrote. Translations and commentaries, no matter how highly respected, still represent one person's informed opinion.

17   That the speaker, though condemning same-sex relations in general, has pederasty specifically in mind is indicated by his mention of Zeus' abduction of Ganymede, which was by this time the standard mythic paradigm for boy-love.

18   Both Xenophon (*Lac.* 1.5) and Plutarch (*Lyc.* 15.5) claim that secrecy and restraint were imposed on spouses so as to make them more eager for sex, which would supposedly cause them to produce more robust children. Pomeroy (1975: 38) suggests that this may have been a form of trial marriage that would allow separation without dishonor if the couple proved infertile.

19   In many parts of Greece, it was customary for freeborn boys of good families to wait upon guests at private symposia and public feasts. Sappho's brother Larichus was an attendant in the town hall of Mytilene, a fact she mentioned repeatedly (Ath. 10.425a), and the young Euripides poured wine for a religious association at Athens (Theophr. fr. 119 Wimmer). Discussion and further examples are in Bremmer (1990: 139–40). Having been abducted and made immortal, Ganymede was assigned the task of pouring wine for the gods on Olympus.

20   We know the Cretan word for this special cup: according to Hermonax (*ap.* Ath. 11.502b), it was made of bronze and called a *chonnos*.

21   Pomeroy observes that the bride-abduction in the Spartan marriage ceremony was part of a complex of procedures, including shaving the girl's head and dressing her as a man, that were also probably intended to ward off malign powers and influences. Assuming the appearance of the opposite sex would deceive spirits jealous of the bride's good fortune (2002: 42–3).

22 The possibility was first broached by Bethe in 1907; it gained additional credibility from the work of researchers who demonstrated the definite existence of Greek male and female initiatory procedures, continuing in some instances into the classical period and beyond (Jeanmaire 1975 [1939]; Brelich 1969; Calame 1977; Dowden 1989). After Dover (1978: 201–3) called attention to the need to explain the Greek valorization of pederasty in sociological terms, Bremmer (1980), Patzer (1982), and Sergent (1986) revived the notion of its initiatory origins.

23 Leitao (1995) proposes that the Ekdusia, a civic festival of initiation held annually at Phaistos, reveals just this kind of adult male anxiety in Hellenistic Crete over the youth's proper transition from the feminine to the masculine domain. At the Ekdusia, graduates of the *agela* were required to don a woman's robe, then strip it off, before taking their oath of citizenship.

24 The ethnographic material for the practice of "ritualized homosexuality" in this region is collected and discussed by Herdt, who notes reports of similar activities among the aborigines of neighboring Australia (1984: 5–6).

25 Aristotle (*Pol.* 1336b.20–22) prescribes that youths not yet of an age to recline at table or drink neat wine should also not attend iambic or comic performances, obviously assuming a correlation between maturity and drinking; Plato (*Leg.* 666a–b) entirely forbids wine to boys under eighteen and permits young men under thirty to drink only in moderation.

26 The fourth letter of this word may have been Greek lambda (Λ), the equivalent of our consonant "l," which was transformed into a delta (Δ) by scratching a line between the two downward strokes: in other words, someone jokingly changed the proper name of Erpetidamus' father into the adjective "boy-lover" (Catalano 1971). If so, the force of the epithet was obviously derogatory. It may chastise the father's over-enthusiasm for boys, inappropriate to his age.

27 The other was Ortheia, a local goddess subsequently identified with Apollo's sister Artemis; she is the divinity honored in Alcman's first *Partheneion* (see below). Most of the Theran inscriptions collected in *IG* XII 3.536–601 are merely proper names, some fragmentary. Combinations of a name

and an adjective (e.g., *IG* XII 3.540, *Lacydidas agathos*, "Lacydidas is good") recall the *kalos*-inscriptions ("so-and-so is beautiful") on Attic vases; see Robinson and Fluck (1937: 21–4).

28 Both fertility gods and satyrs (mythical associates of Dionysos, the god of wine, whom we will meet in Chapter 3) are often represented with penises erect, and dancers imitating satyrs wear large artificial phalloi. The lexicographer Hesychius, in defining *konisalos*, speaks of dancers "inserting their genitals," which indicates that the dance involved a pretense of anal intercourse.

29 Investing bodily fluids with magical properties did occur in antiquity; the elder Pliny catalogues, for example, the special healing powers ascribed to mothers' milk and the alleged blighting effects of menstrual blood (Richlin 1997). However, I can find no ancient Greek or Roman testimony to a popular or medical idea of semen as a masculinizing agent. Indeed, as noted elsewhere, both Aristotle (*Eth. Nic.* 1148b.27–9) and the pseudo-Aristotelian text [*Pr.*] 4.26 claim that boys can be "feminized" into developing a preference for passive anal intercourse by habitual penetration, an outcome that infusions of semen would conceivably have prevented.

30 Dover points out that Ganymede's story is clearly *not* initiatory in origin, for he does not attain maturity but instead remains frozen in adolescence (1988: 130).

31 Kennell (1995: 45–6) states that "girls were considered to be just as much members of the *agôgê* as the ephebes (youths)"; cf. Scanlon (2002: 122). However, Cartledge (1981b: 90–3) and Pomeroy (2002: 3–4) point out that the instructional program, though official, was doubtless less rigorous than that for boys, since it was designed to prepare girls only for their common purpose of motherhood.

32 Sosibius, a Spartan who wrote on the antiquities of his native land, testifies that the songs of Alcman were performed by nude male dancers at the *Gymnopaidia* (Festival of Naked Boys) in his own day, the mid-third century BCE (*FGrH* 595 F5 = *ap.* Ath. 15.678b–c).

33 The name "Hagesichora" means "she who leads the chorus," one piece of support for the possibility that the singers are assuming dramatic roles. The element -*ag*- in the names of both Agido and

Hagesichora, Pomeroy observes, "is common in royal nomenclature and suggests that they were Agiads, related to one line of Spartan kings" (2002: 157). At line 52 the singers refer to Hagesichora as their *anepsia*, "cousin," but this may be an honorary relationship; cf. the use of "sister" and "brother" today to denote someone not a sibling who is closely bonded to the speaker in other ways.

34 An alternative translation of *pharos* is "plough," defended on the grounds that Ortheia is a fertility goddess (Page 1951: 78–9). It is easy to imagine girls marching or even dancing while carrying a mantle, and in fact fifth-century votive plaques from Locri in southern Italy (types 16 and 17, Prückner 1968) show a file of girls in procession carrying a folded piece of cloth and accompanied by a priestess. But dancing while hefting a plough is hard to envision. The Hellenistic woman poet Nossis and her mother dedicate a robe to Hera on the occasion of Nossis' marriage (Nossis GP 3 = *Anth. Pal.* 6.265); see Skinner (1989: 5–6, 1991: 22–3).

35 The most influential formulation of the currently accepted paradigm of Greek sexuality is Halperin (1990: 29–38), but see also Winkler (1990: 45–70), Cohen (1991: 171–202), and Arkins (1994).

36 Ar. *Lys.* 107–10 is an infamous reference to the *olisbos* ("dildo") in classical Greek literature, and jokes about it occur elsewhere in Old Comedy (Henderson 1975: 221–2). Female masturbation fits into the overall comic image of women's licentiousness. *P Oxy.* 2291, a remnant of a third-century CE papyrus, contains a fragmentary word that could be *olisb-*. The poetic fragments it preserves are in the Lesbian dialect and may be by either Sappho (Lobel and Page 1955 ascribe them to her as fr. 99) or her contemporary and fellow countryman Alcaeus. Prostitutes are shown with dildoes on red-figure vases, though they may be playing with them for men's entertainment. However, Side B of a cup by the Pedieus Painter (Louvre G 14, *ARV*² 85/1) features two naked women reaching out to each other while a dildo and a drinking cup hang on the wall between them (see Kilmer 1993: 27, 90–92, fig. R152; Rabinowitz 2002: 142 with figs 5.21 a and b). For references to the *baubôn* (another word for *olisbos*) in the mimes of the Hellenistic author Herodas, see chapter 6).

References

Arkins, B. 1994. "Sexuality in Fifth-century Athens." *Classics Ireland* 1 (www.ucd.ie/~classics/94/Arkins 94.html).

Arthur, M. B. 1984. "Early Greece: The Origins of the Western Attitude toward Women." In J. Peradotto and J. P. Sullivan (eds.), *Women in the Ancient World: The "Arethusa" Papers*. Albany, NY: State University of New York Press, 7–58.

Bain, D. 1991. "Six Greek Verbs of Sexual Congress." *Classical Quarterly* 41: 51–77.

Boedeker, D. D. 2009. "No Way Out? Aging in the New (and Old) Sappho." In E. Greene and M. B. Skinner (eds.), *The New Sappho on Old Age: Textual and Philosophical Issues*. Washington, DC: Center for Hellenic Studies. 71–83.

Brelich, A. 1969. *Paides e Parthenoi*. Rome: Edizioni dell' Ateneo.

Bremer, J. M. 1975. "The Meadow of Love and Two Passages in Euripides' *Hippolytus*." *Mnemosyne* 28.3: 268–80.

Bremmer, J. 1980. "An Enigmatic Indo-European Rite: Paederasty." *Arethusa* 13: 279–98.

—— 1990. "Adolescents, *Symposion*, and Pederasty." In O. Murray (ed.), *"Sympotica": A Symposium on the "Symposion"*. Oxford: Clarendon Press. 135–48.

Burton, J. B. 1998. "Women's Commensality in the Ancient Greek World." *Greece & Rome* 45: 143–65.

Calame, C. 1977. *Les Choeurs de jeunes filles in Grèce archaïque, I: Morphologie, fonction religieuse et sociale*. Rome: Edizioni dell'Ateneo & Bizzarri.

—— 1999 [1992]. *The Poetics of Eros in Ancient Greece*. Trans. J. Lloyd. [Orig. pub. as *I Greci e l'eros: Simboli, pratiche e luoghi*, Roma-Bari: Gius. Laterza & Figli, 1992.] Princeton, NJ: Princeton University Press.

Cantarella, E. 1992. *Bisexuality in the Ancient World*. Trans. C. Ó Cuilleanáin. [Orig. pub. as *Secondo natura*, Rome: Editori Riuniti, 1988.] New Haven, CT: Yale University Press.

Cartledge, P. 1981a. "The Politics of Spartan Pederasty." *Proceedings of the Cambridge Philological Society* 27: 17–36.

—— 1981b. "Spartan Wives: Liberation or Licence?" *Classical Quarterly* 31: 84–105.

Catalano, V. 1971. "La piú antica epigrafe scherzosa ellenica graffita su pithos a Phaistos." *Giornale Italiano di Filologia* 23: 308–24.

Clark, C. A. 1996. "The Gendering of the Body in Alcman's *Partheneion* 1: Narrative, Sex, and Social Order in Archaic Sparta." *Helios* 23.2: 143–72.

Cohen, D. 1991. *Law, Sexuality, and Society: The Enforcement of Morals in Classical Athens*. Cambridge: Cambridge University Press.

Cyrino, M. S. 1995. *In Pandora's Jar: Lovesickness in Early Greek Poetry*. Lanham, NY: University Press of America.

Davidson, J. N. 1997. *Courtesans and Fishcakes: The Consuming Passions of Classical Athens*. New York: HarperPerennial.

Dean-Jones, L. A. 1994. *Women's Bodies in Classical Greek Science*. Oxford: Clarendon Press.

Dover, K. J. 1978. *Greek Homosexuality*. London: Duckworth.

—— 1988. *The Greeks and their Legacy: Collected Papers, Volume II: Prose, Literature, History, Society, Transmission, Influence*. Oxford: Blackwell.

Dowden, K. 1989. *Death and the Maiden: Girls' Initiation Rites in Greek Mythology*. London: Routledge.

duBois, P. 1995. *Sappho is Burning*. Chicago: University of Chicago Press.

England, E. B. 1976 [1921]. *The Laws of Plato*, 2 vols. Manchester: University of Manchester Press; rpt. New York: Arno Press.

Fowler, R. L. 1987. *The Nature of Early Greek Lyric*. Toronto: University of Toronto Press.

Gentili, B. (ed.). 1988 [1985]. *Poetry and its Public in Ancient Greece*. Trans. A. T. Cole. [Orig. pub. as *Poesia e pubblico nella Grecia antica*. Rome-Bari: Laterza & Figli, 1985.] Baltimore, MD: The Johns Hopkins University Press.

Giacomelli, A. 1980. "The Justice of Aphrodite in Sappho fr. 1." *Transactions of the American Philological Association* 110: 135–42.

Golden, M. 1984. "Slavery and Homosexuality at Athens." *Phoenix* 38: 308–24.

Graf, F. 1979. "Apollon Delphinios." *Museum Helveticum* 36: 2–22.

Greene, E. 1996 [1994]. "Apostrophe and Women's Erotics in the Poetry of Sappho." In E. Greene (ed.), 1996, *Reading Sappho: Contemporary Approaches*. Berkeley, CA: University of California Press. 233–47.

—— 2002. "Subjects, Objects, and Erotic Symmetry in Sappho's Fragments." In N. Rabinowitz and L. Auanger (eds.), *Among Women: From the Homosocial to the Homoerotic in the Ancient World*. Austin: University of Texas Press. 82–105.

Hallett. J. P. 1996 [1979]. "Sappho and her Social Context: Sense and Sensuality." In Greene (ed.), *Reading Sappho*, 125–42.

Halperin, D. M. 1990. *One Hundred Years of Homosexuality and Other Essays on Greek Love*. New York: Routledge.

Hanson, A. E. 1990. "The Medical Writers' Woman." In D. M. Halperin, J. J. Winkler, and F. I. Zeitlin (eds.), *Before Sexuality: The Construction of Erotic Experience in the Ancient Greek World*. Princeton, NJ: Princeton University Press. 309–38.

Henderson, J. 1975. *The Maculate Muse: Obscene Language in Attic Comedy*. New Haven, CT: Yale University Press.

Herdt, G. H. 1984. "Ritualized Homosexual Behavior in the Male Cults of Melanesia, 1862–1983: An Introduction." In G. H. Herdt (ed.), *Ritualized Homosexuality in Melanesia*. Berkeley, CA: University of California Press. 1–81.

Hubbard, T. K. 1998. "Popular Perceptions of Elite Homosexuality in Classical Athens." *Arion* 6: 48–78.

Jeanmaire, H. 1975 [1939]. *Couroi et Courètes*. Rpt. of 1939 edn. [Lille: Bibliothèque universitaire]. New York: Arno.

Kennell, N. M. 1995. *The Gymnasium of Virtue: Education and Culture in Ancient Sparta*. Chapel Hill, NC: University of North Carolina Press.

Kilmer, M. F. 1993. *Greek Erotica on Attic Red-figure Vases*. London: Duckworth.

Koehl, R. B. 1986. "The Chieftain Cup and a Minoan Rite of Passage." *Journal of Hellenic Studies* 106: 99–110.

Konstan, D. 1995. *Greek Comedy and Ideology*. Oxford: Oxford University Press.

Kurke, L. 1992. "The Politics of ἁβροσύνη in Archaic Greece." *Classical Antiquity* 11: 91–120.

—— 1999. *Coins, Bodies, Games, and Gold: The Politics of Meaning in Archaic Greece*. Princeton, NJ: Princeton University Press.

Lardinois, A. 2009. "The New Sappho Poem (P.Köln 21351 and 21376): Key to the Old Fragments." In Greene and Skinner (eds.), *The New Sappho on Old Age*. 41–57.

Lefkowitz, M. R. 1976. "Fictions in Literary Biography: The New Poem and the Archilochus Legend." *Arethusa* 9.2: 181–9.

Leitao, D. D. 1995. "The Perils of Leukippos: Initiatory Transvestism and Male Gender Ideology in the Ekdusia at Phaistos." *Classical Antiquity* 14: 130–63.

Lobel, E. and Page, D. 1955. *Poetarum Lesbiorum Fragmenta*. Oxford: Clarendon Press.

Ludwig, P. W. 2002. *"Eros" and "Polis": Desire and Community in Greek Political Theory*. Cambridge: Cambridge University Press.

Mace, S. T. 1993. "Amour, Encore! The Development of δηὖτε in Archaic Lyric." *Greek, Roman, and Byzantine Studies* 34: 335–64.

Merkelbach, R. and West, M. L. 1974. "Ein Archilochus-Papyrus." *Zeitschrift für Papyrologie und Epigraphik* 14: 97–113.

Morris, I. 1996. "The Strong Principle of Equality and the Archaic Origins of Greek Democracy." In J. Ober and C. Hendrick (eds.), *Dêmokratia: A Conversation on Democracies, Ancient and Modern*. Princeton, NJ: Princeton University Press. 19–48.

—— 2000. *Archaeology as Cultural History: Words and Things in Iron Age Greece*. Oxford: Blackwell.

Morrow, G. R. 1993 [1960]. *Plato's Cretan City: A Historical Interpretation of the "Laws"*. Princeton, NJ: Princeton University Press.

Murray, O. 1983. "The Greek Symposion in History." In E. Gabba (ed.), *Tria Corda: Scritti in onore di Arnaldo Momigliano*. Como: Edizioni New Press. 257–72.

Nagy, G. 1996. *Poetry as Performance: Homer and Beyond*. Cambridge: Cambridge University Press.

—— 2007. "Did Sappho and Alcaeus Ever Meet?" In A. Bierl et al. (eds.), *Literatur und Religion. Wege zu einer mythisch-rituellen Poetik bei den Griechen*, MythosEikonPoiesis 1.1. Berlin and New York: Walter de Gruyter. 211–69.

—— 2009. "The 'New Sappho' Reconsidered in the Light of the Athenian Reception of Sappho." In Greene and Skinner (eds.), *The New Sappho on Old Age*, 176–99.

Napoli, M. 1970. *La tomba del tuffatore*. Bari: De Donato.

Ogden, D. 1996. *Greek Bastardy in the Classical and Hellenistic Periods*. Oxford: Clarendon Press.

Page, D. L. (ed.). 1951. *Alcman: The Partheneion*. Oxford: Oxford University Press.

—— 1955. *Sappho and Alcaeus*. Oxford: Clarendon Press.

Parker, H. N. 1993. "Sappho Schoolmistress." *Transactions of the American Philological Association* 123: 309–51.

Patzer, H. 1982. *Die griechische Knabenliebe*. Wiesbaden: Steiner.

Percy, W. A., III. 1996. *Pederasty and Pedagogy in Archaic Greece*. Urbana, IL: University of Illinois Press.

Pomeroy, S. B. 1975. *Goddesses, Whores, Wives, and Slaves: Women in Classical Antiquity*. New York: Schocken.

—— 2002. *Spartan Women*. New York: Oxford University Press.

Prückner, H. 1968. *Die lokrischen Tonreliefs*. Philipp von Zabern: Mainz am Rhein.

Rabinowitz, N. S. 2002. "Excavating Women's Homoeroticism in Ancient Greece: The Evidence from Attic Vase Painting." In Rabinowitz and Auanger (eds.), *Among Women*, 106–66.

Richlin, A. 1997. "Pliny's Brassiere." In J. P. Hallett and M. B. Skinner (eds.), *Roman Sexualities*. Princeton, NJ: Princeton University Press. 197–220.

Robinson, D. M. and Fluck, E. J. 1937. *A Study of the Greek Love-names*. Baltimore, MD: The Johns Hopkins University Press.

Sallares, R. 1991. *The Ecology of the Ancient Greek World*. London: Duckworth.

Saunders, T. J., trans. 1970. *Plato: The Laws*. Harmondsworth: Penguin.

Scanlon, T. F. 2002. *Eros and Greek Athletics*. Oxford: Oxford University Press.

Schaps, D. M. 2003. "Socrates and the Socratics: When Wealth Became a Problem." *Classical World* 96.2: 131–57.

Sergent, B. 1986. *Homosexuality in Greek Myth*. Trans. A. Goldhammer. [Orig. pub. as *L'homosexualité dans la mythologie grecque*. Paris, 1984.] Boston: Beacon Press.

Sevinç, N. 1996. "A New Sarcophagus of Polyxena from the Salvage Excavations at Gümüşçay." *Studia Troica* 6: 251–64.

Sissa, G. 1990a. *Greek Virginity*. Trans. A. Goldhammer. Cambridge, MA: Harvard University Press.

—— 1990b. "Maidenhood without Maidenhead: The Female Body in Ancient Greece." Trans. R. Lamberton. In Halperin et al. (eds.), *Before Sexuality*. 339–64.

Skinner, M. B. 1987. "Greek Women and the Metronymic: A Note on an Epigram by Nossis." *Ancient History Bulletin* 1: 39–42.

—— 1989. "Sapphic Nossis." *Arethusa* 22: 5–18.

—— 1991. "Nossis *Thêlyglôssos*: The Private Text and the Public Book." In S. B. Pomeroy (ed.), *Women's History and Ancient History*. Chapel Hill, NC: University of North Carolina Press. 20–47.

—— 1993. "Woman and Gender in Archaic Greece, or, Why is Sappho a Woman?" In N. S. Rabinowitz and A. Richlin (eds.), *Feminist Theory and the Classics*. New York: Routledge. 125–44.

—— 2002. "Aphrodite Garlanded: *Erôs* and Poetic Creativity in Sappho and Nossis." In Rabinowitz and Auanger (eds.), *Among Women*. 60–81.

Slings, S. R. 1987. "Archilochus: 'First Cologne Epode.'" In. J. M. Bremer et al., *Some Recently Found Greek Poems*. Leiden: E. J. Brill. 24–61.

Snodgrass, A. M. 1977. *Archaeology and the Rise of the Greek State*. Cambridge: Cambridge University Press.

—— 1987. *An Archaeology of Greece*. Berkeley, CA: University of California Press.

Snyder, J. M. 1997a. *Lesbian Desire in the Lyrics of Sappho*. New York: Columbia University Press.

—— 1997b. "Sappho in Attic Vase Painting." In A. O. Koloski-Ostrow and C. L. Lyons (eds.), *Naked Truths: Women, Sexuality, and Gender in Classical Art and Archaeology*. London: Routledge. 108–19.

Spyridakis, S. 1979. "Aristotle on Cretan ΠΟΛΥΤΕΚΝΙΑ." *Historia* 28: 380–4.

Stehle [Stigers], E. 1981. "Sappho's Private World." In H. P. Foley (ed.), *Reflections of Women in Antiquity*. New York: Gordon and Beach. 45–61.

—— 1997. *Performance and Gender in Ancient Greece: Nondramatic Poetry in its Setting*. Princeton, NJ: Princeton University Press.

Thornton, B. S. 1997. *Eros: The Myth of Ancient Greek Sexuality*. Boulder, CO: Westview Press.

Van Gennep, A. 1961. *Rites of Passage*. Trans. M. B. Vizedon and G. L. Caffee. Chicago: University of Chicago Press.

Van Sickle, J. 1976. "Introduction." Special issue on "The New Archilochus." *Arethusa* 9.2: 133–47.

Vermeule, E. 1979. *Aspects of Death in Early Greek Art and Poetry*. Berkeley, CA: University of California Press.

Warland, D. 1998. "Tentative d'exégèse des fresques de la tombe 'du Plongeur' de Poseidonia." *Latomus* 57: 261–91.

West, M. L. 1974. *Studies in Greek Elegy and Iambus*. Berlin: Walter de Gruyter.

—— 2005. "A New Sappho Poem." *Times Literary Supplement*. June 24.

Wilkins, J. 2000. *The Boastful Chef: The Discourse of Food in Ancient Greek Comedy*. Oxford: Oxford University Press.

Williamson, M. 1995. *Sappho's Immortal Daughters*. Cambridge, MA: Harvard University Press.

—— 1996. "Sappho and the Other Woman." In Greene (ed.), *Reading Sappho*. 248–64.

—— 1998. "Eros the Blacksmith: Performing Masculinity in Anakreon's Love Lyrics." In L. Foxhall and J. Salmon (eds.), *Thinking Men: Masculinity and its Self-representation in the Classical Tradition*. London: Routledge. 71–82.

Wilson, L. H. 1996. *Sappho's Sweetbitter Songs: Configurations of Female and Male in Ancient Greek Lyric*. London: Routledge.

Winkler J. J. 1990. *The Constraints of Desire: The Anthropology of Sex and Gender in Ancient Greece*. New York: Routledge.

Yatromanolakis, D. 2005. "Contrapuntal Inscriptions." *Zeitschrift für Papyrologie und Epigraphik* 152: 16–30.

—— 2007. *Sappho in the Making: The Early Reception*. Washington, DC: Center for Hellenic Studies.

Further Reading

Calame, C. 1999. *The Poetics of Eros in Ancient Greece*. Trans. J. Lloyd. Princeton, NJ: Princeton University Press. Insightful study of the symbolic workings of Eros in the archaic and classical Greek community.

Murray, O. (ed.). 1990. *"Sympotica": A Symposium on the "Symposion."* Oxford: Clarendon Press. Collection of essays dealing with history, cultural meanings, and other critical aspects of the symposium.

Nagy, G. 1996. *Poetry as Performance: Homer and Beyond*. Cambridge: Cambridge University Press. Drawing on comparative materials from other oral traditions, this book illuminates the poetics of Greek performance, starting with Homer and continuing through the archaic and classical eras.

Scanlon, T. F. 2002. *Eros and Greek Athletics*. Oxford: Oxford University Press. Explores the connections among athletic competition, religion, and the socialization of young men and women in the ancient Greek world and how sexuality was deeply implicated in athletic culture.

Stehle, E. 1997. *Performance and Gender in Ancient Greece*. Princeton, NJ: Princeton University Press. Discussion of various forms of communal poetic performance and the impact of gender difference on both composition and reenactment.

3

Late Archaic Athens: More than Meets the Eye

Literature is not our only major source of information for ancient sexual ideology.[1] During the "Golden Age" of Attic pottery, from approximately 600 to 400 BCE, workshops at Athens, the hub of the Greek ceramic industry, manufactured fine earthenware for household and religious use. Much of this pottery was decorated with scenes drawn from mythology and the daily life of men and women.[2] The heyday of the craft spanned the era of Athens's hegemony over the Greek world – beginning with Solon's first steps toward the establishment of a democratic system of government in the archaic period, extending through the rule of the Pisistratid dynasty, the Persian Wars, the formation of the Delian League and the consolidation of the Athenian empire during the mid-fifth century, and the brutal **Peloponnesian War** with Sparta, finally ending with Athens's defeat in 404, which resulted in the breakup of its empire. Judging from the degree of craftsmanship, which ranges from exquisite to coarse and shoddy, even the relatively poor could afford painted ware, although ordinary people probably owned only a few display vases.[3] By any definition, though, this was a popular medium, a fact that justifies treating Attic vase painting as a foundation for wide-ranging discussions of attitudes and concepts shared by the general public to which it appealed.

In *Greek Homosexuality* (1978), K. J. Dover assembled a large compendium of erotic scenes on vases to demonstrate certain aspects of the Athenian homosexual ethos, including ideals of youthful beauty, gestures of seduction, favored positions and, by omission, taboo subjects. Subsequently Eva C. Keuls (1985) drew on the same corpus of materials as evidence for her contentions about the treatment of women in Athenian society. Since then, studies of Attic pottery have been at the forefront of work on ancient sexuality. Approaches are often chronologically oriented, with changes in subject matter analyzed as indications of alterations in the preferences, and arguably the mentality, of purchasers (Shapiro 1981, 1992; Sutton 1992; Osborne 1996). For example, scenes of courtship and lovemaking, whether merely suggestive or explicitly sexual, were quite

Sexuality in Greek and Roman Culture, Second Edition. Marilyn B. Skinner.
© 2014 John Wiley & Sons, Inc. Published 2014 by John Wiley & Sons, Inc.

popular during the period 575–450 BCE but are rarely found thereafter. Meanwhile, from the middle of the fifth century onward, representations of respectable women at leisure increase considerably. Determining the cause of such shifts in taste would help to fill in the background needed to interpret the ideological debate about sexual ethics reflected in Athenian texts of the later fifth and fourth centuries.

When working with this body of evidence, however, we must use caution. At first glance it may seem that scenes on vases give us photographic access to life as it was really lived, but that impression would be wrong. For one thing, figures are stylized rather than realistically drawn, and a rich vocabulary of symbolic gestures is employed to convey meaning. Much of this code of pictorial representation, or *iconography*, is still not fully deciphered.[4] Second, content was affected by alterations in technology, most notably the switch from the **black-figure** to the **red-figure** method of vase painting around 525 BCE. The first technique employed figures painted in black upon a red clay background, with bright red and white as secondary colors; details such as patterns on clothing were incised. In the second technique, conversely, figures were outlined on the unfired clay pot, interior details painted in, and the background then covered with a glossy grey slip that turned black during the firing process. Osborne draws a critical distinction between the objectives of each style: black-figure emphasizes action and setting, while red-figure focuses upon the spatial presence and bodies of individuals (1998: 134–9). Although both techniques are used for erotica, the tone of the representations differs: black-figure portrayals of sex tend toward the comic or boisterously obscene, while red-figure, with its greater intensity, attempts to involve the viewer psychologically in the proceedings.

We must also allow for the surroundings in which erotic scenes, especially those with graphic sexual content, were meant to be viewed. Distinct kinds of vases were employed for given purposes, with function often determining decoration (Webster 1972: 98–104): thus figures of women at the public fountain appear on *hydriai*, which were used to fetch water. Sexual scenes are restricted to equipment for the symposium, and symposia were extraordinary occasions on which, under the sway of Aphrodite and the god of wine, Dionysos, participants could engage in activities not normally countenanced. Use of tableware decorated with images of such activities would set the gathering apart from an everyday dining experience. Hence these vases and cups were designed for proper viewing by *specific* individuals under *specific* and *controlled* circumstances. We have to distinguish between intended and unintended audiences, keeping in mind that not everyone who saw the picture of lovemaking on the bottom of the drinking cup would respond to it in precisely the same way. It may be advisable to distance ourselves from these images occasionally by putting ourselves in the place of the female slave who cleaned the tables and washed the dishes the next morning.

Out of Etruria

Speculation about the purpose served by such erotic representations is quite heated. Were they pornographic, meant to arouse the viewer sexually, or instead a stimulus to imaginative fantasy (Kilmer 1993: 199–215)? Looking past their literal content, should we regard ancient sexual images as **apotropaic** (evil-averting) measures or as a mode of symbolic discourse? Did they merely reflect the personal outlook of their consumers or actually mold it (Sutton 1992: 32–4)? Their numbers are small: out of tens of thousands of surviving vases, only about 150 show figures actually engaged in sex, while about two thousand more deal with erotic themes in a more restrained manner.[5] Provenance creates a tremendous problem, for the overwhelming majority of those vases were not found in Athens but recovered from the graves of wealthy **Etruscans** in central and southern Italy. The Etruscans were great admirers and collectors of Greek art who imported vases from Attica along with other luxury artifacts. Aristocratic Etruscan women were publicly more visible than their Greek counterparts, and in their own art the Etruscans did not hesitate to express affection between husbands and wives – cultural factors known to the Greeks, who gave them a sinister interpretation.[6] Some scholars have claimed, then, that explicitly erotic scenes were created only for the export market and reflect Etruscan, rather than Greek, tastes. However, the presence of painted slogans on the vases expressing admiration for young men who were prominent historical figures well known to their Athenian contemporaries (for example, "Leagrus is *kalos* [beautiful]"), argues against that hypothesis because the inscriptions would be meaningless to an Etruscan consumer (Osborne 1998: 139–41, cf. Robinson and Fluck 1937: 1–14). Perhaps, then, the pottery was resold after use; Webster envisioned Greek aristocrats commissioning sets of drinking equipment for particular occasions, then selling them to traders once they had served their purpose (1972: 42–62, 289–300), like a movie actress bringing her Academy Awards gown to the consignment shop. That may be too ingenious. Another expert concludes: "That there was some sort of second-hand trade is perfectly possible. We have yet, however, to recognize or discover the evidence for how it was operated" (Boardman 1979: 34). In short, the question of how these vases got to their resting places in Italian graves is a challenging one. We must keep their find-spots in mind, for it was this selective appeal to members of another culture that ensured preservation.

Erotic scenes fall into three general subject categories. First, there are images of pursuit featuring gods, goddesses, or heroes running after youths or women who look back in alarm. Although sex is the pursuer's implicit goal, representation confines itself to the chase or the moment of capture; with three exceptions, subsequent sexual congress is never shown.[7] Keuls reads these scenes as glorifications of male dominance (1985: 47–55). If so, beholders would be expected to identify vicariously with the pursuing figure, especially in such scenarios as that of Zeus and Ganymede. Abduction, however, can also symbolize a transition to a new mode of existence. When the Athenian hero Theseus, dressed in the costume of an *ephêbos* or youth undergoing military training, pursues a girl, elements in the picture allude to the marriage ceremony that integrates both "uncivilized" young man and "wild" maiden into the community (Sourvinou-Inwood 1987). Figures of Peleus capturing the sea nymph Thetis, and Boreas, the North Wind, swooping down on the Athenian princess Oreithyia, are found on drinking equipment like the *kalyx krater* in fig. 3.1 (Boston 1972.850) and may hint at the intoxicating effects of wine. Yet the same mythic scenes are found on vessels used by brides as they prepare for the wedding.

Fig. 3.1   The Niobid Painter. *Kalyx krater* (mixing bowl) with scenes of abduction or pursuit. Greek, Classical Period, about 460–450 BCE. Place of manufacture: Greece, Attica, Athens. Ceramic, red-figure technique. Height: 48 cm (18 7/8 in.); diameter: 50 cm (19 11/16 in.). Location: Museum of Fine Arts, Boston. Mary S. and Edward J. Holmes Fund. 1972.850. Source: © 2013 Museum of Fine Arts, Boston.

In a funerary context, rape of a mortal is an obvious metaphor for the abruptness of death but may also, through references to the myth of Persephone, hint at salvation and apotheosis. Images of Eos, the dawn goddess, catching up her mortal lovers Tithonus or Cephalos have been read as transgressive fantasies of an adult son's return to the nurturing mother (Stehle 1990: 101–2). Finally, portrayals of Eros as pursuer that show the god pressing up against or forcibly copulating with a captured youth underscore the uncontrollable force of desire by violating a fundamental artistic taboo (Shapiro 1992: 68–70). Consequently, the theme of "erotic pursuit" must be dealt with in context, for it has so many different implications that treating it simply as an expression of gender ideology is overly reductionist.

At the other extreme of unreality, vase painters depicted the sexual practices of **satyrs**. The satyr, a member of Dionysos' entourage, combines donkeylike features – pointed ears, tail, a gigantic and perpetually erect penis – with the snub-nosed, bearded face and crouching posture of a man. With his insatiable appetite for wine and sex, he embodies the bestial element in humanity. Satyrs freely indulge in acts rarely, if ever, performed by human figures on vases, including masturbation, same-sex oral and anal coitus, and couplings with deer and donkeys. The tenor of

Fig. 3.2   Image of satyrs on a red-figure *kylix* by the Nikosthenes Painter (sixth century BCE). Location: Antikensammlung, Staatliche Museen zu Berlin. Source: Bildarchiv Preussischer Kulturbesitz, Berlin/Staatliche Museen zu Berlin/Photo: Johannes Laurentius/Art Resource, NY.

these illustrations is usually humorous: on side B of a red-figure cup (Berlin 1964.4, *ARV²* 1700; fig. 3.2), one pair of satyrs engages in fellatio, a second in sodomy, while the odd satyr out advances on a sphinx who is actually not part of the scene, but instead a feature of the decorative frame.

In scenes of aggression, satyrs brandish huge members as weapons. Their dealings with **maenads**, female worshippers of Dionysos, are complex: in the late archaic period satyrs and maenads are shown dancing together or occasionally engaged in sex, but during the early fifth century relations become strained (McNally 1978). Maenads now flee or defend themselves vigorously (Munich 2654, *ARV²* 462/47, Keuls 1985: fig. 310). A satyr may sneak up on a sleeping maenad, but it is likely that she will wake and fight him off before he consummates his desire (Boston 01.8072, *ARV²* 461/36, sides A and B). Thus the interaction of satyrs and maenads is informed by a dynamic of hostility and, for the former, constant frustration (Lissarrague 1990: 63). All of this is "funny, by Greek standards" (Brendel 1970: 17). Yet the viewer may also have been expected to recognize aspects of himself in the satyrs and ruefully empathize with their plight; comparable self-deprecation is detectable in iambic verse and satyr-dramas (Hedreen 2006).

The satyr's grossly swollen organ epitomizes his shamelessness. Greek men went around in public decently clothed, but artistic practice allowed males, under certain circumstances, to be portrayed either completely nude or at least with genitals exposed.[8] In Greek art the standard of beauty for the male genitals, especially those of attractive youths, was a short, thin, and straight penis with a scrotum of normal size (Dover 1978: 125–35). Gods and heroes conform to the same physical ideal. The aesthetic emphasis given to the penis indicates that its depiction had symbolic ramifications. For a youth, its smaller size relative to that of an adult man suggests modesty and deference, but in its straightness, like that of a sword, it implies suitability to be a warrior. Despicable figures such as slaves and gnarled old men have ugly penises, blunt, clubbed, and twisted. If the satyr's permanent state of arousal makes him ludicrous, the human males who display erections on vases might also be targets of ridicule, since they too exhibit a brutish susceptibility to desire. Nevertheless, we hear of gangs of well-born young men jokingly calling themselves *ithyphalloi* ("hard-ons") and *autolêkythoi* (meaning uncertain, but doubtless crude)[9] as an affront to social norms (Dem. 54.14). Thus, while the satyr served to remind drinkers of the vulgarity of excess, he was also, to use Dover's expression, a convenient trigger for "penile fantasies" (1978: 131).

The third and largest category of sexual motifs comprises homoerotic and heterosexual encounters between human beings, covering all stages of the relationship from courtship to intercourse, and presented in either idealized or vividly frank terms. Since the treatment of this material displays significant variations over time, we must necessarily proceed chronologically in dealing with it. However, it may be helpful at this point to mention one interpretive theory put forward as a framework for approaching the entire corpus of erotic imagery on Attic vases. Calame (1999 [1992]: 72–88) discovers a homology of purpose between the paintings on the tableware used at the symposium and the poetry recited there. In Chapter 2 we saw that sympotic verse falls into two major types: love poetry employed as a vehicle of seduction, or a means of forging camaraderie through an appeal to shared amatory misfortune, and blame poetry, which defines the *hetaireia* as unique and privileged by mocking and expelling outsiders. One can draw a similar iconographic distinction between ritualized love in scenes of courtship and unbridled copulation featuring or imitating satyr sexuality. Thus, according to Calame, the image that pays tribute to the beloved by representing him as an attractive youth wooed by an attentive suitor – perhaps with an inscription remarking upon his beauty – reinforces the message of the love poem that attempts to win him over and persuade him to enter upon a friendship with the *erastês*. Images of drunken excess, on the other hand, were like blame poetry in that they were "designed to pour sexual derision upon symposium drinkers who gradually succumbed to the power of alcohol and would in consequence soon be reduced to the bestial state of satyrs" (1999 [1992]: 87). While this formulation does not cover all instances of erotic imagery – it says nothing of the large role in sympotic scenes played by the courtesan or *hetaira* – a general correlation between love poetry and romantic dalliance, on the one hand, and blame poetry and priapic lust, on the other, may help us to sort out the wide range of images we must consider.

Lines of Sight

Before we begin to analyze erotic subjects on vases, we should briefly investigate Greek theories of erotic arousal in order to grasp the implied connection between sexually provocative visual materials and their reception by the beholder. Sight is the mechanism by which desire is activated. Whether the eye sends out fiery rays that rebound from the object to generate ocular images, as the **Pythagoreans** taught, or the object itself gives out emissions from its surface that strike the eye, an explanation favored by the atomist philosophers, the effect of beauty glimpsed is to inflame the beholder. Both forms of the process are mentioned in the archaic lyricists: in Alcman 3 Astymeloisa's perceived glance melts the onlooker, while in Sappho 31 the speaker is thrown into confusion by her own glance at the beloved. Ibycus, for his part, makes Eros himself cast the fleeting look that provokes desire, a conceit that removes the love object from consideration so as to concentrate exclusively upon the lover's sensations (*PMG* 287).

In Plato's *Cratylus* Socrates ingeniously derives an etymology of "*erôs*" from the verb *eisrheô* "to flow in [through the eye]" (420b). The operations of desire in the *Phaedrus* extend that physiological principle into the realm of metaphysics. According to Socrates, the madness of Eros inspires the soul to perceive eternal realities beyond the world of material bodies. Even if the soul's awareness of its prior experience of the Good has been muddled and distracted in the course of its earthly incarnation, the sight of mortal beauty impels it to aspire once more to the realm of absolutes. Longing (*himeros*) causes the wings by which it had followed in the wake of the gods to sprout again. Despite the resulting pain, "when it looks upon the beauty of the boy, and from thence receives particles [*merê*] that enter and flow into it [which is why *himeros* is so called], it is moistened and warmed, and lets go of its pain and rejoices" (251c). Untranslatable into English, Socrates' pun implies that the stream of material emissions given forth by the boy generates a responsive craving for continued stimulus through its kinetic energy.

Because the eye is so vulnerable and its effects so potent, the gaze is one of the most charged semantic devices on Attic vases. Eye contact denotes an emotional bond between any two individuals – mother and child, for instance – and is instrumental in depicting the nuances of love relationships. Partners feeling mutual desire look deeply into each other's eyes (Berlin F 2269, *ARV*² 177/1; fig. 3.3). Virtuous boys being courted keep their eyes downcast while their lovers gaze fervently at them. Scenes of pursuit (such as fig. 3.1), represent the victim looking back, possibly to entreat the pursuer, but possibly also hinting at consent.

Direct eye contact can also draw viewers into the action. Some pictures show a single participant looking out full face at the spectator. Breaking artistic illusion with its overt recognition of being observed, frontality can be employed for pathos (as when the companion of an abducted maiden gestures outward helplessly), to heighten erotic tension, or to comment ironically upon the action itself. In one homoerotic courtship scene, the *erastês* turns away from his beloved to confront us, displaying great strain in his features (London E74, *ARV*² 965/1; Frontisi-Ducroux 1995: 128 and fig. 105): we sense a patent bid for sympathy. Women bathing or sitting in the protected ambience of the women's quarters stare out at the trespasser who breaches their privacy. Satyrs depicted in the frontal position have grotesque erections, a sign of their own exhibitionism but also a sly dig at the prurience of the audience (Lissarrague 1990: 55–6; Frontisi-Ducroux 1995: 108, 111–12). Bystanders in profile whose looks and gestures direct attention to acts of copulation going on around them also drive home the connection between sex

Fig. 3.3   Red-figure cup by the Kiss Painter (name vase). 521–510 BCE. Young man and girl embracing. From Chiusi. Location: Antikensammlung, Staatliche Museen zu Berlin. Source: Bildarchiv Preussischer Kulturbesitz, Berlin/Staatliche Museen zu Berlin/Photo: Johannes Laurentius/Art Resource, NY.

and spectacle. Such repeated acknowledgments of the viewer's presence remove erotic scenes from the category of mere decoration; they become a key part of the dialogue of the symposium.

Birds of a Different Feather

In the ancient Mediterranean world, the phallos or stylized replica of the male sexual organ was a familiar and potent sign. Because Greeks associated it with fertility, the phallos was a major feature of Dionysiac cult, worn by actors in comedies presented at Athenian dramatic festivals and carried in procession at the Rural Dionysia (Ar. *Ach.* 237–79, Plut. *De cupid. divit.* 527d). Herms, square pillars bearing the head of Hermes, were equipped with phalloi calling attention to their protective function; the mutilation of these figures in 415 BCE, on the eve of the Athenian expedition against Syracuse, triggered fears of a conspiracy against the state (Thuc. 6.27.3). As might be expected, phalloi appear on painted pottery, perhaps as good luck charms, but more often in contexts that leave no doubt of their primary import. On a circular *pyxis* lid from Athens a winged phallos is surrounded by three triangular shapes representing the female genitalia, dotted with black lines to suggest razor stubble. Below the phallos is the inscription "Philonides," a masculine name, while the pudendum to its left is circumscribed by *hê aulêtris anemône*, "the flute-girl Anemone." Scholars see in it a parody of the Judgment of Paris (Kilmer 1993: 194; fig. R1189).

Wings added to the phallos, indicating erection, hint that the gravity-defying member has a mind of its own (Arrowsmith 1973: 136). The conceit became goofy when artists by retracting the foreskin and transforming the *glans* into a staring eye created the phallos-bird. That product of vigorous male imagination is often found in the company of female figures, sometimes ogling them, sometimes being cuddled like a pet (Dover 1978: 133, fig. R414; Kilmer 1993: 193–7; figs. R416, R1192). We occasionally find even more surreal beasts, such as a horse with a phallic head. Surrogates for the onlooker, these beings

reaffirm the male privilege of gazing at women sexually (Frontisi-Ducroux 1996: 93–5). Yet it is noteworthy that the women, far from being offended, are shown treating the phallos-bird with affection. Lewis (2002: 127–8) warns us against inappropriately sexualized readings of women with phalloi and phallos-animals, as they may be a reference to the female citizen's role in fertility cult – though the respectability of figures portrayed in such circumstances may be open to question. Lastly, Vermeule (1979: 173–5) provocatively associates the phallos-bird with other winged creatures, like the Sphinx and Harpies, who bear mortals off to death. If the bird on the vase eyes the viewer, voyeurism, as practiced by this particular surrogate, is uncomfortably self-referential. What at first seems only a joke may have taken on more complicated resonance, then, as the level of wine in the *krater* sank.

Flirtation at the Gym

Sir John Beazley, professor of classical archaeology and art at Oxford University from 1925 until 1956, is remembered for one massive contribution to classical art history: through minute analysis of stylistic details, he single-handedly catalogued and attributed the products of hundreds of black-figure and red-figure vase painters to whom he assigned proper or descriptive names (for example, the Kiss Painter, so called for a well-known picture of a youth and girl about to kiss; see fig. 3.3). It is less widely known, perhaps, that he also pioneered the study of homoerotic courtship scenes on vases (Beazley 1947).

Surveying over a hundred examples of such scenes, Beazley divided them into three schematic groups according to the stage reached in the courtship. In Type α, the *erastês* stands on the boy's left, knees bent, extending his hands in what Beazley termed "the up and down position": with one hand he caresses the *erômenos*'s face beseechingly and with the other he attempts to touch his genitals (Jacksonville AP1966.28.1; fig. 3.4). The boy may react by clutching the *erastês*'s raised wrist, or he may offer no resistance. Other individuals may observe the pair or dance and cavort around them. In Type β the lover bestows presents, usually in the form of animals – fighting cocks, hares, dogs, and so on – upon his beloved (Rhode Island School of Design 13.1479 side A, *ABV* 314/6; fig. 3.5). Both types of scenes are closely paralleled in images of heterosexual courtship. Sometimes, in fact, contrasting scenes on the same vase feature courtship of boys and of women; we will examine one example, a cup by Peithinos, shortly.

Fig. 3.4 Artist unknown (Greek), *kylix*, Attic black-figure Eye Cup, *c*.520–500 BCE. Courtship between man and boy. Source: The Cummer Museum of Art and Gardens, Jacksonville, Florida. Reproduced by permission of the museum.

Fig. 3.5 Greek, Attica. Amphora with male courtship scene, 550–540 BCE. Terracotta, black-figure; h. 11 in. Gift of Mrs. Gustav Radeke. Source: photography by Erik Gould, courtesy of the Museum of Art, Rhode Island School of Design, Providence.

Fig. 3.6 Museum image of Side C of Attic black-figure tripod *pyxis* Mississippi 1977.3.72. Source: Reproduced by permission of the University Museums, University of Mississippi.

Type γ reveals the man and boy engaged, or on the point of engaging, in copulation. While representations of heterosexual congress may be frank, depicting both oral and anal sex and showing more than one partner involved with the woman at the same time, homoerotic sex is discreet. Lovers may be portrayed facing each other wrapped in one cloak. If intercourse is pictured, the sexual position employed is intercrural – the lover stoops to ejaculate between the boy's thighs (Mississippi 1977.3.72, side C; fig. 3.6). Pictorial relations are confined to that single method because penetration would dishonor a free youth, and these scenes depict pederastic interaction in an idealized manner (Dover 1978: 100–9). The upright posture of the boy, in contrast to the bent knees and bowed head of the lover, paradoxically suggests that he is the one in control (Golden 1984: 314–15).

Pederastic courting scenes begin to appear on vases during the early black-figure period and reach their height of popularity after 550; they survive the transition to red-figure but show a steep decline in frequency after 500 and virtually disappear by 475 (Stewart 1997: 157). Beazley's threefold classification holds good for both black-figure and red-figure images, although some thematic differences between products of the two techniques have been noted. It is interesting that the age of the participants grows younger: the mature, bearded *erastês* of black-figure is replaced at the end of the sixth century by a beardless young man, and his partner, correspondingly, is no longer an older adolescent but sometimes a barely pubescent boy (Shapiro 1981: 135). Since black-figure technique is predisposed to render action, stylized representations of the *kômos*, the boisterous march through the streets that ended the evening, greatly outnumber symposium scenes of persons drinking while reclining. Though *kômos* scenes continue to dominate red-figure vases, the number of interior symposium scenes, especially on cups, increases dramatically (Webster 1972: 109–13). Courtship on black-figure vases may occur in a *kômos* setting, with frenzied symposiasts in attendance; red-figure vases place the action in the *palaistra*, the gymnastic wrestling-ground (Kilmer 1993: 12, 16–17). Finally, black-figure has been perceived as less restrictive in subject matter than red-figure, providing rare examples of probable heterosexual cunnilingus and physical arousal on the part of the *erômenos*; in two vases by the Affecter, a sixth-century painter with a highly self-conscious, mannerist approach to his craft, conventions are reversed and the junior partner actively courts the elder (*ABV* 247.90.691, 715; *ABV* 243.45; see Kilmer 1993: 2–3, 1997: 42–4; Lear and Cantarella 2008: 68–71). Red-figure, while engaged with a more limited package of themes, provides a much greater range of variations in detail when handling a given motif.

Explicit erotic acts, involving same-sex and opposite-sex pairs, are seen on pottery for the first time on a set of komastic vases labeled "Tyrrhenian amphorae" and dated to the second quarter of the sixth century BCE. There are about 250 of these amphorae, of which only about eleven show such images of group sex, so the percentage of erotica is admittedly a small one. With their exaggerated erections and acrobatic sexual postures, the rows of human figures copulating resemble satyrs. Earlier depictions of padded dancers with artificial *phalloi*, who may have sung ribald songs at festivals of Dionysos, probably served as the artistic prototype for these designs (Sutton 1992: 9). Thus they appear to be situated firmly within the Greek iconographic tradition. In actuality, however, their indigenous character is contested, with many scholars claiming, again on the basis of find-spots, that they were produced exclusively for the Etruscan market and may therefore be designed to reflect the interests of Etruscan consumers.

Compared with other contemporary Attic vases, Tyrrhenian amphorae are markedly sensationalistic, "specializing in gaudy violence and sexual excess" (Spivey 1991: 142). There are grisly pictures of Trojan War carnage: blood gushes from Polyxena's throat when she is sacrificed (*ABV* 97/27) and the body of the Trojan prince Troilus, ambushed and slain by Achilles, lies decapitated on the ground as Achilles and Hector fight over his head (*ABV* 95/5). Female figures in group copulation scenes participate enthusiastically. One unusual erotic image does not even adhere to the artistic code governing the way sex between two males was normally portrayed at a later date. On the amphora in question (*ABV* 102/100; Kilmer 1997: 44–5 and pl. 7), a bearded man, bent forward, is being penetrated from behind by a younger, beardless man, while to their right an onlooker fondles his own penis. Since it depicts both age-reversal and anal copulation, the vase has been said to challenge the "orthodoxy" of homoerotic representation in Greek art – although, in so far as it inaugurates a tradition, it might not be expected to conform to standards that were only firmed up later. Alternatively, its subject matter may reflect the mores of a foreign people.

This is a good point at which to bring up the whole issue of "orthodoxy" as it is currently debated by art historians working on Athenian materials with graphic sexual content. The notion that Greek painters *never* dealt with particular homoerotic motifs – anal copulation, sexual partners of roughly the same age, junior partners taking

Fig. 3.7   Attic red-figure *kylix*, 85.AE.25. Attributed to the Carpenter Painter. 510–500 BCE. Terracotta. H: 11 ×W (with handles): 38.1 × Diam. (rim): 33.5 cm (4 5/16 × 15 × 13 3/16 in.). Source: The J. Paul Getty Museum, Villa Collection, Malibu, California.

the initiative in courtship or responding to advances with unmistakable excitement – is wrong, as we have already seen. Dover, who is often credited with formulating that strict orthodoxy, himself calls attention to vases that fall outside the norms he has been discussing: among them, two youths who are clearly coevals, one caressing and entwining himself around the other; a youth gripping the buttocks of another, attempting to pull him down upon his penis; a threesome, all of the same age, in which one inserts his penis between the buttocks of two others crouching back-to-back; a black-figure cup featuring two scenes of boys who respond with enthusiasm to a lover's caresses (1978: 86–7, 96; figs R200, R223, R243, and B598). DeVries (1997) collected and published scenes intimating that the *erômenos*, even when not aroused physically, still obtains sensual pleasure from the attentions of his lover and conveys that message through loving gestures; consequently, he should not be considered "frigid." These anomalous instances, however, do not prove that conventions were not in force: rules may be broken deliberately. While the evidence is slight, it could imply that the existence of the established patterns described by Beazley and Dover occasionally induced painters to deviate from them, possibly for favored customers or as special commissions. A red-figure cup much discussed, for obvious reasons, in recent studies

Fig. 3.8 Peithinos, sixth century BCE. Young men and boys in amorous embrace. Athenian red-figure *kylix*, side A. Location: Antinkensammlung, Staatliche Museen zu Berlin. Source: Bildarchiv Preussischer Kulturbesitz, Berlin/Staatliche Museen zu Berlin/Photo: Johannes Laurentius/Art Resource, NY.

of courtship scenes (Malibu 85.AE.25, fig. 3.7) makes this point nicely: it would not amuse us, as it certainly does, if the junior partner were *not* expected to be more self-controlled and undemonstrative than his lover.

Allowing for certain differences in setting or treatment, other red-figure scenes of courtship and preparation for copulation between males conform in general to those already seen. The tone of these scenes is often romantic, privileging the bond between the partners and inviting the viewer to empathize with their feelings. There are, however, very few male homoerotic pictures compared to the large numbers of red-figure vases depicting courtship or sex between men and women. Some vases with exceptional features merit detailed comment because of the large amount of scholarly attention they have generated. We can conclude with an in-depth analysis of each.

The first vase we have already mentioned in passing. Dating from before 500 BCE, it is a **kylix** (drinking cup) signed by the painter Peithinos (Berlin 2279, ARV² 115/1626). On side A (fig. 3.8), four pairs of younger men and older adolescents are engaged in courtship, with a fifth young man at the left standing alone, head bowed. Different phases of seduction are illustrated with great finesse and insight: from left to right, an *erômenos* accepts apples, a traditional love gift, from an admirer; a couple prepare to kiss and the boy, who holds an *aryballos* (another type of oil container), guides his lover's arm and hand toward his genitals; the *erastês* in the next pair meets with determined resistance as he crouches, attempting to insert his erect penis between the boy's thighs; the last pair seem at a very preliminary stage, the lover attempting to embrace the boy's neck while the boy grasps his arm. Strigils, sponges, and *aryballoi* hung on the walls identify the setting as the *palaistra*. On side B (fig. 3.9), three heterosexual couples are in conversation: on the far left,

Fig. 3.9   Peithinos, sixth century BCE. Youths courting young women. Athenian red-figure *kylix*, side B. Location: Antinkensammlung, Staatliche Museen zu Berlin. Source: Bildarchiv Preussischer Kulturbesitz, Berlin/Staatliche Museen zu Berlin/Photo: Johannes Laurentius/Art Resource, NY .

a young man with a dog is greeted by a girl; in the center, a girl offers an apple to a youth; at the right, a young man and a girl are speaking to each other, he leaning on his staff, she gesturing with her left hand and picking (nervously?) at her garment with her right. Under the handle beside them, an elaborately carved stool may define this space as a house interior. Dover remarks on the variation in atmosphere, for the youths and girls do not touch each other at all, but seem "immersed in a patient, wary conversation, in which a slight gesture or an inflection of the voice conveys as much as the straining of an arm in the other scene" (1978: 95). Kilmer proposes that the young men involved in adolescent homosexual relationships on the first side have transferred their allegiance to heterosexual partners on the second (1993: 14–15 and n. 6).

   The **tondo**, or circular painting in the bowl of the cup, confirms that this is a coherent program of pictures, for it represents the hero Peleus wrestling with the goddess Thetis (fig. 3.10). According to the myth, Thetis was fated to bear a son who would be greater than his father; Zeus therefore bestowed her upon Peleus instead of sleeping with her himself. Reluctant to marry a mortal, Thetis attempted to escape from Peleus by transforming herself into various wild creatures, but Peleus proved his mettle by holding her firm. On the cup, Peleus grips Thetis tightly around the waist as she changes shape, symbolized by the snakes wrapped around the limbs of

Fig. 3.10 Peithinos, sixth century BCE. Peleus wrestling with Thetis. Tondo of an Athenian red-figure *kylix*. Location: Antinkensammlung, Staatliche Museen zu Berlin. Source: Bildarchiv Preussischer Kulturbesitz, Berlin/Staatliche Museen zu Berlin/Photo: Johannes Laurentius/Art Resource, NY.

the couple and by the small lion emerging from her right hand. The tale is another paradigm for the "taming" of the bride in marriage, and allusion to it surely indicates that the girls being wooed on side B are respectable citizen maidens, probably the betrothed of the young men who now attempt to get to know them better. The Peithinos cup, Kilmer argues, depicts courtship as a learned procedure, whose lessons, discovered through adolescent pederastic relationships, are ultimately put to use in forging "mature heterosexual relationships."

Another controversial ceramic, the so-called "Eurymedon vase" (Hamburg 1981.173) is an *oinochoê* (wine-pitcher) manufactured in the mid-fifth century. When first published, it was interpreted as a topical memento of Athens's naval and land victories over the Persians in 467 at the mouth of the Eurymedon River in southern Asia Minor (Schauenburg 1975). On one side, a bearded and cloaked youth is running forward, penis in hand (fig. 3.11). On the other, a man in barbarian garb, quiver hanging from his arm, bends forward while raising his hands beside his head in alarm or surrender (fig. 3.12). An inscription between them represents the running figure as saying, "I am Eurymedôn" and the other, "I stand bent over" (Pinney 1984). The stance adopted by the latter figure is the *kubda* position facilitating rear-entry,

Fig. 3.11 Red-figure *oinochoê*, side A. Running youth. Source: Museum für Kunst und Gewerbe, Hamburg, Germany.

Fig. 3.12 Red-figure *oinochoê*, side B. Stooping barbarian. Source: Museum für Kunst und Gewerbe, Hamburg, Germany.

associated with the cheapest form of hasty brothel sex (Davidson 1997: 170). Dover (1978: 105) cites this vase to prove the linkage between anal penetration and dominance in the Greek mind, translating its message as "We've buggered the Persians!" Arguments have been brought against this interpretation – the striding person is not a soldier, the barbarian may not be a Persian, the vase may be making only a general reference to Asiatic decadence (Pinney 1984; Davidson 1997: 170–1, 180–2). None of those alternative scenarios, however, accounts in satisfactory fashion for the specificity and the timeliness of the inscription. As a compromise, Smith (1999) suggests that the bearded youth is a personification of the Battle of Eurymedon itself; if that is the correct explanation, the vase establishes unambiguously that anal penetration was an expression of superior power, considered degrading for the passive partner.

One last vase, attributed to the Dinos Painter and produced around 430 BCE, raises an even more complicated set of problems (London F65, *ARV*² 1154/35; fig. 3.13). It is a bell-shaped *krater* and depicts two young men of about the same age about to have sex while a man and woman look on. At the left, a youth wearing a wreath is seated on a chair, grasping its back with his right hand while he crooks his left arm around his head, elbow up. This odd gesture is a popular one in later Roman representations of lovemaking: it signifies the participant's "openness" to sex (Clarke 1998: 68–70). Another wreathed youth, possibly a little younger, stands before him, steadying himself with a staff as he places his left foot on the chair and prepares to lower himself upon his partner's erect penis. To their right, next to a

Fig. 3.13 Red-figure *krater* by the Dinos Painter, fifth century BCE. Side A. Lovemaking scene. Source: © The Trustees of the British Museum.

column, a bearded man, also wreathed, stares at them, accompanied by a woman, who watches through a half-open door.

The presence of interested non-participants might imply that this is a brothel scene (Keuls 1985: 293). Unusual wreaths worn by the three male figures have been connected to the Anthesteria, a festival associated with youth, wine, and the violation of sexual taboos (von Blanckenhagen 1976: 38–40; Kilmer 1993: 23–4), and that might explain the presence of such unorthodox motifs as male anal penetration and voyeuristic bystanders. Yet the iconography of the sex act on this vase is demonstrably related to that of a slightly earlier work, a vignette of heterosexual intimacy by the Shuválov Painter (Berlin 2414, *ARV*² 1208/41; fig. 3.14). There, the intense eye contact between boy and girl indicates that the artist is primarily interested in conveying their mutual affection; the lovers are rendered as wholly sympathetic characters (Kilmer 1993: 154). One wonders, therefore, whether the Dinos Painter intended a spoof of such tender sentimentality. If so, his slyly lascivious rendering of this male couple would burlesque comparable romantic courtship scenes.

Party Girls

In ancient gender studies, it has become something of a truism that Athenians divided adult women into two antithetical categories: citizen wives, guarded by their husbands, and whores, accessible to anyone willing to pay. Keuls popularized

Fig. 3.14   Red-figure *hydria* by the Shuválov Painter (fifth century BCE). Erotic scene. Location: Antikensammlung, Staatliche Museen zu Berlin. Photo: Johannes Laurentius. Source: Bildarchiv Preussischer Kulturbesitz, Berlin/Art Resource, NY.

this dichotomy by organizing her survey of gender relations around it and emphasizing the "polarization" between wife and whore in the Athenian male's mind (1985: 204–28). Recently, however, a number of scholars have challenged her formulation, arguing that female social status was not that clear cut and determining it in the case of a given woman not always simple. In fact, the supposed conceptual and social split between "nice" wife and "naughty" whore appears to have been all too easily bridged.

Apollodorus, arguing for the prosecution in the forensic speech *Against Neaera* – an indictment of an alleged prostitute to which we will return later – classifies women by three separate functions they perform for a man: "We keep companions [*hetairai*] to give us pleasure, concubines [*pallakai*] to tend our person on a daily basis, and wives [*gynaikai*] to produce legitimate children for us and be trustworthy guardians of our possessions" ([Dem.] 59.122). Although this claim is tendentious, since it implies that each function is exclusive of the other two, it indicates that men did form exclusive, lasting unions with women who were not brides conferred by contractual arrangement with their *kyrios*.[10] Because Athenian citizens were legally debarred from marrying foreigners, concubines were, for the most part, resident aliens.[11] Like a wife, the concubine lived in the man's household and the restrictions upon her sexuality were the same as those of a legally married woman: a statute provided that a *kyrios* who caught a seducer red-handed in his own dwelling could kill the offender with impunity, whether the woman involved was a *gynê* or a ***pallakê*** (Lys. 1.31). For civic purposes, the essential distinction between contractual marriage and concubinage was that children born of the latter arrangement were *nothoi*, "bastards," who were non-citizens and unable to share in their father's estate (Ogden 1996: 34–7, 41–4; Lape 2002–3: 122–6, 130–2). Hence establishing the fact of a mother's valid marriage – through witnesses, as no nuptial registry was kept – became the central problem in numerous Athenian inheritance suits.

Prostitutes, too, were not all of a kind: the flesh market in Athens was sexually diversified (both boys and women were to be had, though females greatly outnumbered males) and complicated in terms of the social standing of its workers. Women who provided sex for money were designated by one of two nouns: ***pornai*** ("whores") and *hetairai* (literally "companions"). The clientele of whores was large, anonymous, and generally of the poorer class, while *hetairai* might enjoy a stable arrangement with one or two men. They operated in distinct environments: the *pornê* stood in an alley or in a row of girls "posted in battle-line" at the brothel entrance (Eub.[?] *ap.* Ath. 13.568e–569d), while the *hetaira*, as her name implies, accompanied a client to a symposium or was hired by the host as an entertainer. Flute-girls, who by law could not receive as a fee more than 2 drachmas (6 obols) a night, were essential to a party, furnishing the music for singing and dancing. Literary and pictorial evidence indicates that some offered sexual services too, but others seem to have been respected professional artists (Lewis 2002: 95–7).[12] In short, then, a whore was paid by the deed, an *hetaira* for an entire evening that might not necessarily include sex, and the status of the latter was therefore considerably higher (Davidson 1997: 94–5). Within this twofold framework there must have been further gradations: for example, free resident aliens working in private establishments would have ranked above slaves kept in state-run brothels, and companions were valued more or less highly based on factors such as age, appearance, talent and education, sexual skills, and personal charisma (Kilmer 1993: 167).

Sites of commercial sexual activity have various names. They may be expressly designated as *porneia*, "brothels," but also, more euphemistically, as *oikiai* or *oikêmata*, "houses" or "rooms," or even as *ergastêria*, simply "workplaces." The last term indicates that what Athenians found contemptible about providing such services was not the nature of the activity – prostitution was both legal and patronized by Aphrodite – but the fact that it was performed under supervision (Cohen 2006). Citizens did not undertake labor, compensated or not, at the behest of another: managed employment was fit only for slaves (Isae. 5.39; Isoc. 14.48). Hence brothel work was synonymous with slavery. Some female staff, then, might have more than one assigned job; when not occupied with customers, they would be set to another kind of productive task, cloth-making. Several Athenian red-figure vases show clients approaching women who either hold wool-working tools or are accompanied by other women carrying such implements (e.g., Chicago 1911.456, *ARV*² 572.88; Keuls 1985: 191 and figs. 175, 176). This inference from vase paintings is confirmed by archaeological evidence.

According to Xenophon (*Mem.* 2.2.4), prostitutes were available throughout the city and not confined to one red-light district. During a noteworthy trial, to which we will return in the next chapter, the prosecutor Aeschines exhorts the jurors: "Look at these fellows there sitting in their cubicles (*oikêmata*), those who openly practice their trade" (1.74). Apparently a house of male prostitution was visible from the law-court located in the **agora**. In the same speech we are told that workshops were defined by the business conducted there, so that a space facing the street could be successively a surgery, a smithy, a laundry, a carpenter's shop, or a *porneion* (1.124). Yet there may also have been purpose-built brothels, if we have interpreted the material remains correctly. Building Z in the Kerameikos, close to the city wall, was quite likely a brothel during some phases of its existence. It was a commodious structure, having two entrances and two courtyards, banquet rooms, a well, and drains indicating copious water use. In the third building stage, a large number of tiny rooms were constructed along its southern side with an entrance giving direct access from the street; these rooms could be locked. Finds from this area of the building, though few, include dining and drinking ware. However, loom weights and underground cisterns that could be employed for washing cloth suggest that it was also a site of textile manufacture (Glazebrook 2011: 39–41, 46). Adjacent to it is another structure, Building Y, whose ground plan, including elaborately decorated dining rooms, may hint at a similar function.

While the standing of the man or woman working on the streets or in a whorehouse is self-evident, a "companion" of either sex occupies a more slippery position. Aeschines can indict his enemy, the influential politician Timarchus, for prostituting himself as a youth because proof of *hetairêsis* (living off lovers) is wholly circumstantial. In terms of gender, the male companion assimilates himself to a female (Aeschin. 1.110–11), while the female herself is even more ambiguous: her position oscillates between femininity and masculinity (Calame 1999 [1992]: 115). If freeborn or freed, she is not under a *kyrios*'s protection; rather, she is *autê hautês kyria*, "her own mistress" ([Dem.] 59.46). Like a man, she can own and manage property and she has a public presence, for her name is heard in gatherings of men (McClure 2003: 68). In documents and speeches, a living woman is not referred to by name if she is respectable; instead, she is designated as "the daughter, wife, or mother of X" (her closest male relative). This is a rule of etiquette, since men addressing men must avoid implying that they are unduly familiar with someone else's female kin (Schaps 1977). The *hetaira*, on the other hand, makes her profits from being notorious, and Apollodorus' offhand references to "**Neaera**" and her supposed daughter "Phano" are intended to leave no doubt of their profession. In the first attested use of the expression *hetaira*, Herodotus, the fifth-century historian, employs it when gossiping about the fabled Egyptian whore Rhodopis – who, contrary to legend, did not, he assures us, erect a pyramid as her monument but did dedicate a tenth of her earnings to Apollo at Delphi, offering a set of iron spits still on view there (2.134–35). By setting up that memorial, Rhodopis was boasting of the distinction she had achieved; in her eyes, fame equaled success. Hence the names of celebrated *hetairai* turn up, along with those of admired youths, in vase inscriptions. On a wine-cooler signed by the painter Euphronius, four naked women, each identified, are drinking together and one, Smikra ("Tiny"), salutes the beautiful boy Leagrus (St. Petersburg 644, *ARV*² 16/15; fig. 3.15). Since a reclining

Fig. 3.15 Red-figure *psykter* signed by Euphronius. Courtesans at a symposium. Source: © The State Hermitage Museum, St. Petersburg. Photo by Vladimir Terebenin, Leonard Kheifets, Yuri Molodkovets.

woman on another vessel, a cup produced about the same time, is similarly designated, the name is probably that of a real person (Peschel 1987: 77).

We should not think of the image as a group portrait, though, for such scenes are "generic sympotic tableaux given particularity through realistic names" (McClure 2003: 70). Furthermore, representations of an all-*hetaira* symposium are also "contrary-to-fact" situations, analogous to Aristophanes' *Lysistrata* and other gender-inversion comedies in which women assume men's roles (Ferrari 2002: 19–20). Euphronios shows his subjects reclining in masculine poses and otherwise behaving in male fashion; when Smikra toasts Leagrus, she acts the part of an *erastês*. Palaesto, another figure in that same scene, gazes directly out at the beholder from over her wine cup; making eye contact, she invites him to identify with her (Kurke 1999: 207–8). Male drinkers can associate themselves with these constructs psychologically because, in throwing their own exclusive party, the women have lost their identity as female "companions" and become figures of indefinite gender. Thus they are vehicles of fantasy capable of mediating the young man's transition from the homosocial sphere of adolescent pederasty to marital heterosexuality. At the same time, their portrayal as humorously immoderate outsiders facilitates bonding among male spectators (Glazebrook 2012).

Hetairai at the very top of the economic pyramid maintained independent establishments, took prominent men as lovers, and were celebrities in their own right: Davidson, employing a term used by Greeks themselves, calls them the **megalomisthoi**, "'big-fee' hetaeras" (1997: 104–7), but we more commonly refer to them as "courtesans." Comic plays were written about them, artists painted and sculpted them, anecdotes about their lives and collections of their witty sayings were compiled, and they even became the subject of scholarly treatises. The great era of courtesan idolatry at Athens came later, between 350 and 250 BCE, so we will revisit these women when we move into the Hellenistic period. But it seems appropriate at this point to talk about the meaning of the *hetaira* as cultural icon, for in that capacity she continues to exercise a spell over modern historians. Earlier in the twentieth century, she was envisioned as an educated and sophisticated "bachelor girl" who conversed with the leading men of Athens, while her sexual life was discreetly played down. Lately she has been applauded for her liberated lifestyle: Garrison portrays her as the incarnation of Athenian "high sexual culture" and surmises that respectable wives adopted her techniques of grooming and lovemaking in order to compete for the attention of their husbands (2000: 121–4, 143–9). How much of this scenario is fact?

Peschel contends that the *hetaira* is a product of the historical circumstances of the late archaic age, a construct invented just when the public visibility of the citizen wife and mother was being curbed (1987: 362–3). For Kurke, her function is that of an ideological stereotype (1996, 1999: ch. 5). As the counterpart of her aristocratic lover, she is dainty, witty, and beautiful; unlike a squalid *pornê*, she is at home in the sympotic gatherings of the *hetaireia*. Her characteristic refinement exemplifies the value attached by the elite classes to a sophisticated hedonism (*habrosynê*). Because she is the ostensible friend and equal of her admirer, she grants sex as a favor in return for gifts, rather than being paid in cash for her services. Representing the economic relations of client and *hetaira* as a form of gift exchange removes them from the commercial realm and sets them at the opposite pole from monetary transactions with whores, emblems of the marketplace frequented by the rising middle class. Though Kurke does not deny that the *hetaira* played a part in Greek entertainments, she believes that the many representations of her in art and literature are not a sign of her actual social importance but instead mark her usefulness as a counter in oligarchic political discourse.

James Davidson's analysis of the grand *hetaira*'s role as fantasy object starts from this same opposition of gift and commodity exchange but approaches it as a marketing strategy. He draws his illustrations from a chapter in Xenophon's *Recollections of Socrates* (3.11). Socrates visits the house of the courtesan Theodote to behold her fabulous beauty himself. Noting the luxury in which she and her mother live, he asks the source of her income. "If someone who has become my friend [*philos*] wishes to do me a kindness, that is my living." Much better than farming, Socrates observes dryly, and proceeds to quiz her about a device (*mêchanê*) for attracting such friends. Appropriating Theodote's own semantic field of "gifts" and "friendship" and conspicuously shying away from vulgar allusion to money or sex, he cynically unpacks her term *philos* and exploits the contradictions inherent in using it as she does. For Davidson, what is revealed by the episode is the subterfuge that underpins the allure of the *hetaira*. Her very language is a tissue of double-meanings in which no firm truth can be pinned down. By pretending to return favor for favor instead of marketing a service, she avoids the laws and taxes that govern commercial prostitution, and by making herself physically inaccessible, even to the point of withdrawing from the public gaze except on rare occasions, she becomes more and more an object of fascination. The courtesan's deliberate seclusion assimilates her to the forbidden wife. It is precisely for those reasons that the male artistic imagination fixates upon her, attempting to capture her elusiveness in paint or writing (Davidson 1997: 120–36).

On vases, pictures of symposiasts courting and making love with *hetairai* – securely identified as such because respectable women by definition did not attend

Fig. 3.16   Douris. *Kylix* (wine cup) with erotic scene. Greek, Late Archaic Period, about 480 BCE. Place of Manufacture: Greece, Attica, Athens. Ceramic, red-figure technique. Height: 7.8 cm (3 1/16 in.); diameter: 21.2 cm (8 3/8 in.). Source: Museum of Fine Arts, Boston. Gift of Landon T. Clay. Photograph © 2013 Museum of Fine Arts, Boston.

symposia – peaked in popularity around 470 BCE, approximately thirty years after the vogue for pederastic courtship scenes began to decline. Indeed, as the Peithinos cup indicates, images of heterosexual courtship adopted the stances and conventions of earlier scenes in which men had courted boys (Stewart 1997: 156–7). In vase paintings, however, the *hetaira* is a more paradoxical figure than the boy, sometimes glamorized, sometimes brutalized, even on the same vase. For all her typological similarity to the male symposiast, she is an alien presence in the *hetaireia*. Lovemaking scenes underscore her inferiority to her sexual partner in significant ways. Although several vases depict face-to-face copulation, with looks exchanged between the partners and the woman taking an active part in the sex act, by far the most common position shown for heterosexual congress is rear-entry – whether vaginal or anal is usually not made clear. While it is true that the position illustrated need not signify a lack of respect for the woman, as prostitutes themselves may have requested anal copulation in order to prevent pregnancy (Kilmer 1993: 33–4), the rear-entry stance requires passivity on her part and implies an emotional distance between her and the man (Sutton 1992: 11). One cup by Douris employing this configuration (Boston 1970.223, *ARV*² 444; fig. 3.16) indicates

Fig. 3.17   Red-figure *kylix* by the Pedieus Painter, *c*.510–500 BCE. Side A, orgy scene. Location: Louvre, Paris. Photo: Chuzeville. Source: Réunion des Musées Nationaux/Art Resource, NY.

through an inscription that the male is fully in control: as he penetrates a woman from the rear, he orders her to "hold still!" (*heche hêsychos*).[13]

Two notorious vases show forced copulation in the surroundings of an orgy. On a cup by the Brygos Painter (Florence 3921, *ARV*² 372/31; Keuls 1985: figs. 167–70; Kilmer 1993: R518), a man penetrates a woman from the rear while apparently shoving her head down toward the penis of another man facing her, and next to them a third man threatens a squatting woman with a stick. The cropped hair of both women suggests that they are slaves. On the more fragmentary reverse, a man beats a crouching woman with a sandal. Side A of the Pedieus Painter's cup (Louvre G13, *ARV*² 86; fig. 3.17) pictures two sexual triads, the woman in each case compelled to perform fellatio on one youth while another enters her from behind. Side B is dominated by a fellation scene in which the youth being serviced seems almost more intent on keeping his drinking horn from spilling. Unlike the slim youthful *hetairai* in other paintings, the women involved are middle-aged and fat, and the wrinkles around their mouths graphically indicate the difficulty they have in accommodating the men's oversized penises (Peschel 1987: 62). Sutton observes that the hierarchy of male over female here is reinforced by control of young over old, free over slave, and employer over employee; it is no wonder that these social inferiors submit without protest (1992: 12).

Several other vases repeat the motif of a threatened or actual beating with a sandal. As enumerated and discussed by Kilmer (1993), these include two, possibly three, male homoerotic scenes (104–7); at least three scenes in which a man wielding a sandal accosts a woman who resists him (108–10); three other scenes of heterosexual foreplay, each with a woman and two men, one of whom brandishes a sandal (110–13); and one instance where a woman uses a sandal on a man with a partial erection (121–4). Except for the scenes in which the male detains a reluctant partner, these images leave it unclear whether the sandal is being employed as a weapon or a mild sexual stimulant, although the one in which the girl swats the man (Kilmer 1993: R192) must involve an attempt at arousal. A last picture, which Kilmer deems "far and away the most violent of the scenes of foreplay" (1993: 113) shows a naked youth yanking a woman's hair with one hand while gripping a sandal with the other (Milan A8037; Kilmer 1993: R530; Lewis 2002: fig. 3.26). The grimace on the woman's face and her pleading gestures indicate that she feels pain and fear; the youth is hauling her forward, probably with the idea of making her fellate him. Like the portrayals of rape on the two "orgy cups" discussed here, this painting leaves no doubt that sadistic force is being exercised against an unwilling victim.

How was the viewer expected to react to these scenes? According to Keuls, they are descriptive, recording what might well have occurred frequently at banquets. She cites an incident reported in *Against Neaera* to demonstrate that "sexual violence was an integral part of the symposium and Athenian society had a high degree of tolerance for it" (1985: 182). There Apollodorus claims that Neaera and her then protector Phrynion once attended a party at which "many had intercourse with her while she was drunk and Phrynion was asleep," including even the servants who waited on tables ([Dem.] 59.33). If vase paintings do reflect conventional reality, an observer would probably associate himself with the dominant male figures rather than their victims. However, the penises of the youths involved in acts of fellatio on the Pedieus Painter's and the Brygos Painter's "orgy cups" are comically exaggerated and resemble those of satyrs, barbarians, and slaves. Caricature puts them into the category of the unsightly and disgusting and may indicate that their conduct is to be regarded with disapproval (Brendel 1970: 27; Kilmer 1993: 156–7).

Because of the great symbolic power attached to the figure of the *hetaira*, scenes in which she appears can also be read as ideological pronouncements. Stewart sees images of sexual violence as visual demonstrations of gender and class supremacy that promote male bonding through fantasy (1997: 165). Kurke (1999: 208–13) agrees that objectification of women is a tactic for fusing the male sympotic group, but points out that the Pedieus Painter's cup showing women abused on its exterior surface contains in its tondo a delightful picture of a young man and a female lyre player strolling along in perfect harmony (see frontispiece). What are we to make of a cup with such an idyllic tondo scene and such external representations of drunken brutality? Some sort of contrast was unquestionably intended: we might bear in mind that the exterior was visible to all, while the interior image would reveal itself only to the drinker, emerging as he drained his wine. Iconography, Ferrari argues, can be as metaphoric as language (2002: 61–86). Perhaps neither the charming interior nor the violence on the exterior was meant to be understood literally. In any case, vase paintings do not chronicle the vicissitudes of the *hetaira*'s life but instead use her as a tool for reaffirming sympotic values and aspirations during an era of intense class conflict. Her treatment in art mirrors the contradictions within that value system.

In the Boudoir

When we move outside the symposium to consider pictures of women in other settings, alone or in company, problems of interpretation are compounded. Even in a non-sympotic situation, one might think, it should at least be easy to tell wives from *hetairai*, but it is not. Indeed, the barrier between the two was apparently permeable in life. Free *hetairai* could enter into long-lasting concubinage relationships and became virtual common-law wives, legally off-limits to other men. Neaera, if we can believe Apollodorus, was once a slave prostitute in Corinth. Her prosecution for attempting to pass herself off as the lawful wife of an Athenian citizen indicates that below a certain social level the boundary separating citizen women from foreigners and respectable from non-respectable women was blurred; this explains why Apollodorus is so anxious to stick females into neat pigeonholes. Naturally, hostile speakers do not bother to draw fine lines but use the pejorative term *pornê* for any woman on whom they wish to cast aspersions. The biographical tradition surrounding Aspasia of Miletus, partner of the influential Athenian politician Pericles, reveals that ambiguity could operate even at the highest levels. Henry (1995: 9–17) constructs an extremely plausible case for her being a resident alien of distinguished background living in a concubinage union with Pericles, yet jokes about her as prostitute and madam were current during her lifetime (Ar. *Ach.* 526–7).

Unless their respectability is unmistakably indicated, one theory holds, all women on red-figure vases, at least until the middle of the fifth century, are supposed to be *hetairai*. Like prostitutes, many vase painters were themselves slaves or foreigners; the Kerameikos, home of the industry, was also a district with numerous brothels; and the aristocrats who bought ceramics purchased equipment for symposia, not gifts for wives. Thus the painters' own social standing, the neighborhood in which they worked, and the market they served created a natural bias toward representing *hetairai* as a class (Williams 1983: 97). Sinister explanations can then be found for the activities in which women are engaged. Obviously female bathers are not respectable because citizen wives would never be shown in the nude. Men approaching a woman purse in hand are about to buy sex; and women spinning in a domestic interior are not hard-working wives but whores in a brothel waiting for customers (Keuls 1985: 258–64).

This sweeping presumption has been challenged. For one thing, the purpose to which an iconographic motif is put may change. Scenes of single naked bathers decorate the interior of wine cups manufactured in the late sixth and early fifth centuries, and accompanying images of dildoes (or, in one instance, a set of disembodied male genitals in the background) leave no doubt that such representations are a kind of "soft porn." Later, however, the same motif of women bathing becomes domesticated. Several women now wash together at a large basin, and the vessel on which the scene appears is a *hydria* or other piece of toilet equipment. These vases were consequently designed for use within the *oikos* by women (Sutton 1992: 22–4). Portrayal of respectable women as desirable reflects a growing tendency to celebrate the presence of *erôs* in married life (Lewis 2002: 149), and putting these sensuous images on household vases serves the interests of the *polis* by presenting female viewers with "appropriate" constructions of their sexuality (Petersen 1997: 44). In both literature and ritual, bathing followed by adornment had long been symbolically associated with the nubility of goddesses (Ferrari 2002: 47–52). By the late fifth century, then, a maiden preparing for her wedding by taking the nuptial bath can be shown naked. The girl's exposure to the viewer's eye is a reminder of her vulnerability during this crucial transition, for in Greek myth and ritual the association between marriage and death, especially for maidens, was a deeply rooted one. Stewart may therefore be right to define the nude female in Greek art as the "liminal female, lacking in or deprived of acculturation" (1997: 41), provided we add that perceptions of what is liminal – prostitutes, brides – can vary over time.

The purse (which Keuls terms an "economic phallus") is an equally ambiguous indicator. Lewis points out (2002: 91–8) that females appear in scenes of commercial life; for example, selling oil (Berne 12227, *ARV*² 596/1; Lewis 2002: fig. 3.1). If a man is talking to a woman with purse in hand, then, she may be a vendor and he a customer, with the purse pointing to an ordinary business transaction. When the woman being approached is represented with veil, distaff, and wool basket, the accoutrements of the virtuous housewife, this iconographic puzzle becomes even more complicated. Since some brothel employees were also wool workers, there was probably a conceptual link between those two activities in the popular imagination (Davidson 1977: 86–90), hence the far-fetched theory that nonrespectable women – so-called "spinning *hetairai*" – posed as matrons equipped with the implements of domesticity in order to arouse customers (Keuls 1985: 258–9). It is much more likely, though, that the purse – if indeed it is a purse – is an abstract symbol of wealth, and as such, appears in different types of domestic scenes, including those where a man of property courts a prospective bride and those in which he is represented as head of a household and is joined by his wife as mistress of the *oikos* (Lewis 2002: 194–9). Alternatively, this pouch could be thought to contain knucklebones, the ancient equivalent of metal or plastic jacks. Playing with them was a child's pastime, but because the activity was associated with youth and charm, knucklebones might be a courting gift. If that is the case, the females in these idealized scenes are marriageable girls, whose wool working testifies to their industriousness, a trait as necessary to the desirable young woman as beauty and modesty (Ferrari 2002: 12–60).

While some pictographic markers are plain and unequivocal – in tableaux of wedding preparation, the bride, with her crown and special sandals, is easy to recognize (Oakley and Sinos 1993: 18) – others give mixed messages. Status, in particular, is hard to determine. Short hair is an indication of slavery, but the hairstyles and headdresses worn by *hetairai* in sympotic scenes vary widely at different periods, with hair sometimes short, sometimes long, perhaps following current fashion (Peschel 1987: 358–9). Literary sources state that the mistress of the household supervises her female slaves, who perform the manual labor. Yet images of domestic work show pairs of women similarly dressed toiling together, with no sign that one is a slave. In late fifth-century pictures of wealthy women at their toilette, the matron is distinguished only by the fact that she is seated, while her attendants are garbed as elegantly as she is (Lewis 2002: 79–81, 138–41).

All-women scenes that appear to have homoerotic implications can be construed differently depending upon the audience projected. Kilmer (1993: 26–30) describes two cups portraying women dressing or perfuming each other; in each picture he finds subtle signs that the women are sexually aroused. Another is more explicit: on one side women are bathing, on the other they play with a phallos-bird beneath dildoes hanging on the wall. These images, he emphasizes, are products of male fantasy produced for men that offer no evidence for real women's homoerotic activities. Yet a hypothetical female viewer might have been gratified by such representations of intimate contact (Petersen 1997: 69). Scenes on vases intended for women's use show female companions expressing fondness by touch. In the picture of women conversing on the late archaic Polyxena sarcophagus (fig. 2.2), the figure on the far left gently places her hand upon the adjoining woman's back; such stroking occurs frequently in scenes set in the women's quarters. Rabinowitz identifies two main contexts: the adorning of the bride, an occasion suffused with romantic intensity, and a musical concert, where one listener expresses the mellow feelings evoked through song by embracing a friend (2002: 117–26). On these vases, she notes, there are no explicit pictures of genital activity, nor should we expect them. Yet vase painters constantly impart shared fondness to women's homosocial environment – evidence, perhaps, that love between women, possibly though not inevitably sexual, was taken for granted by men (2002: 148–9). Though it comes from a much later period, one brief observation about art confirms that men read images of women's physical contact with other women in just that way. In his account of the early fifth-century murals by Polygnotos in the Lesche at Delphi, the second-century CE travel writer Pausanias describes two mythic heroines envisioned in the Underworld: "Below [the image of] Phaedra is Chloris reclining in the lap of Thyia. Whoever says the women when they were alive felt affection [*philia*] toward each other will not be mistaken" (10.29.5).

Bride of Quietness

After 450 BCE, the themes of red-figure scenes involving women change dramatically, perhaps driven by a shift in clientele. Although images of sympotic sexual activity continue to be produced, there are statistically far more scenes of women in domestic surroundings. The usual explanation (though it has been disputed) is that the foreign market, especially in Etruria, had collapsed, and vase painters were now manufacturing more wares for local household use and catering chiefly to feminine tastes (Boardman 1979: 37; Sutton 1992: 24–32). Vases characterized as "women's pots" – vessels specifically used in the wedding ritual as well as perfume containers and cosmetic boxes – are primarily found not overseas but in Attica, where they were preserved as religious or funerary dedications or excavated as fragments from housing sites.

Wedding imagery appears on vases as early as 580–570 BCE and, unsurprisingly, retains its popularity throughout the entire epoch of Attic vase production. During the black-figure period, the marriage procession with the couple in a chariot, escorted by relatives and guests, was the dominant theme: it encapsulated the public side of the occasion, the transfer of the bride from one *oikos* to the other. Closely linked as it was to religious ceremony, such iconography was extremely conservative: for half a century after the introduction of red-figure technique, Oakley and Sinos point out, artists persist in using black-figure for nuptial scenes (1993: 44). Early red-figure vases, while continuing to show the procession, also introduce other themes, such as the ceremonial bath and dressing of the bride. More important, they begin to focus upon the couple's regard for each other as manifested through an exchange of glances. Thus a preoccupation with subjectivity emerges.

While legitimate children had to be born of a contractual marriage, nothing prevented members of the aristocracy from continuing to form valid marriage alliances with leading families of other city-states. Pericles' citizenship law of 451/50 BCE decreed, however, that children with full citizen rights could only issue from the marriage of two Athenian citizens.[14] Technically, those born of a union with a non-Athenian woman, no matter how high her rank, were henceforth children of a *pallakê*. Increased consciousness of the importance of marriage to the state as well as the individual household was subsequently reflected in nuptial imagery. In the new wedding scenes from the second half of the fifth century, "sexuality is shown in a polite but unmistakable manner as the bond that ties together the basic unit of the *polis*" (Sutton 1992: 24). *Erôs* was thought to play a leading part in female acculturation: out of desire for her husband, the bride surrenders and agrees to receive the "yoke." The Washing Painter, who specialized in marriage vases, pictures the god Eros as the bride's companion. Sometimes he assists her as she readies herself for the ceremony (Athens 14790; Oakley and Sinos 1993: fig. 23); his attentions guarantee her loveliness. On vases by other painters, such as the *loutrophoros* intended to hold the water for the nuptial bath shown in fig. 3.18 (Boston 03.802), Eros accompanies bride and groom as they make their way to their new home, an obvious symbol of the mutual physical attraction springing up between the couple. Wedding iconography also features *Peitho*, "Persuasion," as an attendant of Aphrodite and Eros. What insures the fecundity of the *oikos* and the strength of the *polis* is sexual energy channeled into social uses (Thornton 1997: 153; Calame 1999 [1992]: 125–9), as figured by the activities of personified Desire and Persuasion.

Increasingly, however, Eros also becomes a participant in stylized scenes of domestic life, an inconsequential emblem of feminine grace. Although the context may be mundane, Lewis notes, female figures are often given the names of heroines or divine personifications; thus it becomes harder to differentiate real women from mythic personalities (2002: 130). In these scenes, too, "settings are abstract and indistinct, all women look very much the same, and the imagery is dominated by a single ideology of wealth and leisure" (2002: 134). On another set of vases, Aphrodite and her whole retinue become avatars of romance. The Meidias Painter, whose ornate style was much in fashion during the last quarter of the fifth century, places the goddess in an outdoor landscape with her lover Adonis, or presiding

Fig. 3.18 Loutrophoros depicting a bridal procession. Greek, Classical Period, 450–425 BCE. Findspot: Greece (said to have been bought in Athens). Place of Manufacture: Greece, Attica, Athens. Ceramic, red-figure technique. Height: 75.3 cm (29 5/8 in.); Diameter of lip: 25.3 cm (9 15/16 in.); Diameter of body: 18 cm (7 1/16 in.). Source: Museum of Fine Arts, Boston. Francis Bartlett Donation of 1900. 03-802. Photograph © 2013 Museum of Fine Arts, Boston.

over the rape of the daughters of Leucippus by the Dioscouri (London E 224, *ARV*², 1313.5; fig. 3.19). There the abducted girls "put up a token of resistance but not enough to dishevel their delicate transparent gowns and neat coiffures" (Pollitt 1972: 123). As an allegory of marriage, the vase turns the ordeal of the bride's transition from maiden to wife into a palatable fantasy. While tragic poets composing at this time portray Aphrodite as a terrible and irresistible power threatening the community, her role in pictorial art, like that of Eros, has been modified to suit sentimental needs.

Conclusion

To explain revolutionary changes in erotic iconography during the two centuries we have surveyed, art historians have turned to the civic realm. Intercourse scenes first appear about 570 BCE on vases destined for export to Etruria and are then transferred to other kinds of sympotic equipment. Between 560 and 550 the

Fig. 3.19   Late Attic red-figure *hydria* by the Meidias Painter (fl. 410 BCE). Upper register: the abduction of the daughters of Leucippus by the Dioscouri. Lower register: Heracles receiving the golden apples in the garden of the Hesperides. Location: British Museum, London. Source: © The Trustees of the British Museum/Art Resource, NY.

encounter of *erastês* and *erômenos* materializes as a leading theme. Shapiro (1981: 135–6) observes that this time span coincides with the early rise to power of the tyrant Pisistratus, who showed special favor to the prosperous nobility. The frequency of pederastic imagery thus mirrors the economic and social power of the elite under the reign of the despot and his sons. In the late sixth century, scenes of heterosexual congress also increase in popularity, but their implications differ greatly. Through the type of the *hetaira* as "outsider," group orgies celebrate male homosocial bonding (Stewart 1997: 163), while abuse of prostitutes affirms hegemony over inferiors, an indication that class relations were already troubled (Shapiro 1992: 57). It is also noteworthy, however, that some images depict youthful heterosexual pairs with great tenderness, in a manner just as romantic as scenes of homoerotic courtship.

Chapter 4 will show that aristocratic sympotic culture was already losing ground at Athens, as evidenced by the decline in demand for pederastic vases. By the time of the Persian Wars, public opinion had turned against a lifestyle of ostentatious self-indulgence. With the full emergence of the Athenian democracy, a new personal ethic began to take shape: the notion that a head of household must display self-control through rational regulation of pleasures was gradually adopted as a central tenet of democratic egalitarianism. For Stewart (1997: 171), it is the triumph of this mentality that explains the disappearance of erotic vases, except as isolated examples. Other factors may have given rise to the appearance of new motifs. Under the radical democracy, idealization of domestic life as a focus of social stability produced a positive emphasis on female sexuality within marriage (Sutton 1992: 33). Lewis (2002: 133) proposes that the decline in elaborate exported pots allowed ceramics intended for internal household use, which were limited in respect to thematic material, to become more conspicuous. Finally, Pollitt (1972: 125) believes that the extravagances of the Meidias Painter were a response to the difficult moral and political issues posed by the Peloponnesian War, and Burn (1987: 94–6) sees in them a symptom of a deeper existential malaise springing from urbanization. Whatever the plausibility of such conjectures, it seems reasonable to believe that vase paintings do offer glimpses, although fleeting and debatable ones, into the erotic fantasy life of some Athenian consumers, male and, more speculatively, female.

Discussion Prompts

1. Iconography on Athenian vase paintings makes use of individual elements in a scene to convey additional information to the spectator metaphorically. In the illustrations to this chapter, identify specific items that serve that function.
2. The folk art of indigenous peoples is highly valued by North American and European collectors precisely because it reflects the aesthetics and belief-systems of cultures unlike our own. Judging by descriptions of Etruscan culture in the present book, what differences might have led Etruscans to regard Attic pottery as decidedly collectible, so much so that it was used as grave goods?
3. By far the majority of pederastic scenes on Attic symposium ware involve courtship at various stages rather than consummation. Does this fact indicate that consumers were more intrigued by romantic pursuit as opposed to outcome? Or are there other factors that might help to account for the relatively low quantity of explicitly sexual vignettes?
4. "Escapism" is a frequently invoked explanation for the growth in popularity after 450 BCE of interior scenes showing women occupied in domestic pursuits. In this chapter, though, scholars have suggested other possible reasons, economic and political, for this shift in preference. Discuss how they may have worked together to bring about change.

Notes

1 In his pioneering study of Greek and Roman
erotic imagery, the art historian Otto Brendel identifies only five cultures – the classical world, pre-
Columbian Peru, medieval India, Japan during the
seventeenth and eighteenth centuries, and Western
Europe during the eighteenth and nineteenth
centuries – in which art treats sexual subjects explicitly, in a narrative or episodic mode. Allusion to
erotic themes through symbolism is, he observes, far
more common (1970: 6–8).

2 It was a huge industry. Webster (1972: 3) estimates
that "in the great period of the late sixth and early
fifth century there were something like 200 painters
and 50 potters working on fine pottery in the
Kerameikos [the potters' quarter]." The standard
catalogues *Attic Black-figure Vase Painters* and the
second edition of *Attic Red-figure Vase Painters*
(conventionally abbreviated as *ABV* and *ARV*²)
together list over 30,000 surviving vases, dating
from the late seventh to the late fourth centuries,
attributed to specific painters; many other preserved
and published vases remain unattributed. It is estimated that we possess about 1 percent of the total
production of Athenian workshops over three centuries (Beard 1991: 15).

3 Some vases show price marks, but they are notoriously difficult to interpret, since type of vase, size,
workmanship, date of manufacture, and differences
between wholesale and retail or between domestic
and export costs must be taken into account
(Webster 1972: 273–8). One large but not elaborately decorated *hydria* (water jug) from the group
of Polygnotus, dated to 440, has an inscribed price
of 12 obols (London 1921.7–10.2, *ARV*² 1060/138)
and another from the same workshop is priced at
18 obols (St Petersburg 757, *ARV*² 1060/141).
Comparison of prices indicates a fluctuating
market: large vases cost from 4 to 6 obols in the
early fifth century, rose in price by two-thirds at
mid-century, then dropped back to between 3[1/2]
and 7 obols (Johnston 1991: 228). To give a rough
idea of value: in the last quarter of the fifth
century, jurors were compensated for their services
with a stipend of 3 obols a day, half a laborer's
daily wage. A character in Aristophanes' *Frogs*,

staged in 405, remarks that an elegant *lêkythos*
(small oil flask) can be bought for 1 obol (*Ran.*
1236), but this claim, made in a comic context,
may not be historically accurate.

4 For an excellent discussion of pederastic iconography,
its conventions, and its distance from reality, see
Lear's introductory section in Lear and Cantarella
2008: 23–37. Lear observes that *synecdoche*, the
use of a part to represent a whole, is peculiarly
common in vase-painting; thus a hare, a standard
love-gift to an *erômenos*, can symbolize the pederastic relationship itself.

5 An inclusive list of 647 vases containing scenes of
pederastic courtship or other male homoerotic
activity was assembled by the late Keith DeVries
and is now published as an appendix to Lear and
Cantarella's authoritative treatment of pederastic
vase-paintings (2008: 194–233). Although DeVries's
list contains many vases not previously studied, the
number is still a small proportion of surviving
vases overall.

6 Theopompus, a fourth-century BCE Greek historian,
is quoted as saying that the Etruscans share their
women in common, have co-ed gym facilities in
which both sexes exercise without clothing, and
make love openly (*ap.* Ath. 12.517d–f). All of these
statements are inventions derived from the attested
custom of husbands and wives dining together
publicly. A black-figure vase (Oxford, Ashmolean
Museum inv. 1965.97), apparently painted especially for the Etruscan market, shows fully dressed
matrons reclining with their husbands at dinner
(Bonfante 1989: 564–5 and fig. 7).

7 The exceptions are: Boston 95.31, *ARV*² 443/225;
Berlin 2305, *ARV*² 450/31; and Boston 13.94,
*ARV*² 1570/30, all of which show a winged
immortal carrying off a youth and pressing against
or copulating with him in flight. Shapiro (1981:
142–3 and 1992: 64–5), whose interpretation
I follow, identifies the god as Eros; Kilmer (1993:
17–18) thinks he is the West Wind, Zephyrus,
abducting Hyacinthus.

8 Nudity in Greek art and life is widely discussed.
For a history of the question, see Stewart (1997:
24–6). Bonfante (1989) argues that athletic nudity

was a costume, that is, a symbolic mode of dress, originally stemming from ritual initiation. Building upon that thesis, Ferrari suggests that the archaic *kouros* statue represents the initiated youth at the moment he attains *andreia*, "manliness" (2002: 112–26). Contrary to explanations of pictorial nudity as a mark of heroization or abstract idealization, Osborne (1997) demonstrates that the unclothed male body was fixed in geometric and archaic art chiefly as a gender marker but became heavily sexualized in the course of the sixth century. Red-figure painters then began to represent athletes and mature men with penises ligatured, or tied up for protection, as an emblem of sexual restraint. Even satyrs are shown ligatured (naturally a contradiction in terms) on a famous wine-cooler by the painter Douris (London E768, *ARV*² 446/262). By the end of the fifth century only gods and beardless young males are shown nude. Female nudity also has a complex set of meanings, as we will see.

9   The *lêkythos* was an oil container used by athletes (rubdowns with oil were part of the gymnastic routine) and also dedicated at burials. Although it is long and narrow, its shape is not actually reminiscent of a penis, since it has a round flat base and vertical handle. Nevertheless, it figures in a classic comic exchange in Aristophanes (*Ran.* 1200–50) that raises suspicions of indecency. The prefix *auto-*, meaning "self, one's own, same, ideal" is equally hard to unpack. Learned opinion translates *autolêkythoi* as "those who carry their oil flasks themselves [because they are too poor to own a slave]," but in combination with the bluntly obscene *ithyphalloi* that explanation seems pretty lame. Kilmer (1993: 81–9) assembles evidence to show that olive oil was used as a lubricant in anal copulation with male and female partners and by women using leather dildoes; his inference points us in a more likely direction.

10   The technical term for the woman thus given in marriage was *gynê enguêtê*, "pledged wife," and, according to a law of Solon cited in Hyp. 5.16 and Dem. 44.49 and 46.18, only children born of such a marriage were recognized as legitimate (Patterson 1991: 52–3; Ogden 1996: 37–8; Lape 2002–3: 120–7). Since Apollodorus, in order to

support a legal point, is attempting to distinguish the role of "wife" from those of "companion" and "concubine" on a notional basis, his statement should not be taken as evidence that *all* Athenian men kept wives, concubines, and mistresses simultaneously or even sequentially.

11   The case has been made (Sealey 1984: 116–17, on the basis of Isae. 3.35–9) that they may also have been citizen girls whose families were too poor to afford the large dowries customarily handed over at marriage, but a man placing his legitimate daughter in such a situation would have thereby jeopardized the citizenship status of his own grandchildren (Patterson 1991: 58 and n. 61).

12   At the beginning of Plato's *Symposium*, the physician Eryximachus proposes that the guests spend the evening in conversation, sending the hired flute-girl off to perform for the host's female relatives in their own quarters (176e). It is unlikely that a disreputable woman would be given the opportunity to mingle privately with women of good character, even if only to play music.

13   Kilmer (1993: 83–4) argues that the cup (illustrated as his fig. R577) almost certainly depicts anal intercourse, as indicated by several clues: the man's order to the woman, the fact that the couple do not use the bed shown behind them, and the *aryballos* hanging on the wall in front of them.

14   On this law, see Ogden (1996: 59–69). This is one of the main legal points on which the prosecution of Neaera turns. Stephanus, the man with whom Neaera had been living in Athens for thirty years, had four children, three sons and a daughter, whom he treated as Athenian citizens, getting the boys' names inscribed on his tribe's membership register and giving the girl in contractual marriage to another citizen. If they were his children by a citizen wife, whom he presumably had married before becoming involved with Neaera, this would be perfectly permissible. Apollodorus claims, however, that Neaera herself was the children's mother, so that Stephanus had broken the law in passing them off as citizens. Whether the allegation was really true is another matter. Hamel, who subjects the evidence to careful scrutiny, is decidedly skeptical (2003: 47–61, 77–93).

References

Arrowsmith, W. 1973. "Aristophanes' *Birds*: The Fantasy Politics of Eros." *Arion* n.s. 1.1: 119–67.

Beard, M. 1991. "Adopting an Approach II." In T. Rasmussen and N. J. Spivey (eds.), *Looking at Greek Vases*. Cambridge: Cambridge University Press. 12–35.

Beazley, J. D. 1947. "Some Attic Vases in the Cypriot Museum." *Proceedings of the British Academy* 33: 3–31.

Blanckenhagen, P. H. von. 1976. "Puerilia." In L. Bonfante and H. von Heintze (eds.), *In Memoriam Otto J. Brendel*. Mainz: Verlag Philipp von Zabern. 37–41.

Boardman, J. 1979. "The Athenian Pottery Trade." *Expedition* 21.4: 33–9.

Bonfante, L. 1989. "Nudity as a Costume in Classical Art." *American Journal of Archaeology* 93: 543–70.

Brendel, O. J. 1970. "The Scope and Temperament of Erotic Art in the Greco-Roman World." In T. Bowie and C. V. Christenson (eds.), *Studies in Erotic Art*. New York: Basic Books. 3–107.

Burn, L. 1987. *The Meidias Painter*. Oxford: Oxford University Press.

Calame, C. 1999 [1992]. *The Poetics of Eros in Ancient Greece*. Trans. J. Lloyd. [Orig. pub. as *I Greci e l'eros: Simboli, pratiche e luoghi*, Roma-Bari: Gius. Laterza & Figli, 1992.] Princeton, NJ: Princeton University Press.

Clarke, J. R. 1998. *Looking at Lovemaking: Constructions of Sexuality in Roman Art*. Berkeley, CA: University of California Press.

Cohen, E. E. 2006. "Free and Unfree Sexual Work: An Economic Analysis of Athenian Prostitution." In C. A. Faraone and L. K. McClure (eds.), *Prostitutes and Courtesans in the Ancient World*. Madison: University of Wisconsin Press. 95–124.

Davidson, J. N. 1997. *Courtesans and Fishcakes: The Consuming Passions of Classical Athens*. New York: HarperPerennial.

DeVries, K. 1997. "The 'Frigid Eromenoi' and their Wooers Revisited: A Closer Look at Greek Homosexuality in Vase Painting." In M. Duberman (ed.), *Queer Representations: Reading Lives, Reading Cultures*. New York: New York University Press. 14–24.

Dover, K. J. 1978. *Greek Homosexuality*. London: Duckworth.

Ferrari, G. 2002. *Figures of Speech: Men and Maidens in Ancient Greece*. Chicago: University of Chicago Press.

Frontisi-Ducroux, F. 1995. *Du masque au visage: aspects de l'identité en Grèce ancienne*. Paris: Flammarion.

Garrison, D. H. 2000. *Sexual Culture in Ancient Greece*. Norman: University of Oklahoma Press.

Glazebrook, A. 2011. "*Porneion*: Prostitution in Athenian Civic Space." In A. Glazebrook and M. M. Henry (eds.), *Greek Prostitutes in the Ancient Mediterranean 800 BCE–200 CE*. Madison, WI: University of Wisconsin Press. 34–59.

—— 2012. "Prostitutes, Plonk, and Play: Female Banqueters on a Red-Figure Psykter from the Hermitage." *Classical World* 105: 497–524.

Golden, M. 1984. "Slavery and Homosexuality at Athens." *Phoenix* 38: 308–24.

Hamel, D. 2003. *Trying Neaira: The True Story of a Courtesan's Scandalous Life in Ancient Greece*. New Haven, CT: Yale University Press.

Hedreen, G. 2006. "I Let Go My Force Just Touching Her Hair": Male Sexuality in Athenian Vase-Paintings of Silens and Iambic Poetry." *Classical Antiquity* 25: 277–325.

Henry, M. M. 1985. *Menander's Courtesans and the Greek Comic Tradition*. Frankfurt am Main: Peter Lang.

Johnston, A. 1991. "Greek Vases in the Marketplace." In Rasmussen and Spivey (eds.), *Looking at Greek Vases*. 203–31.

Keuls, E. C. 1985. *The Reign of the Phallus: Sexual Politics in Ancient Athens*. New York: Harper & Row.

Kilmer, M. F. 1993. *Greek Erotica on Attic Red-figure Vases*. London: Duckworth.

—— 1997. "Painters and Pederasts: Ancient Art, Sexuality, and Social History." In M. Golden and P. Toohey (eds.), *Inventing Ancient Culture: Historicism, Periodization, and the Ancient World*. London: Routledge. 36–49.

Kurke, L. 1996. "Pindar and the Prostitutes, or Reading Ancient 'Pornography'." *Arion* 4.2: 49–75.

—— 1999. *Coins, Bodies, Games, and Gold: The Politics of Meaning in Archaic Greece*. Princeton, NJ: Princeton University Press.

Lape, S. 2002–3. "Solon and the Institution of the 'Democratic' Family Form." *Classical Journal* 98.2: 117–39.

Lear, A. and Cantarella, E. 2008. *Images of Ancient Greek Pederasty: Boys Were their Gods*. London and New York: Routledge.

Lewis, S. 2002. *The Athenian Woman: An Iconographic Handbook*. London: Routledge.

Lissarrague, F. 1990. "The Sexual Life of Satyrs." In D. M. Halperin, J. J. Winkler, and F. I. Zeitlin (eds.), *Before Sexuality: The Construction of Erotic Experience in the Ancient Greek World*. Princeton, NJ: Princeton University Press. 53–81.

McClure, L. K. 2003. *Courtesans at Table: Gender and Greek Literary Culture in Athenaeus*. New York: Routledge.

McNally, S. 1978. "The Maenad in Early Greek Art." *Arethusa* 11: 101–36.

Oakley, J. H. and Sinos, R. H. 1993. *The Wedding in Ancient Athens*. Madison: University of Wisconsin Press.

Ogden, D. 1996. *Greek Bastardy in the Classical and Hellenistic Periods*. Oxford: Clarendon Press.

Osborne, R. 1996. "Desiring Women on Athenian Pottery." In N. B. Kampen (ed.), *Sexuality in Ancient Art*. Cambridge: Cambridge University Press. 65–80.

—— 1997. "Men without Clothes: Heroic Nakedness and Greek Art." *Gender & History* 9.3: 504–28.

—— 1998. *Archaic and Classical Greek Art*. Oxford: Oxford University Press.

Patterson, C. B. 1991. "Marriage and the Married Woman in Athenian Law." In S. B. Pomeroy (ed.), *Women's History and Ancient History*. Chapel Hill, NC: University of North Carolina Press. 48–72.

Peschel, I. 1987. *Die Hetäre bei Symposion und Komos in der attisch-rotfigurigen Vasenmalerei des 6.-4. Jahrh. v. Chr*. Frankfurt am Main: Peter Lang.

Petersen, L. H. 1997. "Divided Consciousness and Female Companionship: Reconstructing Female Subjectivity on Greek Vases." *Arethusa* 30: 35–74.

Pinney, G. F. 1984. "For the Heroes Are at Hand." *Journal of Hellenic Studies* 104: 181–3.

Pollitt, J. J. 1972. *Art and Experience in Classical Greece*. Cambridge: Cambridge University Press.

Rabinowitz, N. S. 2002. "Excavating Women's Homo-eroticism in Ancient Greece: The Evidence from Attic Vase Painting." In N. S. Rabinowitz and

L. Auanger (eds.), *Among Women: From the Homosocial to the Homoerotic in the Ancient World*. Austin: University of Texas Press. 106–66.

Robinson, D. M. and Fluck, E. J. 1937. *A Study of the Greek Love-names*. Baltimore, MD: The Johns Hopkins University Press.

Schaps, D. M. 1977. "The Woman Least Mentioned: Etiquette and Women's Names." *Classical Quarterly* 27: 323–30.

Schauenburg, K. 1975. "*Eurymedôn eimi.*" *Mitteilungen des Deutschen Archäologischen Instituts (Athenische Abteilung)* 90: 97–122.

Sealey, R. 1984. "On Lawful Concubinage in Athens." *Classical Antiquity* 3.1: 111–33.

Shapiro, H. A. 1981. "Courtship Scenes in Attic Vase Painting." *American Journal of Archaeology* 85: 133–43.

—— 1992. "Eros in Love: Pederasty and Pornography in Greece." In A. Richlin (ed.), *Pornography and Representation in Greece and Rome*. Oxford: Oxford University Press. 53–72.

Smith, A. C. 1999. "Eurymedon and the Evolution of Political Personifications in the Early Classical Period." *Journal of Hellenic Studies* 119: 128–41.

Sourvinou-Inwood, C. 1987. "A Series of Erotic Pursuits: Images and Meanings." *Journal of Hellenic Studies* 107: 131–53.

Spivey, N. 1991. "Greek Vases in Etruria." In Rasmussen and Spivey (eds.), *Looking at Greek Vases*. 131–50.

Stehle [Stigers], E. 1990. "Sappho's Gaze: Fantasies of a Goddess and a Young Man." *differences* 2.1: 88–125.

Stewart, A. 1997. *Art, Desire, and the Body in Ancient Greece*. Cambridge: Cambridge University Press.

Sutton, R. F., Jr. 1992. "Pornography and Persuasion on Attic Pottery." In Richlin (ed.), *Pornography and Representation*. 3–35.

Thornton, B. S. 1997. *Eros: The Myth of Ancient Greek Sexuality*. Boulder, CO: Westview Press.

Vermeule, E. 1979. *Aspects of Death in Early Greek Art and Poetry*. Berkeley, CA: University of California Press.

Webster. T. B. L. 1972. *Potter and Patron in Classical Athens*. London: Methuen & Co.

Williams, D. 1983. "Women on Athenian Vases: Problems of Interpretation." In A. Cameron and A. Kuhrt (eds.), *Images of Women in Antiquity*. Detroit: Wayne State University Press. 92–106.

Further Reading

Ferrari, G. 2002. *Figures of Speech: Men and Maidens in Ancient Greece*. Chicago: University of Chicago Press. Analyzes visual representations on Greek pottery to determine idealized concepts of gender relations.

Kilmer, M. F. 1993. *Greek Erotica on Attic Red-figure Vases*. London: Duckworth. Systematic survey of mainly explicit scenes on this corpus of vases, with many clear photographs.

Lear, A. and Cantarella, E. 2008. *Images of Ancient Greek Pederasty: Boys Were their Gods*. London and New York: Routledge. Thorough presentation of all aspects of pederastic iconography in combination with textual evidence; contains, as an appendix, the most up-to-date list of vases.

Lewis, S. 2002. *The Athenian Woman: An Iconographic Handbook*. London: Routledge. Thematic study of vases as evidence for women's lives, with particular attention to understanding depictions from an archaeological and a cultural standpoint.

Osborne, R. 1998. *Archaic and Classical Greek Art*. Oxford: Oxford University Press. Provides a general historical and cultural context for interpreting the images on Greek pottery in the light of other modes of visual art.

Rasmussen, T. and Spivey, N. J. (eds.). 1991. *Looking at Greek Vases*. Cambridge: Cambridge University Press. Collection of essays by specialists in the field introducing the novice viewer to key approaches and themes.

Webster, T. B. L. 1972. *Potter and Patron in Classical Athens*. London: Methuen & Co. Classic study that set the tone for much current scholarship by examining the interaction between the pottery workshop and the buyer, particularly demands for certain themes.

4

Classical Athens: The Politics of Sex

The reforms of Solon, the early sixth-century lawgiver whom the Athenians regarded as the founding father of their democratic system, included a number of provisions having a direct impact upon the private lives and even bodies of individuals – adult male citizens, citizen youths, **metics** (non-citizen residents), women, and slaves. Laws affecting women included regulations about the marriages of heiresses – fatherless girls without brothers, whose children would succeed to the paternal estate – as well as those prohibiting dowries (later disregarded) and limiting bridal trousseaux, restricting the accessories carried by females in public and their extravagant weeping at funerals, punishing adultery and rape and allowing a father to sell an unchaste daughter into slavery (Plut. *Sol.* 20.2–4, 21.4–5, 23.1–2). Solon is also credited by the comic poet Philemon (fr. 4 *ap.* Ath. 13.569d–f) with establishing a chain of inexpensive brothels, which gave young men the opportunity to relieve sexual urges without molesting virtuous women or embarrassing themselves financially. Furthermore, he was supposed to have founded a temple of Aphrodite Pandemos ("Aphrodite of the Common People") with the proceeds (Nic. *FGrH* 271–2 fr. 9 *ap.* Ath. 13.569d). Scholars doubt Solon's actual involvement in promoting prostitution, but no one denies that in Athens the sex trade was a source of civic revenue: subject to a special tax, it flourished openly.

From his erotic verses ancient readers concluded that Solon himself was privately inclined to the love of boys (Plut. *Sol.* 1.2–3; Apul. *Apol.* 9). Several decrees indirectly attributed to him, styled as "the lawgiver," in Aeschines' speech *Against Timarchus* sought to regulate pederastic practices. Among other provisions, opening and closing hours were imposed upon schools and gymnasia; unauthorized persons were forbidden to enter schools; ages of attendance were specified and accompanying slaves put under supervision; a minimum age of forty was fixed for those who instructed boys in choral dancing (Aeschin. 1.9–11). Still other laws specified a

Sexuality in Greek and Roman Culture, Second Edition. Marilyn B. Skinner.
© 2014 John Wiley & Sons, Inc. Published 2014 by John Wiley & Sons, Inc.

public lashing for slaves who formed liaisons with freeborn boys and prohibited slaves from entering gymnasia (Aeschin. 1.138–9; Plut. *Sol.* 1.4). The latter decree had the effect of sanctioning the gymnasium as a venue for courtship when conducted by freeborn individuals (Scanlon 2002: 272).

Lastly, a law frequently examined by students of Greek sexuality barred an Athenian citizen who had prostituted himself from addressing the assembly, holding public office, or even entering a temple (Aeschin. 1.19–21, 28–30, 32, 40, 73, 195; Dem. 22.21–32, 73). This statute was the one under which Aeschines prosecuted Timarchus in 346/5 BCE, a case discussed at greater length below.[1] It was one clause in a blanket injunction penalizing offenses against the social order, which also included physically abusing parents or failing to support them; evading military service; showing cowardice in battle; and squandering one's estate. The legislative intent was not to regulate private sexual mores, which were thought to be beyond the scope of the law, but instead to protect public spaces from those who had shamefully violated communal standards (Cohen 1991: 72–4). That did not prevent Aeschines, though, from high-mindedly invoking civic morality to win his suit. A corollary law, designed to prevent the disenfranchisement of future citizens, punished relatives and guardians for prostituting citizen boys under their supervision, together with the clients who had paid for the boys' services; under those circumstances the youth was not deemed at fault, since he was a minor. Procuring for a free boy or woman was also condemned (Aeschin. 1.13–14, 184).

None of these regulations made homoerotic behavior itself illegal, as each addressed only the motive for rendering sexual services. If gratifying a lover out of affection was equivocal, doing it for money was indisputably base. Slaves and foreigners might market their bodies with impunity, since they had no stake in government; but a citizen youth who did so, according to Aeschines, gave notice that as a participant in public affairs he would "readily sell out the common interests of the *polis*" (1.29). Unfortunately, the law as written opened up a large gray area because it applied not merely to professional prostitutes registered as such for tax purposes but to amateurs (1.51, 119–20). Thus any citizen, no matter how well-born or well-to-do, who had behaved with less than perfect discretion as an adolescent might be vulnerable to prosecution if he took part in public life as an adult. In addition, appealing to gossip, hearsay, and "common report" to bolster allegations was legal in an Athenian court. Aeschines, who candidly admits the difficulty of proving his charge through witnesses, cites salacious rumor at every turn. The strategy worked, for Timarchus was convicted and his civic privileges abolished (Dem. 19.284).

Whether owed to Solon or not, this corpus of regulations indicates that radical democracy intruded into the personal lives of men and women and imposed some state surveillance on their sexual conduct. In fact, as Halperin (1990: 104) points out, Athenian democracy during the classical period (490–323 BCE) functioned as a gender, as well as a political, system, implicating democratic institutions in conceptual structures of masculinity and femininity. For example, the ideology responsible for suppressing citizen women's visibility in the public sphere (as an ideal, if not altogether in reality) and reducing them to the position of legal dependants was bolstered by democratic goals of curbing ostentatious displays of wealth and guaranteeing status equality among male-headed households, along with legitimate succession (Pomeroy 1975: 57; Fantham et al. 1994: 74–6). In fifth-century Sparta, on the other hand, the military unit, not the *oikos*, was the basis of social organization, competitive instincts found their outlet in combat, and austerity was promoted as an ethical norm. Women therefore continued to be publicly visible and to exercise considerable economic rights. Athenian legislation excluding children of irregular unions from inheriting served the same purpose: it discouraged elites from fathering children with concubines as well as wedded wives and so "put every citizen on the same reproductive footing" (Lape 2002–3: 132; cf. Ogden 1996: 43).

Thus widespread availability of cheap male and female prostitutes and barring the male prostitute from the privileges of public life were "complementary aspects of a single democratizing initiative in classical Athens intended to shore up the masculine dignity of the poorer citizens – to prevent them from being effeminized by poverty – and to promote a new collective image of the citizen body" (Halperin 1990: 102–3). Despite attempts to defuse tensions generated by economic stratification, however, sexual conduct remained embroiled in unresolved class conflicts, for scrutiny of behavior by legal means ran counter to aristocratic traditions of policing social deviations through shame. Consequently, we need to apply both class and gender as complementary analytical categories if we are to grasp the full import of Athenian sexual discourses.

More Equal than Others

The spirit of democratic egalitarianism made slow headway at Athens, for wealthy *oikoi* connected by marriage dominated its politics and retained control of its institutions until the last decades of the fifth century BCE. **Pericles**, the great general and statesman under whose administration the city rose to the height of its power and prestige during the 440s and 430s, was himself a member of one of the noblest of the Athenian propertied families. Extravagance was part and parcel of the elite code. At the beginning of his *History of the Peloponnesian War*, **Thucydides**, writing toward the end of the fifth century, gives a snapshot of proper dress for the oligarchic class of a previous generation (1.6.3–5):

> The Athenians were the first of the Greeks to put aside their weapons and turn to greater luxury through a permissive lifestyle. Indeed, the older cohort of wealthy men who pursued a luxurious way of life only a short time ago stopped wearing linen tunics and binding up the hair on their heads in a knot fastened by golden grasshopper clasps. Spread through kinship ties, the same fashion prevailed for a long time as well among the elders of the Ionians. The Spartans, on the other hand, first began to dress in simple style, the way we do now, and in other respects as far as possible the rich comported themselves similarly to the majority in their standard of living.

Thucydides is speaking of a revolution in taste precipitated by external events and internal tensions within the Athenian *polis*. In the late archaic age, just before the wars between Greece and Persia, Athens had maintained very close ties with the Ionian Greek settlements on the coast of Asia Minor. From Ionia, Eastern luxury goods flowed into Athens to enhance the private lives of aristocrats, making the city a locus of the cult of *habrosynê*. Puzzling red-figure vase paintings from this period depict male symposiasts decked out in Eastern costume, wearing flowing robes, turbans or headbands, and carrying parasols; they are popularly thought to commemorate the lyric poet Anacreon, a native of Ionia then resident in Athens, and his "boon companions" or wealthy patrons (Miller 1992: 96–100). However, Greece's prolonged struggle with Persia from 490 to 479 made imports from the East unpopular, and throughout the fifth century the growing power of the Athenian *dêmos* popularized the notion of all citizens enjoying equal civic rights, whatever their economic status. *Habrosynê* became a term of reproach, associated with effeminacy, as opposed to the manliness of those who had defeated the Persians at Marathon and Salamis.

Two popular assumptions lay behind this disapproving response to the Orientalizing habits of the rich (Kurke 1999: 104). One was economic, a rising conviction that some portion of surplus wealth ought to be earmarked for the common good through private generosity to those less fortunate, or by liturgies – voluntary contributions to the state, like underwriting a chorus for a dramatic festival. By the beginning of the fourth century, when Athens, having lost the Peloponnesian War, was no longer mistress of a tribute-paying empire, such financial support for the *polis* was actually mandated on a rotational basis and supplemented by occasional tax levies. As a corollary to the expectation that the rich should pay their share, a new civic ideology arose: if all citizens were in fact equal under law, the more prosperous should not flaunt their greater means through ostentatious possessions. It is this latter belief that accounts for the change in fashion observed by Thucydides (Geddes 1987).

Yet it would take more than laying aside gold hair ornaments to deflect envy. During the fifth century, the "middling ideology," which defined the citizen body as a homogeneous group of householders possessing moderate resources, emerged as the dominant Athenian political discourse. Male citizen birth made all participants in government equal; other factors such as birth, wealth, education, or occupation theoretically did not matter. "Rich" and "poor" were therefore categories of exclusion (Morris 2000: 113–19). In practice, this ideology glossed over the reality of a very unequal distribution of wealth, which has been identified as the "most politically problematic condition of social inequality" in the city-state (Ober 1989: 192). Only 5–10 percent of the Athenian population lived off the income of their investments; most worked for a living, the vast majority as craftsmen or small farmers. While "rich" and "poor" are relative terms, among the former, the *plousioi*, were approximately 300–400 persons of the "liturgical" class who could afford to fit out a warship or sponsor the performance of a set of plays, and among the latter, the *penêtes*, were those for whom only the modest stipend paid for attending the assembly or serving on a jury – half a workman's daily wage – enabled them to participate in government. Yet there was no property qualification for the exercise of citizenship rights. Hence Aristotle could identify the difference between oligarchy and democracy as that between rich and poor, and characterize democracy as "the rule of the poor" (*Pol.* 1280a.1–4). As noted above, though, the existence of class divisions was seldom acknowledged as such by the Athenians themselves, whose fear of *stasis*, civil disturbance, led them to play down the economic gap – the rich voluntarily foregoing certain conspicuous luxuries such as elaborate housing, and the less affluent often proudly comporting themselves as though they were not at material disadvantage (Davidson 1997: 233–4).

In addition to class, which was defined strictly by wealth, status, as determined by blood and behavior, was the other deciding factor in establishing social rank. Not all wealthy persons were necessarily well-born, for there were affluent metics. An Athenian was an aristocrat if he belonged to one of the clans composed exclusively of families claiming grand lineage. Although some clan members were not rich, those who were continued to pursue activities engaged in by their seventh- and sixth-century ancestors: athletic competition, hunting, horse breeding, participation in symposia, and homoerotic love affairs. Rivalry for distinction was common within this set. At the same time, noblemen as a group attempted to differentiate themselves from the masses and even from prosperous men of lesser birth.

Aristocratic ideology linked high birth to two other desirable attributes: physical attractiveness and moral excellence. The most familiar descriptive term for bluebloods, at least among themselves, was *kalos k'agathos*, "beautiful and good." Because of its poverty, on the other hand, the *dêmos* was morally suspect: the Old Oligarch declares that lack of money is why the masses are more wicked and more ignorant than "the best people" ([Xen.] *Ath. pol.* 1.5).[2] Appreciation of merit, along with beauty, as a defining trait of the nobleman meant that in pederastic discourses exceptional stress was laid upon the lover's virtue, since the example of courage, integrity, and manliness he set for his protégé justified pederasty as a social institution. During the late archaic age, then, the figure of the *erastês* became the embodiment of aristocratic magnanimity, the practitioner of a sacred, as opposed to profane, love, and the freedom-loving patriot, enemy of tyrants.

Oligarchic discourse alleges that the common man is motivated only by greed or lust, but the *kalos k'agathos* is an enthusiast of beauty. In his encomium for Theoxenus (fr. 123 S-M), probably commissioned as a present by the boy's suitor (Hubbard 2002: 260–5), Pindar speaks in the persona of the model admirer of youths. Whoever glances upon the flashing rays from Theoxenus' eyes and does not swell with a wave of longing, he says,

> has a black heart of steel or iron
> forged in a chill fire, and scorned by crescent-browed Aphrodite
> either labors compulsively for money
> or is carried along by female insolence
> down every cold road, enslaved.

The speaker's passionate reaction to the boy's glance is favorably contrasted with the indifference of hypothetical foils distracted by greed and women. Only the concerns of grubbing for a living, which gentlemen do not do, or a degrading obsession with the female sex can explain such apathy. It is noteworthy that what we would call "sexual preference" is here conceptualized as two mutually exclusive tendencies: interest in women is incompatible with attraction to youths. The presence of one or the other inclination, however, is not ascribed to nature or upbringing but is instead determined by the subject's ethical disposition. Although emotionally susceptible to the charm and appeal of boys, the pederast preserves his masculine autonomy, while the womanizer surrenders to impulse and passively subjects himself to a courtesan's will. Implicitly, too, his dealings with *hetairai* involve him in disgusting commercialism as he buys sex. Conversely, the lover presenting tokens of favor to his beloved participates in the honorable economy of gift exchange.

Virtuous admiration for boys is by this reckoning a sublime manifestation of *erôs* quite separate from carnal desire. When we discussed the origins of Aphrodite, we noted that Hesiod and Homer respectively transmit two different accounts of her parentage: in Hesiod, she arises from the severed genitals of Ouranos, and in Homer from the sexual union of Zeus and Dione. Those conflicting myths later gave rise to the distinction between Aphrodite *Ourania*, "Heavenly Aphrodite," and Aphrodite *Pandêmos*, "Common Aphrodite." The domain of the Aphrodite who sprang from Ouranos' member without sexual congress, and therefore partakes only of the male, is chaste homoerotic affection, but her counterpart who participates in the natures of both male and female oversees carnal homoerotic relations as well as all forms of heterosexual relations. Drawn to his beloved by qualities of intellect and soul, the worshipper of Aphrodite Ourania abstains from intercourse because the desire he experiences proceeds from a goddess who "has no stake in *hybris*," that is, physical subjection of another (Pl. *Symp.* 181c). Although it is Plato's spokesman Pausanias who gives classic expression to this doctrine, it was current long before his time as a key element of the discursive code by which the aristocracy attempted to distinguish its way of life from that of the masses.

The bond of *erastês* and *erômenos* was also associated in oligarchic discourse with resistance to despotism. Anonymous drinking songs circulating orally at late sixth-century symposia praised the heroism of the tyrannicides **Harmodius** and **Aristogiton** and celebrated the assassination of Hipparchus, brother of the tyrant Hippias, in 514 BCE. Earlier in the century, their father Pisistratus had staged a series of coups that eventually gave him firm control of Athens, to which Hippias succeeded upon his father's death in 527. Although the Pisistratid dynasty respected Solon's laws and furthered the economic growth he had initiated, Aristogiton and Harmodius, lover and beloved, conspired to kill both brothers. Legend says that they were motivated by an altruistic desire to abolish one-man rule, but Thucydides instead ascribes the conspiracy to private enmities: Hipparchus had made an unsuccessful attempt to seduce Harmodius away from Aristogiton, and, after being spurned, had publicly insulted Harmodius' sister (6.54–59). The pair managed to slay only Hipparchus and were themselves killed in retaliation, and Hippias' rule then proved even more despotic (Hdt. 6.123). Four years later, through the intervention of Sparta, Hippias was expelled from power.

Aristogiton and Harmodius quickly became emblems of the courage and devotion fostered by pederastic *erôs*. With the passage of time, a conceptual opposition between tyranny and homoeroticism arose. Supporters of pederasty advanced the political argument that erotic bonding was more productive of citizen unity than kinship ties (Leitao 2002: 157–62). Men and youths united in friendship were said to be particularly devoted to freedom and the protection of civic institutions. Once again we can call upon Plato's banquet speaker Pausanias to articulate those sentiments (*Symp.* 182b.6–c.7):

> In many parts of Ionia and elsewhere where they live under Persian rule pederasty is thought to be reprehensible. To the Persians it is wrong, along with philosophy and dedication to sport, because they are governed by tyrants. For I do not think it suits rulers that their subjects should conceive high ambitions or form strong bonds of affection and partnership, which those two other institutions and Eros in particular greatly tend to produce. In fact the tyrants here learned that lesson well, since Aristogiton's love [*erôs*] and Harmodius' affection [*philia*] destroyed their regime.

Later in the fifth century, however, the ideological split between mass and elite narrowed as the less privileged began to adopt certain upper-class ways. The symposium, for example, was taken up by a wider public. References to sympotic procedures and etiquette permeate Old Comedy, implying that practices were well known to audiences and that sympotic issues were of enough concern to become a recurrent dramatic theme (Fisher 2000: 358). While the banquet still possesses upper-class associations in comedies such as Aristophanes' *Wasps*, other plays show poorer citizens enjoying the pleasures of formal drinking or dining (Wilkins 2000: 202–13). Incidence of sympotic scenes on cheap tableware may indicate that merchants, artisans, and even rural households participated in such gatherings, on a less lavish scale, of course (Pellizer 1990: 181). Davidson actually posits a "continuum of consumption that parallels the socio-economic continuum": quantity and quality of food, wine, and entertainment would have varied, but conviviality followed the same protocols (1997: 238).

Since institutionalized pederasty was so closely integrated with the symposium as a cultural phenomenon, did pederastic observances trickle down as well? Inscribed potsherds from a dining hall in the *agora*, or civic center, of fifth-century Athens, where officials drawn from all social and economic classes ate together at public expense, indicate that the "discourse of pederasty" was in vogue there, for graffiti designate certain named youths as *kalos*, "beautiful" (Steiner 2002: 357–61). Similarly, references to Aristogiton and Harmodius as founders of the Athenian political system in Aristophanes (*Eq.* 786–7) and the Greek orators (for example, Dem. 19.280, Hyp. 4.3, 6.39) indicate that the tyrannicidal pair were now honored as popular heroes; their pederastic love had become "part of the sexual ideology of the democracy as a whole" (Wohl 2002: 6). Even Aeschines acknowledges them as public benefactors, differentiating their "pure and lawful love" from the base affairs of his adversary (1.140). Yet embracing a convivial tradition or admiring the bravery of a legendary historical couple need not rule out manifestations of disapproval in other contexts.

Pederasty and Class

In the later fifth and fourth centuries there is evidence of considerable objection to the arrogance of the wealthy and well-bred, which, taken to extremes, could result in abusive treatment of other citizens – one of the offenses punishable under the law of *hybris*. Since the oligarchic ideology of entitlement to rule was grounded upon claims of innate moral superiority, democratic rhetoric sought to expose the wickedness of the upper classes. One explicit attack upon the condescending manner and dissolute lifestyle of the nobility is contained in the fourth-century forensic speech *Against Conon*. This is an indictment composed by the orator **Demosthenes** and written for delivery to a panel of jurors by the plaintiff in a trial for assault and battery.[3]

The accuser is Ariston, a young soldier in training, who claims he was physically beaten by the defendant Conon, a man of over fifty, his son Ctesias, and a group of supporters. Ariston describes how Conon, imitating a victorious fighting cock, then flapped his elbows like wings and crowed over him while he lay stunned on the ground (Dem. 54.8–9). Later he accuses his assailants of gross depravity at their symposia: "for these are the people who initiate each other with the rituals of the erect phallos, and do the kinds of things that ordinary human beings cannot even speak of, let alone do, without incurring great shame" (54.17). The witnesses Conon will call to testify to his innocence are tarred, he adds, with the same brush because they are moral degenerates given over to shocking forms of private vice ("men who by day wear dour expressions and affect Spartan airs and put on threadbare cloaks and thin-soled shoes, but when they assemble and are among themselves leave nothing vile or shameful undone"), ready to perjure themselves in order to assist other members of their *hetaireia* (54.34). Finally, Conon's own youthful conduct is advanced as further proof of his godlessness, for he supposedly belonged to a gang of rakes that blasphemously devoured offerings to the underworld goddess Hecate and collected and dined upon the testicles of pigs slain as purificatory sacrifices at the beginning of the Athenian assembly (54.39). Elite exclusivity thus lends support to a charge of impious and unspeakable orgies.

The allegations found in *Against Conon* seem at odds with K. J. Dover's sweeping claim that Greek culture as a whole recognized adult male homosexual desire as natural and legitimate (1978: 1). Though the availability of male prostitutes made sexual gratification quick and easy to obtain for anyone whose tastes lay in that direction, pederasty as a system was class-marked because courtship required leisure and money. Relations of lover and beloved were charged, as we have seen, with considerable moral tension, and not only because of the law concerning self-prostitution. In Plato's *Symposium* Pausanias admits that the code of conduct for the Athenian *erastês*, as opposed to those in force in certain other city-states, is complex and apparently self-contradictory (180c–185c). But, he adds, concerns about pederasty pertain to the welfare of the *erômenos* and not to the intrinsic moral quality of the practice: "it is not clear-cut, but, as I said at the start, pederasty is neither good nor bad in itself, but good when conducted properly and bad when conducted improperly" (183d.4–6). On the surface, however, the rhetoric of *Against Conon* might appear to be condemning same-sex intercourse as something all decent folk denounce and only a lawless minority dare to engage in. Was romantic pederasty, then, a cultural phenomenon accepted by the masses, or was it stigmatized? Those who argue for general social hostility to the custom have recourse to two kinds of evidence: excerpts from Old Comedy and additional speeches from Athenian law courts.

Old Comedy was a state institution that, like the modern political cartoon, mocked civic leaders for conduct deemed inappropriate, helping to mold public opinion of their policies. Playwrights display a self-reflexive awareness of their role as topical commentators, especially in the *parabasis*, an interlude in the middle of the performance when the chorus breaks dramatic illusion and "steps forward" (*parabainein*) to address the spectators on behalf of the author. Comedies were staged under government sponsorship, subject to review by the official appointed to authorize the expenses of production, and presented at either the Great Dionysia or the Lenaia, two annual religious festivals celebrating the communal authority of the Athenian *dêmos*. Thus they can be used as evidence for determining which matters the populace as a whole regarded as urgent or problematical (Henderson 1990: 286–91, 293–307, esp. 296). For his part, the Old Oligarch is grimly cognizant of the institutional character of Old Comedy, its ideological bias, and, most of all, its corresponding propensity to serve class interests ([Xen.] *Ath. pol.* 2.18):

> Furthermore, they [the *dêmos*] do not allow playwrights to satirize or speak poorly of the citizen body, in order that they may not hear bad things about themselves. But if one individual desires to attack another, they encourage him to do so privately, well aware that the satiric victim is for the most part not of the citizenry or the majority, but either a wealthy or a well born or an influential person, and that few of the poor and common folk are lampooned in comedy, and not even those unless it is for meddling in others' affairs and striving to get more than the rest. Hence they are not upset when such figures are ridiculed.

On the basis of the Old Oligarch's testimony, we can assume that the treatment of sexuality in Aristophanes – the only representative of Old Comedy whose plays survive entire – would not be greatly at odds with the sentiments of the general public. The fact that in Aristophanes' plays homoeroticism is never treated in a romantic way, but instead stripped of all emotional coloring and couched in crude physiological terms, therefore requires investigation.

The lofty and self-serving assertions of oligarchic ideology made the protocols of boy-love an easy target of ridicule. It is no surprise, then, that comedy raises a laugh by debunking such pretensions: all professed advocates of chaste pederastic *erôs* are shown as hypocrites, all boys yield out of venality. To cite one example of how

Aristophanes discredits the posturing of aficionados of pederasty: in the central scene of *Clouds* (889–1114), personifications of the traditional and the newfangled ways of training the young, labeled respectively the "Just" (*Dikaios*) and the "Unjust" (*Adikos*) Argument, conduct a debate over education. The conflict is presented from an elite standpoint, with Just Argument defending the time-honored regimen and Unjust Argument attacking it. Just Argument begins with an encomium of old-style *paideia* in the Spartan manner, emphasizing silence, orderliness, rote memorization of traditional songs, self-restraint, and above all modesty. It soon becomes evident, however, that his concern over adolescent decorum veils an unwholesome preoccupation with genitals (973–7):

> When sitting in the gymnasium, the boys had to extend a thigh
> so as never to show anything offensive to outsiders,
> and then, when they stood up again, to smooth the sand,
> taking care to leave no trace of their boyhood for lovers.
> No boy then would ever oil himself below the navel, so that
> dew and down bloomed on his tender parts as on a quince.

As the scene continues, the unmasking of Just Argument becomes more drastic: his moralizing rhetoric is dismissed as wholly outmoded, and his use of mythic examples made to betray itself as self-contradictory. Finally, Unjust Argument crushes him by demonstrating that his most loaded term of reproach, to be "wide-arseholed" (*euryprôktos*) from constant buggering, can be categorically applied to all who set standards of behavior for the community – prosecutors, tragedians, politicians – and finally to most of the spectators.

Costuming and staging enhanced the buffoonery. An ancient commentator on Aristophanes informs us that the two Arguments, dressed as fighting cocks, were brought on stage in wicker cages. An Attic red-figured *kalyx krater* dated to the 420s BCE, formerly in the J. Paul Getty Museum but now repatriated to Italy, portrays two actors costumed as roosters with a flute-player standing between them (fig. 4.1). Both figures are markedly ithyphallic and poised to attack each other. Although the scene was first identified as a contemporary representation of the chorus of Aristophanes' *Birds*, Taplin (1987) makes a good case for it being an illustration of the contest of the two Arguments in *Clouds*.[4] Csapo (1993), who agrees with Taplin, unpacks the symbolic meanings of the fighting cock in ancient Greek culture, including its associations with warfare and specifically with young men of military age, with the erect phallos (another reason for the presence of the phallos-bird in vase-painting iconography), and, in the case of the defeated rooster, with the passive male homosexual. For this reason, he argues, both the "virile" Just Argument and the "effeminate" Unjust Argument are appropriately garbed as cocks. Csapo's analysis helps us realize how viciously Conon had insulted Ariston's manhood: in allegedly crowing over him after knocking him down and beating him, the older man was effectively calling the younger a pathic.

Accusations of passive homosexuality, encapsulated in allusions to the width of the anus and in the stock jibe *katapugôn* (conventionally translated "buggered," but

Fig. 4.1 Attic red-figure calyx *krater* in the collection of the Museo Nazionale di Napoli (inv. no. 205339) and formerly in the collection of the J. Paul Getty Museum, Malibu. Source: Drawing by Christina L. Kolb (CLK in logo).

etymologically summoning up the picture of the rump, *pugê*, offered for penetration), are the most frequent form of abuse in the plays, applied to audiences and public figures alike. One constant running joke is that the most eminent politicians have the most spacious *prôktoi* ("anuses"); it carries a hidden charge of elite nepotism, implying that these leaders have achieved power by calling in favors earned through juvenile sexual submission. Another assumption is that all holders of public office take bribes as a matter of course, having learned to do so when, as boys, they solicited gifts from admirers. In the late play *Wealth* the analogy between receiving courtship presents and prostitution is explicitly drawn. Like courtesans, boy whores ask for money, but good (*chrêstoi*) boys ask instead for a fine horse or a pack of hunting dogs (149–59). Hubbard notes that *chrêstos* is an "aristocratic code word," a synonym for *kalos k'agathos* (1998: 52). Horses and hunting dogs, too, place these *erômenoi* in the circles of the nobility. Comic differentiation of "good boys" from "whores" replicates the ideological dissociation of virtuous *erôs* from ordinary physical desire, satirically aligning it with moralizing rhetoric in which *chrêstoi* designates "ourselves" as opposed to the rude *dêmos*.

The political allegory of *Knights* is grounded on a metonymic fusion of political opportunism and sexual depravity. Old man Demos, who represents the Athenian populace, is in thrall to his cunning slave Paphlagon, a thinly disguised surrogate for

Aristophanes' habitual target, the demagogue Cleon. Frustrated by Paphlagon's sway over their master, two other slaves find a Sausage Seller who is even more of a rogue and cheat and support him in a successful bid to become the new favorite of Demos. Pederastic courtship is a dominant motif in the latter part of the play, since rivalry for influence over the foolish old man is persistently rendered as competition for a pretty boy's affections. Here we must pause to analyze the topical content of that trope.

Pericles himself may have popularized the image of the good citizen as a lover (*erastês*) of his city (Dover 1972: 91). When re-creating his funerary oration over those soldiers who fell during the first year of the Peloponnesian War, the historian Thucydides makes him say at its climax that the survivors must develop an even firmer resolve and daring, not by listening to speeches but rather "by gazing at the genuine power of Athens day by day and becoming her lovers" (2.43.1). In this transferred political context *erastês* is a noun that still retains its prior associations with sympotic, and particularly pederastic, verse (Ludwig 2002: 145–50). Whether Pericles coined it or not, that metaphor would greatly appeal to the average citizen: by invoking erotic literary conventions, it turned the listener, no matter how poor or base, into a manly and honorable subject whose patriotic admiration could reflect his own idealized image of himself (Wohl 2002: 55–62). But Pericles' death in 429 marked a crucial break with the past and the beginning of Athens's long slide toward ruin. Thucydides testifies that Pericles had exercised decisive leadership by relying on his own moral authority, but his successors, jockeying for power, catered instead to the people's pleasure and took direction from them (2.65.8–11). It was thus an easy step for Aristophanes to cast his two scoundrels as self-professed suitors of Athens's collective male governing body.

In *Knights* the figure of the patriotic lover is thoroughly debased (Wohl 2002: 80–92). Paphlagon and the Sausage Seller begin their courtship of Demos by declaring themselves rivals for his affection (732–3). Unfortunately, the Sausage Seller complains, "you are like all these *erômenoi*: you don't accommodate the noble and good [*tous ... kalous te k'agathous*] but give yourself instead to lampsellers, cobblers, shoemakers, and tanners" (736–40).[5] Sexual submission, tricky enough for the beautiful adolescent boy to negotiate, is, of course, utterly disgusting in the case of a senile old man. In a travesty of aristocratic gift-giving, the suitors aggressively lavish delicacies upon their beloved. Comedy sees no dividing line between gifts and payments, so Demos' eager reception of presents brands him a prostitute. His admirers are likewise prostitutes: indeed, the Sausage Seller finally proves he is Paphlagon's destined replacement by confessing how he had made his living: "I dealt in sausages and was fucked some" (1242). "Throughout *Knights*," Wohl observes, "the scandal of prostitution lies close to the surface of the love affair between demos and demagogue, with each party occupying by turns the position of whore and john" (2002: 88).

References to sundry uses for oral and anal cavities pervade the drama. Gratifying the masses with flattery is comically transposed into indulging them with food (they are to be "sweetened with gastronomic phraselets," 215). The Sausage Seller recalls being spotted as a promising politician when he hid a piece of stolen "meat" up his ass (423–6).

Athens's reaction to the doings of its politicians is to gape in stupidity; at 1263 it is labeled "a city of gapers." But the verb "to gape," *chaskein*, is regularly applied to a pathic's stretched anus (Henderson 1975: 211), and Paphlagon is described as standing "with one leg on Pylos, the other in the Assembly … his ass is right among the Chaones [i.e., the 'Gapers']" (75–8). The open mouths of the combatants, polluted with the foul abuse they hurl at each other, are likewise assimilated to the yawning anus. References to buggery are interlaced with scatological humor and jokes about crepitation: about to make his maiden speech in the Assembly, the Sausage Seller is delighted when a pathic (*katapugôn*) farts on his right, taking it for a favorable omen (638–9). The casting of Demos in the subject position of the *erômenos* within a context of anal and fecal imagery underscores the idea of buggery and so breaks the taboo mentioned by the Old Oligarch against depicting the populace in a sordid manner.

In contrast to the negative way in which Old Comedy handles sex between males, heterosexual activity, especially in the context of marriage, is closely associated with such positive Aristophanic themes as peace, abundance, prosperity, rural piety, and celebration. *Acharnians* closes with the hero swaggering off to a party, a pretty girl on each arm, and two other comedies, *Peace* and *Birds*, end with a triumphant wedding procession. The classic affirmation of the societal importance of conjugal relations is *Lysistrata*, not for its farcical treatment of the wives' sex-strike – which blandly ignores other means of relief open to their husbands – but for its siting of the comic action in and around the Acropolis. Athena's symbolic partnership with Aphrodite in furthering Lysistrata's peace process is corollary to their divine collaboration in promoting the continuity of families from one generation to the next (Loraux 1993: 147–83). In this play, as on contemporary vases, marital sexuality is shown as integral to the survival of both the *oikos* and the *polis*.

All scholars agree that the basic orientation of Old Comedy is heterosexual, but they debate how seriously audiences were expected to take the jokes about pervasive sexual degeneracy in these and other plays. Dover (1978: 135–53) can find no passage in which erotic interest in boys per se is castigated, and Henderson (1975: 216–18) maintains that the poet's real intent in choosing to target pederasty was to deflate the moral snobbishness of the nobility. On the other hand, Hubbard (1998: 50–9) maintains that "[h]omosexual acts of any sort tend to be associated with elite self-indulgence and corruption" in Aristophanes because the cult of boy-love, with its web of secret influences and connections, helped the upper class to monopolize power and live well at the expense of the resentful poor. Cantarella understands the playwright's witticisms as historical evidence: she thinks they indicate that the practice of "protracting homosexual relations beyond the proper age limit" was so common that it was creating a hostile reaction against pederasty, exacerbated by concerns over the decline in manpower resulting from the Peloponnesian War (1992: 64–5). The most accurate assessment must fall somewhere between those extremes. In the context of a fertility festival honoring Dionysos, outrageous sexual shamelessness – manifest in the leather phallos worn by comic actors – was ritually meaningful, and pederasty lent itself to particularly blatant and shocking expressions of obscenity. The exploitation of whoring and penetration as controlling metaphors in *Knights* certainly bears out Hubbard's claim, but pejorative references to pederasty in other plays seem more informed by class tensions than by forthright moral opposition. Yet the notorious elusiveness of humor, culturally specific and thus hard to evaluate at a distance of 2,500 years, probably means that we will never be able to agree on the tone of many of Aristophanes' jokes or to identify the groups in the audience to whom they were intended to appeal.

Most of our surviving forensic speeches, an extensive collection including all the canonical Attic orators, were delivered in the early to mid-fourth century BCE, slightly later than the heyday of Old Comedy. Law court speeches had to appeal to a panel of several hundred jurors made up, for the most part, of ordinary citizens. Certain passages have accordingly been cited to demonstrate that the erotic preoccupations of the few were the focus of strong social disapproval among the many (Hubbard 1998: 59–69). In Lysias 3, for example, a wealthy older man, accused of striking his rival Simon in a brawl over a youth, pleads that he himself was the victim of far worse injuries at the other fellow's hands. He did not bring a lawsuit, he explains, because he feared that exposure of his infatuation would make him look stupid and ridiculous (9). One awkward feature of this case is that Simon claimed the boy was hired under contract; if true, the speaker, who had at one point absconded with him, was legally in the wrong (10, 22).[6] Other courtroom opponents are accused of wasting an estate on affairs with boys (Isae. 10.25) or of hiring a citizen boy as a sexual partner (Dem. 45.79). Each time there is a mercenary underpinning to the relationship, in shabby contrast to the rhetoric of virtuous *erôs* promulgated by the aristocracy. Davidson (2007: 447–65) believes that an ethos of commercial sex was encroaching upon traditional ideals of courtship, trailing cynical opinions of all same-sex bonding in its wake. However, none of the examples given here indicates that affairs with boys, free or slave, were themselves censured, for anticipated hostile reactions on the part of the jury would arise from such accompanying circumstances as age-inappropriate conduct, extravagance, and inducing a citizen to prostitute himself. Among addresses to Athenian juries, then, *Against Conon* may be exceptional in its attempt to cast the homoerotic activities of the rich in a menacing and ugly light.

Aeschines' speech *Against Timarchus*, on the other hand, comprises our strongest evidence for approval of institutionalized pederasty among the general citizen population, at least at the time it was delivered (Fisher 2001: 58–62). We must bear in mind that the prosecution case is absolutely circumstantial: Timarchus was not enrolled on the list of prostitutes from whom the authorities collected taxes (Aeschin. 1.119–20), nor were there witnesses to a contract for specified services (160–5). Aeschines is limited to arguing from probability. When pronouncing his indictment, then, he scrupulously distinguishes his opponent's alleged conduct from the behavior of an honorable *erômenos*. First, though owning enough to live moderately, Timarchus freely chose (*proêirêmenos*, 40) to disgrace himself, being addicted (*douleuôn*, "enslaved") to expensive habits, gourmandizing and women (42). There is no insinuation that he was himself inclined toward passivity or even enjoyed the acts performed upon him (Fisher 2001: 173; the nasty implication is summed up by Davidson [2007: 455] as "gay for pay"). Second, he supposedly went with not one but a whole succession of lovers, so that his activities can be categorized not just as *hetairêsis*, "being a (sexual) companion," but as *porneia*, "whoring" (51–2). Third, he is disqualified from exercising his public rights on two counts, for he squandered his patrimony in addition to debasing his body (94–100). Finally, to draw an absolute line between Timarchus' activities and the practice of decent love, Aeschines brings on a straw man, an unnamed "general" seemingly familiar with the pursuits of the gymnasium, that is, a man of considerable leisure (132). This speaker, he says, will defend Timarchus by charging that the prosecution is a hypocritical attack on venerated cultural traditions, including the self-sacrifice of Harmodius and Aristogiton and the splendid friendship of Achilles and Patroclus, by a man notorious for his own pursuit of boys. Into the mouth of this patronizing advocate Aeschines puts an appeal that takes social endorsement of pederasty for granted (133–4):

> For if, he says, some persons malign physical beauty and reduce it to a hardship for those possessing it, will you not be publicly voting against the same thing you ask for privately? It will seem peculiar to him if you all, when about to have a child, pray that your unborn sons be handsome and noble (*kalous k'agathous*) in appearance and worthy of the city; but, persuaded as it seems by Aeschines, you disenfranchise those already born, of whom the city may rightly be proud, if they excel in beauty and youth and arouse passion in some and become objects of strife due to *erôs*.

Clearly the general assumes the jurors share his own conviction that attractiveness in young men, even to the point of sparking off erotic rivalries, is a desirable attribute. Aeschines, who professes himself firmly in agreement, goes on, now speaking in his own voice, to differentiate between self-prostitution and chaste, worthy love (137), drawing on the poets to remind his listeners of what the latter is. That he addresses the distinction at such length (141–59) indicates that there was no litmus test to divide good boys from bad apart from motive, which was not all that easily determined (Ormand 2009: 85). In the absence of hard evidence for Timarchus' actual guilt, the verdict of the jury must be a repudiation of a perceived threat to democratic moral standards (Lape 2006: 144–8). Pederasty, it follows, was felt to have a role to play in the democratic state.

From the admittedly complicated evidence, what conclusions can reasonably be drawn about attitudes toward the institution of pederasty on the part of the *dêmos*? Since homoerotic desire is taken for granted and confessed without apology in forensic speeches, there must have been no stigma attached to interest in boys per se. Yet the rhetoric of pederasty was duplicitous, for it glossed over the physical aspects of the relationship and mystified its inequalities in order to validate elite moral superiority. Aristophanes' plays unmask its apologists as frauds, gleefully allude to the otherwise unmentionable act of anal intercourse, and imply that political preference in return for sexual services was a standard trade-off. Such mockery could achieve its objective only by tapping into a vein of popular cynicism, as diagnosed by Davidson (see above). Closely linked as it was in the ordinary mind to both class privilege and hypocrisy, reference to elite pederasty could summon up corollary impressions of unbridled *hybris*. Ariston dwells upon the debauchery of

Conon and his sons not because the jurors might disapprove of homoerotic activity but because they would react with horror to the subtext of the charge: the old man and his associates, who in the privacy of the dining-room "leave nothing vile or shameful undone" (Dem. 54.34), are equally unscrupulous about riding roughshod over others. Therefore, when aristocratic notions of entitlement clash with the democratic ethic of self-control and restraint, censure unerringly fastens upon the great point of anxiety within the pederastic system – the fear that the junior partner may not make the transition to adult masculinity, becoming a lifelong pleasure-mad effeminate, a despicable *katapugôn* or *kinaidos*.

Interview with the *Kinaidos*

Vampires may not exist, but they are good to think with, and for that reason they dwell among us. Ever since the late nineteenth century, when Sheridan Le Fanu and Bram Stoker first popularized the literary construct of an immortal blood-sucking fiend, vampires, female and male, have prowled our entertainment media – so much so that an extraterrestrial observer monitoring current television programming from a planet circling Alpha Centauri might be forgiven for assuming that such creatures pose a real and present danger to human life. Buffy's adversaries, especially in the early seasons, were chiefly vampires of an old-fashioned stripe. In the last decades of the twentieth century, though, we also witnessed the emergence of the New Vampire, the angst-ridden protagonist of novels and films steeped in morbid eroticism. Expansion of the literary formula to allow for an empathetic and morally complex treatment of vampires was inevitable because as mythic residents of our imaginary they stand for a plethora of terrors – the universal dread of death, obviously, but also culturally specific fears such as formerly unmentionable sexualities (Auerbach 1995: 1–8). In *Dracula*, for example, desire may be "filtered … through the mask of a monstrous or demonic heterosexuality" (Craft 1984: 111), but for its Victorian readers the ghastliness of the novel was intensified by intuitive perception of the Count's secret homoerotic designs upon the protagonist, Jonathan Harker. Thus the monster's spellbinding allure evoked the fascination of what was forbidden, outcast, closeted. When homosexuality became a topic of open discussion, vampires were at last permitted to step into the role of protagonist and even teenage romantic hero. Despite our present-day frankness about the secret they once embodied, however, the Undead have lost none of their potency, as they have simply gone on to attach themselves to yet unrealized areas of the repressed.

That excursus into vampirology was not irrelevant because the **kinaidos** (or, in his Roman incarnation, the *cinaedus*) may have been to the classical world more or less what the vampire was, up until recently, to us. The two Greek stereotypes of aberrant masculinity, as Foucault defined them (1986: 81–2, 84–6), were the tyrant, who, taking advantage of his absolute power, indulges his passions freely, and the effeminate male. In Aristophanes, the latter is a *katapugôn*, but by the fourth century the word *kinaidos* had become the more familiar term (Davidson 1997: 167), and so the one we will use.[7] According to John J. Winkler, that figure is the notional opposite of the hoplite or citizen soldier, whose honor was invested in the inviolability of his body. "The conception of a *kinaidos*," Winkler states, "was of a man socially deviant in his entire being, principally observable in behavior that flagrantly violated or contravened the dominant social definition of masculinity. To this extent, *kinaidos* was a category of person, not just of acts" (1990a: 45–6). As far as real life was concerned, however, the category may have been a null set; it is conceivable, in other words, that there were no actual *kinaidoi*, any more than there are actual vampires. Nor would it matter. As a "scare-image" for enforcing the protocols of manhood and guaranteeing that those in the public eye would observe unspoken rules of decorum, the stereotype, in and of itself, had demonstrable social value. "While the hoplite warrior is the ideal self to which every well-to-do citizen looks, the *kinaidos*, mentioned only with laughter or indignation, is the unreal, but dreaded, anti-type of masculinity behind every man's back" (Winkler 1990a: 46).

Kinaidoi were supposedly recognizable by external signs. Foppish, overelaborate dress was a dead giveaway, as were affected language and gestures and, above all, "feminine" appearance or demeanor. In the comic theater, such characters are true androgynes. Aristophanes' *Women at the Thesmophoria* brings two of the tribe on stage: first the tragic poet **Agathon** (101–265) and, later, the infamous Cleisthenes, pilloried for effeminacy in several other plays (574–654). Agathon is represented as semi-transvestite, wearing a woman's gown but equipped, incongruously, with both male and female accessories, like sword and mirror, which enable him to write parts for both sexes; his fellow tragedian Euripides describes him as "nice-featured, pale, clean-shaven, high-voiced, delicate, good to look at" (191–2). Cleisthenes is also masked as a smooth-cheeked cross-dresser, claiming to be a friend and enthusiastic supporter of the assemblage of Athenian women, whom he addresses as "sisters of my own sort" (*syngeneis toumou tropou*, 573). In a subsequent orgy of gender bending, the play's masculine leads, Euripides and his Old Relative, wind up in drag. The hilarious contrast between their poor efforts to pass as females and the easy gender transgressions of the two "real" effeminates burlesques a fundamental convention of Greek theater – all women's roles in tragedy and comedy were played, as on the Elizabethan stage, by male actors. In the world of comedy, then, the *katapugôn* character collapses the antithesis of male and female, one of the most rigid of Greek conceptual polarities, and in doing so self-consciously calls attention to the artificiality of all theatrical devices (Zeitlin 1996c: 385–6).

Outside comic fictions, though, what did the labels "*katapugôn*" and "*kinaidos*" really denote? Most current work on Greek sexuality follows the lead of Dover, who assigns *katapugôn* the very specific meaning of "allowing oneself to be penetrated anally" (1978: 142–3). Winkler adds a psychological dimension: if sex is construed as competition, with the penetrated always the loser, "the *kinaidos* is a man who desires to lose" and who, like a woman, derives pleasure from being mastered (1990a: 54). As noted above, however, Davidson believes that Dover's and Foucault's power-penetration model has been imposed upon ancient Greek culture erroneously (2001: 7–20; 2007: 101–66). Thus he argues that the terms designate not passivity but lack of self-control. A *katapugôn* is lustful and promiscuous, unrestrained in his pleasure-seeking. The *kinaidos*, too, is sexually insatiable, but he does not necessarily have a preference for the anal position; rather, it is in his inability to attain sexual satisfaction that he resembles women. Still, Dover's and Davidson's explanations are not mutually exclusive, for a slur often can be applied in both a narrow and an extended sense. Thus the epithet "*kinaidos*" seems to function on two planes, conceptualized "not only in anxiously universalizing terms but also in comfortably minoritizing ones" (Halperin 2002: 34, following a formulation by Sedgwick 1990: 1). While it serves to warn each citizen male of the dangers of abject submission to any of the bodily appetites, it can also designate a freakish outsider whose craving for perverse forms of pleasure can be attributed to physiological, mental, and/or moral abnormality.

One text that seems to incorporate both meanings is Plato's *Gorgias* 494a–495a. Socrates is there interrogating Callicles, a young nobleman anticipating an important career in Athenian politics, who eloquently champions the directives of nature as opposed to those of law. Callicles asserts that nature, *physis*, has destined the strongest to rule, justifiably exempting him from conventional constraints (*nomoi*) legislated by the masses to enforce a spurious equality (484b–d). For such a man it is, according to nature, right and proper to gratify all his desires without restraint (491e), and that kind of life will be, in turn, both a virtuous and a happy one. Socrates is attempting to refute the latter tenet:

SOCRATES: … And tell me, do you say such a life involves feeling hungry and eating when you are hungry?

CALLICLES: I do.

SOCRATES: And drinking when you're thirsty?

CALLICLES: Agreed, and that living happily means having all the other desires and being able to gratify them with impunity.

SOCRATES: Good for you, my friend. Carry on as you've begun, and don't hold back out of shame. It appears that I mustn't refrain through shame either. So first tell me if living happily also means itching and scratching, having abundant freedom to scratch, and passing one's life scratching.

CALLICLES: Socrates, you're outlandish and an utter rabble-rouser.

SOCRATES: Callicles, that's just how I both confounded and shamed Polos and Gorgias, but you will not be rattled nor shamed. For you're tough-minded. So just answer me that.

CALLICLES: Very well, I agree that the person scratching himself might live pleasurably.

SOCRATES: And if pleasurably, then also happily?

CALLICLES: Of course.

SOCRATES: And what if he should scratch only his head …? Or need I ask anything further? Look, Callicles, what will you reply if someone should ask you in succession to this question all those that follow? The culmination of all such questions, the life of *kinaidoi*, is it not dreadful and shameful and sad? Or will you dare to say that those persons are happy if they gain what they want with impunity?

CALLICLES: Aren't you ashamed, Socrates, to steer the conversation toward such matters?

SOCRATES: Am I steering it there, noble sir, or is it that man who says expressly that those who gratify themselves, however they gratify themselves, are happy, and does not distinguish among pleasures, which are good and which are bad?

The operative word in this passage is *aischunthênai*, "to feel or show shame," which in Greek cultural terms could come very close to our notion of "losing face." Callicles had previously objected that Socrates' tactics of cross-examination unfairly compelled an adversary into contradicting himself to avoid making a statement that would shame him in the eyes of others, despite his private confidence in its truth. Because shame is a sanction imposed by convention, which Callicles rejects, he deems himself shame-proof. By alluding obliquely to the upsetting topic of *kinaidoi* through the euphemism "scratching one's head," Socrates demonstrates that there are social conventions even a Callicles instinctively respects.[8]

This passage establishes that in Socrates' mind the *kinaidos* is "the paradigm of insatiability, of desire never-to-be-fulfilled" (Davidson 1997: 174). That does not fully explain, though, why Callicles is so disgusted: for him, a *kinaidos* must be something more than a mere symbol of unbridled appetite if decent men do not bring up the subject among themselves. One speaker thus employs the stereotype to represent the antithesis of manly virtue, while the other hears a direct reference to the forbidden subject of anal penetration. The gulf between the two senses of *kinaidos* is bridged by a system of medicine that can ascribe the insatiability of such a person to his physiological makeup. Semen, which in normal men flows into the testicles and penis, causing an erection, passes into the anal region (*hedra*) of those whose natural channels are blocked. The presence of that moisture provokes sexual arousal in the area where it collects. Because the secretion is slight, however, and cannot force an exit, and cools down quickly, pathics are insatiable (*aplêstoi*), like women ([Arist.] *Pr.* 4.26.29–30). Both the *kinaidos*'s desire for anal penetration and his sexual voraciousness are explained by his inability to experience a manly erection and orgasm with its consequent release.[9]

Of course, the scientific postulate that effeminacy results from semen leaching into the fundament is no less alien to human physiology than the superstition that vampires feed on blood. Consequently, we still have not determined whether there were "real" *kinaidoi*, as opposed to a stereotype that could be conveniently trotted out on the stage or hurled as a derogatory term at a political opponent – as today we might call someone who financially preys on the less fortunate a "bloodsucker." The question is a knotty one because cultural differences play an important part. Among Roman social historians one item of debate is whether individuals defined themselves as *cinaedi*, employing the word to categorize their self-perceived sexual identity, like lesbians appropriating the offensive expression "dyke." When depictions of the "*katapugôn*" or "*kinaidos*" turn up in classical Greek sources, though, the contexts are either fictional or pejorative, and therefore suspect as historical evidence. Still, there is one surprising exception, found in what has by now become our casebook for classical Greek sexuality, Plato's *Symposium*.

At this point, we should take a minute to look at the dialogue in its entirety. The *Symposium* purports to be a record of a conversation that took place at the playwright Agathon's house during a celebration of his first tragic victory at the Lenaia festival in 416 BCE. In lieu of the usual entertainment, the guests decide to offer extemporaneous speeches in praise of Eros, and six contributions are recounted verbatim, culminating in an account of the god that Socrates claims he received from the wise woman Diotima. Immediately afterward, the charismatic politician Alcibiades crashes the party and delivers his own drunken eulogy in praise of Socrates. His strained friendship with the philosopher in his youth still chafes him, and he betrays a seething mix of emotions, including obsessive yearning, resentment, and self-pity, which Socrates deflects with his customary noncommittal irony. Plato's deft, urbane sketches of the historical figures present have been used as evidence of their actual personalities, but the validity of his characterizations may not be easy to pin down.

Among the guests is Pausanias, a firm advocate of the elite ideology of pederasty – and, not coincidentally, Agathon's recognized sexual partner (*Symp.* 177d.8, 193b.6–c.5). His speech defending the educational benefits of a noble love expresses a conviction grounded upon his own private experience and vindicated by his protégé's brilliant success (Penwill 1978: 146–7). Some biographical information about Pausanias and Agathon has come down to us.[10] At the time of the party they had already been together for a number of years, ever since Agathon's early adolescence (Pl. *Prot.* 315d–e). They remained constant companions, and when Agathon left Athens some time before 405 to take up residence at the court of king Archelaus of Macedon, Pausanias accompanied him (Ael. *VH* 2.21). Dover (1978: 144) conjectures that jokes about Agathon's transvestitism arose from his practice of trimming his beard close so as to retain the appearance of youth expected of Pausanias' *erômenos*.

Now, it should be obvious from what has preceded that Greek sexual rubrics created burdensome difficulties for partnerships that continued after the junior partner reached adulthood because the latter was understood to remain passive, compliant, and inferior – by observers, to be sure, as we have no idea what went on in the bedroom. Such relationships were discouraged, met either by disapproving silence or by overt hostility directed against the perceived subordinate member (Foucault 1986: 220). Taking his involvement with Pausanias as a given, however, Agathon's friends at the symposium gallantly flatter his looks as though he were still a beautiful boy (at the dramatic time of the dialogue, he is in his late twenties). Agathon, for his part, goes along with the charade, toward the end camping it up with Socrates and Alcibiades, who pretend to be rivals for his affection (222c–223a). When Socrates invites Agathon to change places with Alcibiades and Agathon responds, "Gracious me [*iou iou*], Alcibiades, I couldn't possibly stay here and simply *must* [*pantos mallon*] leave" (223a.3–5), the put-on falsetto is unmistakable; Agathon is playing the *kinaidos* for laughs. From the evidence of the *Symposium*, it appears that a relationship of two grown men, one openly accepting the role of passive partner, might in elite circles be the target of good-natured teasing but no revulsion. This suggests a "disconnect," psychologically and ethically, between the polite conduct of a society where enduring male relationships, though rare, could exist if one partner was willing to brave the consequences, and the ideology of manhood with its disparagement of the *kinaidos*.

In Plato's text, however, the relationship of Pausanias and Agathon is viewed from another, purportedly satirical, perspective by the dramatist Aristophanes, who is among the guests and speakers. (This dinner takes place five years before Aristophanes mounted his production of *Women at the Thesmophoria*. We don't know whether he was ever invited back to Agathon's house afterward.) Aristophanes speaks out of turn, having been temporarily incapacitated by a bout of hiccups. In contrast to the others, who have all delivered abstract eulogies of Eros, the playwright tells a fable (189c.2–d.6).[11] In the beginning, the human race was perfectly spherical, double-bodied with four arms and four legs, and there were three sexes, male, female, and androgyne. As a punishment for their arrogance, Zeus split those ancestral beings in half. The bifurcated creatures, desperately missing their separated other half, neglected to provide for themselves and were in danger of dying off. Out of pity, the god bestowed sexual intercourse upon them so that the race might propagate itself and orgasm bring just enough temporary satisfaction to permit them to go on living. Ever since, we have been searching for our counterparts in an effort to fill the void we suffer because of our incompleteness.

Depending on the original nature of the entire being to which we once belonged, our desires are oriented toward partners of a given sex (191d–192a):

> Any one of those men who are slices from the combined sex, the one previously called the androgyne, are lovers of women. Most adulterers descend from this line. Correspondingly, all those women who are lovers of men and adulteresses also originate from it. But whatever women are cuttings from the female sex do not even think about men, but are instead oriented toward women, and female "companions" are of this breed. Finally, those who are cut from male stock follow after the male, and as long as they are youths, because they are little slices of the male, they are fond of men and enjoy lying together with men and winding their limbs around them, and these are the finest boys and youths, because they are the most manly by nature. However, some say that they are shameless, but that's untrue. For they don't do such things out of shamelessness, but out of daring and manliness and virility, eagerly seeking what is like themselves. There's solid proof for this, as, having grown up, such men are the only ones who enter politics.

Whole arguments for and against the "constructedness" of human sexuality have been based on this paragraph. On a straightforward reading, it appears that Plato's Aristophanes, alone among ancient Greek and Roman sources, is conceptualizing attraction to one or the other sex not as a matter of taste or inclination but as an innate psychological compulsion. Furthermore, he is saying that human beings can be divided into three groups according to sexual preference: heterosexuals, male homosexuals, and female homosexuals. This has been taken to prove the essentialist contention that object-choice categorization is universal (Boswell 1990: 77), or, at least, for the Greeks, *thinkable* (Thorp 1992: 61). Against that hypothesis several objections have been raised. Aristophanes' profession as comic poet is underscored by his hiccups (a gesture toward Old Comedy's preoccupation with bodily functions) and by the obvious cross-reference to his own jokes about "wide-arsed" politicians in *Clouds* and other plays; his typology of sexual preference may be a fantasy no less preposterous than that of spherical hominoids. Again, his class of males attracted to males pointedly conforms to the age-asymmetrical configuration of pederasty: he dwells upon the boys who, at an early age, are attracted to men but says nothing at this point about adult male lovers who are relative coevals. In this his notion of male homosexuality differs radically from ours (Halperin 1990: 20–1). Finally, all of the object-based categories represented here – adulterers and adulteresses, women who prefer women, boys eager to embrace lovers – are transgressive, comprising behaviors that violate Greek social norms. Plato, then, may have invented these essentializing categories of compulsive adulterers and their ilk to further the overall philosophical goals of the dialogue (Carnes 1998: 111–15). What is surely not debatable, however, is that Aristophanes' taxonomy is a means to an end, underscoring his thesis about the homogeneity and universality of sexual longing. Precisely because they are tangential to his main point, and so remain unstated, the ramifications of that categorical paradigm will no doubt continue to generate dispute.

As he draws to a close, the comedian warns his listeners against finding a covert thrust at present company in the myth (193b–c):

> And Eryximachus had better not interrupt me by making fun of the speech and saying that I'm talking about Pausanias and Agathon (although perhaps even they may happen to be of that sort, both male in respect to nature). What I *am* saying – with reference to all, women as well as men – is that as human beings we would be happy if we could achieve our desire and each revert to his original nature by finding his personal beloved.

In the phrase "perhaps even they" (*isôs … kai houtoi*) one might hear an implication that Aristophanes is rising to the couple's defense because their affair "is looked at somewhat askance" by the other guests (Thorp 1992: 60), or, conversely, a snide thrust at two obvious counter-examples to his assertion that partners in homoerotic relationships have the manliest natures (Ludwig 2002: 39–40). Here, again, though, we need to observe the line of argument more closely. Aristophanes declares that he has made a generalization about human psychology, and he goes out of his way to specify that both men and women were included in it. This is not as otiose as it might seem; we saw that in Hesiodic myth women could be treated as a different species, while Hippocratic medicine (discussed in Chapter 5) viewed the female body as fundamentally distinct from that of the male. Consequently, the application of the parable is categorical. Where Pausanias and Agathon fit under its rubrics is simply beside the point. But implicit in the speaker's refusal to consider their case further is the premise that Agathon, unusual as he may be, is *not* an anomaly; his constitution and desires fall within the limits of the normative.

Let me conclude with one last observation about Agathon's characterization in the *Symposium*. He gets a bad press from most commentators, who pronounce him vain and shallow. Admittedly, his panegyric to Eros is elegantly crafted but superficial, and Socrates has no difficulty shooting down its main point (199c.3–201c.9). Even Penwill, who appreciates its verve, finds fault with the artist: Agathon "is attractive, but lacks the true *sophia* ('wisdom') which is a necessary part of virtue" (1978: 162). Although his giddiness is feigned, moralists take it very gravely indeed. In contrast to Socrates, and to the fiery Alcibiades, he is, according to Nussbaum, "without character, without choice … Agathon could stand their blandishments, because he had no soul to begin with" (1979: 168). For an expert in Greek philosophy, as Nussbaum is, it would be hard to say anything more damning. However, a curious incident at the beginning tells another story.

On his way to the dinner, Socrates had summoned along a chance-met friend, Aristodemus. Diffident about showing up without an invitation, Aristodemus agreed to do so, on condition that Socrates invents an excuse for bringing him. But just before they arrive at Agathon's door, Socrates absent-mindedly wanders off, and Aristodemus finds himself suddenly standing, unescorted and embarrassed, in Agathon's dining room. Without waiting for an explanation of his presence, Agathon asks him on the spot to join the company – adding that, on the previous day, he had sought him out, unsuccessfully, in order to invite him. But Agathon is telling a Noble Fib, as he really was at another, boozier celebration (174a.6–7, 176a.6–8).

In reading the dialogue one realizes here for the first time, though not the last, that Socrates, despite all his wisdom, is a problematic figure. From a perspective that sees Alcibiades as a quasi-tragic victim of *erôs*, Nussbaum remarks on the philosopher's impassivity: "It is not only Socrates' dissociation from his body. It is not only that he sleeps all night with the naked Alcibiades without arousal. There is, along with this remoteness, a deeper impenetrability of spirit" (1979: 165). Even in small things – casually pressing an acquaintance to put himself in an awkward position, then leaving him in the lurch – Socrates is not tuned in to others. But Agathon, with sharp intuition and perfect diplomacy – for him, those would be functional survival tools – quickly rescues Aristodemus from looking like a fool in front of his distinguished guests. The clumsy moment is smoothed over.

So much, then, for the scare-figure of the *kinaidos*.

In the Grandest Families

"At first poets recounted all sorts of plots, but today the best tragedies are composed about a few families," Aristotle notes in the *Poetics* (1453a.7). If Old Comedy took advantage of the obscenity traditionally associated with fertility rites to breach norms of communal decency, Athenian tragedy chose the household of the ruling family as its usual setting for case studies in the infraction of natural and divine law. Even when Aeschylus in the *Persians* selected a historical event, the defeat of the Persian army, as his theme, he set the scene outside the palace of Xerxes and dealt with the calamity as seen through the eyes of the Persian royal dynasty. In addition to kinship bonds, spousal connections, reciprocal obligations of host and guest, and suppliant ties, all invested with the same sanctions as kinship, were equally at risk, and violence against such relationships, which may be categorized generally as attachments of *philia*, is characteristic of tragedy as a genre (Belfiore 2000: xvi, 3–9, 13–15).

Crisis within the family unit was thematically arresting because the continuity of the city-state depended upon the productive and reproductive operations of the *oikos* and its corollary supervision of patrilineal inheritance. Because Athenian democracy regarded an ordered and disciplined *erôs* as crucial to those operations, late fifth-century vase painting promotes conjugal love as a stabilizing element in society. Some tragedies, like Euripides' *Alcestis* and *Helen*, also present ideal portraits of the loving and faithful wife. But most instances of tragic *erôs* are disruptive, terminating in bloodshed for the principals. It is left to the chorus, which conventionally does not speak for itself but rather articulates the shared wisdom of the community, to remind audiences that Aphrodite brings joys and benefits when she comes in moderation.

Yet we should not assume that tragedy, even though sponsored by the state and staged, like comedy, at major civic festivals, was composed to justify the value system of democratic Athens. As they probe the established meanings of "key words in the discourse of social order," the plays do as much to question those values as to articulate and reinforce them (Goldhill 1990: 123–4; cf. Foley 2001: 17–18). In ancient debate over the part sex ought to play in human life, the ethical term most frequently invoked was *sôphrosynê* – a compound noun derived from the roots *saos*, *sôs* "safe, sound" and *-phrên* "mind." Although it possessed a large array of meanings, ranging from the strict notion of "physical chastity" to more general notions of restraint and common sense, it is usually translated as "temperance."[12] We associate temperate conduct with moderate consumption of alcohol, but Greek *sôphrosynê* was a virtue with far wider application, for the *sôphrôn* or temperate man was habitually guided in all his conduct by *orthos logos*, "correct reasoning" (Arist. *Eth. Nic.* 1103a.17–18, 1119a.20). When Xenophon, Plato, and Aristotle discuss the wise use of pleasures, they assign to the intellect the job of restraining the passions, determining the proper occasions for moderate indulgence, and recognizing the end to which pleasurable activity should be directed (Foucault 1986: 86–9). Tragic choices made by the individual can therefore be framed in terms of an irreconcilable opposition between *erôs* and *logos*. Heroines such as **Medea** and Phaedra embody this conflict and articulate it most incisively – for in tragedy women can reason as well as men, to their sorrow.

We cannot examine all the plays in which sexuality is deeply implicated in the tragic catastrophe, but we can study one representative work in which the essence of *sôphrosynê* and the limits of rational deliberation are exposed to scrutiny. Our surviving text of Euripides' *Hippolytus* is a revised version of a production that had created a scandal. In an earlier staging, Phaedra, the Cretan-born wife of King Theseus of Athens, approached her stepson **Hippolytus**, with whom she had fallen passionately in love, and openly propositioned him before the audience. Hippolytus fled, covering his head in shame – hence the title of that play, *Hippolytus Kalyptomenos* ("Hippolytus Veiling Himself"). Viewers were dismayed at Phaedra's effrontery, and barbs about Euripides' lewd female characters became a staple of comedy (Ar. *Thesm.* 546–50, *Ran.* 1043–4). Subsequently, in 428 BCE, Euripides put on a revised *Hippolytus*.[13] In this adaptation, Phaedra has the most honorable intentions. She bitterly struggles against her love, characterized throughout as a sickness (*nosos*). It is impossible to overcome, however, for it is a god-sent obsession.

Both Phaedra and her stepson are the victims of Aphrodite. Speaking the prologue, the goddess declares that Hippolytus, who worships chaste Artemis, has offended her by shunning sex and marriage and branding her "the vilest of deities" (13–14). For that blasphemy he must pay, and the means of revenge will be the innocent Phaedra, on whom Aphrodite has already inflicted a violent passion. Horrified by her own desires, the queen shuts herself away in her chambers, resolved to die, but is cajoled by her old Nurse into disclosing her secret. Determined to save her young mistress at all costs, the Nurse, having extracted an oath of silence from Hippolytus, tells him all in the hope that her words will act as a love charm upon him. In his shock and revulsion, he launches into a rabid tirade against women, making it clear that he thinks Phaedra the instigator, the Nurse merely her accomplice (616–68). Phaedra, stung to the quick, retaliates in kind. She had already resolved to commit suicide in a desperate effort to salvage her honor. Because Hippolytus has behaved so arrogantly (*hupsêlos*) in the face of her misfortune, she now decides he will "share in her illness" and himself "learn to be *sôphrôn*" (730–1). Leaving a note accusing him of rape, she hangs herself.

Theseus finds his wife's body and damns Hippolytus using one of three curses bestowed upon him by the god Poseidon, his own father. Before departing into exile, Hippolytus protests his innocence, to no avail: he does not, however, break his oath of secrecy. His father's curse is quickly fulfilled. As Hippolytus drives his chariot team along the shore, a terrifying subterranean rumble is heard, a huge tsunami wave swells up, seething foam, and from it there materializes a monstrous bull. (The abrupt emergence of a bull from the depths of the ocean has been plausibly interpreted as a symbol of repressed sexuality.) Hippolytus' horses bolt, and, as he tries to rein them onto soft sand, the bull heads them off and drives them toward the cliff-side. The chariot capsizes and its driver, tangled in the reins, is dragged by his team. While he is borne back to the palace, barely alive, Artemis appears to Theseus in order to confirm his son's virtue, expose Phaedra's untruth, and lay bare the machinations of Aphrodite. As Hippolytus is carried in, Artemis promises him cult honors from girls about to marry and urges reconciliation between father and son. She departs, and Hippolytus, having forgiven his father, dies in Theseus' arms.

Hippolytus' purity of mind and body is absolute. His first act on stage is to crown Artemis' statue with an "entwined garland from a virgin meadow [*akêratou leimônos*]," which "veneration [*aidôs*] gardens with river waters" (73–8). Paradoxically, this pristine meadow looks back to the erotic meadows and gardens of archaic love poetry into which the maiden ventures at her peril. As he makes his offering, the young man prays only that he may "reach the end of life as I began," maintaining his virginity (87). Critics have struggled to find a motive for Hippolytus' rejection of *ta aphrodisia*; two explanations have been put forth, one psychoanalytic and the other religious. He is, first, a bastard son of Theseus by a *pallakê*, the Amazon queen Hippolyta, now dead. Thus his chastity could be a reaction against his father's domineering sexuality and his worship of the Amazons' tribal divinity a symptom of a sublimated longing for a mother substitute (Segal 1978: 133–9; Mitchell 1991: 103–4). Hippolytus has also been suspected of religious fanaticism (Garrison 2000: 253). When Theseus, believing Phaedra's lie, furiously denounces his son as a hypocrite, he connects him with the so-called "Orphic movement" (952–4):

> Now go pride yourself, through a vegetarian regime
> make a show of your diet, and with Orpheus as your lord
> conduct your rites, honoring the vaporings of many books.

If we could take Theseus' accusation at face value, it would provide insight into the conduct ascribed to members of this mysterious sect. Brief mentions by other authors such as Herodotus, Aristophanes, and Plato give some notion of Orphic beliefs. On the authority of writings attributed to the prophets Musaeus and Orpheus, seers conducted rites known as *teletai* that cleansed participants from the taint of wrongdoing and protected them from the horrors of the afterlife (Pl. *Resp.* 364e.3–365a.3). Believers also abstained from bloodshed (Ar. *Ran.* 1032) and avoided eating the flesh of beasts (Pl. *Leg.* 6.782c). Herodotus (2.81) suggests they went so far as to shun the use of wool garments, at least in burial. Socrates in Plato's *Cratylus* (400c) ascribes to Orphic sources the etymological doctrine that the body (*sôma*) is, like a prison, a place of safekeeping for the soul (*sôizêtai*, "to be preserved") until it pays the penalty for injustice. Combined testimony thus suggests that the Orphics drew an absolute distinction between soul and body, associated the latter with an inherited guilt from which the individual must be ritually cleansed, and prescribed observance of a special way of life that included staying away from animal products. Abstention from sex notionally fits into this framework as one additional way to prevent contaminating the soul with an attachment to things of the body.

However, this neat explanation cannot hold. While there were certainly poems attributed to Orpheus circulating in the fifth century BCE and communities of worshippers who, on the basis of those poems, adopted an ascetic way of life, there was no coherent religious movement properly termed "Orphism" (Dodds 1957: 147–9; West 1983: 2–3). Even if there were, Hippolytus does not comply with what would be one of its cardinal precepts, for he is a huntsman who sheds blood and consumes meat (Linforth 1941: 56–9). Theseus therefore cannot be saying that Hippolytus actually practices Orphic rituals, but is instead speaking hyperbolically: "Go on, profess faith in Orpheus, for all I care." In addition, there is *no* evidence that lifelong sexual abstinence was demanded either of Orphics or of members of related groups, such as followers of Pythagoras in southern Italy or devotees of the Bacchic mysteries associated with Dionysos. We revisit testimony to early sexual asceticism in Chapter 5, but meanwhile we can conclude that it is erroneous to ascribe Hippolytus' conduct to Orphic convictions. If he is a figure whose behavior, even if aberrant, makes sense to fifth-century Athenian spectators, it must be attributed to other causes.

In their entrance hymn, members of the principal chorus, young married women of Trozen, recall their sufferings in childbirth and express gratitude to Artemis for her timely intervention. This is a telling reminder of how limited Hippolytus' appreciation of his patroness really is: in worshipping her only as maiden and huntress, an austere double of himself, he overlooks her societal role in mediating the passage from virginity to marriage and bringing human fetuses, the product of sexual union, to safe delivery (Goldhill 1986: 122; cf. Zeitlin 1996b: 238; Craik 1998: 33). That oversight also clarifies what is wrong with his conception of *sôphrosynê*. Chastity is a praiseworthy asset in unmarried adolescents of both sexes, but it is not a permanent possession, for marriage is the immediate next step (Cairns 1993: 315–19). Hippolytus' protracted virginity is not a positive attribute, as he himself thinks, but instead an ominous mark of failure to make the transition to adult masculinity.

Greek tragedy frequently concerns itself with the precarious psychic condition of the adolescent on the cusp of manhood – Pentheus in Euripides' *Bacchae* and Orestes in Aeschylus' *Oresteia* are good examples (Segal 1982: 164–8). Dionysos, the god of theater, was strongly associated with the Athenian ephebe. Youths undergoing military training are known to have played a large part in the ceremonies of the Greater Dionysia and may even have customarily made up the tragic chorus (Winkler 1990b). Apart from its ritual association with Dionysos, unsuccessful ephebic transition was a predictable topic of drama because of the threat to civic order in a breakdown of generational continuity and the psychological dangers of lasting passivity. The ascetic Hippolytus is, to be sure, at the opposite extreme from the insatiable *kinaidos*, and, as a bastard, he does not have the obligation to perpetuate his father's line that a legitimate son would have. Precisely because those secondary considerations are absent, however, he is an object lesson in the consequences of disobeying the imperatives of nature and presuming oneself superior to the human biological condition. That is a form of *hybris*, and therefore punishable: "I cast down those who think big toward me," says Aphrodite (6). In addition, Hippolytus' conviction that his innate virtue makes him better than others is characteristic of the oligarch who judges most of humankind bad. When brought into conflict with Phaedra's own, no less aristocratic, determination to vindicate herself, that ethical stance leaves no room for negotiation.

Phaedra and Hippolytus are two of a kind. "Both" says Zeitlin, "are concerned with purity of body and soul, both would maintain the integrity of their inner selves at all costs, and both adhere to an outlook of aristocratic idealism" (1996b: 238). Above all, each strives to possess *sôphrosynê*. Though Phaedra aims for it, she herself concedes that she falls short. Yet over and over she betrays a consciousness of sharp eyes around her from whom she must conceal any weakness of character: she does not want her good deeds to pass unnoticed nor to have many witnesses should she commit disgraceful actions (403–4); she will not be caught shaming husband or children (420–1); she will not be shown up as evil in Time's mirror. Her aspiration to virtue is inseparable from a desire for public recognition of that virtue. When the opportunity of doing the right thing is foreclosed by the Nurse's treachery, she is left trying to maintain the appearance of virtue as her last remaining option (Cairns 1993: 335). In that, too, she fails.

What the Neighbors Might Think

Phaedra's obsession with public opinion may seem overly bourgeois, especially for a queen. Anthropological studies have cast light on Athenian social history, however, by suggesting through comparison with contemporary Mediterranean societies that sexual conduct was subject to complicated and informal regulatory mechanisms based upon a politics of reputation. For over half a century, classical Greek society has been categorized as a **"shame culture"** in which losing face before others, subjecting oneself to contempt or ridicule, was considered intolerable (Dodds 1957: 17–18, 28–63). Even critics of the term "shame culture" agree that "Greek ideas of selfhood are mediated through the concept of honour" (Cairns 1993: 432). In the exchange between Socrates and Callicles previously quoted, we observed how acutely sensitive men were to incurring blame, how scandalized they affected to be by improprieties brought into conversation. Athens was likewise a "face-to-face" community where close contact with neighbors was unavoidable. Gossip permeates such communities, holding the actions of others up to public scrutiny and pronouncing collective moral judgment upon them. In doing so, it upholds shared values and promotes conformity with an agreed-upon code of behavior, thereby assuring the relative harmony of communal life (Hunter 1994: 96–7). Through its sanctions, Athenian gossip would have served as a means of social control, discouraging (though not wholly preventing) offenses such as adultery and seduction that threatened not only the purity of the bloodline but also the honor of the household.

The politics of reputation in ancient Athens has been aligned with a present-day cross-Mediterranean code of honor and shame analyzed by numerous social and cultural anthropologists (Pitt-Rivers 1961; Peristiany 1965; Brandes 1987). Although it would be naive to assume that in modern Greece and elsewhere ancient cultural ways have survived intact (Winkler 1990a: 10), and although local variations in the so-called "honor–shame-syndrome" attest to its broad flexibility (Herzfeld 1980; Gilmore 1987), structures of social life, past and present, show certain similarities, and common features of existing systems seem to apply as well to the classical world. Then as well as now, personal honor, one's standing in society, depended upon public opinion; although pedigree and assets counted for a great deal, those advantages could be nullified by disgraceful behavior. Honor was closely affiliated with shame, an internalized sense of failure to conform to norms and expectations prescribed by society. Individuals had a vital stake in maintaining the honor of the family unit, for the reputation of the *oikos* as a whole determined the degree of respect accorded its members. Gender obligations were rigorously differentiated, with males assigned the positive responsibilities of defending family honor and increasing household wealth and females enjoined against doing anything to bring disgrace upon kindred. Because a man's honor was so closely bound up with the chastity of his womenfolk, female sexuality was a constant source of anxiety. Finally, gossip, circulating among both men and women, in the barbershops and markets (Lys. 23.3, 6–7) as well as in homes, must have provided a constant flow of information about real or supposed sexual indiscretions. In such an environment, public statements were made for effect and often contained a good deal of misdirection, requiring that historians weigh their intended purpose carefully instead of taking them at face value.

Hippolytus, in contrast, staunchly lays claim to an inherent *sôphrosynê*. Defending himself before his father, he twice proclaims "there is no man more *sôphrôn* than I" (994–5, 1100) and repeats that statement on his deathbed (1365). We cannot doubt his integrity, for he abides by his principles and keeps his oath under duress, despite the injustice he suffers. At a critical juncture, however, he forgets himself and thereby precipitates the tragic action. It is hard to attribute his misogynistic harangue to anything other than a dearth of *sôphrosynê*: no matter what the provocation, a prudent man should not indulge in a frenzied explosion of temper. Hippolytus' practice of virtue has been so dominated by preserving sexual purity that the wider significance of self-control, as it pertains to mastery of the other passions, momentarily escapes him. For all his aristocratic faith in his innate excellence, he is at last forced to recognize that one can still act contrary to one's moral nature, however fine it is. Speaking of Phaedra's suicide, he regretfully admits: "She did a *sôphrôn* thing, though she could not be *sôphrôn*; I, being *sôphrôn*, did not conduct myself well" (1034–5). This belated distinction between character and deed is evidence of a new maturity, but it comes too late to save him. There is, then, a "violent symmetry" between the two characters: each claims to know what *sôphrosynê* is, finds it wanting in the other, and strikes back even more immoderately – Hippolytus with his burst of spleen, Phaedra by criminally accusing an innocent man before committing suicide (Mitchell 1991: 116–17). Ethical terminology devised to help channel *erôs* into acceptable social forms is not only misunderstood but abused, as neither party, under stress, proves able to employ it in a coherent and rational manner (Goff 1990: 39–48).

Twice in the course of the drama the women of Trozen invoke Eros and Aphrodite in song. As the Nurse enters the house, ostensibly to bring back her therapeutic charm, they pray: "Eros, Eros, you who distill longing upon the eyes and implant sweet grace into the soul of those on whom you make war, may you never appear to me bringing evil, or come in discord" (525–9). In the interval after the messenger's speech and before the epiphany of Artemis, the chorus acknowledges once more that sexuality governs all creatures: "Eros bewitches … the nature of mountain-bred and sea-borne cubs, and whatever the earth nurtures and the fiery sun beholds, and mankind; alone over all these, Queen Cypris, you exercise royal sway" (1280–81). Speaking for the *polis*, they render the goddess the forthright homage Hippolytus refused. These invocations, reminiscent of cult hymns, are counterparts of the Trozenian rituals that enable maidens to cope with the sudden passage from youth to adulthood: making a hair offering, weeping, singing songs that recall Hippolytus' and Phaedra's sufferings (1423–30). Choral odes and the inauguration of cult practices re-establish strategies for controlling *erôs* by celebrating its necessary and constructive workings. Still, memory of the violence consequent upon desire is not easy to blot out.

Criminal Proceedings

Although Athenian law was remarkable for its relative lack of statutes explicitly addressing sexual matters (Cohen 1991: 221–7), some wrongdoing was criminalized. Two offenses that were legally actionable were rape and adultery or seduction (**moicheia**).[14] Forcible rape could be punished in one of two ways. Under a statute ascribed to Solon, the *kyrios* of the victim, woman or minor, could accuse the alleged perpetrator of physical assault. Cases of assault were private, or civil, suits;

should the rapist be convicted, he was required to pay monetary damages to the plaintiff (Lys. 1.32, Plut. *Sol.* 23). If the intent to humiliate could be shown, rape was also actionable under the law of *hybris*, which was treated as a public offense (Cole 1984: 99). Any citizen, not just the *kyrios* of the victim, might bring a lawsuit for *hybris* committed against a free man, woman, child, or even slave. Rape prosecuted under that decree could incur the death penalty (Din. 1.23). Note, however, that this entire set of legal procedures takes no cognizance of marital rape; the concept did not exist. Indeed, female consent to sex, within or outside of marriage, was not recognized in law and did not form the basis for determining a sexual crime; both rape and adultery were offenses against the male guardian (Lape 2011: 22; cf. Eidinow 2011: 89–90).

Stranger rape ordinarily would have taken place outside the *oikos*. Another much-discussed law cited by Demosthenes (23.53–5) lists instances of justifiable homicide, including the killing of a man "caught having intercourse with one's wife or mother or sister or daughter or concubine kept for the purpose of producing legitimate children."[15] This provision removes an intruder seized while engaged in *moicheia* on the premises from the protection of the laws. The Athenian *oikos* and the women it sheltered formed the core of the private sphere. Unauthorized entry was liable to capital punishment. Thieves, kidnappers, and robbers were categorized as a special group of evildoers (*kakourgoi*) who, when apprehended in the act and brought before a magistrate, were summarily executed if they confessed ([Arist.] *Ath. pol.* 52.1). David Cohen explains that these offenses involved the risk of violent confrontation between the intruder and the men responsible for protecting the household (1991: 112–13, 223–4). Investing magistrates with the right to prescribe the death penalty reduced family members' incentive to take the law into their own hands, which might lead to blood feud.

It is possible, but not certain, that adulterers were included in the category of trespassers liable to immediate judicial execution. Our best-documented case of adultery, however, involves a man named Euphiletus who slew his wife's lover himself and was then indicted for murder, the prosecution claiming the killing proceeded from unlawful entrapment. His speech in his own defense (Lys. 1, *On the Murder of Eratosthenes*) gives a detailed glimpse into the domestic arrangements of man and wife in a small household with just one female slave. Because Euphiletus is attempting to persuade the jury that his act was warranted, he tells a vivid, detailed, but not necessarily accurate story, and it is not hard to find places where he stretches the truth or distorts the meaning of the law. One salient example is his assertion (1.32–3) that the Athenian legal code, in supposedly punishing the seducer with death, the rapist merely with a fine, treats the former more harshly because his effect upon the household is more disruptive. The contention itself may or may not be correct (scholars are presently divided) but the brief is full of holes.[16] To win his case, however, the speaker will have to keep the account *plausible*, a consideration that permits us to trust its value as evidence for social history.

According to Euphiletus, he and his wife had been sleeping apart, he upstairs, she downstairs so that she could care for their infant son during the night. He first learned of the affair – which had been going on for some time without his suspicion – when an old woman, sent by a resentful former mistress of Eratosthenes, tipped him off (1.15–16). There we can watch the Athenian gossip machine in operation. Euphiletus interrogates his wife's serving-maid, who confirms the report, and orders her to help him catch Eratosthenes in the act. A few days later, the girl wakens him with the information that his wife's lover is in the house. He sneaks out, leaving her to watch the door, and rounds up several friends:

> Getting torches from the closest shop nearby, we went in through the outer door, which had been left open for us by the maid. We thrust open the bedroom door, and the first to enter saw him still lying beside my wife, the rest standing naked on the bed. I gave him a blow that knocked him down, gentlemen, and, pulling his hands behind his back and binding them, I asked him why he was committing the outrage [hybrizei] of entering my house. He confessed his guilt, and then entreated and begged me not to kill him but to exact a monetary penalty instead. And I said, "It is not I who am about to kill you but the law of the state, which you violated and thought of less importance than your pleasures, and chose rather to commit such an offense against my wife and my children than to obey the laws and be an orderly citizen." (1.24–6)

Dramatic testimony, to be sure, but a district attorney could raise some telling points in closing argument. Granted that the law exempts from punishment the *kyrios* who kills the adulterer, it seems likely that it envisions a situation in which a struggle takes place. Eratosthenes is naked, trussed up, and surrounded; he pleads for his life and offers remuneration; Euphiletus executes him in cold blood. For an aggrieved husband, other courses of action were available: a compensatory payment, privately arranged, but also detainment and public prosecution for *moicheia* ([Arist.] *Ath. pol.* 59.3). The law even protected the accused *moichos*, for he could take legal action against the householder for detaining him illegally. If he proved his innocence, he was set free; if shown to have committed adultery, however, he was handed over to the man who caught him and who, in front of the jurymen, could do with him as he pleased – short of using a knife ([Dem.] 59.66). Finally, if the adulterer was in fact included in the class of *kakourgoi* who could be summarily executed by magistrates, the law might also have restricted the behavior of the husband by prescribing that the trespasser should be turned over to the appropriate officials (Cohen 1991: 115–20). We do not know that this was the case, though.

What would have happened to Euphiletus' wife? Athenian law barred a woman taken in adultery from entering the public temples or attending rituals, and also from wearing any kind of jewelry (Aeschin. 1.183; [Dem.] 59.85–6). If she defied those prohibitions, she might be beaten by anyone with impunity, although she could not be killed. In addition, her husband was compelled to divorce her; if he did not, he lost his civic rights. The latter stipulation was intended to protect the blood-line, as a woman proved unfaithful once could not be trusted in future. But the severity of the sanction implies that some men might be disposed to forgive an errant wife, perhaps because they loved her – perhaps, too, because they would have had to return the dowry upon divorcing her, which could be a financial hardship, or they strongly wanted to avoid the scandal of publicity. Consequently, despite the fact that Aristophanes' comedies paint women as habitual adulteresses, we do not know how frequently the opportunity for sexual adventure presented itself. Certainly *moicheia* was deemed a very grave offense (Carey 1995: 417).

The verdict in this trial has not been preserved. Judging only by his own testimony, Euphiletus appears to have gone much too far, at least in the view of many modern scholars. But it is not easy for products of what Jack Winkler once called "the rather cool culture of NATO Classicists" (1990a: 13) to empathize with the burning heat of outraged male honor. His Athenian peers may well have thought differently.

His and Hers (or His)

No doubt there were solid and mutually satisfying Athenian marriages, but we don't often hear of them. Human happiness seldom makes it into the historical record. Legal testimony gives anecdotal evidence of marital affection (*philia*): a childless woman is reluctant to leave her husband after being urged to take a new mate in hopes of having children (Isae. 2.8–9); a husband does not bring court proceedings because he fears losing his wife (Isae. 10.19). Inscribed gravestones express the grief felt for deceased spouses, but those sentiments, even if presumed to be sincere, are conventionally worded. White-ground *lekythoi*, vases created expressly as offerings for the dead, show poignant vignettes of mourning, but again furnish no information about how people behaved in life. Very few red-figure images are identifiable as interior family scenes because gender conventions prescribed that men spend their time outside the home (Lewis 2002: 177). Conjugal exchanges in Old Comedy are farcical, so Myrrhine's tormenting of her husband Cinesias (*Lys.* 845–958) or Praxagora's hoodwinking of Blepyrus (*Eccl.* 520–70) are hardly examples of the way in which couples regularly conversed. When we speak of normal dealings between man and wife, then, we have to fall back on idealizing fictions in literary texts. Such materials will be tactfully reticent on the subject of marital sexuality, but we can use their overt depictions of gender relations to extrapolate further.

Two of Euripides' tragic heroines, Alcestis and Helen, were mentioned above as epitomes of the perfect wife. Alcestis gives the ultimate proof of female virtue by dying in the place of her husband Admetus. He willingly promises her on her deathbed never to replace her with another woman, but is too obtuse to grasp the long-term consequences of accepting her sacrifice. Only belatedly does he realize that in doing so he has shown himself a coward and thus condemned himself to an ignominious and lonely existence (Eur. *Alc.* 954–7). Luckily, the hero Heracles turns up at the palace. In a quirky act of hospitality, Admetus welcomes him but keeps Alcestis' death a secret. When he finally learns the truth, Heracles tracks Death down, snatches Alcestis away, and restores her to his host – but only after tricking Admetus into breaking his promise by forcing her, disguised as a veiled slave girl, upon him as a gift. The wry overtones of this reunion are intensified because Alcestis, still under obligation to the infernal powers, must stand silent, bound not to speak for three days. Speeding Heracles on his way, Admetus rejoices,

"Now we shall dispose our lives differently, better than before. For I won't deny I've been fortunate" (1157–8). One hopes his optimism is justified. Despite its apparent happy ending, the play strikes many of today's readers as a rather sour comment on male egotism.

In *Helen*, as noted in Chapter 1, Euripides follows an alternative tradition in which his heroine, wholly innocent of adultery, is spirited off from Sparta by Hermes (as she gathers roses like other abducted virgins, 243–5) and detained in Egypt, leaving Greeks and Trojans to battle over a hollow apparition. Meanwhile, she proves her chastity by resisting the advances of the wicked Egyptian king Theoclymenus. The paradoxical demand made on the Greek wife, to be at once sexual, so as to produce children, and pure, to preserve male honor, is resolved by splitting the Helen-figure into the real, faithful spouse and the deceitful *eidôlon* (Foley 2001: 317–18). Helen's exoneration as a virtuous wife, however, is purchased at the cost of her husband Menelaus' military glory, since the prize he had struggled for so long, and for which so much blood was spilt, turns out to be illusory. When he arrives in Egypt, shipwrecked and in rags, an old female gatekeeper shrugs off his grandiose posturing: "Somewhere, maybe, you were somebody, but not here" (455). His life threatened by Theoclymenus, Menelaus cannot act the warrior, but Helen's cunning and feminine charm (*charis*) permit her to trick the king by pretending Menelaus is dead and so effect their escape. Ultimately, Menelaus does engage in pitched battle against a crew of Egyptian sailors, re-enacting history in gory fashion: "The Trojan War is fought again, in miniature. But Helen is now on the right side, cheering on her husband" (Segal 1971: 606). Perhaps, to an Athenian audience, he thus redeems himself, although the stress on carnage ("the ship ran with blood," 1603) is disturbing after what was said about the squander of lives pursuing a phantom. In any case, Menelaus, like Admetus, has to undergo a symbolic failure of masculinity in order to renew his marriage. Both plays impose the bride's loss of identity in changing from one social role to another upon the groom, with unsettling repercussions for gender stability (Foley 2001: 329). Since in each case we are dealing with a couple rejoined after separation, Euripides may be implying that the institution of marriage enforces abrupt transformation upon females but over time also makes imperceptible modifications to the male sense of self; we recall Odysseus' reassumption of his Ithacan identity, likewise confirmed through the marriage bed.

Xenophon's work *On Household Management* addresses gender structures within the household from an administrative standpoint. Although the dialogue is set during Socrates' lifetime, it was written sometime later in the fourth century, well after Athens's defeat in the Peloponnesian War and in the wake of the social and economic crises that protracted conflict had triggered. In response to the growing impoverishment of small farmers and increasing class bitterness, Xenophon defends ownership and maintenance of large private estates: agriculture on that scale benefits the common good, he affirms, by producing virtuous and orderly citizens (Murnaghan 1988: 10). The education of Ischomachus' wife is one of Xenophon's main cases in point. Because her husband is himself knowledgeable about household management, he can mold her into a capable and reliable housekeeper – no easy task, given her youth and inherent female propensity to weakness. With the *oikos* in good hands, its master can spend his time elsewhere, pursuing public affairs.

When his rich but financially strapped friend Critobulus asks for advice on farming productively, Socrates, citing Ischomachus as an example of "a proper gentleman" (*kalos te k'agathos anêr*, 6.12), recalls a dialogue with him on that subject. The first topic discussed was the education of a wife.[17] Like Critobulos, Ischomachus had wedded a girl, not yet fifteen, who had until then had seen, heard, and even said almost nothing – a blank slate, as it were, on which he could inscribe his mandates. Apart from knowing how to weave a cloak from wool, and having seen how spinning is allotted to servants, she had only been educated in *ta amphi gastera*, "matters of the belly" (7.6). Taught how to control hunger, she had developed the rudiments of *sôphrosynê*; for man and wife alike, Ischomachus then confesses to Socrates, that is the most important lesson to be learned. He will repeat this precept to his bride. When she asks in bewilderment how she can assist him, in view of the fact that her mother defined her duty as simply being *sôphrôn*, he responds, "Yes, and my father said the same thing to me. But for both a man and a woman, being *sôphrôn* means making sure their goods are in the best condition and adding to them as much as possible, in a fair and just way" (7.15). Through his spokesman Xenophon radically extends the scope of *sôphrosynê*, associating it, via its connotations of rationality and order, with the science of proper household supervision and assigning it to both sexes as a critical virtue (Pomeroy 1994: 275).

Although his manner in the ensuing discussion may seem condescending, Ischomachus is attempting to educate this immature, sheltered girl half his age to be his colleague in managing the estate. First he needs to explain exactly how he envisions their partnership. Instruction commences "when she was tame [*cheiroêthês*] and had been domesticated [*etetithuseuto*] so as to have a conversation," a tactful reference to the wedding night and the virgin's initiation into married life (7.10). Unfortunately, the English translation carries unavoidable implications of subduing by force and breaking the will, and both Greek words can indeed be used in contexts where one person strives for mastery over another (for example, Dem. 3.31). Yet the joint conversation anticipated indicates that a different meaning must be intended: the "horse-taming" metaphor instead conveys overtones of soothing a nervous animal and calming its fears.[18] Along with the prayers and sacrifices that accompany it, this opening talk, which takes place on the next day, is part of a process aimed at making the bride feel more at home (Scaife 1995: 231–2). Pomeroy (1994: 273) observes its success: as the conversation proceeds, the girl loses her reserve and begins to take a more assertive part in the dialogue.

The concept of marriage as a full partnership with separate but equal functions that Ischomachus outlines is, to be sure, an essentialist arrangement. For Greek society in general, reproduction was the primary objective of marriage. But Xenophon's spokesman defines its main purpose as twofold: raising children, should the god provide them, and managing the *oikos* in common (7.12–13). Male and female perform tasks determined by their natures and attributes – men, more hardy and courageous, laboring outside; women, less strong, more fearful, and fonder of infants, caring for the children, the slaves, and the household stores within. Yet, Ischomachus adds, God gave intellectual endowments, memory and attention, to man and woman in equal measure, since both sexes must use them; and they likewise were given an equal ability to practice self-control. Where one sex falls short, the other makes up for it, and the bond (*zeugos*, "yoke") is more beneficial to each because each has capacities the other lacks (23–8). He then compares his wife to a queen bee presiding over a hive and sending out workers and gives her an account of the duties she will perform – some onerous, like nursing the sick, others, such as managing the staff, giving opportunity for creative fulfillment. Finally, he holds out the possibility that, by showing herself better than him, she can make him her own "second-in-command" (*therapôn*) in the household, earning more and more honor as years go by (41–3). Thinly disguised patriarchy, perhaps, but it is still drastically different, as we will see, from Aristotle's model of permanent male hegemony over wife, children, and slaves.

Ischomachus goes on to recall two occasions where further mentoring was required. In the first, his wife cannot find something he has asked for. Instead of rebuking her, he takes the blame for not showing her where it was to be put, then collaborates with her in a complete inventory of their possessions, reorganization of the storage space, and delegation of responsibilities to a meticulous housekeeper (8.1–9.18). The second incident casts light on the texture of their intimate relations (10.2–13). One day Ischomachus finds his wife wearing cosmetics, white facial powder and rouge, and high heels. He proceeds to give her a sermon on natural beauty. Starting from the principle that lying to her about the amount of his property, which he shares with her, would be wrong, he draws a parallel with their bodies, which they share in intercourse (*tôn sômatôn koinônêsontes allêlois*, 5). If *he* came to bed wearing bronzer to enhance his tan, along with eye makeup, would she find him more deserving of her love? The argument is effective. When she afterward inquires how she might improve her looks through natural means, Ischomachus advises her to exercise regularly by doing housework, which will increase her appetite, health, and complexion. He then indulges in a parenthetic observation to Socrates, man to man:

> Relative to that of a slave, the appearance of a wife who is cleaner and more suitably attired becomes arousing, especially when she is also willing to gratify (*charizesthai*) you instead of being forced to render service. But women who are always arrogantly sitting around leave themselves vulnerable to being compared with painted and deceiving females. (12–13)

Sexual pleasure is a prime component of the marital relationship, at least for the man; for the wife's part in the act, Ischomachus uses the same euphemism, *charizesthai* or "do a favor," that is commonly applied to the *erômenos*'s role in sex. By assimilating her to the boy who obliges his lover out of respect and *philia*, he emphasizes her willingness to please in contrast to the slave's reluctance. Yet, given the collective cultural insistence that the junior partner in pederasty does not experience arousal, is he also imputing to her an absence of sexual desire?[19] I confess I find this incidental remark rather troubling.

Interestingly enough, the narrative of events in *The Murder of Eratosthenes* has certain points in common with Ischomachus' account of his wife's education. When Euphiletus first brought his wife home, he says, he kept a careful eye on her, but after their son was born, he began to trust her and gave his property into her custody (Lys. 1.6). On one occasion after she moves downstairs, the baby begins to fret while the couple are upstairs together; when Euphiletus asks her to go down and see to the child, she accuses him of designs on the maidservant, whom he had molested once before when drunk (12). He understands this as a joke and laughs in response, but the jury would have taken it for granted that the girl was at her master's disposal and heard a note of irritation in the wife's remark. What he did not know at the time, Euphiletus explains, was that Eratosthenes was in the house and the maid was making the baby cry to give his wife a reason to go downstairs. The next morning, he observes that his wife has put on makeup, though her brother had died recently, but he treats this as her own business and says nothing to her (13). Although wife and maid are accomplices, and the latter, when first interrogated, attempts to deny the adultery, she caves in, confesses, and readily assists Euphiletus once he reveals what he knows (19–20). Thus the slave, only interested in saving her own skin, shows no real loyalty to her mistress.

In *On Household Management*, the wife does not have to establish her credentials by bearing an heir; she is accepted as a partner from the outset. Instead of sleeping in separate quarters, husband and wife share a bedroom: they see each other when getting out of bed, before making their morning toilet, which is why cosmetics can fool only strangers (10.8). Euphiletus is fatuously pleased by his wife's resentment of his interest in the slave girl. Ischomachus, for his part, recognizes the owner's right to consort with his slaves, but thinks compulsory sex with someone of mean status not as rewarding as mutual lovemaking, even if his companion does not get the same pleasure he does. He adds that wives who call attention to their privileged place in the *oikos* by having servants wait on them hand and foot are in appearance and demeanor more like *hetairai* than spouses. Exercising full authority over the staff, his wife is empowered to honor those who perform well and to discipline those who do not (9.15), and feels no need to assert her status symbolically through indolence. In Euphiletus' household, a wife he regards as his inferior, to whom he freely gives orders, is represented as dismissive of the maid in turn.

The effect of Ischomachus' program of instruction is to make his wife into his own alter ego (Murnaghan 1988: 12–13). Thanks to his training, he can proudly proclaim that she reasons clearly, reverences order, weighs her actions ethically and disdains certain characteristically feminine behaviors, such as embellishing her physical appearance artificially. Socrates at one point exclaims "By Hera, Ischomachus, you're showing me your wife's truly masculine mind!" (10.1). For progressive thinkers of the period, that was high praise. In Book 5 of the *Republic*, Plato outlines a utopian system of government in which the most gifted boys and girls are given the same program of education and trained to be "Guardians," magistrates and defenders of the community (451c–461e). Far from advocating the liberation of women, however, he sees them as "a huge untapped pool of resources" whose labor could be utilized for the state instead of being squandered on trivial household tasks (Annas 1981: 181–5). Equality for this select group of females is therefore purchased at the cost of domestic life: the nuclear family is abolished, and women Guardians do not even tend their own infants – that job is delegated to nurses (*Resp.* 460d.2–5). Whether functional assimilation to a man, with the consequent eradication of differences gendered as feminine, is too steep a price to pay for access to some, not all, male privileges is a question feminists are still debating.

After the complex questions posed by Xenophon's blueprint of an ostensibly egalitarian marriage, it is almost relaxing to turn to old-fashioned Aristotelian male supremacy (*Pol.* 1259a.37–1260b.20). Here we know where we stand: marriage is a permanently asymmetrical relationship.

> The head [of the household] rules over wife and children. Both are free, but the manner of rule is not the same, for the wife is governed in the fashion of a city-state [*politikôs*], and the children are governed as a king would govern them. For the male is by nature more capable of command than the female ... (1259a.39–1259b.2)

Aristotle goes on to explain what he means by women being governed "in the fashion of a city-state." In most actual *poleis*, the citizens take turns at ruling and being ruled, as there is a presumption of equality among them. Difference in station is signified by protocols surrounding those in office and corresponding titles bestowed upon them: as an analogy, the Marine Band plays "Hail to the Chief" as the President enters the room, and he is addressed as "Mr. President." The male's rule over the female is of this kind, but the inequality is a permanent one, associated with the weighty problem of virtue in the ruled. Aristotle draws a comparison with the soul, in which the rational faculty naturally exercises authority over the irrational part. As the parts of the soul differ, each having its own virtue, so in slave, woman, and child those separate parts are present in different degrees: "for the slave completely lacks a rational faculty; a woman has it, but it is without authority [*akuron*]; a child has it, but it is immature" (1260a.12–14). No effort is made to deny that a woman can reason – she employs that ability in daily life – but the reasoning part of her soul, Aristotle believes, does not have sufficient discretion and so is inferior to that of an adult male. Hence woman must be placed under man's supervision. While both sexes also have the capacity for virtue, he then concludes, the quality of that virtue is specific to each sex: "the *sôphrosynê* of a man and of a woman is not the same, nor is bravery or justice, as Socrates thought; the bravery of the one consists in ruling, the other in obeying, and likewise for the other virtues" (1260a.21–4). In other words, the ability to exert control over oneself is fundamental to the moral nature of human beings. In the Aristotelian scheme of things, woman cannot exert full control over herself, and Greek patriarchy is about control. To be autonomous, or, as a Greek would say, *autê hautês kyria*, "her own mistress," women will have to become more like men. We will see that happening in Chapter 5.

Conclusion

The above account of sexuality in classical Athens by no means exhausts the literary evidence, and some very intriguing testimony has not been discussed. We have not dealt, for example, with the fascinating anecdotal data on sexual conduct provided by other forensic speeches.[20] In undertaking a survey of this kind, one has to work within a particular framework. I have chosen to emphasize the integration of sexuality and class issues, the role of the democratic *polis* in articulating sexual norms, and the degree to which it took cognizance of what we regard as strictly personal matters. With the exception of Aristophanes' *Lysistrata* and, to a lesser extent, Xenophon's *On Household Management*, the sexual relations of husband and wife receive little attention in the literary texts, partly out of discretion, partly because they were seen as relatively unproblematic. Discussion centers rather on potentially disruptive sexual attitudes and behavior.

As a custom identified with the aristocracy, pederastic courtship was deeply implicated in class conflicts and might be targeted in anti-oligarchic discourse. The practitioners of pederasty, conversely, felt threatened enough to formulate an ethical justification for the system and mounted a propaganda campaign in its defense. Cronyism allegedly fostered by homoerotic friendships was a pragmatic political issue, but the moral threat posed to the *erômenos* was of no less concern. Along with egalitarianism, the radical democracy promoted an ethos of restraint and emphasized the importance of stable marital relations for the continuity of the household. However, it also recognized the civic and ethical utility of the training in manliness given to a young man by a praiseworthy *erastês*. Tragedy meanwhile explored the limit cases of interfamilial violence, much of it provoked by forbidden *erôs*.

The politics of reputation, the code of honor and shame, and the state's interest in the preservation of bloodlines all constituted deterrents to rape, seduction, and adultery but also worked at cross-purposes. Since inheritance disputes caused rancor, and ancestral and family cult had to be performed by direct descendants, Athens had legal and religious justification for treating some sexual misconduct as a public crime. On the other hand, fear of disrepute might tempt a family to hush up a scandal, as prosecution of the offense would bring the whole distasteful story to light, providing entertaining gossip even for those who knew none of the parties involved. Finally, domestic relations in stable marriages must have been influenced by the direct dependence of *polis* upon *oikos*, especially among the propertied classes. To a degree that makes contemporary observers somewhat uncomfortable, classical Athenian sexuality in all its forms was implicated in its system of radical democracy. Whether it affords a good model, in terms of either parallels or contrasts, for understanding present-day Western sexual ideology should be one of the key discussion topics in a course in ancient sexuality.

Discussion Prompts

1. This chapter has emphasized the importance of class divisions for understanding how sexual protocols operated in the radical Athenian democracy of the fifth and fourth centuries BCE. What practices served, at least in theory, to reinforce the ideology of egalitarianism? Conversely, what practices might have worked to aggravate class tensions?

2. Recent studies of Aeschines' *Against Timarchus* have been quick to draw parallels between Athenian scrutiny of prominent political figures and the current wave of sexual scandals involving elected or appointed public officials. The rationale for exposing transgressions may appear the same in each case, but there are key differences between the notions of privacy in the minds of Athenian jurors and those possessed by contemporary pundits and voters. Explain.

3. Under Athenian law, the male sexual offender (rapist or adulterer) was subject to severe penalties, up to and including capital punishment, while the adulteress ostensibly suffered lighter consequences – divorce and exclusion from public religious life. What gender assumptions lie behind this apparent inequality? Were the sanctions imposed on the adulteress actually that moderate?

4. Scholars point out that monogamous marriage, and consequently heterosexuality, was fundamentally embedded in the social fabric of the Athenian *polis*, since every head of household was expected to sire an heir to carry on the family line. Putting yourself in the position of that householder, envisage how limitation of nonmarital object choice (boy or woman) to the category of non-reproductive, "recreational" sex might affect sexual subjectivity.

Notes

1   On the historical circumstances surrounding the prosecution of Timarchus, which was politically motivated, see Dover 1978: 19–20 and Fisher 2001: 2–24.

2   The "Old Oligarch" is the nickname given by scholars to the author of an anonymous pamphlet, preserved among the works of Xenophon, which purports to explain the strengths of the Athenian democracy from the viewpoint of an opponent of the system.

3   In addition to addressing the assembly and the law courts themselves, orators like Demosthenes also wrote speeches for others and earned money doing so. The metic Lysias was a successful professional speechwriter although, as a noncitizen, he was not permitted to speak before the populace. At the opening of his speech (54.1), Ariston carefully distinguishes between the civil suit he is bringing, requiring only payment of monetary damages if the defendant should be convicted, and a public indictment for *hybris*, which could carry the death penalty. Though Conon is most certainly liable to prosecution for *hybris*, Ariston assures the jurors, he will follow the advice of friends and kinsman by seeking a guilty verdict on the less serious charge. He is insinuating that his adversary's wealth and influence make it impossible for him to do more.

4   In a later publication (1993: 101–4), Taplin reverses his position, mainly because there is no textual evidence that the Arguments are priapic and no depiction of cages on the vase. The vase painter, however, might have adapted the scene for artistic reasons.

5   Cleon's wealth, Aristophanes never ceases to remind us, derived from ownership of a tanning factory.

6   Written agreements to provide personal sexual services may not have been unusual (Cohen 2000), although we have only one attested case (Dem. 22.23, very likely also referred to at Aeschin. 1.165). They would have protected both parties by finalizing terms while also establishing that the sex was consensual or, in the case of a slave, that the master had authorized it.

7   Strictly speaking, a *kinaidos* was a kind of dancer whose movements, accompanied by the rattle of a tambourine, included suggestive wriggling of the buttocks; an inscription from a temple of Isis (*CIG* 4926) indicates that such dancing might be performed in honor of Dionysos (Williams 2010: 193 and n. 80). A likely parallel, though female, is Syrisca, the sexy tavern-keeper of the pseudo-Vergilian *Copa*, who "skillfully sways her hips to the music of castanets" (2).

8   What was so awful about scratching your head? In Latin, the complete phrase is "to scratch the head with one finger" (*qui digito scalpunt uno caput*, Juv. 9.133). It may allude to the effeminate man's fussiness about his appearance: by using just one finger, he avoids disturbing the careful arrangement of his hair (Williams 2010: 244). It could also have been a coded signal that the man doing so was sexually available for penetration (Taylor 1997: 339).

9   Alternative causes of effeminacy can be found in the ancient sources. As noted in the Introduction, both this passage in the *Problemata* and *Nichomachean Ethics* 1148b.27–9 maintain that desire for anal penetration can be an acquired habit.

10   Collected by Nails (2002: 8–10 and 222); she finds Plato's representation of Agathon "on the whole positive" (9).

11   Dover (1988: 102–14) points out the close resemblance to Aesopic stories.

12   In her definitive study of *sôphrosynê*, North (1966: 32–84) demonstrates how closely individual playwrights' treatments of this concept are related to their notions of what is tragic. Euripides, she finds, uses the word to denote three related but distinct behaviors: self-control in a broad sense, including chastity and modesty; prudence and good judgment; and moderation or observance of limits (1966: 75–8).

13   The tragedian Sophocles also handled the story in his *Phaedra*. We know little about this play, but we can assume Phaedra was less culpable, since in it Theseus was believed dead. The fragments of the lost *Hippolytus Kalyptomenos* and the *Phaedra* are collected, and their relationship to the surviving *Hippolytus* discussed, in Barrett (1964: 15–45).

14   There is no single term for "rape" in ancient Greek; it is instead expressed by verbs denoting the use of force or violence against another or meaning "to shame or violate." Cole (1984: 98) gives a list of these expressions. *Moicheia* is also a controversial word: some scholars (e.g., Cohen 1991: 99–109) restrict it to adultery in the strict sense, but most believe it covers relations with any free woman under the protection of a *kyrios*. See now the discussion of terminology in Eidinow 2011: 90–2.

15   The *pallakê* is included in the class of protected women because this statute, ascribed to the legendary seventh-century lawgiver Draco, antedates legislation circumscribing the inheritance rights of her children.

16   Harris (1990) contends that adultery and rape carried equally harsh penalties, while Carey (1995) thinks adultery was punished more severely. Whatever the facts, Euphiletus cites the Draconian law that merely exempts the killer of the *moichos* from punishment and draws no distinction between rape and seduction as proof that the householder is legally commanded (*hoi nomoi … kekeleukotes [eisi]*, 1.34) to kill the seducer – but not the rapist. He can make this specious argument because there was no judge in an Athenian court to interpret the law impartially to jurors, and because his peers would have been more concerned about the long-term consequences of adultery, which might cast doubt on

the paternity of all the offspring in the *oikos* (Harris 1990: 375; Ogden 1996: 147–8).

17   In accordance with Athenian etiquette, her name is never mentioned, but some scholars (Harvey 1984; Pomeroy 1994: 261–4) identify her with Chrysilla, the real-life wife of a historical figure named Ischomachus (there were several), who, as a widow, became illicitly involved with Callias, her own son-in-law (Andoc. 1.124–7).

18   In his manual *On Horsemanship* (2.3), Xenophon advises that a young horse sent to the trainer should already be "gentle, tractable (*cheiroêthês*), and fond of people," having learned to associate food, water, and relief from pain with its groom; colts so raised, he says, not only like but long for human company. He is not an advocate of bronco-busting.

19   The same hint may be present in the simile of the queen bee at *Oec.* 7.32–9, since bees were an emblem of sexlessness. In Semonides' satire on women, the bee-wife who takes no interest in sexual conversations is the only good one (7.83–93 West[2]). In Xenophon's *Symposium*, on the other hand, Socrates mentions a pair of newlyweds, Niceratus and his wife, who are infatuated with each other: *ho Nikêratos … erôn tês gunaikos anteratai* (8.3). There is no implication that the bride's sexual attraction to her husband is inappropriate.

20   Some are quite bizarre. In Isaeus 6.20, an old man deserts wife and family to move in with his employee, an ex-prostitute who runs his combination rooming-house and wine shop in the Athenian red-light district. Antiphon 1 involves a son who charges his stepmother with poisoning his father, claiming that she had suborned the slave concubine of her husband's friend. About to be packed off to a brothel, the slave administered the poison to both men in the belief that it was a love potion. Of course, these cases feature extremes of behavior; that is why they came before juries.

References

Annas, J. 1981. *An Introduction to Plato's "Republic"*. Oxford: Clarendon Press.

Auerbach, N. 1995. *Our Vampires, Ourselves*. Chicago: University of Chicago Press.

Barrett, W. S. (ed.). 1964. *Euripides' Hippolytos*. Oxford: Clarendon Press.

Belfiore, E. S. 2000. *Murder among Friends: Violation of Philia in Greek Tragedy*. Oxford: Oxford University Press.

Boswell, J. 1990. "Concepts, Experience, and Sexuality." *differences* 2: 67–87.

Brandes, S. 1987. "Reflections on Honor and Shame in the Mediterranean." In D. D. Gilmore (ed.), *Honor and Shame and the Unity of the Mediterranean*. Washington, DC: American Anthropological Association. 121–34.

Cairns, D. L. 1993. *Aidôs: The Psychology and Ethics of Honour and Shame in Ancient Greek Literature*. Oxford: Clarendon Press.

Cantarella, E. 1992. *Bisexuality in the Ancient World*. Trans. C. Ó Cuilleanáin. [Orig. pub. as *Secondo natura*, Rome: Editori Riuniti, 1988.] New Haven, CT: Yale University Press.

Carey, C. 1995. "Rape and Adultery in Athenian Law." *Classical Quarterly* 45: 407–17.

Carnes, J. S. 1998. "This Myth Which Is Not One: Construction of Discourse in Plato's *Symposium*." In D. H. J. Larmour, P. A. Miller, and C. Platter (eds.), *Rethinking Sexuality: Foucault and Classical Antiquity*. Princeton, NJ: Princeton University Press. 104–21.

Cohen, D. 1991. *Law, Sexuality, and Society: The Enforcement of Morals in Classical Athens*. Cambridge: Cambridge University Press.

Cohen, E. E. 2000. "Whoring under Contract: The Legal Context of Prostitution in Fourth-Century Athens." In V. Hunter and J. Edmondson (eds.), *Law and Social Status in Classical Athens*. Oxford: Oxford University Press. 113–48.

Cole, S. G. 1984. "Greek Sanctions against Sexual Assault." *Classical Philology* 79: 97–113.

Craft, C. 1984. "'Kiss Me with Those Red Lips': Gender and Inversion in Bram Stoker's *Dracula*." *Representations* 8: 107–33.

Craik, E. M. 1998. "Language of Sexuality and Sexual Inversion in Euripides' *Hippolytos*." *Acta Classica* 41: 29–44.

Csapo, E. 1993. "Deep Ambivalence: Notes on a Greek Cockfight." Part I, *Phoenix* 47.1: 1–28; Part II, *Phoenix* 47.2: 115–24.

Davidson, J. N. 1997. *Courtesans and Fishcakes: The Consuming Passions of Classical Athens*. New York: HarperPerennial.

—— 2001. "Dover, Foucault and Greek Homosexuality: Penetration and the Truth of Sex." *Past & Present* 170: 3–51.

—— 2007. *The Greeks and Greek Love: A Radical Reappraisal of Homosexuality in Ancient Greece*. London: Weidenfeld & Nicolson.

Dodds, E. R. 1957. *The Greeks and the Irrational*. Boston: Beacon Press.

Dover, K. J. 1972. *Aristophanic Comedy*. Berkeley, CA: University of California Press.

—— 1978. *Greek Homosexuality*. London: Duckworth.

—— 1988. *The Greeks and their Legacy: Collected Papers, Volume II: Prose, Literature, History, Society, Transmission, Influence*. Oxford: Blackwell.

Eidinow, E. 2011. "Sex, Religion, and the Law." In M. Golden and P. Toohey (eds.), *A Cultural History of Sexuality in the Classical World*. Oxford and New York: Berg. 87–106.

Fantham, E., Foley, H. P., Kampen, N. B., Pomeroy, S. B., and Shapiro, H. A. 1994. *Women in the Classical World: Image and Text*. Oxford: Oxford University Press.

Fisher, N. R. E. 2000. "Symposiasts, Fisheaters, and Flatterers: Social Mobility and Moral Concern." In F. D. Harvey and J. Wilkins (eds.), *The Rivals of Aristophanes: Studies in Athenian Old Comedy*. London: Duckworth and the Classical Press of Wales. 355–96.

——, intro. and trans. 2001. *Aeschines: Against Timarchos*. Oxford: Oxford University Press.

Foley, H. P. 2001. *Female Acts in Greek Tragedy*. Princeton, NJ: Princeton University Press.

Foucault, M. 1986. *The History of Sexuality, vol. 2: The Use of Pleasure*. Trans. R. Hurley. New York: Vintage Books. [Orig. pub. as *L'Usage des plaisirs*. Paris: Gallimard, 1984.]

Garrison, D. H. 2000. *Sexual Culture in Ancient Greece*. Norman: University of Oklahoma Press.

Geddes, A. G. 1987. "Rags and Riches: The Costume of Athenian Men in the Fifth Century." *Classical Quarterly* 37: 307–31.

Gilmore, D. D. 1987. "Introduction: The Shame of Dishonor." In Gilmore (ed.), *Honor and Shame*. 2–21.

Goff, B. E. 1990. *The Noose of Words: Readings of Desire, Violence and Language in Euripides' "Hippolytos"*. Cambridge: Cambridge University Press.

Goldhill, S. 1986. *Reading Greek Tragedy*. Cambridge: Cambridge University Press.

—— 1990. "The Great Dionysia and Civic Ideology." In J. J. Winkler and F. I. Zeitlin (eds.), *Nothing to Do with Dionysos?* Princeton, NJ: Princeton University Press. 97–129.

Halperin, D. M. 1990. *One Hundred Years of Homosexuality and Other Essays on Greek Love*. New York: Routledge.

—— 2002. *How to Do the History of Homosexuality*. Chicago and London: The University of Chicago Press.

Harris, E. M. 1990. "Did the Athenians Regard Seduction as a Worse Crime than Rape?" *Classical Quarterly* 40: 370–7.

Harvey, F. D. 1984. "The Wicked Wife of Ischomachos." *Échos du Monde Classique/Classical Views* 28 n.s. 3: 68–70.

Henderson, J. 1975. *The Maculate Muse: Obscene Language in Attic Comedy*. New Haven, CT: Yale University Press.

—— 1990. "The *Demos* and the Comic Competition." In Winkler and Zeitlin (eds.), *Nothing to Do with Dionysos?* 271–313.

Herzfeld, M. 1980. "Honour and Shame: Problems in the Comparative Analysis of Moral Systems." *Man* 15: 339–51.

Hubbard, T. K. 1998. "Popular Perceptions of Elite Homosexuality in Classical Athens." *Arion* 6: 48–78.

—— 2000. "Pederasty and Democracy: The Marginalization of a Social Practice." In T. K. Hubbard (ed.), *Greek Love Reconsidered*. New York: William Hamilton Press. 1–11.

—— 2002. "Pindar, Theoxenus, and the Homoerotic Eye." *Arethusa* 35: 255–96.

Hunter, V. J. 1994. *Policing Athens: Social Control in the Attic Lawsuits, 420–320 BC*. Princeton, NJ: Princeton University Press.

Kurke, L. 1999. *Coins, Bodies, Games, and Gold: The Politics of Meaning in Archaic Greece*. Princeton, NJ: Princeton University Press.

Lape, S. 2002–3. "Solon and the Institution of the 'Democratic' Family Form." *Classical Journal* 98.2: 117–39.

—— 2006. "The Psychology of Prostitution in Aeschines' Speech against Timarchus." In C. A. Faraone and L. K. McClure (eds.), *Prostitutes and Courtesans in the Ancient World*. Madison: University of Wisconsin Press. 139–60.

—— 2011. "Heterosexuality." In Golden and Toohey (eds.), *A Cultural History of Sexuality in the Classical World*. 17–36.

Leitao, D. D. 2002. "The Legend of the Sacred Band." In M. C. Nussbaum and J. Sihvola (eds.), *The Sleep of Reason: Erotic Experience and Sexual Ethics in Ancient Greece and Rome*. Chicago: University of Chicago Press. 143–69.

Lewis, S. 2002. *The Athenian Woman: An Iconographic Handbook*. London: Routledge.

Linforth, I. M. 1941. *The Arts of Orpheus*. Berkeley, CA: University of California Press.

Loraux, N. 1993. *The Children of Athena: Athenian Ideas about Citizenship and the Division between the Sexes*. Trans. C. Levine. Princeton, NJ: Princeton University Press.

Ludwig, P. W. 2002. *"Eros" and "Polis": Desire and Community in Greek Political Theory*. Cambridge: Cambridge University Press.

Miller, M. C. 1992. "The Parasol: An Oriental Status-symbol in Late Archaic and Classical Athens." *Journal of Hellenic Studies* 112: 91–105.

Mitchell, R. N. 1991. "Miasma, Mimesis, and Scapegoating in Euripides' *Hippolytus*." *Classical Antiquity* 10: 97–122.

Morris, I. 2000. *Archaeology as Cultural History: Words and Things in Iron Age Greece*. Oxford: Blackwell.

Murnaghan, S. 1988. "How a Woman Can Be More like a Man: The Dialogue between Ischomachus and his Wife in Xenophon's *Oeconomicus*." *Helios* 15.1: 9–22.

Nails, D. 2002. *The People of Plato: A Prosopography of Plato and Other Socratics*. Indianapolis, IN: Hackett.

North, H. 1966. *Sophrosyne: Self-knowledge and Self-restraint in Greek Literature*. Ithaca, NY: Cornell University Press.

Nussbaum, M. C. 1979. "The Speech of Alcibiades: A Reading of Plato's *Symposium*." *Philosophy and Literature* 3: 131–72.

Ober, J. 1989. *Mass and Elite in Democratic Athens: Rhetoric, Ideology, and the Power of the People*. Princeton, NJ: Princeton University Press.

Ogden, D. 1996. *Greek Bastardy in the Classical and Hellenistic Periods*. Oxford: Clarendon Press.

Ormand, K. 2009. *Controlling Desires: Sexuality in Ancient Greece and Rome*. Westport, CT, and London: Praeger.

Pellizer, E. 1990. "Outlines of a Morphology of Sympotic Entertainment." In O. Murray (ed.). *"Sympotica": A Symposium on the "Symposion"*. Oxford: Clarendon Press. 177–84.

Penwill, J. L. 1978. "Men in Love: Aspects of Plato's *Symposium*." *Ramus* 7: 143–75.

Peristiany, J. G. (ed.). 1965. *Honour and Shame: The Values of Mediterranean Society*. London: Weidenfeld & Nicolson.

Pitt-Rivers, J. A. 1961. *The People of the Sierra*. Chicago: University of Chicago Press.

Pomeroy, S. B. 1975. *Goddesses, Whores, Wives, and Slaves: Women in Classical Antiquity*. New York: Schocken.

—— 1994. *Xenophon, "Oeconomicus": A Social and Historical Commentary*. Oxford: Clarendon Press.

Scaife, R. 1995. "Ritual and Persuasion in the House of Ischomachus." *Classical Journal* 90.3: 225–32.

Scanlon, T. F. 2002. *Eros and Greek Athletics*. Oxford: Oxford University Press.

Sedgwick, E. K. 1990. *Epistemology of the Closet*. Berkeley, CA: University of California Press.

Segal, C. P. 1971. "The Two Worlds of Euripides' *Helen*." *Transactions of the American Philological Association* 102: 553–614.

—— 1978. "Pentheus on the Couch and on the Grid: Psychological and Structuralist Readings of Greek Tragedy." *Classical World* 72.3: 129–48.

—— 1982. *Dionysiac Poetics and Euripides' "Bacchae"*. Princeton, NJ: Princeton University Press.

Steiner, A. 2002. "Private and Public: Links Between *Symposion* and *Syssition* in Fifth-century Athens." *Classical Antiquity* 21.2: 347–79.

Taplin, O. 1987. "Phallology, *Phylakes*, Iconography and Aristophanes." *Publications of the Cambridge Philological Society* 213 n.s. 30: 92–104.

—— 1993. *Comic Angels and Other Approaches to Greek Drama through Vase-paintings*. Oxford: Clarendon Press.

Taylor, R. 1997. "Two Pathic Subcultures in Ancient Rome." *Journal of the History of Sexuality* 7: 319–71.

Thorp, J. 1992. "The Social Construction of Homosexuality." *Phoenix* 46: 54–61.

West, M. L. 1983. *The Orphic Poems.* Oxford: Clarendon Press.

Wilkins, J. 2000. *The Boastful Chef: The Discourse of Food in Ancient Greek Comedy.* Oxford: Oxford University Press.

Williams, C. A. 2010. *Roman Homosexuality.* 2nd edn. Oxford: Oxford University Press.

Winkler, J. J. 1990a. *The Constraints of Desire: The Anthropology of Sex and Gender in Ancient Greece.* New York: Routledge.

—— 1990b. "The Ephebes' Song: *Tragôidia* and *Polis.*" In Winkler and Zeitlin (eds.), *Nothing to Do with Dionysos?* 20–62.

Wohl, V. J. 2002. *Love among the Ruins: The Erotics of Democracy in Classical Athens.* Princeton, NJ: Princeton University Press.

Zeitlin, F. I. 1996a. *Playing the Other: Gender and Society in Classical Greek Literature.* Chicago: University of Chicago Press.

—— 1996b. "The Power of Aphrodite: Eros and the Boundaries of the Self in Euripides' *Hippolytos.*" In Zeitlin, *Playing the Other.* 219–84.

—— 1996c. "Travesties of Gender and Genre in Aristophanes' *Thesmophoriazousae.*" In Zeitlin, *Playing the Other.* 375–416.

Further Reading

Belfiore, E. S. 2000. *Murder among Friends: Violation of* Philia *in Greek Tragedy.* Oxford: Oxford University Press. Crucial study of kin-murder scenarios in Attic tragedy that has implications for the specific threat to familial structures posed by *erôs*.

Cohen, D. 1991. *Law, Sexuality, and Society: The Enforcement of Morals in Classical Athens.* Cambridge: Cambridge University Press. Important analysis of the interaction between legal strictures and informal social mechanisms, such as gossip, in regulating private and public morality.

Halperin, D. M. 1990. *One Hundred Years of Homosexuality and Other Essays on Greek Love.* New York: Routledge. Chapter 5, "The Democratic Body: Prostitution and Citizenship in Classical Athens," 88–112, is a foundational (though controversial) discussion of the relationship between democratic ideology and sexual practices, especially prostitution.

Hamel, D. 2003. *Trying Neaira: The True Story of a Courtesan's Scandalous Life in Ancient Greece.* New Haven, CT: Yale University Press. Accessible and entertaining account of the "back story" behind the trial of the courtesan Neaera, useful for understanding both legal procedures and the social realities of prostitution.

Hubbard, T. K. 1998b. "Popular Perceptions of Elite Homosexuality in Classical Athens." *Arion* 6: 48–78. Influential study arguing for widespread class-based disapproval of institutionalized pederasty among ordinary citizens.

Ober, J. 1989. *Mass and Elite in Democratic Athens: Rhetoric, Ideology, and the Power of the People.* Princeton, NJ: Princeton University Press. Comprehensive treatment of Athenian political institutions and class tensions, focusing on the clash between political equality and social inequality. Chapter 7, "Conclusions: Dialectics and Discourse," 293–339, is highly provocative.

Nussbaum, M. C. 1979. "The Speech of Alcibiades: A Reading of Plato's *Symposium.*" *Philosophy and Literature* 3: 131–72. This interpretation of the *Symposium* focuses on the figure of Alcibiades, an object lesson in the tragic potential of *erôs* directed toward a unique individual, as described in Aristophanes' fable.

Pomeroy, S. B. 1994. *Xenophon, "Oeconomicus": A Social and Historical Commentary.* Oxford: Clarendon Press. Along with an English translation, Pomeroy provides a full historical and social introduction to Xenophon's treatise, with particular attention to gender and the prescribed roles of man and wife.

Winkler, J. J. 1990. *The Constraints of Desire: The Anthropology of Sex and Gender in Ancient Greece.* New York: Routledge. Chapter 2, "Laying Down the Law: The Oversight of Men's Sexual Behavior in Classical Athens," 45–70, supplies additional perspectives on several topics we have discussed, including the construct of the *kinaidos* and the prosecution of Timarchus.

Wohl, V. J. 2002. *Love among the Ruins: The Erotics of Democracy in Classical Athens*. Princeton, NJ: Princeton University Press. Explores the complexities of the metaphor of pederastic *erôs* as applied to transactions between the citizen and the democratic city-state.

5

The Early Hellenistic Period: Turning Inwards

During coverage of the military campaign in Afghanistan against al-Qaeda and the Taliban, occasional news reports surfaced about ethnic minorities in that country, clans and whole communities, who claimed descent from the armies of **Alexander III**, "the Great," king of Macedon. Whether or not those particular claims can be verified, it is true that Alexander in the course of his invasion and conquest of Persia founded numerous cities named after himself in which he may have settled a total of more than 36,000 garrison troops and disabled veterans (Griffith 1935: 21–5; Walbank 1981: 43–5). The most noteworthy of these was **Alexandria** on the Nile delta, later the capital of Egypt under the **Ptolemaic dynasty**. Many of the others were located east of the Tigris; several remote "Alexandrias" preserved elements of Greek civilization for a long time after their founder's death.[1] Although the degree of Hellenic and indigenous cultural interaction may not have been as large as was once supposed (Green 1990: 312–35), in these enclaves the local nobility at least had the opportunity to develop familiarity with the Greek language and the characteristic Greek civic institution, the gymnasium. Lured by the economic possibilities of exploiting native resources, Greek merchants and traders were meanwhile drawn to those areas in increasing numbers, and a regularized form of Greek, the *koinê* or "common" dialect, was widely spoken and used in record-keeping and commerce. To this extent we can still speak of the "Hellenization" of what had been the Persian empire.

The Persian expedition was the result of a radical alteration in the balance of power among the formerly independent Greek city-states. In 360/59 BCE Alexander's father, **Philip II**, succeeded to the kingship of Macedon following the death of his elder brother in battle. Situated north of Thessaly and bordering the Thermaic Gulf of the Aegean Sea (see Map 1), Macedon was a small mountainous kingdom on the periphery of the Hellenic world, continuously under threat of invasion from surrounding tribes. After restructuring the citizen army and pacifying neighboring

Sexuality in Greek and Roman Culture, Second Edition. Marilyn B. Skinner.
© 2014 John Wiley & Sons, Inc. Published 2014 by John Wiley & Sons, Inc.

territories through subjugation or alliance, Philip turned his ambitious eyes south and soon became the dominant player on the mainland Greek political scene. Macedon had long been entangled in Greek political affairs and open to Greek cultural influences; its royal house, the **Argeads**, claimed descent from Heracles and ties to Argos in the Peloponnesus (Hdt. 8.137–39). Those pretensions to Hellenic ethnicity were bitterly contested, however, after Philip began his struggle with Athens and her allies over control of southern Greece.[2] His definitive military victory at Chaeronea in 338 BCE against a coalition led by Athens and Thebes put the Greek peninsula under Macedonian rule, ending the autonomy of the *poleis*.

As *hegemôn*, or leader, of a newly formed League of Corinth made up of the states he had defeated, Philip announced his plans to attack Persia but was assassinated in 336 before he could implement them. Alexander inherited both Philip's crown and his undertaking. After harshly putting down rebellion in Greece, he crossed into Asia two years later at the head of the Macedonian army, never to return. Successive operations took him from the Near East to Egypt, then across the Middle East and central Asia – the full breadth of the Persian Empire – into India, whereupon his troops refused to progress further. Having retraced his journey to Babylon, the Persian capital, he may have been planning a Mediterranean campaign against Carthage (Diod. Sic. 18.4.4) when he died there in 323 BCE.

In the wake of Alexander's death and the ensuing power struggles of his generals, the **Successors**, a cultural transformation took place: Greece entered the so-called Hellenistic Age, a period lasting until the death in 30 BCE of the final descendant of the Macedonian ruling dynasties, **Cleopatra VII** of Egypt. For most of the following century, Athens, once the proud leader of an empire, was under the control of one or another Macedonian dynast, with Macedonian troops billeted in the port area to keep order. Although the people agitated for restoration of democratic rule, the local Athenian oligarchy, in collaboration with its royal masters, maintained a tight grip on both the financial and political systems. Ordinary Athenians were effectively disenfranchised. This does not mean that participation in civic life ceased altogether, but it must have been diminished. Some people redirected their energies toward achieving material success in this age of expanding economic markets; others turned to philosophy for peace of mind. We see a rising emphasis on individualism and one's ethical obligations to oneself.

In mainland Greece certain defining characteristics of the Hellenistic era had already emerged early in the fourth century. Extensive rural poverty resulted from the Peloponnesian War and ongoing quarrels among the Greek city-states. When plantations of slow-maturing vines and olives were destroyed by invading troops, marginal landholders could no longer support themselves; they lost their farms and drifted to urban areas or enlisted as itinerant mercenaries. Wars and internal power struggles also created great numbers of exiles throughout the Greek world, including Italy and Sicily as well as the mainland (McKechnie 1989: 34–78). The political theorist Isocrates pictures a substantial population of rootless and displaced persons wandering around Greece at this time (4.133, 167–9; 5.96, 120–2; 8.24); his accounts may be inflated for rhetorical purposes, but he does call attention to a rising problem (Billows 2003: 197–8). Wealth was concentrated in the hands of fewer individuals; except in some relatively prosperous *poleis* where paid work could be had, tensions between rich and poor became more pronounced.

As a remedy for economic and social distress, Isocrates in a long series of letters and speeches urged first Athens and Sparta and afterward, as Macedon's prominence rose, king Philip himself to mount a campaign against the Greeks' common foe Darius III, the Great King of Persia, in order to acquire the massive wealth of the East for themselves. This "Panhellenic" crusade, justified as revenge for the Persian invasion of Greece and liberation for the Ionian cities still subject to a barbarian overlord (Isoc. 4.182–5), was in reality driven by the anxieties of the property-owning class wanting to rid themselves of the troublesome poor by packing them off as mercenaries. Philip, for his part, used the same Panhellenic propaganda to justify the forced collaboration of the southern Greek states in a war of aggression under his leadership (Pownall 2007: 24–5). Historical analogies between past and present incursions of a Western superpower into the same geographic regions of Mesopotamia and Central Asia can be easily drawn and prove illuminating (Romm 2007).

Alexander's military expedition permanently altered the political and cultural features of the land now known as the Middle East, but its consequences for Greeks left at home were even more far-reaching. As geographic and social mobility increased, older forms of social cohesion broke down, fragmenting kinship ties. Citizen males who had emigrated or become professional soldiers often did not return to their own home towns to marry and have children but instead settled and raised families elsewhere. Tombs and ancestor cult might therefore be abandoned.[3] While the population of major urban centers grew substantially during the Hellenistic era, numbers of persons with citizen rights who were eligible to own land in rural districts apparently fell. In Sparta that problem was especially troubling, for Aristotle ascribes the military weakness of the Spartan state in his day to a lack of manpower, which had slipped below 1,000 male citizens (*Pol.* 1270a.29–34). Such shifts in patterns of settlement had a long-term impact on local agricultural economies. In the second century BCE the historian **Polybius** complains of a grave population crisis (36.17.5): "Childlessness and a general shortage of people have gripped all Greece in our own times, so that cities have been left desolate and destitution has occurred, even though ongoing wars and recurrent plagues have not befallen us." Later authorities, Greek and Roman, continue to describe Greece in comparable terms: the theme of a formerly great nation in decline and ruin becomes a moralizing cliché. Archaeological surveys of select rural environments do suggest a decrease in actual numbers of inhabitants beginning in the late Hellenistic period and continuing under Roman administration, though it seems less catastrophic than the literary sources attest (Alcock 1993: 33–92; cf. Reger 2003: 334–5).

More positive social developments, though, came to pass later in the Hellenistic period after the Successor kingdoms were established. Cities were still subject to far-reaching geopolitical pressures, but, with large-scale instability reduced, local forms of civic life took on renewed importance. Democracy became the accepted mode of government for the majority of Hellenistic cities; inscriptions indicate a substantial amount of electoral participation (Gruen 1993: 354). Even under monarchical oversight, elected or appointed magistrates and public assemblies were kept

busy addressing matters of community interest and providing more elaborate amenities and services for the population. To facilitate these improvements, cities turned
to native benefactors for political and financial support, acknowledging their
assistance with public honors. Such expressions of communal gratitude defused
resentment at the economic gap between rich and poor. "[T]he interaction between
citizen assemblies, civic magistracies and the wealthy elites in taking care of the
cities' infrastructures and needs showed that civic morale and public spirit remained
high despite the reduced independence of the Greek cities in the new world of
Hellenistic Empires" (Billows 2003: 209–12; quotation from p. 212). The great age
of Hellenistic urban culture, centered upon the gymnasium, the training of ephebes,
and the local festival, was now under way.

All these historical occurrences had enormous practical consequences for women.
In some areas, declining numbers of men left poor girls without husbands and
brothers unprotected and vulnerable physically and economically. Female-headed
families of tenant farmers could not cultivate the land, as plowing demanded a
man's strength. If women were compelled to work outside the home, only a few
respectable professions were open: midwifery (though it required a capital outlay
for equipment), wet-nursing, weaving, and selling vegetables from a market garden.
Most, probably, turned to prostitution. Wealthier women, on the other hand,
benefited financially from the loss of male kin, since they alone might be left as
heirs. In the chapter of the *Politics* cited above, Aristotle notes that currently two-
fifths of Spartan land was in the hands of women. Increased economic power, in
turn, could bring with it increased religious and even municipal responsibilities.
Rich women gained greater visibility by serving first as public priestesses and then,
starting in the late Hellenistic period, as honorary magistrates for their cities. During
their terms of office, they donated buildings and sponsored civic events; in thus
putting their resources back into the community, they purchased prestige and gratitude for themselves and their kin (Kron 1996: 171–81; van Bremen 1996: 11–40).

Because, as Polybius tells us, even affluent families had begun to have fewer
children, daughters were more highly valued than before. Those families who could
afford it paid to have their girls educated. Terracotta figurines produced for middle-
class consumers in Egyptian Alexandria include representations of young girls
reading (Pomeroy 1984: 60 and plate 7). Starting in the fourth century, growing
numbers of females moved into the liberal arts and professions: women became
physicians (*IG* II^2 6873), painters, and writers (Pomeroy 1977). By the end of that
century, female poets were starting to exercise artistic influence upon male authors.
Under the patronage of the Ptolemaic queens **Arsinoë II** and Berenice II, writers in
residence at the royal court in Egypt composed works featuring psychologically
credible renderings of women's subjectivity.

Improvement in women's status coincided with a more intense emphasis on
private life. Despite the economic pressures that made it difficult for the less well-off
to support a family, the institution of marriage itself assumed new importance: it
was now considered a primary source of emotional satisfaction for the individual as
well as a strategy for family continuity. At Athens, the New Comedy of **Menander**
and his contemporaries responded to this change in attitudes with sentimental

dramatic scenarios defending romantic love as a motive for choosing a mate. Plutarch accordingly pronounces Menander's plays appropriate after-dinner entertainment for husbands soon to join their wives at home: they contain no pederasty; girls who lose their virginity are in due course properly married; wicked *hetairai* are punished and good *hetairai* rewarded (*Mor.* 712e). Issues of sex and marriage are discussed at length in Plato's last work, the *Laws*, and relationships of affection are a preoccupation of Aristotle's ethical treatises. Whether the wise man ought to marry or even have sex was strenuously debated by adherents of **Stoicism** and **Epicureanism**, the two great philosophical schools of the later Hellenistic period. Other intellectual movements, such as neo-Pythagoreanism, promoted the educated woman's capacity to offer her husband intellectual and emotional companionship and to direct the moral formation of her children. Factors contributing to the materialization of this more pronounced heterosexual ethos, besides the economic and political causes mentioned above, may include medical and scientific considerations, the moral authority of Plato and other political thinkers, and innovative trends in artwork and literature produced in settlements outside mainland Greece. We explore some of those influences in this, and the following, chapter.

Court Intrigues

Before we consider tendencies affecting the wider Greek population, though, let us turn back to Alexander's intimate life. Interest in his campaigns prompted by Western military involvement in the areas he traversed was heightened by the release of Oliver Stone's much-anticipated epic film *Alexander* in November 2004. In the wake of that production, over one hundred books directly relevant to Alexander were rushed into print (Cherry 2007: 306–7). Though ultimately not a box-office success in the United States, Stone's film provoked considerable public comment before and after its release.[4] While faithful in other ways to traditional epic cinematic conventions such as spectacle, it broke new ground by presenting its hero, in keeping with the historical record, as having partners of both sexes: by implication, his childhood friend and comrade Hephaestion and, unambiguously, the Persian eunuch Bagoas, along with the monarch's three wives Roxane, Stateira, and Parysatis. Predictably, this "bisexual" portrayal was deeply offensive to social conservatives and to Greeks and Greek-Americans who looked upon Alexander's exploits as a source of national pride (Paul 2007: 18; Solomon 2007: 43–4). Gay critics, on the other hand, complained that Stone had not gone far enough in his treatment of a hero who had long been a gay icon. His attachment to Hephaestion, for all its emotional intensity, is never given an overtly erotic coloring on-screen, prompting one dissatisfied viewer to dismiss the celluloid relationship as merely a male-bonding "bromance" (Nikoloutsos 2008).

Current scholarship postulates that Alexander's sexual behavior, as far as the historical sources – all non-contemporary and often untrustworthy – allow us to draw legitimate conclusions about it, conformed to that of other male members of the Argead dynasty (Reames-Zimmerman 1999; Cartledge 2004: 228; Ogden

2009: 217). However, the customs of the royal house diverged somewhat from the Athenian protocols we have been examining. Although age-differential relationships were not unusual (Pausanias, the assassin of Philip II, was a former *erômenos* who bore the king a private grudge), erotic liaisons between age-mates are likewise attested, at least among the Royal Pages, a corps of elite adolescents who served as the king's personal attendants (Curt. 8.6.2–10, Arr. 4.13.1–4; see also Ogden 1996: 119–23). Alexander and Hephaestion were coevals, raised together (Curt. 3.12.16). While none of the extant ancient biographers refers to Hephaestion as anything more than Alexander's trusted companion,[5] modern historians grant that the pair may have been lovers when young, though not necessarily as adults (but cf. Lane Fox 1974: 56–7, whose opinion Stone appears to accept when hinting at continued sexual relations). Whatever the truth, no one doubts the strength of their mutual love. Certainly Alexander's extravagant grief at Hephaestion's death, only eight months before his own, was perceived by many if not all ancient writers as excessive (Arr. 7.14.2–3), though some scholars observe that it did follow a normal bereavement pattern (Borza and Reames-Zimmerman 2000: 30; Reames-Zimmerman 2001). Calling attention to the similarity between their friendship and the bond of perfect *philia* Aristotle describes in the *Nicomachean Ethics* (1156b5–35), Reames-Zimmerman remarks that "[i]n terms of affectional attachment, *Hephaistion* – not any of Alexander's three wives – was the king's life partner" (1999: 92; italics are hers). Like Achilles and Patroclus, to whom ancient writers often compared them, Alexander and Hephaestion did not fit the pederastic model but were instead operating within their own set of cultural norms.

Family structure, too, was markedly different from the form it ordinarily took in classical Athens, for the Argeads practiced polygamy. In a famous passage from his lost *Life of Philip*, the biographer Satyrus (*ap.* Ath. 13.557b–e) lists the names and backgrounds of Philip's seven wives – one more than Henry VIII (who, admittedly, is at a disadvantage, since he only engaged in serial monogamy). Satyrus leaves no doubt that these unions served a diplomatic purpose: Philip "married in accordance with his wars," he remarks, citing the peoples each wedding was designed to conciliate. Alexander was born from the fifth of Philip's wives, the Molossian princess **Olympias**, who also produced his full sister Cleopatra. The young prince grew up in the company of several half-siblings: two older sisters and an elder brother, Arrhidaeus, the latter mentally deficient (Plut. *Alex.* 77.5). With a view to his probable destiny, Alexander was given a truly outstanding education, receiving not only physical training in war, athletics, and hunting (fig. 5.1) but also an immersion in literature, in particular Homer, and the sciences, supervised by Aristotle himself. If anyone was prepared by his upbringing to be a king, Alexander was.

By its very nature, however, polygamy in combination with the absence of a fixed principle of legitimacy, also true of the Argead clan, invites strife whenever a regime change occurs (Mitchell 2007). Polygamous societies prioritize the availability of a capable heir (Carney 2000: 24–5). In Macedon the king was the war leader and border disputes were constant, so chances of death in battle were high (Ogden 1999: xvi). Moreover, regicide was surprisingly frequent (Carney 1983). The tendency, then, was to sire even more potential heirs than might be needed. When the ruler

Fig. 5.1 The "Alexander Sarcophagus" from the Phoenician royal necropolis at Sidon, made for Abdalonymos, King of Sidon. Long face: lionhunt, detail: Alexander the Great on his horse, a dog at his feet. Late fourth century BCE. Marble, 195×318×167 cm. Inv. 370T. Location: Archaeological Museum, Istanbul, Turkey. Source: Erich Lessing/Art Resource, NY.

died, whether of natural causes or not, eligible sons, along with uncles and cousins, attempted to seize the throne, competing with half-brothers by other wives. Mothers had strong motives for ensuring a child's succession, since they would enjoy more power as queen mothers than they had as mere queens (Greenwalt 1989). Among the Argeads, therefore, violent and lethal family disputes were the rule. Though he had treated Alexander as heir apparent, Philip's final marriage to a native Macedonian woman, another Cleopatra, raised hopes for a successor of pure Macedonian blood. When the bride's uncle and guardian Attalus drunkenly voiced that sentiment at the wedding feast, Alexander threw a goblet at him; in consequence he and

Olympias briefly fled into exile (Plut. *Alex.* 9.3–5). After Philip was killed, rumors arose that Olympias and perhaps Alexander too were complicit (Plut. *Alex.* 10.4, Just. *Epit.* 9.7.1–2). One present-day historian has actually made a hypothetical case for parricide (Cartledge 2004: 92–6). Olympias herself is also accused of engineering the deaths of the widowed Cleopatra and her infant daughter (Just. *Epit.* 9.7.12; Paus. 8.7.7). That Alexander, in order to strengthen his position, quickly executed certain prominent nobles on the grounds of conspiracy, among them Attalus and, just to be safe, his own cousin Amyntas, is undisputed.

As noted above, Alexander too was polygamous, taking three wives, again for obvious political reasons. None were Macedonians. His alliance in 327 BCE with Roxane, daughter of a Bactrian chieftain, earned him the goodwill of previously hostile local nobles (Carney 2000: 105–7). In 324, during an elaborate mass wedding ceremony at Susa, he married two women from separate branches of the Persian royal line: Stateira, eldest daughter of Darius III, and Parysatis, youngest daughter of Darius' predecessor Artaxerxes. This dual union strengthened his claim to legitimate rule of Persia. Although he postponed marrying until he was almost thirty, Alexander did have an earlier longstanding relationship with the young foreign widow Barsine, who is unaccountably given no part in Stone's film.[6] Product of a mixed marriage between a Persian satrap and the sister of Greek mercenaries, Barsine had probably known Alexander since childhood, for her family was then living in exile at Philip's court; their affair began, however, only after she, together with other female members of the Persian nobility including Darius' mother, wife, and daughters, was captured at Damascus in 333 BCE following the battle of Issus (Plut. *Alex.* 21.4, *Eum.* 1.3). The liaison lasted approximately five years, producing one son, Heracles, named after the reputed ancestor of the Argead line. Though technically having no formal connection with the king, Barsine appears to have enjoyed considerable prestige behind the scenes, since at the mass marriage ceremony in Susa Alexander bestowed two of her sisters and her daughter by a prior marriage upon favored officers (Carney 2000: 103–4).

After Alexander's unexpected illness and demise[7] an ongoing succession crisis lasting decades generated further rounds of bloodshed. Though several months pregnant with the future Alexander IV, a jealous Roxane is alleged (Plut. *Alex.* 77.4) to have personally slain her co-wives Stateira and Parysatis (Plutarch mistakenly terms the latter Stateira's sister) and thrown their bodies down a well. This was supposedly done with the help of Perdiccas, one of Alexander's marshals, who was acting as her guardian; given her condition, it seems more likely that Perdiccas himself, perhaps in collaboration with one or more fellow generals, eliminated the two Persian women in order to clear the way for Roxane's child, the future Alexander IV. Five years later civil war in Macedon resulted in the brutal deaths of Alexander's mentally incompetent brother Arrhidaeus, who as Philip III officially shared his monarchy with the toddler, and Arrhidaeus' wife Adea Eurydice. Joint kingship of two legal minors was an invitation to anarchy. Fearing the future extinction of the dynasty, females from separate branches of the Argead line marshaled armies on behalf of the contender each supported: the matriarch Olympias, who had previously retired to her native Molossia, invaded Macedon to seek sole rule for her grandson, while Eurydice led out troops to defend her husband's claim. War between two women was unprecedented (Duris of Samos *ap*. Ath. 13.560f). Before battle could be joined, however, the Macedonian army went over to Olympias' side, refusing to fight against Alexander's mother (Just. *Epit*. 14.5.1–2, 8–10). After they fell into her hands, Olympias first imprisoned and killed Arrhidaeus and then forced Adea Eurydice to commit suicide (Diod. Sic. 19.11.5). Olympias herself was soon afterward condemned and executed by Eurydice's former ally Cassander, who emerged as de facto ruler of Macedon. Under his orders, Alexander IV and his mother were kept in custody until the boy entered his teenage years, when public opinion began to favor his assumption of the throne; at that point Cassander had Alexander and his mother quietly disposed of (Diod. Sic. 19.105.2–3). A little later (on the chronology, Wheatley 1988: 19 and n. 29), the last possible pretender to the succession, Barsine's son Heracles, was put forward as a candidate, then publicly slain. That was the end of the Argead line.

The moral of the story is that winning an empire is one thing, passing it on another. This lesson too may have contemporary applications.

Who Is Buried in Philip's Tomb?

In 1976 a leading Greek archaeologist, Manolis Andronikos, began excavating a large tumulus near the site of the ancient Macedonian palace at Argae, not far from the modern village of Vergina in northern Greece. During the next two seasons he discovered three fourth-century BCE tombs beneath the mound. Though the earliest, Tomb I, had been robbed in antiquity, a masterful wall painting survives showing Hades' abduction of Persephone, monumental testimony to the shock of sudden death. Nothing else was left apart from pot shards, two broken pieces of a woman's toilet set, and numerous bones, later identified as those of a man, a young woman, and a neonate. All had been inhumed, not cremated (Andronikos 1984: 86–95). Miraculously, the other tombs were intact. Rich grave goods placed in them, including furniture, weapons, and silver and bronze vessels, marked them as royal burials. Tomb II was divided into an antechamber and a main chamber, both containing cremated remains. In the main chamber, investigators found a gold casket, decorated on its lid with a sixteen-point star, the regal symbol that has since become known as the "Star of Vergina." Inside were an exquisite gold wreath and the burned bones of a middle-aged male wrapped in what had been a purple cloth. The antechamber held a

second casket, also containing a wreath, together with the bones of a young woman in a much poorer state of preservation (ibid., 97–197). Tomb III held the cremated bones of an adolescent male placed in a silver *hydria* crowned with a gold oak wreath. From the outset, the excavator insisted that the occupants of Tomb II were Philip II and one of his wives (Andronikos 1984: 226–31). Taken up enthusiastically by his patriotic Greek countrymen, that suggestion launched a controversy that continues to this day.

Because we know the names of all the royal Argead males who died during this period, we can arrive at one, and only one, alternative pair of candidates for the burials in Tomb II: Philip III Arrhidaeus and his wife Adea Eurydice. As stated above, they were killed by Olympias in 317 BCE (Diod. Sic. 19.11.5) and presumably interred hastily. Cassander, however, later cremated their remains and reburied them, according to royal custom, at Argae. Though a non-Argead, he was soon to marry Thessalonicê, daughter of Philip II and half-sister of Alexander, and was "already acting like a king in regard to the affairs of the realm" (Diod. Sic. 19.52.1, 5). Arranging an elaborate funeral for his predecessor would strengthen his own claim to the throne. This explains the presence of so many valuables, especially armor, heaped in the burial chambers. Similarly, Cassander would have been responsible for the interment of the last legitimate member of the Argead line, Alexander IV, son of Alexander by Roxane, who, it is generally agreed, is the youth buried in Tomb III. Even if he had murdered the boy in cold blood, Cassander would not have neglected the final rites: a dead Alexander was more valuable to him as propaganda than a living one (cf., though, Gattinoni 2010).

So who *is* buried in Philip's tomb? Arguments based on the stylistic features of the structure itself, the painted frieze of an animal hunt over the doorway, and the archaeological finds within strongly point toward a date after Alexander the Great's Eastern campaigns (Borza 1990: 261–2, Borza and Palagia 2007) but have not convinced everyone. Resolving the case may depend upon CSI-style labwork on the bone evidence. Cremation, even in present-day mortuaries, does not reduce bone; the ashes we scatter under a tree or across a golf course are the product of subsequent pulverization. In the case of the male Tomb II occupant, enough skeletal material has survived to permit forensic experts to draw conclusions, above all from the skull. We know that Philip II suffered an arrow injury to his right eye, leaving it blind. Several small carved ivory portrait heads, decorations from a couch, were found in the tomb; one is almost certainly a representation of Alexander III, while another shows an older man, bearded, whose right eye appears scarred (fig. 2). With this information in mind, specialists examined the bones of the skull and found irregularities above the right eye socket and on the right cheekbone that they attributed to severe trauma. Using facial-restoration techniques, they created a wax cast of a reconstructed head with mutilated eye that, when hair and beard were in place, looked amazingly like the ivory figure and also resembled supposed coin likenesses and busts of Philip (Musgrave, Neave, and Prag 1984; see further Prag 1990).

However, this accomplishment, impressive as it may seem, has been challenged. Another pathologist has now employed macrophotography to arrive at an opposite set of conclusions: the irregularities thought

Fig. 5.2 Philip II of Macedon, 382–336 BCE Macedonian king. Ivory, fourth century BCE Hellenistic Greek, found in royal tombs, Vergina, fourth century BCE, Greece. Location: Archaeological Museum, Salonica. Source: Gianni Dagli Orti/The Art Archive at Art Resource, NY .

to be caused by trauma are either natural formations or effects of the cremation process along with inaccuracies in reassembling the skull. Examination of the rest of the skeletal material turned up no evidence of other wounds, despite ancient testimony to several more battlefield injuries. Finally, different outcomes occur when bones covered by flesh are cremated, as opposed to dry or degreased bones whose flesh has already decomposed. Long bones cremated dry, according to this report,

> are nearly intact in size and form and show negligible warping; they assume a light brown color and present infrequent and straight transverse fractures. Long bones cremated fleshed are fragmentary with marked warping; they assume a white, blue, and gray color and present frequent and parallel-sided transverse fractures that are either curved (thumbnail) or serrated (Bartsiokas 2000: 513).

(Continued)

Who is Buried in Philip's Tomb? — Continued

Contraction of bone collagen at high temperatures accounts for the peculiar changes in flesh-covered bones. The bones of the Tomb II skeleton, light brown and minimally warped, with straight transverse cracking, are consistent with a dry cremation. These data fit the burial profile of Arrhidaeus, not that of Philip II. Most Anglo-American authorities on Philip and Alexander now believe that the man buried in Tomb II was Alexander's half-brother.

That conclusion does not exhaust the puzzles presented by Andronikos's finds. Viewed through the lens of gender, the grave goods accompanying the woman buried in the antechamber are unusual (Carney 1991: 21). Apart from two items, there was no elaborate jewelry of the sort ordinarily found in a female interment. The gold wreath in the casket indicates that its possessor was a queen (Adams 1980: 70). There was also a gold pin with a chain knotted around it; the pin is foreign, of a type associated with the Illyrians, a tribal population west of Macedon. Instead of other objects of adornment, set against the sealed door to the main chamber (and thus placed there following the male burial) was a collection of armor, including a pectoral or breastplate, ceremonial greaves, and an embossed gold cover for a *gorytos*, a flat Scythian-style quiver. Weapons such as spears were likewise present. While the armor and weapons might have belonged to the male, ancient sources tell us that Cynna or Cynane, daughter of Philip II by an Illyrian wife, had been trained in the use of arms by her mother, for Illyrian women joined battle alongside men. She in turn trained her daughter Adea Eurydice, Philip's granddaughter (Polyaen. *Strat.* 8.60; Duris of Samos *ap.* Ath. 13.560f; see Carney 2000: 128–31). Though her husband Philip III Arrhidaeus was nominally in charge of the Macedonian army, it was Eurydice who organized resistance against Olympias and her invading Epirote forces (Diod. Sic. 19.11.1–2). After Eurydice was captured, she showed great bravery. Ordered to commit suicide by Olympias and given a choice of a sword, a noose, or hemlock, she first laid out and cleansed the body of her murdered husband, then hanged herself with her own girdle, "neither weeping at her own fate nor crushed by the magnitude of her misfortunes," as Diodorus observes (ibid., 7). If the military equipment belonged to her, its presence might indicate that her role as a military leader was being commemorated (Carney 1991: 25; cf. Palagia 2000: 191). While her husband, as king, received the more elaborate burial, she would have been honored for her own part in attempting to defend Macedon.

As for the whereabouts of Philip II, those who assign Tomb II to Arrhidaeus surmise that by process of elimination the osteological remains in the looted Tomb I could be those of Alexander's father, his youngest wife Cleopatra, and their infant daughter (Carney 1992; Borza and Palagia 2007: 82–3, 118; Gattinoni 2010: 115). The historical account supports that possibility, but more labwork may be needed to confirm it.

Medicine and the Sexes

During the late archaic age a number of thinkers in Greek settlements on the Western coast of Asia Minor and in southern Italy and Sicily began to speculate on the composition of the physical universe and to find rational explanations for natural phenomena such as eclipses. Out of this pre-Socratic investigative movement there evolved a theoretical understanding of the human body as made up of various opposing forces that must be kept in equilibrium (Nutton 2004: 44–50; MacFarlane 2010: 46–51). Disease, according to Alcmaeon of Croton

(Kirk-Raven-Schofield 1983: 260 and fr. 310; see Nutton 2004: 47–8 and Holmes 2010: 99–101) arises from some disproportion (extreme heat or cold, excess or deficiency of nourishment) and may be triggered by the impact of external factors on the blood, marrow, and brain. By the late fifth century, medical writers could speak of four bodily fluids or "humors" – blood, yellow bile, black bile, and phlegm – whose balance and mixture varied with the seasons ([Hippoc.] *Nat. Hom.* 4–7) but could be regulated through diet and treatment. For men in the prime of life sexual activity played a part in maintaining health by drying the body through discharge of surplus moisture; this is why, despite its potential risks, it was thought medically necessary.

Sex was vital for women, too, but for quite different reasons. Hesiod's idea that "women are wet," i.e., that their flesh stores up more liquid than a man's, became the basis of the Hippocratic model of female gynecology. While the so-called "Hippocratic corpus" of Greek medical texts – a collection of sixty to seventy treatises credited to the historical physician **Hippocrates** of Cos but probably composed by other anonymous, mostly fifth- and fourth-century, practitioners – sometimes disagrees on the causes and treatments of disease, its basic construction of the female body is consistent, owing much, conceptually, to the myth of Pandora (King 1998: 21, 23–39). Hippocratic writings contain many case histories of male illness, but there was no cluster of diseases recognized during the classical era as specific to men. In contrast, no fewer than ten gynecological treatises address the peculiar health problems of women. Women's pathology is inevitably ascribed to difficulties occurring in the reproductive system ("wombs are the cause of all diseases," [Hippoc.] *Loc. Hom.* 47.1), and the surviving texts reflect a high degree of medical anxiety over a woman's capacity to reproduce. Thus men are regarded as the physiological norm, the subject of "general medicine," while women, with their unique bodily organs, constitute a special case (Dean-Jones 1994: 110–12).

In these medical texts women's physiology is so distinct from that of men that they might well be considered a separate race; because of their biological makeup, furthermore, they are at the mercy of their sexual drives in a way that men are not. Anatomically, the distinguishing feature of the female is the ***hodos***, an uninterrupted internal passageway extending from nose and mouth to vagina.[8] Scent therapies applied to the nostrils could therefore affect organs in the lower parts of the body. Woman's flesh too is of a completely different texture, spongy and absorbent, like wool ([Hippoc.] *Mul.* 1.1). The excess moisture she extracts from food, stored as blood, must be regularly evacuated during the menstrual period or consumed by the fetus in pregnancy; otherwise death can result. The short treatise *On the Diseases of Unmarried Girls* (8.466–70 Littré) warns that virgins are prone to mental illness and suicide if menarche is delayed, for the blood accumulating in their bodies can put pressure on the heart and diaphragm, where consciousness was thought to reside. The only cure is marriage and pregnancy (King 1998: 77–9). The womb or *gastêr*, which the Hippocratics compared to an inverted storage jar, was also a source of female troubles. Because it collected blood to be expelled in menstruation or used to nourish the child, it was unusually susceptible to dryness. It was believed to be an independent organ unattached to the body, and could therefore leave its proper place to travel up the *hodos* searching for moisture, rising to the lungs and neck and producing suffocation ([Hippoc.] *Mul.* 1.7; *Loc. Hom.* 47.1–4). Intercourse, however, irrigated the womb, heated the blood, and made the menses flow more easily. To preserve their health, then, women too needed sex, but unlike men were allowed it only in marriage. The fact that medical writers speak of female sexual experience exclusively in terms of heterosexual penetration suggests a certain societal indifference to any non-reproductive genital activity.

In the *Timaeus* (91b–c), Plato's spokesman characterizes the reproductive organs of male and female alike as autonomous, disobedient animals. The penis, goaded by lust, attempts to master (*kratein*) all things, a decided association of penetration with dominance. Conversely, the womb, "a living creature hungering to create a child," begins wandering through the body if left fallow too long. Although he attributes wandering-womb syndrome to barrenness, not dryness, Plato is following Hippocratic tenets when he represents sexual appetite as a physiological compulsion arising from the organs themselves. Originating in similar fashion, the physical drive in each sex nevertheless pursues distinct goals: the man's impulse to ejaculate is activated by the sight or mental image of an external object, but the woman's craving for pregnancy is a response to her own internal void and the sexual act only a means of relieving that condition. Men could therefore exercise self-mastery by avoiding whatever might stimulate desire; women could not (Dean-Jones 1992: 76–80).

Although Hippocratic medicine considered the physical constitution of the sexes wholly dissimilar, male and female were assigned comparable functions in the reproductive process. Both partners, the author of *On Generation* asserts, produce "male" and "female," that is, strong and weak, sperm during the sex act. These mingle in the womb. The sex of the child depends upon the strength or weakness of the sperm prevailing in quantity ([Hippoc.] *Genit.* 6), and inherited characteristics are also determined by the respective amounts of sperm contributed by father and mother (*Genit.* 8). That hypothesis, which explains why children may not resemble the same-sex parent, also allows for the positioning of gender attributes along a continuum, so that, depending on the potency of the sperm, some biological females will tend toward the masculine, or vice versa (King 1998: 9).

Popular conviction, however, denied the mother a share in the child's heredity: like a farmer sowing seed in a field, a man was instead thought to plant sperm in the woman who served as its passive receptacle, a parallel that would readily occur to an agricultural society (Pomeroy 1975: 65). Feminist classical scholars cheerfully refer to this belief as the "flowerpot theory." With the argument that the mother plays no active part in generation, Apollo in Aeschylus' *Eumenides* successfully defends his client Orestes against a charge of matricide (658–61):

> The so-called mother of the child is not its parent,
> but rather the nurse of the newly-sown embryo.
> The male who mounts begets. She, like a stranger for a stranger,
> preserves the shoot, should the god not harm it.

Fantastic as this assumption may seem, it answered a nagging male fear that woman, who possesses a uterus to house the embryo and can nourish it herself, might also be able to conceive from her own seed without the help of a father (Hanson 1992: 41–3; Dean-Jones 1994: 148–52).[9]

Starting from different premises a century later, Aristotle arrived at a diametrically opposite conclusion: the male possesses the principle of generation, the female that of matter (*Gen. an.* 716a.5–23). Female menstrual fluid, he posited, is a discharge corresponding to semen in males. Both manifest for the first time at puberty, and both are a residue of the normal blood produced by nutriment. Sperm is the vehicle through which the human form is transferred from a living being to inert matter. There is no such thing as female sperm, however, because the production of two discharges at the same time would be a redundancy: "for if there were sperm, there would be no menstrual secretion, but as it is, the existence of the latter indicates that the former does not exist" (*Gen. an.* 727a.29–30). During ejaculation, blood stored in the passages around the testes is concocted, or condensed, into a more potent liquid. Females are colder than males and do not have the vital heat required to manufacture sperm, which is capable of activating matter only when hot and thickened. Hence the mother does not play an active part in conception, but instead contributes matter, in the form of menstrual blood (which, being a residue, is itself richer than ordinary blood), to nourish the resulting embryo.

If women's role in the reproductive process is circumscribed, however, it is precisely because in other ways she has been more closely assimilated to the opposite sex. For Aristotle, woman was a human being, although less perfectly formed than man: famously, he states she is "a defective male, as it were" (*Gen. an.* 737a.28). In so far as her lesser body heat requires her to perform a complementary but different biological function, she must develop complementary but different reproductive organs – the uterus, corresponding to the male penis and testicles. There is, moreover, a formal resemblance between each set of parts, for the uterus, Aristotle adds, has a double chamber, just as the testicles are twofold (*Gen. an.* 716b.32–3). This notion of functionally corresponding male and female sexual organs made a decisive impact on later medical theory. Although we do not know whether Aristotle's views were shaped by changes in the societal position of Greek women, acceptance of his model of female biology has plausibly been linked to contemporary expansion of their communal, legal, and economic activities (Dean-Jones 1994: 20, 249–50).

Subsequently, Hellenistic doctors resident at Alexandria were able to practice dissection and observe the internal features of the human body. Their most important representative, Herophilus, affirmed that the uterus is substantially the same as other organs and denied the existence of conditions specific to women other than those directly concerned with reproduction (Sor. *Gyn.* 3.3). Under the Roman empire, this line of thinking was pursued to its logical end, the **"one-sex" model** of human physiology in which the reproductive organs were seen as essentially the same, differing only in their internal or external positioning. **Galen**, the great second-century CE physician, asks his readers to imagine the male parts turned inside out and placed inside the body, and the converse for the female parts. The scrotum, he claims, would take the place of the uterus, the penis the vagina; meanwhile, the uterus, turned outward, would contain the ovaries in the manner of a scrotum, and the cervix would become the male member. Like the eyes of a mole, which exist in the animal but cannot open, the female organs, already formed within the fetus, are not able to emerge and project outward due to lack of vital heat (*UP* 14.6). While this is an imperfection in the woman, he concludes, it is perfect for human reproduction, since it provides a safe place for gestation. Preserved by Byzantine and Arab physicians, Galen's treatises were handed down to students of medicine in Renaissance and early modern Europe. Until well into the eighteenth century, his anatomical model remained the standard paradigm for Western medicine, not only consulted for diagnosis and treatment but also controlling cultural assumptions about gender (Laqueur 1990: 4–8).

For women, the displacement of the Hippocratic paradigm of "otherness" had both good and bad consequences. Females were no longer treated as a special class of patients whose health was linked entirely to the proper functioning of their reproductive organs. For therapeutic reasons, this development was patently desirable. While regarded as comparable in physical makeup, however, women were perceived as fundamentally inferior to men because of their lesser body heat. At the same time, those aspects of their physiology that were distinctive, like menstruation, began to be seen as insalubrious or disgusting. Herophilus questioned the usefulness of menstruation; by the second century CE, Soranus, a Greek doctor practicing in Imperial Rome, could insist that it actually endangered female health (*Gyn.* 1.29).

On the whole, though, this revolution in medical theory improved women's status because it acknowledged their capacity for self-discipline. Tragic heroines might struggle against Aphrodite's urges, but Hippocratic physicians would consider such efforts doomed from the outset. Woman could not restrain her appetite for intercourse, as it was incited by physiological necessity, so much so that abstinence did her harm. This construction of female desire buttressed the social practice of subordinating women to male authority and rigorously supervising them during their reproductive years. Aristotle's belief in the analogous structure of male and female bodies led him to think in terms of comparable sexual appetites, which in each sex could be regulated through the exercise of self-control, even though woman's innate ability to act as a moral agent was inferior (Dean-Jones 1992: 86). Once it was commonly admitted that women were capable of saying "no," they were allowed more freedom to move beyond the *oikos* and come into contact with strangers.

From Croton to Crete

Theseus' son Hippolytus is an anomaly. No archaic or classical Greek thinker seems to have advocated complete abstinence from sex as a way of life.[10] Strict monogamy, for husband as well as wife, was a different matter: the late sixth-century sage Pythagoras of Samos, who migrated to southern Italy and headed a religious foundation at Croton, imposed that regulation on his followers.[11] Although he promulgated a doctrine of the transmigration of souls and laid down dietary rules similar to those of the Orphics, his remarks on sex as they have come down to us nevertheless do not reflect anxiety over carnal pollution but are instead dictated by commonplace Greek medical and ethical considerations. He is reported as saying that *ta aphrodisia*, though less harmful during the winter months, are not good for a man's health and cause physical debility and that they also weaken self-mastery (Diog. Laert. 8.9, cf. Diod. Sic. 10.9.3–4). On a journey to the underworld Pythagoras allegedly saw men who had been unwilling to have intercourse with their wives undergoing chastisement (Diog. Laert. 8.21). This biographical fabrication (which sounds suspiciously like a fossilized joke from Attic comedy) touches upon the special place occupied by monogamous marriage in Pythagorean ethics.

In accounts of Pythagorean doctrine composed after Plato's time, proponents are made to take a very hard line on sex. A late Hellenistic tract *On the Nature of the Universe* attributed (falsely) to the Pythagorean Occelus states unequivocally that intercourse was designed not for pleasure but procreation (4.1–2). Iamblichus' *On the Pythagorean Life* (209–10) contains precepts against precocious sexual experience (for boys, not before the age of twenty) and against intercourse "contrary to nature and with outrage" (*para physin… meth' hybreôs*), a reference to pederasty; sex instead should be undertaken "in accordance with nature and with *sôphrosynê*" in order to produce a child. The evidence is a mixed bag, and not all of it may be reliable, but the general picture it gives appears consistent: sex within marriage, conducted with restraint and a view to procreation, merits praise; extramarital sex of all kinds is forbidden.

Since Pythagorean thought enjoyed renewed popularity in the Hellenistic age, it may have encouraged growing support of marital fidelity as an ideal for men as well as women. The fourth-century orator Isocrates makes the Cypriot king Nicocles denounce spouses who "through their own indulgences wound those by whom they would not expect to be wounded, and, though they show themselves fair in all other transactions, do wrong in those involving their wives" (3.40). A late fourth-century treatise on household economics attributed to Aristotle, though probably composed by a student, follows Xenophon in its description of the respective work assignments of man and wife but structures the relationship according to Aristotelian hierarchical principles. When it stipulates the husband's duty to his wife, however, it shows the influence of Pythagorean precepts ([Arist.] *Oec.* 1344a.9–12):

> First, the rules in respect to the wife: let him do her no injury. For thus he himself will probably not be injured by her. Even the common law of humanity, as the Pythagoreans say, instructs us in this: one must avoid injuring a wife just as one would not harm the suppliant raised from the hearth. And the husband's extramarital intercourse does her an injury.

This mandate invests fidelity to the marital bond with the sanctity and dignity of suppliant ties. If it is a relic of early Pythagoreanism, it may well reflect the stringent mores of the original fellowship at Croton in which all property was reportedly held in common and women participated on an equal footing with men.

Plato was familiar with Pythagorean doctrine, and its influence may arguably be detected in his injunctions about sex in his last work, the *Laws*, which was probably left unrevised at his death in 347 BCE. In such earlier dialogues as the *Phaedrus* and the *Symposium*, *erôs* is a catalyst impelling the lover to appreciation of the highest truths. Physical chastity is the prerequisite for this encounter with wisdom, but Plato is quite aware that human beings are weak. At *Phaedrus* 256b–d, Socrates envisions a couple, lovers of honor but not given to philosophy, who yield to desire in a moment of frailty and thereafter indulge in sex occasionally, though with misgivings. He pronounces their way of life less worthy, but admits that it still allows for some spiritual growth. In the *Laws*, though, Plato's denunciation of homoerotic acts is sweeping, with no provision made for human shortcomings. His debt to Pythagoreanism is greater in his final dialogues (for example, Timaeus of Locri, his spokesman in the *Timaeus*, voices Pythagorean ideas on number and harmony), and the question, perhaps not fully resolvable, is whether his own stringent pronouncements are borrowed from Pythagoreanism or, alternatively, whether Platonic sexual ethics were instead projected retroactively on to the early Pythagoreans.[12]

In the first two books of the *Laws*, as we saw, the Athenian Stranger critiques the archaic pedagogical institutions of Crete and Sparta. Then he expounds on the lessons of history and the reasons for the breakdown of other political constitutions, including the collapse of Athenian democracy. At the conclusion of the third book, Cleinias, the Cretan, mentions that he is a member of a board of ten overseers charged with drawing up a legal code for a new colony that his countrymen are planning to found (702c–d). With a view to providing a framework for the actual code that Cleinias and his colleagues will eventually fashion, during the remainder of the conversation the three men attempt to formulate a constitution for an imaginary settlement, Magnesia, numbering precisely 5,040 households – a key Pythagorean number (737e). Keeping that background in mind, we can examine what is said about homoeroticism and the other modes of sexual behavior to be addressed in such legislation.

We have already encountered one attack on pederasty in the opening book of the *Laws* (636b–c), where the Athenian Stranger charges that the Cretan and Spartan customs of all-male dining and gymnastic exercise foster homoerotic relations. In contrast to procreative heterosexual relations, they produce pleasure "unnaturally" (*para physin*). Hence persons who perform these acts do so from inability to restrain their appetites, and, in doing so, they thwart the reproductive purpose of sex.[13] This indictment of same-sex intercourse is intended to refute the suggestion that the characteristic military institutions in Sparta and Crete further temperance. As a civic virtue, temperance demands not only moderation in the use of legitimate pleasures but abstention from those that violate communal norms. Since homoerotic relations were an established part of Dorian culture, the Athenian must appeal to the higher law of nature to bolster his claim that debauchery is induced rather than prevented by the all-male ambience of common meals and gymnastic training. We recall Iamblichus' report that sex "contrary to nature and with outrage" was prohibited by the Pythagoreans. Similarity of phrasing may point to Pythagorean influence here.

The lengthier of the two criticisms is part of a later disquisition on curbing licentiousness (835e–841d). The Stranger proposes a practical strategy for discouraging homoeroticism: mustering general public opinion against it by declaring it unholy and contrary to religion, just like incest. Grounded as it is on an appeal to *physis*, however, that prohibition would have to extend beyond same-sex relations to embrace other modes of non-reproductive sex (838e–839a):

> This is just what I was getting at when I said I knew of a way to put into effect this law of ours which permits the sexual act only for its natural purpose, procreation, and forbids not only homosexual relations, in which the human race is deliberately murdered, but also the sowing of seeds on rocks and stone, where it will never take root and mature into a new individual; and we should also have to keep away from any female "soil" in which we'd be sorry to have the seed develop.

To understand the force of this precept, we must turn to a prior law – the very first, in fact, to be laid down. Marriage will be mandatory for all the adult male citizens of Magnesia (and, it goes without saying, for women too). The publicly stated justification is not perpetuation of the household, as one might expect, but self-continuance: producing children is the method provided by nature for the individual to share in immortality, and the man who deprives himself of that opportunity behaves in an unholy manner (721b–d). Since sex is designed for procreation, male–male intercourse is part of a blanket proscription that also rules out onanism and sex with female partners unfit to reproduce as contrary to its natural purpose (Price 1989: 231). In absolute fairness to Plato, though, limitation of sexual relations to reproductive ends seems to apply only until the couple has produced the requisite number of children (ideally two, one of each sex) or exceeded the prime age for reproduction (Gaca 2003: 53, 56–7). After that period, averaging about ten years per couple, discreet and moderate sexual activity for non-reproductive purposes is permissible (784e3–785a3). In no case, however, would homoerotic sex be tolerated.

All this is reminiscent of Pythagorean teaching on marriage.[14] Concentration upon the reproductive purpose of sex is certainly in keeping with its principles. Sanctions against consorting with *hetairai* are attributed to Pythagoras, since we learn from Iamblichus that the inhabitants of Croton sent their mistresses away at his behest (*VP* 50, 132, 195). When the Athenian expresses hope that such a law, apart from discouraging adultery and dissipation, would lead men to be friendly and affectionate (*oikeious kai philous*, 839b.1) toward their wives, he also seems to be endorsing Pythagorean support for companionate marriage. Tellingly, Rist observes that this sentiment is "not a familiar theme in Plato" (1997: 76). Here, I think, the evidence of direct influence is very persuasive.

In concluding his discourse on sexual legislation, the lawgiver admits that the proposals he has put forth, though they would benefit any state if enacted, are highly visionary. Thus he ends by adopting a fallback position involving two options (841d–e):

> However, God willing, perhaps we'll succeed in imposing one or other of two standards of sexual conduct. (1) Ideally, no one will dare to have relations with any respectable

citizen woman except his own wedded wife, or sow illegitimate and bastard seed in courtesans, or sterile seed in males in defiance of nature. (2) Alternatively, while suppressing sodomy entirely, we might insist that if a man does have intercourse with any woman (hired or procured in some other way) except the wife he wed in holy marriage with the blessing of the gods, he must do so without any other man or woman getting to know about it. If he fails to keep the affair secret, I think we'd be right to exclude him by law from the award of state honours, on the grounds that he's no better than an alien.

The first and more preferable alternative would enforce strict sexual monogamy on all citizen males, prohibiting adultery and traffic with prostitutes as well as same-sex relations. The second ordinance makes allowances for surreptitious recourse to paid women at the risk of public shame if the perpetrator is found out. Homoerotic affairs appear to be excluded even if conducted in secret. As Moore (2005: 196) remarks, the second option, which anticipates that not everyone will be capable of complete self-control, "is potentially more suited to the real world of the second-best state." In making this concession, the Athenian Stranger is still mindful of the reproductive function of sex, because extramarital affairs with female prostitutes can produce offspring, however unwelcome. Such affairs are not contrary to the natural purpose of the sexual act, as sterile same-sex activity would be. Introduced obliquely, as a stratagem for convincing the citizen body that homoerotic relations are improper, the objective of siring legitimate children and *only* legitimate children now assumes controlling importance for determining not only the moral quality of a sex act but also, when flagrantly transgressed, the civic standing of the man who has performed it. Belief that the state has a paramount interest in promoting lawful pregnancies while discouraging non-reproductive sex is also affirmed in a second passage of the Pythagorean treatise *On the Nature of the Universe*: "Those who have intercourse with absolutely no intent of creating children commit injustice against the most venerable institutions of society" (4.4). Whether Plato or Pythagoras took the first step, the line dividing the legislative assembly from the bedroom, and from the intentions of those in bed, has been crossed.

Even if the Greek text is occasionally unclear, Plato's import is certain. His belief in *erôs* as a theoretical force for good does not appear to have changed. As he did in the *Phaedrus*, he draws a sharp distinction between feeling or affect toward another human being, which, if unselfish and governed by reason, can lead to virtue (837c), and carnal intercourse with its attendant, all too seductive pleasure. Genital acts between members of the same sex are wrong, he contends, because they afford gratification while impeding the procreative ends to which such pleasure has been attached as an inducement. Plato's line of reasoning starts from the premise that in nature certain measures exist to bring about certain results. This teleological, or end-directed, conception of the material order logically assumes a divine arranger or demiurge that has rationally structured nature so as to fit ends to means. There is an obvious problem as to whether that notion of *physis*, with its latent teleological and theological import, can properly be mapped onto the scientific concept of an evolutionary process driven by the Darwinian principle of natural selection. To say, then, that Plato regarded same-sex *intercourse* (always carefully distinguished from affect) as "contrary to nature" is true enough, but it is a statement that first requires clarification of what the term "nature" means.

Safe Sex

Forced to deal with the momentous changes that transformed Greek society during the fourth and early third centuries, many educated men and a few women sought to develop emotional self-sufficiency through philosophic exercises. Facing threats of war and internal social unrest, instability of wealth and position, and an awareness of themselves as subject to the whims of the goddess Fortune (*Tychê*), they endeavored to form habits of mind enabling them to transcend pain and anxiety and attain private tranquility. Martha Nussbaum has conveniently labeled this enterprise a "therapy of desire," since it adapted a medical model: "Philosophy heals human diseases, diseases produced by false beliefs" (1994: 14). Desire for any number of transient and manifestly unnecessary goods – wealth, power, success – was condemned as a source of mental disturbance, and the philosophic "patient" was taught to look upon such worldly things with indifference. "Living in accordance with nature" became the wise man's aim. Again, much of the force of that precept depends upon the way in which the concept "nature," *physis*, was interpreted. **Cynicism**, a radical movement that arose in the early fourth century, carried the directive to an extreme. Adopting a symbolic uniform of traveling cloak, staff, and knapsack containing all their possessions, its adherents stridently promoted asceticism, poverty, contempt for authority, rejection of the forms of civic life, and disdain for shame and social constraints, which they said inhibited natural instinct. The most notorious Cynic, Diogenes of Sinope, earned the movement its name by relieving his bodily urges with no more self-consciousness than a dog (*kuôn*), ostentatiously defecating and masturbating in public.

Throughout this period Athens maintained its prominence as a center of intellectual activity. Plato had set up the Academy, a "think-tank" for philosophy, and after his death it continued in operation under a long line of successors. Aristotle, who studied at the Academy as a young man, returned to Athens in 335 BCE from Macedon, where he had served as tutor to Alexander, to establish his own school, the Lyceum. Taking advantage of its extensive library, his students embarked on investigative fieldwork and wrote numerous descriptive treatises in the areas of natural history and political science. Both institutions were perceived as breeding grounds of pro-Macedonian sentiment, however; during a brief period of restored popular rule in 307 BCE an attempt was made to ban the establishment of new schools of philosophy, but it was soon revoked. By the beginning of the third century, Zeno of Citium, the originator of Stoicism, and Epicurus of Samos, father of Epicureanism, had made reputations for themselves as lecturers at Athens, attracting many disciples. Their two philosophic foundations, respectively designated the Stoa and the Garden, came to dominate ancient intellectual life from that time forward until well into the imperial Roman era.

While both Stoicism and Epicureanism were comprehensive systems that provided ordered explanations of the workings of the universe, the foundations of human knowledge, and the place of divinity in the cosmos, each specialized in strategies for attaining happiness through rational victory over the passions and willing conformity with nature's laws. Sexual desire, a natural human appetite but also, when misdirected, a source of great psychic distraction, posed an obvious problem in any such ethical system. Depending upon circumstances, *erôs* was a force for both good and ill: it could heighten the lover's perception of self and others, impel him to generous acts of kindness, further the socialization of the young, and strengthen the bonds of community life, but it could also lead to madness, violence, and disregard for the well-being of the beloved (Nussbaum 2002: 60–65; Sihvola 2002: 201–2). Lovers who were themselves decent and altruistic might be hurt by the bad faith of their partner. Aristotle declares that the built-in asymmetry of the pederastic relationship generates unfortunate misunderstandings that subvert its goal of lifelong *philia* (*Eth. Nic.* 1164a.2–8):

> In erotic affairs the *erastês* sometimes charges that his excessive affection is not reciprocated – perhaps there is nothing lovable about him – and meanwhile the *erômenos* often complains that the other had formerly promised everything and now does not live up to his promises. Such things happen when the *erastês* befriends the *erômenos* seeking pleasure and the latter befriends the *erastês* for personal advantage, and neither one can supply what is expected.[15]

Elsewhere in the *Nichomachean Ethics* (1158a.10–13, 1171a.10–13), he defines *erôs* as "an excess [*hyperbolê*] of *philia*" directed to one person exclusively. Given Aristotle's preference for the mean, a notion of desire as excess does not augur well.

The cultural dilemma created by conceptualizing love as such an explosive blend of pleasure and danger, benefits and risk, gave rise to a multiplicity of possible solutions. Fifth-century oligarchic discourse on pederasty waxed enthusiastic about admiration of beauty and manly promise while mentioning copulation only in guarded terms. Plato contended in the *Phaedrus* that chaste passion for another could be a path to spiritual illumination for the couple, while in the *Symposium* the lover's moral ascent is effected through transference of desire to intangible abstract goods. All these approaches identify the affective component of *erôs* as advantageous, the carnal component as bad, or at least potentially injurious. Many Hellenistic thinkers approve a converse strategy: natural bodily impulse is not wrong, but the feelings attached to it can be destructive. Sex without *erôs*, or with a watered-down form of *erôs*, may be enjoyed; fixated passion is to be avoided at all costs.

We can begin with the Cynics Diogenes and Crates, whose positions may seem rather attractive after exposure to the Athenian Stranger's inflexibility. For a Cynic, nature is the only guide to virtue; society, populated by fools, is ridden with senseless prohibitions. While Diogenes practiced masturbation to show that the individual can satisfy his own desires without the help of others, he also advocated that women and children ought to be held in common, and that sexual union should be by mutual consent (Diog. Laert. 6.72). For him, boys and women were as morally capable as men of forming liaisons on the basis of rational choice. His doctrine of self-sufficiency did not mean living in isolation; rather, it enabled the wise man to contract free and independent associations with individuals of both sexes (Rist 1969: 71).

Diogenes refused to recognize marriage, along with other civic institutions, but his pupil Crates entered into an egalitarian marriage with Hipparchia, the sister of one of his students. Crates was ugly, says Diogenes Laertius, and when he exercised unclothed was laughed at (6.92). When he visited Hipparchia's brother, however, she fell in love with his precepts and way of life and threatened to kill herself if she could not marry him (6.96–8). Her parents, at a loss, asked Crates to discourage her. He removed all his clothing and, standing naked before her with cloak, staff, and knapsack lying beside him, said, "Here is your groom and his goods; think about it." Hipparchia agreed to be his partner, and from that time forward lived as he did, dressing in the same fashion, begging for subsistence, and preaching in the market-place. She even accompanied Crates to dinner and put up with coarse mockery from men who did not take her vocation seriously. We are told that the couple attempted to consummate their union in public (Apul. *Fl.* 14), a scandalous allegation, prob-ably untrue, but theoretically proper Cynic procedure. However much of this is romantic invention after the fact, in their own lives Crates and Hipparchia con-firmed the premise that a heterosexual relationship established by full mutual consent could be stable and enduring.

Zeno of Citium was a student of Crates. Stoic morality was shaped by the Cynic vision of living according to nature, which for Zeno was both the goal of life and the measure of virtue (Diog. Laert. 7.87). Reason (*logos*), the defining faculty of the human being, was an extension of the divine reason permeating the material order. Fate laid down the broad pattern of a human life – circumstances of birth, health, progeny, attainments and reversals, date of death – in keeping with a preordained design for the universe. Virtue consisted in voluntarily submitting to the divine plan, choosing things in accordance with nature and rejecting those that were not. Sexual pleasure was attached to behavior that conformed to the natural inclination of the human being. In early Stoic thought, furthermore, sexuality was not purely a bodily experience, for the genital function, like those of the eyes, ears, and other sense organs, was among the parts of the human soul presided over by reason (Gal. *PHP* 3.1.9–15, *SVF* 885). Contrary to Greek popular belief, then, sex was inherently rational and not morally questionable, provided that indulgence was regulated by the higher governing agency in the soul (Gaca 2003: 68–73).

Zeno's *Republic*, his own account of the well-structured state, has come down to us only in fragments, but we have many references to its provisions. Opponents of the Stoics singled it out for attack and later members of the school found it embar-rassing, partly because of its teaching on gender and sexuality. Zeno envisioned a community of the wise brought into accord by Eros, god of friendship and freedom: "Eros," he is reported as saying, "is the divinity who promotes the security of the city" (*ap.* Ath. 13.561c). That seems unexceptionable, except that the wise were expected to consort with the young, seeking out those whose appearance indicated a natural disposition to virtue (Diog. Laert. 7.129), and, through *erôs*, forming friendships, which might well include consensual sexual activity, to cultivate that potential for goodness. The lover was to maintain relations with a beloved until the latter reached the age of twenty-eight, an educational provision laid down because full moral development takes longer to achieve than physical maturity (Schofield 1991: 33–4).

Although his directives are couched in pederastic terms, Zeno's ideal state included female as well as male sages and doubtless allowed for homoerotic pair-bonding between women and girls as well as men and boys. As for heterosexual relationships, he endorsed the Cynic proposal, which drew upon Plato's *Republic*, for a community of wives – supposedly this would forestall jealousy arising from adultery – together with the claim that mutual consent, and *only* mutual consent, was necessary for a valid union. He also advocated unisex dress and exercise in the nude for both sexes (Diog. Laert. 7.33). Indeed, if human beings were to be sexually communal, even incest was permissible (*SVF* 3.753; cf. Gaca 2003: 81). But the Stoics denied that the *erôs* that imbued these civic relations was a passion, for they regarded passions as excessive, disobedient to reason, and contrary to nature (*SVF* 3.378). Passions were the result of mistaken judgments, and someone in the grip of obsessive *erôs*, such as Medea, would find herself in that predicament because she had formed false conclusions about what was required for her happiness. Hence there was one *erôs* for the wise and another for fools (Inwood 1997: 61–8). Later generations of Stoics repudiated Zeno's thinking on sex, gradually arriving, under the influence of upper-class Roman morality, at a position close to that of Plato's Athenian Stranger – permissible only in marriage, employed for procreation. Under its founder and his immediate successors, however, Stoicism came to terms with desire by subjecting it to the tempering effects of rationality.

Epicureanism, the other great Hellenistic belief system, denied the possibility of an afterlife and held that in this one pleasure is the supreme good: seeking pleasure and avoiding pain are natural human tendencies and essential for happiness. Yet Epicurus' definition of "pleasure" does not license unrestrained hedonism. Pleasures are divided into two sorts: the first a combined sense of mental ease (*ataraxia*) and general physical satisfaction; the second a more intense momentary gratification, physical or mental. The former is attained by the removal of pain. "The flesh," he says, "cries out not to be hungry, not to be thirsty, not to be cold. Whoever has these and expects to continue having them could match even Zeus in happiness" (*Sent. Vat.* 33).[16] If you are content with your situation once pain is taken away, desiring nothing further, that is enough for the good life. As for the temporary or "kinetic" pleasures – sipping a cold beer on a hot day, solving a tough math problem – they do not *increase* one's contentment if it exists already but just impart a passing buzz. The latter pleasures, furthermore, often bring pains in their wake (the hangover incumbent on the fifth cold beer), and the wise man should make a rational calculation about which pleasures can be indulged safely without accompanying pain. Desire for those bringing too much pain must be resisted. Sometimes, though, brief pain is wisely endured for the sake of the greater good (for example, the "A" on the test was worth the hours spent solving the math set). Thus Epicurus can assert in his *Letter* to his friend Menoeceus that "sound judgment [*phronêsis*] is more valuable than philosophy" (132).

While food, drink, and sleep are naturally pleasurable and also necessary for survival, sex, though equally natural, is not absolutely necessary. Sexual desire is aroused by a combination of visual stimulus and the physical accumulation of semen in the genitals (Plut. *Amat.* 766e). Being unnecessary, it is easily dispelled if not indulged (*RS* 26); the consequences of indulgence, on the other hand, can be severely painful. A probable excerpt from another of Epicurus' letters warns (*Sent. Vat.* 51):

> I hear from you that the movement of your flesh is too much inclined toward sexual intercourse. As long as you don't break the laws or disrupt well-established customs or cause grief to any of the neighbors or wear out your health or squander your basic goods, indulge your proclivity as you see fit. But it's actually impossible not to be constrained by one of these factors. For sex never does you any good, and you're lucky if it doesn't harm you.

This blunt declaration notwithstanding, there are indications that sex under proper circumstances could be part of the well-ordered Epicurean lifestyle. Gossip about scandalous goings-on among the master and those disciples who lived with him at his estate, the Garden (and who included women, as we will see), can be discounted: Epicureans were tempting targets of smear campaigns. On the other hand, Epicurus does name the pleasure of sexual intercourse, along with those of taste, smell, sound, and vision, among those that come first to mind as goods, adding that mental delight consists in the hope of enjoying them without pain (Cic. *Tusc.* 3.41). Sexual desire apparently can be gratified if its discomforts will be no worse than, say, those occasioned by walking a mile to a friend's house for dinner.

Nussbaum observes that the Garden, with its focus on individual happiness, offered "no strong positive motive for sexual activity," since marriage and child-rearing were very likely discouraged except under unusual circumstances (1994: 152–3). Yet Epicurus also made friendship, *philia*, central to the attainment of the good life and insisted that the wise man will endure pains and hardship, and may even sacrifice his life, for a friend's sake (*RS* 27; Diog. Laert. 10.120). It is conceivable, then, that a relationship of *philia* between man and youth, or man and woman, might include a sexual component, provided that both parties benefited from it and that such intimacy enhanced, rather than endangered, the good will and affection each felt for the other. What was indubitably bad, on the other hand, was *erôs*, which Epicurus defined as "an intense longing for sex accompanied by smarting and distress" (Us. 483). In a move analogous to that of Stoicism, he blamed the sorrows of passionate love on a false belief in the importance of the love object that had attached itself to the sexual impulse (Brown 1987: 112–15). The fundamental difference between the two systems is that the Stoics did originally leave room in the sage's life for a safe brand of vanilla sex. Epicurus suspected that sex, by its very nature, could hardly ever be safe.

Almost all of the philosophic schools and movements flourishing during this period attracted the occasional female student. The investment of time and money attached to a course of study, together with possible residency requirements, ensured that most women students would have been courtesans, although the famous Hipparchia was a girl of good family. Plato is reported to have taught two such women, one of whom dressed like a man (Diog. Laert. 3.46; *P Oxy.* 3656). We do not know the names of any early female Stoics, but, even after Zeno's radical position on sex was abandoned, his corollary tenet of equal education for women continued to be popular and was well received in Rome, where mothers were responsible for their sons' early education. So it is conceivable that some women may have attended the Stoa in Athens. Neo-Pythagoreanism flourished in southern Italy during the Hellenistic period; many of its adherents were respectable women. Several tracts, some purporting to have been composed by members of Pythagoras' family, counsel them on performing their domestic and religious duties. Correspondence going under the name of "Theano," the wife (or daughter) of Pythagoras, advises a mother to stop spoiling her children and preaches tough love (Pythag. *Ep.* 1.1, Thesleff 1965: 195–6). The treatise *On Female Harmony*, ascribed to "Perictione" (Plato's mother), instructs female readers in attaining a virtuous balance and order in the moral life that mirrors the harmonious order of the universe (Lambropoulou 1995: 124–5).[17] Finally, Epicurus' school attracted both courtesans, such as the prominent Leontion, and citizen wives of his followers. Like Epicurus himself, Leontion took up the stylus against a rival philosopher, attacking the views of Aristotle's successor Theophrastus. Though he denounces her for her audacity, a critic of Epicureanism in Cicero's *On the Nature of the Gods* concedes that she wrote polished Attic prose (1.93). Only the Lyceum seems to have excluded women, and the probable reason is that its founder considered them incapable of practical wisdom (Nussbaum 1994: 54). If a delegation of major Hellenistic thinkers were to visit a college classroom, then, Aristotle would be the only one surprised to see women studying alongside men. Zeno, noting the identical T-shirts and jeans on both sexes and the backpacks, reminiscent of Cynic knapsacks, beside the desks, would probably think Utopia had arrived.

Athenian Idol

Apart from seeking answers to her own doubts about life, a successful *hetaira* could have sound business reasons for taking up philosophy. Wealthy and educated clients might enjoy discussing serious intellectual matters over the wine. Accordingly, the grammarian Myrtilus of Thessaly, one of the learned participants in Athenaeus' second-century CE dialogue *Deipnosophistae*, tells us that in Hellenistic Athens there were "*hetairai* who put on airs, embracing education and allotting their time to lessons; for that reason they were also quick at responding to objections" (13.583f).[18] He goes on to recount an anecdote about Stilpo, a sophist, who accused the courtesan Glycera of ruining young men. "We're both guilty of that," she replied. "Your students are hair-splitting fakes, mine are rakes. Whether you or I ruin them makes no difference."[19] This apocryphal story, in which the "bad girl," with her quick repartee, scores one against the smug professor, illustrates what has been called the "discourse on prostitutes" of the fourth and following centuries (Henry 1995: 58). During that era the imaginary whore acquires a heart of gold and the doings of the real-life courtesan are recorded for posterity.

In earlier Greek literature fictional *hetairai* are paid relatively scant attention, almost all of it negative. Portrayals of girlfriends in sympotic lyric are at best ambivalent, and in the iambic verse of Archilochus and Hipponax the prostitute is inevitably characterized as greedy, deceitful, drunken, and lecherous. *Hetairai*, nude or suggestively dressed, are brought on stage in most of Aristophanes' plays simply as mute props to the dramatic action. His *Assemblywomen* of 392 BCE, however, contains a climactic scene in which four whores, one a pretty girl, the others old and horrendously ugly, argue over sexual rights to the young woman's suitor (877–1111). Similarly, an elderly courtesan who keeps a boyfriend has a lengthy part (950–1094, 1197–203) in his last play, *Wealth*. Abuse of the aging prostitute, already a well-worn iambic motif, receives its fullest surviving dramatic treatment in these two episodes, which in their deployment of the *hetaira* as speaking character simultaneously look forward to later developments in comedy.

Middle Comedy, produced in Athens from approximately 390 to 320 BCE, moves the courtesan even closer to stage center (Henry 1985: 33–40). No complete example of this kind of drama has come down to us, but the titles and abundant fragments indicate that she was often a principal figure. Many plays bore the names of fictive or real *hetairai* (Ath. 13.567c), and, though quotations tell us very little, it is a reasonable inference that an individual who gives her name to a play must have been featured in it (Webster 1953: 22–3). Mythological comedy was in vogue and other titles (*Circe, Calypso*) indicate that the *hetaira* was likened to a legendary enchantress. Thus courtesans continued to be portrayed as rapacious and dishonest: Alexis, a leading dramatist of the period, has one of his characters describe in detail the various tricks by which they alter their appearance, including high heels, padding, and makeup (*ap.* Ath. 13.568a–d). At this time, though, two new stock characters are introduced – the youth who defends the virtues of his mistress and the decent girl he loves, who is contrasted with "*hetairai* who spoil the fair name of 'companion' by their conduct" (Antiph. *ap.* Ath. 13.572a). At the end of the play these young women will be recognized as marriageable citizens.

Menander is our only extant representative of New Comedy, which converted the farcical sex-scenarios of the mid-fourth century into character-driven plots set in domestic surroundings. His dramas ring changes on a basic situation in which some obstacle preventing the young hero's union with the girl he loves is removed, usually through an intrigue or a timely revelation of identity. Within that framework, Menander can probe latent strains in familial ideology, often with great finesse. He employs the concubine, whose status is halfway between wife and *hetaira*, to explore those two polarized constructs of "woman" (Konstan 1993). In the *Samia*, he provides us with an unsettling reminder of how tenuous the position of concubine was and how bleak the future might be for those at the bottom of the courtesan class. Returning from a long trip, Demeas, a middle-aged Athenian bachelor, erroneously jumps to the conclusion that his *pallakê* Chrysis, a former prostitute and the "Samian woman" of the title, has seduced his adopted son Moschion and borne

Moschion's child. Outraged, he throws Chrysis and the infant out of the house, cruelly warning her about how she will have to gain her living henceforward (392–6):

> ... earning only ten drachmas,
> girls like you run to dinner-parties and drink wine
> neat until they die, or they starve when they
> don't do these things readily and quickly ...

Happily, Demeas learns that the child is really Moschion's son by Plangon, his next-door neighbor's daughter and the young man's fiancée. Pretending it was a foundling, Chrysis had generously taken the baby in to save a respectable girl's reputation. Although the ending of the play is missing, we can assume that she and Demeas were reconciled. As in several of Menander's other comedies, the actions of a presumed female outsider help to resolve the comic dilemma and restore the unity of the *oikos* (Henry 1985: 112–15).

Thus the fictive stereotype of the *hetaira* becomes more attractive as the Hellenistic era goes on, perhaps because her displaced status evokes the political vulnerability felt by Athenians subject to Macedonian hegemony. Corollary to this development, authors start to indulge a prurient curiosity about the doings of real-life *hetairai*. The trend apparently begins with portrayals of Aspasia by Socrates' former students. Dialogues written by these men, not just Plato and Xenophon but lesser figures such as Antisthenes and Aeschines of Sphettos, use a sensationalized Aspasia – brothel-keeper, counselor to Socrates, expert on love – to advance political and philosophic agendas (Henry 1995: 29–56). For example, Aeschines may have anticipated the new Hellenistic concentration on affective relations within marriage by making his Aspasia wisely endorse mutual *erôs* as a path to virtue for both spouses (Cic. *Inv. rhet.* 1.31.51–2). Although these treatises deploy Aspasia for argumentative purposes and do not purport to tell her life story, they induce readers to speculate about the woman behind the myth.

Apart from Aspasia, who was attacked because of her connection with Pericles (and who may not even have been a *hetaira*), actual courtesans are not often mentioned in Old Comedy. Only three turn up in Aristophanes – Cyrene in *Women at the Thesmophoria* (98) and *Frogs* (1327–8); Cynna in *Wasps* (1032) and *Peace* (755); Salabaccho in *Women at the Thesmophoria* (805); and Cynna and Salabaccho together in *Knights* (763–6). Like Aspasia, they are targeted because of the man whose name is coupled with theirs. Postclassical comedy, however, indulges in lengthy personal attacks on the *hetaira* herself. Several plays bear the names of living women; there were, for example, two dramas entitled *Neaira*, one by Philemon and another by Timocles, which talked about the wealth of Phryne, a younger member of the profession (Ath. 13.567e, 591d).[20] After assailing *hetairai* as a class, a character in Anaxilas' *Neottis* ("Chick," another prostitute name, but probably fictitious) compares them individually to fabled monsters (*ap.* Ath. 13.558a–e):

> Looking at them from the beginning, we can start with Plangon,
> who, just like the Chimaera, assaults barbarians with fire,

but one horseman by himself took away her living,
for he left her house hauling all her furniture with him.
Next, aren't the friends of Sinope now consorting with a Hydra?
She's an old hag herself, but Gnathaena has sprung up near her,
so, when they've got free of the one, there's another twice as bad.

In this passage (which continues with several other comparisons in the same vein), Anaxilas fits current rumors into mythic paradigms. The fire-breathing Chimaera preyed on Asiatic foreigners; Plangon, who does the same thing, was robbed by a Bellerophon in the person of an anonymous cavalry officer. Sinope's lovers, thinking themselves free of her, now have to deal with her neighbor Gnathaena – like Heracles, they are faced with two hydra-heads where one grew previously. Malicious humor of this stripe, which was directed in Old Comedy against leading political and intellectual figures, indicates that courtesans had attained an equivalent celebrity, for it is based on titillating gossip that must have been in fairly wide circulation.

Forensic speeches were doubtless a source of such gossip. Neaera's case was one of several in which courtesans supposedly appeared as defendants, the two most famous being Aspasia's prosecution by the comic poet Hermippus on the double charge of irreverence toward the gods and procuring free women for Pericles (Plut. *Per.* 32.1) and Phryne's indictment for impiety in introducing a foreign cult. Hyperides, who defended Phryne (and reportedly won his case by baring her breasts to the jury, Ath. 13.590d–e) composed two speeches against another *hetaira*, Aristagora (Ath. 13.586a, 587d, 588c). However, it is debatable whether some trials actually happened; Aspasia's court appearance may have been an incident in a comedy by Hermippus (Dover 1988: 138; Henry 1995: 15–16, 24–5), and lost speeches supposed to have been delivered by prosecutors in the legal action against Phryne were most likely composed as rhetorical exercises (McClure 2003: 41). Still, there are enough passing references to notorious women in extant orations (for example, Dem. 22.56; Hyp. 5.1–5) to give us a good idea of how stories that originated as details of an accusation took on a life of their own. Indeed, the basic facts of Neaera's life presented by Apollodorus resurface in Myrtilus' disquisition on harlots (Ath. 13.593f–594a).

Anecdotes of famous prostitutes invaded sober genres such as history and biography, thanks to the eminence of their reputed clients – painters and writers, orators, philosophers, even kings. The legend that Thaïs, an Athenian courtesan and mistress of Alexander the Great's general Ptolemy, instigated the wanton burning of Persepolis at one of Alexander's drunken banquets was disputed even in antiquity (Plut. *Alex.* 38), but it nevertheless set the tone for later stories about the dissolute behavior of monarchs. Demetrius Poliorcetes, ruler of Macedon from 294 to 287 BCE, was closely associated with several *megalomisthoi*, including Leaena, Lamia, Mania, and Myrrhine (Machon 168–87, 226–30 in Gow 1965; Ath. 13.593a). Ptolemy VIII Physcon, a later member of the Egyptian ruling dynasty, wrote *Memoirs* in which he included a catalogue of the female companions of his predecessor **Ptolemy II Philadelphus** (Ath. 13.576e–f). The presence of renowned *hetairai* at

Hellenistic courts can be explained partly as an offshoot of longstanding Eastern tradition and partly as one element in a larger influx of artists, physicians, and philosophers to those centers of leadership and patronage (McKechnie 1989: 153–4). Tales of their activities are highly embellished, however, for their mystique ensured that they would become "the objects of imaginative embroidery and indeed invention" (Ogden 1999: 218).

Many colorful stories, like the one of Stilpo and Glycera, take the form of a conversational exchange in which the heroine puts down a male lover or female rival with a smart retort. Ostensibly the courtesan appears to be celebrated for her sophisticated wit. The anecdotes, however, are free-floating; in the *Deipnosophistae*, where they are preserved, different sources attach the same story to different women. At 13.578e Myrtilus quotes Machon's account of Mania's coarse rejoinder to her colleague Gnathaena, but at 584c he cites Lynceus, who puts the same quip in the mouth of Gnathaena herself. These narratives, then, are stock ingredients of a sympotic oral tradition (McClure 2003: 45–6). Machon, the third-century playwright who collected them in his *Chreiae*, turned them into verse to help storytellers retain them in memory (Gow 1965: 23–4). Their original purpose, we can assume, was not to pay tribute to female cleverness. Instead, they appear to have a subversive content: accounts of prominent men being defeated in repartee or, like king Demetrius Poliorcetes, behaving grossly (Ath. 13.577d–f), encode popular Athenian resentment at the pretensions of its leaders. In these jokes, Kurke (2002: 62) argues, the democratic sympathizer is invited to identify with the *hetaira* who can have the last triumphant word because her marginalized position, as woman and sex-worker, paradoxically allows her to insult kings with impunity.

Epigrams, brief poems in elegiac couplets, were originally inscribed as commemorations on grave markers and votive offerings. During the Hellenistic period, literary epigrams became extremely popular. Convivial themes and settings indicate that many were first recited at symposia and afterward gathered into book form (Cameron 1995: 71–103; Gutzwiller 1998: 117). Imaginary courtesans were very much at home in this developing genre. Elements borrowed from comedy – lovers' conquests and complaints, praises of the beloved, and gibes at gluttonous, bibulous, or aging whores – recur in the epigrammatic collections of a host of third- to first-century BCE poets. Dedications in which a craftsman, upon retirement, offers his tools to his patron god furnished models for risqué takes on prostitutes "hanging up their spurs" (*Anth. Pal.* 5.202–3), an allusion to the exotic *kelês* or "racehorse" position in which the woman rode the man lying beneath her, and similar exercises in double-entendre.

Yet, because the epigram never completely lost its somber association with time and remembrance, the image of the fading courtesan could be imbued with pathos. Laïs of Corinth, whose glamour, distinguished clientele, and exorbitant fees were legendary (Sotion *ap.* Gell. *NA* 1.8), continued to practice her trade until relatively late in life ("relatively," in this context, might be her thirties). For this she became the butt of harsh jokes on the comic stage: Epicrates in his *Anti-Laïs* depicted her as alcoholic, starving, bent with age, and willing to do anything for cash (Ath. 13.570b–d).

In an epigram, however, whose author is unknown (antiquity falsely ascribed it to Plato), the same biographical circumstances are transformed into an object lesson in mutability (*Anth. Pal.* 6.1):

> I who laughed rudely at Hellas, I, Laïs, who once kept
>   a swarm of young lovers encircling my doors,
> to Aphrodite: this mirror, unwilling to see myself as I am,
>   unable to see myself as I formerly was.

Until the end of antiquity, the quatrain inspired follow-up poems (*Anth. Pal.* 6.18–20, 71; 7.218–20) that expanded its nuances. Laïs is a sharply poignant reminder of the human condition. Her arrogance, expressed in scornful laughter at the pleas of her suitors, has met due retribution, but any sense of triumph the reader might feel is cut short by the lapidary finality of the closing line. The mirror she dedicates will bear witness to the merciless contrast between the fragility of mortal endowments and the goddess's enduring beauty. Romanticizing the great femmes fatales of the past in this way was a trend that proved especially congenial to Roman love elegy, which in turn passed the practice on to medieval and Renaissance poets.

By the late third century BCE scholars were getting into the act. In Ptolemaic Alexandria, Aristophanes of Byzantium, director of the library associated with the ancient world's foremost academic institution, the Museum, was the first to compile a treatise *On the Courtesans of Athens* (Ath. 13.567a, 583d). It was probably an offshoot of his research on the plays of his namesake Aristophanes, since by this time readers needed help in identifying the persons referred to in Athenian comedy (Henry 1995: 61–3). Similar studies followed in its wake, adding to the list of 135 *hetairai* Aristophanes of Byzantium had come up with, providing biographical information and racy anecdotes, and attempting to distinguish persons with the same name. That was not easy, as most women used a sexy professional name (like porn stars), and some were given derogatory nicknames in addition (Ogden 1999: 247–52; McClure 2003: 63). Eventually much of this erudition found its way into the thirteenth book of the *Deipnosophistae*, where, along with representative snippets from lyric and elegiac poetry, oratory, history, and Middle and New Comedy, it reveals how much the stereotype of the courtesan, fictitious or real, intrigued the ancient male imagination.

Modern entertainers who become media icons frequently adopt controversial lifestyles or political stances. When cultural rifts intensify, these celebrities turn into lightning rods drawing the censure of unsympathetic factions. For devoted fans, though, the values they represent are as essential to their superstar personas as the entertainment they proffer. Historians and scholars of popular culture can therefore analyze the careers of such figures to determine what broader cultural currents swelled their popularity. In the Hellenistic age, the courtesan performed an analogous symbolic function, for her image as fantasy object of desire was dense with reflections of social malaise. Coming from abroad, possibly as far away as Asia, she displayed a lack of roots indicative of the widespread blurring of geographical and other boundaries. Condemnation of her greed, which consumed inheritances, expressed anxiety over economic disruptions and bitterness about wealth falling into the hands of the undeserving. As the personification of vice who undercut the moralizing of poets and philosophers and the social outcast who might exercise influence over monarchs, she illustrated how conventional standards of decorum had been relaxed, furthering the suspicion that the good citizen was adrift in an unprincipled world. Finally, the man able to keep such an embodiment of conspicuous consumption implicitly boasted of the large gap between his resources and those of the masses (Ogden 1999: 268–9). That adventuresses, however gorgeous in fact or fancy, could become such pivotal figures in the serious discourses of the time is symptomatic of an ongoing crisis of cultural belief.

Conclusion

From the archaic to the late classical era, discourse on sexuality in ancient Greece – itself largely a discourse on sexuality in upper-class Athens – had dealt for the most part with the ethical issues surrounding pederasty. Heterosexual relations, whether for pleasure or procreation, caused little concern. Involvements with *hetairai* created no difficulty unless indulged in to excess. Buttressed by social and political institutions, marital relations, though essential for the continuity of families, were not regarded as problematic in themselves. The major threat to the stability of the *oikos* raised in prescriptive texts was the wife's infidelity, with its consequent risk of contaminating the paternal bloodline. *Sôphrosynê*, which encompassed such a range of meanings when applied to the moral disposition of an adult man, was therefore all but synonymous with chastity when applied to a woman. Xenophon is the only classical author to propose that the ideal partnership of husband and wife requires more than the wife's continence.

Starting in the early Hellenistic age, however, dealings between the sexes grew more complicated. The Macedonian conquest of Egypt, the Eastern Mediterranean, and the Middle East gave rise to a diaspora as mainland Greeks, for the most part male, sought fortunes elsewhere, abandoning old ties. Greater access to education and control over wealth allowed women to participate more visibly in the public sphere. Fixed assumptions about gender came under interrogation as medical discourse found a scientific basis for assimilating women's bodies to those of men. The emotional texture of the marriage bond became denser because it was invested with expectations of companionship and mutual satisfaction. Under the growing influence of Pythagoreanism, moralists encouraged husbands to display respect for their wives, avoiding extramarital affairs as one token of that respect. Changes in women's status created anxieties over maintaining conventional roles within marriage; Menander's characters complain bitterly about well-dowered wives who wear the pants in the family. Philosophers meanwhile warned their followers of the dangers of *erôs* and the risks to self-sufficiency involved in rearing children, who were so vulnerable to misfortune. Celibacy, with sex confined to ephemeral liaisons, was the lifestyle option envisioned for the wise man. At the same time, the courtesan was elevated to an international celebrity, denounced for her greed yet simultaneously idolized for her wit, her beauty, and her ability to charm kings. Thus the expanding world of Hellenistic Greece was witnessing subtle transformations in gender roles both in and out of marriage. Not surprisingly, as we will see in the next chapter, visual art and literature exhibit a corresponding attraction to the feminine.

Discussion Prompts

1. For centuries after his death, fabulous tales of Alexander's further adventures, in which he combines the roles of king, explorer, and magician, circulated orally and in written form among the very peoples he had invaded. Under the modern title of the *Alexander Romance*, these legends are now studied by experts on ancient fiction as prime evidence for the process whereby fact is converted into myth. What particular aspects of Alexander's life and character might have encouraged his transformation into a folk hero?

2. Feminist historians of medicine have demonstrated how nineteenth-century medical beliefs about the limited physiological and mental capacities of women helped to justify denying them access to certain benefits (e.g., the notion that educating a girl would make her less disposed to bear and rear children properly). How did Hippocratic concepts of female physiology reinforce such social practices as early marriage? Does Aristotle's denial of the female partner's contribution to the heredity of the infant potentially weaken the bond of mother and child?

3. While the patriarchal family structure in the Athenian Stranger's hypothetical state of Magnesia resembles arrangements in Xenophon's *On Household Management*, state policing of marital relations and production of children would mean that little concession was made to the traditional privacy and autonomy of the Athenian *oikos*. How might continued oversight by the authorities affect interpersonal relations between Magnesian spouses and among couples and their children?

4. Stories linking Hellenistic kings with prominent courtesans reflect the deeply ingrained Greek association of absolute power with lack of self-mastery: leaders "enslaved" by such women were at the mercy of their passions and therefore unfit to rule. Does this factor add to or detract from the courtesan's allure?

Notes

1 A case in point is the independent kingdom of Bactria, situated in what is now modern Afghanistan, which during the third and second centuries BCE was ruled by Macedonian monarchs. At Aï Khanum, north of Kabul, provisionally identified with the ancient Alexandria Oxiana, archaeologists have found extensive Greek ruins, including a theater, a gymnasium, and a palace complex with a funerary shrine. The latter contained a pillar inscribed with a collection of some 140 Greek maxims from Delphi copied and brought to Aï Khanum by the

philosopher Clearchus of Soli, a pupil of Aristotle (L. Robert, *CR Acad. Inscr.* [1968] 422–57; see Walbank 1981: 60–1).

2   Philip, according to Demosthenes, his zealous Athenian adversary, was "not only not Greek nor related to the Greeks in any way, nor yet a barbarian from a place worthy of mention, but a pestilent native of Macedon, a place where in the past one couldn't buy even a serviceable slave" (Dem. 9.31). Debate over ancient Macedonian ethnicity, still an unresolved scholarly matter (Borza 1990: 77–97; Engels 2010), flared up as a geopolitical issue in the 1990s when the state of Macedonia, formerly part of Yugoslavia, declared itself the "Republic of Macedonia" and adopted the "Star of Vergina," the royal emblem of ancient Macedon, and the figure of Alexander the Great as cultural tokens. Greek nationalists fiercely challenged what they regarded as the illicit appropriation of the Hellenic patrimony by a Slavic people. Even today the very use of the name "Macedonia" continues to be disputed in the courts and occasionally on the streets. Danforth 2010 gives an anthropologist's balanced explanation of the controversy. This is another example of the way questions more than two millennia old, like Plato's view of same-sex intercourse, can explode anew. Throughout this section I purposely refer to Alexander's homeland as "Macedon," not "Macedonia."

3   Pomeroy (1997: 108–14) discusses the appearance of funerary foundations beginning in the late fourth century. As described in inscriptions, the wealthy set up funds to ensure that offerings for the dead would continue to be made for their ancestors and themselves. This had not been the practice earlier because parents could assume that their children would perform due rites.

4   For popular reaction, see materials collected by Tim Spalding and posted on www.isidore-of-seville.com/alexander/14.html#Isthemovieanti-gay? (accessed August 8, 2011).

5   Alexander himself had a special designation for Hephaestion: in contrast to the formal term *philobasileus*, "friend of the king," he was *philalexandros*, "friend of Alexander" (Diod. Sic. 17.114, Plut. *Alex.* 47.5).

6   The historical reality of their affair and the child it produced have been doubted for no satisfactory reason (see Brunt 1975).

7   Malaria and typhus are the favorite candidates for Alexander's fatal illness nowadays, though stories of poisoning, inevitable under the circumstances, have been given serious scholarly consideration (Bosworth 1971).

8   Although Hippocratic sources make no overt mention of such a tube, its existence can be inferred from discussions of female pathology (King 1998: 27–8).

9   In mythology, Gaia engenders her own consort Ouranos (Hes. *Theog.* 126–28), and Hera, piqued at Zeus, independently brings forth Hephaestus and Typhon (ibid., 927–28; *Hymn. Hom. Ap.* 307–52).

10   Hippolytus, an early third-century CE Christian bishop (his name is pure coincidence), who attempted to discredit the heresies of his own time by assimilating them to the teachings of early Greek philosophers, asserts that the fifth-century BCE poet and mystic Empedocles denounced marriage and all sexual relations because immortal souls are thereby entrapped in flesh (*Haer.* 7.29–30). Dodds (1957: 154–5) accepts this testimony, but Zuntz (1971: 261 n.1) pronounces it tendentious. In the surviving fragments of Empedocles there are no explicit moral pronouncements.

11   Much information about Pythagoras' circle at Croton comes from relatively late texts – second- and third-century CE compilations by Diogenes Laertius, Porphyry, and Iamblichus – and may therefore be inaccurate; on the source problems, see Burkert (1972: 97–109). Philip (1966: 138–46) argues that the notion of a religious community is anachronistic, and Pythagoras' followers were more likely a political group. However, Plato (*Resp.* 600b) can already single out Pythagoreans of his day as pursuing a distinctive "Pythagorean manner of life" that marks them out from ordinary Greeks.

12   Although Burkert is speaking of Pythagorean science, he succinctly expresses this dilemma: "The true problem of the Pythagorean tradition lies in Platonism, for Platonizing interpretation took the place of historical reality" (1972: 92).

13   The singular noun *tolmêma*, which Saunders (1970) renders in the plural as "crimes" and I deliberately weaken into the colorless term "act," became, you recall, a point of controversy in *Evans* v. *Romer*. It is derived from the verb *tolmaô*, which has a range of meanings both

positive and negative: to dare or risk something, to endure harsh circumstances, to behave rashly, boldly, shamelessly. While Plato uses the verb well over a hundred times, always denoting bold or daring action, this is the sole occurrence of the noun (Moore 2005: 179–80). Rist thinks some measure of blame should be attached to *tolmêma*, but the exact degree is uncertain (1997: 74). I will refrain from committing myself to any one meaning because that would obviously bias the discussion.

14   Gaca (2003: 94–116) identifies procreationism, the doctrine that one must confine sexual relations to the temperate and lawful reproduction of children, as a specific tenet of the early Pythagoreans, citing the Pythagorean belief that the soul must be guided into embodiment in an orderly and harmonious fashion. Thus Plato, in Gaca's view, is indebted to the Pythagoreans throughout this passage.

15   Similar gloomy observations occur at *Eth. Eud.* 1238b.32–9 and 1243b.15–20. On Aristotle's view of *erôs*, see Price (1989: 236–49) and Sihvola (2002).

16   Epicurus' gods, remote from human cares, enjoy perpetual *ataraxia*. Men cannot, of course, be certain that they will never again be hungry, or thirsty, or cold, but Epicurean teaching instills confidence in being psychologically equipped to surmount what pains may come (Rist 1972: 120).

17   Stob. 4.28.19 (=Thesleff 1965: 142–5). The entire text is conveniently available in Pomeroy (1975: 134–6 and 1984: 68–70).

18   In Athenaeus' *Deipnosophistae*, a group of intellectuals both invented and real – the physician Galen is among the guests – discuss the accoutrements of the symposium, like food, wine, types of vessels, and so on. The thirteenth book, concerning women, features a caustic argument between the Cynic philosopher Cynulcus, an advocate of pederasty, and Myrtilus, an authority on the great courtesans of the past. *Hetairai* are therefore described from conflicting perspectives: "[w]hereas the philosopher portrays them as physically repulsive, rapacious, deceitful, and of low status, the grammarian plays up their importance in shaping and transmitting the cultural legacy of Athens" (McClure 2003: 56). These are some of the things that the fourth-century BCE courtesan meant to Greeks living under the Roman empire. We will attempt to view her through the eyes of her contemporaries.

19   The Greek for what Stilpo teaches is *ta eristika sophismata*, literally "wrangling tactics," and what Glycera teaches is *ta erotika* [*sophismata*]. As McKechnie (1989: 150) notes, the pun had an added bite because the migrant lifestyles of philosophers and *hetairai* were so similar.

20   McClure (2003: 40) believes this play was produced after the trial of Neaera. As she was in her fifties and had been retired for some time, it probably did not cast her as a practicing courtesan; instead, it must have concentrated on the prosecution and its outcome. We would all like to know what happened to Neaera and Stephanus, so it is tempting to speculate that only a verdict of "innocent" would have provoked further comic attacks on her.

References

Adams, W. L. 1980. "The Royal Macedonian Tomb at Vergina: An Historical Interpretation." *Ancient World* 3: 67–72.

Alcock, S. E. 1993. *Graecia Capta: The Landscapes of Roman Greece*. Cambridge: Cambridge University Press.

Andronikos, M. 1984. *Vergina: The Royal Tombs and the Ancient City*. Athens: Ekdotike Athenon S.A.

Bartsiokas, A. 2000. "The Eye Injury of King Philip II and the Skeletal Evidence from the Royal Tomb II at Vergina." *Science* n.s. vol. 288, no. 5465 (April 21, 2000), 511–14.

Billows, R. 2003. "Cities." In A. Erskine (ed.), *A Companion to the Hellenistic World*. Oxford: Blackwell. 196–215.

Borza, E. N. 1990. *In the Shadow of Olympus: The Emergence of Macedon*. Princeton: Princeton University Press.

—— and Palagia, O. 2007. "The Chronology of the Macedonian Royal Tombs at Vergina." *Jahrbuch des Deutschen Archäologischen Instituts* 122: 81–125.

—— and Reames-Zimmerman, J. 2000. "Some New Thoughts on the Death of Alexander the Great." *Ancient World* 31.1: 22–30.

Bosworth, A. B. 1971. "The Death of Alexander the Great: Rumour and Propaganda." *Classical Quarterly* 21: 112–36.

Brown, R. D. 1987. *Lucretius on Love and Sex*. Leiden: E. J. Brill.

Brunt, P. A. 1975. "Alexander, Barsine, and Heracles." *Rivista di filologia e di instruzione classica* 103: 22–34.

Burkert, W. 1972. *Lore and Science in Ancient Pythagoreanism*. Trans. E. L. Minar, Jr. Cambridge, MA: Harvard University Press.

Cameron, A. 1995. *Callimachus and his Critics*. Princeton, NJ: Princeton University Press.

Carney, E. D. 1983. "Regicide in Macedonia." *Parola del Passato* 38: 260–72.

—— 1991. "The Female Burial in the Antechamber of Tomb II at Vergina." *Ancient World* 22: 17–26.

—— 1992. "Tomb I at Vergina and the Meaning of the Great Tumulus as a Historical Monument." *Archaeological News* 17: 1–10.

—— 2000. *Women and Monarchy in Macedonia*. Norman, OK: University of Oklahoma Press.

Cartledge, P. 2004. *Alexander the Great: The Hunt for a New Past*. Woodstock, NY, and New York: The Overlook Press.

Cherry, J. F. 2007. "Blockbuster! Museum Responses to Alexander the Great." In P. Cartledge and F. R. Greenland (eds.), *Responses to Oliver Stone's Alexander: Film, History, and Cultural Studies*. Madison, WI: The University of Wisconsin Press. 305–36.

Danforth, L. M. 2010. "Ancient Macedonia, Alexander the Great, and the Star or Sun of Vergina: National Symbols and the Conflict between Greece and the Republic of Macedonia." In J. Roisman and I. Worthington (eds.), *A Companion to Ancient Macedonia*. Oxford and Malden, MA: Wiley-Blackwell. 572–98.

Dean-Jones, L. A. 1992. "The Politics of Pleasure: Female Sexual Appetite in the Hippocratic Corpus." *Helios* 19: 72–91.

—— 1994. *Women's Bodies in Classical Greek Science*. Oxford: Clarendon Press.

Dodds, E. R. 1957. *The Greeks and the Irrational*. Boston: Beacon Press.

Dover, K. J. 1988. *The Greeks and their Legacy: Collected Papers, Volume II: Prose, Literature, History, Society, Transmission, Influence*. Oxford: Blackwell.

Engels, J. 2010. "Macedonians and Greeks." In Roisman and Worthington (eds.), *A Companion to Ancient Macedonia*. 81–98.

Gaca, K. L. 2003. *The Making of Fornication: Eros, Ethics, and Political Reform in Greek Philosophy and Early Christianity*. Berkeley, CA: University of California Press.

Gattinoni, F. L. 2010. "Cassander and the Legacy of Philip II and Alexander III in Diodorus' Library." In E. Carney and D. Ogden (eds.), *Philip II and Alexander the Great: Father and Son, Lives and Afterlives*. Oxford: Oxford University Press. 113–21.

Gow, A. S. F. (ed.). 1965. *Machon: The Fragments*. Cambridge: Cambridge University Press.

Green, P. 1990. *Alexander to Actium: The Historical Evolution of the Hellenistic Age*. Berkeley and Los Angeles: University of California Press.

Greenwalt, W. 1989. "Polygamy and Succession in Ancient Macedonia." *Arethusa* 22.1: 19–43.

Griffith, G. T. 1935. *Mercenaries of the Hellenistic World*. Cambridge: Cambridge University Press.

Gruen, E. S. 1993. "The Polis in the Hellenistic World." In R. M. Rosen and J. Farrell (eds.), *Nomodeiktes: Greek Studies in Honor of Martin Ostwald*. Ann Arbor: University of Michigan Press. 339–54.

Gutzwiller, K. 1998. *Poetic Garlands: Hellenistic Epigrams in Context*. Berkeley, CA: University of California Press.

Hanson, A. E. 1992. "Conception, Gestation, and the Origin of Female Nature in the *Corpus Hippocraticum*." *Helios* 19.1 and 2: 31–71.

Henry, M. M. 1985. *Menander's Courtesans and the Greek Comic Tradition*. Frankfurt am Main: Peter Lang.

—— 1995. *Prisoner of History: Aspasia of Miletus and her Biographical Tradition*. Oxford: Oxford University Press.

Holmes, B. 2010. *The Symptom and the Subject: The Emergence of the Physical Body in Ancient Greece*. Princeton: Princeton University Press.

Inwood, B. 1997. "'Why Do Fools Fall in Love?'" In R. Sorabji (ed.), *Aristotle and After*. London: Institute of Classical Studies. 55–69.

King, H. 1998. *Hippocrates' Woman: Reading the Female Body in Ancient Greece*. London: Routledge.

Kirk, G. S., Raven, J. E., and Schofield, M. 1983. *The Presocratic Philosophers: A Critical History with a Selection of Texts*. 2nd edn. Cambridge: Cambridge University Press.

Konstan, D. 1993. "The Young Concubine in Menandrian Comedy." In R. Scodel (ed.), *Theater and Society in the Classical World*. Ann Arbor: University of Michigan Press. 139–60.

Kron, U. 1996. "Priesthoods, Dedications and Euergetism: What Part Did Religion Play in the Political and Social Status of Greek Women?" In P. Hellström and B. Alroth (eds.), *Religion and Power in the Ancient Greek World: Proceedings of the Uppsala Symposium 1993*. Uppsala: Acta Universitatis Upsalensis. 139–82.

Kurke, L. 2002. "Gender, Politics and Subversion in the *Chreiai* of Machon." *Proceedings of the Cambridge Philological Society* 48: 20–65.

Lambropoulou, V. 1995. "Some Pythagorean Female Virtues." In R. Hawley and B. Levick (eds.), *Women in Antiquity: New Assessments*. London: Routledge. 122–34.

Lane Fox, R. 1974. *Alexander the Great*. New York: Dial Press.

Laqueur, T. 1990. *Making Sex: Body and Gender from the Greeks to Freud*. Cambridge, MA: Harvard University Press.

MacFarlane, P. 2010. "Health and Disease." In D. H. Garrison (ed.), *A Cultural History of the Human Body in Antiquity*. Oxford and New York: Berg. 45–66.

McClure, L. K. 2003. *Courtesans at Table: Gender and Greek Literary Culture in Athenaeus*. New York: Routledge.

McKechnie, P. 1989. *Outsiders in the Greek Cities in the Fourth Century BC*. London: Routledge.

Mitchell, L. 2007. "Born to Rule? Succession in the Argead Royal House." In W. Heckel, L. Tritle, and P. Wheatley (eds.), *Alexander's Empire: Formulation to Decay*. Claremont, CA: Regina Books. 61–74.

Moore, K. R. 2005. *Sex and the Second-Best City: Sex and Society in the* Laws *of Plato*. New York and London: Routledge.

Musgrave, J. H., Neave, R. A. H., and Prag, A. J. N. W. 1984. "The Skull from Tomb II at Vergina: King Philip II of Macedon." *Journal of Hellenic Studies* 104: 60–78.

Nikoloutsos, K. P. 2008. "The *Alexander* Bromance: Male Desire and Gender Fluidity in Oliver Stone's Historical Epic." *Helios* 35.2: 223–51.

Nussbaum, M. C. 1994. *The Therapy of Desire: Theory and Practice in Hellenistic Ethics*. Princeton, NJ: Princeton University Press.

—— 2002. "*Erôs* and Ethical Norms: Philosophers Respond to a Cultural Dilemma." In M. C. Nussbaum and J. Sihvola (eds.), *The Sleep of Reason: Erotic Experience and Sexual Ethics in Ancient Greece and Rome*. Chicago: University of Chicago Press. 55–94.

Nutton, V. 2004. *Ancient Medicine*. New York: Routledge.

Ogden, D. 1996. "Homosexuality and Warfare in Ancient Greece." In A. B. Lloyd (ed.), *Battle in Antiquity*. London: Duckworth. 107–68.

—— 1999. *Polygamy, Prostitutes and Death: The Hellenistic Dynasties*. London: Duckworth.

—— 2009. "Alexander's Sex Life." In W. Heckel and L. A. Tritle (eds.), *Alexander the Great: A New History*. Oxford and Malden, MA: Wiley-Blackwell. 203–17.

Palagia, O. 2000. "Hephaestion's Pyre and the Royal Hunt of Alexander." In A. B. Bosworth and E. J. Baynham (eds.), *Alexander the Great in Fact and Fiction*. Oxford and New York: Oxford University Press. 167–206.

Paul, J. 2007. "Oliver Stone's *Alexander* and the Cinematic Epic Tradition." In Cartledge and. Greenland (eds.), *Responses to Oliver Stone's Alexander*. 15–35.

Philip, J. A. 1966. *Pythagoras and Early Pythagoreanism*. Toronto: University of Toronto Press.

Pomeroy, S. B. 1975. *Goddesses, Whores, Wives, and Slaves: Women in Classical Antiquity*. New York: Schocken.

—— 1977. "TECHNIKAI KAI MOUSIKAI: The Education of Women in the Fourth Century and in the Hellenistic Period." *American Journal of Ancient History* 2: 51–68.

—— 1984. *Women in Hellenistic Egypt from Alexander to Cleopatra*. New York: Schocken.

—— 1997. *Families in Classical and Hellenistic Greece: Representations and Realities*. Oxford: Clarendon Press.

Pownall, F. 2007. "The Panhellenism of Isocrates." In Heckel, Tritle, and Wheatley (eds.), *Alexander's Empire*. 13–25.

Prag, A. J. N. W. 1990. "Reconstructing King Philip II: The 'Nice' Version." *American Journal of Archaeology* 94.2: 237–47.

Price, A. W. 1989. *Love and Friendship in Plato and Aristotle*. Oxford: Clarendon Press.

Reames-Zimmerman, J. 1999. "An Atypical Affair? Alexander the Great, Hephaistion, and the Nature of their Relationship." *Ancient History Bulletin* 13.3: 81–96.

—— 2001. "The Mourning of Alexander the Great." *Syllecta Classica* 12: 98–145.

Reger, G. 2003. "The Economy." In Erskine (ed.), *A Companion to the Hellenistic World*. 331–53.

Rist, J. M. 1969. *Stoic Philosophy*. Cambridge: Cambridge University Press.

—— 1972. *Epicurus: An Introduction*. Cambridge: Cambridge University Press.

—— 1997. "Plato and Professor Nussbaum on Acts 'Contrary to Nature'." In M. Joyal (ed.), *Studies in Plato and the Platonic Tradition: Essays Presented to John Whittaker*. Aldershot: Ashgate. 65–79.

Romm, J. 2007. "From Babylon to Baghdad: Teaching Alexander after 9/11." *Classical World* 100:4: 431–5.

Saunders, T. J., trans. 1970. *Plato: The Laws*. Harmondsworth: Penguin.

Schofield, M. 1991. *The Stoic Idea of the City*. Cambridge: Cambridge University Press.

Sihvola, J. 2002. "Aristotle on Sex and Love." In Nussbaum and Sihvola (eds.), *The Sleep of Reason*. 200–1.

Solomon, J. 2007. "The Popular Reception of *Alexander*." In Cartledge and Greenland (eds.), *Responses to Oliver Stone's Alexander*. 36–51.

Thesleff, H. (ed.). 1965. *The Pythagorean Texts of the Hellenistic Period*. Åbo: Åbo Akademi.

van Bremen, R. 1996. *The Limits of Participation: Women and Civic Life in the Greek East in the Hellenistic and Roman Periods*. Amsterdam: J. C. Gieben.

Walbank, F.W. 1981. *The Hellenistic World*. Cambridge, MA: Harvard University Press.

Webster, T. B. L. 1953. *Studies in Later Greek Comedy*. Manchester: Manchester University Press.

Wheatley, P. V. 1998. "The Date of Polyperchon's Invasion of Macedonia and Murder of Heracles." *Antichton* 32: 12–23.

Zuntz, G. 1971. *Persephone: Three Essays on Religion and Thought in Magna Graecia*. Oxford: Clarendon Press.

Further Reading

Carney, E. D. 2000. *Women and Monarchy in Macedonia*. Norman, OK: University of Oklahoma Press. Study of the dynastic roles of royal women at the Argead court of Macedon and the successor kingdoms, with biographies of all key female figures.

Cartledge, P. 2004. *Alexander the Great: The Hunt for a New Past*. Woodstock, NY, and New York: The Overlook Press. Among several recent biographies of Alexander, Cartledge's is recommended for its broad scope and its accessibility.

Green, P. 1990. *Alexander to Actium: The Historical Evolution of the Hellenistic Age*. Berkeley and Los Angeles: University of California Press. Comprehensive account of the Hellenistic world from 323 to 30 BCE, focusing on political, cultural, and intellectual developments.

Laqueur, T. 1990. *Making Sex: Body and Gender from the Greeks to Freud*. Cambridge, MA: Harvard University Press. Traces the impact of Galen's "one-sex" model of human biology on the Western medical tradition from the Renaissance to the Victorian period.

McClure, L. K. 2003. *Courtesans at Table: Gender and Greek Literary Culture in Athenaeus*. New York and London: Routledge. Discussion of the courtesan as cultural token in the Greek literary imagination, with particular emphasis on Athenaeus' *Deipnosophistae*.

Moore, K. R. 2005. *Sex and the Second-Best City: Sex and Society in the Laws of Plato*. New York and London: Routledge. Examination of the prescriptions on sexual behavior in the *Laws* in the light of recent work on ancient gender and sexuality.

Nussbaum, M. C. 1994. *The Therapy of Desire: Theory and Practice in Hellenistic Ethics*. Princeton, NJ: Princeton University Press. Analyzes the pragmatic approaches of Aristotle and the schools of Hellenistic philosophy to the individual achievement of psychological health and happiness.

Nutton, V. 2004. *Ancient Medicine*. New York and London: Routledge. Concise but informative survey of the history of ancient medicine from Homer to the seventh century CE.

6

The Later Hellenistic Period:
The Feminine Mystique

Heterosexual *erôs* served different goals during the classical and the Hellenistic eras. In the classical *polis* love between the sexes could be directed into stabilizing the marriage bond, but it was still inherently dangerous, threatening family and state, as the *Hippolytus* warns us. Among displaced and vulnerable individuals, however, in a world where family and state could no longer be taken for granted, romantic love helped overcome isolation. *Erôs* was still violent and disruptive, to be sure. Yet it could also underpin the individual alliances now filling the place previously occupied by sympotic associations, civic institutions, and kinship networks. In the Hellenistic world, Peter Green comments, "nothing so clearly symbolized the shift from public to private life, from civic involvement to personal self-absorption, from duty to hedonism, as the enhanced value placed, at all levels, on personal relationships" (1990: 388). Reflecting the disposition of its consumers, art therefore begins to explore the psychological nuances of encounters between men and women. In the visual arts, the feminine body receives increased attention as an object of aesthetic pleasure; in literature, female desire is now treated empathetically.

Previously the female figure had been, in general, discreetly draped. Naked women on Attic pottery are the exception that proves the rule, for they appear on sympotic ware and other vessels used only under special circumstances. Hellenistic painters and sculptors, however, appropriated the nude female figure for monumental public art and exploited its sensuous features. The first sculpted female nude, Praxiteles' **Aphrodite of Cnidus** (*c.*350 BCE), showing the goddess surprised in the act of bathing, became for the ancients a kind of erotic fetish. Poetry meanwhile seized upon *erôs* as a leading theme, though it distanced itself from sentimentality by also displaying a keen ironic awareness of the prior tradition of writing on *erôs* (Goldhill 1991: 261). Some literary texts still celebrated the charm of male adolescence, but even more paid homage to women's physical allure, praising the beauty of mature women as well as that of nubile girls. Compassionate depictions of women in love became a staple feature of Hellenistic literature.

On a less elevated plane, sex manuals geared exclusively toward male–female intercourse, providing advice on courtship but also explaining the various positions for coitus, came into fashion around this time (Parker 1992). Scholars generally assume that all such treatises (we know of several), were composed by men under female pseudonyms (West 1996: 20–1). To lend them more weight, the handbooks were attributed to practicing courtesans. The most infamous, scraps of which are preserved on papyrus (*P Oxy.* 2891), was supposedly written by the *hetaira* "Philaenis" but in actuality fabricated by a man, the sophist Polycrates of Athens (Aeschrion *ap.* Ath. 7.334b–e). Pretense of female authorship is not as remarkable as the sheer number of these guides to enjoyment: evidently there was an emerging market for them.

Even as the value of emotive heterosexual bonding increased, women's homoerotic desire, formerly ignored, was singled out for explicit censure. One exemplary case is the Hellenistic woman writer's passionate interest in close friendships with members of her own sex, which laid her open to reproach. Female *erôs* therefore continued to be viewed from a man's perspective; whether it was shown as positive or negative depended upon whether it was directed toward male gratification. In this chapter we will track the various changes in creative expression resulting from these large shifts in cultural sensibility.

Disrobing Aphrodite

When Socrates goes to visit the courtesan Theodote, he finds her posing for a painter, so that he and his friends have the opportunity to observe her closely (Xen. *Mem.* 3.11.2). Connections between artists and *hetairai* are well-attested, and in some cases we know the name of the woman who allegedly served as the model for a famous work of art. The classic instance is Phryne, so unconventionally defended by Hyperides at her trial for impiety, who is also said to have posed for both Apelles' painting of Aphrodite Anadyomene ("Aphrodite Rising from the Sea") and Praxiteles' marble Aphrodite of Cnidus (Ath. 13.590f–591a). The attention devoted to that statue in antiquity would have guaranteed Phryne a minor place in history had she never set foot in a courtroom.

It is obviously an exaggeration to say that the female nude did not appear in Greek art before the Hellenistic period. Archaic mirrors of Spartan manufacture – owned, of course, by women – have handles in the shape of naked girls (Stewart 1997: 108–18; Pomeroy 2002: 164–5). We have seen many representations of nude females, and not just *hetairai*, on Attic vases. Confined to pottery and household items, such figures were not on public view. However, the portrayal of females, otherwise clothed, with one or even both breasts exposed became a convention of monumental sculpture during the fifth century in scenes of violence such as the Centaurs' attempted rape of the Lapith maidens on the west pediment of the Temple of Zeus at Olympia or in portrayals of wounded Amazons or dying children of Niobe (Cohen 1997). At the same time, the "wet drapery" style, making its debut

Fig. 6.1   Praxiteles (*c*.400–330 BCE). Cnidian Venus. Roman copy after Greek original, (*c*.350–30 BCE). Location: Museo Pio Clementino, Vatican Museums, Vatican State. Source: Scala/Art Resource, NY.

on the east pediment of the Parthenon, produced the illusion of a thin, clinging veil and was designed to reveal the contours of the female body even while respecting the convention that only the youthful male form could appear nude in monumental art (Salomon 1997: 203; cf. Osborne 1994: 85–6). There was precedent, then, for sculptural studies of elements of the undraped female figure. Nevertheless, the iconography of Praxiteles' "Cnidia" must have been radically innovative.

Unfortunately, the original is lost (transported to Constantinople, it perished in a fire there in 476 CE) and the copies we possess, all Roman, differ from each other in significant respects. The "Colonna" version, found at Hadrian's Villa in Tivoli and now in the Vatican Museum (fig. 6.1), is assumed to be a fairly accurate replica (Havelock 1995: 11–13). Aphrodite stands in a contrapposto position, her weight on her right foot and her head inclined to the left. Her left hand grasps a cloth laid over the top of a *hydria*; the right hand is placed before her pubic area, "surreptitiously concealing her genitals," as one ancient reporter observed ([Luc.] *Am*. 13).

Discussing classic works of art in his encyclopedia of natural history, Pliny the Elder gives the impression that this treatment of Aphrodite stirred up controversy. Praxiteles, he says, carved two studies of the goddess, the other showing her traditionally draped; he offered both for the same price, and the citizens of Cos, who had the right of first refusal, preferred what seemed to them the wholesome one. The inhabitants of Cnidus, a maritime port on the Turkish coast, purchased the rejected piece, which eventually became a major tourist attraction (Plin. *HN* 36.20–21). However, we should not put too much faith in this anecdote: first, it follows a blue-print for stories about unwanted masterpieces that later achieved worldwide renown; and, second, it is much more likely that established artists worked on commission, creating their works on site and tailoring them to the specifications of their patrons. Designed for worship, Praxiteles' Aphrodite was a cult statue that arguably conformed to a local iconographic tradition of portraying fertility goddesses unclothed (Ridgeway 2001). If so, Aphrodite's gesture was a complicated one, combining both Greek and Near Eastern elements, and meant to celebrate her reproductive powers while at the same time screening her modesty (Havelock 1995: 36–7).

Whatever the original meaning of the sculpture, it was sometime later given a sensational re-reading in which the spectator was put in the position of intruding upon the goddess's privacy. Beginning in the first century BCE, epigrammatists wrote verses in which the sight of her own statue takes Aphrodite by surprise. One of the earliest, which we can cite for illustrative purposes, is ascribed to a Plato, naturally not the philosopher (*Anth. Pal.* 16.160):

> Cytherea, the Paphian, came through the billows to Cnidus,
>   wishing to view the image of herself.
> After studying it from every angle in its open shrine
>   she exclaimed, "Where did Praxiteles see me naked?"

For a mortal to look upon a divinity without permission is to invite a terrible retribution (Callim. *Hymn* 5.101–2). Actaeon is torn to pieces by his own hounds after he blunders upon Artemis bathing, and Tiresias loses his eyesight when he glimpses Athena under the same conditions. Praxiteles has not only beheld Aphrodite and escaped without paying the penalty, but has exposed her exactly as she appeared then to the gaze of others, proving himself "antiquity's most successful voyeur and simultaneously its most accomplished craftsman" (Stewart 1997: 104). Now the viewer who approaches the sculpture directly finds himself seeing what Praxiteles saw, and, though Aphrodite's head is turned aside, he (this viewer is by definition a "he") feels a twinge of anxiety when he imagines that she will shift her glance and notice him. The allure of the forbidden doubtless created a frisson that contributed to the image's erotic charge.

From the time of her manufacture and installation until close to the end of the Hellenistic period, neither art nor literature displays any awareness of the Cnidia. About 150 BCE a sudden flurry of interest arises, possibly because the statue had been placed in a more accessible setting where it was visible on all sides. In effect, it was "rediscovered" and converted into a popular icon. More or less faithful copies began to appear. Artists also started to produce a series of other nude or semi-nude Aphrodites inspired by the Cnidia, but varying her pose (Havelock 1995: 64–7, 69–101). Adaptations of Praxiteles' treatment include one in which the goddess assumes the so-called *pudica* or "modest" stance, using both hands to cover herself, her left hand masking her genital area and right arm raised to protect her breasts.

While the tilt of the head is not the same for each and the hair is styled differently, both the Capitoline Aphrodite in Rome and the Medici Aphrodite in Florence conform to this design. An even more suggestive statuette in the Metropolitan Museum of Art in New York (Salomon 1997: fig. 46) shows Aphrodite with one hand on her genital area, the other beside it, as she crouches and turns away fearfully. In such representations, she becomes the epitome of feminine vulnerability (1997: 208–9). These developments imply that the unclothed Aphrodite was conveying a double message: on the one hand, she represented the power and mystery of the sexual impulse, on the other the asymmetry in gender relations unmasked through exposure of women's nakedness.

Havelock argues that it was Roman patrons who were responsible for this new preoccupation with the nude female figure. She notes that peculiarly Roman cultural attitudes toward sex, as reflected in Latin love elegy, included a fascination with the female body as an object of voyeuristic pleasure and a tendency to romanticize the courtesan instead of investing her with political and social meanings. It was then, accordingly, that the torrid love affair of Praxiteles and Phryne was invented, which helped to explain the sensuous appeal of the statue by converting it into a testimonial to passion (1995: 134–6). Perhaps it was Roman sightseers who first turned the Cnidia into a fetish, but learned Greeks followed their lead. Handed down under the name of the essayist **Lucian**, the *Amores* or *Affairs of the Heart* is a discourse on love composed under the later Roman empire. It stages a dispute between an adherent of pederasty, Callicratidas, and a ladies' man, Charicles, over which is the better of the two erotic preferences. The preliminaries to this debate are of interest, as it is set in the precinct of Aphrodite's temple at Cnidus and sparked off by a visit to her shrine. The emotional response of the two adversaries gives us an insight into the powerful meanings attached to this figure in later antiquity.

Accompanying the narrator on a voyage, Charicles and Callicratidas disembark with him at Cnidus to see the statue, although Callicratidas goes along with his friends under protest, as he is not really interested in any image of a female ([Luc.] *Am.* 11). Passing through a luxuriant garden, they first view the sculpture from the front. Charicles is stunned by its beauty and reacts extravagantly, going so far in his admiration as to kiss it. The three then walk to the back of the precinct, enter by another door, and behold it from the rear. Now it is Callicratidas' turn to be overwhelmed as he inspects its "boyish parts," exclaiming over the proportions of the back, the rounding of the hips, and so on, while Charicles, no less impressed, stands frozen weeping (13–14). At that point the visitors notice a mark like a stain on one thigh. When the narrator supposes it a natural defect in the marble, the female attendant tells the visitors that it is instead a trace left by a young man who became obsessed with the statue, hid himself in the shrine overnight, and had sex with it; in punishment for this sacrilege, he afterward committed suicide (15–16). The anecdote is repeated in other sources, and, for all we know, might well have been a story told by tour guides on site; anyone who visits Pompeii is likely to hear even stranger things.

What is worth noting is the extent to which all parties concerned behave as though the Cnidia were not a mere sculpture, but partly a living woman, a courtesan with the magnetism of the famous Phryne, and partly an embodiment of Aphrodite.

Because the statue is the visual realization of a drive common to both men and women, even the confirmed boy-lover Callicratidas finds it arousing. Charicles is moved enough to express his feelings physically by kissing it, something he would not do if he saw it only as marble, but also something he would not dare to do if he felt Aphrodite was actually present within it. On the other hand, the youth who tragically falls in love with the effigy treats it as though it and the goddess are one and the same; that is why his *hybris* is penalized so drastically. This section of the *Amores* has the didactic cast of a fable, and it would be silly to think the conduct of any of the three men a genuine instance of ancient viewer response, but, for all its hyperbole, it assumes a perception of art dissimilar to that of modern viewers. We do not approach our own high-culture icons of sensual beauty, Botticelli's *Birth of Venus* or Michelangelo's *David*, in quite the same way. Otherwise museum guards would have their hands full.

Hellenes in Egypt

During the first two years of his Asian campaign (334–333 BCE), Alexander scored two impressive victories against the Persian army – at the river Granicus near the site of Troy and the following year at Issus in southern Anatolia. Instead of pursuing the defeated Darius, however, he then fought his way down the eastern coast of the Mediterranean all the way into Persian-occupied Egypt, where, in 332, he was welcomed as a liberator and crowned **Pharaoh**. This detour south fulfilled his promise to free Greeks under Persian rule while strategically securing his rear against a possible naval attack. But Alexander may have had personal motives as well: Vasunia (2001: 265–6) suggests that Greek discourses painting Egypt as a realm of wonders had cast their spell upon him. In Homer Egypt's wealth is proverbial (*Il.* 9.381–4; *Od.* 4.127); its soil also produces an impressive range of drugs, and its people are skilled in using them (*Od.* 4.226–32). Throughout his ethnography of the country in Book 2, the fifth-century historian Herodotus emphasizes its antiquity and its monuments, its great religious contributions and the learning of its priests. In the *Phaedrus* (274c–275b), Plato attributes the invention of writing to the Egyptian god Theuth (actually Thoth, patron of scribes). Two late dialogues, the *Timaeus* and the *Critias*, allege that the Athenian statesman Solon brought tales of the lost continent of Atlantis back to his countrymen after hearing them on a visit to Egypt (*Ti.* 20c–27b; *Criti.* 108e–109a, 113b–121c). These and other works of Greek literature in which Egypt was portrayed as a mysterious land of wealth and arcane wisdom generated an ideology that eventually justified its incorporation into a rising Macedonian world empire (Vasunia 2001: 286).

If Egypt was revered for its knowledge, however, it was also disturbingly alien. Herodotus observes that the Egyptians "have established for themselves customs and regulations for the most part contrary to those of all other human beings" (2.35). Their zoomorphic gods and absolute quasi-divine monarchs, their hieroglyphic writing system, their morbid fascination with death epitomized in the practice of mummification, had no analogues in Greek experience. Egypt's famed religiosity, moreover, was permeated with eroticism to an extent that outsiders may well have found troubling. Male sexual potency was viewed as the supreme regenerative force, renewing the physical world each day and actualizing the reanimated human spirit in the afterlife. That vital linkage of sexuality with rebirth was concretely expressed through cosmological and aetiological myths (Cooney 2008: 1–2). The oldest account of creation, devised by the priestly caste at Heliopolis, explained the physical world as coming into being through an act of masturbation performed by the primeval god Atum, from whose semen – swallowed, then spat or coughed out – the next generation of gods arose (Myśliwiec 2004: 5–8). The daily solar cycle involved the impregnation of Nut, the sky goddess, by her male child Re, the setting sun to whom she had given birth at dawn (Allen 1988: 1–7). Likewise, the regenerative power of the Nile flood was personified in the fertility god Hapi, who annually embraced and inseminated the land (Montserrat 1996: 16–17). Of all sacred tales, the most significant was that of **Osiris, Isis**, and their child **Horus**, retold at greatest length in Plutarch's Imperial-age philosophical treatise *On Isis and Osiris*. The plot centers upon the enmity of the brothers Seth and Osiris, the latter's murder and dismemberment, his sister-wife Isis' quest to find his body, the miraculous conception of Horus from Osiris' reinvigorated phallus, Horus' vengeance upon Seth, and Osiris' installation as judge in the next world. Insofar as each Pharaoh, being Horus' successor, held divine office in life and was revered as Osiris after death, this myth was foundational for the kingship. Osiris' resurrection also served as the basis for belief in personal immortality, for he was "the first to rise from the dead, who encompassed within himself every person buried with the proper ritual" (Morenz 1973: 210). Myths of origin thus promulgated the idea that "the universe came into being through autoeroticism and was sustained through sexuality" (Meskell 2002: 62).

Since the notion of rebirth in the hereafter was so fused with that of potency, Osiris and other male divinities were frequently represented with an erection (Myśliwiec 2004: 8–11). The most notable ithyphallic god was Min, emblem of vegetative fecundity, whose key attribute was lettuce, thought to be an aphrodisiac, and whose sacred animal was the bull (Watterson 1984: 187–9). Cult worship of Min, like that of Osiris, was charged with sexual symbolism. His annual festivals, and those of related fertility powers both male and female, were communal events at which participants might engage in sexual acts in order to share in the energy of the god (Montserrat 1996: 163–79). Music, singing, dancing, the sensuous appeal of perfumes, incense, and flowers, and enjoyment of food and drink in the company of an exhilarated crowd would all contribute to an atmosphere of heightened emotion where ordinary taboos were suspended (Meskell 2002: 168–77). Women, as we know from Herodotus, performed ritualized sexual gestures at such times. When journeying by boat to the festival of Bastet at Bubastis, the historian reports, some women play musical instruments or sing and clap, some shout abuse at female bystanders, others dance, still others "stand up and expose their reproductive organs" (2.60).[1] To Greeks, whose temple regulations often defined those having had recent intercourse as ritually impure (Cole 1992: 107–9), mixed-sex orgiastic gatherings in the name of religion confirmed suspicions that Egyptians, for all their putative wisdom, were a libidinous and disorderly people.[2]

Egyptian women's freedom to mingle with strangers at cult celebrations might startle foreigners as well. Such liberty reflected their greater legal and social privileges as compared with those of citizen women in classical Athens. To begin with, an adult Egyptian woman was a **"legal person,"** which means that she was recognized in law as competent to handle her own legal and financial affairs. Unlike Greek women, who needed a *kyrios* to represent them in court, she could act as plaintiff or defendant and testify as a witness (Robins 1993: 136). She also could inherit and manage property, both land and chattels, in her own right; run a small business; make a will and bequeath her goods to whomever she wished. By the same token, she was subject to the same criminal sanctions as men. On the other hand, as Robins (ibid.: 138–41) reminds us, women's legal rights may not have been honored in practice if they had no male protectors. Thus widows figure in texts and inscriptions as conspicuously vulnerable (Graves-Brown 2010: 71–2). Since scribal training was reserved for male members of the bureaucracy and priesthoods, very few women must have been literate. Funerary rites assumed the deceased was male; tombs were mostly owned by men, with women included in them only because of their familial relationship. Consequently, the position of women in dynastic Egypt, insofar as we can speak of them as a single group, was still a subordinate one. Nevertheless, exposure to indigenous gender structures did have an effect on interaction between the sexes among Greek expatriates, as the following passage seems to indicate.

Generalizing from a single case is always risky – remember that on future writing assignments – but can sometimes be allowed, given space constraints and a particularly apt illustration. My example is taken from **Theocritus'** *Idyll* 15, a dramatic skit in which Gorgo and Praxinoa, two wives originally from Syracuse in Sicily but now living in Alexandria with their husbands, go to the palace to view an exhibition in honor of Aphrodite and her mortal lover **Adonis** sponsored by the queen, Arsinoë II.[3] Getting there from their homes involves a harrowing push through city streets teeming with pedestrians and mounted guardsmen. At the palace gate someone steps on the hem of Praxinoa's summer wrap, and the following exchange takes place (70–5):

PRAXINOA: By Zeus, fellow, if you wish for good fortune, look out for my cloak.
FIRST STRANGER: It's not up to me, but nevertheless I'll take care.
PRAXINOA: What a dense mob! They're shoving like pigs.
FIRST STRANGER: Bear up, ma'am, we're all right now.
PRAXINOA: Forever and then some, friend, may *you* be all right for protecting us.
    What a helpful and courteous man!

Several lines later, a second stranger, hardly as nice, overhears the two women marveling at the effigy of Adonis and the tapestries surrounding it and ridicules their broad Dorian accents: "Wretches, stop that endless cooing." Praxinoa stands right up to him: "We're talking in Peloponnesian. It's legal, I suppose, for Dorians to speak Doric?" (87–95). Commentaries note that Theocritus, like his two female characters, was from Syracuse, a colony founded by Corinth in the Peloponnese, and that the entire dialogue, including the snide remark of the stranger, is in the

Doric dialect (Dover 1985 [1971]: 207). Dorians were proud of the way they spoke; no doubt the poet is making fun of the comments his own drawl may have elicited. It is intriguing, though, that he allows a respectable housewife to voice this defense publicly, and to an unknown male at that. Athenians of the classical period were suspicious of casual encounters between unrelated persons of opposite sexes. In Euripides' *Electra*, the old farmer who has married the heroine is upset to find her outside their cottage talking with a visitor – actually her brother Orestes in disguise, though neither knows that (343–4). The speaker in one of Lysias' orations complains that his opponent broke into his house, frightening his kinswomen, who, he alleges, have lived such orderly lives that they blush to be seen even by male relatives (3.6). While the latter claim is patently hyperbolic, and while classical Athenian notions of propriety may not have been shared by all Greeks, Praxinoa's readiness to confront men on the streets marks a real departure from previous gender etiquette. Might it be symptomatic of a general loosening of the rules brought on by the challenges of living abroad?

Greeks, chiefly mercenaries and traders, had of course been making their homes in Egypt for a long time. Evidence suggests that Mycenaean soldiers, ancestors of Homer's warriors, may have served in the army of the so-called "heretic" Pharaoh Akhenaten (Schofield and Parkinson 1994).[4] The earliest Hellenic outpost in the country was Naucratis, founded as a trading station on the Nile delta in the seventh century BCE (Hdt. 2.178–9; Str. 17.1.18; Hanrahan 1961a). During the following century rulers of the Saïte Dynasty relied on Greek troops as they pursued wars of aggression against Assyria and then attempted to stave off the growing power of Persia (Hdt. 2.147–82; Hanrahan 1961b: 41–2). Stephens calls attention to the population of "Hellenomemphites," assimilated Greeks dwelling in Memphis, the ancient Egyptian capital, and comments that by Herodotus' day residents in some areas were numerous enough to constitute "a visible economic group" (2003: 22–3).

However, the real expansion of a Greek presence began after Ptolemy, son of Lagos, one of Alexander's generals, who had been assigned Egypt to govern after Alexander's death, appropriated the territory for himself. He traveled from Babylon to Memphis accompanied by the king's embalmed body, which he had hijacked as the funeral cortege made its way slowly back to Macedon. Perdiccas, regent for the co-rulers Philip III Arrhidaeus and Alexander IV, attempted to retrieve it but was repulsed and killed by his own bodyguard (Str. 17.1.8; Paus. 1.6.3). Alexander's remains were enshrined first at Memphis and later, after the capital was moved to Alexandria, in a splendid tomb adjoining the royal palace (Diod. Sic. 18.28.3), which became a major tourist site until it was destroyed in late antiquity and its location forgotten (Chugg 2002).[5] Possession of the corpse legitimated Ptolemy's proclamation of himself in 304 BCE as monarch of an independent kingdom and successor to Alexander as Pharaoh (Erskine 2002: 173).

While Alexander's other former officers struggled for power in Macedon and the Near East, Ptolemy, now **Ptolemy I Soter**, avoided the worst of the bloodshed. As a precaution against invasion, though, he settled army reservists drawn from many Greek cities on crown land in the Fayum, a potentially rich agricultural area reclaimed from marshes (Walbank 1981: 108–10). This "new garden province," later renamed for Ptolemy II Philadelphus' queen Arsinoë, was soon bringing in huge revenues in the form of rents and taxes, contributing massively to the kingdom's wealth (Thompson 2003: 108–9). In assembling talent Soter was as successful as he was in recruiting mercenaries. Greeks with administrative abilities found desirable employment working alongside Egyptian officials in the complex bureaucracy (Stephens 2005: 229–30). At the same time the ruler set about making Alexandria a center of art and erudition and a magnet for scholars from all over the Greek world. In the vicinity of the palace he established a **Museum** or "Home of the Muses," modeled upon Aristotle's Lyceum in Athens, with its own research library nearby. Eminent scientists and men of letters were invited to reside at the Museum, supported by royal patronage and pursuing their academic projects at leisure. Not surprisingly, the offers were eagerly accepted. Under the early Ptolemies, scholarship, literature and science flourished; with one exception, all of the great names in those three areas belonged to Greek émigrés living in Alexandria (Fraser 1972: 1.52, 68–9). Today their intellectual products are collectively designated "**Alexandrian**," an adjective denoting not only a distinct geographical region and a time frame but also a profound shift in Greek mentalité.

Love among the Pyramids

Literary activity in the postclassical period was geared mainly toward a reading audience, and an extremely well-read audience at that. That does not mean that authors stopped producing texts for religious and secular performance. Choral hymns were often composed for festivals, and itinerant bards competed on a regular circuit of musical contests, singing hymns to local divinities, versifying regional legends, and praising the host city. Original comedies continued to be staged at Athens; mythological burlesques were all the rage in the Greek settlements along the Ionian coast in the extreme south of Italy, known as **Magna Graecia**; and a fragment of earthy popular mime, complete with stage directions, is preserved on an Egyptian papyrus (*P Oxy.* 413). Thus, recital before large groups of listeners still played an important part in the dissemination of literature. Nevertheless, the most influential artists of the time, those who frequented the courts of Ptolemy I Soter and his son Ptolemy II Philadelphus, essentially wrote for a coterie of skilled readers like themselves, scholar-poets who could recognize an obscure Homeric form of a verb or sense the nuances created by deft allusion to Hesiod, Sappho, or Pindar, who relished tales of the origin of strange foreign cults and little-known variants of traditional myths (Bing 2008: 37–47). In addition to self-conscious learning, stylistic polish and experimental narrative technique enhanced the works of the Alexandrian poets. All of those virtues – and they *are* virtues, despite the distaste for such "sterile pedantry" expressed by classicists of previous generations – are often put at the disposal of sentimental or lurid subject matter. When catastrophic passion is being described, the incongruity is disconcerting.

One of the first writers to benefit from royal patronage was the poet Philitas of Cos, who became tutor to the future Ptolemy II. Very little of Philitas' poetry survives, but what remains is recognizably erudite; later authors inform us that he wrote of unhappy love affairs both mythological (Parth. *Amat. narr.* 2) and personal (Ov. *Tr.* 1.6.2; *Pont.* 3.1.58). Since Philitas' influence on later poetry and also on the literary climate at the Museum is considerable (Fraser 1972: 1.309, 556), it is likely that his own compositions furnished models for the poets of the next generation. His pupil Hermesianax of Colophon included accounts of the cyclops Polyphemus' bizarre love for the sea-nymph Galatea (fr. 1 *Coll. Alex.*) and of incest and treason (Parth. *Amat. narr.* 5 and 22) in the first books of his elegiac poem *Leontion*. However, the third book of Hermesianax's poem – named, incidentally, after his mistress – contained a lengthy, tongue-in-cheek catalogue of poets and philosophers said to have endured the pains of unrequited love. Several pairings raise eyebrows: Hesiod was smitten by Ehoie,[6] Homer by Penelope, Socrates by Aspasia. Hermesianax even mentions that Philitas, his own former teacher, sang of "nimble Bittis" after wearing himself out compiling his definitive treatise explaining archaic Homeric words (Hermesian. fr. 7.75–78 *Coll. Alex.*).[7] Already the unlikely application of research to tales of romantic suffering can furnish material for sophisticated parody (Bing 1993).

Epigram, pastoral, narrative elegy, and epyllion, or short epic, were a few of the genres favored by the poets who worked at the Museum. All these productions are heavily imbued with themes of romantic love. One of the first kinds of verse to be practiced was erotic epigram, popular in Alexandria even before Ptolemy II succeeded to the throne (Fraser 1972: 1.556–7). Though doubtless declaimed at symposia, Hellenistic love epigram has unique features that distinguish it from the short sympotic elegies of the archaic period (Gutzwiller 1998: 118–20). Unlike elegy, which is structurally open-ended – one singer picking up the recitation from another – epigram is taut and conclusive, for the last line (as we saw in the Laïs quatrain) sums up the whole. Within the compass of one to four couplets, the lover's discourse constitutes a miniature dramatic performance. His words are usually directed either to himself, in a kind of interior monologue, or to his beloved. If the setting is sympotic (it need not be), no appeal is made to shared experience; instead, the speaker is psychologically divorced from his fellow drinkers, unable to join in their conviviality. Individual epigrams vividly realize discrete, transitory states of emotion, but nevertheless facets of a single coherent persona, whose subjectivity, projected by the author, is revealed in more depth as the recital proceeds or the scroll is unrolled. Lastly, erotic epigram is not didactic, as Theognis' "Cyrnus" elegies are; it does not present a moral lesson, but rather enacts a progression of feelings. Nevertheless, it does comment indirectly on the cultural climate in which it arose. "In a world lacking a civic and political center," Gutzwiller remarks, "the poetic ego who speaks in erotic epigram illustrates, through his constantly frustrated search for reciprocated affection, the perpetual estrangement of Hellenistic man" (1998: 120). Because epigram was such an expressive vehicle for verbalizing that alienation, its amatory topics continued to be worked and re-worked throughout the Hellenistic period, under Roman domination, and down into Byzantine times.

Skilled writers of epigram made use of its corpus of erotic motifs and images in different ways. **Asclepiades** of Samos, the inventor of the amatory epigram, speaks in the persona of an ardent young man (in *Anth. Pal.* 12.46 = GP 15, he says he is not yet twenty-two) who proclaims himself the sport of divine powers indifferent to human happiness. In the next generation, **Callimachus** of Cyrene, a name virtually synonymous with Alexandrian poetics, reacted against Asclepiades' pathos by fashioning pieces that chart the progression of thought as the speaker reflects with calm detachment upon his emotions (Walsh 1990, 1991). While Asclepiades focuses chiefly on relations with women and only secondarily on those with boys, Callimachus' poetry is wholly pederastic; it purposely evokes the sympotic elegies of the Theognidean corpus and the flowering of aristocratic Athenian culture under the Pisistratids (Green 1990: 182–3; Gutzwiller 1998: 214). Because the range of scenarios was limited, succeeding poets demonstrated their ingenuity by returning to well-known models and altering them. Dioscorides, writing toward the end of the third century, imitates the earlier poems of Asclepiades and Callimachus but abandons their restraint, speaking candidly about the bodies of boys and women and describing acts of intercourse in graphic detail. The decisive contribution to literary history made by the late second-century anthologist **Meleager** of Gadara was to excerpt representative pieces of prior epigrammatists from individual collections, arrange them in thematic sequences, the earliest poem in the series followed by its imitations, and then interweave his own variations to create overall coherence and comment upon the whole (Gutzwiller 1998: 276–322). As he compiled his anthology, the *Garland*, Meleager also introduced into the genre a new device, the "cycle" of poems addressed to a single beloved who typifies the artist's craft. His sequences of poems on Heliodora and Zenophila are filled with self-reflexive allusions to garlands, Muses, speech, song and the Graces, the latter emblematic of the charm exerted by poetry (see especially *Anth. Pal.* 5.136–7, 139–41, 143–4, 147–9). Taking a step of enormous consequence for Roman love poetry, Meleager fused aesthetics and erotics into a single programmatic concept.

Although glimpses of the countryside and its rustic pleasures appear in Greek poetry as early as Homer, both in his similes and in the scenes of plowing, reaping, grape-gathering, and herding on the Shield of Achilles (*Il.* 18.541–89), the bucolic *Idylls* of Theocritus are the first to dwell at length upon an idealized world of cowherds, goatherds, and shepherds and foreground their peaceful activities and preoccupations in opposition to the carnage of heroic epic. The chief concern of the herdsmen who populate Theocritus' Sicilian landscape is love. In their songs they retell the sufferings of Daphnis, who, like Hippolytus, perishes at Aphrodite's hands (Theoc. *Id.* 1) and the grotesque misery of Polyphemus (Theoc. *Id.* 6). Needless to say, they themselves also lament their own unrequited passions in delicately crafted verse, filled with artificial tropes and learned references to myth, but piquantly studded with authentic country lore (Theoc. *Id.* 3). All of this might seem to be sheer escapism, the yearning of urban intellectuals for the timeless rhythms of nature and the simplicities of a humble existence – except that pastoral from its beginnings has always been one of the symbolically richest, most politically charged, and artistically most self-conscious of genres. Insofar as the theme of naive and hopeless love can be isolated as one key ingredient of the bucolic *Idylls*, it must operate in ironic counterpoint to the sophisticated intellectual and artistic issues with which they are deeply concerned.

Theocritus' urban mimes (*Id.* 2, 14, and 15) make use of erotic motifs for a different purpose. His characters, who are average people ostensibly drawn from real life, participate in dramatic situations that explore the contemporary experience of living in a cosmopolitan environment with its accompanying sense of cultural dislocation (Burton 1995: 2). In addition to recreating that metropolitan milieu, all three mimes depict circumstances in which the traditional clear-cut, hierarchical alignment of male and female roles has shifted, so that gender dynamics are more equivocal and, as a result, heterosexual relations have become strained. *Idyll* 2 communicates that social friction in a novel way as it views active female *erôs* through the lenses of ethnicity and class.

In an unspecified city, a young woman named **Simaetha**, who apparently shares her house with only a servant girl, falls in love with Delphis, a youthful expatriate from Asia Minor. He is well-to-do, since he belongs to a crowd that frequents the local gymnasium, but she is not: her friends include a wet-nurse and the mother of a flute-girl, both low-status occupations, and, when she wants to dress up to attend a festival, she borrows a wrap from another woman (2.74). After suffering all the pangs of lovesickness for ten days, she sends her maid to fetch Delphis. When he arrives, he makes an impassioned declaration of his own feelings for her. Furtive textual recollections of Homer's crafty Odysseus tell the competent reader that Delphis is fluently inventing a "fiction of desire" to take advantage of this unexpected sexual opportunity (Segal 1984; cf. Goldhill 1991: 265). Too eager to believe him, as she admits later, she assumes the initiative by inviting him into her bed (138–43):

> … Thus he spoke. And I, easily persuaded [*tachypeithês*],
> grasping his hand made him recline upon the soft couch.
> And quickly flesh ripened against flesh, and our faces
> were warmer than before, and we whispered together sweetly,
> and, not to chatter on at length, dear moon,
> we went all the way and satisfied both our longings.

The affair continues for some time, but then he stops coming by. More than a week later she learns from the flute-girl's mother that Delphis, at a symposium, was displaying all the signs of being in love with someone else. In desperation, Simaetha turns to magic to get him back.

The *Idyll* itself consists of two speeches, one a lengthy magical binding-spell (17–63), the other a monologue in which, after her maid leaves to carry out part of the rite, Simaetha gives a full account of her seduction to Selena, goddess of the moon (64–166). That narrative concludes ambiguously. Should her agony continue, Simaetha contemplates poisoning Delphis with evil drugs (*kaka pharmaka*, 161) obtained from a Syrian herbalist. In the meantime, she resolves, "I will bear my suffering as I have endured it" (164), a misleading remark, as she has not in fact dealt with it well up to this point. We are deliberately left in the dark about whether she has worked through her feelings sufficiently to resign herself to circumstances.

For a literary character, Simaetha's position is anomalous. Unlike tragic heroines, she is given no nurse or sister to confide in; had she been a prostitute in training, a madam would have served as her counselor. She seems to be a free citizen woman who might have looked forward to legitimate marriage, for she complains that Delphis left her "dishonored [*kakan*] and no virgin in place of a wife" (41).[8] We are never told why she, a respectable girl, was without the protection of her family. In the absence of such protection, her reputation is already ruined. The affair is common knowledge among Simaetha's acquaintance, for the flute-girl's mother loses no time in telling her what her daughter had observed of Delphis' behavior. Consequently, she has abandoned all sense of shame. Her maid had been sent to the wrestling school to summon Delphis because no decent woman would be seen near a place where youths exercised in the nude. As Simaetha begins her incantation, though, she declares her intention of going to the gymnasium the next day to confront him (8–9). That action would achieve nothing apart from making her a laughing stock in the eyes of the community, and the fact that she can even envision it indicates how bold and indiscreet she has become.

Theocritus' poem is modeled upon a comic mime by the fifth-century poet Sophron of Syracuse; in a papyrus fragment of that mime (*PSI* 1214a), someone gives directions for a purification ceremony, a likely prelude to an attempt to win back a strayed lover (Hordern 2002: 172–3). This scene parallels the opening of *Idyll* 2, where Simaetha issues similar orders to her maid Thestylis. Although her resort to love magic places her in a long literary tradition of witches like Circe and Medea, it also reflects what must have been common practice: books of formulaic erotic spells and charms used against actual people survive, though most of this material comes from late antique Egypt. Yet there are a few curse tablets found in Greece and dating from the Hellenistic period intended either to bind a man or to inhibit the sexual activities of a woman (Dickie 2000: 574–7). Females most likely to practice erotic magic would be those who had professional reasons for doing so, and both the literary and the physical record support an association between prostitutes and sorcery. How Simaetha's enterprise would have struck a contemporary reader is uncertain. In showing a simple working-class girl, no mythic heroine, seeking to exert power over a man by meddling with witchcraft, the poem may express male anxiety over Greek women's increasing independence (Burton 1995: 69). Simaetha, however, is by her own admission overly credulous. When first smitten, she had vainly resorted to spells to cure her affliction, and she has not learned from that failure (90–2). Given such gullibility, her present belief in the fearsome powers of the philters she has obtained may render her pathetic instead of threatening.

Does this fictional scenario of a young woman alone and vulnerable provide any evidence for the realities of women's lives in the Hellenistic period? Pomeroy (1984: 73–5) postulates a class of immigrant females whose kinfolk had died and who were therefore adrift in Alexandria without male control or protection. Asclepiades' epigrams on women, depicting many of them as sexually active and self-reliant without mentioning an exchange of sex for money, might also portray representative members of such a group (Cameron 1995: 494–519). Apart from that equivocal literary testimony, however, we have no documentation for the historical actuality of that class of women. To a Greek reading audience, it would not seem plausible that girls could live on their own, without any visible means of support and unencumbered by relatives and guardians, choosing their own sex partners at will, without being *hetairai*

Fig. 6.2   Gold octodrachm of Ptolemy II and Arsinoë II, Greece. Egypt, Ptolemaic Dynasty, 285–246 BCE. Source: © The Trustees of the British Museum.

(Cairns 1998). The poignant comedy of *Idyll* 2 resides in what Theocritus leaves unsaid because his readers would automatically grasp it: whatever her prior expectations in life, Simaetha will wind up a prostitute but does not have the cunning required to succeed in the profession. For her sake, present-day readers may be inclined to hope the magic spell works instead. Poor Simaetha; even if it should, Delphis is no prize.

Much of the poetry of Theocritus and Callimachus, his fellow resident at the Museum, was written to eulogize their royal patrons. Ptolemy II and his successor Ptolemy III Euergetes were both married to illustrious queens, Arsinoë II and Berenice II of Cyrene, respectively, who had literary interests themselves and pursued their own strategies of sponsorship. Arsinoë was especially concerned with promoting the cult of Aphrodite as patroness of married love and an accompanying ideology of mutual desire between husband and wife.[9] For good reason. Ptolemy Philadelphus (whose name means "sister-lover") and Arsinoë were full brother and sister. Their alliance, entered into for political and economic motives, conformed to the custom of sibling marriage among the Pharaohs, but it shocked their Greek subjects, who regarded it as incestuous.[10] Representing their relationship as a love match, on the model of the consanguineous union of Zeus and Hera (Theoc. *Id.* 17.131–4), was a spin tactic for directing attention away from its irregularity. Not everyone was mollified: Sotades of Maroneia, who made a career of abusing monarchs (Ath. 620f), finally crossed the line when he charged: "You [Ptolemy] are shoving your prick into an unholy hole" (fr. 1 *Coll. Alex.*), a barb that earned him first imprisonment, then execution.

Arsinoë is the earliest living Ptolemaic queen whose profile appears on coins, both alongside her brother and alone; portrayals of the couple together with their deified parents (fig. 6.2) certify the legitimacy of their joint rule (Burstein 1982: 211). Visibly involved in the religious and ceremonial activities of the court in the manner of native Egyptian royal wives, she shared public honors with Philadelphus at home and abroad, employing her own resources to bolster her brother's regime.[11] To counter Greek fears of impiety, the publicity-conscious queen subsidized, among other civic entertainments, a sumptuous commemoration of the Adonia, a traditional women's ritual concerned with the death of Adonis. Surrounding an elaborate tableau in the palace courtyard where Adonis and Aphrodite embraced within a bower of dill, opulent displays of luxury goods and imports sent a heartening message of continued prosperity to all (Burton 1995: 141; Whitehorne 1995). As noted, Theocritus' *Idyll* 15, the *Women at the Adonis-Festival*, applauds that event by re-envisioning it through the eyes of two young housewives. After appreciating the finely crafted tapestries hung around the bower, they are enthralled by the sensuous figure of Adonis and emotionally stirred by a hymn sung in his honor. Their enthusiastic investment in the romantic fantasies evoked by the display underscores the magnitude of the religious tribute that Arsinoë has rendered to Aphrodite as the divine custodian of married women's sexuality. In restaging this informal rite as a "state-supported extravaganza," the queen had proclaimed the reciprocal love of goddess and mortal a paradigm for her subjects to emulate (Gutzwiller 1992: 367). The romantic mutual desire of the royal couple becomes central to Ptolemaic kingship ideology.

New Gods for Old

When Alexander upon his arrival in Memphis sacrificed to the sacred Apis bull, decreed a temple of Isis for Alexandria, then undertook a strenuous journey through the desert to consult the oracle of Zeus-Ammon at Siwah (Arr. 3.1, 3–4), [12] he set the policy for treatment of Egyptian gods by Macedonian Greek rulers: native religious traditions must be honored, for the supremacy of the Pharaoh derived from his capacity to mediate between his subjects and the divine order. Worshipping foreign gods was facilitated by identifying them with existing Greek divinities, as Herodotus had already done: Amun (Ammon in Greek) was Zeus, Osiris Dionysos, Isis Demeter (2.42, 59). Hence **syncretism**, or the fusion of one's own gods with their counterparts in other pantheons, became commonplace during the Hellenic diaspora as outsiders sought to reconcile their rituals with the belief systems they encountered abroad. Once such integration takes place, the "divine personality" of the Greek god and the conventions of portraying him or her can undergo substantial modifications. In Egypt, with its unique theology, the results of this process were sometimes bewildering.

Arsinoë's Adonis is a case in point. In early Greece the Adonia was an unofficial yearly ritual conducted by groups of women who collectively mourned the death of Aphrodite's mortal lover. Fragments of Sappho's formal laments for Adonis survive (frr. 140, 168 V). Passages from fifth- and fourth-century Athenian comedy assert that it was a raucous, all-night-long affair conducted during the summer on the flat roofs of houses (Ar. *Lys.* 387–96; Men. *Sam.* 38–46). Participants sowed quickly germinating seeds in shallow pots containing a small figure of Adonis lying as if on a bier. These "gardens of Adonis," which withered soon after they sprouted, were emblems of Adonis' perishable beauty. While the celebrants engaged in the traditional acts of mourners, wailing, beating their breasts and tearing their garments, they also danced and partied – even to the point of drunkenness, if we can believe our comic informants. Men were not excluded from these occasions, though the Adonia was regarded as a women's ceremony. As such, it may well have afforded citizen women a much-needed opportunity to escape male supervision and release frustrations under circumstances perceived as harmless (Reed 1995: 345–6; Simms 1998: 136–40).

Arsinoë has altered the very nature of the festival. Because it is being held on the palace grounds, it has been purged of its rowdiness and turned into a spectator event. The lament for Adonis is rendered by a prize-winning female singer who paints the scene before her vividly (112–28). Figures of Aphrodite and Adonis recline on an elaborate couch, surrounded by fruits, Adonis-gardens in silver baskets, perfumes, cakes, meats, and greenery. Since Adonis is termed a bridegroom (*gambros*, 129), the setting is their nuptial chamber and the viewers are celebrating a wedding. Mourning is reserved for the following day, when, at dawn, women will carry the effigy of Adonis to the sea and perform dirges there (132–5). While death remains a motif central to the rite, grief is tempered by the certainty of resurrection, for Aphrodite's lover has been transformed into a demigod, the only one of his kind able to commute between the realms of the living and the dead (136–42).

Adonis has taken on some traits of Osiris. The funeral procession to the sea and the act of casting the image upon the water were borrowed from native Egyptian rituals commemorating Osiris' drowning at the hands of Seth or, alternatively, his voyage to the afterlife. Placement of a figure on a bed under a canopy of foliage together with offerings of baked goods and unguents recalls Osirian cult practices specified in a text from Dendera (Reed 2000: 324–34). An intriguing link between Greek and Egyptian traditions is furnished by the custom of leaving "corn-mummies" – effigies of Osiris made of river silt in which barley seeds had sprouted – in burial chambers as tokens of the renewed life of the god. One such life-size figure was found in the tomb of Tutankhamen (Gwyn Griffiths 1980: 167–70). Adonis' gardens, their own symbolic function for Greeks notwithstanding, were a cultural referent familiar enough to Egyptian subjects to be a reassuring indicator of piety and so were prominently featured in Arsinoë's tableau. Associations with regeneration indicated that the Pharaoh's most obligatory duty, maintaining the eternal cyclic order (*Ma'at*) against the forces of chaos, was being steadfastly observed. Integrating the worship of Adonis with that of Osiris allowed Arsinoë to stress the regime's attentiveness to discrete but equally compelling religious systems.

The Ptolemies even popularized their own supernatural invention, **Sarapis**, a divine avatar of themselves. From earliest times Egyptians had nurtured sacred animals as tangible manifestations of godhood; such animals were recognized by certain markings, housed in luxury, given food offerings, and mummified upon their demise (Quirke 1992: 14, 16). At Memphis the most famous of these, the Apis bull, was honored as a surrogate for the god Ptah. Additionally, the Pharaoh, bearing the title "mighty bull," was associated with the living Apis as promoter of agricultural fertility and abundance (Myśliwiec 2004: 76). Alexander, as we saw, made his respect for Egyptian beliefs clear by sacrificing to the bull, while Ptolemy I, for his part, loaned fifty talents, an extravagant sum, to meet the costs of embalming and burying one. Deceased Apis bulls were associated with Osiris under the name "Osorapis." Before Alexander's death Greeks at Memphis were already venerating this posthumous aspect of the divinity (Brady 1935: 9–10). Osorapis was converted, probably as early as the reign of Ptolemy I (Tac. *Hist.* 4.83; Plut. *De Is.* 28), into the Hellenized, fully anthropomorphic god Sarapis, who was then enshrined as the patron of both Alexandria and the dynasty, his divine reign a counterpart to Ptolemy's own sovereignty (Fraser 1972: 1.246–76; Stambaugh 1972: 93–4; Stephens 2003: 15). Canonical statues of Sarapis resembled those of Hades, Greek god of the underworld – seated on a throne, holding a spear or scepter, the three-headed dog Cerberus beside him – but with the addition of a *kalathos*, or basket, on his head, alluding to the productivity of the earth (Stambaugh 1972: 14). As a god of fertility, he was much closer to the benevolent Osiris than to the fearsome Greek king of the dead. Being a chthonic deity, he also possessed the functions of prophecy and healing. Not surprisingly, in view of royal promotion and all his desirable qualities, Sarapis became quite popular; among his Hellenized followers he displaced Osiris as consort of Isis and sire of Horus. Soon the cult of Sarapis and Isis, carried by Alexandrian merchants and former Ptolemaic officials, had spread to many cities in Greece and Asia Minor. Under the Roman emperors it became one of the leading religious sects in the Greco-Roman world (Fraser 1972: 1.275–6; Quirke 1992: 177–8).

Callimachus' greatest poetic achievement, his *Aetia* or "Book of Origins," included several compositions in praise of Arsinoë, who, after her death in 270 BCE, was worshipped as the joint embodiment of Egyptian Isis and Greek Aphrodite. He also extended her propaganda trajectory in a brilliant elegy, the *Lock of Berenice*, which paid homage to the marriage of Ptolemy III and Berenice II in 246 as yet another love match. When Ptolemy departed on campaign shortly after their wedding, the distraught Berenice vowed to offer a lock of her hair to the gods in payment for his safe return. After his successful homecoming, the tress was ceremonially cropped and dedicated in the shrine of Arsinoë-Aphrodite at Zephyrium, but the next day it was nowhere to be found. The court astronomer Conon then announced his discovery of a faint new constellation in the Zodiac belt that suspiciously resembled the missing strand of hair. Callimachus, in turn, wrote a lament uttered by the lock itself in which it praises Berenice's devotion to her husband but complains bitterly of being perpetually separated from her. Even the glory of shining among the stars is no reward: "it does not bring me as much delight as the grief I feel at no longer touching that head" (fr. 110.75–6 Pf.). Ultimately, the lock consoles itself with the thought that Berenice will offer libations of scented oils to it, exalting it even above brighter constellations. Consequently, it "accepts its role as a symbol of the erotic devotion that, as we are to believe, induced the queen to sacrifice her lovely tress and moved Aphrodite to compensate the victim with **catasterism** [stellar immortality]" (Gutzwiller 1992: 384). To this day, astronomers designate the constellation Conon found in the northern heavens the *Coma Berenikes*, a monument to royal love and the enduring influence of courtly encomium.

To Colchis and Back

In the poetry of Theocritus and Callimachus the reciprocal *erôs* of the royal couple is a blessing for their subjects because it evokes the love of the Egyptian divine pair Isis and Osiris, whose harmonious union brings about the annual flooding of the Nile and the enduring fruitfulness of Egypt. It was left to **Apollonius** of Rhodes, who held the post of Royal Librarian under Ptolemy II Philadelphus and may have been the tutor of the future Ptolemy III Euergetes, to confront the negative costs of investing *erôs* with such political consequence. His *Argonautica*, which recounts the quest of the Golden Fleece, is a heroic epic minus a conventional hero. **Jason**, the head of the expedition, comes off poorly: neither a great warrior nor a charismatic leader, in a tight spot he routinely becomes confused and depressed. His *amêchania* ("lack of a plan," or, more flippantly, "cluelessness") is a trenchant reversal of that resourcefulness that earned Odysseus the epithet *polymêchanos*, "of many devices" (Pavlock 1990: 26). On the other hand, he is gifted at diplomacy, as is apparent in his dealings with women, where he can be quite charming and glib while pursuing his own ends. In fact, Beye (1969: 43) asserts that Jason's heroic excellence, or *arête*, resides in his sexuality. This is true, though, only as long as he confines his seductive talents to less formidable victims. When he attempts to make use of the barbarian princess Medea – who, despite her youth, is a priestess of the underworld goddess Hecate and an expert in magic – he unleashes a terrible force for evil that cannot be mastered by persuasion.

At the beginning of the third book of the *Argonautica* the voyagers have arrived at their destination, Colchis on the eastern coast of the Black Sea, now modern Georgia. On Olympus, Hera, Jason's special patroness, and Athena, guardian of epic heroes, contrive to help the Argonauts obtain the Fleece, for its owner, the merciless King Aeetes, will not surrender it easily. The goddesses enlist Aphrodite's aid: she will have her son Eros make Aeetes' daughter Medea fall in love with Jason and assist him with her magic powers. When Jason enters the king's palace to petition for the Fleece, Eros aims his arrow at Medea with instant and shattering results: the bolt sears her heart, her chest heaves with anguish, she loses all memory, and her soul ebbs away with sweet pain (3.286–90). To earn the Fleece, Aeetes decrees, Jason must perform three deadly tasks: yoking a team of fire-breathing bulls to a plough, sowing the teeth of a dragon in furrows, and slaying the warriors who spring up from that seed. That night Medea vacillates between two conflicting impulses, her pity for the man she now loves warring with her fear of the consequences should she thwart her father's plans to destroy him. At the end of an anguished soliloquy (772–801), she resolves to commit suicide, unable to bear the impending disgrace. Although she goes so far as to fetch her casket of poisons and untie its bands, her will to live triumphs, and at last she resolves to give Jason the charm that will enable him to carry out her father's mandates.

All is now set for one of the great seduction scenes in literature. At dawn Medea takes a drug from her casket to make Jason's body invincible, and drives out to meet him at the temple of Hecate. There she sees him striding toward her "like Sirius from the ocean, which rises beautiful and distinct to look upon, but inflicts unspeakable damage on flocks" (957–9). Ominously echoing Homer's description of Achilles advancing upon Hector before their last battle (*Il.* 22.25–32), the simile describes her contradictory impressions: following a rush of admiration, emotional turbulence leaves her paralyzed. Jason picks up at once on her discomfiture, and flattering her (*hypossainôn* – literally, "fawning" like a dog, 974), tries to put her at ease. He throws himself on her mercy, for she is his only hope: all the Argonauts and their wives and mothers will render thanks to her and bless her name for enabling them to return home. To cap his appeal, he introduces a carefully tailored precedent. Ariadne, daughter of Minos, king of Crete, saved Theseus from death at the hands of the Minotaur and sailed away with him to Athens. The gods, for their part, transformed her bridal crown into a constellation as an indicator of divine favor (997–1006). This ***exemplum*** encourages Medea to look forward to marriage, something hitherto undreamt of, as her reward. What Jason has disingenuously omitted is the fact that Theseus, having carried off Ariadne, abandoned her on a deserted island, from which she was rescued by the god Dionysos. The bridal crown fixed in the heavens is the one Ariadne wore when Dionysos brought her to Olympus and made her his wife. Allusions to Ariadne's doomed elopement with Theseus will recur throughout the rest of the epic as a reminder that the bargain struck with Medea was grounded on falsehood. In love not just with Jason but also with the idea of herself as legendary helper-maiden to a brave prince, Medea willingly hands over the magic charm and instructs him in its use.

Until now, the reader's sympathy has been directed toward the hapless princess. In the fourth and final book, however, she learns what kind of man this stranger really is and we see the cruel and destructive side of her personality emerge. When Jason performs the assigned tasks with ease, Aeetes suspects his daughter's connivance. Fleeing the palace one step ahead of her vengeful father, Medea takes refuge with the Argonauts. Before the whole crew, Jason swears to make her his wife, giving her his right hand as a binding pledge (Ap. Rhod. *Argon.* 4.95–100). They steal the Fleece from the sacred grove and flee with the Colchians in close pursuit. Trapped on an island by Medea's brother Apsyrtus, Jason negotiates a treacherous compromise, proposing that the Argonauts should keep the Fleece but hand Medea over for judgment (338–49). Finding herself betrayed, Medea indulges in a furious tirade, and Jason backtracks, pleading that the agreement with Apsyrtus was intended as a ruse.[13] She, in a "lethal pronouncement" (*ouloon … mython*, 410), then promises to deliver her brother into Jason's hands. Though the narrator blames Eros for inflicting upon Medea the "despicable madness" (*stugerên … atên*, 449) that provoked the ensuing deed, he makes no attempt to whitewash it. The girl induces her brother to meet her alone at night in a temple of Artemis. Catching Apsyrtus there unawares, Jason slaughters him at the threshold. The oath he swore to Medea has been reinforced by collusion in murder.

Yet this crime goes unpunished. Although she refuses to receive Jason and Medea as guests, Circe, Medea's aunt, performs a rite that purifies them of blood-guilt (661–752). Arete, queen of Phaeacia, arranges a hasty and inglorious wedding to ensure that her husband, King Alcinous, will not turn Medea over to another delegation of Colchians (993–1222). Occurring under duress and anxiety, the bridal night brings little happiness to either party, but their marriage frees them from the Colchian threat. The Argonauts undergo other difficult adventures on the homeward voyage, and Medea has to save them one last time by overcoming the bronze giant Talos with spells, in the process revealing in full her capacity to harm (638–88). Nevertheless, the crew eventually disembarks on the beach at Pagasae, their trials at an end. Ostensibly the narrative concludes joyfully.

This bare summary hardly does the *Argonautica* justice, for it omits consideration of the many devices – similes, apostrophe, verbal echoes of Homer and other texts – that Apollonius uses to add depth and complexity to his narrative, especially when dealing with Medea. She is not simply a witch; she is a witch who is also a girl painfully awakening to love, and it is her struggle with that love that wins the reader's compassion. Despite our initial good will toward her, and toward Jason as well, though, we observe both main characters progressing through small acts of personal duplicity to an outrageous offense against heroic mores. Their common moral decline is a striking feature of the poem's overall nihilism. Its protagonists "seem to play out their roles in postures of malaise and disaffection, without commitment to the values that underlie the epic tradition, or to anything else, for that matter" (Clayman 2000: 33). Sexual desire fills that ethical vacuum at the heart of the epic, continuing to motivate the conduct of Jason and Medea even after they have attained full understanding of the choices they have made and the resulting circumstances in which they find themselves. One of the fundamental questions the

Argonautica asks, therefore, is whether, in the absence of other frameworks, *erôs* is an adequate tool for forging the bonds of community.

Desiring Women – and their Detractors

Alexandrian writers attempting to portray women sympathetically found models for imitation in contemporary texts composed by women themselves. Hellenistic female poets, who worked primarily, though not exclusively, in the genre of epigram, are often said to have introduced a "gendered" focus into literature, though their subjectivity, insofar as it infuses conventional male genres with innovative elements, might better be deemed "transgendered" (Murray and Rowland 2007). The most influential of this new crop of writers was **Erinna**, assigned by a late antique chronicler to the mid-fourth century BCE. Nothing is really known about her life, which prompted one modern scholar to suggest that her renowned poem the *Distaff*, a 300-line hexameter lament for a dead girlhood companion, was a sophisticated forgery circulating under a woman's name (West 1977).[14] The unanimous testimony of antiquity, however, assigns her a firm place in a canonical list of nine major women poets compiled by Alexandrian scholars (*Anth. Pal.* 9.27 [Antipater of Thessalonica]).

Erinna's artistic innovation was to adapt the epic dirge for the fallen hero, a Patroclus or Hector, to the expression of personal grief, using Sappho's lyrics as a model (Gutzwiller 1997: 203–11). The mutilated lines of a short portion of the *Distaff* (*Suppl. Hell.* 401), which survive on a torn scrap of papyrus, recall a game that the speaker and her friend Baucis had played as girls, mention dolls, a mother, and wool-working, and describe the movements of the dreadful bogey Mormo (15–27). A new section of the poem apparently began with a mention of Baucis' marriage: through the intervention of Aphrodite, she forgot either the childhood activities that were just described or, alternatively, what she had heard from her mother (*matros akousas*, 29). This seems to be a turning point in the speaker's reminiscences, and it is unfortunate that the missing parts of the badly torn papyrus do not allow us to reconstruct what was said with certainty (Snyder 1989: 95). The more legible segment of the text concludes with her complaint that she is not permitted to leave the house, look upon something (possibly a corpse), or mourn with unbound hair for her companion: "shame [*aidôs*] tears my cheeks …" (31–5). From that point on, only line-beginnings survive, including the words "nineteen" and "Erinna," which seem to substantiate ancient testimony that the author represented herself as a nineteen-year-old maiden. A twice-repeated closing invocation of the wedding god Hymenaeus implies a return to the sharp break between girlhood and womanhood marked by initiation into sexuality.

Recent interpretations of this fragment stress its importance as a genuine record of female life, however artistically transmuted (Snyder 1989: 96), its preoccupation with the restrictions imposed upon girls as part of their training for womanhood (Stehle 2001), and its self-reflexive use of weaving imagery as a metaphor for poetic creation (Skinner 2001: 214–15). Ancient male readers, however, were primarily moved by its pathos: in an honorific tribute, Asclepiades describes it as "more compelling [*dynatôteros*]" than many other longer compositions (*Anth. Pal.* 7.11.3). Callimachus, it has been plausibly suggested, modeled his grieving Lock upon the first-person speaker (Gutzwiller 1992: 375–6), and Simaetha's pointed comparison of her body to that of a stiff wax doll (*dagus*, Theoc. *Id.* 2.110) may consciously recall Erinna's reminiscence of playing with dolls (*dagudôn*, *Suppl. Hell.* 401.21). Subsequent influence of the *Distaff* flowed in two directions: late Hellenistic hexameter funerary poems like Bion's *Lament for Adonis* and the anonymous *Lament for Bion* are direct imitations (Bowra 1953 [1936]: 163; Gutzwiller 1997: 207), while the aria of the wronged and abandoned heroine, a standard set-piece of Roman poetry, indirectly traces its descent, through Callimachus' *Lock of Berenice*, back to Erinna (Gutzwiller 1992: 385). Interest in female subjectivity among male poets was therefore sparked off by the timely re-emergence of a female poetic voice narrating female experience.

While Erinna's verses were highly admired in some quarters, they also came under attack, apparently as part of a growing reaction against female homoeroticism. In the archaic and classical periods, as we have seen, women's desire for other women may have been co-opted into a general scheme of acculturation for marriage but was otherwise ignored. In the *Symposium*, Plato's Aristophanes matter-of-factly mentions female "companions" (*hetairistriai*) attracted to other women, but does not elaborate (191e). There is one disputed negative reference to female same-sex appeal in the poetry of Anacreon: the speaker's advances are repulsed by a girl, who, "because she comes from well-founded / Lesbos, finds fault with my hair [*komên*], / for it is white, / and gapes after some other" (*PMG* 358.5–8). "Some other," *allên tina*, being feminine in gender, could mean "another girl," or, taking as its antecedent the feminine noun *komên*, "other hair." On the least obscene hypothesis, the girl is charmed by the comely dark locks of a younger male suitor, but few bother to defend that reading. The information that she hails from Lesbos is interpreted as either an allusion to Sappho, hinting at homoerotic tastes, or a reference to the practice of fellation, which was the peculiar vice imputed to the inhabitants of that island (Jocelyn 1980: 31–4). The verb "gapes," *chaskei*, tips the balance in favor of the latter possibility: the "other hair" is pubic, and Anacreon is accusing the young woman of being an enthusiastic penis-sucker, a charge regularly leveled against whores. This poem, then, is probably not an attack on women's sexual preferences.

In the Hellenistic period silence on the subject of female homoeroticism is abruptly broken. We can observe opposition to love between women developing on several fronts. Fourth-century Attic comedy "heterosexualizes" Sappho, portraying her as the object of pursuit by male poets and the rejected lover, in turn, of the beautiful ferryman Phaon, for whom she commits suicide (Dover 1978: 174). Biographical remarks contained in a papyrus from Imperial Roman times (*P Oxy.* 1800 fr. 1) may allude to scholarly writings from the third and second centuries BCE: Sappho, it is said there, has been accused by some of being *ataktos* ("undisciplined") and a *gynaikerastria* or "lover of women." Together with efforts to normalize Sappho's erotic life or condemn it as licentious, we find female same-sex bonding branded as unnatural not only by Plato (*Leg.* 636c) but also by the normally tolerant

Asclepiades. In *Anth. Pal.* 5.207 (GP 7), he denounces two courtesans who have developed an interest in each other:

> The Samian women Bitto and Nannion are unwilling to frequent
>   the school of Aphrodite according to her rules,
> and desert to other things not good. Mistress Cypris, abhor
>   the fugitives from that intercourse you preside over.

The activities of Bitto and Nannion do not fall under Aphrodite's sphere of influence; by engaging in them, the women make themselves outlaws in the goddess's eyes. This judgment illustrates the ancient tendency to regard *ta aphrodisia* as synonymous with asymmetrical power relations and consequent penetration (Dover 2002: 226). What falls outside that rubric is no longer ignored but has instead become a problem for males. There is a nervous curiosity about what pairs of women actually do; Asclepiades' vague expression *ha mê kala* ("things that might not be nice") invites prurient speculation. Metaphors of desertion, carrying a heavy charge in a culture that identifies masculinity with virtuous deeds on the battlefield, drive home the point that Bitto and Nannion have forsaken their obligations as courtesans. Unless we are missing some humor here, a considerable degree of anxiety about female sexual autonomy is reflected in this quatrain. Far worse than betraying the speaker with another man is betraying him with each other.

Herodas, a mime-writer, mounts the crudest sustained offensive against female homoeroticism, singling out the woman epigrammatist **Nossis** as his special target. A native of Locri on the Ionian coast of Italy, Nossis compiled an album of her own epigrams describing imaginary votive dedications, chiefly encaustic (colored wax) paintings of friends and acquaintances, as they might be viewed by a female observer visiting Aphrodite's archaic temple in that city. In her signature-poem *Anth. Pal.* 5.170 (GP 1) she boldly proclaims "nothing is sweeter than *erôs*" and identifies her book as a collection of Aphrodite's roses. Meleager stated that her "portrait" epigrams were inspired by Eros (*Anth. Pal.* 4.1.9–10). None of Nossis' six surviving physical descriptions of women is overtly erotic, but the speaker's admiration for the beauty of her subjects, expressed in language highly reminiscent of Sappho, is pervaded with homoerotic energy (Gutzwiller 1998: 80). Three of the six are unusual because they speak of courtesans in glowing terms. Here, for example, is *Anth. Pal.* 9.332 (GP 4), on a statue of Aphrodite, a gift to the goddess from a successful *hetaira*:

> Let us go to Aphrodite's temple to see her statue,
>   how finely it is embellished with gold.
> Polyarchis dedicated it, having made a great fortune
>   out of the splendor of her own body.

The audience – made up exclusively of women, as we learn from the feminine participle *elthoisai* in line 1 – is asked to inspect the gilded statue that Polyarchis set up representing herself as Aphrodite and thus advertising the body by which she had earned her living. That warm eulogy of a courtesan, unparalleled in Greek literature, hints at an unusual code of sexual ethics at Locri and a blurring of rigid caste distinctions between respectable and non-respectable women (Skinner 1991: 27).[15]

Three of Herodas' mimes attack Nossis, two outright and one through parody. The subject matter of *Mimiambs* 6 and 7 is dildoes. In the first, one housewife, Metro, visits another, Coritto, to ask about the origins of a scarlet object seen in the possession of a neighbor, "Nossis daughter of Erinna" (6.20–1). This must be a reference to the poet, who identifies her own mother as "Theophilis daughter of Cleocha," using the matronymic (*Anth. Pal.* 6.265.4, GP 3); by calling her Erinna's "daughter," Herodas is asserting the two writers' literary affinity. Coritto, who had loaned the dildo to another friend, is shocked to hear it has fallen into Nossis' hands: "may Nemesis forgive me," she exclaims, "but if I had a thousand, I wouldn't give even a rotten one to Nossis" (34–6). After more persuasion, she confesses that the maker is the cobbler Cerdon, and Metro leaves to seek him out. In *Mimiamb* 7 Metro has made his acquaintance and now brings her friends to examine the products of his craftsmanship – shoes. Cerdon proudly exhibits his handiwork (7.56–8):

> You shall see for yourselves, here are all kinds,
> Sikyonians, small Ambracians, Nossises, unembroidered ones,
> parrot-green ones, hemp-soles, Baukises, slippers …

Greek women's shoes came in all colors and styles, and some of the terms Cerdon employs designate actual footwear: *blautê*, for example, is a common word for "slipper." The Greek proper nouns *Nossides* and *Baukides*, however, are not. Those two names look back to the preceding mime. This unspoken equation between shoes and dildoes becomes a running joke as the customers bargain over and even try on the wares for fit. Meanwhile, the strong attachment to other women displayed in the works of Erinna and Nossis functions as a telltale indicator of aberrant female sexuality. In both mimes, women covet dildoes, lend them out, and help other women obtain them, with the assistance of obliging merchants; their sexual energy aims at self-gratification instead of being directed toward serving male needs. Again there is a comic suggestion that females, in this case outwardly reputable wives, no longer require men for their purposes.

In *Mimiamb* 4, Herodas parodies the fundamental design and theme of Nossis' epigram collection. She had structured her book of verse as a tour of the offerings housed in a temple of Aphrodite. Cynno and Coccale, the two main characters in Herodas' mime, are farm wives who visit a temple of Asclepios, the god of healing, and view the works of art on display there. Much of the humor burlesques class and gender expectations as the sightseers convey their reactions to these sculptures and paintings by parroting the formulas of fourth-century BCE academic art criticism. (Imagine a skit in which two construction workers at a neighborhood tavern discuss the respective merits of Michelob and Bud Light employing the technical vocabulary found in the *Wine Spectator*.)

There are passages, however, in which the author has a definite victim in mind. In lines 19–20, Cynno tells Coccale to set a votive tablet or *pinax* next to a statue of the deity Hygeia ("Health"). The paintings Nossis depicts in verse are also tablets, *pinakes*, bearing an encaustic image of the sitter, and they too would have been placed beside the effigy of the god to whom they were dedicated. A few lines later, Coccale admires a statue of a woman (4.35–8):

> Don't you see, Cynno, how this statue stands –
> the one of Batale, daughter of Myttes?
> If someone has not seen Batale herself,
> looking on this figure, he would not need the original.

Herodas once more uses the matronymic, Nossis' well-known way of identifying herself, to specify whom he is targeting. The names of both mother and daughter have obscene connotations, the former associated with "anus," the latter with words for sexual indulgence and a woman's private parts; no respectable women would bear them (Cunningham 1971 *ad loc.*). One recurrent motif of Nossis' epigrams is the artist's skill in capturing distinctive traits of the sitter's personality. When Coccale calls attention to the pose of the statue and remarks that someone who had never seen Batale could form a correct impression of her from this likeness, she implies that the stance is a suggestive one. It seems reasonable to conclude that these lines make fun of Nossis' epigrams on courtesans (Skinner 2001: 219).

Overall, the relationship between the leading characters in the mime travesties the dealings between Nossis' first-person speaker and her implied addressee. The epigrammatist recreates a "women's world" of artistic elegance that permits a male reader who identifies with the subject position of her constructed female listener to experience vicariously the intense emotive undercurrents of women's interaction. Herodas' Cynno also briskly shepherds Coccale around a temple, supplying information about artists and dedicants, while her friend repeatedly gasps in naive wonder at the lifelike qualities of the art. Through his mocking sketches of wives conversing, here as in *Mimiambs* 6 and 7, Herodas deflates the tender atmosphere of Nossis' private world and the emotionality of women's intimate contact with each other.

Conclusion

As we noted in the introduction, romantic love could at least temporarily fill the vacancy left by the disappearance of other social institutions that once facilitated male bonding. At Athens, for example, the decline of the old propertied families and the concentration of power among plutocrats in league with Macedonian royalty had displaced pederasty from its former privileged position. Meanwhile, in those Greek cities of Asia Minor that had been recently Hellenized and, above all, in Ptolemaic Alexandria, emigrants found themselves in an alien environment, without the support of kinfolk networks or the familiarity of the civic rituals they had known as children. Cultural diffusion consequently worked both ways, exposing Greek colonizers to exotic beliefs and practices even as they themselves instructed subalterns in Hellenic usages. In Egypt, where restrictions on the public activities of respectable women had always been much less stringent than in classical Athens, such contact inevitably led to shifts in gender arrangements – and thus to differences in the way in which even casual affairs were presented in litera- ture. There was clear mythic and poetic precedent for portraying Medea as a woman who takes desertion badly, but when Simaetha is seen following in her footsteps something has changed.

Although our overview of sexuality in Alexandrian poetry has concentrated upon the representation of heterosexual relationships, pederasty continued to be prominent in the literature of the time. Apart from Asclepiades' and Callimachus' homoerotic epigrams, the album of verse handed down under the name of Theocritus contains several poems in that vein. *Idyll* 6, for example, features a singing match between two shepherds, formerly lover and beloved, now estranged; their hostility, inflated of course for comic purposes, would justify Aristotle's skep- ticism about the positive outcomes of pederastic liaisons. In *Idyll* 13 Theocritus, like Apollonius, tells the story of Heracles' love for Hylas and his fruitless search for the boy, who had been abducted by nymphs. This popular episode exemplifies the Hellenistic tendency to portray mythic heroes in a less-than-heroic light, handling their amorous adventures sentimentally or ironically. In reality, decreased opportunity to participate directly in civic government was reducing the impor- tance of pederasty as a tool of socialization and cross-generational bonding among the elite. Consequently, the boy's conduct was no longer implicated in a nexus of communal concerns about his present self-restraint and future moral development. With those ethical components removed, literary treatments of the unattainable beloved blame his refusal to comply upon willfulness, arbitrariness, and greed. As objects of a frustrated passion, boys and women thus come to resemble each other more and more, for the lover's obsession will no longer have ramifications for anything outside his own life.

By the second century BCE, the Roman senatorial class was profoundly caught up in Greek affairs, first as conquerors of the failing Macedonian kingdoms, then as governors of provinces, patrons and purchasers of art, and students of learning. We have already observed how Roman cultural assumptions may have affected Greek artistic production by imposing new sexual meanings upon one existing work of sculpture, the Cnidia. Although popular descriptions of the erotic art of classical antiquity frequently start from the unstated premise that those materials reflect "Greco-Roman" habits of thought persisting in uniform manner across cultures and centuries, we lose something when we process the distinctive flavors and textures of Greek and Roman thought into a bland purée. In the next two chapters we will first try to pinpoint the uniquely Roman aspects of ancient sexu- ality and then observe how they are expressed in literature of the middle and late Roman Republic. After that, we will be in a position to investigate how conflicting elements in class and gender systems may have contributed to the volatile sexual climate of imperial Rome.

Discussion Prompts

1. The popularity of the female nude in Western painting and sculpture is, as art historians frequently note, a comparatively modern phenomenon; in antiquity the male nude was instead the norm. Now that you have had opportunities to compare Greek concepts of sex and gender with our own, what differences in gender assumptions might help to explain this disparity in artistic conventions?

2. Although Osiris was connected by Greek authors to various other gods, including Zeus (Diod. Sic. 1.25.2), he was most consistently associated from Herodotus onward with Dionysos. Consequently worship of Dionysos was also promoted by the early Ptolemies: Ptolemy Philadelphus, for example, mounted a stupendous procession in honor of Dionysos, perhaps to celebrate his accession in 285 BCE (Callixeinus *ap*.Ath. 196a–203b). What facets of Dionysos would encourage syncretism with Osiris?

3. Scholarship on Alexandrian poets stresses that they wrote for the court and for other learned readers. All the same, many works of that time took the lives of ordinary, non-heroic individuals as their subject: besides Theocritus' shepherds and Simaetha, we find Callimachus writing a short epic, the *Hecale*, about an old woman who offers the hero Theseus shelter for the night. Based on what you have learned about the experiences of Greeks in Egypt, can you think of reasons why such a readership might be interested in the activities of common people?

4. One point developed in the last section of this chapter is the growth of hostility toward female homoeroticism as expressed in women's writing. What changes in gender attitudes might help to explain why female professions of erotic or quasi-erotic feelings for other women, tolerated if not actually admired in Sappho's poems, would provoke such reactions during the Hellenistic age?

Notes

1 Exposing the genitals (*anasyresthai*) can be deliberately offensive (Theophrastus uses the verb of a male "flasher," *Char*. 11.2). Performed by women, however, it is explained as an act to induce fertility or turn away evil. In Greek myth it is associated with Baubo, who by doing so makes the grieving Demeter laugh. Terracotta figurines of a woman's head mounted directly above her exposed genitals have been found in a temple precinct of Demeter and Kore at Priene (Olender 1990: 83–4).

2 To be sure, Herodotus couples the Egyptians with the Greeks as cultures in which temple precincts

are sacrosanct, sexual activity on the premises is prohibited, and worshippers who have had relations must wash before entering (2.64). Such sanctuary restrictions, however, would not necessarily preclude intercourse elsewhere during festivals.

3 Critics (e.g., Whitehorne 1995: 63; Foster 2006: 133–5) refer to the two as "matrons" or "ladies," implying they are in their mid-thirties or so. From internal clues – such as the fact that Gorgo seems to have no children, Praxinoa's one boy is a toddler, and an old woman addresses them as "pretty girls" (*kallista paidôn*, 62) – I would guess they are

still adolescents, not long married. Think of them as teenagers from Queens or the Bronx visiting Rockefeller Center to look at the Christmas tree. On Arsinoë's celebration itself, see below.

4   Akhenaten, who reigned *c.*1352–1335 BCE, rejected worship of the traditional Egyptian pantheon in favor of one god, the Aten, that is, the light from the sun-disc giving existence to the world each day. This religious innovation did not survive his reign, and after his death he was execrated as a criminal (Montserrat 2000: 14–29). Odysseus' lies about his adventures in Egypt (*Od.* 14.257–86) might reflect historical memories of pre-Homeric mercenary engagements under the Pharaohs.

5   Periodically some hopeful archaeologist or treasure hunter announces its rediscovery; the story always turns out to be false, but good for five minutes on CNN.

6   This far-fetched joke is hard to explain, but bear with me. In addition to the *Theogony* and *Works and Days*, Hesiod composed a *Catalogue of Women* recounting tales of mythic heroines. Each new entry was there introduced with the phrase *ê hoiê*, "or such a one as she …" Hence the poem was also known as the *Ehoiai*. Hermesianax turns the formula into a girl's name and declares that Hesiod composed his *Catalogue* while courting her, leading off each segment by invoking "Ehoie" (fr. 7.21–6 *Coll. Alex.*).

7   Instead of "Bittis," it has been proposed, we should actually read "Battis," meaning "gloss, verbal explanation," on the assumption that Hermesianax converted Philitas' interest in rare words into his metaphorical "mistress." Scholars disagree on the merits of this suggestion. Whatever the case, we are probably right to suspect another joke.

8   Some scholars (for example, Faraone 1999: 153–4) contend that Simaetha is a young courtesan left on her own after the death of an older woman who had trained her. In that case, her aggressive pursuit of Delphis followed by his rejection of her would diminish her sexual charm by making her look foolish in the eyes of prospective clients.

9   The queen's identification with Aphrodite was so close that Callicrates, admiral of the royal navy, built a temple dedicated to Arsinoë-Aphrodite on a headland called Zephyrium; the divinity became widely known under the cult title

Zephyritis (Posidippus 12 GP [*PDidot.*]). See Fraser (1972: 1.239–40); Kron (1996: 172).

10   Egyptologists have long debated the motivation for sibling marriages within the royal families of Dynastic Egypt. One now-debunked theory is that the throne descended through the female line, so that each new Pharaoh had to legitimize his claim by marrying the "heiress," usually a sister. In actuality, though, we know of several principal queens of the Eighteenth Dynasty who were non-royals. The fact that the king was thought to be a god affords a better explanation: marrying a sister would ensure that divine blood was not diluted, and the regal pair could thereby be assimilated to the supreme couple Osiris and his sister-wife Isis (Robins 1993: 26–7).

11   Arsinoë personally controlled vast amounts of wealth coming from gifts to her by her first husband, king Lysimachus of Thrace. After her death she was deified, temples were erected to her, and cult practices established. The so-called "Chremonides decree," part of an ill-starred attempt on the part of Athens and Sparta, backed by Ptolemy II, to overthrow Macedonian rule (268/7–262/1 BCE), specifically mentions her support for Greek freedom (IG II2 687.16–18). These and other considerations lead some historians to believe that Arsinoë was the de facto ruler of Egypt. Burstein argues that this claim is exaggerated but admits that the extraordinary tributes she received both during her lifetime and posthumously indicate that she played a "prominent and popular role in the life of Egypt during her brother's reign" (1982: 212).

12   Greeks in the classical period were already seeking advice from the oracle (Plut. *Cim.* 18). Biographers of Alexander, who provide detailed narratives of the hazardous trek to the shrine, agree that there Zeus-Ammon accepted Alexander as his own son, not Philip's (Curt. 4.7.25–7, Diod. Sic. 17.51.1–3, Just. *Epit.* 11.11.7–11, Plut. *Alex.* 27.3). From a Greek perspective, Zeus' paternity would further the comparison with Heracles, whom Alexander was trying to emulate (Edmunds 1971: 374–6). For Egyptians, the god's acknowledgment was crucial because the reigning Pharaoh was thought to be the product of a union between an earthly mother and Amun-Re in human form (Robins 1993: 37–8, 41). The fictive version of Alexander's conception

in the *Alexander Romance* provides him with yet another father, the last native Pharaoh of Egypt Nectanebo II, giving him a hereditary right to the throne; see Stephens 2003: 65–71.

13   Whether Jason had planned to kill Apsyrtus all along or abruptly seizes on this possibility in order to placate Medea is unclear; his real intentions are completely opaque. Hunter notes (1993: 14–15) that at this and other critical moments the reader observes Jason only through Medea's eyes and thus cannot be sure, any more than she is, of whether he can be believed.

14   In what is now the most authoritative treatment of Erinna's fragments, Neri (2003: 30–4) concedes the economy of West's hypothesis while noting that our limited knowledge of literary production in peripheral areas of the Greek world leaves open the possibility of an authentic female poet.

15   Fifth-century BCE material evidence for cult practice seems to corroborate that absence of discrimination against the prostitute, refreshingly at odds with other ancient Greek sources. The "Ludovisi throne" housed in the Palazzo Altemps in Rome – securely attributed on artistic grounds to a Locrian sculptor and even believed to come from the archaic temple of Aphrodite at Locri – depicts the birth of the goddess in its central panel. A female worshipper is portrayed on each side. One, a heavily draped matron burning incense, symbolizes the legitimate exercise of sexuality within marriage. The other, a naked *hetaira* playing an *aulos*, obviously represents non-marital, non-reproductive sexuality. Their functions are not hostile but complementary. At Locri, then, Aphrodite seems to have been officially venerated under both aspects.

References

Allen, J. P. 1988. *Genesis in Egypt: The Philosophy of Ancient Egyptian Creation Accounts.* Yale Egyptological Studies 2. New Haven, CT: Yale University Press.

Beye, C. R. 1969. "Jason as Love-hero in Apollonios' *Argonautika.*" *Greek, Roman, and Byzantine Studies* 10: 31–55.

Bing, P. 1993. "The *Bios*-tradition and Poets' Lives in Hellenistic Poetry." In R. M Rosen and J. Farrell (eds), *Nomodeiktes: Greek Studies in Honor of Martin Ostwald.* Ann Arbor: University of Michigan Press. 619–31.

—— 2008. *The Well-read Muse: Present and Past in Callimachus and the Hellenistic Poets.* Rev. edn. Ann Arbor: Michigan Classical Press.

Bowra, C. M. 1953 [1936]. "Erinna's Lament for Baucis." In *Problems in Greek Poetry.* Oxford: Clarendon Press. 151–68 [= *Greek Poetry and Life.* Oxford: Clarendon Press. 325–42].

Brady, T. A. 1935. *The Reception of the Egyptian Cults by the Greeks (330–30 B.C.).* University of Missouri Studies 10.1. Columbia: University of Missouri.

Burstein, S. M. 1982. "Arsinoë II Philadelphos: A Revisionist View." In W. L. Adams and E. N. Borza (eds.), *Philip II, Alexander the Great and the Macedonian Heritage.* Washington, DC: University Press of America. 197–212.

Burton, J. B. 1995. *Theocritus's Urban Mimes: Mobility, Gender, and Patronage.* Berkeley, CA: University of California Press.

Cairns, F. 1998. "Asclepiades and the Hetairai." *Eikasmos* 9: 165–93.

Cameron, A. 1995. *Callimachus and his Critics.* Princeton, NJ: Princeton University Press.

Chugg, A. 2002. "The Sarcophagus of Alexander the Great?" *Greece & Rome* 49.1: 8–26.

Clayman, D. L. 2000. "The Scepticism of Apollonius' *Argonautica.*" In M. A. Harder, R. F. Regtuit, and G. C. Wakker (eds.), *Apollonius Rhodius. Hellenistica Groningana* 4. Leuven: Peeters. 33–53.

Cohen, B. 1997. "Divesting the Female Breast of Clothes in Classical Sculpture." In A. O. Koloski-Ostrow and C. L. Lyons (eds.), *Naked Truths: Women, Sexuality, and Gender in Classical Art and Archaeology.* London: Routledge. 66–92.

Cole, S. G. 1984. "Greek Sanctions against Sexual Assault." *Classical Philology* 79: 97–113.

—— 1992. "*Gynaiki ou themis*: Gender Difference in the Greek *leges sacrae.*" *Helios* 19.1–2: 104–22.

Cooney, K. M. 2008. "The Problem of Female Rebirth in New Kingdom Egypt: The Fragmentation of the Female Individual in Her Funerary Equipment." In C. Graves-Brown (ed.), *Sex and Gender in Ancient*

Egypt: *"Don your wig for a joyful hour"*. Swansea: Classical Press of Wales. 1–25.

Cunningham, I. C. (ed.). 1971. *Herodas: Mimiambi*. Oxford: Clarendon Press.

Dickie, M. W. 2000. "Who Practised Love-magic in Classical Antiquity and in the Late Roman World?" *Classical Quarterly* 50: 563–83.

Dover, K. J. 1978. *Greek Homosexuality*. London: Duckworth.

—— (ed.). 1985 [1971]. *Theocritus: Select Poems*. Bristol: Bristol Classical Press.

—— 2002. "Two Women of Samos." In M. C. Nussbaum and J. Sihvola (eds.), *The Sleep of Reason: Erotic Experience and Sexual Ethics in Ancient Greece and Rome*. Chicago: University of Chicago Press. 222–8.

Edmunds, L. 1971. "The Religiosity of Alexander." *Greek, Roman and Byzantine Studies* 12.3: 363–91.

Erskine, A. 2002. "Life after Death: Alexandria and the Body of Alexander." *Greece & Rome* 49.2: 163–79.

Faraone, C. A. 1999. *Ancient Greek Love Magic*. Cambridge, MA: Harvard University Press.

Foster, J. A. 2006. "Arsinoe II as Epic Queen: Encomiastic Allusion in Theocritus, Idyll 15." *Transactions of the American Philological Association* 136: 133–48.

Fraser, P. M. 1972. *Ptolemaic Alexandria*, 3 vols. Oxford: Clarendon Press.

Goldhill, S. 1991. *The Poet's Voice: Essays on Poetics and Greek Literature*. Cambridge: Cambridge University Press.

Graves-Brown, C. 2010. *Dancing for Hathor: Women in Ancient Egypt*. London and New York: Continuum.

Green, P. 1990. *Alexander to Actium: The Historical Evolution of the Hellenistic Age*. Berkeley and Los Angeles: University of California Press.

Gutzwiller, K. J. 1992. "Callimachus' *Lock of Berenice*: Fantasy, Romance, and Propaganda." *American Journal of Philology* 113: 359–85.

—— 1997. "Genre Development and Gendered Voices in Erinna and Nossis." In Y. Prins and M. Shreiber (eds.), *Dwelling in Possibility: Women Poets and Critics on Poetry*. Ithaca, NY: Cornell University Press. 202–22.

—— 1998. *Poetic Garlands: Hellenistic Epigrams in Context*. Berkeley, CA: University of California Press.

Griffiths, J. Gwyn. 1980. *The Origins of Osiris and His Cult*. Leiden: E. J. Brill.

Hanrahan, M. 1961a. "Naucratis, and the Relations between Greece and Egypt during the VIIth and VIth Centuries B.C., Part One." *University Review* 2.5: 46–57.

—— 1961b. "The Relations between Greece and Egypt during the VIIth and VIIIth [*sic*] Centuries B.C., Part Two." *University Review* 2.7: 33–45.

Havelock, C. M. 1995. *The Aphrodite of Knidos and her Successors: A Historical Review of the Female Nude in Greek Art*. Ann Arbor: University of Michigan Press.

Hordern, J. H. 2002. "Love Magic and Purification in Sophron, *PSI* 1214a, and Theocritus' *Pharmakeutria*." *Classical Quarterly* 52: 164–73.

Hunter, R. 1993. *The "Argonautica" of Apollonius: Literary Studies*. Cambridge: Cambridge University Press.

Jocelyn, H. D. 1980. "A Greek Indecency and its Students: *ΛAIKAZEIN*." *Proceedings of the Cambridge Philological Society* 26: 12–66.

Kron, U. 1996. "Priesthoods, Dedications and Euergetism: What Part Did Religion Play in the Political and Social Status of Greek Women?" In P. Hellström and B. Alroth (eds.), *Religion and Power in the Ancient Greek World: Proceedings of the Uppsala Symposium 1993*. Uppsala: Acta Universitatis Upsalensis. 139–82.

Meskell, L. 2002. *Private Life in New Kingdom Egypt*. Princeton and Oxford: Princeton University Press.

Montserrat, D. 1996. *Sex and Society in Graeco-Roman Egypt*. London and New York: Kegan Paul.

—— 2000. *Akhenaten: History, fantasy, and ancient Egypt*. London and New York: Routledge.

Morenz, S. 1973. *Egyptian Religion*. Trans. A. E. Keep. Ithaca: Cornell University Press.

Murray, J. and Rowland, J. M. 2007. "Gendered Voices in Hellenistic Epigram." In P. Bing and J. S. Bruss (eds.), *Brill's Companion to Hellenistic Epigram*. Leiden and Boston: E. J. Brill. 211–32.

Myśliwiec, K. 2004. *Eros on the Nile*. Ithaca: Cornell University Press.

Neri, C. 2003. *Erinna: Testimonianze e frammenti*. Bologna: Pàtron Editore.

Olender, M. 1990. "Aspects of Baubo: Ancient Texts and Contexts." In D. M. Halperin, J. J., Winkler, and F. I. Zeitlin (eds.), *Before Sexuality: The*

Construction of Erotic Experience in the Ancient Greek World. Princeton, NJ: Princeton University Press. 83–113.

Osborne, R. 1994. "Looking on – Greek Style. Does the Sculpted Girl Speak to Women Too?" In I. Morris (ed.), *Classical Greece: Ancient Histories and Modern Archaeologies*. Cambridge: Cambridge University Press. 81–96.

Parker, H. N. 1992. "Love's Body Anatomized: The Ancient Erotic Handbooks and the Rhetoric of Sexuality." In A. Richlin (ed.), *Pornography and Representation in Greece and Rome*. Oxford: Oxford University Press. 90–111.

Pavlock, B. 1990. *Eros, Imitation, and the Epic Tradition*. Ithaca, NY: Cornell University Press.

Pomeroy, S. B. 1984. *Women in Hellenistic Egypt from Alexander to Cleopatra*. New York: Schocken.

—— 2002. *Spartan Women*. New York: Oxford University Press.

Quirke, S. 1992. *Ancient Egyptian Religion*. London: British Museum Press.

Reed, J. D. 1995. "The Sexuality of Adonis." *Classical Antiquity* 14.2: 317–47.

—— 2000. "Arsinoe's Adonis and the Poetics of Ptolemaic Imperialism." *Transactions of the American Philological Association* 130: 319–51.

Ridgeway, B. S. 2001. "Some Personal Thoughts on the Knidia." In N. Birkle (ed.), *Macellum: Culinaria Archaeologica. Robert Fleischer zum 60. Geburtstag von Kollegen, Freunden und Schülern*. Mainz. www.archaeologie-sachbuch.de/Fleischer/index.htm. (accessed 18 March 2013).

Robins, G. 1993. *Women in Ancient Egypt*. Cambridge, MA: Harvard University Press.

Salomon, N. 1997. "Making a World of Difference: Gender, Asymmetry, and the Greek Nude." In Koloski-Ostrow and Lyons (eds.), *(Naked Truth)*, 197–219.

Schofield, L. and Parkinson, R. B.. 1994. "Of Helmets and Heretics: A Possible Egyptian Representation of Mycenaean Warriors on a Papyrus from El-Amarna." *The Annual of the British School at Athens* 89: 157–70.

Segal, C. P. 1984. "Underreading and Intertextuality: Sappho, Simaetha, and Odysseus in Theocritus' Second Idyll." *Arethusa* 17: 201–9.

Simms, R. 1998. "Mourning and Community at the Athenian Adonia." *Classical Journal* 93.2: 121–41.

Skinner, M. B. 1991. "Nossis *Thêlyglôssos*: The Private Text and the Public Book." In S. B. Pomeroy (ed.), *Women's History and Ancient History*. Chapel Hill, NC: University of North Carolina Press. 20–47.

—— 2001. "Ladies' Day at the Art Institute: Theocritus, Herodas, and the Gendered Gaze." In A. Lardinois and L. McClure (eds.), *Making Silence Speak: Women's Voices in Greek Literature and Society*. Princeton, NJ: Princeton University Press. 201–22.

Snyder, J. M. 1989. *The Woman and the Lyre: Women Writers in Classical Greece and Rome*. Carbondale, IL: Southern Illinois University Press.

Stambough, J. E. 1972. *Sarapis under the Early Ptolemies*. Leiden: E. J. Brill.

Stehle [Stigers], E. 2001. "The Good Daughter: Mothers' Tutelage in Erinna's *Distaff* and Fourth-century Epitaphs." In Lardinois and McClure (eds.), *Making Silence Speak*, 179–200.

Stephens, S. A. 2003. *Seeing Double: Intercultural Poetics in Ptolemaic Alexandria*. Berkeley, Los Angeles, and London: University of California Press.

—— 2005. "Lessons of the Crocodile." *Common Knowledge* 11.2: 215–39.

Stewart, A. 1997. *Art, Desire, and the Body in Ancient Greece*. Cambridge: Cambridge University Press.

Thompson, D. J. 2003. "The Ptolemies and Egypt." In A. Erskine (ed.), *A Companion to the Hellenistic World*. Oxford: Blackwell. 105–20.

Vasunia, P. 2001. *The Gift of the Nile: Hellenizing Egypt from Aeschylus to Alexander*. Berkeley, CA: University of California Press.

Walbank, F. W. 1981. *The Hellenistic World*. Cambridge, MA: Harvard University Press.

Walsh, G. B. 1990. "Surprised by Self: Audible Thought in Hellenistic Poetry." *Classical Philology* 85: 1–21.

—— 1991. "Callimachean Passages: The Rhetoric of Epitaph in Epigram." *Arethusa* 24: 77–105.

Watterson, B. 1984. *The Gods of Ancient Egypt*. London: B. T. Batsford Ltd.

West, M. L. 1977. "Erinna." *Zeitschrift für Papyrologie und Epigraphik* 25: 95–119.

—— 1996. *Die griechische Dichterin: Bild und Rolle*. Stuttgart: B. G. Teubner.

Whitehorne, J. 1995. "Women's Work in Theocritus, Idyll 15." *Hermes* 123: 63–75.

Further Reading

Bing, P. 2008. *The Well-Read Muse: Present and Past in Callimachus and the Hellenistic Poets*. Rev. edn. Ann Arbor: Michigan Classical Press. Influential analysis of the ways in which Alexandrian literature responded to the reality of a reading public.

Hutchinson, G. O. 1988. *Hellenistic Poetry*. Oxford: Clarendon Press. Standard treatment of major Alexandrian poets, their distinct themes and approaches, and their influence upon Roman poetry.

Meskell, L. 2002. *Private Life in New Kingdom Egypt*. Princeton and Oxford: Princeton University Press. Incorporates a rich body of archaeological and textual evidence to offer a detailed picture of private life among ordinary Egyptians, with an excellent chapter on romantic love, eroticism, and sexuality.

Montserrat, D. 1996. *Sex and Society in Graeco-Roman Egypt*. London and New York: Kegan Paul. Although this book covers a slightly later time period, it is one of the best introductions to sexual concepts and practices among ancient Egyptians.

Quirke, S. 1992. *Ancient Egyptian Religion*. London: British Museum Press. Accessible schematic explanation of key Egyptian religious beliefs.

Robins, G. 1993. *Women in Ancient Egypt*. Cambridge, MA: Harvard University Press. Brings together evidence from texts and material culture to present a comprehensive picture of women's lives.

Snyder, J. M. 1989. *The Woman and the Lyre: Women Writers in Classical Greece and Rome*. Carbondale, IL: Southern Illinois University Press. The best general introduction to women writers in antiquity, with a good discussion of the Hellenistic female poets.

Stephens, S. A. 2003. *Seeing Double: Intercultural Poetics in Ptolemaic Alexandria*. Berkeley, Los Angeles, and London: University of California Press. Examines the presence of motifs from Egyptian myth, ritual and tradition in Alexandrian poetry.

Vasunia, P. 2001. *The Gift of the Nile: Hellenizing Egypt from Aeschylus to Alexander*. Berkeley, CA: University of California Press. Surveys representations of Egypt in classical Greek literature in order to demonstrate their impact upon Alexander's imperial goals.

7

Early Rome: A Tale of Three Cultures

Academics' ingrained habit of compartmentalizing the history of classical antiquity as separate "Greek" and "Roman" segments can mislead students into thinking that the two peoples knew nothing of each other until Rome, having defeated **Carthage** in the Second Punic War (218–201 BCE), started looking around for somebody else to conquer. Yet archaeological evidence indicates that almost four centuries earlier the Romans were already well acquainted with Greek mythology and art. For example, the shrine of the Niger Lapis, or Black Stone, in the **Forum** was sacred to **Vulcan** (Hephaestus), and a votive deposit placed there in 580–570 BCE contained a fragment of an Attic black-figure cup illustrating the myth of Hephaestus' return to Olympus. A late sixth-century monumental grouping from the roof of an archaic temple in the Area Sacra di Sant'Omobono, now on display in the Montemartini Museum in Rome, portrays the apotheosis of Hercules, the Greek hero Heracles, who is being escorted to Olympus by Minerva (Athena). Both figures are immediately recognizable by their distinctive attributes of lion-skin and helmet, as seen on Attic vase paintings of the same period (Cornell 1995: 147–8, 162–3). Religion, art and artifacts, and other elements of Greek culture were introduced into archaic Rome either through Etruscan intermediaries or directly, via commerce with the Euboean colonists of Pithecusae (modern Ischia) and Cumae and the settlements of southern Italy (Magna Graecia). To commence an account of Roman Hellenization with the first diplomatic contacts between Rome and the Greek East in the third century BCE is therefore to begin too late: from its origins Rome had always known Greek influence in one form or another.

Isolating what is distinctly Roman in Greco-Roman constructions of sexuality cannot be done, then, by going back historically to a pristine pre-Greek era. Accounts of very old cults, like the Lupercalia, describe odd practices but offer no indication that underlying beliefs about human fertility differed from contemporaneous beliefs in mainland Greece.[1] At an early date, Roman gods were so closely identified with

Sexuality in Greek and Roman Culture, Second Edition. Marilyn B. Skinner.
© 2014 John Wiley & Sons, Inc. Published 2014 by John Wiley & Sons, Inc.

their more robust Greek counterparts that we are unable to turn to mythology to extract indigenous notions of Cupid or Venus. Literature, which is our best witness to patterns of thinking, was Hellenized from the outset: our earliest surviving texts, **Plautus'** comedies, written and produced between 205 and 184 BCE, are adaptations of Attic New Comedy. Lastly, the "Roman art" familiar from Pompeian wall paintings and statuary is for the most part a late Hellenistic art: fashioned by Greek craftsmen, it pleased the eye of Roman purchasers but, with certain exceptions, did not radically depart from the themes and styles of earlier Greek art. Many of the pieces found at **Pompeii** and Herculaneum are, in fact, reproductions of Greek works created in the fifth or fourth centuries BCE.

The impact of Etruscan culture is another complicating factor. Although the origin of the Etruscans was a disputed matter in both antiquity and earlier modern times, archaeologists now concur that their civilization developed out of the indigenous Villanovan culture of the thirteenth to eighth centuries BCE. By the sixth century, several confederations of major Etruscan cities had been established, extending from Northern Italy down to the Bay of Naples (Barker and Rasmussen 1998: 43–4, 141–78). The **Tarquin dynasty**, which ruled Rome until its expulsion in 510 BCE, had Etruscan ties. According to legend, its patriarch Tarquinius Priscus had been born in Etruscan Tarquinii, the son of a Corinthian immigrant; his mother was a native of that city and he himself had married Tanaquil, an Etruscan woman of high rank (Liv. 1.34.1–5). From the late seventh through the sixth centuries, when the Tarquins were once thought to be in power, the Roman populace had supposedly adopted a wide array of Etruscan institutions, including architecture, religious practices, ceremonials such as the triumph awarded a victorious general, military tactics, social organization, dress and magisterial insignia, the alphabet, and the calendar (Ogilvie 1976: 30–61). Recent scholarship, however, questions both the fact of Etruscan domination and the extent of Roman borrowing, positing instead a cultural amalgamation of "Greek, orientalising and native Italic elements" shared by all communities in this area of central Italy (Cornell 1995: 171–2). Whatever the case, it seems worthwhile to look briefly at Etruscan art for evidence of attitudes toward gender and sexuality that differ from those we have observed among classical and Hellenistic Greeks. Surviving Etruscan texts are of no help here, for most are funerary inscriptions and the rest religious.

We noted previously that the public visibility of aristocratic Etruscan wives scandalized Greek observers. Engraved metal goods fashioned for such women – mirrors and bronze chests – served as conspicuous markers of their status and provide inscriptional evidence for their literacy; the elaborate designs frequently show women and men interacting in mythic and real-life situations. Bonfante (1986: 240) notes the remarkable emphasis on groups of older women and younger men, sometimes lovers, sometimes identified as mother and son. The wealth and luxurious tastes of upper-class Etruscan women are reflected in detailed depictions of their fashionable dresses, shoes, hats, and jewelry on metalwork and in tomb paintings. All these representations emphasize leisure and enjoyment. They clash not only with classical Greek idealizations of the circumspect mistress of the household but also with Roman ideology valorizing the industrious matron.

Fig. 7.1 Sarcophagus and lid with husband and wife. Italic, Etruscan, Late Classical or Early Hellenistic Period, about 350–300 BCE. Findspot: Italy, Lazio, Vulci. Place of Manufacture: Italy, Lazio, Vulci. Marble. Height × width × length: 93.3 × 117.4 × 213.8 cm (36 3/4 × 46 1/4 × 84 3/16 in.). Source: Museum of Fine Arts, Boston. Museum purchase with funds donated by contribution and the Benjamin Pierce Cheney Fund. 86.145a–b. Photograph © 2013 Museum of Fine Arts, Boston.

As for sex, its symbolic presence in Etruscan funerary art is particularly striking. The front panel of a cinerary urn from Chiusi, now in the Louvre, depicts satyrs engaging in wild copulation at a banquet (Brendel 1970: 28 and fig. 21). Some tombs, such as the sixth-century Tomb of the Bulls in Tarquinia, contain paintings of intercourse, both same-sex and heterosexual; motifs in other tombs include a phallus, a man farting or excreting, and a scene of a woman being whipped. These have been interpreted as apotropaic images protecting the dead from harm and, in the case of the last picture, a Dionysiac allusion to suffering and rebirth. Other tomb paintings show married couples warmly conversing at dinner. Sarcophagi display husband and wife reclining in an embrace, as in the famous "Sarcophagus of the Spouses" from Cerveteri, now in the Louvre, or nude and lying together under a single blanket, "making eye and body contact" (Hallett 1988: 1267) in the sensuous manner shown here (fig. 7.1).

Bonfante argues that this use of erotic imagery in familial burial contexts is life-affirming, since it insists upon the continuity of affection beyond the grave and may also work to ensure the fertility of surviving descendants (1996: 155, 166).

Roman funerary art, in contrast, does not make use of overt sexual symbolism. We will see, though, that the employment of the phallus as an apotropaic charm was ubiquitous in Roman daily life, and it is arguable that other household decorations from Pompeii and Herculaneum with seemingly prurient sexual content (only recently put on display in the National Archaeological Museum at Naples) may have been intended to bring the beholder good luck rather than arouse him.

The Pecking Order

Bearing in mind that some aspects of a Roman model of eroticism may be of Etruscan origin, can we isolate any conspicuous departures from the patterns we have identified in Greek materials? In Latin literature produced between approximately 200 BCE and 14 CE, that is, during the last two centuries of the Republic and extending into the **principate** of **Augustus**, the first Roman emperor, the conceptual framework of sexual relations seems much the same as the one prevailing in Greek art and literature from the archaic to the Hellenistic period: sex is, in essence, a dominance–submission relationship. Although the "penetration model" does not cover the full spectrum of sexual acts performed in those Roman texts, a hierarchy of dominance and submission is assumed even in circumstances where participants deviate from the norm.

However, factors determining sexual dominance were not assigned the same degree of weight in the Greek *polis* and the Roman megalopolis because social configurations were not the same. In the classical Greek city-state, where the male citizen population was relatively small and homogeneous, the crucial requirement for dominance over boys, women, and non-citizens was adult manhood.[2] Roman social stratification was far more complex. In one specialist's words (Fredrick 2002: 9–10):

> Rome in the first century BCE presents a finely nuanced social hierarchy from elite senators and knights down to the freeborn; "beneath" them, freed slaves of low political status but considerable economic opportunity (many enjoyed economic superiority over freeborn citizens); "beneath" them, cadres of domestic and rural slaves carefully graded in status and function (many slaves enjoyed better living conditions and more responsibilities than free citizens).

Owing to these paradoxes of stratigraphy, rank and class were more decisive in calibrating sexual power relations than physiological manhood. During the Republic, the body of the Roman **vir**, the adult citizen male, was regarded as inviolable, legally protected from sexual penetration, beating, and torture. Thus biological sex would appear to confer bodily immunity. In actuality, though, the word *vir* was applied selectively to adult freeborn citizen males in good standing and positioned at the top of the hierarchy; slaves, freed persons, and "disreputable" individuals did not enjoy the same protections from assault as the well-born did. What seems a distinct physiological term is actually a description of "gender-as-social-status," involving factors such as birth, citizenship, and respectability that to our way of thinking have nothing to do with gender (Walters 1997: 32). For the Romans, they did, because the male who did not enjoy such bodily protection was automatically effeminized.

The institution of **patronage**, which created vertical networks of authority and influence, complicated existing social asymmetries. Patronage is a system in which two individuals of unequal status, the higher-ranking patron and his lesser client, trade goods and services on a personal basis, each according to his means (Saller 1982: 1). The democratic ideology of classical Athens was hostile to personal patronage, since it undercut notional political equality by calling attention to disparities in wealth and social standing (Millett 1989: 17). In Rome, however, patronage relations permeated all levels of society. Former masters and mistresses automatically became patrons of their freed slaves, who were expected to provide part-time assistance to them and show ongoing respect. Because the system was based on social advantage rather than sex, high-ranking women could have male clients of good, though inferior, birth.[3] Attention to intricate gradations of social position spilled over into sexual relations and became a controlling factor in the construction of Roman sexuality. The slave's body was wholly at his master's disposal; ex-masters might even continue to obtain sexual services from freed slaves, though whether they could demand them is debatable (Sen. *Controv.* 4 pr. 10; Butrica 2005: 210–21). Consequently, a freeborn client's public deference to his great patron might be scandalously distorted through rumor and innuendo into a quasi-sexual mode of servitude (Oliensis 1997: 154–5). Roman social and sexual hierarchies are two interrelated systems that "can hardly be understood independently" of each other (Richlin 1993: 532).

Social standing is so closely tied in the Roman imagination to exercise of sexual privilege that writers regularly employ phallic imagery as a concrete metaphor for the workings of power. The poet Catullus, having served on the staff of Memmius, governor of Bithynia in 57–56 BCE, vents his annoyance at his former boss: "O Memmius, while I lay on my back you slowly rammed me in the mouth with that whole beam of yours well and at length" (28.9–10). In actuality, Memmius had done nothing more than impose restraints on his subordinates to prevent them from financially exploiting the natives, thereby disappointing Catullus, who had gone to Bithynia hoping to make money. Greek authors restricted such use of obscenity as a symbolic code to genres such as iambic verse and Old Comedy, but in Latin materials it appears more frequently, and differences in genre only govern whether the activity is vividly represented, as in Catullus' complaint, or implied through euphemism. This troping strategy accounts for many of the racy tidbits about the private lives of Roman women and emperors that found their way into ancient history and biography and are still regarded by some as credible fact.

Apart from the Roman tendency to sensationalize political and social transactions between unequals by painting them in lurid hues, three other areas of cultural dissimilarity have been pinpointed. The first is a salient difference recently explored in considerable depth. Although sexual attraction to youths was regarded as completely normal, just as it was in Greece, Roman men were rigorously prohibited by law as well as custom from sexual contact with freeborn citizen boys. Violation of the physical integrity of a citizen youth was treated as the equivalent of unlawful relations with unmarried women and punished as ***stuprum***, a criminal sexual act (Fantham 1991; Williams 2010: 103–36). In Plautus' *Curculio*, the hero, infatuated with a courtesan owned by a pimp, receives the following advice from his slave (35–8):

> Nobody forbids anyone to walk on the public street;
> as long as you don't cut a path through a fenced area,
> as long as you keep away from the bride, the widow, the virgin,
> the young man, and freeborn boys, love whom you please.

Pederasty, as an institutionalized cross-generational relationship of two Roman citizens, thus becomes unthinkable. Furthermore, because slaves and prostitutes were the only legitimate objects of male homoerotic desire, relationships with boys were often treated as trivial even by those who viewed them in a favorable light.

A second difference in attitudes has to do with concerns surrounding the chastity of the ***matrona***, the married woman of respectable status. Elite matrons were publicly visible representatives of their natal, even more than their marital, families (Hallett 1984); their legal and economic position assured them a central role in religious observance and a key part in the workings of the patronage networks that permeated the social structure. That visibility, however, made women's sexual behavior a sphere of unease for the community as well as for their kinfolk. The prosperity and power of the state, the ***res publica***, depended upon the continued good will of the gods, who were profoundly offended, it was thought, by the wickedness of the ruling classes. If sexual immorality was rampant (and in Roman moralizing speech it always is), the fault was not laid at the door of the adulterer, as in Greece, but at that of the irresponsible, pleasure-seeking woman (Liebeschuetz 1979: 45–7). Adultery was therefore a serious ethical issue in both Greece and Rome, but with different causes and consequences in each society.

Finally, a more tenuous contrast has been perceived: Roman society is variously described as "sadistic" (Kiefer 2000 [1934]: 75–117), "macho" (Davidson 2001: 28–9), or "Priapic" (Richlin 1992; Williams 2010: 18) to a degree that Greek society was not. According to this hypothesis, a "hyper-masculine identity," to borrow Craig Williams's phrase, was publicly demonstrated by aggression – verbal, as in attacks upon political or legal opponents, or even physical, if the other party was of low status. Hostilities took place before witnesses because power relations had to be acknowledged openly. Sex, violence, and spectacle are thus securely linked together in the Roman mentality. The popularity of gladiatorial games, with their accompanying slaughter of wild beasts and brutal punishments of condemned criminals, might be explained in this fashion (Lilja 1983: 135). Whether there was, in fact, a greater propensity toward violence in Roman culture and, if so, what factors might account for it are questions that deserve much fuller investigation. In the remainder of the chapter, we will consider each of the three areas of diversity listed above in greater depth, turning to literature, art, history, and law to bring such elements of Roman sexual ideology into better focus.

Imported Vices

According to the late first-century BCE historian **Sallust**, Rome fell from grace once she became mistress of the world (Sall. *Cat.* 10–13). Formerly her people had been virtuous, frugal, and self-disciplined, but the temptations of leisure and riches proved too much. Avarice and ambition began to erode morality. Under the dictatorship of Sulla, who seized control of Rome in 82 BCE, greed instigated property confiscations and massacres of Roman citizens. Roman armies had meanwhile been exposed to the softening effects of Eastern luxury. Disposable wealth invited degeneracy (13.3):

> But the appetite for sexual offenses, gluttony, and other refinements had advanced to an equal degree: men played the woman's role [*viri muliebria pati*, literally "men endured things done to women"], women made their chastity available; for dining they sought out all the products of land and sea; they slept before they felt a desire for sleep; they did not wait upon hunger or thirst, or cold, or fatigue, but by soft living anticipated all these things.

Here moral depravity manifests itself through a perversion of natural appetites, including those for food, drink, and sleep as well as sex.

That narrative of decline is one to which most concerned Romans would have subscribed, although they might have located the point of collapse earlier. In the middle decades of the second century BCE, traditionalists like **Cato the Censor** were already castigating fellow members of the nobility for their uncontrolled self-indulgence. Polybius, a Greek eyewitness of events in the capital city, reports that young men who had been exposed to Hellenistic opulence during the recent campaign (171–167 BCE) against King Perseus of Macedon were setting such a fashion for extravagance that outrageous sums were being paid for slave catamites and jars of imported smoked fish. Infuriated, Cato protested in a speech before the Roman people that "they could most readily recognize that the state was going to the bad, when pretty boys being sold fetched more than fields and jars of smoked fish more than ox-drivers" (Polyb. 31.25.5). In this and other moralizing texts, the same progression of events can be traced: money permits its possessors to wallow in pleasure, addiction to pleasure leads to even more heinous conduct, and the destabilization of the Roman state follows. Self-evident as this complex of ideas seemed to Roman writers, its assumptions require unpacking. For now we will let them stand, but you might want to pencil in a question mark beside Sallust's and Cato's statements.

In constructing such accounts, the Romans laid the blame for their deterioration on exposure to Greek ways. They represented native ancestral customs, or the ***mos maiorum***, as strict and austere; debauchery was a foreign import. This contention encouraged scholars of a quarter-century ago to envision archaic Rome as a puritanical society where "acceptable sexual behavior was limited to heterosexual marital intercourse" (Hallett 1988: 1268) because the manpower demands of agriculture and warfare required procreation (Lilja 1983: 134). All forms of same-sex congress were supposedly disapproved, and homoeroticism only became a cultural practice after the upper classes began to adopt a Hellenized mode of life in the third century BCE. Ramsay MacMullen cites the number of Greek loan-words in what he calls the Roman "vocabulary of homosexuality"[4] (*paedico*, the verb for anal penetration, derived from Greek *pais*, "boy"; *pathicus* and *cinaedus*, two Latin equivalents for *kinaidos*; *catamitus*, a young male sex object) and suggests that these, like similar Graecisms for items of luxury such as cosmetics, garments, and edibles, point to "a way of life imported as a package, and on occasion repudiated as such" (1982: 486). Citing the pronouncements of the Stoic philosophers **Seneca the Younger** and **Epictetus**, one can then argue, with MacMullen, that this aberrant way of life, which was confined to a minority, continued to be bitterly denounced by the rest of society; or one can declare, on the basis of the picture given by poets of the **Augustan Age**, that upper-class Romans had become so thoroughly Hellenized by the end of the first century BCE that relations with boys were "both very common and very lightly viewed" (Griffin 1986: 25). Either way, that is an impressionistic method of doing history, for the answer to the question of whether elite Roman males were converted to pederasty through contact with Greece will depend on the type of evidence one selects.

Later studies have clarified this issue by drawing the line between traditionally permitted and forbidden sexual objects. In Rome no blame was attached to the man who indulged in sex with either his own male slave or a male prostitute, provided that he took the active role and that financial expenditure, if any, was kept within reasonable limits (Cantarella 1992: 101–4; Williams 2010: 20–9). The poet **Horace**, who adopts an admonitory stance in his *Satires*, asks his addressee whether, when dying of thirst, he would demand a golden goblet to drink from, or disdain everything except peacock and turbot when starving. No? Well, then,

> ... when your groin bulges,
> if a servant-girl or estate-born boy is handy, whom you can jump on
> right away, would you prefer being ruptured by the swelling?
> Not me; I want my sex ready and accessible. (*Sat.* 1.2.114–19)

To make his point, Horace strips away the romance of desire, picturing coitus as a process for relieving a bothersome physical urge and using one's own property as the simplest and easiest way of doing it. The absolute indifference to the sex of the object in this quasi-ethical pronouncement should indicate that the act of copulation with a male slave was not, for the slave-owning population, a moral issue. As for the elder Cato, when he inveighs against the purchase of boys for sexual use, is he denouncing pederasty? Not in itself, any more than he is denouncing smoked fish. Rather, his anger is directed at rich young men who lavish enormous amounts of cash on personal gratification rather than earmarking wealth for productive agricultural projects. That waste of resources, in his view, is what threatens Roman stability (Edwards 1993: 177). Such feelings would be entirely characteristic of Cato; his frugality was legendary, and his sole criterion for judging something good was its use–value.[5]

Citizen youths were strictly off limits, though, and in fact the chastity of the freeborn boy was an area of considerable social concern. Below the age of puberty, such boys wore special clothing, a purple-bordered toga and a golden amulet (*bulla*) to mark their status. Matrons and boys were protected by law from unwanted attention; following them on the street, suborning their attendants, or pestering them was legally actionable (Ulp. *Dig.* 47.10.15.15–23). Another law, the *Lex Scatinia* or *Scantinia*, may have punished actual sexual congress with protected minors, but the provisions of that law are so unclear and so debated (see Cantarella 1992: 106–14; Richlin 1993: 569–71; Williams 2010: 130–6) that it is best left to one side. What is absolutely beyond doubt is that Roman jurists put unmarried women and boys on the same footing, defining intercourse with them as a sexual offense, *stuprum*, and, by the third century CE, prescribing capital punishment for an accomplished seduction (Paulus *Dig.* 47.11.1.2). Consequently, there was no provision for courtship of free citizen youths in the Roman scheme of sexual morality. Anecdotal evidence indicates that seductions of boys occurred, but concerns about adultery with matrons were far more prevalent.

Can we speak of "pederasty" at all when dealing with Roman practices of boy-love? Since the power dynamics in the relationship were so distinct from those courtships figured on Greek vases and imagined in the dialogues of Plato, it is hard to relate one to the other. Slave boys who were special favorites were known as ***delicati***, "pets" – yet, no matter how indulged, were at the mercy of their owner. As for the prostitute, his client bought what services he wanted. Some pantomime actors were much in demand, like Bathyllus, reputed to be the favorite of Augustus' friend **Maecenas** (Tac. *Ann.* 1.54), but even so were stigmatized and suffered legal disabilities because of their profession (Edwards 1997). In such relations there was no room for the flexibility and negotiation theoretically possible in the encounter of the Greek *erastês* and *erômenos*, with its moral demands on both citizen participants.

In literary renderings of homoerotic affairs, Roman poets adopted the romantic conventions of Hellenistic epigram, praising the boy's beauty and lamenting his coyness, avarice, infidelity, and so on. Catullus teases us by addressing pederastic verse to a Juventius, the offspring, it is hinted, of a genuine old Roman family (poems 24 and 81; on the family itself, of Etruscan origins and consular rank, see Cic. *Planc.* 19 and 58). Yet the name, derived from *iuvenis* ("youth"), is implausibly apt; though its owner is real, we can guess at a private in-joke in which a friend is humorously written into a stock situation (Macleod 1973). Horace and **Tibullus** give the beloved a Greek name to signal that they write in the tradition of Alcaeus and Anacreon. Latin authors, then, handle these pederastic motifs in an artificial way. Perhaps one attraction of such poetry was its evocation of a fantasy situation that could glamorize the mechanics of sexual transactions with slaves and hired partners.

Bringing Women under Control

Greeks and Romans were fascinated analysts of divergences in each other's customs. Matters of sex and gender drew the attention of observers on both sides. Polybius, the product of a culture in which respectable women, even after the social transformations of the fourth and third centuries, were still expected to be relatively unobtrusive, was struck by the ostentation of the female relatives of his Roman friend Scipio Aemilianus. Here is his recollection of how Scipio's aunt Aemilia paraded her wealth when attending women's cult ceremonies (31.26.3–5):

> It happened that Aemilia, for this was the name of the aforementioned woman, had a magnificent cortege in women's processions, because she had shared the life and fortune of Scipio [Africanus, the adoptive grandfather of Scipio Aemilianus] at its height. For, apart from the ornamentation of her person and her mule-cart, all the baskets and the cups and the other paraphernalia of sacrifice were of silver or gold, and all the objects accompanied her on these conspicuous outings, and there were a corresponding number of slave-boys and maidservants following along.

When Aemilia died, Polybius goes on, Aemilianus, who inherited her estate, bestowed these trappings on his own mother Papiria. Though of high birth, she had been divorced and was living on modest means. Up until then, Papiria had not participated in public pageants, but at the next festival, sure enough, she turned up with the retinue that had been Aemilia's. Female spectators recognized the muleteers, team, and wagon, and, impressed by her son's generosity, called down blessings upon him (6–8).

It was customary for aristocratic Roman ladies to advertise the achievements of male kin through their luxurious clothing and appointments; these were, as a speaker in Livy's history affirms, the equivalent of men's magistracies and badges of office (Liv. 34.7.8–9). The fact that the populace was familiar with Aemilia's vehicle indicates that such displays made quite an impression on bystanders. However, the man who funded them might view them in a different light: "I don't much like these highly connected women, their airs, their huge dowries, their loud demands, their arrogance, their ivory carriages, their dresses, their purple, who reduce their husbands to slavery with their expenses" (Plaut. *Aul.* 167–9). Cato, needless to say, was of the same mind. Attempting to defeat the repeal of a sumptuary law restraining women's extravagance, he is made to argue: "Whoever can pay from her own means, will; she who can't will ask her husband. That poor man – both the one who consents and the one who doesn't, since what he hasn't given he'll see given by someone else" (Liv. 34.4.16–17). Adultery is always one step behind luxury in this way of thinking.

Cornelius Nepos, who wrote Latin biographies of eminent men, observes in his preface that different peoples judge different things honorable and shameful, evaluating them according to ancestral tradition. To illustrate: the Athenian Cimon married his half-sister on his father's side, a criminal act by Roman standards; in Crete it is praiseworthy for adolescents to have many lovers; Spartan widows take paramours; and Greeks see no disgrace in being an athlete or actor. "Many things, on the other hand, which we deem proper they would pronounce appalling – specifically, the conduct of our women" (Nep. 6–7):

> For what Roman man is ashamed to escort his wife to a dinner party? Or what lady of the manor does not sit in the forecourt of the house and venture out in public? In Greece it's very different, for a woman is not summoned to dinner unless it's with

relatives, nor does she reside anywhere but in the interior part of the house, which is called the "women's quarters," where no one goes except those connected by close ties of blood.

Despite Nepos' bland assurances that Roman husbands were comfortable with their wives' presence in society, however, the activities of women outside the home, especially among the upper classes, were perceived as a weak point in the ethical system and a potential danger to the collective order.

The story of the **rape of the Sabine women**, one of Rome's founding myths, provides archetypal justification for the elite Roman wife's participation in men's affairs. Romulus and his band of fugitives and outcasts, seeking wives, invite the neighboring Sabines and their families to attend a festival, then, at a given signal, kidnap the young women present. When the Sabines, having assembled a coalition, march on Rome to rescue their daughters, the women run between the two armies, holding up their babies (it took a while to assemble that coalition), and negotiate a peace between Sabine fathers and Roman sons-in-law. Given in marriage, the daughter of a leading senatorial family was expected to follow the Sabine women's example of maintaining a dual loyalty (Pomeroy 1975: 186). Marriage was a practical medium for cementing political and economic alliances between two such families. Wives, who remained closely bonded to their fathers (Hallett 1984: 76–110), could serve as intermediaries when strategies were being formulated, and, if differences arose between members of the natal and marital families, were expected to help resolve them. Their political interests were notionally, therefore, an extension of a praiseworthy readiness to assist the men related to them by blood and marriage.

There were, however, two distinct forms of marriage. Roman fathers maintained permanent control, *patria potestas*, over their adult sons and daughters, which in theory extended to possessing rights of life and death over them (Just. *Inst.* 1.9). Yet custody was transferable, and under one arrangement the bride became subject to the authority (*manus*) of her husband. Whatever property she owned was reassigned to him as dowry (Cic. *Top.* 23). Legally, she entered his family on the same basis as a daughter: if he died intestate, she shared in his estate equally with her children (Treggiari 1991: 28–9). In the other type of marriage, the bride and her property remained under the authority of her own father while he lived. If she died without making a valid will her natal family, parents or siblings, would automatically inherit. Should her father predecease her, she became independent, although permission of a male guardian, or *tutor*, often a member of her paternal family, was required for important legal and economic transactions. Tutelage allowed her kinfolk to keep an eye on her estate, for she would need her guardian's approval to bequeath an inheritance to any outsiders, including her own children – who were part of her husband's family, not hers (Treggiari 1991: 32). Because upper-class women had become very wealthy by the end of the Republic, owning considerable property and managing it on a day-to-day basis themselves, this latter marriage arrangement came to prevail, as it was in the best financial interests of blood kin. However, marriage without *manus* meant that a husband technically could not restrict his wife's person or her business dealings, whereas her father or guardian, who could, lived in a different household and was not in a position to supervise her. This gave women considerable personal freedom and allowed them to operate on their own initiative, even in the public sphere (Pomeroy 1975: 154–5).

Although the activities of elite Roman women as patrons, investors, creditors, and benefactors are under-reported compared with those of their male counterparts, enough documentation exists to indicate that they were well integrated into wide commercial and economic networks. They were also energetically involved in conferring favors and lobbying. The Romans would not have understood our insistence upon intrinsic merit and lack of favoritism in appointments: for them, a candidate was especially well qualified for a job if someone close to power was able and willing to pull strings on his behalf. Wives and mothers of magistrates, provincial governors, and military officers were strategically placed to do so and their assistance was regularly sought. If pressure of this sort was applied to help male relatives, it was usually condoned, since female kin were expected to support the careers of family members. Thus Seneca, later to become Nero's chief advisor, publicly thanks his mother Helvia for financial resources and benefits that furthered his advancement but notes quite pointedly that she had not called in that debt by taking advantage of his own station to ask favors for others, as many mothers would do (*Helv.* 14.2–3).[6]

The problem with women's involvement in dealings of this kind, where gifts, loans, benefits, and legacies greased the wheels of patronage by creating reciprocal obligations to be repaid, was that by its very nature it was more ambiguous than men's (Dixon 2001: 100–6). Pulling strings could be commendable, as when a son's career was being launched, or sinister and corrupt, as when wives of governors were accused in the Roman senate of using their presence abroad to enrich themselves (Tac. *Ann.* 3.33–4). When influence was underhandedly applied, men feared the subversion of legitimate decision-making power. Even if a woman did not play for such high stakes, and was only interested in getting a good return on her capital, loans and investments involving men other than her kin could be misinterpreted as sexually motivated. The classic instance is the loan the noblewoman **Clodia Metelli** made to M. Caelius Rufus, at that time an associate of her brother P. Clodius Pulcher (Dixon 2001: 102). When Caelius was later prosecuted on a charge of street violence and Clodia appeared as a prosecution witness, Caelius' lawyer Cicero maliciously twisted help for her brother's confederate into proof of sexual intimacy (Cic. *Cael.* 31). Cicero himself once considered borrowing money from a certain Caerellia, elderly enough to be above suspicion, yet he was still warned that for a man of his stature being in debt to a woman made a bad impression (Cic. *Att.* 12.51.3).

Adultery was an extremely important matter in Roman society, as the number and variety of sources on the topic attest (Richlin 1981). Although the honor of fathers, brothers, and husbands was not as compromised by a woman's misconduct as it was in Greece (Treggiari 1991: 311–12; Edwards 1993: 54–5), men must still have been troubled by the possibility of public scandal and consequent notoriety.[7] Jokes in Martial (6.39) and **Juvenal** (6.76–81, 597–601; 9.86–90) on children not sired by their putative fathers indicate that husbands may have been nervous about spurious offspring.[8] In addition to those issues, such unease seems an obvious way of displacing vague misgivings about wives' independent conduct of their business and social affairs onto a tangible area of concern.[9] Lastly, anxieties over societal changes in late Republican Rome precipitated by continued civil unrest, including a loss of confidence in patronage ties and the weakening of accepted class boundaries, appear to find concrete expression in tales of well-born adulteresses attracted to social inferiors (Edwards 1993: 52–3). Adultery therefore may be a metaphor for a number of broader worries that had nothing to do with female sexual conduct.

Male alarm about a woman's associations with other men was not, of course, completely unfounded: opportunities for wrongdoing were available especially for someone like Clodia Metelli, a widow who lived in her own house on the **Palatine Hill** and was no longer subject to a father's jurisdiction. Few seriously doubt that she did have an affair with the poet Catullus (see below). However, we cannot know how much of what Cicero said to discredit her was sheer invention (Skinner 1983; Dixon 2001: ch. 9; see now Skinner 2011: 96–116). That has not stopped scholars, even in these more mistrustful times, from swallowing his allegations wholesale and regurgitating them as historical "facts" about Roman noblewomen.

When Julius Caesar's nephew and adopted son **Octavian**, later the emperor Augustus, defeated Antony and Cleopatra at Actium in 31 BCE, it marked the end of a century of civil war and internal discord. Roman thinkers had been quick to assign blame for the sufferings experienced by the peoples of Italy and the provinces during this period to the arrogance, covetousness, and ambition of powerful leaders – the Gracchi, Marius, Sulla, Pompey, Caesar, Marc Antony, and their friends and supporters. The struggles they engaged in were considered virulent symptoms, however, of a graver disease, the flagrant immorality of the elite. Justification of Rome's rule over the rest of the world was based on her ability to impose a fair and stable peace on warring nations, which required that she herself had to demonstrate her own moral capacity to govern (Galinsky 1981: 134–8). Leading families' neglect of religion, resistance to marriage and reproduction, and tolerance of adultery were thought to have provoked divine wrath, endangering Rome's claims to empire. Already in 46 BCE Cicero had urged Julius Caesar, then dictator, to shore up a collapsing society through strict laws that, among other things, would repress license and further the propagation of children (*Marcell.* 23). In January of 27, after annexing Egypt, discharging his veterans, and celebrating a triple triumph, Octavian proclaimed the restitution of the Republic. In return, he obtained from the Senate a grant of proconsular ***imperium*** ("military command") and accepted the title of *Augustus* ("venerable") in recognition of his capacity for principled leadership (Galinsky 1996: 15–16). From that point on, he undertook the long-term task of sponsoring a program of civic and moral renewal that would restore religion and family to a central place in Roman aristocratic life.

In the year 28 BCE, as the ***princeps*** ("leading citizen," another of his titles) informs us in an inscription, the ***Res Gestae***, summing up his achievements, he began repairs on eighty-two urban temples (Aug. *RG* 20.4), a first step toward reconciliation with the divine order. Attempts, probably a year later, to impose legal penalties on unmarried men of the upper classes met with determined resistance (Suet. *Div. Aug.* 34). The love elegist **Propertius** may refer to that abortive project when he represents himself and his mistress Cynthia rejoicing at the withdrawal of legislation that would have compelled him to marry a woman of his own station. One couplet of his elegy expresses sour cynicism about the military needs driving efforts to boost the declining birthrate: "Why should I supply sons for patriotic triumph-processions? No child of my blood will be a soldier" (Prop. 2.7.13–14). That reaction would be only too predictable for a generation of young men born during the late 50s and early 40s who had lived all their lives under the cloud of civil war.

Perhaps in response to protests such as these, the concluding poem in Horace's sequence of "Roman Odes," published in 23 and addressing the ethical and political conflicts of the preceding decade, mounts a direct attack on the stereotype of the sexually daring woman popularized by Propertius and his fellow love elegists. *Ode* 3.6 begins by warning the present generation of punishments to come should the shrines neglected by predecessors continue to decay (*lines* 1–4). Roman rule is grounded on piety toward the gods, and recent military defeats hint at divine wrath not yet expiated (5–16). In the central stanzas, Horace traces the source of Rome's evils to the home and the future bride who learns seductive wiles even before her marriage (21–32):

> Generations pregnant with wrongdoing
> first defiled marriage and offspring and the household;
>   flowing from this source a river of bloodshed
>   has saturated our country and its people;   20
> the ripe virgin is pleased to learn Ionic dances
> and is trained in coquetry and now already
>   thinks upon unchaste adventures
>   at a tender age;
> soon she is seeking younger lovers   25
> while her husband drinks, nor does she select
>   someone to give illicit delights to
>   furtively, while the lights are dim,
> but openly sought, with her spouse's knowledge
> she rises, whether a shopkeeper bids her,   30
>   or the captain of a Spanish freighter,
>   a profligate buyer of shame.

Why should this young woman and her easygoing husband be held responsible for Rome's military reversals? Because, Horace goes on, the men who defeated Carthage and the monarchs of the East were not born of such parents. Sons of soldiers, raised in the Sabine hills, while their fathers were away at war they toiled until sundown performing hard farm work – breaking ground with mattocks, hauling cut wood – at the bidding of a strict mother (33–44). Moral authority resides in the forceful woman who, in her husband's absence, trains her sons in obedience and accustoms them to strenuous physical labor:

The salient role of the women portrayed admiringly in Latin literature was as disciplinarians, custodians of Roman culture and traditional morality. The familiar modern contrast between the authoritative father-figure and the gentle (and powerless) mother is strikingly absent. The ideal mother of Latin literature is a formidable figure. (Dixon 1988: xiv)

If Horace's errant virgin is incapable of instilling such principles in her children, they in turn will be even more lax with their own children; the process is cumulative (Liebeschuetz 1979: 93). For this reason, and in spite of the hopes raised by endorsing Augustus' scheme of temple renovation, the poem concludes on a note of despair: "the age of our parents, worse than our grandfathers, brought us forth, who are worse than they were and are soon to give birth to offspring even more degenerate" (46–8). Of all the late Republican-era sermons preached on the topic of moral decline (and there were quite a few), it is this poem that articulates most plainly the tight conceptual linkage between religious piety, military courage, and a stern maternal integrity far more rigorous than mere chastity.

Augustus succeeded in passing his legislation on marriage and children in 18 BCE (Cass. Dio 54.16.1–2). It comprised two statutes, the **Lex Iulia de maritandis ordinibus** regulating marriages among the elite classes – including both senators and equestrians, well-born individuals not directly involved in politics – and the **Lex Iulia de adulteriis coercendis** attempting to discourage adultery. The former, which was supplemented by the *Lex Papia Poppaea* in 9 CE, imposed legal disabilities upon men and women who remained unmarried during their reproductive years and rewarded parents of three or more children with benefits – preferential career advancement for men, exemption from tutelage for women. It also forbade senators and their descendants to marry freedwomen and actresses (Paulus *Dig.* 23.2.44 pr.) but recognized freedwomen's marriages to freeborn men of the lower classes as valid, provided such women were not of bad character. Prostitutes could form a valid marriage only with freedmen. Bans on senators marrying freedwomen were probably not necessary, as snobbery discouraged the practice. Politicians might slander each other by alleging that their enemies were products of such *mésalliances*, but factual evidence to support those allegations is lacking.

The Julian law on adultery made the act of consorting with a married woman a public offense to be tried before a standing criminal court (McGinn 1998: 140–7). The husband, who was compelled to divorce his wife once he harbored suspicions of her, had the exclusive right, along with her father, to initiate a prosecution for sixty days after commission of the putative offense; after that, any qualified third party might do so. Since a successful prosecutor received a share of the property confiscated from those found guilty, both the incentive to bring an accusation and the possibility of false accusation existed. The alleged adulterer was tried first; if he was convicted, the wife was tried. Parties found guilty were both subjected to severe financial penalties and relegated to separate islands, perhaps for only a stipulated period of time. They also incurred civil disabilities: the adulterer lost his civic privileges, including the right to serve in the army; the woman involved was forbidden to remarry. There were provisions for those who took the law into their own hands. A father catching his daughter in bed with a lover either in his own house or in that of her husband could kill both offenders with impunity, even if he had previously handed his daughter over to the *manus* of her husband (Treggiari 1991: 282). A husband might kill a lover of low status: a slave, a freedman of the family, or someone whose profession made him disreputable, such as a gladiator or actor. Under no circumstances could he kill his own wife. Husbands also could not collude in their wives' misdeeds: if a man knew that adultery had taken place and did not divorce his spouse and initiate a prosecution, he too could be charged with criminal conduct (Paulus *Dig.* 2.26.1–8).

Prior to the passage of the Julian law, accusations of adultery brought against a woman would have been dealt with by a council of kinfolk most likely composed of representatives of both families (Treggiari 1991: 267–8). The matter might have been treated leniently, since, from the offended husband's point of view, a quiet divorce was usually the best solution. Criminalization of sexual misbehavior sought to replace flexible attitudes of family members weighing the practical consequences of various options with an uncompromising ideological rationale for discouraging marital infidelity. Giving the father permission to kill his daughter was a concession to *patria potestas*, but otherwise the Julian law completely removed jurisdiction over the adulteress from her family. Whether that regulation had the deterrent outcome intended is unclear. In the historical record, there are certainly numerous prosecutions for adultery, but some were undoubtedly politically motivated. Those were the sensational cases, remembered because of the prominence of the parties involved. Treggiari points out that, in comparison with other kinds of criminal accusations, the number of possible defendants was greater – men and women of all classes could be charged – and so was the pool of third-party prosecutors (1991: 298). Wealthy philanderers were doubtless the likeliest targets of accusation. The massive discussion of legal issues surrounding adultery in the writings of late imperial jurisconsults may indicate that actual trials of non-senatorial parties were common, or that the technical problems posed by the statute gave rise to an endless stream of hypotheticals.

The Julian legislation had the pragmatic corollary effect of creating a caste of sex workers (McGinn 1998: 156–71). While the respectable matron was distinguished by her costume of long robe and hair ribbons, the prostitute customarily wore a man's toga (this cross-dressing, certainly symbolic, may mark her degraded condition as a "public" woman). Augustus' legislation formalized the existing dress code and required the convicted woman to wear the prostitute's garment, a stipulation that conflated adultery with venal promiscuity. At the same time, the statute defined certain groups of women as exempt from its jurisdiction: slaves, whores and madams, foreigners not married to Roman citizens, the latter because their private activities were of no interest to the state (McGinn 1998: 194–9). Later jurists placed the condemned adulteress herself in the same category. Men could have sexual relations with such women without fear of committing *stuprum*. However, prostitutes were obligated to register as professionals with the authorities. When Vistilia, a member of a high-ranking family, attempted in 19 CE to avoid impending prosecution by registering, the Senate closed that loophole by passing a decree that no woman of the upper classes would be allowed to prostitute herself (Tac. *Ann.* 2.85). "Respectable" and "non-respectable" women were not only distinguished outwardly but also legally distanced from each other by social rank.

Butchery for Fun

Studying late Republican Rome, T. P. Wiseman thinks, is "like visiting some teeming capital in a dangerous and ill-governed foreign country" because its mores were not ours. As he embarks upon an exposé of Roman brutality, he warns that what will follow "is not for the squeamish" (1985: 4–5). References to instruments of torture taken for granted in ancient sources – lashes, the rack, red-hot metal plates – are made grimmer by the awareness that such penalties were inflicted publicly, at least in the imperial era. Slaves and lower-class criminals were most liable to be tortured; by the end of the second century CE, as we will see, a formal status distinction between the "more distinguished" (**honestiores**) and the "less distinguished" (**humiliores**) exempted the former group from corporeal punishment but defined it as proper to the latter. Fear was the recognized means of keeping a gigantic slave population under control.

During the late Republic, prominent men went about with armed bodyguards, for mob violence was a frequent occurrence and dignitaries themselves shrank at nothing to maintain their honor. As for sex, Wiseman remarks, the notion that penetration involved disgrace prompted the use of sexual assault as punishment for intruders, especially adulterers, an exercise all the more humiliating if inflicted by a householder's slaves. Suggestive images were visible everywhere: ithyphallic statues of **Priapus**, the garden god; lewd mimes, which upper-class women attended; semi-naked harlots in the streets (Wiseman 1985: 5–14). These observations on cruelty and sex are juxtaposed without being integrated, but the inference is plain. In a culture where sex was so unashamedly on display, where violence was accepted as routine, and where bodily penetration was synonymous with dominance, brutality may have been erotically stimulating. In fact, such a claim has been made: according to Otto Kiefer, harsh practices of educating children, dealing with women and slaves, and punishing criminals were all manifestations of a Roman will to power that turned on itself once it lost its object, the pursuit of empire, and exhausted itself in "wild orgies of sadism" at gladiatorial games (2000 [1934]: 78–9).

Kiefer's and Wiseman's horror is that of outsiders repelled by an unthinkable way of life. Yet escalating bloodshed in entertainment media has lately brought scholars to try to understand a seemingly comparable phenomenon, the Roman arena, "from the inside" (Kyle 1998: ix–x). Gladiatorial bouts were originally a funeral ritual presented as an offering to the dead. By the late Republic they were socially institutionalized as entertainment, termed **munera** ("gifts") because they were generally sponsored by magistrates bidding for popular favor. Combatants, who walked into the arena knowing that they might well die to pleasure the crowd, became trendy celebrities. Their reputed sexiness is easily documented; graffiti from Pompeii mark the hot reputations of two local stars, Celadus and Crescens (*CIL* 4.4342, 4353), and Juvenal retells with relish (6.82–113) the scandal of Eppia, the senator's wife who eloped to Egypt with her scarred and middle-aged lover Sergius – a far cry from Russell Crowe.[10] "It's the sword women love," the satirist jeers in a not-so-subtle double entendre that actually displays considerable socio-logical insight (112). Rome was a warrior society in which military prowess remained vital to the notion of masculinity even after the age of the citizen-soldier was long past. Once war was "converted into a game" (Hopkins 1983: 29), the gladiator's combat skills, bravery, and self-possession in the face of death turned him into an emblem of virility, in contrast to the aristocrat who led a sedentary and, possibly in his own eyes, ignoble life (Wiedemann 1992: 34–7; Barton 1993: 27). Even though gladiators were, for the most part, slaves or condemned criminals, it is therefore not difficult to understand why they possessed such erotic appeal. It was, however, a paradoxical sensuality because they were simultaneously regarded with profound contempt; the Christian apologist **Tertullian**, who inveighs against the arena in his pamphlet *On Spectacles*, thinks it perverse that "men hand over their souls, women their bodies" to those very persons whom they stigmatize with disrepute and loss of civic status (22.2).

What a Piece of Work Is a Man!

Cultures conceptualize masculinity along a surpris-ingly broad spectrum. Many books have been writ-ten, for example, on the Latin American notion of *machismo*, which is not easy for observers of Northern European stock to grasp. (Conversely, swarthy laborers from rural Mediterranean societies might have a hard time understanding why being labeled a "metrosexual" is in some circles a compli-ment.) Ancient ideas of masculinity transformed themselves in response to a changing cultural envi-ronment, as the following chapters on Rome will show. Here is a preview of what to expect.

We can start, as always, with Homer. In epic poetry, war is the activity that defines a man (*Il.* 6.490–3). Captains urge troops to show "manliness" (*ênoreê*, derived from *anêr*, "man") in support of comrades, but too much individual daring (*agênoriê*), such as Achilles displays, is condemned because it puts fellow soldiers at risk (Van Nortwick 2008: 77). Penelope's intrusive suitors are also characterized by *agênoriê*, testosterone overload, as it were (Graziosi and Haubold 2003). To classical Greek thinkers, manliness, which they call **andreia** (likewise from the root *anêr*), is a civic and philosophical virtue equated with courage and defined by Aristotle as a mean between cowardice and rashness (*Eth. Nic.* 1107b, 1115a). In both periods, the essence of

Greek masculinity is agonistic: it involves valor in battle alongside one's companions and competitive zeal for the esteem bestowed by the army or *polis* (Sluiter and Rosen 2003: 14–15).

Roman masculinity may be more complex than that, for the number of academic studies attempt-ing to dissect it is steadily growing. In Latin the word for "manliness" is **virtus**. Cognate with *vir*, "man," this noun, too, is regularly used of martial prowess. According to Myles McDonnell, that was, in fact, its original meaning; the ethical overtones found in the English derivative "virtue" accrued only after *virtus* was equated with Greek *aretê*, "excellence" (2006: 59–71, 105–41). Other philol-ogists believe the word may have acquired a moral dimension at a very early stage in its history (Eisenhut 1973: 219–22). The fact that *virtus* is a fully adequate translation for both *andreia* and *aretê*, concepts quite separate in the Greek langu-age, shows that its extension is somewhat elastic.

Although *andreia* and *virtus* both denote the quality essential to being a "real man," they reflect genuine cultural differences in conceptions of gender. One notable distinction between the two is that Greeks perceived something off-key about female *andreia* (Goldhill 1995: 137–43), while Roman women might rightfully aspire to *virtus* and were praised for achieving it (e.g., Cicero speaks of his wife's "astonishing *virtus*," *Fam.* 14.1.1). Romans were inclined to grant their womenfolk a share in masculinity because, unlike the archaic and classical Greeks, they never saw it as something a man was born with. In the early Hellenic belief-system, as encapsulated in the **Pythagorean Table of Opposites** (Arist. *Metaph.* 986a.22–9), the antithesis of male and female was axiomatic, a fundamental polarity that could organize secondary categories of experience like right and left, hot and cold, dry and wet. Because each of those dyads consisted of a positive and a negative quality, the superior element (right, hot, dry) was assigned to the male, the inferior to the female (Lloyd 1966: 48–65). So metaphysically entrenched was this principle of gender opposition that theorists like Aristotle found it necessary to invent physiological or circumstantial explanations for the perverse "femininity" of the *kinaidos*. However, under the influence of the "one-sex" biological model, which gained ground, we recall, during the early Roman empire, Greek intellectuals began to regard themselves as a composite of masculine and feminine traits, either set of which might prevail regardless of anatomical sex (Gleason 1995: 58–60). They came around, in other words, to a Roman way of thinking.

Romans held manhood to be an achieved state, one the biological adult male (*mas*) had to attain through struggle and self-discipline before testing it on the battlefield and in the forum. Rhetorical training, with its emphasis on generating an authoritative public presence, was the vehicle for producing the *vir bonus*, the good man who was by definition also a good soldier and good citizen (Gunderson 2000: 7–9). What was gained at great cost to self might be readily lost, though, and was perpetually open to question. Failure and defeat impugned virility unless counteracted by a prodigious display of resolve in the face of death. "Because it did not come naturally for a male to have *virtus*, it was no less natural for the Romans to attribute *virtus* to a female, who, equally unnaturally, showed exceptional will and energy" (Barton 2001: 41). The suspicion that masculinity is persistently vulnerable accounts for the many examples of "gender slippage" that we will encounter in subsequent pages as ancient men articulated and in certain cases acted out their worst fears.

However psychologically conflicted the Romans were in their attitude toward gladiators, they felt no remorse over the slaughter of beasts or the torture and killing of felons. Scheduled in the afternoons, as the last event on the program, gladiatorial matches were preceded by trained animal shows and staged hunts of wild animals (**venationes**) and then by mass executions that served up the deaths of the condemned as a diversion.[11] In contrast to gladiators, who offered spectators a model of fortitude with which they might identify, hunts and executions were one-sided demonstrations of Roman might and authority. There is no way to determine an accurate body count of victims, animal and human, killed in this fashion, but recorded totals are shocking (Kyle 1998: 76–9). Animals perished in the greatest numbers.[12]

Emperors reaffirmed the power of empire by exhibiting creatures imported from remote provinces and manifested their own generosity through the destruction of costly specimens. Victories of hunters over ferocious beasts demonstrated human mastery of nature (Wiedemann 1992: 55–67). Insofar as watchers in the amphitheater felt themselves distanced as a species from the creatures on the sand below, they experienced no pathos in their suffering (Brown 1992: 207–8). Punishments of criminals, involving both extreme pain and degradation, were used as deterrents and also looked upon as a restoration of social order, for the wrongdoers suffered in proportion to the injuries they had committed. The Roman spectator did not regard them as proper objects of sympathy either, because human offenders, like predatory animals, were viewed as potential threats to the community as a whole. In each case, there was a clearly articulated rationale of expediency for the death meted out. We should distinguish, then, between the callousness toward putatively deserved suffering shown even by the educated upper classes and a sadistic delight in inflicting suffering on the undeserving, which Roman upper-class morality rejected (Lintott 1999: 44, 50–1).

From a self-justifying position of ethical superiority, elite authors do ascribe a sordid bloodlust to the masses. **Petronius** makes one of his municipal freedmen characters, anticipating a coming show enthusiastically, say of the donor: "He will provide a first-class contest, fights to the death, with the butchery in the middle so the amphitheater can see it" (*Sat.* 45.6). In a letter to his student Lucilius (*Ep.* 7.2–4), the philosopher Seneca charges that attending executions in the arena blunts moral sensitivity because the barbarity of the multitude is infectious. When he went there at midday hoping for some relaxation, he says, he was exposed instead to "pure slaughter" (*mera homicidia*), men without protection forced by attendants to slay each other with the audience urging them on: "Kill him, whip him, burn him!" Most viewers prefer that kind of thing to regular gladiatorial matches and specially arranged bouts, he adds, because they are not interested in skill but revel in carnage for its own sake.[13] Such cruelty was believed to be instantaneously addictive. **Augustine**, bishop of Hippo and major Christian theologian, recalls that his young friend Alypius, while studying law at Rome, was hauled off to the arena by acquaintances despite his protests. At first he refused to watch, but when the crowd roared and he opened his eyes, overcome by curiosity, he was transfixed: "when he saw that blood, he at once drank in the brutality, and did not turn away but trained his eyes on the sight, and swallowed madness without knowing it, and was excited by the intensity of the contest and inebriated with bloody pleasure" (*Conf.* 6.8). From that time on, Augustine testifies, he became a passionate fan of the games.

How can we account for the Romans' pleasure in witnessing the inflicting of pain? One current explanation views gladiatorial spectacles as "a ritual of empowerment" (Barton 1993: 35). Rooting for the underdog was not a Roman tradition; audiences preferred the psychological security of locating themselves on the winning side. Besides reaffirming collective order, punitive action against outlaws and beasts assured even the socially marginal of their superiority to such "others." Compensatory violence was thus an outlet for the frustration experienced by subjects of an increasingly more autocratic and oppressive government (Futrell 1997: 48–9). Gladiatorial shows, furthermore, functioned as political theater. With the emperor watching, citizens might engage in mass demonstrations against individuals or public policies; audiences would also be flattered by an emperor's efforts to solicit their goodwill (Hopkins 1983: 14–20; Gunderson 1996: 126–33). Finally, decisions about whether a defeated gladiator would live or die were determined by the attitude of the crowd. In a collective act nostalgically reminiscent of its vanished political sovereignty, the assembled populace could grant life to a game

Fig. 7.2   Exterior of bull ring, Merida, Spain. Source: photograph © 2008 Marilyn B. Skinner.

but defeated fighter and freedom to an impressive one (Wiedemann 1992: 165). Self-respect was accordingly purchased at the cost of others' agony, and gratification followed in its wake.

Explaining the popularity of the games as being due to their unique cultural operations within Roman society is attractive because it treats audience demand for violent spectacle as a historically contingent phenomenon divorced from present-day reality. In contrast, one new investigation, while acknowledging the validity of a culturally specific approach, draws upon social psychology to stress the similarities between the arena and other cross-cultural instances of collective bloodlust (Fagan 2011). Public executions, often involving torture and protracted suffering on the part of the victims, attracted great crowds in Europe, Britain, and the United States until the mid-nineteenth century; extreme combat sports in which participants risk serious injury have their eager followers even today. Though dog fighting is illegal in the USA, it is widely practiced throughout the country in conjunction with other forms of criminal conduct; in Hispanic societies the bullfight is a communal ritual, with bull rings located in all major cities (used, however, for a variety of events—see Fig. 7.2). As students of history, we may disapprove of the following the games enjoyed in the Roman world, but as students of human behavior we should recognize that many of the satisfactions they provided are today furnished by related forms of mass entertainment, from summer blockbuster action films to the Super Bowl.

Conclusion

This chapter has attempted to identify some of the idiosyncratic features of Roman sexuality, compared with Greek and, to a certain extent, Etruscan notions of eroticism. Like classical Athenians, the Romans conceptualized sex as a hierarchical relationship in which the male penetrator assumed the dominant role. However, they aligned this construction of sex with an intricate system of social relations in which the ascendancy of the free person over slave or former slave, rich over poor, well born over base, and even man over woman did not always line up as neatly in practice as such inequalities should have done theoretically. They also imposed strict sanctions on violating the integrity of a citizen youth and laid the blame for adultery on the errant wife, not her lover, defining it as a matter of civic concern even more than family honor. If Seneca and other witnesses are telling the truth, they were mesmerized by the spectacular brutality of the arena and took a sadistic delight in the terror and suffering of those slain. Such factors are enough to ensure the distinctiveness of Roman sexual protocols. Yet this does not mean that Roman mores were not deeply colored by Hellenic thinking, or even vice versa: introduced into the Greek East, gladiatorial games and beast-hunts became as popular as they were in Italy.

From the second century BCE onwards, wealth had been flowing into Rome from its conquered territories. Social change, inevitable under the circumstances, was blamed by Roman authors on exposure to Greek decadence, and, more immediately, on the selfish choices of individuals stemming from an unmanly lack of self-discipline. Disquiet over late first-century BCE unrest took the form of jeremiads against a perceived epidemic of luxurious living. No attempt was made to distinguish among the immoral behaviors practiced by the hedonist – the man guilty of one was presumably guilty of the rest as well (Corbeill 1996: 128–73). Accusations of squandering money are accompanied by charges that the offender has likewise been dancing and singing, feasting sumptuously, getting drunk, committing adultery, and playing the passive role in homoerotic coupling, vices linked together in a metonymic chain because each one was connected to an overabundance of wealth. Fantasies of criminal copulation and bizarre departures from gender roles were a natural outgrowth of the notional integration of sexuality, dominance, and social rank.

Discussion Prompts

1.   Democratic systems in contemporary first-world countries laud individual attributes such as talent and determination when explaining academic, vocational, athletic, or artistic success. Elite young Roman men instead relied greatly on personal connections as they launched political or military careers. Why was patronage such a critical factor in Roman society as opposed to our own?

2. Roman moralists blamed the wickedness they observed on exposure to Greek customs, especially those of the Eastern Mediterranean. Projecting negative qualities on members of another class, ethnic group, or religion in order to hold them responsible for perceived social ills is, according to many psychologists, a defense mechanism by which we avoid confronting our own weaknesses. What does the tendency to fault Greeks for luxurious living suggest about Roman ambivalence regarding wealth and its uses?

3. The Julian laws regulating marriage, encouraging childbirth, and imposing sanctions on adultery have been described by ancient historians as an unprecedented intrusion of government into the private sphere. What features of Roman culture as described in this chapter would render such legal intervention possible, if not palatable? In other words, where did the Romans draw the line between strictly personal interests and those of the state? Do current-day social conservatives operate from the same general premises?

4. When discussing the popularity of beast-hunts and gladiatorial matches, we surveyed attempts by scholars to show how those particular pastimes met Roman cultural needs. Using the same method of inquiry – investigating how entertainments respond to audience fantasies and desires – explain the psychic attractions of summer action flicks, particularly franchises repeatedly involving the same cast of good guys in roughly the same predictable set-up.

Notes

1   The Lupercalia, held on February 15, was closely connected with the legend of the she-wolf who suckled the twins Romulus and Remus (Ov. *Fast.* 2.381–424). Following the sacrifice of a goat to a divinity (variously designated as Faunus or Lycaean Pan), naked young men ran about the Palatine striking whomever they met, especially women of childbearing age, with thongs made from the skin of the goat. Although the celebration itself was thought to date back from before the founding of Rome, the rite of flagellation was introduced in the third century BCE in response to an epidemic of miscarriages (Liv. fr. 63 Weissenborn = Wiseman 1995: 19 no. 13).

2   How large were Athens and Rome, comparatively? Herodotus (5.97.2) gives a figure of 30,000 Athenian male citizens in the early fifth century BCE. If we multiply by four to account for wives and children, we get a total citizen population of 120,000 plus slaves and metics. Some doubt that the population of Athens was that high. According to the emperor Augustus' head counts for recipients of money and wheat distributions (Aug. *RG* 15), approximately 250,000 male Roman citizens received allotments on five occasions between 44 and 12 BCE; the number rose to 320,000 in 5 BCE, then sank to 200,000 in 2 BCE. Those rapid fluctuations must reflect variations in accounting procedure rather than actual population shifts. Estimating numbers of women, children, resident aliens, soldiers, and slaves, Hopkins (1978: 96–8) arrived at a total of 800,000 to one million during the reign of Augustus, a figure now widely accepted (Scheidel 2001: 51). The quick and dirty answer, then, is that Augustan Rome was three to four times larger than classical Athens.

3   An example is the prominent noblewoman Caecilia Metella, who in 80 CE arranged for Cicero, then beginning his oratorical and political career, to defend her hereditary client Sextus Roscius on a charge of murdering his father (Cic. *Rosc. Am.* 27). See Dixon (1983).

4   Before Dover's and Foucault's work altered scholarly thinking, confusion frequently resulted from the mistaken categorization of pederasty or passivity (or both) as "homosexuality." For example, Boswell (1980: 87) concludes a survey of evidence for homoerotic practices in Rome with the contention that "none of its laws, strictures, or taboos regulating love or sexuality was intended to penalize gay people or their sexuality ... they were fully integrated into Roman life and culture at every level." By imposing a modern cultural category on sexual acts in Latin texts, he arrives at the misleading generalization that Rome, in contrast to Christian Europe, was "tolerant" of gay persons as a minority group.

5   In his treatise *On Agriculture*, Cato advises farm owners to sell off old and sick slaves along with other superfluous chattels (2.7). This counsel prompts an extraordinary outburst of disapproval from his Greek biographer Plutarch, who condemns it as inhumane and protests that one should not behave so callously even toward animals, though he ends by saying that readers must make up their own minds about that side of Cato's character (*Cat. Mai.* 4–5). Defenders would argue that the censor's ostentatious frugality was a reproof to the profligacy of his contemporaries.

6   Cf. *Helv.* 19.2, where Seneca also acknowledges his aunt Marcia's role in obtaining his quaestorship. The line between proper intercession and undue interference in public affairs was, as Dixon (2001: 103) remarks, "all a matter of perspective."

7   A popular mime, whose plot was apparently well known, involved a dapper adulterer, a clever wife, and a foolish husband. Ovid, exiled for having written the "immoral" *Art of Love*, reminds Augustus that he had sponsored this no less risqué skit at his own games (*Tr.* 2.497–516). In one stock scene, to which both Horace (*Sat.* 2.7.59–61) and Juvenal (6.42–4) allude, the lover is hidden in a chest when the husband returns home unexpectedly. The mockery directed at him implies that in a real-life situation a deceived husband might also incur ridicule.

8   Strictly speaking, under Roman law a child was illegitimate only if he or she was not born of a valid Roman marriage; such children had no legal father and took their status (slave or free) from that of their mother (Paulus *Dig.* 2.24.1). If a child was born to a woman who was married, her husband was considered the father unless he refused to recognize the child as his own. There are actually relatively few surviving jokes about someone's paternity, although Cicero, whose wit could be tactless, is credited with a pair (Plut. *Cic.* 25.4, 26.6). It is important to recall that in classical Athens biological paternity was not a joking matter.

9   Cicero, whose financial position was often overextended, worried about decisions made by his wife Terentia regarding her holdings but could do nothing except plead with her (*Fam.* 14.1.5).

10 Classicists, for their part, recount with equal relish that, when the armory of the gladiatorial barracks at Pompeii was excavated, archaeologists found eighteen skeletons, including one of a woman wearing considerable gold jewelry and an emerald necklace and carrying a cameo in a casket (Mau 1982 [1902]: 163). Innocent explanations are seldom proposed, although there might well be one: it seems unlikely that a rich lady would wear all her valuables to a tryst with her boyfriend in a barracks while a volcano was erupting.

11 We have abundant testimony to the attraction of "fatal charades" in which criminals done up as mythological heroes suffered the hero's fate: a man costumed as Hercules, for example, might be burnt alive (Lucill. *Anth. Pal.* 11.184; Tert. *Apol.* 15.5). Coleman explains the psychological appeal of viewing such executions as a combination of righteous interest in justice, horror, the element of unpredictability when a beast was employed as the means of destruction, and a morbid fascination with the actual moment of death (1990: 57–9).

12 Kyle confronts the gruesome practical question of how "literally tons of human and animal flesh" (1998: 159) were disposed of. Gladiators who died well might be provided with decent burial, although some public cemeteries debarred them (1998: 160–2). During the Republican period, carcasses were dumped into pits on the Esquiline Hill, but the practice would have ended when the area was reclaimed and turned into a pleasure garden by Augustus' advisor Maecenas (1998: 164–8). Animal remains, Kyle suggests, were distributed to the populace as meat (1998: 190–4)

and the corpses of criminals were thrown into the Tiber, because water would flush away the pollution of death, while the body was insulted by being denied burial (1998: 213–28).

13 Seneca's many references to the technicalities of gladiatorial combat indicate that he attended the games regularly and appreciated the expertise displayed by a well-matched pair of opponents (Wistrand 1992: 20; Cagniart 2000: 609). His interest in gladiatorial combat as sport was not incompatible, it appears, with his professed Stoic reverence for human life.

References

Barker, G. and Rasmussen, T. 1998. *The Etruscans*. Oxford and Malden, MA: Blackwell.

Barton, C. A. 1993. *The Sorrows of the Ancient Romans: The Gladiator and the Monster*. Princeton, NJ: Princeton University Press.

—— 2001. *Roman Honor: The Fire in the Bones*. Berkeley and London: University of California Press.

Bonfante, L. 1986. "Daily Life and Afterlife." In L. Bonfante (ed.), *Etruscan Life and Afterlife*. Detroit: Wayne State University Press. 232–78.

—— 1996. "Etruscan Sexuality and Funerary Art." In N. B. Kampen (ed.), *Sexuality in Ancient Art*. Cambridge: Cambridge University Press. 155–69.

Boswell, J. 1980. *Christianity, Social Tolerance, and Homosexuality: Gay People in Western Europe from the Beginning of the Christian Era to the Fourteenth Century*. Chicago: University of Chicago Press.

Brendel, O. J. 1970. "The Scope and Temperament of Erotic Art in the Greco-Roman World." In T. Bowie and C. V. Christenson (eds.), *Studies in Erotic Art*. New York: Basic Books. 3–107.

Brown, S. 1992. "Death as Decoration: Scenes from the Arena on Roman Domestic Mosaics." In A. Richlin (ed.), *Pornography and Representation in Greece and Rome*. Oxford: Oxford University Press. 180–211.

Butrica, J. L. 2005. "Some Myths and Anomalies in the Study of Roman Sexuality." In B. C. Verstraete and V. Provencal (eds.), *Same-Sex Desire and Love in Greco-Roman Antiquity and in the Classical Tradition of the West*. Binghamton, NY: Harrington Park Press (co-published simultaneously as *Journal of Homosexuality* 49. nos. 3/4 [2005]). 209–69.

Cagniart, P. 2000. "The Philosopher and the Gladiator." *Classical World* 93.6: 607–18.

Cantarella, E. 1992. *Bisexuality in the Ancient World*. Trans. C. Ó Cuilleanáin. [Orig. pub. as *Secondo natura*, Rome: Editori Riuniti, 1988.] New Haven, CT: Yale University Press.

Coleman, K. M. 1990. "Fatal Charades: Roman Executions Staged as Mythological Enactments." *Journal of Roman Studies* 80: 44–73.

Corbeill, A. 1996. *Controlling Laughter: Political Humor in the Late Roman Republic*. Princeton, NJ: Princeton University Press.

Cornell, T. J. 1995. *The Beginnings of Rome: Italy and Rome from the Bronze Age to the Punic Wars (c.1000–264 BC)*. London: Routledge.

Davidson, J. N. 2001. "Dover, Foucault and Greek Homosexuality: Penetration and the Truth of Sex." *Past & Present* 170: 3–51.

Dixon, S. 1983. "A Family Business: Women's Role in Patronage and Politics at Rome 80–44 BC." *Classica et Mediaevalia* 34: 91–112.

—— 1988. *The Roman Mother*. Norman, OK: University of Oklahoma Press.

—— 2001. *Reading Roman Women: Sources, Genres and Real Life*. London: Duckworth.

Edwards, C. 1993. *The Politics of Immorality in Ancient Rome*. Cambridge: Cambridge University Press.

—— 1997. "Unspeakable Professions: Public Performance and Prostitution in Ancient Rome." In J. P. Hallett and M. B. Skinner (eds.), *Roman Sexualities*. Princeton, NJ: Princeton University Press. 66–95.

Eisenhut, W. 1973. Virtus Romana: *Ihre Stellung im römischen Wertsystem*. Munich: Wilhelm Fink.

Fagan, G. G. 2011. *The Lure of the Arena: Social Psychology and the Crowd at the Roman Games*. Cambridge: Cambridge University Press.

Fantham, E. 1991. "*Stuprum*: Public Attitudes and Penalties for Sexual Offences in Republican Rome." *Échos du Monde Classique/Classical Views* 35 n.s. 10: 267–91.

Fredrick, D. 2002. "Introduction: Invisible Rome." In D. Fredrick (ed.), *The Roman Gaze: Vision, Power, and the Body*. Baltimore, MD: The Johns Hopkins University Press. 1–30.

Futrell, A. 1997. *Blood in the Arena: The Spectacle of Roman Power*. Austin: University of Texas Press.

Galinsky, K. 1981. "Augustus' Legislation on Morals and Marriage." *Philologus* 125: 126–44.

—— 1996. *Augustan Culture*. Princeton, NJ: Princeton University Press.

Gleason, M. 1995. *Making Men: Sophists and Self-Presentation in Ancient Rome*. Princeton, NJ: Princeton University Press.

Goldhill, S. 1995. *Foucault's Virginity: Ancient Erotic Fiction and the History of Sexuality*. Cambridge: Cambridge University Press.

Grazioni, B. and Haubold, J. 2003. "Homeric Masculinity: ΗΝΟΡΕΗ and ΑΓΗΝΟΡΙΗ." *Journal of Hellenic Studies* 123: 60–76.

Griffin, J. 1986. "Augustan Poetry and the Life of Luxury." In *Latin Poets and Roman Life*. Chapel Hill, NC: University of North Carolina Press. 1–31.

Gunderson, E. 1996. "The Ideology of the Arena." *Classical Antiquity* 15: 113–51.

—— 2000. *Staging Masculinity: The Rhetoric of Performance in the Roman World*. Ann Arbor: The University of Michigan Press.

Hallett, J. P. 1984. *Fathers and Daughters in Roman Society: Women and the Elite Family*. Princeton, NJ: Princeton University Press.

—— 1988. "Roman Attitudes toward Sex." In M. Grant and R. Kitzinger (eds.), *Civilization of the Ancient Mediterranean: Greece and Rome*, 3 vols. New York: Scribners'. II: 1265–78.

Hopkins, K. 1978. *Conquerors and Slaves*. Sociological Studies in Roman History, vol. 1. Cambridge: Cambridge University Press.

—— 1983. *Death and Renewal*. Sociological Studies in Roman History, vol. 2. Cambridge: Cambridge University Press.

Kiefer, O. 2000 [1934]. *Sexual Life in Ancient Rome*. Trans. G. and H. Highet. London: Kegan Paul International.

Kyle, D. G. 1998. *Spectacles of Death in Ancient Rome*. London: Routledge.

Liebeschuetz, J. H. W. G. 1979. *Continuity and Change in Roman Religion*. Oxford: Clarendon Press.

Lilja, S. 1983. *Homosexuality in Republican and Augustan Rome*. Commentationes Humanarum Litterarum 74. Helsinki: Societas Scientiarum Fennica.

Lintott, A. W. 1999. *Violence in Republican Rome*, 2nd edn. Oxford: Oxford University Press.

Lloyd, G. E. R. 1966. *Polarity and Analogy: Two Types of Argumentation in Early Greek Thought*. Cambridge: Cambridge University Press.

Macleod, C. W. 1973. "Parody and Personalities in Catullus." *Classical Quarterly* 23: 294–303.

MacMullen, R. 1982. "Roman Attitudes to Greek Love." *Historia* 31: 484–502.

Mau, A. 1982 [1902]. *Pompeii, its Life and Art*. Trans. F. W. Kelsey. New edn., revised and corrected. Rpt. New Rochelle, NY: Caratzas Brothers.

McDonnell, M. 2006. *Roman Manliness: Virtus and the Roman Republic*. Cambridge: Cambridge University Press.

McGinn, T. A. J. 1998. *Prostitution, Sexuality, and the Law in Ancient Rome*. Oxford: Oxford University Press.

Millett, P. 1989. "Patronage and its Avoidance in Classical Athens." In A. Wallace-Hadrill (ed.), *Patronage in Ancient Society*. London: Routledge. 15–47.

Ogilvie, R. M. 1976. *Early Rome and the Etruscans*. Hassocks, Sussex: Harvester Press.

Oliensis, E. 1997. "The Erotics of *Amicitia*: Readings in Tibullus, Propertius, and Horace." In Hallett and Skinner (eds.), *Roman Sexualities*. 151–71.

Pomeroy, S. B. 1975. *Goddesses, Whores, Wives, and Slaves: Women in Classical Antiquity*. New York: Schocken.

Richlin, A. 1981. "Approaches to the Sources on Adultery at Rome." *Women's Studies* 8: 225–50.

—— 1992. *The Garden of Priapus: Sexuality and Aggression in Roman Humor*, rev. edn. Oxford: Oxford University Press.

—— 1993. "Not before Homosexuality." *Journal of the History of Sexuality* 3.4: 523–73.

Saller, R. P. 1982. *Personal Patronage under the Early Empire*. Cambridge: Cambridge University Press.

Scheidel, W. 2001. "Progress and Problems in Roman Demography." In W. Scheidel (ed.), *Debating Roman Demography*. Leiden and Boston: E. J. Brill. 1–81.

Skinner, M. B. 1983. "Clodia Metelli." *Transactions of the American Philological Association* 113: 273–87.

—— 2011. *Clodia Metelli: The Tribune's Sister*. New York: Oxford University Press.

Sluiter, I. and Rosen, R. M. 2003. "General Introduction." In R. M. Rosen and I. Sluiter (eds.), Andreia: *Studies in Manliness and Courage in Classical Antiquity*. Leiden: E. J. Brill. 1–24.

Treggiari, S. 1991. *Roman Marriage: "Iusti Coniuges" from the Time of Cicero to the Time of Ulpian*. Oxford: Clarendon Press.

Van Nortwick, T. 2008. *Imagining Men: Ideals of Masculinity in Ancient Greek Culture*. Westport, CT: Praeger.

Walters, J. 1997. "Invading the Roman Body: Manliness and Impenetrability in Roman Thought." In Hallett and Skinner (eds.), *Roman Sexualities*. 29–43.

Wiedemann, T. 1992. *Emperors and Gladiators*. London: Routledge.

Williams, C. A. 2010. *Roman Homosexuality*. 2nd edn. Oxford: Oxford University Press.

Wiseman, T. P. 1985. *Catullus and his World: A Reappraisal*. Cambridge: Cambridge University Press.

—— 1995. "The God of the Lupercal." *Journal of Roman Studies* 85: 1–22.

Wistrand, M. 1992. *Entertainment and Violence in Ancient Rome: The Attitudes of Roman Writers of the First Century AD*. Studia Graeca et Latina Gothoburgensia 56. Göteborg: Göteborg University.

Further Reading

Barker, G. and Rasmussen, T. 1998. *The Etruscans*. Oxford and Malden, MA: Blackwell. Comprehensive introduction to major issues in Etruscan cultural studies, incorporating much recent work in archaeology.

D'Ambra, E. 2007. *Roman Women*. Cambridge: Cambridge University Press. Compact, accessible summary of the place of women, elite and non-elite, in the Roman gender system and in public and private life. Many illustrations.

Fagan, G. G. 2011. *The Lure of the Arena: Social Psychology and the Crowd at the Roman Games*. Cambridge: Cambridge University Press. Contextualizes crowd reactions to events in the Roman amphitheater by examining comparable effects of violence on audiences in other times and places.

Futrell, A. 1997. *Blood in the Arena: The Spectacle of Roman Power*. Austin: University of Texas Press. Fine introduction to gladiatorial combat as a Roman social institution, with attention to the construction and operation of the amphitheater in Italy and the provinces.

Hallett, J. P. and Skinner, M. B. (eds.). 1997. *Roman Sexualities*. Princeton, NJ: Princeton University Press. Collection of influential essays on various aspects of Roman sexual norms directed toward distinguishing and explaining cultural specificities.

Skinner, M. B. 2011. *Clodia Metelli: The Tribune's Sister*. Oxford: Oxford University Press. This biography, which attempts to extract some historical facts about Clodia from the welter of allegations surrounding her, incidentally offers accounts of the lives and activities of several noblewomen of the late Republic.

Wiedemann, T. 1992. *Emperors and Gladiators*. Another good introduction to the subject, covering the place of gladiatorial games in Roman culture, the origins and development of the *munera*, and the social background of gladiators themselves.

Williams, C. A. 2010. *Roman Homosexuality: Ideologies of Masculinity in Classical Antiquity*. Rev. 2nd edn. Oxford: Oxford University Press. Authoritative discussion of the protocols of proper male conduct and all aspects of gender-deviant behavior, with commendable attention to differences between Greek and Roman practices.

8

Republican and Augustan Rome: The Soft Embrace of Venus

"To some extent, the Roman male was condemned to a life of maleness," says Eva Cantarella (1992: 220). Her quip calls attention to the difficulties citizen men, especially those of the upper classes, may have experienced in obeying a cultural injunction ceaselessly to perform masculinity, showing no hint of **mollitia**, "softness," in conduct, dress, or demeanor. To be a Roman *vir*, a "real man," was to be *hard* in every sense – physically to be impervious to pain or fatigue, mentally to be stern and unyielding, and, of course, always to take the insertive position in sexual congress (Veyne 1978: 50–1). Assertions that adult males are behaving in womanish fashion imply willing assumption of the passive or receptive role, a breach of the first protocol of Roman manhood (Williams 2010: 18, 180). With the right amount of malice, any behavior could be construed as womanish. The Roman *vir* is always poised precariously on a slippery slope leading to loss of manhood.

"Passivity," as Romans understood it, also involved more than a simple yearning to be penetrated. It was a failure of willpower. The inviolable body of the elite Roman man was the external projection of his resolute and indomitable spirit. Moralists' attacks on Greek decadence exhibit a fear of its softening effects on character. Luxurious living leads to decay of moral fiber and a corollary pursuit of more and more extreme forms of pleasure. Men turn to "feminized" modes of sex as control over the body's boundaries and recesses dissipates in a frenzy of self-indulgence. The broader meanings of *mollitia*, then, encompass a breakdown of self-discipline that annihilates social, not just sexual, manhood (Dupont and Éloi 2001: 89–91). Passivity was a bankruptcy of will and nerve and only secondarily a sexuality.

Nevertheless, it *was* a sexuality, though not an easy one to pin down, as it was not distinguished by object-choice or even by the act committed. The Romans borrowed from the Greeks the word *kinaidos*, denoting a man who allowed himself to be entered anally. In Greek, this term was always associated with anal penetration, though in an extended sense it also connoted an inability to curb appetite with reason.

Sexuality in Greek and Roman Culture, Second Edition. Marilyn B. Skinner.
© 2014 John Wiley & Sons, Inc. Published 2014 by John Wiley & Sons, Inc.

Latinized as *cinaedus*, it meant the opposite of *vir*; thus Romans could be assigned to one of two categories, "man" (*vir*) or "not-man" (*cinaedus*). *Viri* might or might not exhibit a preference for a particular kind of penetrative activity, oral, anal, or genital, but the preference itself did not define them further. By contrast, as remarked at the opening of this book, "not-men" were often characterized as addicted to specific practices – presenting themselves for sodomy or servicing men or women through oral contact. Yet the more unmanly someone was considered, the more inclined he supposedly was to engage in all of those unnatural practices, perhaps simultaneously.[1] Being sexually passive, moreover, did not exclude being active at other times. Villains could be reproached as defiled in every orifice of their bodies and, in the next breath, accused of criminal *stuprum* involving boys and women.

That might seem merely the broad brush of invective painting outside the lines, but the testimony of the fifth-century CE physician Caelius Aurelianus is applicable here, since it presents a digest of later medical theory on the state of effeminate men (*molles*). Such men, Caelius argues, suffer from a mental affliction (*corruptae mentis vitia*) that engenders limitless desire without hope of satisfaction (Cael. Aur. *Morb. Chron.* 4.9.131–2). Although the most direct expression of abnormality is their adoption of female dress and mannerisms, out of fear or respect for others' good opinion they can channel desire into a display of virility. Here too, though, they go overboard, give way to excess, and involve themselves in greater misdeeds.[2] As they age, Caelius warns, their mental state worsens and their lust becomes stronger, and after they can no longer play an active role because of senility, "all their appetitive energy is turned in the other direction" (*Morb. Chron.* 137). Boys are, like old men, prone to passivity; the former because they are not yet capable of functioning in a virile manner, the latter because that capacity has deserted them. According to this model, then, the active role is only a stage in the male life-cycle. From the evidence of Caelius and other sources, C. A. Williams concludes that the *cinaedus*, instead of being defined by his practices, is a "gender-deviant" or, better, liminally gendered individual, one who straddles the boundary between masculinity and femininity (2010: 232–3). I would say, rather, that being a *cinaedus* is the zero-degree condition out of which manhood emerges, given a sane and healthy mind, and into which it must eventually sink back. Some potential men never make it.

This more flexible idea of the *cinaedus* is only one of the ways in which Roman sexual mores varied from those of the Greek world. Other divergences have been identified. From a Roman perspective, no blame attached to using adult male slaves or prostitutes, not boys, as passive partners; the emperor Galba, according to Suetonius (*Galb.* 22) had a predilection for "extremely butch and over-age" lovers. Indeed, there was a special category of Roman male prostitutes known as **exoleti**, "the over-aged" (see now Butrica 2005: 223–31). This practice was distasteful to Greeks, as it ran counter to the romantic dream of pederasty: we recall that readers of Zeno's *Republic* objected to the proposal that *erastai* should continue their relations with *erômenoi* until the latter turned twenty-eight. Again, as might be expected from their humorous glorification of Priapus, the phallic god, and their tendency to use the phallus as an amulet, the Romans, both men and women, were said to admire the well-hung male: "Whatever bath you hear applause in, Flaccus, know that Maro's dick is there" (Mart. 9.33). On this point, the cultural difference between Greeks and Romans is essentially one of attraction as opposed to identification (Williams 2010: 86). Gazing at the slim, athletic youth with modest penis, the classical Athenian felt desire; looking at Priapus, or at his well-endowed neighbor in the steam room, the Roman vicariously thrilled at the paraphernalia of domination.

These conjectures about Roman male sexual subjectivity were extrapolated from statements in a late antique medical treatise and clues furnished by epigrams and phallic tchotchkes. All might be souvenirs of single historical moments, so we need to cast the net wider. Let us now turn to what Roman men – and one woman – actually did say about themselves as gendered beings, beginning with testimony from the late Republic and early decades of the Augustan principate and proceeding on, in subsequent chapter installments, to the high Imperial period and into late antiquity. Despite this lengthy time span, textual witnesses are remarkably consistent. Almost without exception, they appear to proclaim the contrary of what we have just hypothesized: priapic power is what the other guy has.

Only Joking

The model of joke telling set forth in Freud's *Jokes and their Relation to the Unconscious*, which leagues the speaker (A) and the listener (C) in sympathy against the comic butt (B), permits a reading of Roman sexual humor as fundamentally aggressive in its purposes (Richlin 1992a: 57–63). Abusive wit invites audiences to relax their inhibitions against expressing feelings of hostility, in much the same way that pornography, according to feminist researchers, arouses in its consumers a greater propensity to use force against women and children (ibid., 78–80). If that is the case, literary obscenity would have been complicit in the culture of violence to which Romans were acclimatized. We can assess two very different genres of humor, Plautine drama and Catullan invective, to discover whether that formulation is always true.

Plautus' rowdy farces correspond to their Attic Greek models about as much as a *Saturday Night Live* impression of a politician resembles the genuine article. We saw in Chapter 5 that Athenian New Comedy explored changes in family dynamics by presenting believable characters in conflict over domestic issues, with a socially sanctioned love match the desired resolution. In Plautus, the hero's interest in the girl is only a peg on which to hang the plotting of the clever slave, whose machinations on behalf of his young master defeat a blocking figure – domineering father, pimp, or wealthy rival – and establish the girl's citizen identity or facilitate her purchase from the slave dealer (Segal 1968: 70–98). Comic business rare or nonexistent in Menander, like slapstick turns, flights of fantastic wordplay, and slanging matches, is a staple of Plautine humor. Much of the verbal sparring, and even some of the byplay, is risqué to say the least. Half of the surviving plays, for example, contain jokes about sexual submission, usually a gratuitous dig at the services a male slave performs for his master (Lilja 1983: 28–33). Since the insulting remark, made by another slave, often includes a Latin pun with no equivalent in Greek, such passages are probably inventions of the Roman playwright corresponding to nothing in the original (Williams 2010: 36–8). Other joking, also at the expense of slaves, involves threats of torture and crucifixion. While there are no actual instances of slaves being abused on stage (apart from blows clownishly given and exchanged), the frequency of references to physical punishment, featuring extravagant metaphors for beating or execution, makes it clear that audiences thought those bits funny (Parker 1989; Fitzgerald 2000: 36–40). Again, this is a motif found infrequently in Greek drama and then, for the most part, only in Old Comedy.

If humor directed at slaves aimed only at degrading them further, it would surely be pointless, for slaves as a class were already the most oppressed group in Roman society. Tendentious jokes about their susceptibility to sexual penetration, beating, and capital punishment must have served a purpose other than the pure expression of hostility. Taking Freudian theories of humor one step further invites the supposition that Plautine mockery was directed at what was feared. In the same way that present-day "horror jokes" about AIDS, cancer, or terrorism "allow us to dispel some of our immense fear of random harm or death," comic jokes about slave torture silently acknowledge but then allay the constant dread of slave uprisings (Parker 1989: 235–8; quotation from p. 236). At the same time, the clever slave is working for the benefit of the youth rebelling against his father's will. "Splitting" the figure of the son defying *patria potestas* into two characters, the one dependent upon the wily tricks of the other, permits a final reconciliation between parent and child. Guilt is deflected on to the slave, who is brought to heel by a threat of punishment even if he escapes the punishment itself. "The wish for rebellion is indulged," Parker observes, "but the fear of rebellion is pacified" (1989: 246).

A complementary approach to Plautine humor starts from the premise that Roman comedy, performed on festive occasions, creates a privileged space of reversal, a "*Saturnalian*" moment, in which prevailing rules of hierarchy and decorum are temporarily eased. This is the reason for the comic slave's impunity; as the quintessential avatar of festive license, he will get away with his mischief today, but not tomorrow (Segal 1968: 140–4). It is also why Plautus' slaves normally remain slaves even after performing exceptional services for their youthful masters. At the end of the play, the topsy-turvy world in which underlings drive the action is restored to proper order so that authority figures can take up the reins again. Emancipation, on the other hand, would mean an irrevocable shift in the relations of owner and slave.[3]

Extending this reading of Roman comedy as a "Saturnalian" exercise of imagination, one can then ask what pleasures the fantasy reversal of slaves' and masters' roles (along with other hierarchies, such as those of husband and wife, age and youth, rich and poor) offered to audiences (McCarthy 2000: 17–29). Funded by the government and mounted at public festivals, productions catered to the tastes of the dominant class and mirrored its ideology. As pointed out in Chapter 7, though, relations of dominance were not homogeneous but instead formed a complicated network of inequalities due to the fact that some status indicators might offset others. Not only were relative rankings of people on the same political or economic level very hard to fix, but status itself, so crucial to the functioning of the system, was persistently contested among ostensible equals. McCarthy therefore postulates that masters felt anxiety arising from "the constant need to jockey for position in the many minutely gradated hierarchies that ordered Roman society" (2000: 20). Involvement in such a web of domination meant that each participant would at some point feel insecure because someone else out-ranked him. While remaining a slave (and thereby underscoring the futility of slave revolt), the character of the clever slave invites the citizen population to identify sym-pathetically with him and take pleasure in his cynical management of his betters. Vicariously assuming the subject position of fictional slave provided masters with short-term release from both the hard work of maintaining an authoritative presence in the company of real slaves and social inferiors and the difficulties of fending off the impositions of those perched on a more lofty rung of the ladder (ibid., 25). If we accept McCarthy's theory, then, jokes in which slaves are the butts of ribald humor negotiated the opposition between "higher" and "lower" status by having one menial remind an uppity fellow servant of his vulnerability to sexual penetration.

The most enthusiastic mockery in Roman comedy, however, is directed not at subalterns, slaves and the like, but at imperious spoilsports who attempt to thwart the Saturnalian resolution. In a like vein, cheeky ridicule of those in power was the aim of such widespread subliterary forms of expression as scurrilous lampoons and anon-ymous graffiti. In fact, the production of all literature during the Republican period, including elevated modes of writing, was pervaded by an ethos of strenuous social competition. Composed by and for the upper class and often recited in the presence of live audiences, history, poetry, and other genres became, at an early date, handy platforms for defining aristocratic male identity and promulgating a desired image of the self (Habinek 1998: 34–68). Consequently, they were implicated in open jostling for political advantage throughout the late Republican era and into the principate. Cicero's eagerness to have the events of his consulship recorded for posterity (*Fam.* 5.12) illustrates the perceived value of texts as a vehicle for increasing one's prestige. Caesar's dispatches or *Commentaries* were likewise tailored to give domestic audi-ences the most favorable picture of his controversial military operations in Gaul and Britain. Augustus' attempt to muster the talents of contemporary poets and historians to plead the necessity of social reform and articulate the essential features of his program is the most conspicuous instance of asking literature to serve political ends. Whether the *princeps* fully succeeded in winning the hearts and minds of artists is still contested, but there can be no doubt that his policies set the tone for most Augustan age writing.[4] Even after the emperor's hegemony was securely established and the restoration of the Republic became an impossible dream, production and recital of literary work continued to play a role in more nuanced rivalries for social prominence, as documented in the letters of the younger **Pliny**. Though freedom of speech had been curbed, meanwhile, traditions of public mockery persisted into the imperial era in the form of anonymous squibs poking fun at emperors.

Awareness of the extent to which the composition and recital of poetry was bound up with the Republican political rat race is necessary for understanding the thrust and verve of Catullan invective. Catullus, the younger son of a wealthy Veronese family, came to Rome in his twenties around 60 BCE. During the last decades of the Republic, ambitious scions of important provincial households migrated to the metropolis in large numbers in pursuit of military and social advancement. In the elevated circles in which Cicero and other leading political players moved, such newcomers were at a profound disadvantage, for they were snubbed as interlopers and branded "uncouth rustics." Catullus is acutely self-conscious of his non-Roman origins and, alas, goes too far in making up for them. On the one hand, he proudly proclaims himself a "Transpadanus" or native of the northern territory beyond the Po River (39.13); on the other, he is determined to show himself as cool and supercilious as any aristocrat born on the Palatine. With his political verse lambasting eminent personalities he must have meant to make a name for himself, for it aims at provoking gasps of shocked laughter and applause at his daring. We can draw an intriguing parallel between that strategy and a present-day competitive ethos in rural Mediterranean villages that encourages adult males to "perform manhood" by verbally inflicting public shame on others (Wray 2001: 113–60). Catullus' obscene abuse is attention-grabbing.

If such fierce assaults were merely self-serving, they would doubtless be ethically questionable. However, the premise that Catullus turned his poetic talents to personal advantage does not necessarily deprive his invective of moral content. Blunt obscenities serve satiric ends by figuring political corruption as depravity, as in poem 57, a harsh attack on Julius Caesar and his deputy Mamurra:

> Two dirty fags have a sweet deal going,
> Mamurra the pathic and pathic Caesar.
> No wonder: corresponding stains on both,
> the one from the city, the other at Formiae,
> are firmly set in and won't be bleached out:
> equally diseased, twin organs of vice,
> two little eggheads in one little bed,
> neither one nor the other the keener seducer,
> chummy rivals for and of girls.
> The two dirty fags have a sweet deal going.

Catullus strikes at the jugular by imputing an unhealthy egalitarianism to Caesar and Mamurra's purported liaison: each serves as the *pathicus*, turn and turn about. Because taking the active sexual role is a metonym for "natural" exercise of rank and privilege, allegations that Caesar reciprocally services his henchman cancel out his patrician birth and his authority as proconsul, reducing him to the level of his creature. Translated into a political indictment, the poem charges that the commander responsible for policing his functionaries is instead conniving in their guilt by using his clout to protect them – a serious accusation, all the grimmer for being conveyed in such searing language. Indeed, Caesar complained that Catullus' verses on Mamurra left an indelible blemish on his own name (Suet. *Div. Iul.* 73). Yet he nevertheless maintained a friendship with Catullus' father back in Verona and forgave the young man himself when he finally apologized. Like politicians today, Caesar knew that angrily responding to an insult dignifies it; perhaps he also appreciated Catullus' effrontery because he was something of a posturer himself (Suet. *Div. Iul.* 45; Plut. *Caes.* 4). Following Caesar's lead, we ought to regard Catullan polemic as bold and imaginative rather than mean-spirited, granting the poet the same artistic license we would give a stand-up comedian who specializes in outrageous, politically incorrect humor.

For all his blistering attacks on politicians, Catullus frequently abandons his polemic stance to portray himself as victimized by those who, like his former chief of staff Memmius, are in a position to do him damage. Privations he endured may, as we saw, also be represented in sexual terms. By posing as a dupe, he is able to diagnose gross malfunctions in the patronage system and deplore a climate of opportunism in which double-dealing is only to be expected. Yet he also assumes part of the blame for the humiliations visited upon him and those friends with whom he sympathizes, making it clear that their own "unreflective collusion" with the Roman establishment laid them open to disgrace (Nappa 2001: 105). If he suffered indignities in Bithynia, it is because he had dreamed of quick and painless enrichment by milking the province, and because his job as a staff member was obtained by currying favors, "seeking noble friends" as he describes it (28.13). The sexual imagery that casts doubt on Catullus' manhood by depicting him acquiescing in oral sodomy makes that larger point unforgettably: hoping to get ahead, he bought into a rigged scheme and thus surrendered his integrity. The sporadic frustrations of the Catullan speaker as he attempts to rise within the patronage network anticipate the deeper and lasting sense of alienation expressed by prominent men under the empire, when birth and wealth in themselves put one at risk and being too close to the seat of power induced perpetual nervousness. Catullan sexual polemic must therefore be understood in a wider public context: like Plautine humor, it does not simply aim at demeaning its object but instead grapples with recurrent anxieties surrounding the speaker's or the audience's own social standing.

Young Men(?) in Love

It may seem perverse to introduce Catullus to readers by way of his satiric and invective pieces when he is chiefly known as one of Rome's greatest love poets. Doing so, however, makes it possible to locate the gender slippages of Republican and Augustan erotic elegy within a broader framework in which centuries-old patterns of elite male behavior were disintegrating. Much of Catullus' lyric and elegiac verse traces his unhappy affair with "Lesbia" – a pseudonym, recalling Sappho of Lesbos, which almost certainly conceals the name of Clodia, the socially prominent wife of Metellus Celer (see Chapter 7). Accordingly, his poems reverse gender expectations by casting a grown man, not an inexperienced girl, as the betrayed lover. In the oligarchic rhetoric we have been discussing, adulterers were stereotypical examples of dissipation, and being at a woman's beck and call was a flagrant sign of unmanliness. Catullus undermines such facile moralizing even as he explores the thorny consequences of a self-confessed violation of ethical principles. Emotionally ravaged by his fixation upon a promiscuous adulteress, the first-person speaker of the "Lesbia cycle" earns our compassion when he finds himself trapped in a grey area between masculinity and effeminacy, honor and culpability.

Catullus represents his adulterous affair as the equivalent of a legitimate marriage.[5] Commemorating an initial night of love with Lesbia, poem 68 depicts her entering his house – borrowed for the purpose from a friend – as a bride escorted by Cupid (70–2, 131–4). Her act of crossing the threshold is envisioned as an awesome divine epiphany. Later in the poem, though, he faces up to the folly of that romantic illusion, reluctantly admitting that, while Lesbia's behavior is discreet, he is not her only partner. The most he can hope for is that she will regard him as her favorite (143–8):

> In any case, she did not come to me led by her father's hand
>   into a house fragrant with Assyrian perfume,
> but at midnight gave stealthy little tokens taken   145
>   from the very embrace of her own husband.
> And so that is enough, if to me alone is granted
>   the day she marks with a brighter stone.

This paradox of treating a clandestine affair as marriage involves the speaker in a double bind, for the fidelity he desires in his mistress presupposes her own infidelity to her marriage vows (Rubino 1975: 291). Consequently, he himself has no right to demand any exclusive commitment from her, as he finally admits to himself. The sober-minded resignation he arrives at in 68.147–8 will not last long, however, for he has already invested far too much in this relationship.

In the absence of other sanctions, Catullus, in pleading with his beloved, appeals to the code of honor that had once underpinned binding agreements between members of the aristocracy. This strategy desexualizes the liaison, converting it into a contractual bond (**foedus**) between two gentlemen. He loved her, he tells Lesbia in poem 72, "not just as a common fellow loves his girlfriend, but as a father loves his sons and sons-in-law" (3–4). In his eyes, theirs was an enduring alliance marked by the familial affection that unites generations. Elsewhere he describes his own conduct toward her with such value-charged terms as *fides* ("credibility"), *officium* ("service, obligation"), *pietas* ("consciousness of duty") and justifies the use of that language by designating their love as "this eternal compact of holy friendship," *aeternum hoc sanctae foedus amicitiae* (109.6). All his efforts to redeem her are in vain, though, as she sinks further and further into degradation.

In poem 75 Catullus admits the hopelessness of imposing a code of reciprocal obligation upon the actual circumstances of the affair:

> To this point, my Lesbia, has my mind been brought through your fault
>   and has itself so ruined itself by its own service [*officium*],
> that it could not now bear you goodwill, were you to turn all virtuous,
>   nor cease to love you, whatever you might do.

By forging ties of intimate friendship, **amicitia**, with his mistress, he had attempted to define a private sphere of relations grounded upon a steadfastness banished from the larger political realm with its self-serving friendships (*amicitiae*) and flimsy alliances of convenience. Yet his claim to virtue as a lover, and his righteous anger at her perfidy, were of course already undercut by his disregard for the inviolability of marriage, an institution even more fundamental to an ordered community than friendship. That untenable position gives his bitter complaints all the more poignancy. Worse: his appropriation of a vocabulary of social obligation to shore up his irregular union would have been futile in any case, since its imposition was arbitrary and unilateral, backed by no consensus of society. In fact his hopes of true affection were a pipe dream. "In light of the increasing fragility of aristocratic political and social relations in the closing years of the Republic as Rome heads toward civil war, the Catullan lover's irrational dedication to an irreplaceable beloved is also a fantasy of absolute commitment possible only in some other world" (Fitzgerald 1995: 134).

Insofar as "Lesbia" herself was so thoroughly caught up in the power transactions of the ruling elite, the weak foundations of Catullus' erotic world had always been exposed to the vicissitudes of current political events. It is fitting, then, that when he finally breaks with her in poem 11, he conflates her sexual hunger with the relentless progress of Roman imperial expansion. Furius and Aurelius, two characters who elsewhere appear in his corpus as false friends, have apparently tried to bring about a reconciliation with Lesbia, meantime professing, perhaps as an alternative, their own willingness to accompany the speaker to the ends of the earth:

> Furius and Aurelius, comrades of Catullus
> whether he shall penetrate into the farthest Indies,
> where the long-resounding shore is beaten
> by the Eastern wave;
>
> or among the Caspians and spineless Arabs,   5
> or the Scythians or quiver-bearing Parthians,
> or to the flat plains the seven-mouthed
> Nile discolors;
>
> or march over the lofty Alps,
> viewing the trophies of mighty Caesar,   10
> the Gallic Rhine, the rough straits, at world's end
> the British;
>
> all these, wherever the will of the gods
> should take him, prepared to endure with him –
> go, tell my girl a few things   15
> unkindly said.
>
> May she live and prosper with her lovers,
> three hundred of whom she embraces at once,
> loving none truly, but again and again
> breaking the loins of all.   20
>
> Nor let her look back on my love as before,
> which through her fault perished just like the flower
> on the edge of the meadow, once it is touched
> by the passing plough.

Here Lesbia's predatory dealings with her partners are equated, by implication, with Roman military expansionism, undertaken, as Catullus charges elsewhere, not for reasons of national security but rather to feed the eager ambition of army commanders (Konstan 2000).

In the opening stanzas, the speaker envisions hypothetical options for adventure abroad, calling to mind actual military campaigns begun in 55 BCE: Crassus' ill-fated expedition against Parthia, Gabinius' intervention in Egypt, Caesar's first invasion of Britain. Scholars have often remarked that the verb "penetrate" (*penetrabit*) and the condescending description of the Arab enemy as unmanly (*molles*, "soft") paint military aggression as erotic domination. Paradoxically, as he runs through this catalogue of foreign settings, Catullus' own scope of activity narrows. By the third stanza he is reduced to a tourist, a simple witness to Caesar's heroic exploits (Putnam 1974: 72); in the fourth he relinquishes control over his life to the gods. When he refuses Furius and Aurelius' offer of companionship and instead packs them off to tell Lesbia what he is too disgusted to say to her directly, he turns his back on the whole martial enterprise. In startling contrast to the carefully regulated obscenity of the preceding stanza, he finally appropriates and applies to himself the poignant Greek nuptial image of the flower plucked in the meadow, symbolizing the bride's loss of virginity. This flower, though, was not gathered by a maiden, but instead cut down by a plow moving inexorably on. If the speaker's love was the flower, Lesbia becomes the plow – and plowing a furrow to define settlement boundaries was the main ritual action involved in founding a Roman colony (Cic. *Phil.* 2.102, Verg. *Aen.* 5.755; see Skinner 1991: 9). Thus the poem comes full circle. At its outset, current unilateral offensives against "feminized" tribes were described as priapic assaults; in the last stanza, Lesbia's insatiable sexual appetite is assimilated to Rome's territorial encroachment. In all this, Catullus' own sense of masculine integrity has been heedlessly destroyed by forces beyond his control, like the flower on the meadow's verge or the peoples in the way of the imperial machine.

Succeeding decades witnessed the development and popularity of Latin erotic elegy, a genre in which the poet, embellishing upon Catullus' predicament, portrays himself as a lover totally enslaved by a capricious beauty. For her sake he endures crushing humiliation: "[n]o duty is too low, no punishment too degrading for him to suffer in the service of love" (Copley 1947: 291). Propertius opens his earliest book of elegies by announcing: "Cynthia first snared poor me with her eyes, I who before was touched by no desire," then describing how Love had cast down his proud glance and trampled his head underfoot (1.1.1–4). Tibullus, his contemporary, fantasizes himself as his mistress Delia's slave attendant, clearing a path for her through the crowd (1.5.61–6) or guarding her person while meekly accepting lashes and chains (1.6.37–8). Later he is in thrall to an even more cruel **domina**, Nemesis, at whose bidding, he says, he would sell his ancestral estate or drink poison (2.5.53–60). Ovid, the last practitioner of Augustan elegy, who busies himself exploding the conventions of an already exhausted genre, runs the "slavery of love" conceit into the ground. In the *Art of Love*, ostensibly an instructional manual on choosing and winning a mistress, he advises the aspiring elegiac lover to demonstrate obedience to his lady's will: adapt your mood to hers, let her win at dice, hold her parasol and clear her way through the crowd, place a footstool under her feet, help her remove or put on her shoes, warm her cold hand in your lap, hold a mirror for her (2.199–216). The submission of these lovers, then, ismore profound and melodramatic than Catullus', whose struggle to salvage his own personal dignity is evident throughout the cycle of epigrams in which he protests his ill treatment.

Meanwhile, the status of the elegiac poet's mistress – the **docta puella** or "learned girl" – is left unclear, in fact deliberately blurred. Contradictory aspects of her characterization puzzle critics. She has had access to considerable education and is therefore able to appreciate the poet-lover's verse and compose verse herself (Prop. 2.3.21–2). Sometimes she is represented as under the control of a *vir*, also a common word for "husband," which gives the impression that she is a married citizen woman. Indeed, we find implications of high rank: in Propertius 1.16 a personified house door complains that it formerly welcomed triumphs, but now witnesses the drunken brawling of its mistress' suitors (1–8), and in another elegy (3.20.8), a girl, who may or may not be Cynthia, is reminded of the brilliant fame of her learned grandfather. However, from the evidence of Propertius 4.7.15–16, Cynthia at one time dwelt in the Subura, a poor and not very reputable district. Both Cynthia and Delia are said to be worshippers of Isis, whose cult was associated with prostitutes (Prop. 2.28.61–2, 4.5.33–4; Tib. 1.3.23–32). Often the *puella* is depicted as free to make her own sexual choices, selecting among her lovers and favoring the man who brings the most gifts. In those contexts, she is obviously a woman of easy virtue: by the late Republic, in fact, the word *puella* could be a euphemism for "whore" (Adams 1983: 346–8). Tibullus (1.6.67–8) states outright that Delia is not entitled to the long robe and headband of the decent married woman. Finally, Ovid candidly advises at the beginning of his *Art of Love* that the girls his addressee will pursue are not reputable (1.31–4). Having disingenuously warned matrons off, he presents himself as singing of safe congress and permitted deceits, "and in my poem there will be no wrongdoing." Much good this disclaimer did, however, when the *Art of Love* drew Augustus' wrath down upon him for promulgating adultery. Mixed signals were obviously being given.

Cornelius Gallus, the recognized inventor of love elegy, wrote poems about a "Lycoris," who was actually the freedwoman Volumnia Cytheris, a mime actress. Imagining the heroine of elegy as an independent, expensive courtesan such as Cytheris – a **meretrix** like the Greek *hetaira*, as opposed to the **scortum** or common prostitute – permits us to define a witty underlying tension when the pleas of the poetic lover are viewed from her perspective. As a woman on her own, she must provide for her old age by soliciting gifts from admirers before youth and beauty fade. The lover, on the other hand, can offer her nothing but his talent. He eloquently promises that their union will be immortalized in verse, a far finer present than material goods. Perhaps so, but she herself is aware that literary glory buys no bread. This irreconcilable disparity of interests has been termed the "elegiac impasse" (James 2003: 14). Vows of eternal devotion on the lover's part attempt blithely to gloss over economic considerations, though they would inevitably occur to a reader living in money- and class-conscious Rome. The speaker's dogged refusal to acknowledge those material facts of the relationship, and his futile railings against what he sees as his mistress' fickleness and avarice, obliquely poke fun at the blindness of romantic fixation.

There are, however, other meanings attached to the *docta puella*, and the workings of elegy have much more complex repercussions. It is now a truism that on one level the elegiac woman stands for the author's poetry, a self-referential metaphor that can be traced back to the Hellenistic epigrammatist Meleager. Beginning with Lesbia, almost all Roman literary mistresses bear names indicating their association with literature or aesthetics. Cynthia's name is derived from an epithet of Apollo, god of music, employed only by Callimachus; it signals Propertius' adherence to a Callimachean poetics of learned, elegant, highly polished verse (Clausen 1976). "Delia" is a straightforward reference to Apollo's birthplace, the island of Delos. Ovid sings of "Corinna," the name of a real Boeotian woman poet and, by a happy coincidence, also a calque or bilingual pun, for *korê* (girl) is the Greek equivalent of *puella*. The most transparent use of this device is "Cerinthus," the woman elegist Sulpicia's designation for her beloved. His name is the Greek word for "bee-bread," a substance manufactured by bees. Its close ties with honey remind us of the "sweetness" of verse, and its connection with wax (Greek *kêros*, Latin *cera*) points directly to the tablets covered with wax on which the poet composes (Roessel 1990). By calling her partner "Wax-man," Sulpicia makes it very clear that he is a poetic fiction allowing her to address questions of gender and writing under the guise of a love affair. When the male poet, meanwhile, proclaims his undying desire for his beloved, he celebrates his own imaginative control over his subject matter. Ovid's fable of Pygmalion, the sculptor who falls in love with the statue he makes (*Met.* 10.243–97), has consequently been interpreted as a comment on the inherent gender asymmetry in the elegiac metaphor of art as mistress (Sharrock 1991).

Sulpicia Unveils Herself

The most provocative instance of an elegist using erotic metaphors as tools for investigating curbs on personal autonomy is that of Sulpicia, niece of the eminent statesman Messalla, who headed a literary circle to which Tibullus and Ovid belonged. Transmitted to us as part of Tibullus' collection, her cycle of six elegiac epigrams begins with a programmatic poem in which she protests against the constraints imposed on the woman writer ([Tib.] 3.13.1–2 = 4.7). "At last love has come," she announces, a love of such a kind that to her the rumor (*fama*) of covering it (*texisse*) would be a source of greater shame (*pudor*) than the rumor of baring it (*nudasse*). Because of her social visibility, a young Roman woman would be expected to behave circumspectly, and writing love elegy, even about an imaginary affair, exposed her to

risk. Accordingly, the contrast between publication and silence is here figured as a difference between clothing and nakedness, and the use of *pudor* in this context reinforces the bold suggestion of a striptease. Kristina Milnor skillfully unpacks the metaphor: "a woman who offers her words to the reading public has notionally prostituted herself; in body and spirit, she no longer belongs only to herself but to anyone who might pick up a book" (2002: 260). Indeed, Sulpicia goes on to invite anyone denied the experience of love to participate vicariously in her affair, refusing even to seal her tablets so that her lover might first read them, and closing with the announcement that her literary reputation as a love poet requires complete honesty: "It's a pleasure to trespass, and tiring to put on a face for

(Continued)

Sulpicia Unveils Herself — Continued

reputation's sake: I, a worthy woman, will be said to have been together with a worthy man" ([Tib.] 3.13.9–10). The expression *esse cum* "to be with" is a delicate equivalent of "to have sex." Thus the last line breaks two taboos: it affirms the physical nature of the female speaker's relationship and, in a striking departure from the elegiac convention of erotic slavery, promises that the affair will be one of moral and social equals.

In her signature poem 3.16 (= 4.10), Sulpicia defines her poetic identity as *docta puella* against that of the generic elegiac mistress, revealing herself as the offspring of a noble house. Cerinthus, it seems, has presumed upon her affection by becoming involved with a disreputable woman, and she sarcastically reproaches him: "Let your attraction to a toga-clad creature, a whore laden with a wool-basket, mean more to you than Sulpicia, daughter of Servius" (3–4). By unmasking herself publicly in this way, she metapoetically pulls rank on the fictitious courtesan figure: male poets may play it safe by writing of their sordid "Cynthias" and "Delias," but she is an aristocrat with a good name to lose. Accordingly, she reintroduces into elegy the consequences avoided by depicting the *docta puella* as a permissible sex object, for she proceeds to warn Cerinthus that there are persons who fear that she might "yield to a base bed," *cedam ignoto ... toro* (5–6). Yet scholars have noted the irony with which this haughty affirmation of rank and class is undercut. *Servi filia* means "daughter of Servius," that is, her patrician father Servius Sulpicius Rufus, but it could equally well mean "daughter of a slave," *servus* (Hinds 1987: 44–5). Furthermore, the wearing of masculine dress, which marks the prostitute as a marginalized figure, could be symbolically imputed to Sulpicia herself because she has assumed the role of poet-lover generically assigned to the male partner (Flaschenriem 1999: 47–8). In this epigram, then, Sulpicia rings changes on elegy's inherent ambiguities of gender and status, adopting the victimized posture of the male speaker, identifying herself as an upper-class woman whose sexuality is not beneath public notice, and daringly trying on,

just for an instant, the character of slave-prostitute herself. It is a bravura performance.

In the Introduction to this book, I quoted in full the last poem of the preserved sequence (3.18 = 4.12), in which Sulpicia explains to Cerinthus that she left him the night before, not because she did not desire him, but because she was afraid to confess how much she did. Even in English translation, the complex structure of this declaration is apparent; it is a perfect example of the poet's notoriously difficult and labored syntax (Lowe 1988: 198–9). Instead of striving for clarity, the rhetoric retards full expression until the very last line, when meaning bursts forth in a rush: "wanting to conceal my own passion." Recent criticism has traced the psychological undercurrents: "Here, it is almost as if she restages, in the rhetorical organization of the poem, her former hesitation – her impulse to hide her ardor – but then firmly renounces such concealment and evasion" (Flaschenriem 1999: 51). The issue resolved in this final epigram can be traced back to the anxieties about propriety raised in Sulpicia's programmatic poem, which on first reading apparently has to do with whether a decent young Roman girl may write about her own sexual adventures. But we see now that *stuprum* was a peripheral matter: Sulpicia's verse is scandalous because it makes use of an obviously fabricated love affair to protest conventional strictures forcing women to lie and dissimulate their feelings (Hallett 1992: 352). To accomplish this critique of patriarchy, the poet must adopt a masculine perspective, invoking, in spirit if not in words, Catullus' notion of love as *amicitia* and condemning her previous dishonesty as a violation of the trust Cerinthus deserves as her equal. In this closing poem, and in fact throughout the sequence, disruptions of gender role are no affectation but a real and inherent consequence of female artistic expression. Thus the effeminacy affected by the male speaker of elegy has opened up space for a woman writer to assume a corresponding transgendered position (Wyke 1994: 114–15) and, in doing so, to speak forthrightly of the restrictions imposed upon her sex.

Although the poet exercises discursive mastery over the *puella* as art object, he nevertheless insists on his servility to her as love object, and therefore puts himself into a "feminized" subject position. His erotic stance is so unmanly that elegy has been said to make use of three genders: the masculine, the feminine, and the effeminate (Wyke 1994: 125). That concession to female dominance implicitly alludes to the increasing constriction of freedoms formerly enjoyed by the senatorial and equestrian classes. From the second century BCE onward, the figure of the controlling woman had stood for a disordered society in which the *mos maiorum* had been turned on its head. Elegists found this metaphor of male subjection useful for voicing feelings of impotence and marginalization as Rome passed under the control of one man. At the same time, the lover declares his unwillingness to participate in military service abroad or laments his misfortunes when actually engaged in that service, refuses to turn his talents to epic celebrations of Roman might and power, revels in his indolence, and disrupts conventional social arrangements by questioning a rival's right to exclusive possession of a woman – who may, it is suggested, be a legitimate wife. All these behaviors are symptomatic of a crisis in the Roman male subject's conception of himself as a social and political agent (Miller 2004: 16–30). As a medium of literary protest, elegy is not only subversive but narcissistic.

Apparent contradictions in the status of the *puella* seem to reflect current moral pressures on elite men. In politicizing love poetry, the elegists followed the lead of Catullus, who took advantage of his mistress' involvement in backstairs political intrigue to color the poetic affair with topical overtones by presenting it as an exploitative relationship of social unequals. In an atmosphere of increasing hostility to adultery and other forms of sexual immorality, however, writing first-person accounts of liaisons with married noblewomen would have been indiscreet. Thus the elegiac mistress, on the surface, becomes a courtesan, and the *vir* who stands in the way of the poet-lover's happiness is ostensibly her wealthy protector. This means that male status anxiety, which elegy wishes to explore in depth, cannot be symbolically justified by any extra-literary distinction of the beloved or by her influence and connections in the real world. Propertius and Tibullus disguise this weakness in the plot of love elegy with the claim that they have been captivated by the girl's beauty and accomplishments, though they also try to blur the line between courtesan and matron through ambiguous language. Because a woman's personality, however charismatic, seems inadequate to explain the lover's utter submission, though, elegy's inversion of gender and power dynamics may strike the reader as contrived. The fact that love elegy relies upon far-fetched scenarios hints that the genre is not really concerned with such scenarios – nor, for that matter, with the notion of romantic love. What is truly being negotiated between the first-person speaker and his mistress is best understood in socio-political terms.

Mother of All Empires

Venus, goddess of love and sexuality in the Roman pantheon, is an equivocal figure. On the one hand, she occupies a crucial place in state religious cult and ideology: among her titles is that of ***Venus Genetrix***, divine ancestress of the Roman nation through Aeneas, her child by Anchises (see discussion of the *Homeric Hymn to Aphrodite* in Chapter 1). The patrician family of the Julii traced their lineage back to Iulus, son of Aeneas. When Julius Caesar became master of Rome after defeating his rival Pompey, he began construction on a new Forum Julium as an extension of the old market and civic meeting place. The centerpiece of Caesar's architectural project, dedicated on September 26, 46 BCE (Cass. Dio 43.22.2), was a temple of his hereditary patron divinity Venus worshipped under the epithet "Genetrix." This cult title celebrated the goddess as mother of not only the Julian clan, but, by extension, all the people of Aeneas (Weinstock 1971: 80–90). A generation later the epic poet **Vergil** created the canonical image of Venus as protective ancestress of the Roman race in his *Aeneid*, which retold the story of Aeneas' flight from Troy and eventual settlement in Italy. Early in its opening book she tearfully complains to Jupiter about the sufferings of the Trojans: "What end do you give to their labors, great king?" (*Aen.* 1.241). Jupiter reassures his anxious daughter by prophesying Aeneas' settlement in Italy, the later founding of Rome by Romulus, and Rome's ultimate leadership of the world (1.254–96). The chief impression made on the reader is the goddess' passionate concern for her descendants, and that impression still dominates scholarly discussions of her role in the epic.

Yet, for all her importance in state cult, Venus could nevertheless be viewed as a formidable agent of disruption because she was the immediate source of those unlawful pleasures that had supposedly sapped the moral fiber of men and women and were thus to blame for present ills. In the hands of two great poets, **Lucretius** and Vergil, that tension between her "beneficial" and "destructive" aspects reveals flaws in human nature that militate against the achievement of tranquility and lasting peace for individuals and nations alike.

Lucretius' *On the Nature of Things*, a didactic epic in six books summarizing Epicurean science and moral teaching, begins by invoking the divine ancestress of the Romans, *Aeneadum genetrix*, as the supreme creative force in nature (1.1–9)

> Mother of Aeneas' tribe, delight [*voluptas*] of gods and men,
> nurturing Venus, who under the gliding signs of the sky
> propagates the ship-bearing sea, the crop-bearing land,
> since through you all the host of living things
> is conceived and, brought to birth, looks on the light of the sun: 5
> you, goddess, you put to flight the winds and clouds of the sky
> at your coming, for you the dexterous earth sends forth sweet flowers;
> for you the plains of the sea sparkle
> and the calm sky glitters with extended light.

As soon as spring winds blow, the poet continues, Venus, personification of a newly awakened earth, manifests herself in the natural world. Heralded by birds and causing beasts to follow her enraptured, she strikes "alluring desire" into their breasts to make them produce offspring species by species (10–20). Her creative powers are so absolute and far-reaching that they overflow into the sphere of artistic invention, envisioned as an analogous creative act (Clayton 1999: 70). Accordingly, Lucretius calls upon her to be his ally (*socia*, 24) in writing his descriptive account of the world she governs and asks her to endow his poetry with an enticing charm, *lepos*. So far, his picture of Venus is wholly benign and not altogether inconsistent with Epicurus' teachings on divinity. Though Lucretius follows his master in repeatedly insisting that actual gods are remote from human affairs, have no need of mankind, and do not intervene, for good or ill, in our business (2.167–81, 646–51; 5.110–94, 1194–240), it is easy to read this opening invocation as allegorical praise of the awesome processes of Nature, the productive dynamics of the sexual instinct, and Epicurean pleasure (*voluptas*, 1) as the motivating goal of the wise man (Brown 1987: 92–4).

Unorthodox overtones creep in, however, as the poet continues his prayer. Venus alone is in a position to end hostilities on sea and land (1.29–42). The operations of war are the domain of bellicose **Mars**,

> who often casts himself back on your lap
> constrained by the eternal wound of love,
> and thus looking up, his rounded neck pillowed,   35
> feeds his starved eyes with love gazing open-mouthed,
> and his breath, when he reclines, hangs on your lips.
> Bending over him from above as he lies on your holy body,
> goddess, pour forth from your mouth sweet blandishments
> seeking tranquil peace for the Romans, renowned lady.   40
> For I am not able to write with easy mind
> during this treacherous time for my country …

This tableau of Mars lying in Venus' embrace is heavily weighted with literary and pictorial antecedents. One of Lucretius' models is a poem on nature by Empedocles, a fifth-century follower of Pythagoras, who in his own proem may have depicted his two primary cosmic principles, Love and Strife, in a comparable anthropomorphic pose (Sedley 1998: 26–8). Iconographically, Mars' attitude is immediately reminiscent of Hellenistic representations of male divinities leaning back on the bosom of a female companion, such as the well-known scene of Bacchus/Dionysos reclining on his wife Ariadne's lap in the center of the great fresco of initiation in the **Villa of the Mysteries** at Pompeii (Room 5, East Wall, fig. 8.1; Edmunds 2002: 346–8). Similarly, the male speakers of Hellenistic erotic epigram imagine themselves reposing on the lap of a mistress (for example, *Anth. Pal.* 5.25.1–3 by Lucretius' contemporary Philodemus).

In art, however, this particular "erotic schema" (Edmunds 2002: 351) is a good deal older than the Hellenistic period: it can be traced back to Attic Greek vase painting, as on a late fifth-century hydria attributed to the Meidias Painter (Florence 81948; *ARV*² 1312.1). There, Adonis is embraced by Aphrodite, his languid relaxation rendering him both vulnerable and effete. Similarly, the centerpiece of Arsinoë's lavish display celebrating the Adonis festival in Ptolemaic Alexandria was the effigy of the boyish Adonis lying on a couch in Aphrodite's arms (Theoc. *Id.* 15.84–5, 131). This iconographic scheme had apparently become the traditional way to portray the goddess and her young consort. For Lucretius to describe the Roman war-god, sire of Romulus, in a posture originally associated with the youthful Adonis is unsettling. It suggests that Venus' relationship to her lover is that of a pampering mother,

Fig. 8.1 Silenus and satyrs, Marriage of Dionysos and Ariadne. Fresco. Location: Villa of the Mysteries, Pompeii, Italy. Source: Scala/Art Resource, NY.

a disturbing notion to a Roman whose ideological construction of "motherhood" instead saw the female parent, in the father's absence, as a strict disciplinarian. Furthermore, Mars bears a telling similarity to the hapless suitor mocked in the powerful diatribe against the illusion of romantic love that closes the fourth book of the poem (Brown 1987: 97). Like that lover, he is gripped by obsessive, frustrating desire for what he cannot possess, while his emotional dependency makes him profoundly susceptible to Venus' wheedling words. Since she is pressing the cause of peace, this seduction scene is doubly disquieting because the liaison of the adulterous divine couple ironically serves to promote human good. Not only is Mars unmanned and painted as a libertine, but the fusion of the erotic and the maternal in the goddess' stance also infantilizes him (Clayton 1999: 71–3). Although it is not to be taken as a straightforward prayer, this passage is equally hard to explain as an allegory of the generative powers of nature triumphant over forces of negativity and violence, as has been argued by Monica Gale (1994: 222–3). Too many adverse elements stand in the way of such a reading. We will shortly see that Vergil picks up Lucretius' characterization of Venus as eroticized mother and makes her display the same combination of nurturing and seductive traits in dealings with her son. The outcomes are no less troubling.

Let us turn briefly to Book Four of *On the Nature of Things* to study its concluding diatribe against romantic love, which deconstructs this evocation of a sublime and numinous presence. The first thing to bear in mind is that sex and love are not identical phenomena: the latter, in Lucretius' view, is an unhealthy perversion of the former, permeated by false illusions. He leads up to the topic of sex through an analysis of the mechanism of dreaming. Dreams contain the residue of daily experience; the images seen are predetermined by waking pursuits or by the physiological condition of the speaker. Three examples of dreams occasioned by bodily appetites are cited: the thirsty man dreams of drinking from a river; someone needing to urinate supposes himself using a chamber pot, but actually wets the bed and its expensive coverlets; adolescent boys ejaculate in the course of an erotic dream (*DRN* 4.1024–36). From the last instance, Lucretius moves into a description of the biological and psychological workings of the sexual drive. The transition is skillfully contrived as an anticipation of his forthcoming point: the frustrating or embarrassing dream event is the product of a real corporeal need overlaid by mental error (Nussbaum 1994: 166–7). Romantic love is similarly explained, though it takes place in conscious life.

In the atomistic universe of Epicurus, sense perception always involves physical contact between entities: sight, for example, is the impression made by material particles shed by an object, which strike the eyes and then enter the consciousness of the beholder. Male sexual desire is the impulse to discharge semen into an attractive body whose visual impact upon the mind has biologically triggered the production of that fluid: "the body seeks that by which the mind has been wounded with love" (4.1048). This is a natural physical response; for us, *this* is "Venus" (*haec Venus est nobis*, 1058). Erotic urges are not inflicted by some mysterious divine agent but instead have a simple mechanistic explanation.

In the denunciation of romantic love that follows, Lucretius employs the noun "Venus" as a metonym for physical desire (1061, 1084, 1101, 1107, 1148, 1172), for the human object of such desire (1071, 1157), and for the act of intercourse (1073, 1113, 1128), using this troping strategy to demonstrate how a mere physiological process is foolishly elevated into a supernatural force. If the psyche fixates upon one person and she becomes the sole object of an infatuated hunger to possess, the lover, even in the actual course of lovemaking, suffers cares, pains, and cruel disappointments (1076–120). His urge for complete union with the beloved can never be satisfied, since the only thing his body can take in are the flimsy images (*simulacra*, 1095) given off by her body. Orgasm brings only momentary relief. Consequences of fixation include the ruin of health, fortune and reputation, as well as guilt, anxiety, and jealousy (1121–40). The lover deludes himself about the beloved's appearance, ascribing to her a superhuman beauty, turning her corporeal shortcomings into virtues, even refusing to admit that she performs the same physical functions as other women and therefore exudes foul odors (probably a reference to the menstrual period). Were he to enter her house at that time, one whiff would send him packing, damning himself for his own stupidity "because he would see that he had endowed her with more than it is correct to grant a mortal" (1183–4).

Our "Venuses," Lucretius adds ironically, are aware of that fact and attempt to preserve their suitors' illusions by concealing such behind-the-scenes features of human life (*vitae postscaenia*, 1186). You, however, can conjure them up in imagination to purge yourself of fantasy, and then, if the woman is a decent sort, accept her for what she is, an ordinary human being (*humanis concedere rebus*, 1191). He proceeds to demonstrate that women too derive enjoyment from the sexual act, paving the way for a "new understanding of intercourse, one that makes its aim the giving and receiving of pleasure on both sides" (Nussbaum 1994: 183). The remainder of Book Four concerns itself with the procreative aims of marriage: it explains the processes of conception and transmission of biological traits and the physical causes of infertility, advising wives to avoid harlots' lascivious movements employed for contraceptive purposes (1268–77). At the close, Lucretius observes that a "little woman" (*muliercula*, 1279), of no particular beauty but well groomed and accommodating, can bring a man to love her through daily habit, like dripping water wearing away a stone. However we are to take that last dubious simile, a relationship of intimacy developed over the course of years, characterized as *consuetudo* (1283), the Epicurean term for friendship (Betensky 1980: 294), is held up as the prosaic but rational alternative to the torments of passion.

The centerpiece of Lucretius' attack on love is a grim picture of unsatisfying sexual intercourse whose dominant element is sadistic aggression. In the very moment of possession lovers do not know what to enjoy: they injure the desired body by pressing down upon it and biting the lips they kiss, because "the pleasure is not pure, and there are underlying goads compelling them to hurt that very thing, whatever it is, from which those sprouts of frenzy arise" (1076–83). Immediately before climax they greedily affix their bodies, mingle salivas, and gasp while clenching the other's lips with their teeth, "in vain, for they are not able to scrape away anything, nor to penetrate and disappear into that flesh with their entire flesh" (1105–11). Conversely, a woman's responsive lovemaking is genuine and aims at giving as well as receiving pleasure: "seeking shared gratification she urges him to run the course of love" (1195–6). On the one hand, Robert D. Brown comments, we have "an affectionate act leading to mutual satisfaction"; on the other, "a one-sided and desperate act of near violence, the pleasure of which is swamped with frustration." The woman's movements are instinctive, the lover's driven by unnatural expectations (1987: 65–6). Recent feminist studies of Lucretius commend his contemporary-sounding valorization of female sexual response and shared pleasure (Nussbaum 1994: 184–5) and even suggest that his polemic against romantic obsession forms part of a broader critique of Roman structures of masculinity (Gordon 2002). One might note, though, that Lucretius' therapeutic model of sex is curiously biased. Despite Epicurean assumptions about the intellectual and moral parity of the sexes, it seems essentialist in its polarization of "unhealthy" male and "natural, healthy" female libido. It does not admit the possibility that a woman, too, might experience obsessive desire.

With the character of **Dido**, the Carthaginian queen who falls desperately in love with Aeneas and commits suicide when he abandons her, Vergil in his *Aeneid* reverses the gender roles in Lucretius' account of erotic madness. Widow of the former king of Tyre in Phoenicia, Dido had fled her home with a group of supporters after her brother slew her husband in a palace coup. When the Trojan survivors are driven by a storm to the coast of Africa, they seek aid from her at her new settlement, Carthage. Like Aeneas, Dido is a political refugee who has experienced personal trials and bereavement. As a girl, she had heard about the fall of Troy while living in her father's house. Generous, warm, and compassionate, she is psychologically predisposed to be swept off her feet by a hero with whose story she is familiar. On their first meeting she is astounded at seeing him in the flesh: "Are you *that* Aeneas ...?" she asks (Verg. *Aen.* 1.617). In addition to feeling genuine admiration for a celebrated figure and personally empathizing with his misfortunes, Dido is in a lonely and precarious position as the female ruler of a small city surrounded by hostile peoples. Thus her spontaneous attraction to Aeneas is understandable in purely human terms.

But Venus is only too eager to get involved. Fearing the designs of Jupiter's wife Juno, whose hatred of the Trojans is the most formidable barrier to Aeneas' mission, and mistrusting the Carthaginians' motives, since Juno is their patron goddess, she sends her son Cupid, disguised as Aeneas' own son Iulus, to kindle a consuming passion for Aeneas in Dido's heart. When Dido, attracted to the boy because of his father, takes Cupid unknowingly upon her lap, the god obligingly begins, little by little, to efface her commitment to her former husband – for whose sake she had sworn never to remarry – and stimulate her dormant heart with a quickening love (1.717–22). It is possible to think of Cupid as an external realization of the queen's own feelings. By involving Venus, however, Vergil ensures that her desire for Aeneas has been, as the psychologists say, overdetermined: what might have been resisted as mere human impulse is all the more inescapable because it is supernaturally inflicted.

In Book Four, the tormented and miserable queen at length confides in her sister Anna, who encourages her to follow her heart, not least because of the military advantages of such a dynastic alliance (4.35–49). The political connection is also at the forefront of Juno's mind when she approaches Venus to cut a deal, proposing a merger of Trojans and Carthaginians and joint divine custody of Carthage, with Dido's people subject to Aeneas as their king (4.102–4). Her hidden purpose, as Venus quickly intuits, is to delay or prevent the fated arrival of the Trojans in Italy. With only token hesitation, and thick-skinned indifference to the well-being of the two principals, Aeneas' mother consents to the plan, knowing full well that Jupiter will never approve. Juno arranges a storm that conveniently forces Dido and Aeneas while out hunting to take shelter together in a cave, apart from their companions. The upshot is a travesty of a wedding ceremony: primal Earth and Juno, as matron of honor, attend; lightning flashes in heaven, sole witness to the conjugal rites; nymphs howl on the mountain tops. "That was the first day of death and the first cause of evils," remarks the narrator. "Dido is no longer moved by appearances or reputation nor contemplates a secret love: she calls it marriage; with this name she covers her fault" (169–72). No mention is made of Aeneas' feelings, although, as the tragedy unfolds, we learn that the queen's affection was reciprocated. Jupiter eventually hears of the affair and sends Mercury down to remind the errant hero of his duty to his son and their descendants. Mercury comes upon an Aeneas clad in purple and gold, occupied with constructing new buildings – a sign that he has willingly taken on the role of royal consort (259–64). Awed by the god's epiphany and the cutting rebuke he delivers, the Trojan leader gives orders to ready the ships in secret. He will wait, he tells his men, for just the right moment and seek the most diplomatic way to tell *optima Dido* (287–94). It is really an excuse to put off a painful scene, one this hero does not have the guts to cope with.

Dido finds out on her own, of course, and, in an emotionally draining speech, confronts him with what she perceives as his breach of faith and pleads with him to stay (305–30). Pathos gives way to fury when Aeneas, making a steely effort to remain impassive (*obnixus curam sub corde premebat*, 331), attempts to reason with her; she mounts a disjointed tirade against him, threatening him with vengeance and promising that her ghost will hunt him down (365–87). Her hysteria at this point is a sign of incipient madness. When, upon further pleas from Anna, Aeneas refuses even to delay his departure, Dido, hounded by awful nightmares, resolves to commit suicide (450–73). As she beholds the Trojan fleet departing, she curses Aeneas and his bloodline and, in a final prayer, calls for eternal enmity between his people and hers (607–29). She then mounts a pyre she has prepared in the inner chambers of the palace and stabs herself with the sword her lover had left behind. Much later, on a journey through the Underworld, Aeneas meets the ghost of Dido, and, moved by compassion and guilt, finally confesses the truth: "Unwillingly, o queen, I left your shores" (6.460). It is too late. She remains icily silent, then shrinks from him, fleeing away to the embrace of her former husband Sychaeus.

Discussion of the Dido episode has generally centered upon which of the two protagonists is more responsible for the catastrophe: Dido, because she broke her vow of chastity and deceived herself with false expectations, or Aeneas himself, because he allowed an impossible situation to get out of hand, then, to avoid the agonizing consequences, coldly repressed his emotions and fled. While it is tempting to take sides, the ethical dilemma as it is presented to the reader makes it hard to form facile judgments. Both lovers are to blame, and Aeneas' sin of omission – his inability to let himself identify with Dido and share her pain – contributes as much to the sorry outcome as her loss of womanly virtue. Hence their final meeting in the Underworld wholly reverses their prior roles; for Aeneas, weeping as he confronts the queen's pitiless inflexibility, now experiences what she herself had suffered at his hands. Indeed, the fact that Dido receives consolation from Sychaeus, while Aeneas can only continue his journey burdened by regret, makes it clear that his long-term punishment will be greater and may hint that in Vergil's eyes there are worse crimes than loving too much.

If any character in the epic should be condemned for malicious mischief, it is Venus. Shortsighted as she appears to be, she may not have foreseen any lasting harm resulting from her manipulation of Dido's emotions or her cynical pact with Juno. Nevertheless, her actions strike one perceptive critic as "a case of cruel, divine irresponsibility, a piece of irresponsibility which not only contributed to Dido's death, but had nearly disastrous implications for her son" (Lyne 1987: 26). This is not the only place in the *Aeneid* where she shows unattractive qualities, but her selfish caprice is most evident here. Had she left well enough alone, the human protagonists might have handled their own difficulties better.

Is Venus merely Aeneas' interfering mother, or something more? It has long been customary to conceptualize divine agency in the *Aeneid* as a clash between two primal forces at work in the cosmos: Juno, the embodiment of anarchy and ***furor*** ("madness"), whose obsessive attempts to eradicate the Trojan race drive the narrative action (Keith 2000: 67), and Jupiter, catalyst of order, bent on establishing Rome as a stabilizing imperial power. When Juno bows to her husband's will at the end of the poem, renouncing her vendetta against Aeneas in return for the abolition of the Trojan name (12.791–842), it seems a victory for peace and rationality, though critics point out that her deeper grievances remain unresolved (Feeney 1991: 147–9). Yet viewing action on the divine plane solely in terms of the polarization of Jupiter and Juno may be reductionist. That approach overlooks the workings of Venus, who supports her father's long-range objectives but has no qualms about temporarily collaborating with the enemy, whatever the cost. If Jupiter and Juno are cosmic principles, so is she. On the metaphysical level, Venus mediates between order and chaos: amoral and impetuous, she triangulates what might otherwise have been a clear-cut struggle between good and evil. She is the incarnation of elemental human passion, treacherous because unpredictable.

As mother of the Roman race, she is a wild card, for her demeanor is often, to say the least, unmotherly. True, she often intervenes in Aeneas' life as an invisible helper. Because she comes to his rescue on those occasions, we think of her as a caring figure. Yet her face-to-face contacts with her son are few and strained, and his unsatisfying interaction with her is puzzling. Although their emotionally distanced association reflects Roman constructions of maternal behavior (Leach 1997: 364–5), some have noted, in addition, an unhealthy seductiveness in Venus' conduct, especially during an encounter in the woods near Carthage (1.314–410). There she appears to her son disguised as a young maiden huntress, bare to the knee and with loosened hair, to tell him Dido's story and reassure him that his fleet is safe. As she turns away, her neck glows, her hair breathes out fragrance, her dress ripples down to her feet, and, goddess-like, she walks majestically off. Recognizing his mother, Aeneas calls out bitterly as she vanishes (407–9):

> "Why do you tease your son so often with false phantoms,
> you, cruel as well? Why can't we clasp our right hands
> and hear and return earnest words?"

There is a touch of lighthearted mockery in Venus' deception, which, as we infer from *totiens* ("so often") has happened before. Yet there are also undertones of eroticism throughout the passage, both in the goddess' disguise as nubile, scantily dressed virgin and in the mature sensuality (ruddy flush, perfumed hair, rippling dress) she projects when leaving (Reckford 1995–6).[6] Presenting herself as a Punic huntress, a doublet of Dido (who will, of course, join Aeneas on the fatal hunt), Venus stirs her son's latent sexuality and prepares him to be receptive to Dido's advances. Incestuous overtones are compounded by patent echoes of Aphrodite's seduction of Anchises, Aeneas' own father, in the archaic *Homeric Hymn* (Reckford 1995–6: 16–22; Oliensis 1997: 306). Thwarted longings aroused by this seductive mother must have contributed to his inability to express his heartfelt feelings to Dido: if Venus refuses to deal honestly with him, how can he fully trust anyone else he cares for?

In the last six books of the *Aeneid* Vergil makes it evident that forcibly repressed eroticism, on the part of Aeneas and others, manifests itself in violence. Linkages between sexuality and aggression in the narrative include the speaker's seemingly incongruous prayer to Erato, the muse of love poetry, to assist him in recounting the battles between the Trojans and their Italian opponents (7.37–44); the sterile virginity of the Fury Allecto, who, at Juno's behest, incites the war (Mitchell 1991: 222–4; Keith 2000: 69, 72–4); the "feminization" of young men slain in battle and the assimilation of the blood they shed to that shed by the deflowered bride (D. Fowler 1987); the romanticized treatment of Nisus and Euryalus, a homoerotic couple whose heroic, if futile, deaths are followed by an extraordinary promise of poetic immortality from the narrator (9.446–9); suggestive hints of Aeneas' sexual attraction to the young warrior Pallas, whose death at the hands of the opposing commander Turnus he brutally avenges in the last lines of the poem (Gillis 1983: 53–83; Putnam 1985); the highly eroticized description of the death of the warrior maiden Camilla, killed by a spear thrust beneath her bared breast (11.803–4); and, finally, the fact that Aeneas is provoked to slay a wounded Turnus pleading for mercy by the sight of Pallas' baldric, worn as a trophy, which depicts the Danaids' murder of their bridegrooms on the wedding night (12.940–52).

The most blatantly erotic incident in the poem is also the most explicit conflation of militarism with sex. Venus approaches her husband Vulcan to get him to manufacture a set of weapons for Aeneas (8.370–406). In a scene deliberately reminiscent of Lucretius' encounter between Venus and Mars, she cajoles him, embraces him when he hesitates, inflames him with desire, and so obtains his consent:

> "... Therefore I am come as suppliant to beg the power I reverence
> for armor, a mother for her son. The daughter of Nereus,
> the wife of Tithonus were able to move you with tears.
> Look at what nations are assembling, what towns with barred gates   385
> sharpen their weapons seeking me and the death of my people!"
> Thus the goddess spoke, and on both sides with her white arms
> she clasped him in soft embrace as he struggled. Suddenly he
> caught the customary spark, and the well-known heat
> entered his vitals and ran through his trembling bones,   390
> just as when torn out by rolling thunder a fiery streak
> passes gleaming with light through the clouds.
> His wife happily sensed this, aware of her beauty and wiles.

When she presents the weapons to her son, she finally appears undisguised and permits him to embrace her (8.608–16). "She must seduce Vulcan at the creation, Aeneas at the acceptance, of the arms," Putnam remarks (1985: 16). Thus sexuality, far from being incidental to the events of the last half of the *Aeneid*, permeates the poem in a muted and displaced form and lends it a bleak pathos.

Not all poets found Venus' duplex personality troubling. In his fourth volume of *Odes*, Horace glides easily from addressing the love-goddess as "savage mother of sweet Cupids" in the opening poem (*Carm.* 4.1.4–5) to a vision of peace in the final poem of the book (15.25–32). There the speaker, on behalf of all Romans, promises first duly to invoke the gods in the company of wife and children and then to celebrate "Troy and Anchises and the offspring of nourishing Venus." By alluding to Lucretius' proem through the epithet he gives Venus (*alma*, "nourishing"), Horace implies that the prayer at the beginning of *On the Nature of Things* has finally been answered: Venus has calmed Mars' warlike temper, and the suffering she once inflicted on the speaker has been transmuted into familial blessings and joy at the revival of civic community (Putnam 1986: 295–9; Feeney 1998: 101–4).

Meanwhile, the imperial family's claim to descent from Venus furnished ample fodder for Ovid's irreverence. If Caesar is her descendant, then Cupid must be his kinsman (*Am.* 1.2.51). Had Venus, like Corinna, sought an abortion when pregnant, "the future world would have been bereft of its Caesars" (*Am.* 2.14.17–18). In the *Metamorphoses*, Julius Caesar's impending assassination is the occasion for a pastiche of the scene between Venus and Jupiter in *Aeneid* 1: Venus again complains of the wrongs inflicted on her progeny, and Jupiter affirms the unchangeable decrees of fate, predicts the avenging triumphs of Caesar's son Augustus, and bids Venus transform the soul of Caesar into a star (15.760–842). *Alma* Venus – there is that epithet again – catches it up as it leaves his body and bears it aloft, and, "as she carried it, felt it glow and catch fire and released it from her bosom" (847–8). No doubt we should imagine her dropping it like a hot brick. In his open letter to Augustus defending his poetry after his relegation to Tomis, discussed below, Ovid protests that it is impossible to keep spicy literature out of the hands of a matron. As soon as she reads Lucretius' opening words *Aeneadum genetrix*, "mother of Aeneas' tribe," she will want to know just how that might have happened (*Tr.* 2.261–2). Even in exile, he cannot resist a sly dig at the Caesarian myth of origins.

Yet it is true enough that we make jokes about things we fear. And the fortuitous constellation of poetic motifs surrounding Venus – adultery with Mars and Anchises; passion, madness, and brutality arising from thwarted desire; parentage of the race, its empire, and the imperial house – spoke to very dark elements in the collective psyche.

Domestic Visibility

When Augustus undertook his mission to reform the morals of upper-class society and bring back the piety of an earlier, happier time, he did not neglect the visual arts as a communicative medium. One of the familiar iconographic, as well as literary, themes of the Augustan period is the expectation of an imminent Golden Age with its accompanying promise of fertility and abundance (Zanker 1990: 172–83; Galinsky 1996: 106–21). Images of prosperity may be balanced by the warning that the Golden Age will not be attained without struggle ("relentless labor has conquered all," Verg. *G.* 1.145–6), but they nevertheless permeate contemporary Roman

Fig. 8.2   Saturnia, Tellus, Goddess of the Earth, Air and Water. Panel from the Ara Pacis, 13–9 BCE. Location: Museum of the Ara Pacis, Rome, 13–9 BCE, Italy. Source: Nimatallah/Art Resource, NY.

art. The classic illustration is the famous *Ara Pacis Augustae* in Rome, the "Altar of the Augustan Peace" constructed by the Senate from 13 to 9 BCE, deemed the most representative monument of its time (Galinsky 1996: 141; Severy 2003: 104–12). With its luxuriant decorative motifs of tendrils, flowers, vines and branches, the altar complex is itself a testimonial to the productivity of the land and its people under the imperial order. Emblematic of this promise of future blessings is the richly symbolic panel of Peace or Mother Earth (the identity of the figure is disputed) on the southeast side of the precinct wall (fig. 8.2).

A mature deity sits on a rocky throne embracing two chubby infants who reach up toward her breasts. Fruits lie in her lap; grain, poppies, and reeds grow beside her; two domestic animals, a cow or ox and a sheep, rest at her feet; and personifications of favoring breezes, their garments billowing, flank her on either side. Whoever this mother goddess is, it is noteworthy that she is depicted with the sensual qualities of Venus. Her garment slips from one shoulder; her breasts are prominent, one nipple faintly visible under thin, clinging drapery, which is also drawn tightly across her rounded abdomen.[7] This is female sexuality openly acknowledged, but properly put to use in generation and nurturing.

Meanwhile, the two long friezes of the wall feature religious processions: the north frieze shows senators and their families; the south frieze (fig. 8.3) the imperial family, including women and children, assisting at a sacrifice conducted by Augustus and the

Fig. 8.3 Marcus Agrippa with imperial family (south frieze). Detail from the Ara Pacis. 13–9 BCE. Location: Museum of the Ara Pacis, Rome, Italy. Source: Scala/Art Resource, NY.

major colleges of priests. The group is led by Marcus Agrippa, husband of Augustus' daughter Julia, the tall man shown with head covered on the far left. This is the first time adults and children are depicted interacting on a state monument, and the connection between the overall iconographic program of fertility and the concrete representation of actual Roman families, however idealized, is readily understood (Milnor 2005: 56–7). While the distinguished officials on the north and south friezes perform their public duties, the presence of their women and children beside them indicates that they also have reproductive and familial obligations no less vital to the state (Kleiner 1978: 772–6; Kampen 1994: 123). In this respect, the family of Augustus himself serves an exemplary purpose, the children holding out the prospect of continued political stability and a secure imperial line of descent.

That line of descent was not, however, a strict patrilinear succession. Augustus had no sons and only one daughter. His female kin were consequently called upon to provide him with male heirs. Being crucial to the legitimate transmission of his legacy, Augustus' wife, sister, and daughter assumed great significance in the political sphere (Corbier 1995: 192). **Livia**, his wife, became the key figure linking the Julian and the Claudian houses when in 4 CE the *princeps* adopted his stepson **Tiberius**, her son by her previous marriage to Ti. Claudius Nero, as his own son and ultimate successor. Livia had already been the recipient of earlier public honors (Cass. Dio 49.38.1, 55.2.5) and had played a key role in sponsoring religious cults for married women, thus assuming the informal role of mother of the Roman state (Severy 2003: 131–8). Because of her dynastic position as sole link between her husband and son, she now had to be included in monuments to the imperial family (Flory 1996: 296–7).

When Tiberius became emperor in 14 CE, representations of Livia multiplied, showing her in sacerdotal dress as the priestess of the newly deified Augustus and investing her with the tokens of female divinities, particularly Ceres. Association with the Roman goddess of agriculture continued the theme of prosperity and abundance first sounded under Augustus' reign and also accentuated her maternal honors, assuring the propriety of Tiberius' accession (Bartman 1999: 102–12). Public recognition of her dynastic consequence set the pattern for the subsequent use of female members of the imperial household in statuary and reliefs, and especially on coinage, as markers of the vitality of the ruling house and the domestic program of the emperor. Conservative qualms about showing women, traditionally identified with the private sphere, in state-sponsored art were alleviated not only by stressing their domestic roles but also by assimilating them to personifications such as *Concordia* ("harmony") and divinities who oversee the performance of female duties (Kampen 1991). The imperial woman is a presence in official art not as a historical subject but as a sign of familial and reproductive concerns.

Going Too Far

Sensationalism is more arresting than sober fact, but to a Roman listening audience it was more entertaining as well. From the Augustan era onward, public readings were a popular diversion, and a great number of literary texts, even prose texts, were produced with recitation in mind. Ancient oratory privileged the impact of language over its referential content; that is, it was regarded primarily as an instrument for captivating listeners and not a means of communicating accurate information. Authors trained in schools of rhetoric imbued their writing with an exhibitionistic, "over-the-top" quality, striving to outdo their colleagues in point and verbal brilliance while hooking listeners with striking, sometimes grotesque images. This fashion for staginess affected different genres differently, but it is already present in late Republican poetry and becomes more pronounced in works produced toward the close of Augustus' reign and afterward.

Ovid, who belonged to the generation after Propertius and embarked on a poetic career during the late twenties BCE, is the strategic forerunner of imperial-age poets who score points by going to extremes. In numerous ways he signals his intent to be rebellious, most obviously when retelling mythic incidents of sex or violence or both. Consequently, Ovid's many (suspiciously many?) rape scenes have been exhaustively scrutinized. Ostensibly, the narrator expresses great sympathy for his hapless victims (Curran 1984). Indeed, the opening set-piece in the *Art of Love* on the Rape of the Sabine Women (1.101–34) has been read allegorically as a denunciation of Roman militarism because so much weight is placed on the terror of the abducted maidens (Hemker 1985).

Critical analysis, though, uncovers a grim subtext in such scenes: the author eroticizes the victim's suffering or, worse, trivializes it (Richlin 1992b). Thus the beauty of the Sabine captives is said to be enhanced by fear (*potuit multas ipse decore timor*, 126). Rounding off his story, the preceptor lightheartedly identifies himself with Romulus and his gang of rapists: "Romulus, you alone knew how to give largesse to your soldiers; give me such largesse, I'll be a soldier too" (*Ars am.* 1.131–2). Later on in the poem, he advises the enthusiastic lover that using force is "pleasing to girls" (1.673). To make the latter point, he recounts the tale of Deidamia, violated by Achilles disguised as a woman (681–706):

> … she by this sexual offense [*stupro*] learned he was a man [*virum*].
> In fact, she was conquered by force [*viribus*], so you ought to believe;
>   but she wished to be conquered by force [*voluit vinci viribus*] anyway.   700
> Often she cried "Wait!" when Achilles was now hurrying off;
>   for he had donned heroic armor, distaff put aside.
> So where's that "force" [*vis*] now? …

Here the flippant punning on *vir* "man" and *vis* "rape" appears to hint that rape is what genuine men do, with the supplemental wordplay on the verbs *volo, velle* "to wish" and *vincere* "to conquer" reinforcing the claim that women want them to do it.

   Physical transformations in Ovid's *Metamorphoses*, a panoramic catalogue of myths about change of form, repeatedly stem from threatened or realized atrocities. In the first book, the attempted or actual rapes of Daphne, Io and Syrinx are followed by **metamorphosis** into a laurel tree, a cow, and a clump of reeds, respectively (1.452–746). This chain of permutations is programmatic for the epic itself. Rape is not the only danger; at times Ovid uses mutilation of the body to stand in for the genital act he does not depict overtly. When the Thracian king Tereus, having despoiled his sister-in-law Philomela, cuts out the tongue with which she has reviled him, the reader is given an appalling picture of the severed member lying on the floor, quivering, muttering, twitching toward the feet of its mistress as it dies (*Met.* 6.557–60). "Is it decorum that makes the poet omit the details of the rape?" Richlin asks. "If so, it is a decorum that allows him to show us what the inside of [Philomela's] mouth looks like with the tongue cut out of it. This is a conflation of violence with sex" (1992b: 164). Cruelty begets cruelty: having learned of her husband's crime, Tereus' wife Procne joins with her sister in butchering the king's son, Itys, and serving him up to his father at dinner. That grisly impasse reached, the transformation of the three principals into birds (667–74) is tacked on abruptly, seeming an afterthought.

   Elsewhere in the *Metamorphoses*, stories dwell upon the step-by-step change of the human form into that of animal or plant. By evoking horror, such disfigurement supposedly opens up space for the intersection of violence and pleasure (Richlin 1992b: 165). The pleasure would be that of the male reader gratified by observing the degradation of someone other than himself, which in complementary fashion heightens and reaffirms his own status. The satisfaction he enjoys can be equated with the visual gratifications experienced by spectators of public entertainments. Richlin compares Ovid's plots to the erotic scenarios of pantomime – a ballet on a mythic theme, usually a melodramatic account of rape or seduction, performed by a single male dancer (1992b: 174–6). Ovid embellishes his narrative with rhetorical effects that either cleverly distance the action or intensify its repulsiveness. Pantomime atrocities were similarly stylized, formalized by the theatricality of masks and flowing silk costume and elegantly conveyed through gesture. Men found effeminate dancers sexually attractive and women, too, were said to be feverishly aroused by their movements when they enacted the plight of suffering heroines (Juv. 6.63–6). In both poetry and dance the combination of sophisticated art and thematic brutality may be a prurient turn-on.

That feminist indictment of Ovid is a heavy one and, if applicable, would taint the delight modern readers take in this wittiest of all Roman poets. Yet Ovid's rape scenes must be approached with due attention to their topical implications. His pre-exilic works react against both the histrionics of their elegiac predecessors and the Augustan climate of religious and moral earnestness. That does not mean they are politically "anti-Augustan," but they purposely transgress boundaries. The *Art of Love*, for example, spoofs the emperor's program of family values, and the preceptor's facetious approval of rape as courtship tactic contributes to its ludicrousness. Treatments of rape in the *Metamorphoses* jar the sensibilities when given a comic twist or when they fuse gruesomeness with narrative flourishes, as in the tale of Philomela discussed above.

In a key episode of the *Metamorphoses* (6.5–145), the author may indicate why he employs sexual violence as a reiterated motif. There the mortal Arachne pits herself against the goddess Pallas Athena in a weaving contest. Pallas creates a balanced, orderly, "Augustan" composition depicting her own gift of the olive to the Athenians as witnessed by the Olympians in majesty and, in each of the four corners, a cautionary tale of a mythic sinner's punishment. Arachne, in turn, produces a tapestry showing in chaotic fashion a whole succession of divine assaults on human women. The goddess can find no fault in the work but destroys it anyway, then beats Arachne with a shuttle; she hangs herself in despair, and Pallas, finally pitying her, transforms her into a spider doomed to weave for all time to come. Like Helen's weaving in the *Iliad*, which figures the epic itself (3.125–8), Arachne's textile is an emblem of the whole *Metamorphoses*, its design a justification of Ovid's subject matter. Rape scenes critique the surface decorum of Augustan art and poetry. There is a patent intention to shock and even offend, but their shock value requires the reader's underlying agreement that rape is an ugly business.

When Augustus reacted to years of poetic impudence by relegating Ovid to distant Tomis on the Black Sea in 8 CE, he gave as one pretext the immorality of the *Art of Love*. Addressing the emperor from his place of exile, Ovid defends himself by pleading that the message of his work was distorted and taken far more seriously than it was meant (*Tr.* 2.241–4, 277–8, 357–60). But that excuse after the fact may itself be disingenuous. Like Oscar Wilde, Ovid affected a nonconformity (in his poems, that is – we don't know how he dressed and acted) that called the prevailing temper of his times into question. Like Wilde, he paid the penalty. Foes of sanctimoniousness inevitably do.

Conclusion

Trained by Freud to look for latent sexual content beneath the surface of dull or neutral discourse, we may find it hard to grasp that Roman sexual discourse, wholly uncensored as it frequently is, has a latent content all its own, dealing with matters more disturbing to its original audience than mere libido. In this chapter we have probed beneath the use of sex and gender as symbolic counters in literature of the Republican and Augustan eras.

Correlations in the Roman mind between phallic display and claims to hegemony inspired poets to give concrete expression to hierarchical tensions by representing them as metaphorical sexual congress. In such texts, the unspoken referent to be inferred, the dirty little secret, as it were, is the ethical problem posed by unrestricted power. The slave is at once a tool doing his master's bidding and also, the moment his humanity is recognized, capable of exercising free will and demonstrating virtue (Fitzgerald 2000: 6–8). Discomforts in the relation of master and trusted household slave might be relieved, on the part of both, by laughing at a rude Plautine joke about slaves sexually obliging their owners. Catullan invective is all the more biting for its use of obscenity to encode charges of political corruption. Mocking the contention that men such as Caesar and Pompey have earned their position through their superior courage, wisdom, and achievements and their services to the Roman state, it presents collusion with subordinates as literally "being in bed together" – a trope that underscores the self-interest of the superior's motives.

The gender inversions of Latin love poetry convey multiple messages. Culturally, the Roman female was not the simple antithesis of the male, a place that woman occupied in the Greek symbolic universe. Her communal, financial, and familial responsibilities endowed her with male gender traits: she was a combination of "Sameness" and "Otherness" (Hallett 1989). If the poetic beloved is aligned with the oligarchy, as Catullus' "Lesbia" was, her insatiable sexual lust can stand for the ambition and greed motivating military expeditions. Social masculinity, moreover, always ran the risk of being "feminized." Elegiac writers took advantage of built-in instabilities in Roman gender structures to create erotic fictions that expressed concerns about the position of elite men in a changing political environment, both in the fast-paced and dangerous last decade of the Roman Republic and during the Augustan age, when the rules of the power game were completely rewritten. These figurative repercussions are most evident in the short epigrammatic cycle of Sulpicia, who uses the scandal of an erotic intrigue to protest the social constraints imposed upon her sex.

Meanwhile, the epic poets Lucretius and Vergil saw that the contrary image of Venus, at once amoral temptress and protective mother of the Roman nation, could reveal social tensions. The introductory lines of *On the Nature of Things* depict her interceding with her paramour Mars on behalf of her people, her intentions doubtless good but the circumstances questionable. Lucretius' analysis of erotic obsession in Book Four then pictures human "Venuses" turning the same cajolery on their own hapless lovers. In the *Aeneid*, Venus is positioned halfway between the cosmic forces of order and chaos; her character, implicated in violence to a profound degree, gives a flickering glimpse into the mindset responsible for a century of civil wars. Those pessimistic visions of the goddess of love anticipate the private anxieties about sex that were to surface during the imperial period.

On public monuments of the Augustan age the female figure, allegorical or drawn from life, proclaims the centrality of both dynastic succession and renewal of communal and domestic propriety. Propertius and Tibullus had already shown themselves indifferent to the civic and military goals of the regime. Ovid took resistance one step further. With the same vigor he had displayed in mocking the silliness of elegiac clichés, he lampooned moral proclamations in his *Art of Love* and *Metamorphoses*. Rape in those works calls attention to the real abjection of citizens under the Augustan regime, above all as sexual subjects (Johnson 2008: 69–71). The trope operates – feminist readers are correct here – by eroticizing a vulnerability to violence. That explains its metaphoric thrust, for under the Augustan marriage laws, it implies, responsible sex is coercive.

Discussion Prompts

1. Because Plautine comedies are adaptations of Greek New Comedy, they are set in Greece even after translation into Latin, and the characters themselves retain their Greek personal names and identities. Many plot devices, too, assume Greek laws and customs: thus to be eligible for legitimate marriage a girl must turn out to be a citizen by birth. Superimposed upon this Greek background, the plays contain current allusions and in-jokes that only Romans would understand. How would this nominal Greek setting add to the comic flavor of the plays?

2. In their portrayals of the poet-lover and his mistress, to what extent did the Latin love elegists modify Catullus' depiction of an ideal love relationship as a compact of friendship (*amicitia*)? What might have been their reasons for doing so?

3. Find parallels, if you can, between Lucretius' account of sexual obsession in Book Four and Vergil's representation of Dido's state of mind in the *Aeneid*. Can Dido's madness be explained in Epicurean terms?

4. Ovid's *Metamorphoses*, though unquestionably an epic poem, strikingly departs from classical epic conventions. Thematically, for example, it does not concentrate upon the adventures of a single hero but instead reports the circumstances and outcomes of hundreds of physical transformations, most involving shifts in grades of existence (human beings become animals or plants; less commonly, the reverse occurs). For that reason, some critics approach Ovid's poem as a kind of anti-*Aeneid* (though admittedly there are metamorphoses in the latter poem too). Are there ways in which the perspectives of the one epic might be said to differ from that of the other?

Notes

1 With a liveliness that would do credit to any pornographer, the philosopher Seneca tells the horror story of Hostius Quadra, who was given to sexual threesomes and mirrors. If you really want to know the details, there's a Loeb translation (*Q Nat.* 1.16).

2 Caelius may mean that, in efforts to prove their virility, they engage in penetrative relations with forbidden partners such as married women (Williams 2010: 234–6). If so, this is an interesting anticipation of the notion that a Don Juan overcompensates for latent doubts about his masculinity.

3 In *A Funny Thing Happened on the Way to the Forum*, Larry Gelbart and Burt Shevelove's brilliant adaptation of Plautus for Broadway (1963), the scheming slave Pseudolus is motivated throughout by his young master's promise of manumission in exchange for helping him get the girl; in fact, Pseudolus' freedom is the "happy ending" toward which the dramatic action aims. This is a fundamental modification of the ancient plot-scheme that patently reflects American, not Roman, values. Malamud (2001: 39) notes the edginess imparted by assigning the part to an actor with a marked ethnic/racial identity: in the first production, the Jewish comedian Zero Mostel, who had been blacklisted as a Communist sympathizer during the McCarthy era; in a recent revival, the black actress Whoopi Goldberg.

4 Belief about the degree to which Augustus (or his advisor Maecenas) dictated the literary agenda is liable to be influenced by the scholar's own political milieu. Sir Ronald Syme's classic account of Augustus' skilled organization of intellectual attitudes (1939: 460–8) was composed on the eve of the Second World War and shaped by the effectiveness of Fascist propaganda. Frank expositions of "anti-Augustan" elements in Horace, Vergil, and Propertius, on the other hand, became popular during and immediately after the war in Vietnam. Recent work insists that authors themselves took the lead in exploring issues surrounding Augustus' principate (White 1993: 206–8) and participated creatively in continuing discussions about ideals and values (Galinsky 1996: 225–6). Hence, the facile opposition of terms such as "Augustan" and "anti-Augustan" is probably misleading (Kennedy 1992).

5 The Catullan speaker's fantasy of marrying "Lesbia," however, does not prove that the historical Catullus ever aspired to marry the original of "Lesbia." The idea of "autobiographical" or "confessional" poetry faithfully recording the events of the author's life – to say nothing of his actual feelings – was foreign to ancient poetics. Creating and projecting a speaker to whom an audience could relate was a vital part of rhetorical training. That speaker might be endowed with a certain autobiographical color for verisimilitude but could equally well be a constructed figure bearing no resemblance to the author whatsoever. The only fact Catullus provides about his poetic affair is that in one epigram, poem 79, he drops a transparent hint that "Lesbia" was a sister of the radical demagogue P. Clodius Pulcher. On the grounds of probability, we may then infer that he means the wife of Metellus Celer, the most visible of Clodius' three sisters. Whether the writer gives an accurate picture of her character and personality is anyone's guess. It is remotely conceivable that he might even have invented their affair out of whole cloth because her public image could be conveniently fashioned into such a rich symbol of aristocratic villainy. Probably not, but a good dash of skepticism is still a trait useful in a Catullan scholar.

6 In fact, as Reckford (1995–6: 2–3) observes, the Latin words *pedes vestis defluxit ad imos* ("her garment flowed down to her feet," 404), might be alternatively construed to mean that her clothing slips down to her feet, leaving her naked. Even if we exclude that implication, we still sense, he maintains, the presence of "a sexuality so considerable that, even when 'minimized' (if that is the right word), it is still disturbing" (1995–6: 8).

7 The subtle erotic allusion of showing drapery slipping off a goddess' shoulder is already manifest in the portrayal of Aphrodite ("Figure M") on the east pediment of the Parthenon.

References

Adams, J. N. 1983. "Words for 'Prostitute' in Latin." *Rheinisches Museum* 126: 321–58.

Bartman, E. 1999. *Portraits of Livia: Imaging the Imperial Woman in Augustan Rome*. Cambridge: Cambridge University Press.

Betensky, A. 1980. "Lucretius and Love." *Classical World* 73.5: 291–9.

Brown, R. D. 1987. *Lucretius on Love and Sex*. Leiden: E. J. Brill.

Butrica, J. L. 2005. "Some Myths and Anomalies in the Study of Roman Sexuality." In B. C. Verstraete and V. Provencal (eds.), *Same-Sex Desire and Love in Greco-Roman Antiquity and in the Classical Tradition of the West*. Binghamton, NY: Harrington Park Press (co-published simultaneously as *Journal of Homosexuality* 49 nos. 3/4 [2005]). 209–69.

Cantarella, E. 1992. *Bisexuality in the Ancient World*. Trans. C. Ó Cuilleanáin. [Orig. pub. as *Secondo natura*, Rome: Editori Riuniti, 1988.] New Haven, CT: Yale University Press.

Clausen, W. 1976. "CYNTHIVS." *American Journal of Philology* 97: 245–7.

Clayton, B. 1999. "Lucretius' Erotic Mother: Maternity as a Poetic Construct in *De Rerum Natura*." *Helios* 26: 69–84.

Copley, F. O. 1947. "*Servitium amoris* in the Roman Elegists." *Transactions of the American Philological Association* 78: 285–300.

Corbier, M. 1995. "Male Power and Legitimacy through Women: The *Domus Augusta* under the Julio-Claudians." In R. Hawley and B. Levick (eds.), *Women in Antiquity: New Assessments*. London: Routledge. 178–93.

Curran, L. C. 1984. "Rape and Rape Victims in the *Metamorphoses*." In J. Peradotto and J. P. Sullivan (eds.), *Women in the Ancient World: The "Arethusa" Papers*. Albany, NY: State University of New York Press. 263–86.

Dupont, F. and Éloi, T. 2001. *L'Érotisme masculine dans la Rome antique*. Paris: Belin.

Edmunds, L. 2002. "Mars as Hellenistic Lover: Lucretius, *De rerum natura* 1.29–40 and its Subtexts." *International Journal of the Classical Tradition* 8.3: 343–58.

Feeney, D. C. 1991. *The Gods in Epic: Poets and Critics of the Classical Tradition*. Oxford: Clarendon Press.

—— 1998. *Literature and Religion at Rome: Cultures, Contexts, and Beliefs*. Cambridge: Cambridge University Press.

Fitzgerald, W. 1995. *Catullan Provocations: Lyric Poetry and the Drama of Position*. Berkeley, CA: University of California Press.

—— 2000. *Slavery and the Roman Literary Imagination*. Cambridge: Cambridge University Press.

Flaschenriem, B. L. 1999. "Sulpicia and the Rhetoric of Disclosure." *Classical Philology* 94: 36–54.

Flory, M. B. 1996. "Dynastic Ideology, the *Domus Augusta*, and Imperial Women: A Lost Statuary Group in the Circus Flaminius." *Transactions of the American Philological Association* 126: 287–306.

Fowler, D. 1987. "Vergil on Killing Virgins." In M. Whitby, P. Hardie, and M. Whitby (eds.), *"Homo Viator": Classical Essays for John Bramble*. Bristol: Bristol Classical Press. 185–98.

Gale, M. 1994. *Myth and Poetry in Lucretius*. Cambridge: Cambridge University Press.

Galinsky, K. 1996. *Augustan Culture*. Princeton, NJ: Princeton University Press.

Gillis, D. 1983. *Love and Death in the "Aeneid"*. Rome: L'Erma di Bretschneider.

Gordon, P. 2002. "Some Unseen Monster: Rereading Lucretius on Sex." In D. Fredrick (ed.), *The Roman Gaze: Vision, Power, and the Body*. Baltimore, MD: The Johns Hopkins University Press. 86–109.

Habinek, T. 1998. *The Politics of Latin Literature: Writing, Identity and Empire in Ancient Rome*. Princeton, NJ: Princeton University Press.

Hallett, J. P. 1989. "Women as *Same* and *Other* in Classical Roman Elite." *Helios* 16: 59–78.

—— 1992. "Heeding our Native Informants: The Uses of Latin Literary Texts in Recovering Elite Roman Attitudes toward Age, Gender and Social Status." *Échos du Monde Classique/Classical Views* 36 n.s. 11: 333–55.

Hemker, J. 1985. "Rape and the Founding of Rome." *Helios* 12: 41–7.

Hinds, S. 1987. "The Poetess and the Reader: Further Steps towards Sulpicia." *Hermathena* 143: 29–46.

James, S. L. 2003. *Learned Girls and Male Persuasion: Gender and Reading in Roman Love Elegy*. Berkeley, CA: University of California Press.

Johnson, P. J. 2008. *Ovid before Exile: Art and Punishment in the* Metamorphoses. Madison, WI: University of Wisconsin Press.

Kampen, N. B. 1991. "Between Public and Private: Women as Historical Subjects in Roman Art." In S. B. Pomeroy (ed.), *Women's History and Ancient History*. Chapel Hill, NC: University of North Carolina Press. 218–48.

—— 1994. "Material Girl: Feminist Confrontations with Roman Art." *Arethusa* 27: 111–37.

Keith, A. M. 2000: *Engendering Rome: Women in Latin Epic*. Cambridge: Cambridge University Press.

Kennedy, D. F. 1992. "'Augustan' and 'Anti-Augustan': Reflections on Terms of Reference." In A. Powell (ed.), *Roman Poetry and Propaganda in the Age of Augustus*. London: Bristol Classical Press. 26–58.

Kleiner, D. E. E. 1978. "The Great Friezes of the Ara Pacis Augustae." *Mélanges de l'École Française de Rome Antiquité* 90.2: 753–85.

Konstan, D. 2000. "Self, Sex, and Empire in Catullus: The Construction of a Decentered Identity." In C. Fernández Corte, F. Pordomingo, V. Bécares Botas, and R. Cortés Tovar (eds.), *La intertextualidad griega y latina*. Madrid: Ediciones Clásicas. Published on the *Diotima* website (www.stoa.org) with permission of the editors, February 2000.

Leach, E. W. 1997. "Venus, Thetis and the Social Construction of Maternal Behavior." *Classical Journal* 92.4: 347–71.

Lilja, S. 1983. *Homosexuality in Republican and Augustan Rome*. Commentationes Humanarum Litterarum 74. Helsinki: Societas Scientiarum Fennica.

Lowe, N. J. 1988. "Sulpicia's Syntax." *Classical Quarterly* 38: 193–205.

Lyne, R. O. A. M. 1987. *Further Voices in Vergil's "Aeneid"*. Oxford: Clarendon Press.

Malamud, M. 2001. "A Funny Thing Happened on the Way from Brooklyn: Roman Comedy on Broadway and in Film." *Arion* 8.3: 33–51.

McCarthy, K. 2000. *Slaves, Masters, and the Art of Authority in Plautine Comedy*. Princeton, NJ: Princeton University Press.

Miller, P. A. 2004. *Subjecting Verses: Latin Love Elegy and the Emergence of the Real*. Princeton, NJ: Princeton University Press.

Milnor, K. 2002. "Sulpicia's (Corpo)reality: Elegy, Authorship, and the Body in [Tibullus] 3.13." *Classical Antiquity* 21: 259–82.

—— 2005. *Gender, Domesticity, and the Age of Augustus: Inventing Private Life*. Oxford: Oxford University Press.

Mitchell, R. N. 1991. "The Violence of Virginity in the *Aeneid*." *Arethusa* 24: 219–38.

Nappa, C. 2001. *Aspects of Catullus' Social Fiction*. Studien zur klassischen Philologie 125. Frankfurt am Main: Peter Lang.

Nussbaum, M. C. 1994. *The Therapy of Desire: Theory and Practice in Hellenistic Ethics*. Princeton, NJ: Princeton University Press.

Oliensis, E. 1997. "Sons and Lovers: Sexuality and Gender in Virgil's Poetry." In C. Martindale (ed.), *The Cambridge Companion to Virgil*. Cambridge: Cambridge University Press. 294–311.

Parker, H. N. 1989. "Crucially Funny or Tranio on the Couch: The *servus callidus* and Jokes about Torture." *Transactions of the American Philological Association* 119: 233–46.

Putnam, M. C. J. 1974. "Catullus 11: The Ironies of Integrity." *Ramus* 3: 70–86.

—— 1985. "Possessiveness, Sexuality and Heroism in the *Aeneid*." *Vergilius* 31: 1–21.

—— 1986. *Artifices of Eternity: Horace's Fourth Book of Odes*. Ithaca, NY: Cornell University Press.

Reckford, K. J. 1995–6. "Recognizing Venus (I): Aeneas Meets his Mother." *Arion* 3.2–3: 1–42.

Richlin, A. 1992a. *The Garden of Priapus: Sexuality and Aggression in Roman Humor*, rev. edn. Oxford: Oxford University Press.

—— 1992b. "Reading Ovid's Rapes." In A. Richlin (ed.), *Pornography and Representation in Greece and Rome*. Oxford: Oxford University Press. 158–79.

Roessel, D. 1990. "The Significance of the Name *Cerinthus* in the Poems of Sulpicia." *Transactions of the American Philological Association* 120: 243–50.

Rubino, C. A. 1975. "The Erotic World of Catullus." *Classical World* 68: 289–98.

Sedley, D. 1998. *Lucretius and the Transformation of Greek Wisdom*. Cambridge: Cambridge University Press.

Segal, E. 1968. *Roman Laughter: The Comedy of Plautus*. Cambridge, MA: Harvard University Press.

Severy, B. 2003. *Augustus and the Family at the Birth of the Roman Empire*. New York and London: Routledge.

Sharrock, A. R. 1991. "Womanufacture." *Journal of Roman Studies* 81: 36–49.

Skinner, M. B. 1991. "The Dynamics of Catullan Obscenity: cc. 37, 58 and 11." *Syllecta Classica* 3: 1–11.

Syme, R. 1939. *The Roman Revolution*. Oxford: Oxford University Press.

Veyne, P. 1978. "La Famille et l'amour sous le haut-empire romain." *Annales (ESC)* 33: 35–63.

Weinstock, S. 1971. *Divus Julius*. Oxford: Clarendon Press.

White, P. 1993. *Promised Verse: Poets in the Society of Augustan Rome*. Cambridge, MA: Harvard University Press.

Williams, C. A. 2010. *Roman Homosexuality*. 2nd edn. Oxford: Oxford University Press.

Wray, D. 2001. *Catullus and the Poetics of Roman Manhood*. Cambridge: Cambridge University Press.

Wyke, M. 1994. "Taking the Woman's Part: Engendering Roman Love Elegy." *Ramus* 23: 110–28.

Zanker, P. 1990. *The Power of Images in the Age of Augustus*. Trans. A. Shapiro. Ann Arbor: University of Michigan Press.

Further Reading

Fantham, E. 2004. *Ovid's* Metamorphoses. Oxford: Oxford University Press. Interpretive survey of major themes and topics in the epic, with useful bibliographies after each chapter.

Gaisser, J. H. 2009. *Catullus*. Malden, MA, and Oxford: Wiley-Blackwell. Up-to-date introduction incorporating the latest scholarship and covering the most essential facets of Catullus' verse and its ancient and modern receptions.

Galinsky, K. 1996. *Augustan Culture: An Interpretive Introduction*. Surveys numerous aspects of the Augustan age, including its art, literature, and religion, in order to identify unifying themes and characteristics.

Johnson, P. J. 2008. *Ovid before Exile: Art and Punishment in the* Metamorphoses. Important discussion of passages in the epic that respond to a climate of increasing artistic restraint.

Johnson, W. R. 2000. *Lucretius and the Modern World*. London: Duckworth. Excellent overview of Lucretius' thought and its relevance for the twenty-first century student of science and technology.

Kennedy, D. F. 1993. *The Arts of Love: Five Studies in the Discourse of Roman Love Elegy*. Cambridge: Cambridge University Press. Theoretical, provocative reading of love elegy as a genre with special attention to its rhetoric and conventions.

McCarthy, K. 2000. *Slaves, Masters, and the Art of Authority in Plautine Comedy*. Princeton, NJ: Princeton University Press. Stimulating analysis of the cultural purposes served by the comedies and the reasons for their appeal to multiple audiences.

Perkell, C. (ed.). 1999. *Reading Vergil's* Aeneid: *An Interpretive Guide*. Norman, OK: University of Oklahoma Press. Collection of essays by leading Vergilian scholars providing a book-by-book explanation of the poem together with studies of key themes.

Zanker, P. 1988. *The Power of Images in the Age of Augustus*. Trans. A. Shapiro. Ann Arbor: University of Michigan Press. Full account of Augustus' employment of stylistic elements in the visual arts to convey the aspirations and ideals of the Principate.

9

Elites in the Empire:
Self and Others

Images of debauched Roman emperors are part of our mental picture of the ancient world. For generations, Hollywood has delighted in juxtaposing breathtaking vistas of Rome in all its imperial majesty with interior scenes of despots behaving badly. The camera first pans over temples, basilicas, and colonnades gleaming with marble and gold, S·P·Q·R in bronze capitals everywhere, before entering the great halls of the *Domus Aurea*, Nero's fabulous palace in the Esquiline valley, or the *Domus Augustana* atop the Palatine. There, an autocrat clad in purple is terrorizing counselors, decreeing a massacre of Christians, hosting a disgusting though lovingly filmed orgy, or blackmailing his own sister into having sex with him. These cinematic clichés are morality plays for our own time, but they reflect, if not historical reality, at least elements of the historical tradition. **Tacitus**, **Suetonius**, **Cassius Dio** and the ***Historia Augusta***, to name a few surviving accounts of the high imperial period, all devote a good deal of space to the misdeeds of emperors and their womenfolk, interspersed with portents, mentions of natural catastrophes, and Roman military struggles on the frontier. From the pages of these authors, a more generalized myth of imperial Rome as a civilization of almighty power and frantic hedonism has passed, via novels, movies, and television mini-series, into Western popular culture – to culminate in America, for example, in the architectural glitz of Caesars Palace and its adjoining Forum Shops in Las Vegas or, on a lesser note, the frat toga party last weekend.

By now you should have an inkling of why such stories circulated in antiquity. If the Roman people believed that its good fortune and right to govern other nations came directly from the gods and was contingent upon the acts of those in authority, disasters of any kind could be blamed upon the excesses of the ruling house. Furthermore, an emperor whose grip on the throne was still shaky – who had gained it, perhaps, through revolt or assassination – would want to justify his regime by blackening the image of his predecessor. Yet even when government, at home and

Sexuality in Greek and Roman Culture, Second Edition. Marilyn B. Skinner.
© 2014 John Wiley & Sons, Inc. Published 2014 by John Wiley & Sons, Inc.

abroad, was orderly and responsible, charges of vice and tyranny were still used to discredit the *princeps*. Throughout the reign of the **Julio-Claudian** dynasty, which ended with the death of **Nero** in 68 CE, and at intermittent periods thereafter, Roman emperors found themselves at odds with the senatorial aristocracy.

The fundamental issue was one of dignity. Rank and reputation had become increasingly significant to the upper classes in a society in which officials were appointed and free competition for magistracies was no longer possible. The emperor had to maintain and defend his own honor at all costs if he was not to incur contempt (Lendon 1997: 113–29). The senate, though, still played a key legislative and judicial role in government and saw itself as the body that formally conferred legitimacy on a new sovereign. If the emperor did not treat the senate with sufficient respect, or took actions of which it disapproved, prominent members might openly manifest their displeasure, causing him to lose face. For that reason, a law originally intended to punish treason was extended under Augustus' successor Tiberius to cover actions that injured imperial dignity (**maiestas**), including slander and libel. Considerable numbers of *maiestas* prosecutions took place under the Julio-Claudians, subsequently under **Domitian**, and into the later empire. Nevertheless, subversive rumors and anecdotes circulated, some based on fact, others sheer invention, and this "fossilized invective" eventually found its way into the works of historians, who, writing for an audience of elites, took no pains to debunk it.

In their reports of what had transpired under "bad" emperors, those writers created an atmosphere of relentless oppression and terror. Tacitus' evocation of Domitian's reign (81–96 CE) is a case in point:

> If, during fifteen years, a large span of mortal life, many died by accidental means, but all the most vigorous through the cruelty of the emperor, we few are, so to speak, the survivors of not only our friends but also ourselves, with so many years taken from the prime of our lives, in which we adult men reached old age and we elders almost the very limits of a full life while keeping mute. (*Agr.* 3)

Paranoia was a constant. Even if someone did not play an active part in politics, we are told, merely being wealthy posed its risks, for men and women might be condemned on a trumped-up charge – adultery or violation of the *maiestas* law – and their property confiscated (for example, Tac. *Ann.* 11.1–3 [Valerius Asiaticus]; 12.22 [Lollia Paulina]). When a suspected conspiracy was unearthed, like that of Calpurnius Piso against Nero in 65 CE, executions followed. Whatever the likelihood of guilt, the killings were painted as wholesale bloodbaths. After Nero's death, and again after the assassination of Domitian in 96 CE, "martyr tales" heroizing courageous nobles who died because they had defied tyranny were retold over and over. Those who had not just survived but even prospered under the alleged monster, such as the younger Pliny, accordingly presented themselves as clandestine supporters of the freedom fighters (Freudenburg 2001: 215–34).

One particular cause of friction between the senate and certain emperors was their popularity with the common people. Attempts to court the favor of the masses might earn applause at the games, but they dismayed the aristocracy whose self-image involved maintaining their distance from the "mob." **Caligula**, Nero, and, in the next century, **Commodus** were castigated by historians for their enjoyment of chariot racing or gladiatorial combats, as such indulgences won approval from the poor (Edwards 1993: 194). Cassius Dio prefaces his report of Commodus' gladiatorial exhibitions with the assertion that he, as a senator, was an eyewitness to them (73.18.3–4). He even confesses his fright when one day the emperor, sword in one hand and lopped-off head of an ostrich in another, pantomimed doing the same to the assembled audience of senators. Dio's spontaneous reaction was a sudden nervous fit of the giggles, and he had to chew on laurel leaves from his garland to suppress them, since laughing aloud, he believed, would have meant immediate death (73.21.1–2).

For the nobility, was life under the empire really that dreadful? The record is so clouded with calumny and propaganda that sorting out facts from fiction, especially in the case of controversial figures such as Nero, would be a lengthy task. This is not to deny that emperors were ever brutal or debased; some may have been. Yet the sexual practices attributed to the *princeps* by hostile sources are the predictable ones found in earlier polemic: incest, sadism, promiscuous adultery, flagrant effeminacy. It is the degree of sensationalization that sets those allegations apart. Likewise, the vices of imperial women differ from those attributed to Clodia Metelli only in the amount of imaginative color applied – as a group, these women are consistently portrayed as adulterous, cruel, and treacherous, but the escapades of some, such as **Claudius'** wife **Valeria Messalina**, receive spectacular treatment (Tac. *Ann.* 11.1–4, 12, 26–38). The truth about Messalina's behavior will never be known, but it is plausible that the figure of an empress out of control serves as a trope for "the nature of imperial autocracy," power exercised without restraint (Joshel 1997: 244). That historical construct is then elaborated by the satirist Juvenal in his astonishing fantasy of Messalina the *meretrix Augusta* ("imperial whore"), creeping out at night to service customers in a brothel and returning to the palace reeking of sex but still unsatisfied (6.115–32). History must adhere to a semblance of fact, but satire is authorized to give rein to the prurient imagination.

Because narratives of palace debauchery are so laden with topical meaning and so rhetorically embellished, a discussion of sexuality among the upper classes will be more fruitful if it confines itself to examining general changes in mind-set, as far as we can recover them. The evidence is scrappy but it will allow us to trace some trends. We can begin with Foucault's hypothesis that those modifications in the structure of government that concentrated power in the hands of an absolute ruler also caused high-ranking individuals to dread the vicissitudes of political life. Free-floating anxiety then created greater moral unease over the circumstances of the sexual act; at the same time it induced a need for the emotional comforts of marriage.

Risky Business

The second and third volumes of Michel Foucault's *History of Sexuality* were published together in French (1984), but independently in English translation (1986, 1988). Foucault had been working on both at the same time and employing the conclusions reached in the second volume, *The Use of Pleasure*, as the point of departure for the third, *The Care of the Self*, which continues his investigative trajectory into the Roman empire. Although the latter study has not unleashed the fierce dispute among classicists stirred up by his pronouncements on classical Greek sexual mores, one of its basic contentions has been widely, and rightly, questioned. Yet there is also some truth to the overall picture he presents.

During the epoch of Rome's greatest prosperity, Foucault theorizes in *The Care of the Self*, men of the upper class began to devote increased energy to the preventative maintenance of their bodies and the oversight of their souls. Pursuing a regime of exercise and moderate diet while seeking spiritual tranquility, they were attentive to discourses that cast sex as a source of disturbance:

> A whole corpus of moral reflection on sexual activity and its pleasures seems to mark, in the first centuries of our era, a certain strengthening of austerity themes. Physicians worry about the effects of sexual practice, unhesitatingly recommend abstention, and declare a preference for virginity over the use of pleasure. Philosophers condemn any sexual relation that might take place outside marriage and prescribe a strict fidelity between spouses, admitting no exceptions. Furthermore, a certain doctrinal disqualification seems to bear on the love for boys. (1988: 235)

This moral system, Foucault hastens to add, is not identical with early Christian sexual ethics, where the non-marital sex act is a sin and pederasty is condemned as contrary to natural law. It is instead a fine-tuning of pre-existing concerns about sexuality – concerns already articulated, as we ourselves have seen, by Greek philosophers and physicians during the classical and Hellenistic periods – that now become more intense in response to changes in the social environment.

Among a number of possible reasons for this development, Foucault singles out and explores two. The first is a new emphasis on the importance of the matrimonial bond and the relationship of man and wife (1988: 72–80; cf. 147–85). As a Roman institution, he argues, marriage was at first a mere contractual agreement entered into for political, economic, and dynastic reasons, and so of interest chiefly to those with property to transmit. Those without wealth had no inducement to marry, and instead formed short-lived concubinage unions.[1] However, marriage lost its function of validating family alliances under the emperors, since distinction in the political sector was no longer achieved by winning elections and now depended on influence at court. Private, affective motives for forming a union took the place of familial and pragmatic ones. Following the example of their social superiors, the urban poor began to regard marriage as a source of psychological support and mutual assistance and to enter into it in larger numbers. As a result of these new realities, he concludes, the emotional ties between the couple assumed greater importance, especially for the husband, while the wife's role, though still subordinate, became more equivalent to his.

Foucault identifies the Roman version of Stoicism, a philosophy popular among the educated orders during the first two centuries of the Christian era, as a decisive factor in promulgating this new attitude toward marital relations. Reversing the theoretical position of its founder Zeno, who had abolished marriage in the ideal state, Roman Stoicism advocated marriage as natural and necessary; moreover, it encouraged a corresponding chastity in husband and wife and emphasized their reciprocal obligations to each other. One of its adherents, **Musonius Rufus**, prominent under Nero, argued that the intrinsic link between sexual pleasure and procreation rules out seeking pleasure wholly for its own sake, even in marriage; the man who has relations with a courtesan or slave, though he might seem to be injuring no one (no one who counts, that is), is therefore degrading himself (XII, Lutz 85–9). Musonius also maintained that the companionship of husband and wife, considered as a goal of marriage, was even *more* important than procreation, which could, after all, result from any kind of union (XIIIa, Lutz 89). Since the conventional Roman view of marriage defined its purpose as the begetting of legitimate children (*liberorum quaerundorum causa*), Musonius' privileging of spousal affection in its place is indeed a step in ethical reflection toward the modern Western concept of companionate marriage.

However, the premise that a decisive change in thinking about marriage occurred at this particular time in Roman history has been painstakingly interrogated. Specialists in Roman studies object to Foucault's uncritical employment of testimony from Greek authors as evidence for Roman attitudes and values (Richlin 1991: 171). When he summons Plutarch, a second-century CE Greek essayist from Boeotia, to bear witness to recommended conduct for the wife (Foucault 1988: 174–5, 180–2), he is definitely on shaky ground, for Greek and Roman notions about the wifely role were, as we have seen, very different. The claim that the rationale for marrying altered over time has also been contested. Sources show that concerns over property and succession did not abate, but continued to play a large part in marriage decisions among the elite throughout the imperial period (Cohen and Saller 1994: 46). Conjugal affection, moreover, was not a phenomenon that surfaced for the first time in the decades after Augustus (Dixon 1991). As early as the late Republic there existed, alongside the legal view of marriage as a vehicle of property transmission, a sentimental ideal of spousal love, seen, for example, in Lucretius' poignant sketch of mourners lamenting a husband whose premature death has snatched him from wife and children (*DRN* 3.894–99). Cicero's heartsick letters to Terentia during his exile express longing for her presence: "Take care of yourself and believe that nothing is nor ever has been dearer to me than yourself. Farewell, my Terentia, whom I seem to behold and am therefore dissolved in tears, farewell" (*Fam.* 14.3.5). Finally, tombstones indicate that members of the working class entered into marriage relationships well before the imperial period (Garnsey and Saller 1987: 136). Apart from its snobbish cast, the notion that a new regard for marriage trickled down from the educated classes to the commons flies in the face of epigraphical evidence.

Foucault also fails to observe that the moralizing discourses on marriage he draws upon to support his contentions were not written in a vacuum. Instead, they participate in a long-standing dialogue over the desirability of marriage (Cohen and Saller 1994: 47–9). Augustus, to make the case for his marriage legislation, read to the Senate a speech by Metellus Macedonicus, censor in 131–130 BCE, urging citizens to take wives: "If we could live without a wife, gentlemen, we would all do without this nuisance; but, since nature has decreed that we can neither live with them satisfactorily enough, nor without them in any manner, one should take thought for his lasting welfare rather than for momentary pleasure" (*ap.* Gell. *NA* 1.6.1–2). Macedonius' contemporary, the satirist **Lucilius**, had meanwhile composed a poem laying out a catalogue of women's flaws, including extravagance and sexual infidelity, as grounds for rejecting marriage outright (frr. 678–86 Marx). Reacting to Augustus' program, the poet-lover Propertius in elegy 2.7 expresses his determination to remain a bachelor and continue in his stormy relationship with Cynthia (see Chapter 8).

Well into the era on which Foucault concentrates, the debate continued. At approximately the same time that Pliny the Younger, another of his informants, was confessing his passionate feelings for his bride Calpurnia ("it is unbelievable how much I am gripped with longing for you," *Ep.* 7.5.1), Martial was composing raunchy epigrams on lustful wives and Juvenal was denouncing women in his sixth satire, a monstrous list of female vices, crimes, and follies posing as an effort to dissuade the addressee, Postumus, from marrying. That this theme reappears during the imperial era in Martial's sallies and Juvenal's gargantuan (well over 650 lines) harangue should not be surprising. Just as Lucilius' satire seems to have been a sardonic reply to Metellus Macedonicus' exhortations, Juvenal and Martial, in turn, are probably reacting to the spiritually uplifting presentation of wedlock and procreation in Stoic writings. The notion that marital values changed radically during the empire is therefore erroneous.

As a second factor impacting elite male sexual subjectivity, however, Foucault points to the increasing complexity of the political power grid and speculates about a shift in the conditions under which individuals holding office might exercise agency (1988: 81–95). Dealings among those endowed with power were now more convoluted. Within a network of circumscribed authority, where extrinsic pressures were constantly felt from all sides, a placeholder was exposed to the intrigues of others and he had to acquire a finely tuned sense of danger to avoid reversals of fortune. Stoic moralists never tire of pointing out the risks and humiliations associated with ambition for public office. As an illustrative text, Foucault cites the younger Seneca's advice to a correspondent (*Ep.* 14.3–4). We fear three kinds of evils, the philosopher says: poverty, disease, and injury at the hands of a superior. "Of all these nothing distresses us more than what threatens us through the power of another [*ex aliena potentia*], for it arrives with great clamor and disturbance." Again, Seneca warns in his treatise *On the Tranquility of the Soul*, there is no rank whose trappings are not accompanied by "lawsuits and censorial black marks and a thousand stigmas and utter scorn" (11.9). Another Stoic writer, Epictetus, who had been the slave of Nero's personal secretary and observed first-hand the pitfalls of life at court, scornfully asks an official whose hand he had kissed, whose chambers he haunted, on whom he bestowed gifts in order to obtain his post (*Disc.* 3.7.31). The man who becomes Caesar's friend, he observes elsewhere, does not sleep as well or dine with as much enjoyment as before. What does he fear? That which goes along with his high position: being beheaded (*Disc.* 4.1.47–8). Employees of large American firms at the level of middle management and above may recognize a form of that malaise of which Epictetus speaks: for "beheaded" read "downsized."

Such anxieties may have elicited two kinds of response. One, of course, was an intensified attention to badges of class and the adoption of behaviors that underscored social superiority, including deliberate insults to underlings (MacMullen 1974: 110–11). But some, Foucault believes, went to the opposite extreme, retreating into a preoccupation with the inner life that left them relatively indifferent to status concerns. Greater self-consciousness on the part of the individual, who increasingly saw himself as fragile and exposed, would entail uneasiness about sexual desire as a likely threat to detachment and self-control. Moral trepidation was reinforced by the pronouncements of doctors, who warned against the excessive expenditure of semen. Moderate sexual intercourse might still be thought advantageous: the learned physician Galen challenges Epicurus' opinion that it had no health benefits whatsoever (*Ars med.* 24.9, 1.371 Kühn). Yet Galen also prescribes attentiveness to the exact balance of humors within the body – themselves conditioned by climate, diet, and condition of the soul – before indulging in sexual activity, so that the convulsive effects of intercourse and the resulting expulsion of moisture will not disturb the constitution unduly. On the whole, he thinks, it is better to err on the side of caution. In medical science, then, Foucault notes a certain tendency to view sexual activity as a source of disease. "The sexual act is not an evil," he sums up, but "it manifests a permanent focus of possible ills" (1988: 142).

Here, I believe, a plausible case has been made. Galen's medical treatises construct the physical body as a complex mechanism prone to instability, whose workings required constant monitoring (Perkins 1995: 165–6; Shaw 1998: 63). If political stresses did take their toll on the confidence of upper-class men, their worries may well have been displaced onto the body, resulting in a growing overall concern about health. Misgivings about the proper place of sex in the physical regimen would then induce a disposition toward greater sexual austerity and in some cases motivate abstinence. The amount of medical attention paid to regulating sperm production and sexual desire indicates that among Galen's readers self-imposed restraint was not atypical (Rousselle 1988: 19–20).

We must always remember that Foucault was dealing with public discourses, not diaries or confessions. He cannot therefore claim that elite Roman men experienced sexual anxiety, only that the works he examines seem to reflect that phenomenon. Moreover, he is primarily engaged with ethical treatises and, to exemplify prevailing medical ideas of male physiology, the writings of physicians. Thus, as his critics often rejoin, a whole spectrum of explicitly sexual material, for the most part misogynistic and xenophobic – from graffiti scrawled on walls at Pompeii to salty light verse and satiric prose and poetry – is left out of account (Richlin 1991: 170; 1992: xvi). But the coexistence of those aggressive and obscene discourses alongside the medical and ethical documents Foucault relies upon does not invalidate the conclusions he draws from the latter. It is reasonable to assume that the very anxiety he posits might have given rise to literature that permitted its subjects to vent feelings of hostility and frustration in a safe manner by identifying with a speaker attacking what was seen as alien. Moreover, obscenity could also have had a "therapeutic" application: breaking of discursive taboos would release tension through laughter, all the more within a culture in which the physical expression of sexual desire was, at least ideologically, under firmer constraint. In a sense, then, the vituperative and gross materials to which we now turn corroborate the evidence furnished by more sober literature.

Boys Named Sue

Reminiscing about the great debating champions of the past, the rhetorician L. Annaeus (**Seneca the Elder**, *c*.55 BCE to *c*.37–41 CE) complains to his three sons toward the end of his life that eloquence "has gone to the dogs" (*se retro tulerit*, *Controv*. 1 pf. 6). The reason is not far to seek. Look at the current generation, grumbles the old man – lazy, unable to focus on an objective, and, worst of all, effeminate. "Disgusting enthusiasms for singing and dancing grip these pansies; to crimp their hair, pitch their voice to a womanly warble, vie with women in the softness [*mollitia*] of their bodies and adorn themselves with the foulest fineries is the blueprint for our youth" (*Controv*. 1 pf. 8). It takes a *man* to be a public speaker: didn't the great Cato define the orator as "a good man skilled at speaking" (*vir bonus dicendi peritus*, 9)? Thus he scornfully dismisses the present lot of aspirants: "Go now and seek orators among these plucked and polished fellows, men only in their lusts" (10).

Some two decades later, his son and namesake the philosopher Seneca pronounces judgment along similar lines, but now targeting literary flamboyance (*Ep*. 114). Bad taste in oratory becomes popular, he argues, because the Greek proverb is true: as a man lives, so he speaks. If a nation is given over to luxury, it will also admire stylistic extravagance, for the moral disposition (*animus*) is bound up with the creative intellect (*ingenium*) and reveals itself in the intellectual product as clearly as in the movements of the body (*Ep*. 114.1–3). To illustrate, Seneca takes Augustus' friend Maecenas as a case in point. Maecenas, he alleges, was a byword for foppishness, affectation, and self-indulgence, and his writing was just as loose (*soluta*, 4) as his dress. Seneca picks out several examples of what he considers an overwrought eloquence, paralleling them with instances of unconventional public conduct. "These words so indecorously arranged, so whimsically thrown out, so constructed in defiance of common usage indicate that his personal habits too were no less novel and perverse and unique" (7). Maecenas' greatest virtue was his mildness of temper, for he refrained from force and displayed his power in no other way than by his flagrant behavior; but he spoiled that praise by this artifice of thoroughly unnatural style, proving himself "not mild [*mitis*] but soft [*mollis*]."

At about the same time, Seneca's younger contemporary, the satirist **Persius**, is denouncing the literary creations of the Neronian age, which pander, he says, to corrupt tastes. That no one reads Persius' own dense works is understandable, seeing what Roman audiences actually prefer (1.13–23):

We write in solitude, that one in verse, this one in prose,
some grandiose thing that the lung swelled with breath may exhale.
Of course you will eventually recite it from a high seat in public,   15
barbered and dazzling in a fresh toga, wearing your birthday sardonyx,
having rinsed your supple throat with a shrill warble,
languidly casting a come-hither glance.
Then you might see great Tituses tremble
in no decent manner and with no dulcet sounds, when the poetry   20
enters their loins and their recesses are tickled by quavering verses.
Are you, you old queen, framing tidbits for others' little ears,
tidbits to which you, arthritic and wrinkled, would say, "No more!"?

Both reciter and audience are tarred with the brush of unwholesomeness. The poet, who takes the active role in this episode of "intercourse," penetrates his brawny listeners with titillating sounds and rhythms that induce an orgasmic response. He, however, is already so decayed and wrecked by past physical depravity that even such a sublimated form of sex becomes too much for his own brittle constitution.

In the complaints of the Senecas, father and son, and in Persius' lubricious denunciation of modern verse, a semiotic pattern emerges. When imperial authors decry effeminacy – whether they choose to fasten on alleged sexual passivity, on foppish dress and conduct, or on an affected speaking and writing style – they are speaking of violations of the code of social masculinity. Such lapses were deemed appalling because the framework of manliness had become wobbly. Privileged Romans of the time could not automatically base claims to superiority upon birth, wealth, office, or military record; even male sex carried no firm guarantees. Too many rungs of the social ladder were broken or occupied by upstarts. The only way to establish one's own gender securely was to degender another. As a result, very few real men are attested as living in imperial Rome – most of the time there are only two, you and I, and I'm not quite sure of you. Nevertheless, both of us can comfortably hide our mutual suspicions of each other by scoffing at a third person. That is where satire comes in.

Satire is the only ancient literary genre the Romans claimed as their own preserve (Quint. *Inst.* 10.1.93). Its recognized inventor was Lucilius, a wealthy second-century BCE nobleman, friend of Scipio Aemilianus and other worthies. In his thirty books of *Satires*, which exist now only in fragmentary form, Lucilius appropriated the hexameter, the lofty medium of epic verse, to present the underside, as it were, of epic – caustic glimpses of the banal, often sordid happenings that epic ignores. Whether the Roman satirist is, like Horace, mildly and ironically critical of his surroundings, or fiercely disapproving, like Juvenal, modern readers are inclined to view him as an alienated observer genuinely outraged by what he beholds. In actuality, however, he is very much part of the power elite (even Horace, who positions himself as an "outsider" by virtue of being a mere freedman's son, is still a close friend of Maecenas and associate of Augustus), and he addresses an audience of rich educated men, those best equipped to appreciate his elaborate parodies of serious literature. Since targeting folly or vice and denouncing offenders justify his energetic display of wit and eloquence, satire licenses the ancient author to misrepresent reality by exaggerating its darker side. Like the archaic Greek lyric poets, moreover, the satirist adopts a **persona** – which means he is speaking in character even when he uses his own name (Anderson 1982: 3–10). Consequently, we should be extremely careful about taking both his grim pictures of urban life and his claims of moral indignation at face value. The satirist is an entertainer, not an evangelist. Yet the sniggering he provokes seems to be of a nervous kind. Nothing illustrates that tendency better than reports of a vast secret subculture of closet pathics.

Them

To a social historian the Roman lampoonist's choice of victim is revealing. These are types his audience expects him to abuse, for on various grounds they already have been defined as beyond the pale of acceptability. Women continued to be an obvious target of aggressive sexual humor and to serve, when needed, as the defining case of "Otherness." As the culture became more polyglot, persons of distinct ethnicity – Greeks, Egyptians, Jews, and Syrians – were likewise vilified (for example, Juv. 3.60–80; 14.96–106; 15 *pass.*). Economic opportunities multiplied under the empire for those who did not share aristocratic prejudices against manual labor or commerce, and some freedmen entrepreneurs became as affluent as members of the senatorial class. Concern arose about former slaves not knowing their place: during Nero's reign, the Senate debated a proposal allowing patrons to revoke the manumission of those who behaved insolently (Tac. *Ann.* 13.26–7). Satire accordingly lumps jumped-up freedmen into the same category with government informers and notorious criminals. Because foreigners and freedmen, no matter how affluent, were still regarded as inferior to the freeborn citizen male, members of each group could be stigmatized as effeminate.

At Nero's court the novelist Petronius, author of the now-fragmentary and infamous *Satyrica*, was hailed as an *elegantiae arbiter* ("expert on refinement," Tac. *Ann.* 16.18) before his enforced suicide in the aftermath of the Pisonian conspiracy – an end confirming Epictetus' point about Caesar's friends. The longest surviving episode in the novel is devoted to a dinner party at the house of a prosperous but vulgar freedman named **Trimalchio**. He and his associates make no bones about their value system; everything is appraised in economic terms, and the highest praise bestowed upon anyone is that "he grew (financially) from small beginnings" (*ab asse crevit*, *Sat.* 43.1; cf. Trimalchio's own self-epitaph, *ex parvo crevit*, *Sat.* 71.12). Uneducated themselves, they pretend to culture, yet think the rhetorical training of the narrator and his friends a useless frippery (*Sat.* 58.7–8).[2] What was surely more disgusting to Petronius' audience than Trimalchio's venality or ignorance is his unabashed admission that he used sex for advancement (*Sat.* 75.10–76.2). He arrived in Rome from Asia when he was only as high as a candelabrum, he tells his guests, and at the age of fourteen was Himself's (*ipsimi*, i.e., his owner's) darling. "No shame in what the master orders," he avows. But he also performed services for Herself (*ipsimae*). "You know what I'm saying; I'll be quiet, I'm not a boaster."

Bedroom activities were the key to his success, for he eventually became lord of the house (*dominus in domo*), and his master, when he died, left him a senator's fortune. Some social reality lies behind this caricature. Well-off families often had difficulty in reproducing and, when the line died out, the beneficiaries might be trusted freedmen and slaves (Garnsey and Saller 1987: 110, 123–5). Testamentary dispositions could give rise to gossip about why dependants had been so favored. In Julio-Claudian Rome, then, social structures were changing. For a select group, rapid upward mobility had become thinkable, and there was an emerging, and upsetting, disconnection between rank or lineage and money.

Although order and class were proclaimed more visibly than they had been during the Republic, appearances could be deceiving. Trimalchio hijacks insignia to which he is not entitled.[3] Martial spots a man sitting in the reserved front rows at the Theater of Marcellus wearing a sardonyx ring, a purple cloak, and the lunette-buckled sandals of a senator, the brands marking him as a former slave covered by patches (2.29). These are comic exaggerations, but they hint that persons on the rise were dressing above their station. Authors consequently devote an enormous amount of attention to elite male self-presentation. Careful monitoring of image had always been essential in a society that believed hidden defects of character, and even male gender deviance, could be inferred from irregularities in gesture, dress, body carriage, and gait (Cic. *Fin.* 5.47, *Off.* 1.126–31; cf. Sen. *Ep.* 52.12). Some individuals, however, deliberately flouted the rules. During the Republic, leaders who courted popular approval, like Julius Caesar, seem to have adopted a flamboyant style of dress and oratory in deliberate contrast to the restraint of conservative adversaries (Corbeill 2002). The orator Hortensius was legendary for his prissy over-attention to the folds of his toga (Macrob. *Sat.* 3.13.4).[4] Such transgressions of the code of masculinity were promptly branded "effeminate" and the perpetrators denounced as *cinaedi*.[5] In the imperial age, suspicion still fastened upon the fastidious dandy who wore perfume and plucked body hair in order to be more attractive to women (Ov. *Ars am.* 1.505–24). But phobia also attached to the stereotype of the unrecognized *cinaedus* – the man who showed all the hallmarks of masculinity but was a hidden pervert.

It will come as no surprise to the cynically minded that Stoic moralists were portrayed as given to secret vice. Speaking vaguely, but in language pointing to that sect, the rhetorician **Quintilian** complains that philosophers use their countenance, stern demeanor, and nonconformist dress to mask extremely bad conduct (Quint. *Inst.* 1. pr. 15). Publicly harsh though privately self-indulgent, they "gain credibility through contempt for others" (*Inst.* 12.3.12). What Quintilian professes as fact Martial frames as a clever joke (1.24):

> Decianus, you see that fellow with uncombed hair,
>   whose frowning eyebrow you yourself fear,
>   who invokes Curii and Camilli, champions of liberty?
>   Don't trust his looks. He was a bride [*nupsit*] yesterday.

The speaker's addressee, a personal friend and fellow Spaniard (1.61.10), is himself an adherent of Stoicism (1.8). This epigram, then, is aimed at charlatans who adopt its external trappings to conceal their degeneracy. Martial's unnamed subject has solemnized a union in which he will play the submissive partner; the punch line takes advantage of the lexical circumstance that Latin *nubere* "to marry" can be used only of a woman, for her status is the one that formally undergoes change (Treggiari 1991: 5, 439).[6] Behind hallmarks of virtue – careless grooming, forbidding manner, patriotic nostalgia – the epigrammatist detects a pathic. In Martial as in Quintilian, the controlling motif is hypocrisy.

Juvenal's second satire develops that motif further. He borrows the figure of the Stoic *cinaedus* from Martial, sketching out a bristly preacher whose smooth buttocks and piles inform the grinning doctor of his covert sex-life (2.11–13). When such a one begins to denounce adulterous women, calling upon the *Lex Iulia*, Juvenal summons his female counterpart, a woman named Laronia, to their defense. Her speech scathingly dissects the philosopher's pretensions to virtue (38–63). After she routs him, the satirist takes back the reins to steer his tirade in a new direction, foreshadowed by her charge that effeminates protect each other. He predicts the decline and fall of Creticus, a prosecutor of adulteresses whose only indiscretion so far is to wear finely woven, transparent clothing in court, ostensibly because of the July heat. Because contact breeds contagion, Creticus will soon join the company of those who, clad in sky-blue and green and heavily made up, perform an obscene travesty of the rites of the Bona Dea, a matronal cult from which men were excluded (65–116). This juicy peek at a secret society of *cinaedi* is followed by the example of a priest of Mars, Gracchus – a name redolent of Republican nobility – who weds a horn-player (and brings him a considerable dowry) before a company of well-wishers. "How could Mars permit it?" the speaker fulminates. Such events are becoming an accepted part of social life; soon they will take place openly, and the couple will want a mention in the official registry (117–36). As the final step in his degradation, Gracchus "comes out" by giving a gladiatorial exhibition before the emperor as a **retiarius**, or net-and-trident man (143–8).[7] "Gracchus's public engagement in an activity appropriate to slaves simply makes manifest the consequences of his posturing as a female" (Konstan 1993: 14). Thus the trajectory of Juvenal's satire moves inexorably from concealment to open confession, implying that depravity so extreme cannot help but make itself known.

That there were rigid Roman protocols for correct male behavior, and that some individuals, for political or personal reasons, attempted to test them, is indisputable. But what about the possibility of an effeminate lifestyle – of men who self-identified as having an alternative sexuality (whatever they might have called themselves) and banded together in a support network? Juvenal's Laronia states emphatically that their kind hang together ("there is great solidarity among the soft [*molles*]," 2.47). Do the specificities of dress, grooming (all-over depilation), mannerisms, and ways of speaking attributed to *cinaedi*, many attested in a broad range of sources, confirm the extra-literary reality of individuals distinguished from other males by such visible signs, and even offer evidence of group cohesion? Some scholars have argued that case (Richlin 1993: 542–3; Taylor 1997: 339). Though we may dismiss Martial's and Juvenal's accounts of publicly solemnized marriages between two men as fictions, allegations that the emperors Nero and **Elagabalus** (reigned 218–222 CE) became "brides" might indicate that private rituals of the sort were not unknown.[8] Juvenal's account, however distorted, of a men-only religious ceremony has been thought to tally with what we might expect of a passive male Roman subculture (Richlin 1993: 548). Indeed, the increasing number and virulence of literary attacks on pathics during the high empire has been attributed to the growing visibility of that subculture. In the same texts, a new tendency to ascribe aggressiveness and omnivoracity to the *cinaedus* supposedly emerges because relations between its adult members were challenging the paradigm of sexual dominance and submission by permitting role interchange (Taylor 1997: 349–57).

But all this is conjectural. Given the vehement bias of our sources, it is risky to construct any historical picture from the vignettes contained in them. As in the case of his Greek analogue, we cannot know whether the *cinaedus* – the Roman sexual category of men who preferred to be penetrated by other men and/or to service women orally – had any material existence or was just a fabulous construct (Parker 1997: 60–2). Even if we grant that *cinaedi* did exist, we cannot swallow literally the appearance and conduct imputed to them. Finally, while arguing that negative evidence is admittedly weak, looking for a glimpse of an alternative subculture in nonliterary sources unearths nothing. Casual networking might well have taken place among friends, and bathhouses and taverns were undoubtedly pickup places, but no record of those activities survives (except for crude graffiti at Pompeii). The most likely venue for organized supportive activity would indeed be a religious association (*sodalitas* or *sodalicium*), but my own informal survey of cult inscriptions found no trace of any fraternity that might be construed as having that particular purpose. For the moment, we must conclude that the question is unanswerable.

During the same time-frame, however, a corollary stereotype appears, one whose physiological aberrations expose her as an undeniable figment of the lewd imagination. The **tribas** is the female version of the *cinaedus*, a woman who transgresses gender roles by playing the man's part. She can do so because she is endowed with a clitoris large enough to serve as a penis: "your huge sex organ fakes manhood" (Mart. 1.90.8). Thus she can penetrate not only boys and women but even men – or so the younger Seneca assures us. In addition to assuming the insertive function, this virago gorges, swills drink, and exercises like a man, though, according to Seneca, she also pays the price, because she suffers from men's afflictions, baldness and gout (*Ep.* 95.20–1). Martial rings a final change on gender inversion when he portrays the tribad Philaenis ending her day with a spot of cunnilingus because she believes giving head is unmanly: "May the gods give you back your mind, Philaenis, if you think it's manly to lick cunt" (7.67.16–17). For Philaenis, the pseudo-man, to take an interest in female genitalia proves that she is not a man after all and can never hope to be one (Brooten 1996: 47–8).

The creation of such a freak, in defiance of biological and social reality, is a reflex of the peculiarly Roman fascination with the phallus. For a woman, abandoning the passive role requires the physical equivalent of a male organ. Yet that postulate runs counter to the very meaning of the Greek word *tribas*, which is derived from a verb "to rub" and thus implies that women can pleasure each other in the absence of a penis (Hallett 1997 [1989]: 267–8). That may be the sardonic point of a vignette by

Lucian, a Greek satirist from Syria writing during the second century CE. In his *Dialogues of the Courtesans* he provides fifteen light sketches of *hetairai* pragmatically exchanging information on men and seduction techniques. The fifth dialogue, however, involves one woman, Clonarium, interrogating a second, Leaena, about her newest client, a wealthy lady named Megilla. As Leaena tells the story, when she was approached by Megilla and her partner Demonassa, she had no idea what they wanted, even after the two began kissing and fondling her as they slept three in a bed. Megilla pulls off her wig to reveal her shaven head and proclaims herself a man, "Megillus" the husband of Demonassa, but Leaena is still confused. First she supposes that Megilla is an actual man masquerading as a woman, then a hermaphrodite, and lastly a man who had magically changed sex, like the mythical Tiresias. All of these conjectures Megilla denies: she is instead a woman with "the mind and the appetite and all the other things of a man." She then offers to show Leaena that she is as good as a man in every respect, having "something instead of a man's organ" (5.4). Bribed with a necklace and a dress, Leaena consents. "But what did she *do*?" inquires Clonarium, "and how?" That is the question she has been asking all along. "I won't tell you the details," replies Leaena, "they're shameful [*aischra*]." The reader, avid to learn the great secret, is left flat. Shaggy-dog story, second century CE.[9]

Alternatively, one might deny that sexual activity between women could happen at all. This seems to be a tongue-in-cheek motif invoked to amuse a sophisticated audience. When Ovid in the *Metamorphoses* recounts the plight of Iphis, a girl infatuated with another girl (*Met.* 9.666–797), he makes his high-minded heroine declare her passion unheard-of, atrocious, and novel (727–8). But his earlier imaginary letter from Sappho to Phaon, a youth with whom she has fallen in love, paints the archaic Greek poet as a classic *tribas* and self-confessed former lover of girls (*Her.* 15.15–20; Gordon 1997). Roman writers therefore distance women's homoerotic relationships from everyday reality (Hallett 1997 [1989]: 259–60). Yet, as we will see in Chapter 10, magical spells, medical and astrological texts, handbooks of dream interpretation, and other imperial and late antique sources prove that love between women, while universally condemned, was known to occur (Brooten 1996: 359–62). Imperial-age textual depictions of the phallic woman should be studied in conjunction with the much wider range of nonliterary evidence for female erotic relations.

Like the *cinaedus*, the figure of the *tribas* has been interpreted as a symptom of social disquiet, indicating that additional strains were being placed on relations between men and women. During the first century CE, male oversight over women's economic activity lessened, first because of the Julian legislation exempting women who had borne the proper number of children from tutelage and afterward through the emperor Claudius' removal of automatic guardianship by paternal kin in cases of intestacy (Gai. *Inst.* 1.157, 171). It is likely that affluent women took advantage of their increased financial freedom, a development that might have been perceived as threatening. Moralists and humorists may have attached the masculine organ to the female who apes all of a man's sexual and social behaviors to make the point that women were getting out of hand (Sullivan 1991: 197–207, esp. 205–6). It is also possible that the satiric caricature of the tribad became popular at this moment because upper-class males, including members of the imperial family, had begun to delegate some quasi-public responsibilities to their wives. Woman as a gender construct had taken on characteristics formerly monopolized by men. Consequently, a new category of bad women – the "illegitimate man," usurper of phallic privilege – had to be invented.

Roads to Romance

Outside Italy, imperial administration relied upon the collaboration of leading citizens of provincial communities for the day-to-day management of local affairs (Ando 2000: 49–70). Elites were co-opted into the project of maintaining empire-wide stability through grants of Roman citizenship, patronage and kinship affiliations, and opportunities for political and social advancement in a new cosmopolitan order. Greek-speaking cities in the eastern half of the empire enjoyed increased prosperity under Roman rule, and, with local economies thriving, a fresh sense of Greek cultural identity emerged. Festivals featuring athletic or artistic contests, a vital component of civic life since the archaic period, were inaugurated or revived all over the Eastern Mediterranean, financed for the most part by private sponsors (van Nijf 2001). More important still in the construction and promotion of a transnational Hellenism was literary education, *paideia*. Replacing the old polarity by which Greeks defined themselves against "barbarian" nations, a "new-style Hellenism, the pluralist, multicultural, Roman-inspired web that embraced the entire civilized world" (Whitmarsh 2001: 25) took form, enrolling all who, regardless of ethnicity, had had the advantage of an intense (and expensive) training in classical literature, rhetoric, and oratory. Writing blossomed in the wake of self-awareness. Greek prose reached its zenith during the Imperial age as learned authors generated an enormous volume of historical, biographical, oratorical, philosophical, scientific and medical treatises.

Rock-star Rhetoric

The outstanding Greek orators of the Imperial age would doubtless think present-day political candidates' stump speeches and prepared debate statements – ghostwritten, run past focus groups, airbrushed and memorized – awesomely flat. *Their* orations had no prefabricated talking points. Instead, a renowned public speaker was expected to hold forth for several continuous hours impromptu. Cities turned to the ranks of these skilled declaimers, the so-called "**sophists**" (from Greek *sophia*, "wisdom"), to represent them as ambassadors because a rigorous course of learning was expected to instill not only fluency in extempore communication but also correct habits of mind and physical self-presentation. As a

high road for the ambitious provincial, therefore, oratory was so extensively pursued that instructors were in great demand. Flavius Philostratus, author of the collected *Lives of the Sophists*, designates the epoch between 50 and 250 CE the "**Second Sophistic**," in homage to a former phase of sophistic activity in fifth-century BCE Athens when rhetoric had first become an object of specialized study (VS 491). Today the scholarly label, while admittedly imprecise, serves to identify both that period of Greek history and the cultural and literary fashions that dominated it.

Sophists were renowned as professional performers as well as teachers. They competed before

(Continued)

Rock-star Rhetoric — Continued

peers and students, improvising elaborate speeches on set themes proposed by the audience. The rules were complicated and demanding. While topics could be fictional or mythic, they were frequently drawn from the Golden Age of Athenian history (Swain 1996: 92–6). The orator needed to speak in character – for example as Demosthenes defending himself against blame for the Greek defeat at Chaeronea – with due respect for recorded facts. Furthermore, he had to declaim in pure Attic Greek: not the *koinê*, the simplified vernacular that had become the ordinary language of commerce throughout the eastern Mediterranean, but an archaizing literary dialect based, lexically and syntactically, on recognized classical models. Employment of this artificial dialect marked out its speakers as designated heirs to past Athenian greatness as well as urbane, educated men who were superior to the masses (Swain 1996: 17–21). In addition to perfect command of ideas and language, champion sophistry required an imposing theatrical presence: grooming, costume, body language gauged for maximum audience appeal. Yet oratorical performance was also "a forum in which issues of gender and identity were fought out" (Whitmarsh 2005: 29–30) and too much lack of restraint, verging on the exhibitionistic, might expose the performer to the charge of effeminacy. Identity, so constructed, was as much about manhood as it was about class or, for that matter, Hellenism (Whitmarsh 2001: 96–108, 116–29). Orators had to present themselves as the flawless Greek male.

One man who prided himself on doing so was **M. Antonius Polemo**, illustrious citizen of his adopted city Smyrna, distinguished advocate and friend to emperors, and the subject of a long biography by Philostratus (*VS* 530–44). His style of eloquence is described as "heated, contentious, and sharply ringing like a trumpet at the Olympic games" (*VS* 542), and a colleague, Herodes Atticus, advised a fan praising Herodes' own delivery to "read Polemo's declamation and know a *man*" (*eisesthe andra*, *VS* 539). In an incisive study of

gender and public image during the Second Sophistic (1995), Maud Gleason selects Polemo as her paradigmatic type of hyper-masculinism, not only for his own daunting personality but also for his self-proclaimed expertise in judging inward disposition from outward show. Polemo was the author of a major treatise on physiognomy, the putatively scientific discipline of reading character from signs imparted by eyes, mouth, and other parts of the body, stance, gesture, and voice. Because masculinity was seen as "an achieved state, radically underdetermined by anatomical sex" (Gleason 1995: 59), and gender deviance was such a hazy, if odious, charge, ferreting out and exposing disguised effeminates was one of the main uses to which Polemo put his technique.

In a culture that policed gender so energetically, though, public blurring of sexual boundaries created its own delicious frisson. Polemo's greatest adversary was **Favorinus** of Arles in France, a celebrity lecturer who had been born, we are told, a hermaphrodite (perhaps his testicles were undescended, a medical condition known as cryptorchism). As an adult he was beardless, with a high-pitched voice, but genital abnormality did not stop him from having a busy sex life and even from being arraigned on a charge of adultery – with a consul's wife, no less. He also quarreled with the emperor **Hadrian**, though Hadrian magnanimously let it pass. Hence, says Philostratus, he presented himself as the embodiment of three paradoxes: he was a Greek-speaking Gaul, a eunuch tried for adultery, and someone who had disagreed with an emperor and lived (*VS* 489). These paradoxes, says Gleason, "are notable for the way they emphasize his power to transcend the limitations of his birth (whether provincial origins or anatomical deficiencies)" (1995: xxviii). Rather than attempting to overcome his congenital features, he exploited them, to the point of enchanting audiences with his modulations of tone, animated glances, and rhythmic expressions (*VS* 492), and, Whitmarsh adds, with a "counter-intuitive mixture of manliness and unmanliness" (2001: 115). His rivalry with

Polemo, which escalated into a public feud, involved vicious abuse on both sides. Polemo's physiognomical tract contains a wicked caricature of Favorinus (unnamed, but identified as a Celtic, i.e., French, eunuch), a creature physically repellent and morally disgusting, steeped in magic arts and a poisoner on the side (Gleason 1995: 7). He is also the figure behind the satirist Lucian's sketch *The Eunuch*, which presents him, under the pseudonym Bagoas (shades of Alexander!), as one of two finalists for a lucrative chair of philosophy at Athens. When the other candidate objects that a eunuch is not a fit candidate to instruct boys, a bystander suggests that Bagoas prove himself a man by stripping. Revealing that he has the required equipment would qualify him for the academic appointment. However, since he had once been caught in adultery but pleaded incapacity in order to get off, it might also put him into legal jeopardy again (*Eun.* 10). With this *reductio ad absurdum* Lucian spoofs the cult of virility surrounding the practice of oratorical competition.

We see a completely distinct side of Favorinus in anecdotes preserved by his Roman friend Aulus Gellius, for whom he is first and foremost a philosopher. In his frequent appearances in the *Attic Nights*, he comes across as a formidable expert in both Greek and Latin philology (*NA* 2.22, 26), readily familiar with the literature in each language, and an engaging conversationalist (4.1.19). Though he crosses swords with many erudite disputants, no one, Gleason notes, ever engages in an *ad hominem* attack upon him or mentions his physical imperfections (1995: 143–4). In a book of memoirs that would be unseemly. Still, it is fascinating to watch him circumambulate the highest levels of Roman society with such aplomb – as when he condescends to lecture a senator's mother-in-law on the advantages of maternal breastfeeding (*NA* 12.1). "Taking title to the philosophical persona with an imperturbable authority, and adopting the sententiousness and frank speech, if not the shaggy grooming, of the traditional role, Favorinus was able to carry off many contentious social encounters that might otherwise have exposed him to personal ridicule" (Gleason 1995: 144).

Could a charismatic, eloquent politician who somehow tested the canon of masculinity (in ways apart from sexual preference) be elected to the US Congress or the British Parliament these days? It's worth considering.

The most characteristic literary product of that intellectual movement, however, is the **Greek novel**, at least if we concentrate upon issues of identity (Swain 1996: 101–31). Five specimens of lengthy prose fiction, collectively termed the "ideal novels," survive intact; others are known from papyrus fragments. The genre, which originated, as far as we can tell, precisely at this time (though dates of particular texts are disputed), contains several exceptional features. All of the novels make use of a standard plot, although it is varied in inventive ways. A young man and woman fall passionately in love but are soon separated, either before or immediately after marriage; the two, while parted, attempt to remain faithful to each other as they endure kidnapping, shipwreck, incarceration, enslavement, and other catastrophes. Their adventures take them to various exotic locales in and near the Greek East. (In the one departure from the above paradigm, Longus' *Daphnis and Chloe*, the adolescent protagonists, nobly born children raised by shepherds, do not leave their native Lesbos, confronting the encumbrances of sexual ignorance in place of the vicissitudes of fortune.) Finally, the lovers are reunited, and, amidst great popular jubilation, restored to their rightful place in society. Elegant prose style, high literary tone, sophisticated deployment of allusion and irony, and extreme rhetorical self-consciousness indicate that these compositions were directed toward an erudite reading public (Bowie 1994).

The rise of interest in ancient sexuality is responsible for much of the novels' current academic popularity (Morales 2008: 39). The most conspicuous factor in all five is their unique model of heterosexual relations. Although same-sex unions may play a minor part elsewhere in the narrative, the bond central to the plot is that of a young man and woman enamored of each other.[10] Hero and heroine are both of free status and eligible to wed, but their alliance is formed through mutual consent rather than initiated by their parental households. *Erôs*, contrary to its operations in lyric poetry or Attic tragedy, is not a disruptive force but instead inseparable from marriage (Haynes 2003: 156–7). Female desire as displayed by the heroine is likewise represented in a positive light. David Konstan's designation for this relational model as "sexual symmetry" seems, at first glance, quite accurate. Challenges faced by the boy and girl are much the same, and the strategies of resistance they employ do not differ: "sighs, tears, and suicide attempts are as characteristic of the male as of the female in distress; ruses, disguises, and outright violence in defense of one's chastity are as much the part of the female as of the male" (Konstan 1994: 8). In Achilles Tatius' *Leucippe and Cleitophon*, the male protagonist even claims to have "imitated (*memimêmenon*)" the virginity of his beloved, though he immediately qualifies that assertion: "if there is such a thing as virginity in men as well" (5.20.5). One or the other party is always courted by rivals, many of whom, motivated by genuine love rather than lust, tender him or her an offer of honorable marriage. This rival is in a superior social position, so the egalitarianism of the core relationship is confronted with alternatives that involve an unequal balance of power. Lastly, Konstan observes, the hero of the Greek novel does not perform the modern hero's job of saving the endangered heroine, for that would upset the convention of symmetry, which imposes the part of victim on male and female alike (1994: 34).

Foucault proclaimed this phenomenon of symmetrical sex roles a "new erotics" based upon the voluntary decision to maintain virginity until its fulfillment in marriage. "Love, virginity, and marriage form a whole," he states; "the two lovers have to preserve their physical integrity, but also their purity of heart, until the moment of their union, which is to be understood in the physical but also the spiritual sense" (1988: 231–2). So described, love in the ancient novel does not appear that far removed from a Christian sexual ethics, even though Foucault tries hard to differentiate them. More recent work, however, finds such a description too simplistic. Goldhill (1995: 109–11) protests that Foucault's reading overlooks the place of these narratives as part of a complex contemporary discourse on the desiring male subject and neglects the humor and irony with which they treat sexual matters. Morales (2008: 42–3) observes that a Foucauldian analysis concentrates upon outcomes at the expense of the way readers might engage with internal tensions produced by plot shifts and digressions.

One can add that the experiences of the male and female lovers are not, in fact, truly "symmetrical." Prominence in the story is normally given to the heroine, who frequently possesses greater intelligence and resolution than the hero. Because of her exceptional beauty, though, it is she who is unwillingly subjected to the male gaze (Elsom 1992), who is more often objectified or commodified, and who also bears the brunt of physical and mental distress. Pathos is evoked by placing her in a hopeless situation where she can only lament her fate bitterly. While her beloved may likewise feel pain of mind or body and certainly laments as bitterly as she does, he is at greater liberty to act rather than endure passively. Consequently we may suspect that, as alleged in the case of Ovid, the anticipation of witnessing female suffering might be part of the novels' appeal. Yet we will see in Chapter 10 that female suffering, in the novels as in Christian martyr texts, actually conveys a comforting message, although the motif is embedded in two different figurative systems.

How do the novels cast light on the meaning of "Greekness," and what is their relationship to contemporary Greek civic ideology? The first question is easily answered. In these fictional worlds, the essential constituent of Hellenic cultural identity is knowledge of the Greek language (Stephens 2008), while *paideia*, as might be expected, is the badge of social pre-eminence. Yet there is no mention of Rome, whose presence would remind Greeks of their subordinate status. Instead, Hellenic customs are contrasted with those of "barbarian" peoples encountered in a pre-Roman era – Egyptians, Ethiopians, Persians, and Phoenicians – always to the detriment of the latter. It is possible, then, that the heroine's successful defenses of her chastity against foreign suitors are coded declarations of elite superiority and integrity (Haynes 2003: 79–80, 161–2). Ways in which these romances perform their domestic ideological tasks, if any, are less obvious. One can read the lovers' commitment to each other as protection against a capricious universe, their submissiveness and thoughts of suicide as actions characteristic of an individual "who perceives a certainty of the future as hopelessly blocked" (MacAlister 1996: 52). The hero's marginality could reflect a further weakening of those traditional male communal responsibilities, marriage and the propagation of children. Accordingly, then, the novels tout passionate love, as opposed to duty, as the basis of a stable union (Konstan 1994: 229–30). On the other hand, it is equally possible to view such texts as the ebullient affirmation of the values of a Hellenized and urbanized elite (Perkins 1995: 41–76). Their historical setting looks back to the glory days of classical Greece; encounters with other peoples make plain the virtues of Greek urban society; and the protagonists' attachment to one another simply constitutes a bright new rationale for directing sexuality into socially mandated arrangements. Romance could even have been enlisted in support of the dynastic ambitions of provincial aristocracies: being induced to identify with the desiring hero, a male reader might have been more readily persuaded to marry, despite economic constraints that made setting up a household and playing a leading role in civic life less attractive (Cooper 1996: 20–44; Swain 1996: 129–30). All these hypotheses are arguable, but none has produced consensus because a lack of direct testimony makes it impossible to determine the emotive effect of these curiously modern-sounding tales on their ancient audiences.

'Greek Love' under Rome

Anyone who visits more than one collection of Roman statuary will quickly get to recognize a familiar face – not Augustus, or Nero, or Marcus Aurelius, but that of a young man, somewhere around twenty, whose features are unmistakable, even when he is masquerading as the gods Dionysos or Hermes. This was **Antinous** (fig. 9.1), the beloved companion of the emperor Hadrian, who drowned in the Nile under mysterious circumstances while the imperial court was touring Egypt in 130 CE. His lover, in an excess of grief, founded a city named Antinoöpolis on the spot where he died and erected images of him as of a god; Hadrian was later persuaded that a new star had appeared in the sky, an emanation of Antinous' immortal soul (Cass. Dio 69.11.2–4).

Yet all the honors bestowed did not stop questions from being asked. Antinous' death in late October coincided with the festival of the Nile and services for the supreme male divinity Osiris, who ritually died and was resurrected each year. Ancient writers speculated that the young man had freely offered up his own life to preserve that of the emperor.[11] The facts of the case trouble modern scholars, who have imagined sinister court intrigues. Still, the distinguished novelist Marguerite Yourcenar (*Memoirs of Hadrian*, 1951) and popular historians (Lambert 1984: 141) have gone with a presumption of voluntary sacrifice, even as they suggest that Antinous might also have had private reasons for taking his own life. Or it may have been just a senseless accident.

What cannot be debated is that the new cult of divine Antinous immediately gripped the imagination of the populace. Even when we take imperial promotion and encouragement into account, its rapid spread appears to have been a spontaneous response – impelled, perhaps, by sentimental or erotic recollections of other doomed mythic youths such as Hyacinthus and Narcissus (Vout 2007: 100–6). In a short time Antinoöpolis became a holy city to which pilgrims flocked to be cured or hear oracles pronounced. From Egypt, worship of Antinous as a savior god expanded rapidly across the Roman world. In Greece, Asia Minor, and along the North African coast, and to a lesser but still sizable extent in Italy, Spain, and northwestern Europe, images and dedicatory inscriptions attest to formal or private veneration (Lambert 1984: 3–5, 184–5, 187–8). Scattered traces of his worship have been found from Britain to the Danube. Cities struck coins and medallions in his honor. Out of countless sculptures produced during the eight remaining years of Hadrian's reign – posthumous representations of the new god in one or another of his divine aspects – approximately a hundred still exist.[12] Their survival is remarkable because worship of Antinous provoked the rage of Christian apologists, who cited the apotheosis of a disgusting catamite as proof of the moral bankruptcy of paganism. Hatred of this rival cult (which, in celebrating a young man's sacrifice and supposed rebirth, was curiously analogous to Christianity) guaranteed that its temples and icons would be targeted for obliteration when the latter creed finally triumphed.

The significance of the deified Antinous as a role model may be inferred from a double funerary portrait now in the Egyptian Museum at Cairo (Inv. CG 33267)

Fig. 9.1 Colossal bust of Antinous. Location: Museo Pio Clementino, Vatican Museums, Vatican State. Source: Scala/Art Resource, NY.

found at Antinoöpolis and dated on archaeological and art-historical grounds to the 130s or 140s CE. Two males, a light-skinned, smooth-cheeked adolescent and a darker-skinned, bearded adult man, stand side by side, the younger figure on the viewer's left. He wears the crimson cloak of the Greek citizen youth, while his companion is attired in a toga-like garment. Above the outer shoulder of each is the gilded statuette of a Greco-Egyptian deity: the god accompanying the youth has been recognized as Osirantinoos, a local conflation of Osiris and Antinous, and the one beside the man as Hermanubis, produced by syncretizing the Greek Hermes Psychopompus, conductor of souls to the underworld, with Anubis, the jackal-headed Egyptian god who also led the dead to judgment (Parlasca 1966: 70–1). Despite the marked differences in skin tone, the two have traditionally been identified as siblings, but a recent study argues on contextual and iconographic grounds that they are more likely to have been lovers. Not only was this tondo discovered in urban surroundings consecrated to a romantic bond of man and youth, but the lighter complexion of the adolescent, his dress, and his positioning to the left are all reminiscent of the way in which wives are depicted in portraits of married couples (Haeckl 2001: 67–8, 70–6). Most significant is the Egyptian date inscribed above the young man's shoulder, corresponding to our May 10. Haeckl suggests it is the day on which he died – the beloved, like Antinous, thus predeceasing the lover

(2001: 70–1). If so, the existence of the joint portrait may mean that a caring relative had chosen to leave the tondo intact as a memento of the relationship rather than separating it into two individual mummy portraits after the older man passed away.

For some persons, worship of Antinous may have been meaningful because it bestowed religious endorsement on man-boy love as part of a Hellenizing lifestyle. The elite gymnasium culture that flourished in the Greek-speaking parts of the Roman empire still advocated the socialization of adolescents through participation in pederastic relationships. Although Roman concern for the welfare of citizen youths might cast a shadow of doubt upon that way of life, it was not yet under threat. Hadrian himself was a fervent philhellene and generous benefactor of Greek communities. Literature praising the charms of boys was being produced in great quantities during his reign: **Strato**, who specialized in pederastic epigrams, compiled and published a whole collection of them now included in the *Palatine Anthology*. At the end of that book of verse, though, he dissociates himself from its contents, circumspectly pleading that he composes simply to meet customer demand (*Anth. Pal.* 12.258):

> Someone in future, perhaps, hearing this light verse of mine,
>   will think the sufferings in love were all my own.
> But I am always scratching out poems for various lovers of boys
>   because a god has endowed me with this gift.

Should we infer from Strato's closing poem that homoerotic matter required explanation? Evidence from other genres may point in that direction.

Starting around the same time, according to Foucault, there is a change in the temper of Greek philosophic discourses on *erôs* (1988: 189–92). Pederasty is not condemned, but it is no longer privileged, as it was in fifth-century BCE Athens, as a training ground for virtue. During the Imperial period staged debates over the merits of loving boys as opposed to women, or vice versa, become a literary commonplace. Heterosexual intercourse is championed in these contests as part of the design of nature; pederasts answer that relations between males are impelled by feelings more sublime than "natural" brute instinct. In Plutarch's *Dialogue on Love*, however, the two modes of sexuality are opposed in an innovative way. Love of boys is contrasted with the union of man and wife, and the pederastic relationship is found wanting because of the limitations enjoined upon it by custom.

We have seen that society has an ideological stake in denying carnal pleasure to the citizen youth due to fears that he might become habituated to the passive role. That, of course, means that sex has no place in romantic friendship, or, if it does, that the lover gets satisfaction only because the beloved has submitted either voluntarily, which reflects on his masculinity, or through force, a boorish act. "But how," Plutarch's advocate for marriage asks, "can Eros exist without Aphrodite?" (*Amat.* 752b). If the aim and end of passion is sexual consummation, any love which excludes the physical expression of desire is doomed to fizzle out quickly. Conversely, the narrator himself adds, the same can be said for Aphrodite without Eros: sex in the absence of love is self-indulgence purchased for a drachma (759e–f). True intimacy is the work of both gods in combination. It is a state that can be attained only through conjugal love because pederasty is one-sided, satisfying just the adult partner. The joint pleasure of intercourse between husband and wife, on the other hand, engenders "reverence, consideration, mutual affection and trust," and consequently friendship (769a). Hence Plutarch's dialogue promulgates a "Platonizing" doctrine in which man and woman are equally active celebrants of Eros, and pederasty is deemed inadequate because it "lacks the internal relation and the stability of the couple" (Foucault 1988: 209).

That some radical rethinking of Greek gender arrangements was in the air may seem even more likely after we examine the dialogue's framing story. Attending a festival of Eros at Thespiae in Boeotia, the newly married narrator Plutarch, his bride and his friends learn of a bizarre situation creating a hullabaloo in the town. Ismenodora, a wealthy widow, had taken on herself the responsibility of negotiating a marriage between a girl related to her and a young man named Bacchon, who was still a minor, handsome, and much courted by potential *erastai*. During their interviews, Ismenodora had fallen in love with the youth and, instead of furthering the marriage with the girl, was offering to marry Bacchon herself. Her proposal had caused a rift between two men entrusted with the boy's welfare – his cousin Anthemion, who favored an alliance with the well-off Ismenodora, and his principal admirer Pisias. This state of affairs inspires the dispute among Plutarch's acquaintances over the respective advantages and shortcomings of pederasty and marriage.

One issue that concerns Pisias and his side is the likelihood that Ismenodora might dominate her young husband because of her fortune, her age (she is probably thirty to his nineteen or so), and her lack of decorum in assuming the initiative (*Amat.* 753a–b). Plutarch, as a participant in the dialogue, meets the objection by remarking that wealth is all to the good if a woman is of good character, as Ismenodora is, and for her, a sensible older woman, to manage a young man – why, what is so bad about that? (753d–754e). On cue, a messenger turns up to report that Ismenodora has taken matters into her own hands. Suspecting that Bacchon himself had no objection to marrying her, she arranged for a group of her friends to kidnap and carry him bodily into her house, where preparations for the wedding are taking place even as the news is brought. Bacchon's *erastês* Pisias storms off to appeal to the magistrates, while Ismenodora sends for her own ally Anthemion. Plutarch, for his part, delivers a long eulogy of Eros and marriage to those left behind as they head back more slowly toward Thespiae. When they arrive, they find that the disagreement is already resolved. Pisias has in the meantime consented to the marriage and is all dressed up to take part in the wedding procession. Thanks are given to the god, and everyone, we presume, lives happily ever after.

Ismenodora's abduction of her beloved may be the most extreme instance of gender-bending in Greek literature. By representing her as mature, of excellent repute, concerned for the welfare of her young charge, and proactive in the affair, Plutarch casts her as the male *erastês*. Her enterprise is apparently sanctioned by the outcome of events. Foucault argues that she is given attributes of the senior male partner to show that Plutarch is not rejecting the ethical values traditionally associated with pederasty but instead subsuming them under his own conception of a single unified love fully realizable only in marriage (1988: 196–7). That reading, however, may again overlook some of the ambiguities present in the text. Plutarch the speaker asks a rhetorical question about the evils of female agency and is answered with the news that the infatuated widow has bypassed communal authority. "How like an *erastês*," Goldhill muses, "can a woman be?" (1995: 155) The end may justify the means, but the novelistic frame of the dialogue, he continues, still tests "the limits of the move towards reciprocity, symmetry, and sharing" exhibited in Greek novels of the Imperial period and intrinsic to Plutarch's notion of conjugal love. Even in an essay ostensibly celebrating the power of Eros and its fulfillment in matrimony, recognition and acceptance of autonomous female desire is fraught with misgivings. As in the novels, then, any philosophic debate over modes of sexuality is better viewed as "a site of engagement and negotiation" (ibid., 161), instead of a vehicle for ethical commentary.

Roads to Nowhere

While Greek writers were reflecting upon the nature of *erôs*, Romans were composing their own prose fictions likewise dealing with lengthy journeys. Though influenced by the Greek romance, surviving novels in Latin nevertheless do not resemble Second Sophistic narratives. It is not simply a matter of plot but also of tone and thematics. Both Petronius' incomplete *Satyrica*, which we have already encountered, and **Apuleius'** *Metamorphoses* are picaresque novels – that is, they follow the random adventures of a main figure on the fringe of society, in Spanish a *picaro* or rogue. Instead of containing a causal sequence of events unfolding logically toward a foreseeable conclusion, the story-line of such novels is episodic. Incidents are raffish, often involving deception or criminal activity; sometimes the hero is the author of the misdeed, at other times a mere observer. Romantic love is conspicuously absent, sex is coarse, and humor tends to be bawdy or sadistic.[13] The picture of human experience presented is "fragmented, disjointed, and unstable" (Zeitlin 1971: 652). If the hero at last finds a safe haven and ceases his wanderings, it is not through his own efforts: deliverance is either a pure stroke of luck or the product of supernatural agency.

The narrator of the *Satyrica*, a twentyish youth named Encolpius (in Greek conjuring up the meaning "Crotch"), quite literally embodies the incoherence of the world around him, not least in the chaotic frustrations of his sexual life. As the lacunose text begins, he, along with two companions, Ascyltus and the boy Giton, is in a municipality on the Bay of Naples, most likely the harbor town of Puteoli (modern Pozzuoli). Their ramblings take them down mean streets and into very seedy brothels and rooming houses. Encolpius fancies himself passionately in love with Giton, to the point of subsequently vowing double murder when the latter abandons him for Ascyltus (*Sat.* 81.6). Their stormy pederastic liaison may therefore burlesque the comradeship of hero and heroine in the Greek romance. Encolpius has already had previous affairs with men and women, including a pair who reappear later in the narrative, the shipmaster Lichias and the adventuress Tryphaena. At one point he was also involved with Ascyltus, now his rival for the boy's affections. When the two companions quarrel viciously, Giton and Ascyltus refer to Ascyltus as Encolpius' *frater*, "brother," a term that Encolpius himself applies to Giton (9.2–3, 4, 10; 10.7; 11.4). In the context it cannot be anything other than euphemistic, although its connotations of familial intimacy contrast harshly with the spitefulness of the insults the rivals heap on each other. Soon afterward Encolpius and his friends suffer mortifying sexual abuse at the hands of Quartilla, priestess of Priapus, and her entourage, ostensibly because they have violated the god's secret rites. For the first time in the surviving text the hero experiences sexual impotence (20.2), his recurrent affliction in the remainder of the novel.

After journeying to the city of Croton, Encolpius catches the eye of Circe, a high-born lady of randy tastes, and is invited to a tryst only to disappoint her. He tries his luck with Giton but fails again. Apologetically, he confesses to the insulted boy that he has, in effect, lost his identity: "Believe me, brother, I don't know I'm a man, I don't perceive it. That part of my body that once made me an Achilles is dead and gone" (129.1). Folk remedies for impotence have no lasting effect, and, after a second fruitless encounter with Circe, Encolpius is beaten and ignominiously ejected from her house. In a scene of high parody he threatens his flaccid member with steel and inveighs against it (132):

> Upright and leaning on my elbow, then, I denounced my stubborn part in words like this: "What have you to say for yourself, you disgrace to all men and gods? For it is blasphemy even to allude to you in serious talk. Have I deserved this of you, that you should drag me down from my place in heaven to the nether world? That you should disrespect my years in their burgeoning prime and impress upon me the torpor of extreme old age? I beg you, give me a perfunctory show of support." As I poured out these angry remarks,
>
> > she, turned away, kept her eyes fixed on the ground,
> > by the opening speech is no more moved in face
> > than supple willows or poppy with drooping stem.[14]

Finally Encolpius resorts to witchcraft for a cure and in the process kills Priapus' sacred goose, which only intensifies the god's anger toward him (139.2). Just before the fragments give out, he shows the poet Eumolpus (140.12–13) that Mercury has fully restored him to health, for reasons we do not know; we also have no idea whether the cure was permanent.

Sexual unions in the *Satyrica* blur the distinctions of age and role clearly drawn elsewhere in literature and art. Encolpius is sometimes the passive, at other times the active, partner. Although he penetrated the stronger and more domineering Ascyltus (9.10), neither seems conscious of any real division between *erastês* and *erômenos*, and their sexual dealings with each other are in fact cold-blooded and unsentimental (Richardson 1984: 113). Ascyltus, whose physical equipment is prodigious, is certainly not averse to obliging a rich pathic (92.10). Even the teenage Giton can be pressed into service to deflower Quartilla's serving-girl Pannychis (25–6) and subsequently dallies willingly with Tryphaena (113.5–8). Yet this polymorphic and hectic sexual activity cannot conceal the abyss at the heart of things: the Quartilla scene defines all three characters, and especially Encolpius, as victims to whom unpleasant sex happens. The pattern of thwarted desire in the protagonist's life – one frustration, emotional or physical, after another – may therefore be viewed, metaphorically, as a quest for meaning under circumstances where meaning can never be determined (Slater 1990: 241–51).

Encolpius' impotence also figures the hollowness of his intellectual posturing. Unemployed vagabond though he is, he prides himself on his superior education and, as narrator, constructs from the flow of events epic and tragic plots in which he, naturally, plays the mythic hero (Conte 1996: 37–72). Just as his exposure to freedmen society at Trimalchio's dinner affords an ironic comparison between him, the educated parasite, and men whose values center upon food and money instead of learning, so his constant humiliations subvert his efforts to give a veneer of novelistic romance to casual couplings. The putatively obscene episodes of the *Satyrica* are an incisive means of exposing the weakening cultural authority of elite schemes of education in the Neronian age.

References in the novel to witchcraft, particularly when interwoven with the theme of sexual dysfunction, reflect popular belief that erotic desire and its expression were vulnerable to supernatural influence (McMahon 1998: 61–97). Encolpius readily blames his trouble on sorcery (128.2). Magic, broadly defined as the employment of occult means to affect the natural world, had always been part of ancient belief systems, but under the Roman empire its practice was severely punished. Literature also took increased cognizance of magical practices, depicting them in ghastly colors and associating them, as in the past, with the figure of the witch who employs her craft to exert sexual power over men. However, the traditional association between witchcraft and sexuality had become even more sinister and was now colored by the lure of the forbidden. Inquiry into the esoteric might therefore be represented as the product of a morbid and prurient curiosity.

Writing a century or more after Petronius, Apuleius of Madaura, a city in northern Africa, creates in his *Metamorphoses* (otherwise known as the *Golden Ass*) a puzzle that continues to engage scholars because it maps carnality onto the craving for occult knowledge and takes an equivocal position on involvement with arcane mystery religions. Apuleius was a public intellectual, widely traveled, who himself had been the target of a legal prosecution for witchcraft in his youth. That came about, he explains in his speech of self-defense (*Apol.* 68–101), only because he had married Pudentilla, a wealthy widow (no, she did not kidnap him), and other members of her family were attempting to gain control of her fortune. From both the brilliance of the speech and the fact that his career continued to prosper, we assume that he was acquitted, but whether this incident shaped his subsequent attitude toward magic is impossible to say.

The *Metamorphoses*, probably composed late in Apuleius' life, grafts an ostensibly personal record of spiritual conversion upon a ribald story of a man changed into an ass. His apparent source for the latter was a Greek narrative, now lost, but an abridgement, also in Greek, hints at its flavor. The *Onos* ("Ass"), dubiously attributed to the Greek satirist Lucian, is a first-person account by a young man named Lucius. He travels to Hypata in Thessaly, a backwoods region of northern Greece reportedly thick with witches. In Hypata he discovers that the wife of his host is a witch, and wheedles the maid, with whom he is having a steamy affair, to let him peek at her mistress while she conducts her rites. When he sees the lady transform herself into a bird, he wishes to do the same, but the maid by mistake brings the wrong salve. Instead he becomes an ass, though he retains his human consciousness. The girl tells him not to worry, as eating roses will immediately change him back into a man. While still in ass shape, though, Lucius is stolen by robbers and from that point on undergoes a series of painful, degrading, and even life-threatening adventures.

Ultimately he is bought by a rich man's cook. After he is caught consuming human delicacies, the cook's master brings him into the dining room, has him recline at table, and shows him off to friends. A distinguished and beautiful woman wonders if Lucius' accomplishments extend to other matters as well. The experiment proves successful; his master learns of it and decides to exhibit him in the amphitheater copulating with a female criminal sentenced to be thrown to the beasts. Lucius and the condemned woman are taken into the arena and forced to lie together on a banquet couch. He is not only ashamed but terrified of being mauled by a bear or lion, so, when someone passes by carrying roses, Lucius leaps off the couch, bolts them down, and transforms back to human form in front of the crowd. He is in danger of being burnt to death as a sorcerer, but the provincial governor, who is attending the games, happens to know his parents and, believing his story, releases him. Before returning to his native city, Lucius decides to revisit the lady who had been his lover, sure that she will now find him even more handsome. When she sees him naked, however, she throws him out because he no longer possesses the endowments he enjoyed as an ass.

The *Onos* is a "**Milesian tale**" – it belongs, that is, to a fictional genre considered pleasurable and entertaining ([Luc.] *Am*. 1.1) but also judged obscene (Plut. *Crass.* 32; Ov. *Tr.* 2.413, 443–4). Its most well-known representative is the story of the "Widow of Ephesus" retold in Petronius (*Sat.* 111–12). There, a grief-stricken wife renowned for her chastity sets out to starve herself to death at her late husband's tomb, but is instead persuaded to live by a soldier who had been stationed nearby to guard the body of a crucified criminal. While he is consoling the widow, relatives steal the convict's corpse. To prevent her new love from killing himself because he had neglected his duty, the widow offers her husband's corpse to take the place of the abducted one. Both the *Onos* and the "Widow of Ephesus" affect an utterly cynical stance on morality. Women's lust is a symbol of human appetite in general, which respects no civilized limits; in a closing plot twist, the notion that it can be controlled through cultural sanctions is exploded. The sheer outlandishness of the Milesian tale made it scandalously funny.

Apuleius twice indicates to the reader that his novel is of that type: once in the prologue, where he says he will "join various stories for you into this Milesian discourse" (*Met.* 1.1.1) and again in the fable of "**Cupid and Psyche**," where, breaking the narrative illusion, he jokes that Apollo, though Greek and Ionian, gave his oracle in Latin "to oblige the author of the Milesian work" (4.32.6). The *Metamorphoses* borrows much from the *Onos*, including the character of Lucius and the exotic northern Greek locale; with minor modifications, the plot-line follows it closely. Some passages of the *Metamorphoses* even reproduce the Greek word for word, although Apuleius develops details mentioned only in passing that amplify his major themes (Sandy 1999: 87–8). Such similarities would doubtless lead a first-time reader who knew the *Onos* or its predecessor to assume that Apuleius' work would also have a bawdy ending.

The chief differences between the *Onos* and the *Metamorphoses* are the inclusion of numerous "inset tales" that the Apuleian narrator hears in the course of his travels and the denouement, which veers off in an unexpected direction. Stories embedded in the narrative frame fall into three principal groups: tales of witchcraft and the supernatural, placed in the first three books to underscore Lucius' credulity and characterize his absorption with magic as a kind of inappropriate desire; the long central fairy-tale of Cupid and Psyche (4.28–6.24), in which Psyche, like Lucius, comes to grief because of a rash craving for prohibited knowledge; and, in Books 7–10, depressing accounts of adultery, jealousy, and murder instigated by a string of evil wives, interwoven into the main narrative in which Lucius in ass form is subjected to sadistic beatings and repeatedly witnesses the brutality and depravity of those around him. Apuleius places these fantastic incidents in realistic settings that indirectly offer us "a complex and significant portrait of a provincial society" (Millar 1981: 74). The sordid atmosphere of the tales in the last books mirrors the grim picture of rural Greece seen through the narrator's eyes: a region from which the policing authority of the Roman government is far removed, where wealth coexists alongside extreme poverty, soldiers commandeer the few resources of the underprivileged, robbery and assault are frequent occurrences, and public order is maintained only through local self-help. The combination of the inset stories, which create an overriding impression of institutional breakdown, the random violence inflicted on the ass, and the bleak social setting indicates that Lucius' world is one from which escape, through religion or other means, might well be sought.

The oppressive ambience of Books 7–10 thus paves the way for the conversion tale of Book 11, which departs from the *Onos* just at the point where the protagonist is about to be exhibited in the arena. Stealing away from the amphitheater, Apuleius' Lucius, still an ass, gallops to the seashore several miles off, where he collapses in exhaustion. Woken just before midnight by the rising moon, he purifies himself in the sea and prays for deliverance. The goddess Isis appears in a resplendent vision, gives him instructions for regaining his true mortal shape, and commands him to dedicate himself to her service, with the understanding that she will protect him thereafter in life and in death (11.5–6). The next day, during a rite of Isis marking the opening of the sailing season, Lucius, as bidden, eats a wreath of roses held out by her priest and becomes human once more. The priest, who has been forewarned of events by the goddess, draws what seems a suitable moral (15.1–2):

> Neither your birth nor even your rank or that very learning in which you excel helped
> you in any circumstances, but, having slipped into servile pleasures on the slick footing

of robust youth, you earned the harmful prize of luckless curiosity. But in any event the blindness of Fortune, even while it tortured you with critical dangers, led you on, through its thoughtless malice, to this state of religious beatitude.

The remainder of the book is taken up with Lucius' initiation into the cult of Isis, his removal to Rome and two further initiations there, and his eventual pursuit of a prosperous legal career.

Readings of the *Metamorphoses* as an allegory of transcendental enlightenment based upon Apuleius' private experience are encouraged by a passage in which another priest predicts the subsequent literary fame to be achieved by a "man of Madaura" (Apuleius' own native city, remember), a reference that Lucius takes to apply to himself (11.27.9). In doing so, however, he seems to overlook the fact that he had earlier designated the mainland Greek city of Corinth as his home town (2.12.3). If, as the "man of Madaura," the author Apuleius has suddenly usurped the place occupied by the narrator, does that mean that the *Metamorphoses* is no longer fiction but a kind of religious autobiography? It is tempting to think so, and no less an authority than Augustine of Hippo (himself the author of a classic spiritual memoir, the *Confessions*) was in doubt over whether Apuleius was recounting actual events or making them up (*De civ. D.* 18.18).

Yet contemporary readings have challenged that easy conflation of hero and author. One sophisticated analysis of the novel presents it as a carefully wrought challenge to a trained audience, provocatively laden with ambiguities, false leads, and playful ironies (Winkler 1985). On this interpretation, Lucius the devotee of Isis, though genuinely fervent, remains as naive as before, duped by visions produced through autosuggestion, while seeds of doubt about the motives of the Isiac clergy, centering upon that threefold series of redundant and very costly initiations, are deftly planted in the reader's mind. The conclusion that he is being fleeced by unscrupulous priests can be left open or firmly endorsed. If the latter option is chosen, the *Metamorphoses* can be deemed "an amusing satire on religious mania and youthful gullibility" (Harrison 2000: 248). Should the reader instead suspend judgment, it becomes "a philosophical comedy about religious knowledge" that concedes the inscrutability of belief (Winkler 1985: 124). Alternatively, one can still defend it as a novel of conversion, albeit intellectual rather than moral – one in which the narrator appropriates a religious system as a metaphysical center of truth and coherence in the wake of cognitive crisis (Shumate 1996: 285–328). That interpretation permits admission of the dubious honesty of the Isiac priests while taking a sympathetic stance toward Lucius' faith. Yet whether we understand the final book as receptive to or dismissive of religious phenomena, the novel appears to chart allegorically a process of loss and recovery of self that is symptomatic of its time.

In that allegory, as in the earlier *Satyrica*, the "natural" integration of sexual agency, social ascendancy, and adult manhood is unraveled. Like Encolpius, Lucius is a product of an elite system of education that should have prepared him for leadership in civic life. Both men, however, wind up outside the precincts of society.

Encolpius' periodic experiences of sexual exploitation and his continued incapacity to perform as a man are patent metaphors for his social impotence. As for Lucius, the ass is culturally a "preeminently phallic animal," yet in that form he is constantly abused, humiliated, and threatened with castration (Winkler 1985: 173–8). Even in his earlier life as a human being he was dominated by the servant girl Photis, who set the agenda for their lovemaking and gave him orders he obeyed; when the wealthy matron of Book 10 desires him as her lover, she too takes the initiative in bed and forces herself upon him (32.3–4). If in the Greek novel the hero's failure to assert his social masculinity is problematic, a symptom of the cultural insecurities involved in being Greek under Rome, in narratives produced for a reader of Latin the sense of lack is more nebulous, more pervasive, and inscribed on the male body itself.

Conclusion

Whether the shocking accounts of palace intrigue and misconduct handed down to us by historians are grounded in fact or only vestiges of senatorial smear campaigns, they do convey the impression that under the empire the aristocratic class in Rome saw itself as threatened. Even if life and honor were not at stake, status anxiety was increasing as old families died off, while imperial freedmen rose to influential positions at court and still other former slaves were amassing fortunes. That anxiety, deflected into a fixation on health, may underlie growing worries about the debilitating effects of sexual indulgence on the fragile male body. Concerns about social propriety were meanwhile incorporated into moralists' discourses on vice: as a shorthand term, "unmanliness" was now being applied to a gamut of behaviors deemed inappropriate, all the way from wearing dinner garments of the wrong color to writing best-selling epics. Anxiety also led to the rise of urban legends, conspiracy theories about secret societies of pathics and the monstrous phallic woman. Finally, fictional works in Latin explore an insidious sense of disempowerment by following the tribulations of compromised main characters at the mercy of fortune.

In the Eastern Mediterranean, meanwhile, educated Greeks were reaping the rewards of empire by taking a leading part in local affairs as civic magistrates and philanthropists. Prose fiction produced for their consumption assured them of the advantages of Hellenic culture in a diversified world by depicting sympathetic young people confronting and triumphing over hazards encountered in distant lands. Accomplished orators vied for recognition with virtuoso rhetorical performances. At the same time, philosophical critiques of conventional morality, including the age-old double standard, may have furthered the promotion of marriage as a route to erotic and emotional satisfaction and a corresponding decrease in praise for pederasty as a means of character formation. Still, the evidence does not allow us to treat these developments as anything more than possible trends. If Greeks sensed a nascent external threat to their way of life, they left no record of it.

Discussion Prompts

1. In times of social uncertainty, it is understandable that individuals might try to maintain a sense of security by exerting tight control over their own bodies. Today one area of anxiety for many people is obesity: great amounts of time and money are spent in often fruitless efforts to become thin(ner). Among the Roman upper classes, if Foucault is right, food consumption was not as intense a source of worry as sexual expenditure. What have you learned about the construction of sexuality in antiquity that might explain a possible displacement of other fears on to sex? (By analogy, can you think of cultural reasons why contemporary anxieties would be displaced on to food?)
2. Satire is still a favorite medium of entertainment, but its formal conventions, its audiences, and the purpose of the satirist have all changed appreciably since the Romans invented the genre. In our society, what are the most frequent targets of satirical treatment? What is the relationship between those objects of satire and the audience, and what psychological rewards does the audience receive as it witnesses the operations of satire?
3. Works of prose fiction seem, in antiquity as in the modern world, to have a close connection with the larger concerns of a society. Keeping that principle in mind, give reasons why, in the Greek novel, it is necessary for the heroine and hero to be constantly exposed to physical danger. In the Roman novel, on the other hand, why is the well-educated hero regularly brought into contact with persons of sub-elite status?
4. While categorical human boundaries like gender are still enforced today, entertainers are one select group permitted to strain them, though often at personal cost (here you might think of examples). How did Favorinus' status as a crowd-pleaser give him certain immunities against the kinds of sexual insults commonly lodged against Roman emperors and leading political figures?

Notes

1   Here Foucault follows the lead of the ancient historian Paul Veyne, who appears to have accepted the statements of Roman moralists at face value when he posits that in Republican times incentives to sexual fidelity in marriage and personal investment in childrearing were dismissed by the aristocracy and immaterial to other classes (Veyne 1978: 35–43).
2   Elites justified their disdain for wealthy freedmen by scoffing at their lack of education. Trimalchio's abysmal grasp of Greek mythology (*Sat.* 59.3–5) is paralleled in the younger Seneca's real-life anecdote about Calvisius Sabinus. During dinner Sabinus kept slaves who had memorized the Greek classics at his elbow to prompt him with fitting quotations, but after quoting half the tag he would forget the rest (*Ep.* 27.6).
3   On the doorposts of his dining room Trimalchio exhibits a trophy (presented by his treasurer Cinnamus, sucking up to the boss) that commemorates

his membership in the college of *seviri Augustales*, a lesser priestly office open to freedmen (see Chapter 10), with the rods and axes displayed by a consul and the bronze ship's beak emblematic of a victory in a naval battle (*Sat.* 30.1–2). Senators and magistrates wore a toga edged with a purple stripe and freeborn rich men a gold ring; Trimalchio sports a tasseled purple-striped napkin and two rings, one gilt, the other gold with iron stars soldered onto it (*Sat.* 32.2–3).

4 Macrobius relates (*Sat.* 3.13.5) that Hortensius sued a colleague for assault (*iniuria*) because the man had inadvertently jostled him and disturbed his toga arrangement; that sounds like a line from something akin to a Jay Leno monologue that made it into the historical record. One anecdote about Hortensius has lately received a great deal of attention from students of Roman sexuality. When Torquatus, the opposing lawyer in a trial, mocked his purported effeminacy by addressing him as "Dionysia," the name of a well-known female dancer, Hortensius responded mildly, "I would frankly prefer to be Dionysia, yes, Dionysia, than such as you, Torquatus: artless, loveless, witless" (Gell. *NA* 1.5.3). The last three words, spoken in Greek, culminate in *aprosdionusos*, an untranslatable pun underscoring Torquatus' boorishness. Hortensius' riposte suggests that effeminacy was not necessarily considered an "unqualified disgrace" and that "the game of masculinity might not always be worth playing in its entirety" (Williams 2010: 174).

5 One generation later, Maecenas was performing official duties for Augustus wearing loose flowing garments. Though that contributed to his reputation for effeminacy, it is likely that he was sending a political message, for the anonymous author of two *Elegies* in his honor defends Maecenas' mode of dress by arguing (with extended mythological examples) that leisurely attire was appropriate after Augustus' victory at Actium had ensured universal peace (1.49–102).

6 In Mart. 12.42 the scenario is expanded. Callistratus, who is pointedly described as "bearded," becomes Afer's bride, complete with all the trappings: torches, veil, ritual cries of "Talassio!" and dowry. "Enough already, Rome?" asks Martial. "Surely you're not waiting for him to give birth?"

7 The lightly armored *retiarius*, who dodged and parried rather than thrust, was predictably conceptualized as "effeminate": see Juv. 6.9–12.

8 Applied to an emperor this is probably a stock libel, although Vout (2007: 136–40) finds plausible implications of Roman hostility toward philhellenism. Nero is alleged to have gone through two wedding ceremonies, one in which he played the groom to the eunuch Sporus, whom he had had castrated (Suet. *Ner.* 28; Cass. Dio 62.28.2–3a, 63.13), and one in which he was the bride. Sources disagree on the name of the male "husband" involved in the latter ceremony (Pythagoras, Tac. *Ann.* 15.37 and Cass. Dio 62.28.3, 63.22.4; Doryphorus, Suet. *Ner.* 29). Likewise, the name of Elagabalus' "husband" is variously given as Zoticus, nicknamed Magirius or "Cook" (*SHA Heliogab.* 10.5) and Hierocles (Cass. Dio 79.15). In Dio's version, Hierocles, the established consort, employs an anti-aphrodisiac to ensure that Zoticus, despite his considerable physical endowments, does not replace him in Elagabalus' affections (79.17). That seems an imaginative effort to reconcile two separate slanders.

9 Brooten notes the paradoxical effect of making Megilla's masculinization central to the vignette while explicitly denying her a penis: the missing organ is constantly present to the reader's imagination (1996: 51–3). Haley, however, argues that Lucian's treatment of female homoeroticism, though admittedly voyeuristic (2002: 298), may be viewed positively because it destabilizes fixed categories of female sexual identity.

10 In Xenophon of Ephesus' *Ephesian Tale*, the hero Habrocomes' great friend is a bandit named Hippothous, whose own loss of Hyperanthes, his beloved, explains his willingness to help Habrocomes get back his wife Anthia. Similarly, Cleinias, cousin and friend of Cleitophon in Achilles Tatius' *Leucippe and Cleitophon*, quite early in the novel loses his boyfriend Charicles in a riding mishap, while another acquaintance, Menelaos, later reveals that he accidentally slew his youthful partner while hunting. In the novels, according to Perkins (1995: 72), pederastic relations end tragically because they are impelled by personal desire and serve no larger social purpose.

11 Cassius Dio (69.11.2) first reports Hadrian's official pronouncement, "he fell into the river," then

adds, "but the truth is, he was sacrificed [*hier-ourgêtheis*]." After mentioning that possibility, the fourth-century CE *Historia Augusta* obscurely hints at another explanation involving Antinous' beauty and Hadrian's obsessive lust (*SHA* Hadr. 14.6). Aurelius Victor, writing at about the same time, elaborates on the "willing sacrifice" theme (Aur. Vict. *Caes.* 14.8): to prolong Hadrian's life, another had to die in his place, and Antinous was the one person willing to do so. Euripides' *Alcestis* must have exerted some influence on that story-line.

12 Not all portraits identified by art historians as "Antinous" may be the genuine article. On the problems of attribution and authenticity see Vout 2007: 74–96.

13 On the basis of what survives, however, we should not conclude that Greek fiction fans preferred soft-focus sentiment while only tough-minded Romans went in for the grittier stuff. Scrappy papyri preserve fragments of two picaresque novels in Greek, Lollianus' *Phoenician Story* and the anonymous *Iolaus*, each recounting sensational events in lurid detail. Parsons, editor of the latter text, compares it to the *Satyrica* (1971). On Lollianus, see Winkler 1980.

14 "She" because the unexpressed antecedent *mentula* ("prick") is feminine. The first two lines of verse are quoted directly from Vergil's *Aeneid* 6.469–70, where Dido in the underworld refuses to respond to Aeneas' apology. The concluding phrase of the last line is from *Aen.* 9.436, in which young Euryalus, slumping in death, is compared to a poppy weighted down by heavy rain. Courtney 2001: 199 calls this "the wittiest joke in Petronius."

References

Anderson, W. S. 1982. *Essays on Roman Satire*. Princeton, NJ: Princeton University Press.

Ando, C. 2000. *Imperial Ideology and Provincial Loyalty in the Roman Empire*. Berkeley: University of California Press.

Bowie, E. 1994. "The Readership of Greek Novels in the Ancient World." In J. Tatum (ed.), *The Search for the Ancient Novel*. Baltimore: The Johns Hopkins University Press. 435–59.

Brooten, B. J. 1996. *Love between Women: Early Christian Responses to Female Homoeroticism*. Chicago: University of Chicago Press.

Cohen, D. and Saller, R. 1994. "Foucault on Sexuality in Greco-Roman Antiquity." In J. Goldstein (ed.), *Foucault and the Writing of History*. Oxford: Blackwell. 35–59.

Conte, G. B. 1996. *The Hidden Author: An Interpretation of Petronius's "Satyricon"*. Berkeley, CA: University of California Press.

Cooper, K. 1996. *The Virgin and the Bride: Idealized Womanhood in Late Antiquity*. Cambridge, MA: Harvard University Press.

Corbeill, A. 2002. "Political Movement: Walking and Ideology in Republican Rome." In D. Fredrick (ed.), *The Roman Gaze: Vision, Power, and the Body*. Baltimore, MD: The Johns Hopkins University Press. 182–215.

Courtney, E. 2001. *A Companion to Petronius*. Oxford: Oxford University Press.

Dixon, S. 1991. "The Sentimental Ideal of the Roman Family." In B. Rawson (ed.), *Marriage, Divorce, and Children in Ancient Rome*. Oxford: Clarendon Press. 99–113.

Edwards, C. 1993. *The Politics of Immorality in Ancient Rome*. Cambridge: Cambridge University Press.

Elsom, H. E. 1992. "Callirhoe: Displaying the Phallic Woman." In A. Richlin (ed.), *Pornography and Representation in Greece and Rome*. Oxford: Oxford University Press. 212–30.

Foucault, M. 1986. *The History of Sexuality, vol. 2: The Use of Pleasure*. Trans. R. Hurley. New York: Vintage Books. [Orig. pub. as *L'Usage des plaisirs*. Paris: Gallimard, 1984.]

—— 1988. *The History of Sexuality, vol. 3: The Care of the Self*. Trans. R. Hurley. New York: Vintage Books. [Orig. pub. as *Le Souci de soi*. Paris: Gallimard, 1984.]

Freudenburg, K. 2001. *Satires of Rome: Threatening Poses from Lucilius to Juvenal*. Cambridge: Cambridge University Press.

Garnsey, P. and Saller, R. 1987. *The Roman Empire: Economy, Society, and Culture*. Berkeley, CA: University of California Press.

Gleason, M. 1995. *Making Men: Sophists and Self-Presentation in Ancient Rome.* Princeton, NJ: Princeton University Press.

Goldhill, S. 1995. *Foucault's Virginity: Ancient Erotic Fiction and the History of Sexuality.* Cambridge: Cambridge University Press.

Gordon, P. 1997. "The Lover's Voice in *Heroides* 15: Or, Why is Sappho a Man?" In J. P. Hallett and M. B. Skinner (eds.), *Roman Sexualities.* Princeton, NJ: Princeton University Press. 274–91.

Haeckl, A. E. 2001. "Brothers or Lovers? A New Reading of the 'Tondo of the Two Brothers'." *Bulletin of the American Society of Papyrologists* 38: 63–78.

Haley, S. P. 2002. "Lucian's 'Leaena and Clonarium': Voyeurism or a Challenge to Assumptions?" In N. S. Rabinowitz and L. Auanger (eds.), *Among Women: From the Homosocial to the Homoerotic in the Ancient World.* Austin: University of Texas Press. 286–303.

Hallett, J. P. 1997 [1989]. "Female Homoeroticism and the Denial of Roman Reality in Latin Literature." In Hallett and Skinner (eds.), *Roman Sexualities.* 255–73.

Harrison, S. J. 2000. *Apuleius: A Latin Sophist.* Oxford: Oxford University Press.

Haynes, K. 2003. *Fashioning the Feminine in the Greek Novel.* London and New York: Routledge.

Joshel, S. R. 1997. "Female Desire and the Discourse of Empire: Tacitus' Messalina." In Hallett and Skinner (eds.), *Roman Sexualities.* 221–54.

Konstan, D. 1993. "Sexuality and Power in Juvenal's Second Satire." *Liverpool Classical Monthly* 18.1: 12–14.

—— 1994. *Sexual Symmetry: Love in the Ancient Novel and Related Genres.* Princeton, NJ: Princeton University Press.

Lambert, R. 1984. *Beloved and God: The Story of Hadrian and Antinous.* London: Weidenfeld & Nicolson.

Lendon, J. E. 1997. *Empire of Honour: The Art of Government in the Roman World.* Oxford: Clarendon Press.

MacAlister, S. 1996. *Dreams and Suicides: The Greek Novel from Antiquity to the Byzantine Empire.* London: Routledge.

MacMullen, R. 1974. *Roman Social Relations: 50 BC to AD 284.* New Haven, CT: Yale University Press.

McMahon, J. M. 1998. *"Paralysin Cave": Impotence, Perception, and Text in the "Satyrica" of Petronius.* Leiden: E. J. Brill.

Millar, F. 1981. "The World of the *Golden Ass.*" *Journal of Roman Studies* 71: 63–75.

Morales, H. 2008. "The History of Sexuality." In T. Whitmarsh (ed.), *The Cambridge Companion to the Greek and Roman Novel.* Cambridge: Cambridge University Press. 39–55.

Parker, H. N. 1997. "The Teratogenic Grid." In Hallett and Skinner (eds.), *Roman Sexualities.* 47–65.

Parlasca, K. 1966. *Mumienporträts und verwandte Denkmäler.* Wiesbaden: Franz Steiner.

Parsons, P. 1971. "A Greek *Satyricon*?" *Bulletin of the London University Institute of Classical Studies* 18: 53–68.

Perkins, J. 1995. *The Suffering Self: Pain and Narrative Representation in the Early Christian Era.* London: Routledge.

Richardson, T. W. 1984. "Homosexuality in the *Satyricon.*" *Classica et Mediaevalia* 34: 105–27.

Richlin, A. 1991. "Zeus and Metis: Foucault, Feminism, Classics." *Helios* 18: 160–80.

—— 1992. *The Garden of Priapus: Sexuality and Aggression in Roman Humor,* rev. edn. Oxford: Oxford University Press.

—— 1993. "Not before Homosexuality." *Journal of the History of Sexuality* 3.4: 523–73.

Rousselle, A. 1988 [1983]. *"Porneia": On Desire and the Body in Antiquity.* Trans. F. Pheasant. Oxford: Blackwell.

Sandy, G. N. 1999. "Apuleius' *Golden Ass*: From Miletus to Egypt." In H. Hofmann (ed.), *Latin Fiction: The Latin Novel in Context.* London: Routledge. 81–102.

Shaw, T. M. 1998. *The Burden of the Flesh: Fasting and Sexuality in Early Christianity.* Minneapolis, MN: Fortress Press.

Shumate, N. 1996. *Crisis and Conversion in Apuleius' "Metamorphoses".* Ann Arbor: University of Michigan Press.

Slater, N. W. 1990. *Reading Petronius.* Baltimore, MD: The Johns Hopkins University Press.

Stephens, S. A. 2008. "Cultural Identity." In T. Whitmarsh (ed.), *The Cambridge Companion to the Greek and Roman Novel.* 56–71.

Sullivan, J. P. 1991. *Martial: The Unexpected Classic.* Cambridge: Cambridge University Press.

Swain, S. 1996. *Hellenism and Empire: Language, Classicism and Power in the Greek World AD 50–250*. Oxford: Clarendon Press.

Taylor, R. 1997. "Two Pathic Subcultures in Ancient Rome." *Journal of the History of Sexuality* 7: 319–71.

Treggiari, S. 1991. *Roman Marriage: "Iusti Coniuges" from the Time of Cicero to the Time of Ulpian*. Oxford: Clarendon Press.

van Nijf, O. 2001. "Local heroes: athletics, festivals and elite self-fashioning in the Roman East." In S. Goldhill (ed.), *Being Greek under Rome: Cultural Identity, the Second Sophistic, and the Development of Empire*. Cambridge: Cambridge University Press. 306–34.

Veyne, P. 1978. "La Famille et l'amour sous le haut-empire romain." *Annales (ESC)* 33: 35–63.

Vout, C. 2007. *Power and Eroticism in Imperial Rome*. Cambridge: Cambridge University Press.

Whitmarsh, T. 2001. *Greek Literature and the Roman Empire: The Politics of Imitation*. Oxford: Oxford University Press.

—— 2005. *The Second Sophistic*. Oxford: Oxford University Press.

Williams, C. A. 2010. *Roman Homosexuality*. 2nd edn. Oxford: Oxford University Press.

Winkler, J. J. 1980. "Lollianos and the Desperadoes." *Journal of Hellenic Studies* 100: 155–81.

—— 1985. *"Auctor" and "Actor": A Narratological Reading of Apuleius's "The Golden Ass"*. Berkeley, CA: University of California Press.

Zeitlin, F. I. 1971. "Petronius as Paradox: Anarchy and Artistic Integrity." *Transactions of the American Philological Association* 102: 631–84.

Further Reading

Champlin, E. 2003. *Nero*. Cambridge, MA, and London: The Belknap Press of Harvard University Press. If the observations about bad emperors at the beginning of this chapter simply whetted your desire to know more, you should enjoy Champlin's biographical study of the archetypal bad emperor.

Gleason, M. 1995. *Making Men: Sophists and Self-Presentation in Ancient Rome*. Princeton, NJ: Princeton University Press. In addition to further information about Polemo and Favorinus, Gleason's monograph contains provocative chapters on aspects of oratorical training and their relation to concepts of gender.

Reardon, B. P. (ed.). 1989. *Collected Ancient Greek Novels*. Berkeley, Los Angeles, and London: University of California Press. Highly readable translations of all the Greek novels and fragments, with a fine general introduction and excellent notes.

Richlin, A. 1992. *The Garden of Priapus: Sexuality and Aggression in Roman Humor*. 2nd edn. New York: Oxford University Press. Authoritative demonstration of how Roman satire and invective work to assure (male) audiences of their social superiority by denigrating "outsider" groups.

Vout, C. 2007. *Power and Eroticism in Imperial Rome*. Cambridge: Cambridge University Press. Imaginative discussion of the part played by fantasies of an emperor's private life, inspired by statuary, panegyric, or even gossip and slander, in the formation of power relationships between the ruler and his subjects.

Whitmarsh, T. 2005. *The Second Sophistic*. Oxford: Oxford University Press. Short but informative introduction to Second Sophistic performance culture and literature, including a provocative chapter on "figured speech" conveying hidden meanings.

10

The Imperial Populace: Toward Salvation?

Civilizations have characteristic strategies for coming to grips with intangible realities, and the way such realities are conceptualized reveals basic facts about the way in which a society operates. In the United States and Britain, we normally resort to quantitative models when speaking of long-term historical trends because of our fundamental belief that scientific data, properly processed and analyzed, are closest to "truth." Consequently, we are most likely to ascribe realignments of the political or social infrastructure to measurable economic and demographic forces. To graph those forces, we make calculations and create tables using complex mathematical equations. The Romans, on the contrary, did not ground reality on numbers. Aside from interventions of nature – earthquakes, weather – they attributed the flow of events to an individual agent, namely the Great Man in power. This notion of historical causation meant that consequences perceived as injurious were ascribed to the moral failings of the emperor.

Under the Julio-Claudians, for example, the day-to-day machinery of administration was concentrated in the imperial household and managed by a staff made up of the *princeps*'s own former slaves. There were two pragmatic reasons for this development (Millar 1977: 70). As one might expect in a patronage system, government business had always been conducted mainly through personal contact, by means of petitions and favors – often in the private residence of the magistrate, as there were few public buildings designated for such purposes. Furthermore, the state did not equip its office-holders with a body of civil servants; except for certain paid staff (**apparitores**, see next section, 'The 99%'), executives organized their own teams of functionaries. Freedmen were placed in sensitive positions and entrusted with confidential matters because of the debt of loyalty they owed their former masters. During the reign of Claudius (41–54 CE) the freedmen Narcissus and Pallas were appointed to the highest offices in the imperial secretariat and served as the emperor's private advisors, becoming scandalously rich as a result. The wealth and

Sexuality in Greek and Roman Culture, Second Edition. Marilyn B. Skinner.
© 2014 John Wiley & Sons, Inc. Published 2014 by John Wiley & Sons, Inc.

influence of these upstarts infuriated the Senate. To convey the outrageousness of the situation, ancient historians go to defamatory extremes. Claudius is alleged to be the puppet of his wives and freedmen, conducting himself "as their servant rather than their emperor" (Suet. *Div. Claud.* 29) while they themselves make decisions of state (e.g., Narcissus orders Messalina's execution, Tac. *Ann.* 11.37). That is moralizing anecdote functioning as political allegory. We would put the same content into a graph and run it on the front page of *USA Today*: "Growth of Palatine Bureaucracy, AD 40–50." (Opinion page: "Is the Palatine Bureaucracy out of Control?" *Pro*: "Bureaucracy Should Answer to Representatives of Roman People," by P. Clodius Thrasea Paetus, *vir clarissimus. Con*: "Imperial Secretaries Must Report Only to Princeps," by Ti. Claudius Narcissus, *ab epistulis*.) Employed as they are for didactic purposes, then, historical anecdotes are not reliable sources of fact. Yet we can uncover patterns of collective thinking in such tales because, read with due caution, they offer clues to elite ideology (Saller 1980).

If we wish to proceed beyond ideology, though, we can attempt to devise our own quantitative measures for the ancient Roman world. That is a very tricky proceeding, as it greatly depends on accidents of survival. Statistical details such as prices or tax records are relatively scarce and limited in scope; almost all documentary information comes from Egyptian papyri, but Egypt was not a typical province. Archaeology can provide material evidence – settlement remains, for example – to corroborate notional projections such as population density within a defined geographical area. Numbers transmitted in literary or historical accounts, on the other hand, are prone to scribal error even when they are not grossly distorted; most population tallies, for example, are dismissed by one authority as "no more than symbolic values" inserted to add vividness or emphasis (Scheidel 2001: 49). By themselves such figures, even if they seem accurate and correctly transcribed, may still be virtually meaningless unless treated in context.

Nevertheless, certain data, taken in conjunction with other evidence, can supply parameters to guide further inference. One area of inquiry where that approach has been successfully adopted is ancient **demography** – crucial because of its underlying impact on social and economic institutions. In contrast to modern developed countries, where, as a result of the demographic transition, both birth and death rates are low,[1] high mortality rates in pre-industrial societies required production of more than two children to ensure that couples replaced themselves. Using model life tables and comparative data from later periods along with ancient source material (including an early form of actuarial table cited by the jurist Ulpian, *Dig.* 35.2.68 pr.), demographers calculate that Roman mortality rates were unusually elevated even by premodern standards, with an average life expectancy of only twenty-five years at birth (Frier 2000: 788–91). Estimates of fertility in adult Roman women are correspondingly high. For freeborn girls, universal marriage at an early age was conditioned by demands on reproductive capability: to maintain population at existing levels, and taking childhood mortality into account, the average woman reaching menopause must have borne a total of at least five to six children (ibid., 797). Even so, not all women produced that number of offspring, as many died in childbirth and others had no partners for some of their fecund years. Accordingly, marital fertility was doubtless even higher, ranging from six to nine children per female (Scheidel 2007: 41). Thus the patriarchal structures we have studied, with their resulting gender asymmetry, are best understood as responses to unremitting demographic pressures. That in turn will help explain why celibacy became a religious flashpoint in early Christian communities.

Census returns from Roman Egypt provide our sole quantifiable evidence for family reproductive strategies (Bagnall and Frier 1994: 137–59). When corrected statistically, they establish that the average age of maternity was a little over twenty-seven years. Divorcees or widows tended not to remarry after reaching thirty or thirty-five, placing an even greater burden of expectation on younger women. On the other hand, female fertility rates peak in the late twenties because of the prevalence of a "**natural fertility**" pattern in which married couples kept on having children as long as they were physically able, well into their thirties and forties. Although methods of contraception and abortion were known to physicians, there is no sign that families intentionally stopped procreation after a given number of births; instead, pregnancies were spaced out by "dampening" post-partum fecundity through prolonged breastfeeding. Although these data pertain to Egypt, and we cannot ascertain that a "natural fertility" pattern held good for the entire Roman empire, Scheidel, citing parallels in similar pre-transitional populations, believes its overall existence is the "most economical" conclusion (2001: 34).

Neither Augustus' marriage legislation nor satirists' attacks on selfish rich and childless women (e.g., Juv. 6.592–601) should lead us to think that family limitation as we know it today was practiced. True, ancient sources give the impression that child exposure was common, most frequently among the poor (Harris 1994). At the opposite end of the economic scale, competitive elites may have deliberately restricted childbearing to avoid partitioning inheritable assets (Muson. XV, Lutz 97–101; Scheidel 2007: 70). Ensuing declines in numbers and extinction of family lines then forced the ruling classes to provide avenues of upward mobility that allowed controlled infusion of qualified new blood. Yet the behavior of the affluent few was unrepresentative of the population as a whole and had no effect on demographic levels; whatever caused the decline of the Western Roman empire, it was not, despite comparisons drawn by modern doomsayers, a suicidal embrace of childfree independence in defiance of the common good. In fact, Frier has raised the possibility that overpopulation put a strain upon the "carrying capacity" of certain regions, with inevitable Malthusian consequences: "a rising population, as it outstrips available resources, gradually leads to increased mortality rates as a positive check on population growth, until a kind of demographic equilibrium is established at a level of mortality that is sufficiently high to counterbalance the upward surge in population" (2001: 155–6). In a worst-case situation where food became locally scarce, prices had risen because demand outweighed supply, and the poor were slipping below subsistence level, undernourishment would increase vulnerability to the catastrophic plagues that broke out in later centuries.

Study of demographic patterns is an instance of one of the strategies we must employ when dealing with the imperial populace, where we confront gradual and measured alteration in *mentalité* and habit. These long-term changes require us to formulate other sets of questions. Instead of concentrating upon the inner lives of those in power, as we have generally done so far when speaking of Rome, we need to envisage mass responses to an environment shaped by external factors beyond personal control. In the following pages, we will first survey the legal constraints placed upon non-elites from the beginning of the imperial period through the second century CE and estimate, as well as we can, relative prosperity among levels of the general population. Then we will review inscriptional and archaeological evidence from the Western empire, especially Pompeii, to gain insights into the domestic lives of the working classes during the principate and also into the cultural meanings ordinary people attached to erotic art and artifacts. Turning to the religious sphere, we will analyze the quest for greater surety in life and death driving the spread of interest in astrology, the occult arts, and numerous non-traditional cults including Christianity. With such background knowledge in place, we can conclude by assessing the sociological implications of Christian asceticism and Christian martyrdom. All these components arguably come into play as causal factors for the paradigm shift that resulted in the world of late antiquity.

The 99%

That the richest 1% of Americans control approximately 40% of the nation's wealth became an "Occupy" movement protest slogan in the fall of 2011. Ancient historians cite a comparable statistic for the Roman empire: what we have been calling the elites, those educated persons who possessed significant material resources and formed the governing class in Rome or smaller urban locales, constituted more or less one percent of the empire-wide population, lately estimated to be around 70 million at its demographic height during the mid-second century CE (Scheidel and Friesen 2009: 66).[2] Imperial legislation divided this cohort of individuals, designated by third-century jurists the *honestiores* ("more distinguished"), into three **ordines** or ranks determined by heredity and property qualifications: the 600 members of the senatorial order, with estates of at least one million sesterces each; the order of **equestrians**, freeborn Roman citizens possessing a minimum of 400,000 sesterces; and the **decurions**, or members of town councils, whose strength and property thresholds may have varied from one district to another.[3] Though approximating their numbers is extremely complicated, the economic historian Walter Scheidel has calculated that the three ranks combined embraced a minimum of 350,000, but not more than 500,000, persons including their families. In addition, perhaps 100,000 discharged veterans, some more well-off than others, were counted among the *honestiores* in recognition of army service (Scheidel 2006: 41–2).

All individuals outside this advantaged set, the 99% as it were, from the late second century on were termed *humiliores* ("less distinguished"). In the eyes of the law, they were subject to graver punishments for the same criminal act (*Dig.* 48.19.9.11 [Ulp.]). Penalties took corporeal form: a member of the *humiliores* might be sentenced to hard labor or executed by the cruelest methods imaginable, being crucified, thrown to the beasts, or burned alive, while those of honorable rank would instead be exiled. During the Republic even the poorest citizens had technically enjoyed bodily impunity, but Augustus extended the coercive powers of the urban prefect, the magistrate charged with keeping order, to controlling riotous citizens as well as slaves (*qui coerceret servitia et quod civium audacia turbidum*, Tac. *Ann.* 6.11.3). By this directive, he subsumed slaves and free non-elite citizens into a single group to be managed by threats of force (*vis*) and instituted a legal distinction based on status rather than civil privilege (Perkins 2009: 97). Over the next two centuries this discriminatory judicial system steadily took final form. Penalties inflicted on the lower class grew harsher as the conflation of slave and free broadened and irregular sanctions, once thought suitable only for slaves, came into wider use (Garnsey 1970: 152).

In practice, though, the financial and social structures were not as dichotomized as the legal division of *honestiores* and *humiliores* might imply. While historians avoid using the term "middle class" to designate those occupying an economic station below the wealthy elites but above the masses struggling at subsistence level, some segments of the population fit that description. One writer hypothesizes the existence of three economic classes, applying "class" in the popular (not the Marxist) sense: on top, the wealthy with access to power and education, living off the toil of others; below them, working households owning the means of production such as land or a shop, and dependent for income on family effort rather than on slaves; and at the bottom, laborers, some hired, mostly slave (Harris 1988: 604–5). Alternatively, Scheidel and Friesen, having deployed a mix of statistical models to chart the interfaces among economic indicators, arrive at percentage-based conclusions regarding class hierarchy (2009: 84–5):

> in the Roman Empire as a whole, a 'middling' sector of somewhere around 6 to 12 per cent of the population, defined by a real income of between 2.4 and 10 times 'bare bones' subsistence or 1 to 4 times 'respectable' consumption levels, would have occupied a fairly narrow middle ground between an élite segment of perhaps 1.5 per cent of the population and a vast majority close to subsistence level of around 90 per cent. In this system, some 1.5 per cent of households controlled 15 to 25 per cent of total income, while close to 10 per cent took in another 15 to 25 per cent, leaving not much more than half of all income for all remaining households.

These two formulations agree with earlier ones in envisioning a tremendously steep social pyramid where differences between extremes were immense and stratification was "pronounced" (MacMullan 1974: 89–90, 94). They nuance overly binary schemes, however, in arguing for gradation among the middling groups rather than stark polarization of rich and poor (Scheidel 2006: 43–5) and in acknowledging the economic contribution of such groups. Though reiterating that "'middling' incomes" were the exception, subsistence the norm, Scheidel and Friesen conjecture that households with some disposable income enhanced the supply of goods and the earnings of purveyors by complementing elite spending power (2009: 90–1). Harper (2011: 38–60) refines this tripartite model by grouping slave-owning households into four categories: the Illustrious and the Elite, again making up the wealthiest 1–1.5% of Roman society;

the Bourgeois, or sub-elite working population in towns; and the largest class, the Agricultural holdings of rich peasants and villagers in the countryside, where 80% of residents dwelt. Slaves themselves, by his reckoning, formed approximately ten percent of the entire fourth-century imperial population – just under 5 million souls.

Who were those folks in the middle? Epigraphical evidence drawn from Rome confirms the existence of thriving urban businesses (Joshel 1992: 106–12); archaeological investigations have unearthed traces of small and medium-sized family farms in all regions of the empire; papyrological records from Egypt attest to many functioning trades and professions (Lewis 1999: 134–55). Furthermore, although land holdings might remain unchanged over generations and sons follow fathers into a shop or a trade, there were avenues of upward mobility. Roman citizens of humble birth could enlist in the army, serve for the regulation twenty-five years, and upon discharge receive a substantial cash bonus; with their accumulated savings, this could be enough to qualify them for decurion status. Unlike veterans, prosperous freedmen legally remained *humiliores*, but they too might play a leading part in their communities. In the Western empire, wealth permitted them to serve as **Augustales**, officers of the imperial cult, paying high membership fees and making voluntary benefactions. Sponsoring sacrifices and entertainments and constructing public amenities were among the philanthropic duties expected of them. In return, they enjoyed privileges during their terms of office comparable to those of magistrates, including honorific emblems and special seating at the games. Inscriptions refer to them collectively as an *ordo* (*ILS* 6190 [Bovillae]; *ILS* 6141 and 6164 [Ostia]).

Apparitores, salaried attendants on Roman magistrates, were another, more heterogeneous, group, some of whom were freeborn and others former slaves.[4] Appointed through patronage, these public employees held continuing positions and often achieved conspicuous success, financial and social, by networking within their own professional associations. For ambitious freedmen and municipals, apparitorial posts were a critical first step in upward mobility, providing "access to society for those who had been excluded from it" (Purcell 1983: 121). Ostrow notes the similarities in social function between the orders of *Augustales* and *apparitores*: each gave competent individuals (or, in the case of freedmen, their freeborn sons) the opportunity to gain rewards, including equestrian status or local political honors (1990: 372–3). During the opening centuries of the empire, then, a select fraction of individuals not born into wealth could aspire to raise their fortunes through these means. Limited but ongoing social mobility was one building block of the social stability that distinguished an age in which the Mediterranean world enjoyed the **pax Romana** – an unprecedented time of foreign and domestic peace.

Gravestones and Walls

For the Roman world, as for few other ancient cultures, we are fortunate in having a large body of written materials that allow us a glimpse into the life experiences of non-elites. Documentary papyri and *ostraca* (inscribed pottery shards) from Egypt preserve tax records and receipts, petitions, wills, and other legal documents, even

Fig. 10.1 Marble grave relief showing a husband and wife. Rome, Italy *c*.80 BCE. Source: © The Trustees of the British Museum.

private letters. Inscriptions from widespread parts of the Empire record vows and offerings made by living individuals or memorialize the deceased. Tombstones, in fact, account for about three-quarters of the entire corpus of Latin inscriptions (Saller and Shaw 1984: 124). In addition to preserving names, social status, and occupations, they are an invaluable primary source for investigating the family unit. Here a key distinction between the higher and lower orders emerges. Among the propertied classes, marriages were arranged by adult relations to safeguard the orderly transmission of assets and advance familial goals. Divorce and remarriage were common in elite circles; and, while conjugal affection was valued, overall there was a relative absence of emotional investment (Bradley 1991). In contrast, non-elites frequently chose their own partners and formed bonds out of affection, and with a view to mutual aid. This was particularly true of slaves, who legally could not marry. Despite the formidable problems of maintaining ties that were not recognized in law and liable to be disrupted through sale or the master's sexual claims on a partner, slaves formed de facto marriages known as **contubernia** (literally "tent-sharing") and worked together to obtain manumission for themselves and any children born into slavery. The texture of married life in such "companionate unions" was very different from that in aristocratic households, and inscriptions, although formulaic, reflect the many ways in which partners depended upon each other for material and emotional support.

A Republican-era commemorative stele (*CIL* 1.2.1221, *ILS* 7472) set up in honor of his wife by a butcher on the Viminal Hill in Rome, now in the British Museum (GR 1867,0508.55), well illustrates that point (fig. 10.1). In the center the couple is depicted in relief, the wife kissing her husband's hand in a farewell gesture. On the left side, the man, Lucius Aurelius Hermia, praises her continence, loyalty, affection, and dutifulness. On the right, his spouse responds:

> In life I was named Aurelia Philematium; I was chaste, modest, unfamiliar with the crowd, faithful to my husband. He, whom I lack, alas! was a fellow-freedman of the same master and was truly a parent and more to me. He took me to his bosom when I was seven; at the age of forty I am stronger than death. Through my devotion he constantly flourished in the sight of all.

Both partners had been slaves, originally named just Hermia and Philematium, in the establishment of one Lucius Aurelius, who may have been connected with the consular **gens** *Aurelia*, a prominent Republican clan. Upon attaining their freedom, they became Roman citizens, each taking their former master's name as an emblem of their new social identities. Philematium came under the protection of Hermia when she was only seven years old and thus speaks of him as a parent as well as a husband. He may in fact have purchased her freedom in order to marry her once he, too, was free; the relatively low ratio of female to male slaves in aristocratic households meant that the latter had difficulty finding wives (Harper 2011: 72). Since Hermia gives his occupation as "butcher," his former master could have helped him set up a small business in return for a share of the profits; as it was thought demeaning for nobles to engage in commerce directly, third-party investments through freedmen were not unusual. In such a situation Philematium lived with her older spouse for thirty-three years, first as a fellow slave and then as his lawful wife, perhaps helping out in the butcher's shop. No children are named on the relief; none may have survived.

In passing under a man's protection at an early age, Philematium was relatively fortunate. Sexual use of slaves was institutionalized in Roman society. Unlike the wives and daughters of free men, female slaves were put on the same conceptual level as prostitutes in terms of sexual accessibility, since, like prostitutes, they were outside the bounds of public protection. Assault or violation of a slave was merely a crime against ownership, like injuring a draft animal (Harper 2011: 281–325, 426–31). In the Empire, furthermore, the primary source of new slaves was natural reproduction (Scheidel 1997; Harper 2011: 69–78). Slave pregnancy worked to the owner's financial advantage: the agronomist Varro discusses propagation of human beings under the same rubric as animal husbandry (*Rust.* 2.1.26, 10.6–7). In law the child of a slave mother was deemed to increase the value of an estate and had to be surrendered if a suit for recovery was brought (*Dig.* 5.3.27 pr. [Ulp.]). Columella, author of another agricultural manual, recommends that, as an incentive to procreation, a woman who has reared four children should be given her freedom (*Rust.* 1.8.19). It follows, obviously, that masters would not be likely to manumit females still capable of childbearing; such women, especially if employed as domestic servants, would also have few opportunities to amass the sum needed to buy themselves out of slavery (Treggiari 1976: 91–2). Their best hope of obtaining freedom was through entering into *contubernium*. Though technically illegitimate, children born of unions between a freed mother and a slave father were themselves freeborn citizens, as they followed maternal status. Hence we find inscriptions in which a freed wife's name precedes that of her still enslaved spouse because the couple wished to stress the highest social level they had so far achieved. Giving future offspring a better start in life meant that improving the mother's legal position took precedence (Flory 1984: 217–18).

Among the free poor, too, marriage was regarded as a desirable state. From the late Republic onward, as we saw, gravestones attest to its popularity. In the city of Rome at least, there is no evidence for two freeborn persons who had the right to marry forming an informal living-together arrangement instead (Rawson 1974: 289). Even soldiers on active service, until the third century CE ineligible to marry, still entered into lasting relationships; when the soldier was discharged, such previously existing bonds were legitimized. Instances in which the female partner is referred to as a concubine as opposed to a wife involve differences in rank – a freeborn man and a freed woman, for example – and suggest that marriage between the two was either legally impossible or socially unacceptable, although the partners use the same terms of love and respect toward each other that spouses do (Dixon 1992: 93).

Some unusual family arrangements do surface. The epitaph of Allia Potestas (*CIL* 6.37965 = *CLE* 01988) pays tribute to a freedwoman said to have lived with two lovers at once, creating an attachment between them like that of the mythical friends Orestes and Pylades. The dedicator, her patron, praises her as hard-working and chaste, as though she were a respectable *matrona*, then oversteps propriety by describing her physical attributes (eyes, hair, breasts, legs, not to mention her "hard hands") with devastating frankness. In *CIL* 6.26451, where the thirty-year-old Servilia Successa is commemorated by her *contubernales* ("partners") Primus and Secundio, we again seem to have a polygamous union – unless these are the pseudonyms of Servilia's "first" (*primus*) and "second" (*secundus*) husbands. While successive partners might conceivably have honored her jointly, it is difficult to think of a reason why false names would be put on the monument. Other inscriptions in which a woman designated as a *contubernalis* is commemorated by two men might only mean that a family friend had joined the bereaved husband in erecting the tombstone (for example, *CIL* 6.6647 and 6.28534).

Servilius Rufus, a former slave, commissioned a funerary monument for himself and, named in the following order, his wife (*uxor*), a concubine who, he indicates, has passed away, and then another wife (misspelled *uxsor*), all of freed status (*CIL* 6.1906). It is unclear whether the unions were contracted in the order listed, or whether the concubine was concurrent with one or the other of the wives. (If so, Rufus may have broken the law, as a late legal source dictates that a man cannot take a woman as his concubine while still married [Paulus *Sent.* 2.20.1].) However, the concubine could have been the earliest; in that case, the first wife's name, because of her higher status as a legally married spouse, precedes that of the concubine. The second wife's name may have been added later, after the monument was already erected, for the variant spellings of *uxor* hint at two different carvers (Rawson 1974: 292–3).

What about commemorations of same-sex partnerships? Slaves who had been boyfriends are warmly remembered. M. Ulpius Vannius, a centurion, erects a monument (*AE* [1929] 106) to the sixteen-year-old Diadumenus, the son of his freedman Felicio, whom he designates his "foster child" (**alumnus**) and "home-born slave" (**verna**); the youth was probably his bed-mate as well, for Ulpius also refers to him affectionately as *delicatus*, a term for the passive slave partner (Phang 2001: 274). Thus no stigma attached to the young slave who had served his master in that way. But it is significant that there is no Latin equivalent for the "long-time companion" of contemporary obituary notices (significant, too, that this very term has emerged into use among us only recently). *Contubernalis*, which when applied to opposite-sex partners indicates a sexual relationship in which at least one party is or had been a slave, usually has the literal meaning "fellow soldier" when one man sets up a memorial to another. Marked language may express special ties. An inscription from Dalmatia (*ILJug.* 3.02617 = *AE* [1934] 00284) honors Thelonicus, a former *retiarius*, who was awarded his freedom by the people. The dedicants are Xustus, his friend (*amicus*), and Pepticius, his comrade (*sodalis*), presumably both slave gladiators too. Does the distinction in terminology imply a difference in the relationships? We will never know. A funerary relief from the Augustan period depicts two women, their right hands clasped in the traditional marriage gesture (British Museum Sculpture 2276, *CIL* 6.3.18524; Brooten 1996: fig. 7). The inscription beneath the relief identifies them as Fonteia Eleusis and Fonteia Helena, former slaves in the same household. Much later, another party recut the marble relief to transform the figure on the left into a man – and perhaps disguise the real nature of their attachment (Brooten 1996: 59–60). This interpretation is not the only possible one, however, and it is the most controversial. The only certain conclusion we can draw is that epigraphical evidence of coeval same-sex unions, if it exists at all, is extremely scarce. Thus the absence of explicit testimony tells us something.

Other kinds of inscribed records capture more ephemeral moments. The fourth volume of the *Corpus of Latin Inscriptions* is given over to messages painted or scratched on walls from Pompeii, Herculaneum, and Stabiae. Prices of male and female prostitutes are listed (as low as two *asses*, or about the cost of a cup of passable wine, *CIL* 4.1679 and 4024). References to sex are ubiquitous. Scribblers declare their affection, boast, trade insults and make raunchy jokes (for examples, see Williams 2010: 291–301). On the walls of the notorious "purpose-built brothel" now visited by busloads of tourists (building VII.12.18–20), low-status customers engaged in a competitive discourse on masculinity, affirming their own prowess, questioning the virility of other patrons, and exaggerating the lubricity of the women serving there (Levin-Richardson 2011). Some of the brothel writers' names have been found in additional neighborhood contexts, indicating a localized clientele who knew and frequently interacted with each other (Franklin 1986).

Unless a writer signs her name, we have no way of determining sex. There are a few inscriptions apparently composed by females (e.g., *CIL* 4.1679 and 8873; see Woeckner 2002). Still, it is a safe bet that men were responsible for most of the graffiti, as the literacy rate among non-elite women was no doubt low. Two erotic inscriptions, however, invite special consideration of authorial gender. The first (*CIL*

4.5092), found in the peristyle, or inner courtyard, of house IX.5.11, is a six-line poem in iambics, apparently broken off before it was finished:

> If you were feeling the fires of love, mule driver,
> you would be hurrying more, so that you might see (your) Venus.
> I love a good-looking [boy] youth. Strike the whip, I beg, let's go.
> You're drunk. Let's go. Take up the reins and shake them.
> Bring me to Pompeii, where love is sweet.   5
> You are mine ...

Pompeians were avid theatergoers, as physical facilities, house decoration, and, naturally, graffiti all attest (Franklin 1987). Throughout the Empire, popular culture was song-oriented: even persons with little formal education were trained from infancy to memorize and could readily pick up music by ear (Horsfall 2003: 11–17). Ovid pictures the Roman masses, the **plebs**, picnicking at the festival of Anna Perenna, drinking, singing "whatever they have learned at the theaters," and clapping in rhythm (*Fast.* 3.535–6). With their flattering allusion to Pompeii as an erotic playground, the verses above might come from a skit performed by a traveling troupe. They seem to have been adapted to the writer's private circumstances through the alteration in the third line, where he or she first inscribed *puerum*, "boy," then inserted *iuvenem*, "youth," above it. Since the two terms are metrically identical, it is possible that a misremembered word was corrected or that the line was simply changed for euphony (*iuvenem* assonates pleasantly with the surrounding Latin words). Yet *puerum* carries lingering homoerotic connotations, implying a male speaker and presumably also a male writer. With *iuvenem*, applied to adolescents on the brink of manhood and thus partners more suitable for girls, one can posit that the maker of the graffito (if not the song composer) might have been female (Stevenson 2005: 50–1). Whether or not the argument is compelling, it has at least been broached.

A better case has been submitted for the female authorship of another graffito, *CIL* 4.5296. Like the above inscription, it was scratched onto a painted wall, in this instance the far corner of a passageway between a narrow street and the interior of a small house containing just two rooms and a courtyard. The dwelling (house IX.9.6) is located next door to that of a professional sign-painter, and the economic level of the household was apparently upper working-class. Visitors passing through the entrance hallway (surprisingly well decorated and well secured) would have been fewer in number than those attending the wealthy civic grandees in their atrium houses. Most of them, perhaps, were relatives and close friends.

CIL 4.5296 is a poem of nine lines in irregular meter. Milnor, in a comprehensive discussion of the inscription and its surroundings (2013: Ch. 4), translates as follows:

> Oh, would that it were permitted to grasp with my neck your little arms
> as they entwine [it] and to give kisses to your delicate little lips.
> Come now, my little darling (**pupula**), entrust your pleasures to the winds.
> (En)trust me, the nature of men (*virorum*) is insubstantial.
> Often as I have been awake, lovesick (*perdita*), at midnight,   5

you think on these things with me: many are they whom Fortune lifted high;
these, suddenly thrown down headlong, she now oppresses.
Thus, just as Venus suddenly joined the bodies of lovers,
daylight divides them and if (?)

Care was taken to make the text legible and attractive. The lettering is neat,
Milnor points out, with consistent spelling overall and words separated by dots
("interpuncts"). In addition, the graffito was marked on a white panel framed by a
decorative border, positioned in order to blend in with, not interrupt, the painted
decoration.[5] The lines are a tissue of romantic commonplaces: longing to embrace
and kiss the beloved, plea for reciprocity, warning against other suitors' fickleness,
complaint of sleeplessness – and lastly a four-line reflection upon Fortune's volatility
and the precariousness of love. What is exceptional is the gender of the parties.
Since the person addressed as *pupula* in line 3 and the speaker's self-characterization
as *perdita* in line 5 are both grammatically feminine, the poem appears to be an
erotic message from one woman to another. Sexual difference seems deliberately
invoked by the admonition that male nature is "insubstantial [*levis*]," an express
twist on a charge ordinarily aimed at capricious elegiac mistresses. Against Copley's
contention (1939) that the passage is a continuous quotation in hexameters, Milnor
posits that it, like some other instances of Pompeian graffiti, is a cento of elegiac
snippets intended to be read as a single poem. Dramatic shifts in tone achieved
through juxtaposition of formerly unrelated extracts convey a complicated range of
meanings, including the ironic redirection of misogynist sentiments. Within a literary
culture ferociously opposed to same-sex female desire, such a profession of
homoerotic constancy would be unparalleled – but, as a verbal collage, possible.

In the Eye of the Beholder

The relative ease with which we grasp the ideological implications of female gender
on state monuments and statuary (Chapter 8) might lead us to suppose that the
sexual content of Roman visual art conveys equally straightforward meanings. That is
not the case, for many representations, including models of organs and actual images
of copulation, had other connotations than those our culture would assign to them.
Some images that we would categorize as suggestive or even lewd were apparently
not intended to elicit a prurient response from Roman viewers: unexpurgated images
may have been created for humorous purposes or, alternatively, to project an aura of
luxury, elegance, and high status (Clarke 1998: 12–13, 275–8). If we postulate a
cultural understanding that sex could be "read" in various metaphoric senses, we can
examine visual art from the early and middle empire to learn what graphic sexual
content expressed to viewers who were, for the most part, of the "middling" classes.
Let us consider a few examples of unexpected cultural messages.

Portraits of deceased citizen women as goddesses were popular in affluent circles
during the first and second centuries CE. Allegorical court art supplied a visual
language for endowing human figures with divine attributes. When a woman is

represented as a bountiful Ceres her nurturing capacity is aptly commemorated. Nude portrayals of respectable Roman matrons as Venus, however, raise questions of decorum, to say nothing of kitsch. First, they break with official Julio-Claudian iconography, for female members of the imperial family are modestly draped when shown as Venus. Second, the imposition of a portrait head of a mature woman upon a youthful and idealized body strikes the modern beholder as ludicrous. Neither the nudity of the statue nor the incongruity between the head and the torso created a problem for ancient audiences, though, because the messages transmitted by these statues were not literal ones. Instead of shaming the matron by showing her naked, the divine body represented her as fertile, a fitting corollary to the participation of respectable wives in Venus cults that encouraged the harnessing of sexuality to the goals of the family and the state (D'Ambra 1996: 221). Moreover, the women so portrayed were chiefly freedwomen, for whom borrowing the pose of the Capitoline Aphrodite was a claim to classical learning as well as a way of imitating the artistic practices of the imperial house. Nude female portrait statues remind us that, conditioned as it was by a different set of cultural expectations, the ancient viewer's aesthetic response to something that to us appears scandalous may have been blasé.

Ancient replicas of male genitalia are another example of objects with social meanings distinct from those we would attach to them. We noted earlier that the phallus was a standard good-luck charm and a protection against malign influences. As a cultural symbol, it was also a source of preposterous fun, as art and literature dealing with the phallic god Priapus indicate. Priapus is the protector of gardens and orchards, and his most noteworthy feature is his gigantic sexual organ. With this he threatens to rape intruders anally, orally, or vaginally, depending on age and sex. The *Carmina Priapea* is a collection of eighty anonymous poems on that theme, some coarse, others witty and extremely learned, most attempting to be downright hilarious whether we find them so or not. A good deal of the humor lies in the sophistication of the verses that treat such unpromising material.

Visually, a painting of Priapus weighing his member (fig. 10.2) from the **House of the Vettii** at Pompeii tells an analogous joke: the counterweight to the god's organ is a large sack of coins, and the two are nicely in balance. The phallus is worth its weight in gold (Williams 2010: 100), or, to reverse the idea, money and potency – sexual, social, or political – amount to the same thing. This painting is right in the entrance hall of the house, where no visitor would miss it. It is apotropaic, of course, a spectacular defense against the Evil Eye, but it is also an in-your-face declaration of having arrived. The house belonged to the brothers A. Vettius Restitutus and A. Vettius Conviva, former slaves who had amassed a considerable fortune and spent a good deal of it turning their large home into a showplace of offbeat, sometimes elegant, more often quirky, visual design. Self-made men just like the fictional Trimalchio, the Vettii indicated through this remarkable painting that wealth had been their passport to standing and respect in the community.

Phalluses are an ornamental motif in Roman art. They appear by themselves in reliefs and mosaics from Pompeii, Herculaneum, and Ostia, and they can also form part of a larger decorative ensemble (Johns 1982: 64–72, with figs 46 and 47, 52–4). Examples of the latter include wind-chimes (***tintinnabula***) in which the phallus, the

Fig. 10.2   Priapus weighing his penis. Roman wallpainting. Photo: George Tatge. Location: Casa dei Vettii, Pompeii, Italy. Source: Alinari/Art Resource, NY.

key element, is strung with bells, themselves apotropaic devices. Often the phallus is given features of an animal, such as wings, legs or a tail, to endow it with bestial sexual vigor. A bronze *tintinnabulum* from Pompeii (fig. 10.3) takes this conceptual flight of fancy to the extreme, for it represents a beast-fighter about to slay the savage animal that is his own penis. In doing so, he will castrate himself. For Carlin Barton (1993: 73), the artifact epitomizes the strange ideological contradiction at the core of the gladiator's masculinity. Sexual desire at its most extreme turns aggressively upon the desiring subject, triggering a corresponding rage at one's own body. This icon accordingly marks the ultimate fusion of sexuality with violence.

But would a Roman passer-by, confronting this object as it hung in an entryway, have regarded it that gravely? It may simply have been designed to provoke startled amusement (Johns 1982: 68). Discussing the work of the classical Greek painter Parrhasius of Ephesus, Pliny the Elder observes that in his spare time he painted miniature sexual scenes, "getting recreation from this kind of impertinent joke" (Plin. *HN* 35.72). Laughter is itself apotropaic; and for the likelihood that sexual imagery could be a source of mirth, releasing tension and anxiety, we can cite a recently discovered series of paintings in the changing room (*apodyterium*) of Pompeii's Suburban Baths. These baths were a private facility with considerable luxury features, used by both men and women, though possibly at separate times of the day. In the dressing room, above the shelf supporting numbered wooden boxes

Fig. 10.3 Ithyphallic bronze *tintinnabulum*, gladiator figure fighting a wild-cat shaped phallus with bells. Pompeiian. Location: Museo Archaeologico Nazionale, Naples, Italy. Source: Fotografica Foglia/Scala/Art Resource, NY.

where bathers would have stored their clothes, a painter has depicted first the shelf and boxes themselves in a *trompe l'oeil* illusion, and then, in the register above that, a series of erotic vignettes. Although the pictorial program is incomplete, being preserved on only one wall, the scenes, several of them unique, increase in shock value as the viewer progresses: after two pictures of male–female lovemaking, in one of which the woman mounts the man, they successively depict a woman performing fellatio, a man performing cunnilingus, two women copulating, apparently using a dildo, a sexual threesome of two men and a women, a foursome of two men and two women, and a nude man, perhaps a poet, with grotesquely exaggerated and deformed testicles (Clarke 1998: 212–40, with plates 9–16). Because they are placed so as to take the visitor by surprise, and because they are to be found in a room where a bather, having undressed, would first feel exposed to the Evil Eye (and the judgmental assessments of other bathers), their presence is best explained as a tactic for dispelling self-consciousness: these images violate Roman sexual acculturation so outrageously that laughter is the only conceivable response (Clarke 2002: 155, 156). What we have here, quite literally, is locker-room humor. Shortly before the eruption of Vesuvius in 79 CE, incidentally, the series of little pictures was painted over with simple decorative motifs – possibly, Clarke suggests, at the behest of a new and more prudish owner of the establishment.

Beginning in the Hellenistic period, and continuing well into the imperial Roman era, representations of sexual congress are also employed as decorative motifs in wall paintings and on household artifacts. The persistence of the iconography is noteworthy (Brendel 1970: 54–69). Although there are exceptions to the rule, including homoerotic ones, the usual composition features a man and woman on a bed coupling in one of several positions. This repertoire of standard positions (**figurae**) may have originated, Brendel thinks, with Greek how-to manuals explaining sexual techniques visually as well as textually. We learned earlier that sex handbooks were produced by Hellenistic writers (probably by men for men, despite their attribution to female authors) as part of a burgeoning interest in feminine psychology and the emotional dynamics of heterosexual affairs. Certainly, the mood of these erotic scenes is soft and romantic, even when they appear on mass-produced goods. Crafts borrow images from each other, creating an art that bridges class boundaries. The same images, and variations upon images, are reproduced in frescos, cameo glass, expensive gold and silver vessels, and ordinary terracotta ware for the general population. Despite the homogeneity of the representations, however, their purpose differed, depending upon whether they were being manufactured for the elite or the less wealthy consumer.

In *Tristia* 2, his poetic epistle addressed to Augustus from Tomis, Ovid defends the content of his verse by citing other erotic materials, literary and visual, that circulate at Rome exposed to matrons' eyes without incurring the emperor's displeasure. "In our houses," he points out emphatically, "just as the ancient figures of heroes are conspicuously described by an artist's hand, so there is in another place a little tablet that reveals the various conjunctions and postures for sex" (521–4).[6] Archaeological evidence confirms Ovid's testimony by disclosing that at this period bedrooms (**cubicula**) in the homes of the wealthy might contain panels of men and women in intimate situations. The decorative scheme of the surviving bedrooms in the Villa Farnesina, a luxury villa on the bank of the Tiber dated to approximately 20 BCE, includes small paintings in the upper registers depicting the preliminaries to intercourse: servants make preparations while the couple exchange glances or kiss. Nowhere is actual coitus depicted, although Ovid states that it could be.

What would scenes of sexual congress be doing in a respectable bedroom? Even if they did copy illustrations in sex manuals, it is unlikely that they served the practical aim of cementing marital relations by teaching young couples new ways of making love. Myerowitz suggests that erotic pictures simultaneously mirrored, enlarged, and theatricalized the activities taking place in their surroundings, so that the people who performed them would think consciously about what they were doing (1992: 147–52). Sexuality was thus "domesticated" by becoming the object of critical reflection rather than instinctive response – the precise opposite of our own culturally encouraged predisposition to lose ourselves in the sheer physicality of the act. John Clarke contends, however, that the Villa Farnesina images must have been purely decorative, for they are simply one ingredient in a complex iconographic ensemble that reproduced the experience of visiting a picture gallery (1998: 96, 106–7).

Cities on the Bay of Naples destroyed by the eruption of Vesuvius in 79 CE were centers of feverish social mobility, where private houses – in their size, programs of decoration, and furnishings – played a crucial part in establishing the relative status

Fig. 10.4 Fresco of erotic scene from Pompeii, House of Caecilius Iucundus. Location: Museo Archeologico Nazionale, Naples, Italy. Source: Erich Lessing/Art Resource, NY.

of the owners by proclaiming their resources and refinement (Wallace-Hadrill 1994: 183–6). In Pompeii, erotic art has moved from the upper zone of the wall fresco to the center of the wall and from the bedroom to the reception areas.[7] When the freedman banker L. Caecilius Iucundus (of *Cambridge Latin Course* fame) remodeled his house after a major earthquake in 62 CE, he commissioned an opulent fresco (fig. 10.4) for a prominent place on the wall of a colonnaded portico. A servant approaches a bed on which a reclining man entreats a seated, reluctant woman, seen only in profile, her back turned to the viewer and one arm stretched out behind her. This is an unusually evocative composition: will the hesitant woman yield, or no? Its expensive detail, which included applied gold leaf, and its distinctive location indicate that Caecilius Iucundus wanted visitors to stop and inspect it. Similarly, the wealthy proprietor of the House of the Centenary equipped one room in a lavish dining suite with two central panels, one on either side, showing couples engaged in intercourse.

Even the poor opted for such displays. Although elsewhere he used shoddy construction methods and sparse decoration, the occupant of one tiny home (house I.13.16) turned half of his ground-floor footage into a garden with a dining room whose back wall contained an eclectic mix of images. In the company of a clumsy rendering of statues of Venus and Priapus with a live peacock between them, a sketchy landscape, two salvaged marble heads of Hercules and Bacchus fitted into improvised niches, and an array of phalluses (two ejaculating), was a scene of a man and woman copulating. All these representations of erotic congress, from the most sophisticated to the crudest, were claims to status. What had begun as a fashion among the elite at Rome was now diffused among the population of smaller towns, where it marked aspirations, however naive, to upper-class chic. The shabby "purpose-built brothel" catering to the poor, with small cubicles and masonry platforms for beds, featured paintings above the doors of the individual cribs showing couples making love in luxurious settings, on comfortable couches. These scenes "encode fantasies of upper-class sexual luxuries for viewers who could not afford them" (Clarke 1998: 205).

One scene in the brothel (1998: 201–2 and fig. 83) does not portray a couple having intercourse, but instead focuses upon a picture within the picture. A naked man reclines on a bed and points to a tablet hanging on the wall, while a woman, fully clothed, stands beside the bed and follows his gaze. While the loss of color in the fresco makes it difficult to decipher what they actually view, evidently they are drawing inspiration from the tablet before them. Even more indicative of the circumstances in which such art could be viewed is a bronze mirror cover from the first century CE showing a man and an elegantly coifed and bejeweled woman making love on a couch: above their bodies hangs a painting of a couple also engaged in sex but using a different position (Johns 1982: fig. 35). The ambience, presented in fascinating detail, is wholly domestic: a puppy sits on a stool by the bed. Still, it is unlikely that this is a scene in a private home, for the revealing frontal position of the woman, who is nude except for a necklace and armbands and a long chain or garland that follows the contours of her body, is almost certainly that of a courtesan.

Among extant depictions of sexual acts, images of heterosexual intercourse predominate, but a few portrayals of male same-sex coupling have survived. Some are found, interestingly enough, on mass-produced glazed terracotta ware, known as **Arretine pottery**, which was manufactured in the Italian town of Arretium (modern Arezzo) during the Augustan period. Arretine ware was widely exported all over the empire and thus furnishes a standard of popular taste; in another attempt to copy the fashions of the wealthy, its designs imitate those on embossed gold and silver vessels. Explicit sexual images are relatively infrequent among the pottery fragments. However, we possess pieces of both clay vase molds and actual vases that show men penetrating boys, alternating in the same composition with portrayals of man–woman intercourse in which the woman squats above the man's erect penis.

The Warren Cup

From workaday Arretine pottery we can segue, as a kind of case study, to the illustrations of male–male lovemaking most frequently discussed by Roman art historians today, those on the so-called Warren Cup (GR 1999.4–26.1) purchased by the British Museum in 1999 for £1.8 million. This is an exquisitely worked silver *kantharos* (drinking cup) named after its first modern owner, the American-born antiquities collector Edward Perry Warren (1860–1928). Decorated silverware was produced for prosperous members of the middle class, and an unusual design suggests a private commission (D. Williams 2006: 35–6). The Warren Cup displays two *repoussé* (embossed) reliefs with smaller details incised. Side A (fig. 10.5) shows a pair of adult males making love on a bed. The bearded

older man, garlanded with a laurel wreath, penetrates the younger man lying atop him, who supports himself by clutching a strap with one hand; with the other he presses his lover's hand against his hip. There is a lyre poised on an open chest above and behind the bed. A slave boy with close-cropped curly hair, standing in a doorway, glances at the couple while entering or leaving the room. Although the motif of the observing slave occurs in other erotic paintings (such as the fresco from the House of Caecilius Iucundus in fig. 10.4), the iconography of the scene as a whole, with its relatively grown-up partners, is unparalleled.

Side B (fig. 10.6), conversely, features a pederastic composition also found on Arretine ware and expensive cameo glass: a young man enters a much

Fig. 10.5 The Warren Cup, side A. Lovemaking, man and youth. Source: © The Trustees of the British Museum.

Fig. 10.6 The Warren Cup, side B. Lovemaking, man and boy. Source: © The Trustees of the British Museum.

(Continued)

The Warren Cup — Continued

younger partner, clearly a boy, who lies on his left side fully exposed to the viewer's eye. However, there is one telling difference between this and other examples of the pattern. Instead of gazing affectionately at one another, as couples do elsewhere, the man looks down and the boy (whose long lock of hair, falling down his back, designates his status as feminized slave, *delicatus*) stares out into space as though distancing himself from what is happening. On the wall of this room, a double flute (*aulos*) hangs as a pendant to the lyre on Side A, and two long folds of drapery separate the scenes.

The Warren Cup was reportedly found at Bittir in Judaea, near Jerusalem, along with coins of the emperor Claudius. Stylistically, experts date its manufacture to the early first century CE, but, because it shows signs of heavy wear, it may have remained in use over two generations (Williams 2006: 45–9). At first glance, the panels on its sides offset each other. Both conform to the protocols of ancient sexuality by showing a younger receptive partner, but the difference in ages is greater on Side B. Are we meant to understand that the age gaps differentiate two varieties of sexual practice, as the

paired coitus of same-sex and opposite-sex couples does on Arretine ware? What about the careful teamwork between the partners on Side A, in opposition to the inert and detached compliance of the boy on Side B? Visual cues – the beard worn by the older partner, his laurel wreath, and the elegant lyre – give the Side A vignette a "Hellenizing feel" and may be intended as a contrast to the more conventionally Roman encounter on Side B, with its explicit anal penetration of a non-citizen boy (C. A. Williams 2010: 101–2).[8] Yet other iconographic correspondences – the convivial wreaths, the musical instruments – may indicate that both scenes take place in a Greek fantasy world. In any case, the modeling of all the heads is highly indebted to Augustan-era portraiture (Clarke 1998: 71–2, 87). Even if given Greek trappings, the participants are thus denoted as Roman types. Furthermore, although erotic scenes occur on other silver vessels, the craftsmanship of the Warren Cup is so elegant, and the images so distinctive, that drawing conclusions about general sexual attitudes from the evidence it presents may be ill-advised. It is one of a kind.[9]

Such pederastic scenes are quite unlike those on classical Greek vases, and the implications of the differences are well worth noting. First, the act of penetration is distinctly pictured: the man is entering his boy partner from the rear. Second, the boy welcomes his lover's embraces, for in one variant (Clarke 1998: 76, fig. 26) he grasps the man's arm, presumably to draw him closer, and in another (1998: 77, fig. 27) the couple are kissing. As the Greek ideological construction of boy-love required the citizen youth to take no pleasure in the passive role, pederastic anal intercourse is almost never shown on Attic pottery, and resistance to courtship is far more frequent than receptivity. Roman art is not caught in that ideological bind because it is assumed that the penetrated boy is a slave or prostitute (Williams 2010: 101). Consequently, artists are free to convey a mood of mutual tenderness between males (Clarke 1998: 78). Furthermore, the fact that images of pederastic copulation alternate on the same vase with heterosexual scenes confirms that the practices were regarded as equivalent. In the published record, finally, pictures of heterosexual congress far outnumber homoerotic ones, but that does not necessarily indicate that the latter theme was comparatively unpopular. Instead, it may hint that many depictions of man–boy intercourse either remain unpublished or were selectively destroyed upon discovery (Williams 2010: 351 n. 150). When analyzed circumspectly, then, Arretine ware can provide some evidence, although restricted, for ordinary users' reception of homoerotic artistic matter.

"O Isis und Osiris ..."

Despite a thick overlay of Masonic symbolism, Tamino and Pamina's ordeal in Mozart's opera *The Magic Flute* corresponds to the basic initiatory pattern informing the **mystery religions** of antiquity. Freed at last of prior erroneous beliefs about the wicked intentions of Sarastro and his college of priests, the young couple and their bird-catcher friend Papageno are subjected to trials in which their mutual devotion, courage, and obedience are tested. Upon passing those tests (Papageno with a "D"), all receive rewards – for the bird-catcher, a little wife to cherish and for Tamino and Pamina, enrollment in the fellowship of Sarastro's temple. Through struggle, terror and ignorance have been replaced by firm knowledge.

Ancient mysteries likewise rewarded the worshipper with knowledge and experience of the sacred not available through participation in civic rituals. This does not mean that state cult was hollow or perfunctory. Indeed, the Romans prided themselves, as a people, on their religiosity. In a treatise exploring current theological doctrines, Cicero makes his Stoic adherent Balbus assert: "If we choose to compare our mores with those of foreigners, we will find that in other things we are merely their equals or even their inferiors, but in religion – that is, the veneration of deities – we are far superior" (*Nat. D.* 2.3.8). As his subsequent remarks indicate, however, Balbus has in mind the meticulous attention to portents and augury demanded of those priests or magistrates charged with determining the will of the gods and maintaining favorable rapport with them. Religious scruple, in this sense, aimed at the communal, not the personal, good; it was left up to individuals to work out their own relationships with the divine. For many, the official succession of annually recurring festivals and mundane activities, coupled with family prayers at a household shrine, might well have been enough. Someone with strong spiritual leanings could take a given deity as a patron. The emperor Domitian was zealously devoted to Minerva who, before his assassination, supposedly warned him in a dream that she was unable to protect him further because she had been disarmed by Jove (Suet. *Dom.* 15.3). At times of crisis one could seek supernatural aid by making or vowing an offering. Sanctuaries were filled with terracotta objects donated by petitioners of modest means; inscribed stone and marble altars commemorated favors received from all the major Olympian figures and innumerable local gods. Increasingly during the Empire, though, people turned for both help and spiritual satisfaction to the so-called "mystery cults" that promised deliverance, here and in the afterlife, to the select few.

Mysteries differed from other religious observances by requiring candidates to undergo an initiation whose content was kept secret from outsiders. Like coming-of-age rituals, they effected a change of status; the worshipper, whose mental disposition had been altered through contact with holy things, entered into a special bond with the divinity (Burkert 1987: 8). Mysteries were by no means an exclusively Imperial-epoch phenomenon. In antiquity the paramount and most esteemed mysteries were those of Demeter and Persephone at Eleusis, already celebrated during the archaic era (*Hymn Hom. Cer.* 270–74). Closely integrated with the Orphic movement, Dionysiac ("Bacchic") orgiastic rites were introduced in classical times into Magna Graecia, from there spreading to Etruria and other parts of Italy. Some cults of Eastern derivation took on an intense Greek coloring in the Hellenistic period before arriving in Rome. These include veneration of Isis and her Ptolemaic consort Sarapis and likewise of **Mithras**, originally an ancient Persian deity; Mithraic mysteries, inaugurated, according to Plutarch (*Pomp.* 24.5), by pirates from Asia Minor who pillaged Mediterranean sanctuaries in the early first century BCE, were afterward infused with Greek astrological lore and brought to Rome, arguably in the entourage of the Hellenized dynasty of Commagene (Beck 1998). Other foreign divinities were syncretized (see Chapter 6) with familiar members of the Roman pantheon and adored as composite deities; thus Ba'al, the god of Doliche in northern Syria, was amalgamated with Jupiter and, as Jupiter Dolichenus, cultivated by initiates in a sanctuary on the Aventine hill (Beard, North, and Price 1998: 1.275 and 2.295–7).

Rumors of debauchery and criminal behavior naturally attached themselves to exclusive religious movements. Certain mystery cults therefore met with state opposition, at least initially. Coupled with fear of seditious plotting, such rumors led the Roman Senate in 186 BCE to issue a decree (*CIL* 1².581 = *ILS* 18; Liv. 39.8.3–19.7) abolishing Bacchic shrines and imposing strict restrictions on votaries. Yet groups of Bacchic followers remained active, as attested by the great frieze in Pompeii's Villa of the Mysteries, dated to the first century BCE. Similar efforts were made during the late Republic and the early Empire to prevent the construction of sanctuaries to Isis and Sarapis within the city boundary. During the turbulent 50s BCE Isiac agitators disrupted state sacrifice and erected shrines to the Egyptian divinities right in the center of Rome; their religious insurgency has been plausibly linked to concurrent political strife over the regulation of workers' associations (Malaise 1972: 365–77). Humorous allusions to that struggle appear in Catullus' poems, where a "little whore" (*scortillum*) characteristically worships Sarapis (10.25–6) and statues of the divine child Harpocrates (= Horus) as a boy with a finger to his lips commanding silence prompt dirty jokes (74.4 and 102.4). Memories of Cleopatra's intimate association with Isis (on coinage she had styled herself *thea neotera*, "the younger goddess") colored Augustus' distaste for the cult, which he and his second-in-command Agrippa more than once attempted to repress (Cass. Dio 53.2.4, 54.6.6). In 19 CE, Tiberius expelled foreign religions from Rome, singling out Egyptian and Jewish believers (Tac. *Ann.* 2.85; Suet. *Tib.* 36.1). Yet by the reign of Caligula an imposing temple of Isis had been erected in the Campus Martius. When the building was destroyed by fire in 80 CE, Domitian, then *princeps*, reconstructed it munificently, a sign that the Egyptian goddess was now welcome in Rome.

In contrast, the Anatolian cult of Meter (Cybele), like Dionysos a divinity known to inflict madness (Eur. *Hipp*. 141–4; Catul. 63), was officially imported by senatorial directive in 204 BCE as a measure to expel Hannibal from Italy. Under the title **Magna Mater** ("Great Mother") the goddess received a temple on the Palatine and a key festival, the Megalensia, was instituted in her honor. Controls were meanwhile put in place to stop Roman citizens from participating in traditional gruesome ceremonies in which her native priests, the *galloi*, flagellated and castrated themselves. Even while the aristocracy promoted an austere, sanitized version of Magna Mater as civic protectress, though, the populace invoked her in its own way. Archaeological investigations have exposed a large cache of terracotta votives beneath a subsequent temple, including many statuettes of the goddess's mortal lover **Attis**, whose self-castration and death were indispensable parts of her sacred tale (Roller 1999: 274–80). Such figurines functioned as surrogates for the donors. Under the later Empire, finally, Attis became the divine hero of mystery rites characterized by the *taurobolium*, in which candidates for initiation were drenched in the blood of a bull slaughtered above their heads (Burkert 1987: 6, 98).[10] This ritual was of course limited to those who could afford bulls.

Mithraism, well established by the second century CE, firmly reinforced public values. Various late authors – Celsus, Tertullian, Porphyry – allude to its tenets (sources in Beard, North, and Price 1998: 2.311–16) and archaeological work on its shrines or *mithraea* yields further insights into its myths and practices. Because it is relatively well documented, we can treat it as an exemplary type of mystery cult. Membership, restricted to men, entailed progression through seven grades of initiation from Raven, or catechumen, to the supreme rank of Father, who presided over cult activities. Small congregations conducted services and shared communal meals in secluded locations, often underground crypts. The elaborate mythology dealt with the career of the savior-god Mithras, most notably his primordial bull-slaying, an emblem of resurrection (Tert. *De praescr. haeret.* 40). Because it promoted brotherhood among its enthusiasts, Mithraism was highly popular with soldiers; outside Italy, in both the western and eastern halves of the Empire, evidence of worship emerges wherever Roman troops were stationed (Turcan 1996: 207–15). Inscriptions tell us that imperial freedmen were also among the god's devotees (*ILS* 4198, 4203, 4204). Military service and government administration were both regulated environments in which obedience to superiors and acceptance of one's place in the hierarchy were necessary for advancement. By replicating those conditions in the religious sphere, Mithraism reinforced proper behaviors outside it. Hence Gordon deems the cult "a fairly sophisticated contribution to the maintenance of social control" (1972: 104).

For students of ancient sexual mores, the most pressing task in dealing with the first two centuries of the Empire is to account for a large-scale shift toward asceticism not only among elites, as discussed in Chapter 9, but within the general population. We may ask, then, whether mystery religions enjoined sexual continence. Some did, but just for brief periods. Abstinence (*castimonia*) for ten days was required of prospective Bacchic initiates according to Livy (39.9.4, 10.1), though this detail may be only a plot device. In preparation for her rites, female worshippers of Isis also remained chaste for ten days, an inconvenience deplored by their poet-lovers (Tib. 1.3.25–6, Prop. 2.33.1–6) and ridiculed by Juvenal (6.535–6). On the other hand, Apuleius' Lucius, urged by the goddess to undergo initiation, procrastinates because of the demands her service would make upon him, specifically "the very strenuous practice of chastity" (*castimoniorum abstinentiam satis arduam*, *Met.* 11.19). The Stoic philosopher Chaeremon, himself a priest, reports that ministers of the Egyptian gods fasted and abstained from intercourse for varying lengths of time before performing holy rituals (fr. 10 van der Horst *ap*. Porph. *Abst*. 4.7). Summarizing the same passage of Chaeremon, the Christian apologist Jerome goes even further, making his source say that the priests had no traffic with women at all; but Jerome is at pains to prove that extreme self-denial is admired even among pagans (*Adv. Iovinian*. 2.13). Still, celibacy was not expected of ordinary members of Isis' cult; indeed, we have inscriptions in which married couples jointly declare themselves her votaries (*CIL* 11.574 = *ILS* 4410).

Historians have long sought reasons for popular interest in esoteric religions, not least because they might in turn shed light on Christianity's appeal to roughly the same segments of the population. Not surprisingly, one early explanation was that the so-called "Oriental" religions had more to offer: they satisfied on an emotional, an intellectual, and even an ethical level in a way that institutionalized state worship did not (Cumont 1911: 20–45). Dodds, a half-century later, added a psychological dimension: he called the late second and third centuries CE an "Age of Anxiety" in which a loss of confidence in conventional beliefs triggered intense pessimism and a frenetic search for new absolutes (1965: 3–5). While both generalizations contain an element of truth, neither is fully adequate, and present-day specialists caution us that there may have been a wide range of factors involved in the selection of religious options. Some deny that mysteries were a religion in the strict sense (Burkert 1987: 3–4) and focus instead on the extraordinary impressions created by the initiatory experience. Others note the sense of community generated by cult membership, which extended to changes in everyday life (Beard, North, and Price 1998: 1.287–9). Promise of a better existence after death was a feature of certain, but not all, cults, and only Christianity held out the hope of future bodily resurrection. One should bear in mind, finally, that none of the above reasons necessarily precluded other possibilities.

During the same period, numbers of seekers dabbled, like Lucius, in fringe pursuits. Access to arcane wisdom, part of the attraction of the mysteries, contributed on a more sinister plane to the lure of magic (Rives 2007: 159–65). To invest themselves with fuller authority, practitioners (**magi**) appropriated the divine apparatus, the terminology, and the conceptual frameworks of various Eastern mystery religions as well as Judaism (Betz 1991: 249–53). Consequently, there was an extensive grey area where mystery observances and magic were hard to differentiate, for in cults apart from Christianity there was no body of sacred ordinances to define unsanctioned religious practice (Phillips 1991: 266). That is a key consideration because, in a parallel legal development, the application of a Republican-era law initially designed to punish poisoning (*veneficium*) was gradually extended to cover related uncanny and malicious acts and ultimately acts of religious deviance (Rives

2003). Administration of abortifacients and love potions, performing spells to enchant or bind, sacrificing human beings or drawing omens from human blood, profaning shrines, even possession of magical treatises – by the fourth century CE almost all are treated as capital crimes, and *magi* themselves are condemned to be burned alive (Paulus *Sent.* 5.23.14–19). Literally, magic was taboo.

Despite these brutal sanctions, the large corpus of Greek magical papyri from Egypt, ascribed to late antiquity but employing centuries-old phraseology, shows that individuals continued to use such means to exert control over their own lives and those of others. The papyri contain handbooks of prescriptions and generic recipes into which the names of agent and victim were to be inserted. In the particular sphere of our interest, erotic magic, strategies include curses designed to separate couples, binding spells (*agôgai*) to inflame someone with *erôs* for the petitioner, and *philia* spells to strengthen an existing relationship (Faraone 1999: 55–69, 119–31; examples in Ogden 2002: 227–9, 231–6). Winkler observes that male customers who commissioned *agôgai* project what seem to us sadistic fantasies upon the female object of desire, wishing upon her their own inner torment, anxiety, and sleeplessness; on a pragmatic level, he surmises, imagining the designated victim afflicted by identical pains might have served as a form of client therapy (1990: 71–98). We do have specimens of two, possibly three, binding spells in which one woman seeks to attract another woman, and they too employ the language of erotic enslavement: "inflame the heart, the liver, the spirit of Gorgonia, whom Nilogenia bore, with love and affection for Sophia, whom Isara bore" (*Suppl. Mag.* 1.42.A.12–13, trans. Brooten 1996: 87). Although she was a paying customer (and the spell, which is lengthy, was perhaps not cheap), Sophia would have had little choice in the wording, because in order to work the charm had to employ set formulae.[11] Its language mirrors cultural ideology, not her private subjectivity. The key contribution of this and the other two spells, Brooten rightly notes, is that they document the existence of actual women wanting other women as partners and taking steps to bring it about, as opposed to behaviors of that fictional creature the *tribas* (ibid., 105).

Along with occultism, astrology and dream prediction gained in appeal during the first few centuries CE as people attempted, if not to gain their desires, at least to know in advance what lay in store for them. Handbooks of astrology such as those of Claudius Ptolemy (second century CE) and Firmicus Maternus (fourth century CE), and **Artemidorus'** *Oneirokritika*, a manual of dream analysis from the second century CE, provide answers to the kinds of questions average persons might ask about money, health, marriage, work, business transactions, legal difficulties, and many other events of ordinary life (Foucault 1988: 7; T. Barton 1994: 175–6). Consequently, these treatises have lately been mined as sources for popular assumptions about gender and sexuality, as opposed to formulations biased toward the elite.

Astrological texts postulate that character traits and fixed sexual orientations are predetermined by stellar conjunctions. To give a brief causal explanation: the signs of the zodiac themselves and the seven planets that occupy those locations (the modern term is "houses") are gendered. Thus Aries and the Sun are male, Virgo and the Moon female, and, yes, men are under Mars and women under Venus (Beck

2007: 60, 77, 83–4). However, the gender of a given planet can be modified or reinforced at any one moment by its position in the zodiac, its aspect, or geometrical relation, relative to the Sun, and its ascending or descending place in the heavens. When a planet's normal masculinity is enhanced by position, men born under its influence are hypermasculine, women mannish and inclined to take the sexual initiative; when the femininity of a planet is intensified, female natives are endowed with "proper" womanly qualities (docility, modesty), but males are at best soft and apprehensive, at worst eunuchs. Some planets, moreover, are helpful ("benefic") and others harmful ("malefic"); extreme gender deviance, that of the pathic and the *tribas*, is the product of malign planetary influence. Despite the fact that the stars are ultimately responsible, gender transgression is still presented as morally culpable behavior (Brooten 1996: 115–41).

Bound up as it was with the destinies of leading men, astrology became politically significant just as the Roman Republic entered its closing decades. Cicero's good friend P. Nigidius Figulus, an expert amateur astrologer, is said to have pronounced upon learning the hour of Augustus' nativity in 63 BCE that the ruler of the world had been born (Suet. *Div. Aug.* 93.5). As *princeps*, Augustus would later publish his horoscope and put his birth sign, Capricorn, on coinage in order to bolster his claim to power (ibid., 93.12). In 11 CE, however, he forbade astrological conferences in private and responses to inquiries about someone's death (Cass. Dio 56.25.5). Under later emperors, astrological speculation regarding a present or potential ruler was considered treasonous; imperial edicts prohibited consultations, expelled practitioners, and punished the guilty with exile or death. Nevertheless, ancient sources are filled with anecdotes concerning successful predictions of a *princeps*'s rise or fall, and repeated expulsions and show trials seemingly did little to reduce inquisitiveness (T. Barton 1994: 44–52).

Like astrology, ancient dream interpretation was a complex technique aimed at predicting the future. In this it differed entirely from psychoanalytic approaches designed to unearth past trauma buried in the unconscious. That dreams could give either accurate or misleading information was taken for granted in antiquity: Vergil (*Aen.* 6.893–6) describes "twin gates of Sleep" in the underworld, one made of horn, by which true dreams exit, and the other of glowing ivory, through which false dreams are sent. (Aeneas leaves through the *ivory* gate, a point that has perplexed generations of critics.) For his part, Artemidorus distinguishes at the beginning of his manual (1.1) between true **oneiroi** or prophetic dreams and *enhypnia*, dreams prompted by pressing personal concerns, which to him, unlike Freud, are of no interest. In a passage from a later book he explains why *enhypnia* should be disregarded: as the product of irrational fears or desires and of present bodily conditions, they are valueless; men in control of their passions do not experience them (4 pr.: 239.14–20 Pack). Predictive dreams, on the other hand, may be either transparent or allegorical, thus calling for interpretation. Allegorical dreams do not come true immediately and require the interpreter to seek out similarities between what is dreamed and what is portended (2.25: 145.11–12 Pack). Some of the similarities Artemidorus finds are commonsensical, others strained: for example, to dream of entering a bordello may presage death, since whorehouses and cemeteries are common to all (1.78). In making his evaluation, an expert must also apply what Foucault calls an "analogy of value" (1988: 15) to the dream matter. According to Artemidorus, "it is a general principle that everything that seems to conform with nature, law, custom, technique, terminology, and timing is good, everything contrary to these bad and inauspicious" (4.2: 245.2–4 Pack).

Among these predictive dreams are explicitly sexual ones, including dreams of fulfilled incest. In Freud's system, the latter can never get past the dream censor, because they divulge the repressed desires masked by "innocent" imagery. Artemidorus, conversely, assigns incestuous dreams a social import, as they foretell changes in the dreamer's station or happenings that will befall a member of his family (1.78–9). While both Freud and Artemidorus assume that dreams communicate meaning through a symbolic language drawn from the dreamer's immediate associations, then, the culturally determined weight each assigns to sex is very different. For Freud, past sexual wishes or traumas are the hidden message to be deciphered, while for Artemidorus sex is one of a number of symbolic schemes for conveying information about future practical success or misfortune:

> Sex, like food and clothing, provides material with which the soul can talk to us about the truly important things in life, such as whether we will come into money, whether my son will recover from an illness, whether my wife will be faithful and hard-working, whether I will win or lose a lawsuit. These are issues that matter. (Winkler 1990: 27)

In fact, Artemidorus' model of interpretation, by seeking out predictions rather than causes, inverts Freud's actual objectives in addition to reversing his notion of overt and latent dream content (Price 1990: 383).

Sexual activity, like any other dream activity, should agree with nature and convention in order to be propitious. Hence good and evil outcomes are aligned with ideas of normative masculinity and femininity. If the dream content conforms to proper social hierarchy – in matters of sex, the male dreamer playing the active and superior role, the woman, boy, or slave taking the passive, inferior position – the prognosis is favorable, otherwise generally not. Artemidorus' negative readings of dreams containing oral sex reflect the culturally shared conviction that it pollutes the mouth, though he makes an exception for those who earn their livings with their mouths, like flute players and public speakers (1.79: 96.6–12 Pack). Incest, which he categorizes as "against convention," may mean diverse things depending upon the blood relationship, the part taken by the subject, and the age and sex of the other participant. While having intercourse with one's child is frequently ominous, the dreamer's union with his own mother may be very favorable, depending upon what position he uses and whether his mother is still living.[12] The most terrible of all dreams is for a mother to fellate her son, as it foretells death of children, property loss, and grave illness for the dreamer himself. Finally, intercourse between two women falls into the category of acts against nature, since Artemidorus conceives of sex exclusively in terms of penetration, which under the circumstances is accomplished only through artificial means (Foucault 1988: 24–5). Moreover, he does not differentiate female partners according to relative wealth, age, or status, as he does when speaking of male–male sex acts. Women are all alike, and in this case too much alike (Brooten 1996: 184). Absence of sexual hierarchy, here as in other situations we have examined, is in itself regarded as unnatural.

Christian Continence

Though derived from Judaism, whose antique traditions commanded respect, Christianity, in contrast with ostensibly similar cults, was alarming to Roman observers because of its perceived unsavory beginnings and rapid spread. In explaining why Nero fixed upon the Christians as scapegoats for the Great Fire of Rome in 64 CE, Tacitus (*Ann.* 15.44.3) emphasizes the recent execution of its founder under Tiberius and paints the "deadly ***superstitio***" as a kind of viral disease.[13] His contemporary Pliny the Younger, governor of Bithynia and Pontus, requests advice from the emperor Trajan on dealing with the same *superstitio*, which has infested the countryside as well as cities (*Ep.* 10.96.9). Why did the authorities find the new sect so threatening? Comparison between Mithraism and Christianity as they operated within their respective social contexts is illuminating. Both made their initial appearance in Rome during the first century of the principate. Both promulgated distinctive doctrines, advocated a comprehensive ethical system, employed baptism as an initiatory rite, and commemorated through sacramental re-enactments a divine act of salvation – for one, the killing of the cosmic bull, for the other, the passion and death of Jesus. After that they part company. While traditional Greco-Roman divinities could be found in Mithraic and other pagan sanctuaries, Christianity was uncompromisingly monotheistic. In the minds of non-believers, its refusal to worship the national gods and participate in civic rituals invited divine retribution against the community as a whole and aroused popular wrath whenever natural disasters occurred: "If the Tiber floods its banks, if the Nile does not flood the fields, if the sky stands still or the earth moves, if there is famine or plague, at once the shout goes up: 'Christians to the lion!'" (Tert. *Apol.* 40.2). Public feeling demonstrably played a large role in motivating government persecution, though magistrates themselves may also have been offended by believers' obstinate rejection of ancestral religion (de Ste. Croix 1963).

One more fundamental contrast between Mithraism and Christianity must also be kept in mind. Mithraism was, in Gordon's words (1972: 112), "world-affirming rather than world-denying." By providing a vertical structure for religious advancement that paralleled secular gradations and reinforced behaviors contributing to success in daily life, the cult implicitly assured its members that the existing social order had value. Conversely, early Christian worshippers lived in the constant expectation of a "new heaven and new earth" and sought ways to speed the arrival of God's kingdom. Immured as they were in the material realm, however, subject to the linear progression of time, the rotation of the seasons, and the ultimate indignity of death and corruption, how could weak human beings bring about their promised deliverance? One exercise of free will presented itself:

> Sexuality was based on a drive that was widely spoken of as irresistible ... This drive, furthermore, was the known cause of the one irrefutably unidirectional process to which human beings freely contributed – procreation. Without human collaboration, that layer, at least, of the somber landslip of the "present age" would not continue. If sexual activity could cease among human beings, the tumultuous cascade of the human race from copulation, through birth to the grave, would come to a halt. (Brown 1988: 84)

In view of the relentless childhood and adult mortality rates, which we have discussed, the refusal of the eligible young to take part in the socially indispensable process of procreation was indeed a blow against the "present age" as represented by the communities in which they lived.

Sexual abstinence appeared to have scriptural and apostolic authority. Jesus himself had endorsed making oneself an eunuch "for the kingdom of heaven's sake" (Matt. 19: 12) and distinguished the children of this world, who "marry, and are given in marriage" from those worthy of the resurrection, who "neither marry, nor are given in marriage; neither can they die any more: for they *are equal unto the angels*" (Luke 20: 34–6). What he proclaimed as true for the future blessedness of his followers could effortlessly be construed as applicable to existing conditions as well (Lane Fox 1987: 363). **Paul** the apostle, in his authoritative teaching on Christian marriage in the first Epistle to the Corinthians, had likewise begun with the flat assertion, "It is good for a man not to touch a woman," before warning that celibacy was not appropriate for everyone. His advice was directed to a congregation at Corinth rent by status distinctions (Theissen 1974) in which some members, presumably in response to internal disagreements, were experimenting with extreme forms of renunciation. Paul wished to deter them from going to such excess (Brown 1988: 53). While he did not disown marriage, his lukewarm endorsement of it as a practical alternative ("better to marry than to burn," 1 Cor. 7: 9) left open the door for more stringent readings. Over the following centuries, prominent church fathers produced commentaries on this scriptural passage making it exalt virginity above marriage; allow sexual relations within marriage only for the sake of procreation; prohibit remarriage after the death of a spouse; and, in the view of radicals such as Origen and Pelagius, ban the incontinent, even if married, from prayer and reception of the Eucharist (Clark 1999: 259–329).

Accordingly, the practice of asceticism, particularly in sexual matters but also in the related areas of eating and drinking, accelerated from the first to the fourth and fifth centuries CE as believers sought to recapture a purity enjoyed by Adam and Eve before sinning (T. M. Shaw 1998: 161–219). Promoted as the holiest of earthly states, virginity not only allowed men and women to maintain a singleness of purpose in worshipping God but also served as a symbolic rejection of the world even after most Christians had started to think the apocalypse was no longer imminent. By taking a vow of chastity, girls evaded their obligation to bear children, with its attendant physical risks, and attained a degree of autonomy envied by their married sisters – or so the patristic authors of treatises on virginity argued. Wedded couples could aim at greater perfection by undertaking to live together in perpetual abstinence. The heroines of Greek romance striving to remain faithful to their lovers were supplanted by the fictional **Thecla**, protagonist of the apocryphal *Acts of Paul and Thecla*, who abjures marriage after overhearing Paul preach and becomes his follower, successfully thwarting the efforts of family and fiancé to bring her to the altar. The parents and magistrates who threaten Thecla with death for her disobedience are emblems of secular power; her defiance of them is "a patently antisocial vision of religious heroism at the expense of civic duty" (Cooper 1996: 67).

Celibate lifestyles eventually led to the invention of new social institutions: consecrated female communities and organized monasteries. The emperor **Constantine**'s edict of 320 CE, which officially abolished the Julian penalties for celibacy in force until then, removed an oppressive burden from the wealthier classes and made it possible for those who would otherwise have been subject to financial sanctions to renounce marriage (Evans-Grubbs 1995: 131–9). Although many Christian writers opposed the extremist ascetic movement, the Church had a financial stake in its popularity among the aristocracy, for wealthy women who adopted that life, having no descendants, willed massive amounts of money to ecclesiastical and charitable projects (Clark 1995: 373–5). These women might gather dozens of virgins from less affluent backgrounds under their protection, taking them into their households (Brown 1988: 265). In the deserts of Egypt, meanwhile, monks from all walks of life struggled to purge their bodies and minds of sexual desire, at first in solitary cells and later in dedicated confraternities (Clark 1999: 18–19, 24). In monastic literature, women figure as inexorable sexual temptresses threatening the chastity of even the most resolute holy man; such misogyny, a holdover from pre-Christian times, defines the ascetic as the inhabitant of a landscape no longer attached to the settled world (Brown 1988: 242–4).

If sex within marriage could be denigrated as "fornication" (admittedly by Tatian, an author later pronounced heretical), all forms of extramarital sex were by definition anathema to Christian moralists. Homoeroticism, male and female, was singled out as especially depraved. Even before the conversion of Constantine, there were sporadic governmental attempts to discourage passivity. Efforts to get rid of male prostitutes were at least contemplated by the mid-third-century emperor Severus Alexander (*SHA Alex. Sev.* 24.4)[14] and undertaken by a subsequent ruler, Philip the Arab (Aur. Vict. *Caes.* 28.6). In a late compilation of legal opinion ascribed to the jurist Paulus, voluntary submission to penetration earned confiscation of half the guilty man's property and ineligibility to make a will disposing of the other half (*Sent.* 2.26.13). For Christians, meanwhile, intolerance of homoeroticism was a natural outgrowth of Old and New Testament injunctions against same-sex intercourse (OT, Lev. 18: 22 and 20: 13, defining male anal intercourse as an "abomination"; NT, 1 Cor. 6: 9 and Rom. 1: 26–7, in which Paul pronounces same-sex genital activity, both male and female, "unnatural").[15] Attitudes derived from Judaism were reinforced by Greek philosophical declarations about the natural procreative purpose of sex. After Christianity became the established state religion official disapproval hardened: in 342 CE passive sexual behavior was outlawed by a decree of the emperors Constantius and Constans preserved in the Theodosian Code (9.7.3) and, in 390 CE, another imperial decree provided that male prostitutes from Roman brothels should be rounded up and burned alive. In 438 the punishment was extended to every man found to have allowed himself to be penetrated; then, in 533, **Justinian** prescribed in his *Institutes* (4.18.4) that the active male partner was also guilty and must suffer death by the sword.[16] Through further decrees Justinian confirmed the practice of punishing male–male sexual activity without role distinction, castigating it as a religious crime, an act abhorred by God (Cantarella 1992: 181–6). As the epitome of sex willfully turned to non-procreative and therefore vicious ends, the practice was henceforward subject to harsh secular as well as religious penalties, penalties that endured almost up to the twentieth century.

Things Fall Apart

One final set of observations takes us back to where this chapter began, when we noted the existence of a great legal and economic gap between the empowered classes and the populace. As long as living conditions within the Empire remained relatively untroubled overall, social structures and wealth distribution, though top-heavy, were not wobbly. However, the interdependence of many elements contributing to the *pax Romana*, including political stability, military security, agricultural production, tax policy, commerce, and the monetary system, meant that if large problems arose in one sphere they would automatically spill over into related areas. The crisis of the third century resulted from many separate but cohering institutional failures.

Catastrophe began with the so-called "Antonine plague" during the reign of Marcus Aurelius, which broke out in Macedonia in 165/6 CE and spread to Rome in the following year. From descriptions of symptoms by Galen, who encountered and treated it in the army camp at Aquileia (*Libr. propr.* 19.18 Kühn), it has plausibly been diagnosed as smallpox (Littman and Littman 1973: 245–52). The epidemic persisted for twenty-three years with occasional irruptions and a second major outbreak in 189 (Cass. Dio 73.14.3). While not as lethal as the medieval Black Death, it is conservatively estimated to have caused 7–10 million fatalities above the normal mortality rate (Littman and Littman 1973: 255). Reminding us that there were probably pockets of high and low incidence, Duncan-Jones accepts a figure of 25–33% mortality in some locales (1996: 116 n. 88). Further outbreaks of plague during the next two centuries took additional tolls, particularly among urban residents and the military.

Political unrest contributed to disorder. With the assassination of Commodus, Marcus Aurelius' son, in 192 CE, the succession of Antonine emperors came to an abrupt end. After an interlude of civil disturbance, Septimius Severus gained the throne, expanded the army, and spent the rest of his reign (193–211) securing the frontiers. In order to pay his troops, Severus debased the silver coinage, precipitating a trend that led to currency collapse after subsequent emperors attempted to meet soldiers' demands, despite inadequate supplies of precious metals (Duncan-Jones 2004: 43–7). Rather than being motivated by egalitarianism or generosity, his heir Caracalla's extension of Roman citizenship to the whole population of the empire in 212 CE may have simply aimed to increase the tax base (Cameron 1993: 9). When the last emperor of the Severan dynasty, Severus Alexander, was slain in 235, government fell into anarchy. Civil war was endemic as legitimate rulers struggled with usurpers. During a period of forty-seven years twenty-five emperors held power, only one of whom died a natural death (Brown 1971: 24). On every front, meanwhile, defenses crumbled. In 251, while fighting the Goths near the Danube, the emperor Decius was killed; nine years later, the Persian king Shapur I defeated a Roman army already weakened by plague and took its imperial commander Valerian prisoner. Breakaway empires sprang up in Gaul and the Near East. Diocletian (284–305) finally ended the chaos by bringing the armies to heel and instituting a tetrarchy – that is, a junta in which four absolute monarchs, two co-emperors and two designated successors, shared power and responsibility for defending separate geographical regions. The tetrarchy did not long survive Diocletian's abdication and retirement, but those events go beyond the limits of our history.

According to a widely accepted "taxes and trade" model (Hopkins 1980), the Roman state, through a variety of measures – setting up efficient transport networks on land and sea, establishing a common monetary system, imposing a unified body of commercial laws – had facilitated a vigorous trans-Mediterranean trade in commodities during the first centuries of the principate. Taxes were probably kept low because provinces paying tribute could raise sufficient money by selling products directly or indirectly to regions where government revenues were primarily spent, namely Rome and the military frontiers. Depopulation following the Antonine Plague reduced agricultural production, manufacture, public building, and minting of coins (Duncan-Jones 1996: 120–34). Following drops in productive activity and trade, the tax burden necessarily increased (Lo Cascio 2007: 646). Soon taxation was on its way to being the heavy encumbrance it was in the late empire, when evasion and flight to avoid payment were common and decurions were held responsible for making up municipal revenue shortfalls out of their own pockets. Thanks to the ruinous monetary policies of the central government, price increases became a corollary hardship. Diocletian's well-known Price Edict of 301 CE sought to curb rampant inflation by fixing maximum costs for commodities, but financial distress was too pervasive to be resolved by fiat. For tax purposes payment in kind was allowed to supplant coinage.

Different parts of the Empire were differently affected by plague, war, and financial stress. Archaeological surveys suggest that in the West, especially Italy, decline in numbers of rural settlements occurred (Duncan-Jones 2004: 27–38, 49–50). Egypt also saw the abandonment of farms and villages, the privatization of formerly public holdings, and the assimilation of more land into large estates (Rathbone 2007). Africa prospered because it was protected by the Mediterranean from civil war and invasion, but public construction still declined, possibly because of increased tax demands or expropriations (Duncan-Jones 2004: 38). Eastern regions were more robust, exhibiting a period of shallower erosion followed by a rebound in the fourth century. Because it was not homogeneous, the Empire was able to survive the turmoil, but the middling and poor population, most broadly exposed to risks of disease and violence, also suffered the harshest consequences of economic upheaval and the cruelest punishments of the law should they fall foul of it.

During this era, though, Christian martyrs were confronting pagan observers with a different perception of the relations between soul and body (Brown 1988: 26–32). Instead of being, as Platonic and Stoic thought avowed, mere temporary housing ideally governed by the rational soul, the body in their eyes had been transformed by Christ's incarnation and was now potentially destined for resurrection. Martyrdom, accordingly, was a demonstration of what this redeemed body might achieve in triumphing, aided by the Spirit, over pain, suffering, and death. Though not necessarily a prerequisite for martyrdom, virginity was part of the same ensemble of freedoms, as it marked a body liberated from the biological constraints of reproduction. The lesson was not lost on contemporaries. Galen, in his lost commentary on Plato's *Republic*, is said to have remarked:

> For their [the Christians'] contempt of death [and of its sequel] is patent to us every day, and likewise their restraint in cohabitation. For they include not only men but also women who refrain from cohabiting all through their lives; and they also number individuals who, in self-discipline and self-control in matters of food and drink, and in their keen pursuit of justice, have attained a pitch not inferior to that of genuine philosophers. (Walzer 1949: 15)

Although the numbers the Christians among the unphilosophical masses to whom rational demonstration of truth is a closed book, Galen concedes that they have in their own way achieved a high degree of moral virtue, manifested by their fortitude in the face of death, their absolute mastery over corporeal desires, and their commitment to justice.

The last of these attributes requires more exposition. In the midst of state opposition and even organized persecution, how could Christians strive after justice? Theories differ, but one answer proposed is that their celebration of martyrdom and their belief in the material resurrection of the body countered the inequities of the Roman criminal justice system with its differential punishments involving bodily humiliation. Greek novels, as discussed earlier, titillate elite readers with the prospect of well-born heroes and heroines subjected to physical degradation and ghastly deaths, but the point is that such threats are never fulfilled. Because the lovers are the equivalent of *honestiores*, their miraculous escapes from torture and bondage affirm class invulnerability just as firmly as does their preserved chastity – especially since slaves and other social nobodies have no such immunity, often dying as substitutes for the protagonist (Perkins 2009: 55–7). Martyrs, on the other hand, die in earnest after judicial condemnation, but the amphitheater in which they brave the wild beasts is a performance venue in which Roman power dynamics are subverted.

Gender, too, is reversed: the resolute female martyr acquires "a sort of virile honor" (Shaw 1993: 7). Thus in her prison diary the twenty-year-old matron Vibia Perpetua, scheduled to die in the arena the next day, records a dream in which she, transformed into a man (*facta sum masculus*, *Passio Perp.* 9.7), wrestles with and defeats an Egyptian, hideous in appearance: upon waking, she identifies her dream adversary as the devil (ibid., 14). The narrative of her actual death, composed by an anonymous eyewitness, emphasizes that none of the tactics used to dishonor Perpetua and her companions – including stripping them almost naked before the crowd – had its desired effect. Rather, spectators were appalled to see a respectable young woman so mistreated, even while facing execution, and demanded she be clothed decently. Turned back upon the spectators, shame loses its power to browbeat the sufferer.

Martyr trials themselves are portrayed as only the prelude to an ultimate divine judgment in which the outcomes will differ: "what you do to us, God likewise [will do] to you" (*tu nos ... te autem Deus*, *Passio Perp.* 18.8). Since the deeds for which the soul will be rewarded or punished were committed "not without the flesh" (Tert. *Apol.* 48.4), according to Christian doctrine the two components, united again at the resurrection, will together partake in the possessor's eternal state. To outsiders this scheme might appear more equitable than Roman judicial proceedings with their hierarchical protocols and their metonymic association of the lower social orders with the infamy and disgust attached to the body:

> Christian resurrection discourse seems to challenge the juridical fictions and symbolic networks that position the upper stratum, those identified with the soul/mind, as superior and too refined for harsh physical punishment. Christian texts stress that there are no exceptions; everyone's body must be presented at court and, if guilty, endure equal penalties. (Perkins 2009: 101–2)

It is true that legal punishments after the establishment of Christianity became, if anything, much harsher, particularly for sexual offenses such as adultery, rape, and seduction as well as male homoeroticism, all now capital crimes (MacMullen 1986: 333–6, 342). That development is plausibly attributed to reformist zeal, the conviction that means justify ends and pain must be inflicted to discourage proliferation of truly heinous sins. Earlier, however, during the upheavals of the third century, insistence upon the value of every human body ran counter to notions that some bodies, those of the elite, were by nature more worthy of respect even as they reinforced the claim that a body disciplined by abstinence was a temple of sanctity. Among the marginalized, such principles heightened the attractions of austerity.

Conclusion

Apuleius' second-century CE Thessaly is not Periclean Athens, but most features of the elite milieu described in the initial books of the *Metamorphoses* – including underlying structures of sex and gender and expectations about the conduct of men and women – would not have surprised a time-traveler from the fifth century BCE. True, mainland Greece had in the meantime become part of a cosmopolitan world swept by global economic and political cross-currents. Yet its social and familial structures seem to have undergone relatively little change, and the behavior of the upper classes in particular – their dynastic goals, inheritance strategies, and group solidarity over geographical distances – might appear destined to continue on indefinitely.[17] As for the conditions of life in rural areas, among the poor, they would surely have been timeless.

Within two centuries after the *Metamorphoses* was written, though, the mores it takes for granted were hugely altered. Lucius' conversion and transformation into a celibate minister of Isis foreshadows the growth of an ascetic movement that renounced sexual activity and the general comforts of the body in pursuit of spiritual deliverance. Although this trend is rightly associated with the spread of Christianity, it is rooted to some degree in certain pre-Christian attitudes extending all the way back to sixth-century BCE Pythagoreanism. Notions of a fundamental split between soul and body, of the medical and ethical problems associated with the sexual act, and of the natural and necessary connection between sexuality and reproduction – which, in its most drastic form, took the stance that sex may be performed *only* for procreative purposes – were freely circulating in Greece by the Hellenistic era. Pederasty as a practice, though culturally accepted, had long been questioned as well, particularly where changes in civic institutions had made the formation of friendships between older and younger male citizens politically insignificant. Pythagorean doctrine on the duties of husband to wife, including fidelity, was originally the teaching of a marginal sect, but, by the early imperial era, mainstream Roman and Greek writers were stressing the value of the affective bond within marriage and the reciprocal spousal obligation of monogamy. While all of these attitudes predate Christianity, they were easily subsumed under a compatible ascetic outlook, with a particular emphasis on celibacy, which Christians had inherited from certain radical Jewish cults, such as the Essenes (Plin. *HN* 5.15.73) and the authors of the Dead Sea Scrolls (Brown 1988: 33–44). Once ecclesiastical thinkers like Clement of Alexandria started integrating the tenets of classical philosophy into their own creed during the early second century CE, the Christian code of sexual austerity became an amalgamation of biblical Jewish, apostolic, and Hellenistic Greek traditions.

The question of whether that code marks a decisive break from Greek and Roman sexual principles or, on the other hand, continues and extends them is an extremely complicated one. Foucault, who intended to explore it thoroughly in the fourth volume of his projected *History of Sexuality* – for which his studies of classical Greek and imperial Roman sexual ethics were basically a preparation – died in 1984 before that book was completed. At the conclusion of *The Care of the Self*, he adopts a position that straddles the divide: Christian dogmas on sex closely resemble those found in Greco-Roman philosophy, but they are embedded in a different way of thinking about oneself as a moral subject (Foucault 1988: 235–40). In interviews and lectures Foucault had suggested that the new Christian continence demanded rigorous self-scrutiny and confession in order to root out even involuntary impure thoughts and motions of the flesh; it was not any more a matter of obeying reason but of suppressing libido. Such a shift had deep-seated consequences for the modern West, because postulating a wellspring of forbidden desires within the soul would ultimately lead to the identification of the homosexual as a particular category of human being, "the most central argument of Foucault's *History*" (Boyarin and Castelli 2001: 361).

Before his death, however, Foucault had encountered in the writings of John Cassian, a fourth-century theoretician of monastic life, a systematic technique for dissociating the will from movements of thought tending towards impurity. In a late essay, published posthumously, he surprisingly concludes that even these "new fashions in monastic sexual mores" had pre-Christian roots in guidelines for mental discipline fostered by Stoicism and Neoplatonism, so that the supposed "massive rupture with earlier moralities" posed by Christianity "is barely noticeable" (Foucault 1985: 25). Thus it is not altogether clear what his final position would have been. Foucault's ultimate failure to provide a definite answer ensured that the question of rupture or continuity would continue to be heavily debated by students of late antiquity and historians of religion – as it is now, three decades after his death (Gaca 2003: 4–11). In the current absence of consensus, the issue must provisionally be set to one side. Instead, we have turned our attention to charting the most obvious manifestations of an emerging atmosphere of sexual rigor. It should be enough if we have located that broadly based trend within its immediate sociological and historical contexts, so that it can be understood as a coherent amplification of pre-existing conditions.

Discussion Prompts

1. At the beginning of the first section, you were reminded of the "Occupy" slogan "We are the 1%." Scheidel and Friesen's study of economic stratification cited on page 354 concludes that around 10 or 11% of the population controlled between 30% and 50% of the yearly *income* of the Roman empire, which is, of course, not the same thing as its wealth. Keeping in mind that for antiquity all such figures are approximations, and that there are vast differences between an agriculturally-based economy and an information society, is it valid to speak of parallels between the stratification of assets in the empire and the concentration of capital in the hands of a minority today?

2. The practice of recording events (deaths, honors, decrees) on stone was a distinctive feature of the Roman way of life, adopted in many regions only after incorporation into the empire. In a famous 1982 article, Ramsay MacMullen pinpointed a change in what he termed "the epigraphic habit": inscriptions of all kinds in the Latin-speaking world peak during

the reign of Septimius Severus and then decline abruptly. In contrast, papyri from Egypt, especially private documents, continue to be produced throughout the third and fourth centuries. MacMullen ascribed this difference to the fact that texts on papyri address a specific reader and have practical utility, while inscriptions on stone are directed to the world at large. What further conclusions can you draw, assuming that MacMullen is right? (The article is cited in the references, in case you want to look it up on JSTOR.)

3. When reading about the popularity of astrology during the high Empire and the incorporation of astrological doctrine into religious cults such as Mithraism, you should bear in mind that in both scientific and popular ancient belief the earth was the center of the cosmos, with the sun, moon, and planets revolving above it and the zones of the fixed stars and the empyrean lying beyond. Copernicus' heliocentric model of the solar system, introduced in 1543, was not fully accepted until the eighteenth century. How would the notion of an earth-centered universe reinforce the credibility of astrology?

4. The example of the Warren Cup reminds us that museums have always been fiercely competitive about acquiring impressive works of ancient art. Since the implementation of the 1970 UNESCO convention prohibiting illicit trafficking in cultural property, however, countries of origin have succeeded in repatriating many such items acquired illegally and often through looting. Consequently, archaeologists, museum curators, foreign governments and private collectors have been embroiled in a fierce argument over "who should own antiquity?" Investigate and discuss the positions taken by representatives of each of those interest groups.

Notes

1 Economists, geographers, and other social scientists employ a "democratic transition model" to study the effects of population change in industrialized nations from the late eighteenth century onward. In those nations declining death rates due to increased agricultural productivity and modifications in public sanitation were ultimately followed by a decline in birth rates as well. While populations in countries at an advanced stage of the transition have stabilized, in many developing countries fertility rates remain high despite larger numbers of children surviving to reproductive age. World population growth has consequently been explosive.

2 Imperial population size is a heavily debated question; the authors concede that their approximation may be too low (Scheidel and Friesen 2009: 66 n. 21). Harper, who accepts that peak estimate for the second-century CE, posits a society of 50 million in later antiquity (2011: 23 and n. 97). Readers should bear in mind that my summary of demographic and economic conditions

draws upon several competing postulates and that a great number of other variables come into play. For an overview of the many problems involved in providing a realistic account of the imperial Roman economy, see Bowman and Wilson 2009. My deepest thanks to Bruce Frier for walking me through the complexities of demographic extrapolations for ancient societies.

3   A *sesterce* (abbreviated HS) was the basic Roman monetary unit. Its buying power in Rome is hard to assess because, outside Egypt, we have no actual records of daily wages and considerable variation in the recorded prices of basic commodities like wheat (Scheidel and Friesen 2009: 69–72). What it was worth in our money is impossible to say, not only because the relative value of any two currencies fluctuates (as anyone who has done a study abroad program knows), but also because, starting in the reign of Nero, coinage was periodically debased (i.e., the amount of precious metal was reduced). Deterioration of the currency during the crisis of the third century CE was a key cause of economic collapse.

4   The major kinds of *apparitores* included messengers, heralds, *lictores* – who carried the insignia of magistrates and also served as bodyguards – and scribes, the most socially distinguished of these careers. Minor posts included porters and *pullarii*, keepers of the sacred chickens. The epitaph of one *apparitor* states that he attained a superior grade as chicken-keeper before going on to become a scribe (*ILS* 1886).

5   Archaeologists identify houses in Pompeii first by neighborhood (*regio*, with a Roman numeral), then by block (*insula*) and finally by entrance number; hence this location is *regio* IX, *insula* 6, door 6. Pompeians, by the way, would not share our opinion of graffiti, even those found inside a building. Today someone caught scratching a message onto, say, a painted mural in a high school corridor would be regarded as vandalizing it. By defacing an aesthetic object, the perpetrator,

we assume, is venting hostility. Inhabitants of Pompeii seem to think of inscribed graffiti as a form of conversation: one passer-by makes a comment, another adds to it, and so on. Thus graffiti clusters inside houses are found in well-lit and greatly trafficked places. Williams (2010: 298) suggests that their presence attests to a construction of public and private space at odds with the one current in European and American cities. Benefiel (2010: 89) sensibly comments that domestic staff would have deterred visitors from writing on the walls, especially on highly visible surfaces, had it been an egregious offense. We must presuppose that graffiti were not considered injurious to the decorative scheme and were possibly even thought to enhance the impression made on visitors.

6   There is a conflict in the manuscripts of Ovid between *nostris* "our," which, as a generalizing plural, would mean that such paintings are commonly found in all upper-class houses, and *vestris* "your," laying the charge at Augustus' own doorstep. I have opted for the more conservative reading. If the other is accepted, and if scholars are correct in identifying the owner of the Villa Farnesina as Augustus' daughter Julia, Ovid would be telling the truth: erotic images could be seen in the emperor's very residences.

7   The following paragraphs are heavily indebted to Clarke (1998: 145–94 and 196–206), which contains fine photographs of all these buildings and images, as well as several other comparable sites not discussed here.

8   Butrica (2005: 236–8) advances a unified reading of the iconographic scheme: the slave boy peering through the door sees his own future progression as an object of desire from *delicatus* to mature *exoletus*. That interpretation transforms it into a poignant reflection upon the human life-course, one that might well occur to an ancient viewer.

9   In fairness, I must note that the authenticity of the Warren Cup has been questioned. Sox, Warren's biographer, does not mention the

object when discussing the collector's acquisitions but refers to "a silver bowl" in the context of other erotic *curiosa* once owned by Warren and now suspected to be fakes, including Arretine pottery moulds with related decorations (1991: 252–3). On the other hand, Dyfri Williams cites "corrosion products that remain in the cracks even after both its twentieth-century cleanings" as proof of its antiquity (2006: 7). Many distinguished experts on Roman art believe it genuine, as my references indicate. Vout (2007: 74) is singularly cautious. Marabini Moevs (2008) mounts an attack based on stylistic incoherencies arising, she argues, from the artisan's attempts to incorporate ancient design elements into a modern pastiche.

10   The *taurobolium* protected the initiate against evil for twenty years (Burkert 1987: 18). Fans of the HBO series *Rome* may remember Atia, Octavian's mother, indulging in one, although the practice is not otherwise attested prior to the second century CE. In Atia's day, presumably, it was still an experimental procedure.

11   Evidence that the spell is formulary is provided by the names of Sophia and Gorgonia, which are not given grammatical endings prescribed by the syntax but merely inserted into the text at appropriate points (Brooten 1996: 88–9). Use of the matronymic is common in magic rituals in order to insure that the desired individual, and not some like-named person, will be affected, for mistakes can be made about paternity but never maternity.

12   Upset after dreaming of incest with his mother, Julius Caesar was reassured by interpreters that it portended his conquest of the world, since the earth is the mother of all (Suet. *Div. Iul.* 7.2).

13   *Superstitio*, the descriptive category imposed by Roman authorities upon Christianity, connotes not merely "superstition" but nefarious activities, spilling over into magic (Beard, North, and Price 1998: 225–7). Christian apologists themselves deplore accusations of cannibalism and similar iniquities.

14   In a later chapter of the same biography (34.4), Severus is actually said to have deported male prostitutes and drowned some favored by his predecessor Elagabalus. The doubtful factuality of the *Historia Augusta* reassures us that we need not fret too much about the contradiction. Scholars of ancient sexuality until recently thought that mentions of *spintriae*, initially as participants in Tiberius' notorious amusements on Capri (Tac. *Ann.* 6.1, Suet. *Tib.* 43) and subsequently banished under Caligula (Suet. *Calig.* 16.1), referred to "rent-boys." However, Champlin 2011 plausibly contends that they were free and well-born adolescents of both sexes who engaged in suggestive amateur group charades. Suetonius also records that Caligula himself, while staying on Capri during his uncle's reign, dressed in costume and eagerly took on theatrical roles (*Calig.* 11). Perhaps the new emperor's motives for ridding Rome of his fellow thespians were something other than high-minded.

15   Reference to these biblical passages is the equivalent of stepping into a theological and scholarly minefield. The rationale for the prohibitions in Leviticus is contested: is this a purity regulation forbidding the mingling of two defiling substances (semen and excrement); a denunciation of the passive male as unnatural; an injunction against the waste of male seed; or a condemnation of practices associated with foreign cults? All these possibilities and others have been broached (Olyan 1994: 197–206). Brooten (1996: 189–372) presents an extensive exegesis of Romans 1: 18–32, the immediate context in which the verses on male and female homoeroticism occur, their relationship to natural law theory and Jewish law, their subsequent influence on ancient Christian attitudes toward homoeroticism, especially between women, and an annotated bibliography of recent studies of Romans 1: 26ff. and biblical perspectives on homosexuality.

16   Justinian disingenuously cites the *Lex Iulia de adulteriis coercendis* – Augustus' adultery law of 18 BCE – as his authority for punishing the active partner. Of course, the Julian law said nothing of male–male relations.

17   One difference from classical Athenian custom is self-evident: Lucius' foster-mother Byrrhena hosts an elegant dinner party attended by the cream of local society (*Met.* 2.18–31).

References

Bagnall, R. S. and Frier, B. W. 1994. *The Demography of Roman Egypt.* Cambridge: Cambridge University Press.

Barton, C. A. 1993. *The Sorrows of the Ancient Romans: The Gladiator and the Monster.* Princeton, NJ: Princeton University Press.

Barton, T. 1994. *Ancient Astrology.* London and New York: Routledge.

Beard, M., North, J., and Price, S. 1998. *Religions of Rome.* 2 vols. Cambridge: Cambridge University Press.

Beck, R. 1998. "The Mysteries of Mithras: A New Account of Their Genesis." *Journal of Roman Studies* 88: 115–28.

—— 2007. *A Brief History of Ancient Astrology.* Malden, MA, and Oxford: Blackwell.

Benefiel, R. R. 2010. "Dialogues of Ancient Graffiti in the House of Maius Castricius in Pompeii." *American Journal of Archaeology* 114: 59–101.

Betz, H. D. 1991. "Magic and Mystery in the Greek Magical Papyri." In C. A. Faraone and D. Obbink (eds.), Magika Hiera: *Ancient Greek Magic and Religion.* New York and Oxford: Oxford University Press. 244–59.

Bowman, A., and Wilson, A. 2009. "Quantifying the Roman Economy: Integration, Growth, Decline." In A. Bowman and A. Wilson (eds.), *Quantifying the Roman Economy: Methods and Problems.* Oxford Scholarship Online, 2009. 3–84. http://lib.myilibrary.com.ezproxy1.library.arizona.edu?ID=234896 (accessed 22 March 2012).

Boyarin, D. and Castelli, E. A. 2001. "Introduction: Foucault's 'History of Sexuality': The Fourth Volume, or, a Field Left Fallow for Others to Till." *Journal of the History of Sexuality* 10.3–4: 357–74.

Bradley, K. R. 1991. "Dislocation in the Roman Family." In K. R. Bradley, *Discovering the Roman Family: Studies in Roman Social History.* New York and Oxford: Oxford University Press. 125–55.

Brendel, O. J. 1970. "The Scope and Temperament of Erotic Art in the Greco-Roman World." In T. Bowie and C. V. Christenson (eds.), *Studies in Erotic Art.* New York: Basic Books. 3–107.

Brooten, B. J. 1996. *Love between Women: Early Christian Responses to Female Homoeroticism.* Chicago: University of Chicago Press.

Brown, P. 1971. *The World of Late Antiquity AD 150–750.* London: Thames & Hudson.

—— 1988. *The Body and Society: Men, Women and Sexual Renunciation in Early Christianity.* New York: Columbia University Press.

Burkert, W. 1987. *Ancient Mystery Cults.* Cambridge, MA, and London: Harvard University Press.

Butrica, J. L. 2005. "Some Myths and Anomalies in the Study of Roman Sexuality." In B. C. Verstraete and V. Provencal (eds.), *Same-Sex Desire and Love in Greco-Roman Antiquity and in the Classical Tradition of the West.* Binghamton, NY: Harrington Park Press (co-published simultaneously as *Journal of Homosexuality* 49 nos. 3/4 [2005]). 209–69.

Cameron, A. 1993. *The Later Roman Empire: AD 284–430.* London: Fontana Press.

Cantarella, E. 1992. *Bisexuality in the Ancient World.* Trans. C. Ó Cuilleanáin. [Orig. pub. as *Secondo natura*, Rome: Editori Riuniti, 1988.] New Haven, CT: Yale University Press.

Champlin, E. 2011. "Sex on Capri." *Transactions of the American Philological Association* 141: 315–32.

Clark, E. A. 1995. "Antifamilial Tendencies in Ancient Christianity." *Journal of the History of Sexuality* 5: 356–80.

—— 1999. *Reading Renunciation: Asceticism and Scripture in Early Christianity.* Princeton: Princeton University Press.

Clarke, J. R. 1998. *Looking at Lovemaking: Constructions of Sexuality in Roman Art.* Berkeley, CA: University of California Press.

—— 2002. "Look Who's Laughing at Sex: Men and Women Viewers in the *Apodyterium* of the Suburban Baths at Pompeii." In D. Fredrick (ed.), *The Roman Gaze: Vision, Power, and the Body.* Baltimore, MD: The Johns Hopkins University Press. 149–81.

Cooper, K. 1996. *The Virgin and the Bride: Idealized Womanhood in Late Antiquity.* Cambridge, MA: Harvard University Press.

Copley, F. O. 1939. "A Paraclausithyron from Pompeii: A Study of C.I.L., IV, Suppl. 5296." *American Journal of Philology* 60: 333–49.

Cumont, F. 1911. *The Oriental Religions in Roman Paganism.* Chicago: Open Court Publishing.

D'Ambra, E. 1996. "The Calculus of Venus: Nude Portraits of Roman Matrons." In N. B. Kampen (ed.), *Sexuality in Ancient Art*. Cambridge: Cambridge University Press. 219–32.

de Ste. Croix, G. E. M. 1963. "Why Were the Early Christians Persecuted?" *Past & Present* 26: 6–38.

Dixon, S. 1992. *The Roman Family*. Baltimore, MD: The Johns Hopkins University Press.

Dodds, E. R. 1965. *Pagan and Christian in an Age of Anxiety*. Rpt. 1970. New York: W. W. Norton.

Duncan-Jones, R. P. 1996. "The Impact of the Antonine Plague." *Journal of Roman Archaeology* 9: 108–36.

—— 2004. "Economic Change and the Transition to Late Antiquity." In S. Swain and M. Edwards (eds.), *Approaching Late Antiquity: The Transformation from Early to Late Empire*. Oxford: Oxford University Press. 20–52.

Evans-Grubbs, J. 1995. *Law and Family in Late Antiquity: The Emperor Constantine's Marriage Legislation*. Oxford: Clarendon Press.

Faraone, C. A. 1999. *Ancient Greek Love Magic*. Cambridge, MA: Harvard University Press.

Flory, M. B. 1984. "Where Women Precede Men: Factors Influencing the Order of Names in Roman Epitaphs." *Classical Journal* 79: 216–24.

Foucault, M. 1985. "The Battle for Chastity." In P. Ariès and A. Béjin (eds.), *Western Sexuality: Practice and Precept in Past & Present Times*. Trans. A. Forster. Oxford: Blackwell. [Orig. pub. as *Sexualités occidentales*. Paris: Editions du Seuil/Communicationes, 1982.]

—— 1988. *The History of Sexuality, vol. 3: The Care of the Self*. Trans. R. Hurley. New York: Vintage Books. [Orig. pub. as *Le Souci de soi*. Paris: Gallimard, 1984.]

Franklin, J. L., Jr. 1986. "Games and a *Lupinar*: Prosopography of a Neighborhood in Ancient Pompeii." *Classical Journal* 81: 319–28.

—— 1987. "Pantomimists at Pompeii: Actius Anicetus and His Troupe." *American Journal of Philology* 108: 95–107.

Frier, B. W. 2000. "Demography." In A. K. Bowman, P. Garnsey, and D. Rathbone (eds.), *The High Empire, A.D. 70–192*. Cambridge: Cambridge University Press. 787–816. Cambridge Histories Online. Cambridge University Press. 09 August 2012. DOI:10.1017/CHOL9780521263351.028.

—— 2001. "More Is Worse: Some Observations on the Population of the Roman Empire." In W. Scheidel (ed.), *Debating Roman Demography*. Leiden and Boston: E. J. Brill. 139–59.

Gaca, K. L. 2003. *The Making of Fornication: Eros, Ethics, and Political Reform in Greek Philosophy and Early Christianity*. Berkeley, CA: University of California Press.

Garnsey, P. 1970. *Social Status and Legal Privilege in the Roman Empire*. Oxford: Clarendon Press.

Gordon, R. L. 1972. "Mithraism and Roman Society." *Religion* 2: 92–121.

Harper, K. 2011. *Slavery in the Late Roman World AD 275–425*. Cambridge: Cambridge University Press.

Harris, W. V. 1988. "On the Applicability of the Concept of Class in Roman History." In T. Yuge and M. Doi (eds.), *Forms of Control and Subordination in Antiquity*. Leiden: E. J. Brill. 598–610.

—— 1994. "Child-Exposure in the Roman Empire." *Journal of Roman Studies* 84: 1–22.

Hopkins, K. 1980. "Taxes and Trade in the Roman Empire (200 B.C.–A.D. 400)." *Journal of Roman Studies* 70: 101–25.

Horsfall, N. 2003. *The Culture of the Roman Plebs*. London: Duckworth.

Johns, C. 1982. *Sex or Symbol: Erotic Images of Greece and Rome*. Austin: University of Texas Press.

Joshel, S. R. 1992. *Work, Identity, and Legal Status at Rome: A Study of the Occupational Inscriptions*. Norman, OK, and London: University of Oklahoma Press.

Lane Fox, R. 1987. *Pagans and Christians*. New York: Alfred A. Knopf.

Levin-Richardson, S. 2011. "*Facilis hic futuit*: Graffiti and Masculinity in Pompeii's 'Purpose-Built' Brothel." *Helios* 38: 59–78.

Lewis, N. 1999. *Life in Egypt under Roman Rule*. Atlanta, GA: Scholars Press.

Littman, R. J. and Littman, M. L. 1973. "Galen and the Antonine Plague." *American Journal of Philology* 94: 243–55.

Lo Cascio, E. 2007. "The Early Roman Empire: The State and the Economy." In W. Scheidel, I. Morris, and R Saller (eds.), 619–47. Cambridge Histories Online, (accessed 19 August 2012). DOI:10.1017/CHOL9780521780537.024.

MacMullen, R. 1974. *Roman Social Relations: 50 BC to AD 284*. New Haven, CT: Yale University Press.

—— 1982. "The Epigraphic Habit in the Roman Empire." *American Journal of Philology* 103: 233–46.

—— 1986. "What Difference Did Christianity Make?" *Historia* 35: 322–43.

Malaise, M. 1972. *Les conditions de pénétration et de diffusion des cultes égyptiens en Italie*. Leiden: E. J. Brill.

Marabini Moevs, M. T. 2008. "Per una storia del gusto: riconsiderazioni sul calice Warren." *Bollettino d'Arte* 146: 1–16.

Millar, F. 1977. *The Emperor in the Roman World (31 BC–AD 337)*. Ithaca, NY: Cornell University Press.

Milnor, K. 2013. *Graffiti and the Literary Landscape in Roman Pompeii*. Oxford: Oxford University Press.

Myerowitz, M. 1992. "The Domestication of Desire: Ovid's *Parva Tabella* and the Theater of Love." In A. Richlin (ed.), *Pornography and Representation in Greece and Rome*. Oxford: Oxford University Press. 131–57.

Ogden, D. 2002. *Magic, Witchcraft, and Ghosts in the Greek and Roman Worlds: A Sourcebook*. Oxford: Oxford University Press.

Olyan, S. M. 1994. "'And with a Male You Shall Not Lie the Lying Down of a Woman': On the Meaning and Significance of Leviticus 18: 22 and 20: 13." *Journal of the History of Sexuality* 5: 179–206.

Ostrow, S. E. 1990. "The *Augustales* in the Augustan Scheme." In K. A. Raaflaub and M. Toher (eds.), *Between Republic and Empire: Interpretations of Augustus and His Principate*. Berkeley, Los Angeles, and London: University of California Press. 364–79.

Perkins, J. 2009. *Roman Imperial Identities in the Early Christian Era*. London and New York: Routledge.

Phang, S. E. 2001. *The Marriage of Roman Soldiers (13 BC–AD 235): Law and Family in the Imperial Army*. Leiden: E. J. Brill.

Phillips, C. R., III. 1991. "*Nullum Crimen sine Lege*: Socioreligious Sanctions on Magic". In Faraone and Obbink (eds.), *Magika Hiera: Ancient Greek Magic and Religion*. 260–76.

Price, S. R. F. 1990. "The Future of Dreams: From Freud to Artemidoros." In D. M. Halperin, J. J. Winkler, and F. I. Zeitlin (eds.), *Before Sexuality: The Construction of Erotic Experience in the Ancient Greek World*. Princeton, NJ: Princeton University Press. 365–87.

Purcell, N. 1983. "The *Apparitores*: A Study in Social Mobility." *Papers of the British School at Rome* 51: 125–73.

Rathbone, D. W. 2007. "Roman Egypt." In Scheidel, Morris, and Saller (eds.), 698–719. Cambridge Histories Online, 19 August 2012. DOI:10.1017/CHOL9780521780537.027.

Rawson, B. 1974. "Roman Concubinage and Other *de facto* Marriages." *Transactions of the American Philological Association* 104: 279–305.

Rives, J. 2003. "Magic in Roman Law: The Reconstruction of a Crime." *Classical Antiquity* 22: 313–39.

—— 2007. *Religion in the Roman Empire*. Oxford and Malden, MA: Blackwell.

Roller, L. E. 1999. *In Search of God the Mother: The Cult of Anatolian Cybele*. Berkeley, Los Angeles, and London: University of California Press.

Saller, R. P. 1980. "Anecdotes as Historical Evidence for the Principate." *Greece & Rome* 27: 69–83.

Saller, R. P. and Shaw, B. D. 1984. "Tombstones and Family Relations in the Principate: Civilians, Soldiers and Slaves." *Journal of Roman Studies* 74: 124–56.

Scheidel, W. 1997. "Quantifying the Sources of Slaves in the Early Roman Empire." *Journal of Roman Studies* 87: 156–69.

—— 2001. "Progress and Problems in Roman Demography." In Scheidel (ed.), *Debating Roman Demography*. 1–81.

—— 2006. "Stratification, Deprivation and Quality of Life." In M. Atkins and R. Osbourne (eds.), *Poverty in the Roman World*. Cambridge: Cambridge University Press. 40–59.

—— 2007. "Demography." In Scheidel, Morris, and Saller (eds.), 38–86. Cambridge Histories Online, (accessed 13 August 2012). DOI:10.1017/CHOL9780521780537.004.

—— and Friesen, S. J. 2009. "The Size of the Economy and the Distribution of Income in the Roman Empire." *Journal of Roman Studies* 99: 61–91.

Shaw, B. D. 1993. "The Passion of Perpetua." *Past & Present* 139: 3–45.

Shaw, T. M. 1998. *The Burden of the Flesh: Fasting and Sexuality in Early Christianity*. Minneapolis, MN: Fortress Press.

Sox, D. 1991. *Bachelors of Art: Edward Perry Warren and the Lewes House Brotherhood*. London: Fourth Estate.

Stevenson, J. 2005. *Women Latin Poets: Language, Gender, and Authority from Antiquity to the Eighteenth Century*. Oxford: Oxford University Press.

Theissen, G. 1974. "Soziale Integration und sakramentales Handeln: Eine Analyse von 1 Cor. XI 17–34." *Novum Testamentum* 16: 179–206.

Treggiari, S. 1976. "Jobs for Women." *American Journal of Ancient History* 1: 76–104.

Turcan, R. 1996. *The Cults of the Roman Empire*. Oxford and Malden, MA: Blackwell.

Vout, C. 2007. *Power and Eroticism in Imperial Rome*. Cambridge: Cambridge University Press.

Wallace-Hadrill, A. 1994. *Houses and Society in Pompeii and Herculaneum*. Princeton, NJ: Princeton University Press.

Walzer, R. 1949. *Galen on Jews and Christians*. London: Oxford University Press.

Williams, D. 2006. *The Warren Cup*. London: British Museum Press.

Williams, C. A. 2010. *Roman Homosexuality*. 2nd edn. Oxford: Oxford University Press.

Winkler, J. J. 1990. *The Constraints of Desire: The Anthropology of Sex and Gender in Ancient Greece*. New York: Routledge.

Woeckner, E. 2002. "Women's Graffiti from Pompeii." In L. J. Churchill, P. R. Brown, and J. E. Jeffrey (eds.), *Women Writing Latin: From Roman Antiquity to Early Modern Europe*. New York: Routledge. 67–84.

Further Reading

Beck, R. 2007. *A Brief History of Ancient Astrology*. Malden, MA, and Oxford: Blackwell Publishing. Star lore is a complicated subject, even for those of you who read your newspaper horoscopes daily, but Beck explains the theoretical aspects with humor and grace. One neat feature of the book is the section showing you how to replicate a real ancient horoscope using an astronomical computer program.

Boyarin, D. 1993. *Carnal Israel: Reading Sex in Talmudic Culture*. Berkeley, Los Angeles, and London: University of California Press. Space limitations for this textbook did not permit a treatment of notions of sexuality in rabbinic Judaism, but Boyarin's volume is a fine starting point for anyone wishing to investigate that topic.

Brown, P. 1971. *The World of Late Antiquity, AD 150–750*. London: Harcourt Brace Jovanovich Inc. Beautifully illustrated concise guide to the civilizations and cultural developments in the Mediterranean world from the Antonine age to the rise of Islam.

Brown, P. 2008. *The Body and Society: Men, Women and Sexual Renunciation in Early Christianity. Twentieth-Anniversary Edition with a New Introduction*. New York: Columbia University Press. Comprehensive answer to the "why" of early Christian sexual asceticism, tracing the expanding movement from the Pauline epistles to Augustine's concept of original sin. Noteworthy for its sober and illuminating introductory essay looking back on the development of the scholarly field over the past two decades.

Cameron, A. 1993. *The Later Roman Empire: AD 284–430*. London: Fontana Press. With less of a geographic and temporal sweep than Brown's 1971 history, Cameron explores key periods and topics in greater depth.

Lewis, D. L. 2009. *God's Crucible: Islam and the Making of Europe, 570–1215*. New York: W. W. Norton & Company. Lewis discusses the rise of Islam in the context of the struggles between Rome and the Persian empire in late antiquity and traces its later impact upon Visigoth Spain and, ultimately, the Frankish peoples.

Rives, J. B. 2007. *Religion in the Roman Empire*. Malden, MA, and Oxford: Blackwell Publishing. Sound introduction to the topic, beginning with a fundamental explanation of what "religion" meant to the Romans (not the same thing it means to us). Excellent on imperial-age mystery cults and their attractions.

Shaw, T. M. 1998. *The Burden of the Flesh: Fasting and Sexuality in Early Christianity*. Shaw explains the medical basis of ascetic practice, including the relationship between diet, human physiology, and sexual desire.

Afterword: The Use of Antiquity

If, as Robin Lane Fox contends, "the transition from pagan to Christian is the point at which the ancient world still touches ours directly" (1987: 11), current legal disputes over gay rights are the sphere in which confrontations with pre-Christian sexual protocols are most likely to occur. In 1993, as we saw in the Introduction, condemnations of same-sex intercourse by the main speaker in Plato's *Laws* were cited in *Evans* v. *Romer* to prove that disapproval of such activity is not specific to the Judeo-Christian religious tradition but instead justified under natural law as defined through reason. While the first edition of this book was being written, the United States Supreme Court heard yet another case involving the civil rights of homosexuals: in its landmark ruling in *Lawrence* v. *Texas* (02–102, 41 S.W. 3d 349, reversed and remanded), it overruled a Texas law criminalizing sodomy when practiced by two persons of the same sex. By a 6 to 3 decision, handed down on June 26, 2003, the Court affirmed that the rights of liberty and privacy guaranteed under the Due Process clause of the Fourteenth Amendment to the Constitution include the right of two consenting adults to engage in such acts within the home. The majority opinion, written by Justice Anthony Kennedy, states that sodomy laws "seek to control a personal relationship that, whether or not entitled to formal recognition in the law, is within the liberty of persons to choose without being punished as criminals."

There were further ramifications to this ruling. In extending the protection of the Due Process clause to the private consensual behavior of same-sex adults, the Supreme Court also reversed its 1986 decision in *Bowers* v. *Hardwick*, which had upheld the constitutionality of a Georgia statute defining sodomy as a criminal offense. Although the Georgia law was itself gender-neutral, the person charged in the case was a gay man, and the legal question in *Bowers* was framed in terms of whether the Constitution provides for "a fundamental right to engage in homosexual sodomy." Writing for the majority, Justice Byron White refused to consider

Sexuality in Greek and Roman Culture, Second Edition. Marilyn B. Skinner.
© 2014 John Wiley & Sons, Inc. Published 2014 by John Wiley & Sons, Inc.

such a possibility: "Proscriptions against that conduct," he noted, "have ancient roots" (478 US 186 [1986], at 192). Chief Justice Warren Burger emphatically concurred:

> Decisions of individuals relating to homosexual conduct have been subject to state intervention throughout the history of Western civilization. Condemnation of those practices is firmly rooted in Judaeo-Christian moral and ethical standards. Homosexual sodomy was a capital crime under Roman law. See Code Theod. 9.7.6; Code Just. 9.9.31 .... To hold that the act of homosexual sodomy is somehow protected as a fundamental right would be to cast aside millennia of moral teaching. (478 US, at 196–7)

Like the defenders of Colorado's Amendment 2, Chief Justice Burger reaches all the way back to antiquity for an authoritative precedent. When he claims that criminalization of homosexual behavior is inherent in the Western legal tradition, he appeals to the late antique codifications of Roman law under Theodosius and Justinian, which by metonymy implicitly stand for the whole Greco-Roman past. Human sexuality is thus always and everywhere the same, and homosexuality always and everywhere wrong. The Supreme Court decision in *Bowers* rests upon this essentialist assumption.

When it reversed that decision in *Lawrence*, the Court rejected both the central finding in *Bowers* and the premise on which the finding was based. It determined that the Bowers Court had buttressed its argument with inferences drawn from a historical model of sexuality called into doubt by subsequent research. Justice Kennedy notes that there are "fundamental criticisms of the historical premises relied upon by the majority and concurring opinions in Bowers." To demonstrate that point, he embarks upon a survey of the intent behind early modern laws against sodomy. In Renaissance England and colonial America, he observes, such laws applied to relations between men and women as well as between men and men. Wrongdoing was inherent in the act, not determined by the sex of persons committing the act, because no separate category of such persons yet existed: "The absence of legal prohibitions focusing on homosexual conduct may be explained in part by noting that according to some scholars the concept of the homosexual as a distinct category of person did not emerge until the late 19th century." What was criminalized under such laws was not *homoerotic* sex, the jurist reasons, but all forms of *nonprocreative* sex. Later, during the nineteenth century, sodomy laws were chiefly used to punish assault and offenses against minors; rules of evidence then in force would have made it very difficult to prosecute consenting adults for acts committed in private. Far from possessing "ancient roots," therefore, criminalization of the activities of same-sex couples under existing sodomy laws did not begin to occur until the 1970s, and a significant number of such prosecutions involved conduct in a public place. "In summary," Kennedy concludes, "the historical grounds relied upon in *Bowers* are more complex than the majority opinion and the concurring opinion by Chief Justice Burger indicate. Their historical premises are not without doubt and, at the very least, are overstated."

To historians of sexuality, the implications of Justice Kennedy's logic were astonishing: the Supreme Court had found for social constructionism. Classicists immediately began to trace possible interconnections between the sexual frameworks of antiquity and the legal principles set forth in the *Lawrence* majority opinion. Jeffrey Carnes pinpoints one crucial area of overlap. While the studies cited by Kennedy in order to validate his reading of the historical record are not themselves works of classical scholarship, the approach taken by those secondary sources applies premises drawn from Foucault's analysis of Greco-Roman sexuality. The radical theory of the formation of the modern subject used to undercut the essentialist position assumed in *Bowers* is thus grounded in ancient cultural history. Meanwhile, the class of homosexuals, which, according to *Lawrence*, did not exist at the time sodomy laws were being formulated (and so was not envisioned as falling within the purview of sodomy laws) is now recognized as "an identity that marks out a class of citizens deserving of equal protection under the laws" (Carnes 2003: n.p.). The categories of homosexuality and heterosexuality as they are *presently* socially constructed have been reified by the Supreme Court, and the cultural specificity of those constructions is confirmed not only by their prior absence from historical discourses, but also by the discrete manner in which same-sex relations, between men and between women, were conceptualized in antiquity. Hence, further consideration of constitutional issues affecting homosexuals may well have to take ancient sexual constructs into account.

One such issue may already have occurred to you – at least, it occurred to Supreme Court Justice Antonin Scalia, who spoke about it at length in his dissent. He believed the *Lawrence* ruling was tantamount to throwing the door wide open to gay marriage:

> Today's opinion dismantles the structure of constitutional law that has permitted a distinction to be made between heterosexual and homosexual unions, insofar as formal recognition in marriage is concerned. If moral disapprobation of homosexual conduct is "no legitimate state interest" for purposes of proscribing that conduct … and if, as the Court coos (casting aside all pretense of neutrality), "[w]hen sexuality finds overt expression in intimate conduct with another person, the conduct can be but one element in a personal bond that is more enduring," … what justification could there possibly be for denying the benefits of marriage to homosexual couples exercising "[t]he liberty protected by the Constitution" …? Surely not the encouragement of procreation, since the sterile and the elderly are allowed to marry.

The momentum this question speedily gathered attests to the correctness of Scalia's perception. In the decade since *Lawrence* was decided, the right of gay couples to marry has gradually been recognized at the state level, initially through court rulings and legislative action and most recently by voter approval in statewide referendums. At the time of writing (May 2013) twelve states and the District of Columbia issue marriage licenses to same-sex couples. President Barack Obama has given the movement his personal endorsement and has affirmed the equality owed to "our gay brothers and sisters" in his Second Inaugural Address. The constitutionality of the 1996 Defense of Marriage Act (DOMA), which prohibits the federal government from recognizing same-sex unions, is now before the Supreme Court. At the same time, the Court is also scheduled to rule on California's Proposition 8, a ballot initiative banning same-sex marriage. Decisions on both cases are expected in June 2013, though whether the anticipated rulings will fully decide the main legal issues is uncertain. In the United Kingdom, meanwhile, same-sex couples may enter into civil partnerships granting most of the legal rights of marriage, and the first steps have been taken toward legalizing gay marriage itself. Canada, for its part, had already enacted same-sex marriage into nationwide law in 2005. Whatever the outcomes of pending legislative and judicial processes in the United Kingdom and the United States, though, the passionate convictions of both supporters and opponents will ensure that the topic of gay unions continues to be disputed for many years to come.

Whenever debate arises, ancient notions of marriage may well come into play, for they have shaped the Christian view of marriage as a union of one man and one woman that gay marriage, as many argue, threatens to subvert. Bringing in the reports of Nero's weddings, or Martial's and Juvenal's accounts of male brides, would prove nothing either way, since that tactic naively confuses conventional motifs of polemic and satire with reportage. However, the threefold purpose of Christian marriage as encapsulated in the Anglican *Prayer Book* can be traced back to classical sources (Treggiari 1991: 11–13). Marriage, it is there stated, was ordained for the procreation of children, as a remedy against sin, and as a means of mutual support. Greeks and Romans alike defined reproduction as the notional purpose of marriage; here their influence is patent. Again, the idea of marriage as a partnership and source of mutual assistance is already inherent in the *homophrosynê* prized by Odysseus, but it receives its strongest affirmation from Musonius Rufus, who maintains that it is even more central to the purpose of marriage than producing children. Lastly, Paul's defense of marriage as a safeguard against fornication in 1 Corinthians 7, though itself arguably derived from the Septuagint, later formed the basis of Clement of Alexandria's conflation of scriptural and Greek philosophical tenets into an austere sexual ethic of procreation in the Lord (Gaca 2003: 247–72). As in Paul, so subsequently in Clement, the marriage of Christ and his church is integrated with Christian marriage. This means that a sexually active wedded Christian performs his or her faith in marriage – a principle still basic to Christian fundamentalism and the rationale for its commitment to preserving what is regarded as the sanctity of the institution. Awareness of how marriage was conceptualized in the classical world would appear to be a first step toward formulating the arguments for and against same-sex marriage.

Nevertheless it should be evident that, appealed to as a basis of judgment, ancient sources themselves leave room for dispute. If marriage is fundamentally for procreative ends, gay marriage is automatically ruled out; sterile marriages might be allowed to continue, on the grounds that they were entered into with the hope of having children, but marriage of those in their post-reproductive years would theoretically need to be specially justified. (The *Lex Iulia de maritandis ordinibus*, which imposed penalties upon the celibate, did not apply to women over 50 and men over 60.) On the other hand, nothing in that conception of marriage precludes either polygamy or concubinage in conjunction with marriage. Alternatively, if Musonius is right, and it is the stable social bond that is most central to marriage and presumably of most interest to the state, the right of forming a legally recognized union would have to be extended to gay couples – and it would be in the best interests of the state to permit them to do so. (Musonius thought same-sex intercourse unnatural, so he would be horrified by that remark, but it *is* the logical consequence of his postulate.) Whatever the outcome of this present controversy, we must acknowledge that sexual intercourse did not begin, after all, in 1963 – nor has it always been the same as it is now. Yet the forces that persist in shaping it well up from ancient springs.

References

Carnes, J. S. 2003. "Certain Intimate Conduct: Classics, Constructionism, and the Courts." Unpublished paper.

Gaca, K. L. 2003. *The Making of Fornication: Eros, Ethics, and Political Reform in Greek Philosophy and Early Christianity*. Berkeley, CA: University of California Press.

Lane Fox, R. 1987. *Pagans and Christians*. New York: Alfred A. Knopf.

Treggiari, S. 1991. *Roman Marriage: "Iusti Coniuges" from the Time of Cicero to the Time of Ulpian*. Oxford: Clarendon Press.

Glossary of Terms

Achilles: hero of Homer's *Iliad*, whose wrath at an insult to his honor brings about the tragic deaths of his companion Patroclus and the Trojan defender Hector

Aeneas: hero of Vergil's epic the *Aeneid*; son of Aphrodite and Aeneas who led Trojan survivors to Italy after the fall of Troy

Adonis: Greek demigod, lover of Aphrodite slain by a boar, celebrated in women's cult

Aeschines: fourth-century BCE Athenian politician, prosecutor of lawsuit against Timarchus

Agathon: fifth-century BCE Athenian tragic poet, host of dinner gathering in Plato's *Symposium*

Agela: "herd," in Dorian societies a cohort of youthful age mates educated together

Agôgê: Spartan age-based educational system

Agora: marketplace and civic center of a Greek *polis*

Alcaeus: archaic Greek poet, native of Lesbos and contemporary of Sappho, composer of pederastic and political songs for the symposium

Alcman: archaic Greek poet, composer of choral songs for Spartan girls

Alexander III of Macedon: known as "the Great," conqueror of the Persian empire

Alexandria: city founded by Alexander, capital of Egypt under the Ptolemies and Romans

Alexandrian: designation for cultural and literary products created in Hellenistic Alexandria under the patronage of the early Ptolemies

Alumnus, pl. ***alumni:***   a slave child or foundling fostered by his master and treated as a favorite

Amicitia: "friendship," applied by Catullus to his idealized relationship with Lesbia

Anacreon: archaic Greek poet, composer of love poetry and drinking songs

Anchises: Trojan prince, lover of Aphrodite and father of Aeneas

Sexuality in Greek and Roman Culture, Second Edition. Marilyn B. Skinner.

Andreia: Greek concept of masculinity, associated particularly with competitiveness

Andreion: men's dining area, either a public building or a room in a private house

Antinous: companion of the emperor Hadrian deified after his death

Aphrodisia, ta: "the matters of Aphrodite," Greek term for "sex" or "sexuality"

Aphrodite: Greek goddess of love and sexual activity; Roman equivalent is Venus

Aphrodite of Cnidus: fourth-century BCE marble statue by Praxiteles, first monumental nude female figure

Apollodorus: fourth-century BCE Athenian politician, prosecutor of lawsuit against Neaera

Apollonius: Hellenistic Greek poet, Royal Librarian under Ptolemy II Philadelphus and author of the *Argonautica*

Apotropaic: "turning away," applied to a device, formula, or gesture intended to avert evil

Apparitor, pl. *apparitores*:   paid staff serving Roman magistrates and priests

Apuleius: second-century CE Roman orator and novelist, author of the *Metamorphoses*

Archaic Age: period from approximately 750 to 490 BCE in which the *polis* culture and the characteristic institutions of classical Greece took shape

Archilochus: archaic Greek poet, composer of iambic or "blame" poetry ridiculing outsiders

Aretê: "excellence" of any kind, but especially moral excellence

Argead dynasty: ruling house of Macedon

Aristogiton: tyrannicide who, together with his beloved **Harmodius**, killed Hipparchus, brother of the sixth-century BCE Athenian autocrat Hippias

Aristophanes: fifth-century BCE Greek comic playwright, author of the only completely surviving examples of Old Comedy

Aristotle: fourth-century BCE Greek philosopher, author of influential treatises on biology, ethics, and politics

Arretine pottery: mold-produced terracotta tableware reproducing designs on more expensive precious metal vessels

Arsinoë II: wife and sister of Ptolemy II Philadelphus of Egypt

Artemidorus: second-century CE dream interpreter, author of the *Oneirokritika*

Asclepiades: Hellenistic poet, inventor of the amatory epigram

Athena: virgin goddess, patron and defender of the city of Athens; Roman equivalent is Minerva

Athenian Stranger: chief spokesman of Plato's last dialogue, the *Laws*, generally regarded as a surrogate for the philosopher himself

Attis: originally in myth the mortal lover of the goddess Meter or Cybele, later the divine hero of a mystery cult

Augustales: officials of the imperial cult in the Western Roman empire, generally recruited from the ranks of freedmen

Augustan Age: period (27 BCE to 14 CE) during which Rome was governed by Augustus

Augustine (Aurelius Augustinus):   fourth-century CE bishop and theologian, author of the *Confessions*

Augustus (C. Julius Caesar Octavianus): nephew and adopted son of Julius Caesar and first Roman emperor

Black-figure: Greek vase painting technique in which figures are painted in black upon the natural clay background, with red and white as secondary colors

Butler, Judith (1956–): American philosopher and feminist theorist who regards gender as a script for performance, realized through repetition

Caesar, C. Julius: first-century BCE Roman politician and general, conqueror of Gaul and, following his civil war with Pompey, dictator, assassinated in 44 BCE

Caligula (C. Iulius Caesar Germanicus): successor to Tiberius as *princeps*; ruled 37–41 CE

Callimachus: Hellenistic Greek poet, patronized by the second and third Ptolemies and their queens, proponent of a learned and restrained poetics that greatly influenced later Roman writers

Carthage: city in Northern Africa, founded by the Phoenicians, thrice defeated by Rome in the Punic Wars

Cassius Dio: second-century CE Greek senator and author of a partially surviving comprehensive history of Rome

Catasterism: transformation into a star or a constellation

Cato, M. Porcius (Cato the Censor): second-century BCE Roman statesman, orator, and historian

Catullus, C. Valerius: first-century BCE Roman poet, famous for love poems to his mistress Lesbia and invective against prominent politicians

Charis: "grace," the manifestation of external beauty and attractiveness

Cicero, M. Tullius: first-century BCE Roman orator, statesman, and philosopher

Cinaedus: "gender-deviant male," Latin equivalent of *kinaidos*

Circe: mythic witch, lover and helper of Odysseus

Claudius (Ti. Claudius Nero Germanicus): successor to Caligula as *princeps*, added Britain to Roman empire; ruled 41–54 CE

Cleopatra VII: last Ptolemaic ruler of Egypt, defeated by Octavian at Actium in 31 BCE

Clodia Metelli: first-century BCE Roman noblewoman, thought to be "Lesbia," the mistress of the poet Catullus

Commodus, L. Aurelius: son of and successor to emperor Marcus Aurelius; ruled 180–92 CE

Constantine: first Christian emperor, whose victory over Maxentius in 312 CE led him to promote Christianity aggressively

Constructionism: belief that gender and/or sexual behavior is chiefly or exclusively the product of cultural factors such as language and must be regarded as specific to its particular culture

Contubernium, pl. *contubernia*: a union between a Roman couple, at least one of whom was a slave, held to be invalid in law but treated as a legitimate marriage by the partners themselves

Cubiculum, pl. *cubicula*: small interior room in a Roman house, often used as a bedroom

Cupid and Psyche, tale of: a long narrative insert within Apuleius' *Metamorphoses* telling of Psyche's struggle to win back her lover Cupid

Cynicism: philosophical school that advocated poverty and rejection of social constraints

Cypris: poetic name for Aphrodite

Cyrnus: boy to whom Theognis' elegiac love poetry is addressed

Decurion class: propertied individuals, Greek and Roman, who were members of municipal councils

Delicatus, pl. *delicati*: a slave boy with whom a Roman master has a continuing sexual relationship

Demography: study of the quantitative aspects of human populations

Dêmos: the common people of a Greek city-state, as opposed to the aristocracy; alternatively, the community as a whole

Demosthenes: fourth-century BCE Athenian orator, opponent of Philip II of Macedon

Didactic poem: in antiquity, a long poem in hexameters composed in an elevated style and purporting to give instruction upon a subject

Dido: queen of Carthage in Vergil's *Aeneid*, who commits suicide after Aeneas, obeying a divine mandate, leaves her

Dildo: leather phallos putatively used for female masturbation

Dionysos: Greek god of wine and the theater; Roman equivalent is Bacchus

Docta puella: "learned girl," technical term for the elegiac beloved as the embodiment of the poet-lover's writings

Domina, pl. *dominae*: Latin word for the mistress of a house and, by extension, the demanding beloved of Roman love elegy

Domitian (T. Flavius Domitianus): last emperor of the Flavian dynasty, ruled from 86–96 CE

Dorians: Cultural and linguistic subgroup of Greeks inhabiting Crete, Sparta, and other territories

Dover, K. J. (1920–2010): British classicist, author of *Greek Homosexuality*

Elagabalus (M. Aurelius Antoninus): third-century CE priest of the Syrian sun god Elagabalus, proclaimed Roman emperor in 218 and assassinated four years later

Elegiac poetry: poetry consisting of successive hexameter and pentameter couplets

Enkrateia: self-control, especially in reference to bodily pleasures

Ephêbos, pl. *ephêboi*: Greek youth undergoing military training

Epic poem: in antiquity, a long narrative poem in hexameters composed in an elevated style and dealing with a mythical or historic theme

Epictetus: Greek first-century CE Stoic philosopher, former slave

Epicureanism: leading Hellenistic and Roman philosophical school founded by Epicurus

Erastês: "lover," the older male partner in a Greek pederastic relationship

Equestrian class: in Rome, wealthy individuals of good families outside the senatorial order

Erinna: Hellenistic Greek female poet, author of the *Distaff*, a 300-line hexameter lament for a dead friend

Erômenos, pl. *erômenoi*: "beloved," the younger male partner in a Greek pederastic relationship

Eros: Greek god of desire; as abstract noun *erôs*, desire or passion; Roman equivalent is Cupid

Essentialism: belief that gender and/or sexual behavior conforms to inherent natural patterns common to all human beings

Etruscans: indigenous pre-Roman population of Italy whose culture flourished from the eighth to the fifth centuries BCE

Euripides: fifth-century BCE Athenian tragic playwright, author of the dramas *Alcestis*, *Helen*, and *Hippolytus*

Exemplum: mythical or historic precedent

Exoletus, pl. ***exoleti:*** "superannuated," a term applied to adult male prostitutes

Favorinus: second-century CE Greek orator and sophist

Figura, pl. ***figurae:*** illustration, specifically of a sexual position used as decoration

Foedus: in Roman society, a binding agreement between equals

Forum: civic center of a Roman town or city

Foucault, Michel (1926–84): French philosopher and social historian, author of the *History of Sexuality*

Furor: "madness," characteristic trait of Juno in Vergil's *Aeneid*

Galen: second-century CE Greek physician, author of a widely influential corpus of medical treatises

Gallus, C. Cornelius: first-century BCE Roman military commander under Octavian and first prefect of Egypt, forced to commit suicide after being recalled; inventor of Latin love elegy

Gastêr: Greek word for both "belly" and "womb"

Gender: the social and cultural constructions of masculinity and femininity associated with biological sex

Gens, pl. ***gentes:*** "clan," a collective term for a Roman kin-group that shared the same family ("gentile") name and claimed descent from a common ancestor

"Greek love": modern euphemism for the social institution of pederasty practiced in ancient Greece

Greek novel: one of five existing specimens (others are known) of Imperial-age prose fiction narrating the adventures of two nobly-born young lovers

Gymnasium: Greek public building designated for athletic training and exercise

Gynê, pl. ***gynaikes:*** wife, married woman

Habrosynê: luxury and refined sensuality, celebrated by the Greek oligarchic class

Hadrian (P. Aelius Hadrianus): second-century CE Roman emperor, known for his philhellenism, reigned from 117–138 CE

Hêbê: "ripeness," sexual maturity

Hera: Greek queen of the gods, wife and sister of Zeus; Roman equivalent is Juno

Helen: wife of Menelaus, king of Sparta, whose abduction by Paris caused the Trojan War

Heracles: mythic Greek hero whose successful performance of the Twelve Labors earned him immortality; Roman equivalent is Hercules

Hermaphrodite: a being possessing the physical characteristics of both sexes

Hermes: Greek messenger god; Roman equivalent is Mercury

Herodas: Hellenistic Greek poet, author of mimiambs or satiric skits, several of which attack female poets

Herodotus: fifth-century BCE Greek historian of Egypt and the Persian Wars

Hesiod: Greek epic bard, composer of the didactic poems the *Theogony* and the *Works and Days*

Hetaira, pl. *hetairai*: "companion," Greek courtesan

Hetaireia: a group of male sympotic participants

Hippocrates: fifth-century BCE Greek physician to whom the corpus of Hippocratic medical treatises is ascribed

Hippolytus: mythic son of Theseus, king of Athens, punished by Aphrodite for excessive dedication to chastity

Historia Augusta: fourth-century CE collection of biographies of the later emperors from Hadrian on; parts are of very dubious authenticity

Hodos: in Hippocratic medicine, an uninterrupted passage in women's bodies extending from the head to the vagina

Homer: Greek epic bard, composer of the *Iliad* and the *Odyssey*

Homeric Hymns: a collection of Greek hexameter poems from the archaic and classical periods celebrating various divinities

Homoerotic: having to do with same-sex attraction or lovemaking

Homophrosynê: "like-mindedness," ideal trait of the Greek married couple

Honestiores: under imperial Roman law, those who because of their status were exempt from corporal punishment

Hoplite: Greek citizen soldier, heavily armored infantryman

Horace (Q. Horatius Flaccus): Roman first-century BCE lyric and satiric poet, friend of Maecenas

Horus: divine child of Osiris and Isis, whom each living Pharaoh embodied

House of the Vettii: dwelling at Pompeii known for its highly original decorative schemes, including a large fresco of Priapus

Humiliores: under imperial Roman law, those of lesser status who could be subjected to bodily punishment, including execution

Hybris: "arrogance," an action that trespasses upon the rights of another, especially a god

Hydria, pl. *hydriai*: Greek vase used to carry water

Iambic poetry: abusive poetry, usually humorous, composed in various meters

Iconography: code of pictorial representation conveying information through attributes, costume, gesture, and other symbolic means

Imperium: Roman military command, invested in senior magistrates and governors of provinces

Initiation: formal ceremony incorporating a youth or a religious adherent into a community

Isis: major Egyptian goddess, sister and wife of Osiris, later revered as supreme female divinity

Ithyphallic: having an erection

Jason: mythic Greek hero, leader of the expedition to recover the Golden Fleece and husband of the Colchian princess and witch Medea

Julio-Claudian dynasty: the first imperial dynasty, whose members were affiliated with the Julian and the Claudian families; the line ended with Nero's death in 68 CE

Juvenal (D. Iunius Iuvenalis):   early second-century CE Roman satirist

Kinaidos: Greek stereotype of the dissolute and effeminate male, intimating a preference for passive sexual activity

Koinê: Greek "common" dialect, language of commerce in the Hellenistic and Roman eras

Kôma: trance-like sleep, possibly supernatural in origin, an after-effect of intercourse

Kômos: rowdy procession through the streets following a symposium

Krater: container used to mix wine and water at a Greek symposium

Kylix: wide, shallow Greek drinking cup equipped with handles, popular at the symposium

Kyrios: male citizen head of a Greek household, guardian of its women, children, and slaves

Lex Iulia de adulteriis coercendis: law passed in 18 BCE making adultery a criminal offence

Lex Iulia de maritandis ordinibus: law passed in 18 BCE regulating marriage among Roman upper classes, encouraging production of children, and penalizing celibacy

Livia: wife of Augustus, mother of his adopted son and eventual successor Tiberius

Lucian: second-century CE Greek sophist, author of satirical essays and dialogues

Lucilius, C.:   second-century BCE Roman nobleman, inventor of satire

Lucretius (T. Lucretius Carus):   first-century BCE Roman poet, composer of the didactic epic *On the Nature of Things*, setting out the principles of Epicurean philosophy

Lyric poetry: poetry composed in stanzas of various kinds made up of short rhythmic phrases

Maecenas, C.:   friend and close associate of Augustus and numerous poets, including Horace

Maenad: female follower of Dionysos

Magna Graecia: collective name for Greek colonies in the south of Italy founded during the archaic period

Magna Mater: title under which the Asian goddess Meter, together with her mortal lover Attis, was honored in Rome

Magus, pl. *magi*:   a professional practitioner of magic

Maiestas: "dignity," originally that of the Roman people, which it was criminal to injure; later extended to that of the emperor, which could be harmed by slander and libel

Manus: authority of father or husband over Roman married woman

Mars: Roman god of war, paramour of Venus and father of the Roman people; Greek equivalent is Ares

Martial (M. Valerius Martialis):   late first-century CE Roman epigrammatist

Matrona: respectable Roman married woman

Matronymic: identification by mother's, rather than father's, name

Medea: mythic Colchian princess and archetypal witch brought to Greece by Jason, who subsequently kills her own children to punish his infidelity

Megalomisthos, pl. *megalomisthoi*:   courtesan who could command extravagant prices

Meleager: second-century BCE Greek anthologist and epigrammatist, composer of the *Garland*

Menander: Hellenistic-era Athenian playwright, author of romantic comedies of manners

Menarche: first menstruation, sign that a girl is ready for marriage

Menos: the potency of an adult man, imagined as a finite supply of spermatic liquid

Meretrix, pl. *meretrices*:   Latin word for courtesan, the equivalent of the Greek *hetaira*

Metamorphosis: change from one mode of physical existence into another

Metic: non-citizen resident of Athens

Mêtis: "cunning intelligence," characteristic virtue of both Odysseus and Penelope

Milesian tale: a genre of ancient fiction characterized by short humorous and obscene anecdotes

Minoans: Bronze Age non-Greek inhabitants of Crete whose civilization flourished between 3500 and 1500 BCE

Mithras: Persian savior god, slayer of the cosmic bull, whose mysteries, restricted to men, spread throughout the empire during and after the first century CE

Moicheia: sexual intercourse with a woman under the protection of another *kyrios*

Mollitia: "softness," Latin word connoting effeminacy and lack of discipline when applied to a man

Mos maiorum: "the customs of the ancestors," or traditional Roman beliefs and behaviors

Munera: "gifts," term for gladiatorial games because they were presented by emperors or local magistrates

Museum: artistic and scholarly center established by Ptolemy I in Alexandria, to which the famous library was attached

Musonius Rufus, C.:   first-century CE Roman Stoic philosopher

Mycenaeans: Bronze Age Greek-speaking inhabitants of peninsular Greece and the Aegean islands, who reached the height of their power between 1450 and 1200 BCE

Mystery religion: salvation cult requiring prospective members to undergo secret initiatory rites that established a personal relationship with a deity

Natural fertility pattern: reproductive pattern in which married couples continue having children until no longer physically capable of doing so

Natural-law theory: belief that human morality is governed by inherent principles discoverable by reason

Neaera: fourth-century BCE Greek *hetaira*, prosecuted in Athens for allegedly passing herself off as a citizen wife

Nepos, Cornelius: first-century BCE Roman biographer

Nero (Nero Claudius Caesar):   *princeps* from 54–68 CE, popular with Greeks and the common people but detested by the senatorial class; known for his musical and artistic interests

Nomos: "law, convention," the sphere of human experience determined by culture, opposite of *physis*

Nossis: Hellenistic Greek female epigrammatist who celebrated the women of her native city Locri in southern Italy

Octavian: see Augustus

Odysseus: mythic Achaean hero, famous for his cunning, whose return home from Troy is the theme of Homer's *Odyssey*

Oikos, pl. *oikoi*: "household," basic unit of society in the Greek city-state

Olympias: wife of Philip II of Macedon and mother of Alexander the Great

Oneiros, pl. *oneiroi*: prophetic dream

One-sex model: medical notion that male and female reproductive organs were essentially the same but positioned differently

Ordo, pl. *ordines*: in Rome, a group of persons having the same rank or social status, for example, the senatorial order

Orphic cult: archaic Greek religious practices, akin to later mystery cult, emphasizing ritual purity and salvation in the afterlife

Osiris: major Egyptian god, brother and husband of Isis, king of the dead in the afterlife

Ovid (P. Ovidius Naso): first-century BCE Roman elegiac and epic poet, relegated by Augustus for writing the "immoral" *Art of Love*

Paidagôgos: "pedagogue," slave attendant of Greek boy

Paideia: Greek program of education and socialization

Palaistra: wrestling area at the Greek gymnasium, frequent site of courtship scenes on vases

Palatine Hill: exclusive residential district of Rome, overlooking the Forum; later the site of imperial palaces

Pallakê: Greek concubine under the protection of a man whose children were legally ineligible to share in his estate

Pandora: mythic first woman, created by Zeus in retaliation for Prometheus' theft of fire

Paris: son of Priam, king of Troy; favorite of Aphrodite because he awarded her the golden apple in a divine beauty contest; elopement with Helen was pretext for Trojan War

Partheneion, pl. *partheneia*: song composed for a chorus of girls

Pathicus: Latin term for adult male who prefers the passive or receptive role

Patria potestas: Roman fathers' control over adult sons and daughters, theoretically extending to power of life and death

Patronage: a social system in which patron and client, individuals of unequal status, exchange personal services according to each partner's means

Paul: "Apostle to the Gentiles," an early convert from Pharisiac Judaism to Christianity whose directives on sexuality and marriage have greatly influenced subsequent Christian teaching about sexual morality

Pax Romana: the 200-year period of relative freedom from military turmoil at home and abroad lasting from the accession of Augustus in 27 BCE to the death of Marcus Aurelius in 180 CE

Pederasty: sexual attraction to a pre-adolescent boy on the part of an adult male; in ancient Greece, the institutionalized practice of adult male courtship of citizen youths

Pedophilia: attraction to prepubsecent or pubescent children as sexual objects

Peloponnesian War: military struggle between Athens and Sparta and their respective allies from 431–404 BCE, ending in Athens's defeat

Penelope: wife of Odysseus, proverbial for her fidelity

Penetration model: the model of ancient sexuality popularized by K. J. Dover and Michel Foucault in which sexual relationships are said to mirror the hierarchical structure of social relationships and the dominant role is assigned to the male penetrator

Pericles: fifth-century BCE Athenian statesman, author of law restricting citizenship to children born of two citizen parents

Persius (A. Persius Flaccus):   first-century CE Roman poet, composer of satires advocating a Stoic morality

Persona: "mask," a first-person character assumed by authors of some ancient genres of literary works, for example satire

Petronius: first-century CE Roman novelist, author of the *Satyrica* and plausibly identified with a member of Nero's court forced to commit suicide

Phallos, pl. *phalloi*:   model of male genitalia (Latin *phallus*)

Pharmakon, pl. *pharmaka*:   herb or drug having a magical and/or medical effect

Pharaoh: Egyptian king, quasi-divine mediator between the people of Egypt and the gods

Philia: friendship or affection

Philip II of Macedon: conqueror of mainland Greece and father of Alexander the Great

Physis: "nature," the sphere of human experience not subject to social control, opposite of *nomos*

Pindar: fifth-century BCE Greek lyric poet, best known for composing athletic victory odes

Pisistratid dynasty: the family of Pisistratus and his sons Hippias and Hipparchus, rulers of Athens during the sixth century BCE

Plato: fourth-century BCE Athenian philosopher, author of numerous Socratic dialogues

Plautus: second-century BCE Roman playwright, author of farcical comedies loosely based on Greek originals

Plebs: collective term for the Roman masses

Pliny (C. Plinius Caecilius Secundus, Pliny the Younger):   first and early second-century CE senator, governmental official, and letter-writer

Plutarch: second-century CE Greek biographer, essayist, and moralist

Polis, pl. *poleis*:   Greek city-state, distinctive mode of urban life from the archaic period onward

Polybius: second-century BCE Greek historian who chronicled Rome's rise to power

Polemo, M. Antonius: second-century CE Greek sophist, orator, and author of a treatise on physiognomy

Pompeii: town on the Bay of Naples destroyed by the eruption of Vesuvius in 79 CE

Pornê, pl. **pornai:**   "whore," Greek female sex worker, paid by the act

Priapus: ithyphallic Roman god, protector of gardens and subject of obscene poetry

Princeps: "leading citizen," title bestowed on Augustus by the Roman Senate and assumed by succeeding emperors

Principate: form of Roman governance established by Augustus

Propertius, Sex.:   first-century BCE Roman poet, composer of four books of love elegy celebrating his affair with Cynthia

Ptolemaic dynasty: Macedonian rulers of Egypt who traced their ancestry back to Ptolemy I Soter

Ptolemy I Soter: former Macedonian general of Alexander, later king of Egypt and founder of the Ptolemaic dynasty

Ptolemy II Philadelphus: successor of the above, under whose rule Alexandria became a panhellenic cultural center

Pythagorean Table of Opposites: Pythagorean conceptual system preserved by Aristotle that organizes elementary human experience into opposing categories

Pythagoreans: followers of the sixth-century BCE religious teacher Pythagoras of Croton, renowned for both ethical and mathematical contributions to philosophy

Queer: as a political term, "queer" denotes a theoretical stance that rejects heteronormativity, or the traditional conceptual dominance of the male–female gender dichotomy, as well as traditional gender identities such as "gay," "Lesbian," "bisexual," and "straight"

Quintilian (M. Fabius Quintilianus):   first-century CE Roman teacher of rhetoric, author of a standard treatise on training the orator

Res publica: the Roman state

Red-figure: Greek vase painting technique in which a figure with details painted in retains the color of the unglazed clay and appears against a black background

Retarius, pl. **retarii:**   a gladiator armed with a net and trident, not a sword

Res Gestae: an autobiographical narrative of the emperor Augustus' achievements stressing the legality and constitutionality of his position

Sallust (C. Sallustius Crispus):   first-century BCE Roman historian, author of *Catiline* and *Jugurtha*

Sabine women, rape of: Roman founding myth justifying intermarriage with neighboring peoples and female participation in public affairs

Sappho: archaic Greek woman poet, native of Lesbos, composer of songs celebrating female desire

Sarapis: Hellenized consort of Isis popularized by the Ptolemies

Saturnalian: referring to the *Saturnalia*, a Roman festival of several days in mid-December during which presents were exchanged and slaves were allowed greater license

Satyr: mythical companion of Dionysos with both human and bestial features, symbolic of excess

Scortum, pl. **scorta:**   Latin term for common whore, male or female; equivalent of Greek *pornê*

Second Sophistic: period between 50 and 250 CE when Greek sophists flourished

Seneca, L. Annaeus (the Elder): first-century BCE Roman author of treatises on declamation

Seneca, L. Annaeus (the Younger): first-century CE Roman Stoic philosopher and advisor of Nero

Sex: possession of female or male physiological sexual characteristics, primary and secondary

Sexuality: 1) the quality of being sexual or having sex; 2) possession of sexual powers, or capability of sexual feelings; 3) recognition of or preoccupation with what is sexual; 4) appearance distinctive of sex; 5) the culturally specific set of meanings placed upon sex; 6) sexual inclinations, specifically object preference, as a determinant of identity

Shame culture: a culture in which behavior is primarily motivated by the desire to preserve honor and avoid shame within the surrounding community

Simaetha: heroine of Theocritus' second *Idyll* who resorts to magic in order to win back her lover

Sociobiology: a generalizing theory of human conduct in which universal patterns of gendered behavior are explained as evolutionary strategies for procreative success

Socrates: fifth-century BCE Athenian public figure executed for corrupting youth, featured in Plato's dialogues and in the *Memorabilia* of Xenophon

Solon: early sixth-century BCE Athenian magistrate, proponent of democracy and putative author of laws regulating pederastic courtship and conduct of women

Sophist: in the Imperial age, a professional teacher of Greek rhetoric and practiced declaimer

Sôphrosynê: moderation, temperance

Stoicism: leading Hellenistic and Roman philosophical school founded by Zeno

Strato: second-century CE Greek author and compiler of pederastic epigrams

Stuprum: in Roman law, the criminal sexual violation of a citizen youth or unmarried female

Successors: generals of Alexander who carved up his empire among themselves after his death

Suetonius (C. Suetonius Tranquillus): second-century CE biographer of the Julio-Claudian and Flavian emperors

Sulpicia: first-century BCE Roman noblewoman and author of elegiac epigrams on her affair with "Cerinthus"

Superstitio, pl. *superstitiones*: derogatory term applied to religious creed deemed not only irrational but morally suspect

Symposium, pl. *symposia*: banquet and drinking party attended by Greek elite males and *hetairai*

Syncretism: the practice of assimilating the gods of one culture to those of another

Tacitus, Cornelius: first- to early second-century BCE Roman historian of the early principate, author of the *Annals* and the *Histories*

Tarquin dynasty: legendary Etruscan kings of Rome in the seventh and sixth centuries BCE

Tertullian (Q. Septimius Florens Tertullianus):   second-century CE Christian apologist and polemicist

Thiasos: Greek religious organization, usually honoring a particular divinity

Thecla: fictive heroine of the *Acts of Paul and Thecla* who rejects marriage in order to become a disciple of Paul and undergo Christian baptism

Theocritus: Hellenistic Greek poet, active in Alexandria during the reign of Ptolemy Philadelphus, author of *Idylls*, bucolic poems in hexameters

Theognis: archaic Greek poet, composer of elegiac songs for symposia

Thucydides: fifth-century BCE Athenian historian, author of history of Peloponnesian War

Tiberius (Ti. Iulius Caesar Augustus):   successor to Augustus as *princeps*, ruled from 14–37 CE

Tibullus, Albius: first-century BCE Roman poet, author of two books of love elegies describing his affairs with Delia, Marathus, and Nemesis

Tintinnabulum, pl. *tintinnabula:*   wind-chimes, frequently incorporating the phallus as an artistic element

Tondo: circular painting in the bowl of a drinking cup

Tribas, pl. *tribades* (English equivalent is "tribad"):   stereotype of female who transgresses gender roles by actively penetrating females and even males

Trimalchio: main character in Petronius' *Satyrica*, a stupendously wealthy but vulgar freedman

Tutor: guardian assigned to independent adult Roman woman to exercise oversight over her legal and financial affairs

Tychê: Greek goddess of fortune; Roman equivalent is Fortuna

Tyrannos, pl. *tyrannoi:*   sole ruler who has gained control of the *polis* unconstitutionally

Valeria Messalina: wife of emperor Claudius, accused of committing flagrant adultery and forced to commit suicide in 48 CE

Venatio, pl. *venationes:*   wild-beast hunts presented in Roman amphitheaters

Venus Genetrix: title of Venus as divine mother of the Roman race through her son Aeneas

Vergil (P. Vergilius Maro):   first-century BCE Roman poet, author of the *Eclogues*, the *Georgics*, and the *Aeneid*

Verna, pl. *vernae:*   a slave child born on the estate

Villa of the Mysteries: a suburban villa outside Pompeii containing a large room (possibly a dining room) with a continuous frieze depicting an initiation into Bacchic rites

Vir: Roman adult citizen male

Virtus: Roman concept of masculinity, connoting both bravery and moral virtue

Vulcan: Roman god of metalworking, husband of Venus; Greek equivalent is Hephaestus

Xenophon: fourth-century BCE Athenian prose writer, author of the *Memorabilia* and the *Oikonomicos*

Zeus: Greek king of the gods; Roman equivalent is Jupiter

Index

Sexuality in Greek and Roman Culture, Second Edition. Marilyn B. Skinner.
© 2014 John Wiley & Sons, Inc. Published 2014 by John Wiley & Sons, Inc.

Printed in the USA
CPSIA information can be obtained
at www.ICGtesting.com
JSHW060726261223
54130JS00003B/18